African Literatures in English
East and West

Longman Literature in English Series

General Editors:
David Carroll, University of Lancaster
Michael Wheeler, University of Southampton
Chris Walsh, Chester College of Higher Education

For a complete list of titles see pages viii–ix.

African Literatures in English

East and West

Gareth Griffiths

An imprint of **Pearson Education**

Harlow, England · London · New York · Reading, Massachusetts · San Francisco · Toronto · Don Mills, Ontario · Sydney
Tokyo · Singapore · Hong Kong · Seoul · Taipei · Cape Town · Madrid · Mexico City · Amsterdam · Munich · Paris · Milan

Pearson Education Limited
Edinburgh Gate
Harlow
Essex CM20 2JE
England

and Associated Companies throughout the world

Visit us on the World Wide Web at:
www.pearsoneduc.com

First published 2000

© Pearson Education Limited 2000

ISBN 0-582-08926-3 PPR
ISBN 0-582-08925-5 CSD

British Library Cataloguing-in-Publication Data
A catalogue record for this book is available from the British Library

Library of Congress Cataloging-in-Publication Data
Griffiths, Gareth, 1943–
    African literatures in English : East and West / Gareth Griffiths.
        p. cm. — (Longman literature in English series)
    Includes bibliographical references and index.
    ISBN 0–582–08925–5 (csd) — ISBN 0–582–08926–3 (ppr)
    1. African literature (English)—History and criticism. I. Title. II. Series.

PR9340.G75 2000
820.9′96—dc21   99–053636

Set in 10/12pt Sabon
Typeset by 35
Produced by Pearson Education Asia Pte Ltd.
Printed in Singapore

Contents

Editors' Preface	vii
Series List	viii
Acknowledgements	xi
Publisher Acknowledgements	xii
Introduction	1

Part One
PATRONAGES AND THE DEVELOPMENT OF EAST AND
WEST AFRICAN ENGLISH WRITING — 5

1 Eighteenth- and Nineteenth-Century Slave Narratives of the Black Diaspora — 7

2 Nineteenth- and Early Twentieth-Century Histories, Travel Accounts, Political Writing and the Beginnings of Fiction — 25

3 Nineteenth- and Twentieth-Century Missionary Writing-Testaments and Writing by Africans Produced under Missionary Auspices and Control — 50

4 Twentieth-Century Secular Patronage: Literature, Education, Control — 71

5 Self-Help: Indigenous Traditions, Popular Literatures and Twentieth-Century Local Patronages — 91

Part Two
DOMINANT THEMES AND PATTERNS IN EAST AND
WEST AFRICAN ENGLISH WRITING — 107

6 Alternatives: Contrasting Themes and Patterns in Post-Independence African English Writing — 109

7 Self-Criticism and Post-Independence Disillusion — 143

8 Opposition, Resistance and Decolonisation — 172

9 Internal Discord — 225

Part Three
ALTERNATIVE VOICES IN EAST AND WEST AFRICAN
ENGLISH WRITING — 245

10 Minority Voices: English Writing in Non-Anglophone East and West African Countries — 247

11 Women's Voices: Gendered Pasts, Liberated Futures   281

12 New Transcultural Voices in East and West African Writing   308

Part Four
FURTHER REFERENCES   337

Chronology of Literary and Historical/Cultural Events   339

General Bibliography   351

Individual Authors: Notes on Biography, Important Works
and Criticism   362

Index   399

Editors' Preface

The multi-volume Longman Literature in English Series provides students of literature with a critical introduction to the major genres in their historical and cultural context. Each volume gives a coherent account of a clearly defined area, and the series, when complete, will offer a practical and comprehensive guide to literature written in English from Anglo-Saxon times to the present. The aim of the series as a whole is to show that the most valuable and stimulating approach to the study of literature is that based upon awareness of the relations between literary forms and their historical contexts. Thus the areas covered by most of the separate volumes are defined by period and genre. Each volume offers new and informed ways of reading literary works, and provides guidance for further reading in an extensive reference section.

In recent years, the nature of English studies has been questioned in a number of increasingly radical ways. The very terms employed to define a series of this kind – period, genre, history, context, canon – have become the focus of extensive critical debate, which has necessarily influenced in varying degrees the successive volumes published since 1985. But however fierce the debate, it rages around the traditional terms and concepts.

As well as studies on all periods of English and American literature, the series includes books on criticism and literary theory and on the intellectual and cultural context. A comprehensive series of this kind must of course include other literatures written in English, and therefore a group of volumes deals with Irish and Scottish literature, and the literatures of India, Africa, the Caribbean, Australia and Canada. The forty-seven volumes of the series cover the following areas: Pre-Renaissance English Literature, English Poetry, English Drama, English Fiction, English Prose, Criticism and Literary Theory, Intellectual and Cultural Context, American Literature, Other Literatures in English.

David Carroll
Michael Wheeler
Chris Walsh

Longman Literature in English Series

General Editors:
David Carroll, University of Lancaster
Michael Wheeler, University of Southampton
Chris Walsh, Chester College of Higher Education

Pre-Renaissance English Literature
* English Literature before Chaucer *Michael Swanton*
  English Literature in the Age of Chaucer
* English Medieval Romance *W. R. J. Barron*

English Poetry
* English Poetry of the Sixteenth Century *Gary Waller (Second Edition)*
* English Poetry of the Seventeenth Century *George Parfitt (Second Edition)*
  English Poetry of the Eighteenth Century, 1700–1789
* English Poetry of the Romantic Period, 1789–1830
  J. R. Watson (Second Edition)
* English Poetry of the Victorian Period, 1830–1890 *Bernard Richards*
  English Poetry of the Early Modern Period, 1890–1940
* English Poetry since 1940 *Neil Corcoran*

English Drama
* English Drama before Shakespeare *Peter Happé*
* English Drama: Shakespeare to the Restoration, 1590–1660
  Alexander Leggatt
* English Drama: Restoration and Eighteenth Century, 1660–1789
  Richard W. Bevis
  English Drama: Romantic and Victorian, 1789–1890
* English Drama of the Early Modern Period, 1890–1940 *Jean Chothia*
  English Drama since 1940

English Fiction
* English Fiction of the Eighteenth Century, 1700–1789 *Clive T. Probyn*
* English Fiction of the Romantic Period, 1789–1830 *Gary Kelly*
* English Fiction of the Victorian Period, 1830–1890
  Michael Wheeler (Second Edition)

* *Already published*

* English Fiction of the Early Modern Period, 1890–1940 *Douglas Hewitt*
English Fiction since 1940

English Prose

* English Prose of the Seventeenth Century, 1590–1700 *Roger Pooley*
English Prose of the Eighteenth Century
* English Prose of the Nineteenth Century *Hilary Fraser with Daniel Brown*

Criticism and Literary Theory

Criticism and Literary Theory from Sidney to Johnson
Criticism and Literary Theory from Wordsworth to Arnold
* Criticism and Literary Theory, 1890 to the Present *Chris Baldick*

The Intellectual and Cultural Context

The Sixteenth Century
* The Seventeenth Century, 1603–1700 *Graham Parry*
* The Eighteenth Century, 1700–1789 *James Sambrook (Second Edition)*
* The Romantic Period, 1789–1830
* The Victorian Period, 1830–1890 *Robin Gilmour*
The Twentieth Century: 1890 to the Present

American Literature

American Literature before 1880
* American Poetry of the Twentieth Century *Richard Gray*
* American Drama of the Twentieth Century *Gerald M. Berkowitz*
* American Fiction, 1865–1940 *Brian Lee*
* American Fiction since 1940 *Tony Hilfer*
* Twentieth-Century America *Douglas Tallack*

Other Literatures

Irish Literature since 1800
* Scottish Literature since 1707 *Marshall Walker*
Australian Literature
* Indian Literature in English *William Walsh*
* African Literatures in English: East and West *Gareth Griffiths*
* Southern African Literatures *Michael Chapman*
* Caribbean Literature in English *Louis James*
* Canadian Literature in English *W. J. Keith*

* *Already published*

Map of Africa

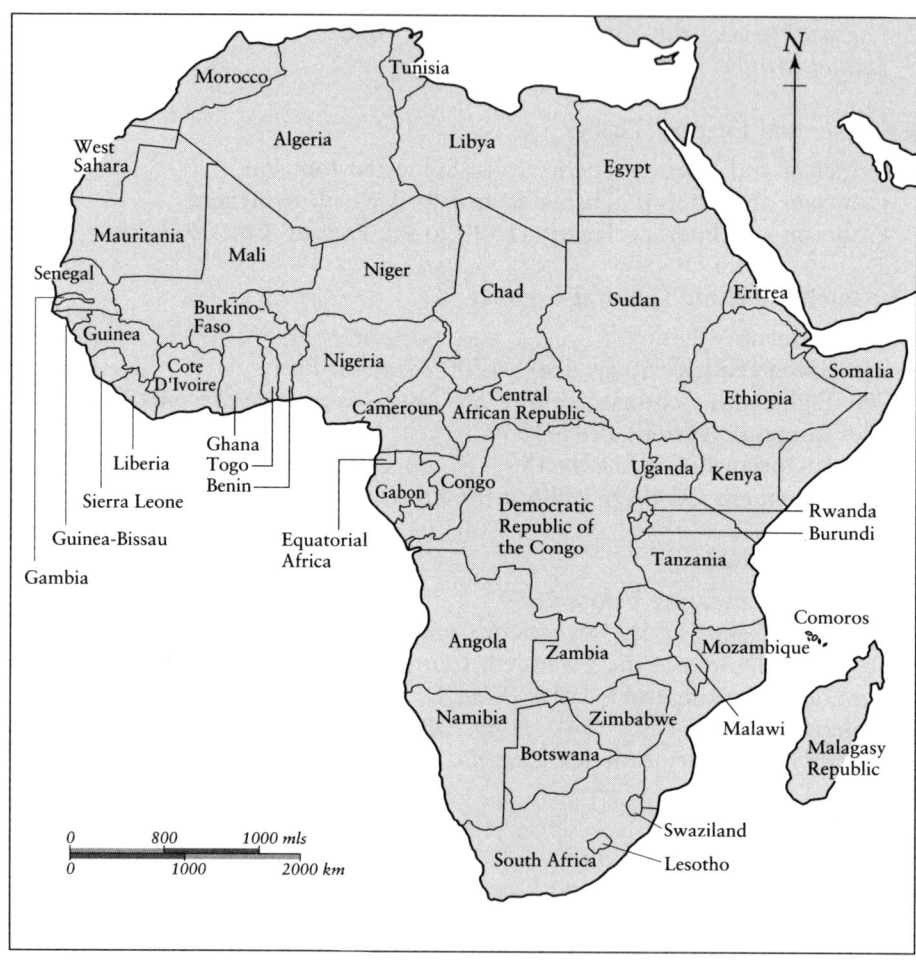

Acknowledgements

I am grateful to David Carroll for persuading me to undertake this task, though there have been many moments when I regretted saying yes. I very much regret that illness prevented this pioneer of the field from participating in the final editorial process, and so deprived me of his great expertise and knowledge of African literatures. Thanks, too, to Michael Wheeler for taking up the task at short notice, though it is far outside his own area of expertise.

I have been indebted to many people for answering queries and offering other help in completing this book. I particularly want to thank the library staff at the Reid Library, University of Western Australia, Perth, especially Peter Limb, who has an inexhaustible passion for all things African, and who helped locate a number of crucial texts; the Melville J. Herskovits Africana Library, Northwestern University, especially my good friend Metta Shayne, who for a Francophone bibliographer is remarkably charitable and helpful to we Anglophonic researchers; and the staff of SOAS Library, University of London, for their unfailing friendliness and courtesy.

Special thanks to Bernth M. Lindfors, who read the final draft, and thus saved me from many factual errors. He bears no responsibility for those which remain. Thanks also to Tony da Silva for his invaluable assistance in the final stages of manuscript preparation.

Once again, this book is dedicated to my loving family, Carolyn, Michael and Aneurin, with all my gratitude for their tolerance and support.

Publisher Acknowledgements

We are grateful to the following for permission to reproduce copyright material:

The author, Kofi Awoonor for 'A Dirge', extracts from 'Songs of Sorrow' and a poem about 'Allotey . . .' from *The House By The Sea* (1978); East African Educational Publishers for poetry extracts from *Song Of Lawino* by Okot p'Bitek; Heinemann Educational Publishers, a division of Reed Educational & Professional Publishing Ltd for extracts from *Efuru* (1996) by Flora Nwapa, for poems 'Heaven's Gate' and 'Whatever happened to the Elephant' by Christopher Okigbo from *Labyrinths With Path Of Thunder* (1971) and for extracts from *Petals Of Blood* (1977) by Ngũgĩ wa Thiong'o; the author, David Maillu for an extract from his verse novel 'After 4.30'; Pearson Education for the lyric 'The Stage' from *Cascades* by Jared Angira published by Longman Group Ltd 1979 and for extracts from *The Poet Lied* by Odia Ofeimun published by Longman 1980; Saros International Publishers for poem by Ken Saro-Wiwa from *Songs In The Time Of War* (1985) and Zimbabwe Publishing House for poems from *The Cows Of Shambat* by Taban lo Liyong.

We have been unable to trace the copyright holders of *Uganda Crisis* by Akena Adoko; *Juices* and *Silent Voices* by Jared Angira; and *A Harvest Of Our Dreams* by Kofi Anyidoho; *Concerto For An Exile* by Syl Cheney-Coker; *I Wan Bi President* by Ezenwa-Ohaeto; the poem 'Witch' by Joe de Graft from *Beneath The Jazz And Brass*; *Sufferhead* by Aig-Imoukhuude; *Hand On The Navel* and *Highlife For Caliban* (1995) by Lemuel Johnson; the poem 'The Drummer in his Times' by A. Kayper-Mensah; *Franz Fanon's Uneven Ribs* by Taban lo Liyong; *A Handle For The Flautist* by Odia Ofeimun; *Labyrinths Of The Delta* (1986) by Tanure Ojaide; 'Poetry Is' by Niyi Osundare, and would appreciate any information which would enable us to do so.

Introduction

African writing in English began in the eighteenth century and was well established by the second half of the nineteenth century. Fictional works were in existence from the 1890s onwards. It would be impossible to attempt an overview of such a long period of writing, from such a diverse body of countries and cultures, without drastically and arbitrarily limiting both the kinds of texts examined and the methodology by which they are selected and discussed. Many and various, external patronages acted to develop African writing in English throughout its different historical phases. It is, of course, obvious that at no time did these patronages constitute the only forces influencing the development of African writing. From the earliest period African intellectuals also created their own patronage structures and means of publication, as the history of local publishing shows. Africans owned and ran newspapers and printing houses during the nineteenth and early twentieth centuries in Sierra Leone, Ghana and Nigeria. This has continued into the present day, with newspapers still acting as a conduit for publication of literature and literary criticism. Local publications sponsored by universities such as student magazines offered a training ground for younger writers, and Africa has always been and continues to be the home of numbers of vital 'little magazines' which have nurtured local writing. Local pamphlet and book publishing from the Onitsha Market Literature phenomenon in the 1940s to the recent upsurge of popular publishing in East and West Africa has had a strong influence in modern times too. Nevertheless, any account of African literatures in English must deal with the powerful, external patronage structures which acted on the majority of the texts produced in English in Africa. The history of these texts is, in a number of significant and neglected ways, the history of the struggle of Africans to wrest the colonial language of English to their own ends, and to do so within institutions and practices which often sought to determine how and what Africans could or should write. As such, the struggle for the expression of African voices within these constraints is a powerful part of the story of the African struggle for self-determination and for self-identity – a struggle which took place in the face of such powerful determining forces as slavery, colonisation and ongoing neo-colonial control. This is the emphasis of Part One of this book.

Part Two seeks to group texts around some of the dominant themes which have been identified in African English writing. Of course such groupings are also necessarily arbitrary and disputable, and they are also extremely slippery, with texts frequently being eligible for discussion under various themes and through various contrasting lenses.

Part Three acknowledges this in developing accounts of various 'voices' which demand to be heard outside the generalising context of thematic criticism.

These include the writers of the various countries where English has been practiced as a minority language for writing, and also women writers who have been neglected in many earlier accounts. The decision to place these women's voices in a separate section is not an easy one, since it could be read as an attempt to ghettoise this writing. For this reason I have also made extensive reference to women writers in the thematic sections. Nevertheless, there is an increasing awareness that women African writers have produced a powerful body of work which has a distinctive history and tradition. In this section I also address the growing number of writers who by origin, by theme, or by their publishing patterns emphasise the increasing internationalisation of African English texts in recent years. That these come at the end of the text does not imply that this is a fitting or proper culmination, nor does it imply that their work is to be preferred over writers with other concerns, although these texts may serve to remind us of the increasing difficulty of constructing accounts of writing on a simple cultural or even geographical basis in an increasingly globalised world. Whether we find this a good or a bad thing is, of course, a separate issue. That these writers are now in the forefront of those to whom an international audience pays attention, however, has considerable consequences for the future of English writing in Africa. It is also significant that they may not be at the forefront of those writers in English being read by many people in Africa itself, as the growth in local popular texts in the same period shows.

The fact that this volume is located in a series entitled Longman Literature in English defines both what it sets out to do and what it does not attempt. It is not a comprehensive critical introduction to all West and East African literatures. Such an undertaking would be vastly greater in scope, and even if, as in the case of Albert Gérard's pioneering comparative language studies, only secondary sources on many of the languages and literatures involved were used, it would require a breadth of scholarship and reading which would daunt all but the bravest heart. This volume claims no such scope. It does not even purport to be a critical introduction to all colonial language literatures in Africa, since an examination of the range of differences between Anglophone, Francophone and Lusophone writing would be precluded by the more limited aim of this series. This is an introductory history of writing in English in those territories of West and East Africa where English was used at some time during the period from the eighteenth to the twentieth century. It seeks to place these writings in relationship to the development of English as a mode of expression by Africans in the varying social, political and cultural contexts which evolved during that period. To this extent it is as much an attempt at initiating a sociology of the text written in English in Africa as a literary history in the traditional sense. To this extent also it inevitably concentrates mainly on the interrelationship between the European forms, structures and poetics imported along with the notion of a literature in English, and less on the equally important effect of the many and diverse local oral traditions, although in places I have sought to acknowledge the interactive use of the practices of writing and printing introduced by the Europeans with local languages to produce indigenous writing from the mid-nineteenth century onwards in many African languages. Occasionally texts and writers in these languages are featured, especially where they have had an obvious and ongoing influence on the practice of African writing in English.

The methodological limitations are those of any broad, comparative study. The project of reading individual texts and traditions within the frame of specific 'local knowledges' is important, but it is clearly the task of those who can bring that local knowledge to bear. No single writer, African or non-African, can hope to have that kind of local expertise across the whole range of African writing, not even restricting this to the effect on writing in English in Africa. The answer might be not to seek to produce any general accounts at all at this time. It would certainly be the prudent answer. But prudence is a niggardly virtue, and, as I have argued above, the continuation of a partial and proximate attempt at constructing not an authoritative or exhaustive history but a limited, partial and corrigible comparative account may help us at this stage of the unfinished larger task to understand a little better one set of the many forces which acted on these texts to make them what they are. It is to this limited but I hope still useful end that this volume is directed. It is for others to correct, extend and complete its inevitable absences, inadequacies and silences.

Part One

PATRONAGES AND THE DEVELOPMENT OF EAST AND WEST AFRICAN ENGLISH WRITING

Chapter 1

Eighteenth- and Nineteenth-Century Slave Narratives of the Black Diaspora

The earliest forms of writing in English by black Africans were the narratives of the slaves captured and transported by the European slave-traders who thronged to the West African coast in the eighteenth and early nineteenth centuries. The masters of these slaves were only rarely concerned with the welfare of their charges, and in the plantation context of much slavery during the period the relationship of slave and master involved only the most limited association and the most cursory of language exchanges. Nevertheless such exchanges formed the basis for a powerful subversive language known as 'massa talk'. This referred to the way the black slaves hid a rebellious meaning beneath a deliberately obsequious and naive response to their 'massa'. Whilst it would certainly be more than ironic to see these brutal exploiters as cultural patrons, it might at least be said that they provided the first forced contacts between enslaved Africans and the language of their new masters in the slave plantations.

But not all Africans sold as slaves ended up as plantation hands. Many slaves in the eighteenth century, in particular those who were sold to owners in Europe, or who ended up in the northern states of the USA, occupied a role which was as much decorative as functional. In such an environment their symbolic purpose was dominant. As David Dabydeen has argued, the African slave's social role in eighteenth-century Britain was not unlike that of the domestic dwarf or jester of earlier periods. They offset the condition of the dominant master, and emphasised his or her privileged being. In portraits of the time black slaves often shared the same role and the same iconography as domestic pets such as dogs and parrots.[1] In this context the ability of these slaves to engage in such 'human' activities as speech, writing, music-making and other artistic forms functioned parodically. These transplanted and dis-located human beings, deprived of their indigenous cultural contexts, their language and even their names, were reconstituted as figures occupying a profoundly ambiguous expressive space. The ability of privileged, domestic slaves to speak and write English was seen as a charming diversion, and so tolerated. But slave-owners who used slaves as work objects and chattels per-ceived their ability to speak, let alone write, English as a threat to be discour-aged. One of the most significant of such early African slave narratives, that of Olaudah Equiano, records how on the occasion of his sale by the 'liberal' Captain Pascal, who had taught him to speak and write English, his new owner's reaction to Equiano's vocal assertion of his rights was to tell him that he 'talked too much English'. It is significant too that the liberal Pascal had no qualms in selling Equiano to the far less liberal Captain Doran.

Until the mid-eighteenth century, before the institution of slavery was widely or seriously questioned, the interest in African narratives was often a consequence of the wider Enlightenment interest in the *beau sauvage*. It was the product of the success of earlier representations of the noble savage, such as Mrs Aphra Behn's novel *Oroonoka* (1688). By the mid-eighteenth century this interest had led to a flourishing genre in both England and on the Continent of what the French termed *romans africains*.

The development of a strong emancipationist movement in the late eighteenth and early nineteenth centuries gave a fresh and different impetus to the production of such narratives. Slaves, some of whom had succeeded in obtaining their freedom by purchase, or as a gesture of liberality on the part of emancipationist owners, were frequently engaged by the anti-slavery movement to produce accounts of their travail and suffering. Some of these accounts, for example those of Briton Hammon (1760), James Gronniosaw (*c.* 1770), or Venture Smith (1798), are ghosted accounts, versions of their lives 'as told to' a literate European writer. The role of the amanuensis in such accounts, and the degree to which they intervened in the construction of the text, makes the authenticity of these texts rather questionable.[2] Such was the demand for such narratives in the period, however, that, as Philip D. Curtin has noted:

> The nature of European curiosity has itself given a peculiar bias to the body of surviving narratives. In the eighteenth century, the romantic view of the noble savage aroused the European interest in Africans – if they were thought to have had high status in their own societies. Later, in the nineteenth century, the romantic interest in Africa was replaced by the humanitarian concern of the anti-slave movement. Both motives, however, prompted Europeans not only to record slave narratives, but also to manufacture them out of whole cloth. In all, European writers probably have set down more fictitious accounts of Africans in the slave trade than the whole body of genuine narratives.[3]

It is against this background that we need to consider the genuine narratives by slaves who wrote in the tongue of their new masters and mistresses. These texts are a witness to the diligence, strength of character and skill of their authors, and also to their ability to negotiate the requirements of their patrons and their audience. This negotiation with the power of existing patronage structures led to the complex rhetoric of such early writing as the letters of Philip Quaque (*c.* 1750–1816), the *belles-lettres* of Ignatius Sancho (1782), and the poetry and letters of the freed slave Phillis Wheatley (1793).[4] The degree to which the patronage of their liberal masters exercised a controlling influence, directly or indirectly, over the content and form of these early slave narratives varies from text to text.

The Letters of Ignatius Sancho (1782), for example, contain little internal evidence of a tension between his identity as an African and the requirements of the eighteenth-century *belles-lettres* tradition into which he fitted with seeming ease. Many eighteenth-century slaves had left Africa at so young an age as to be effectively European in their culture. Ignatius Sancho, for example, was brought to England from the West Indies as a child, and his culture was, as a result, 'completely Western'.[5] Sancho's prose is a direct imitation of the eighteenth-century style and themes he had been taught to admire and reproduce. It contains no internal evidence that it was written by an African, nor does he show any concern with recording his experiences as a transported slave.

The Poetry and Prose of Phillis Wheatley (1773), on the other hand, poses a more complex case. Like Sancho she was born in Africa in or about 1753, and arrived in America as a child of about seven years old in 1761. Unlike him she appears to have retained a conscious memory of her place of origin, though she refers to it only infrequently in her poetry:

> I, young in life, by seeming cruel fate
> Was snatch'd from Afric's fancy'd happy seat:
> What pangs excruciating must molest,
> What sorrows labour in my parent's breast?
> Steel'd was that soul and by no misery mov'd
> That from a father seiz'd his babe belov'd:
> Such, such my case. And can I then but pray
> Others may never feel tyrannic sway.[6]

Despite the kind of passage quoted above, earlier critics, operating with the purity of criteria which perhaps only hindsight can provide, have seen her work as lacking sympathy with her people's struggle for freedom. It has also been criticised for being over-dependent in style and subject matter on conventional eighteenth-century American and English literary texts. However, modern editors have argued that she retains, through her imagery, links with the religious and cultural practices of her African origins and that her poetry contains powerful images of freedom.[7]

More convincing is the argument that Wheatley's conscious choice of the elegiac form and the strong emphasis in her poetry on the pleasures of the after-life are a poetic means of 'escaping an unsatisfactory, temporal world', in line with the long religious tradition of black American writing and of the Negro spiritual.[8] The Christian elegy, with its conventional themes of the after-life as a freedom attained by the Christian soul after earthly suffering, offers the chance for an imagery of spiritual freedom, earthly enslavement, and metaphorical chains and fetters which incorporates the deeper longings of the young African poetess:

> He sought the paths of piety and truth,
> By these made happy from his early youth!
> In blooming years that grace divine he felt,
> Which rescues sinners from the chains of guilt. (231)

No doubt the expectations of the liberal slave-owners, among whom she lived and died, prevented any more explicit exploration of these themes. The texts produced under such controlling patronages frequently contain a potential for subversive themes which cannot fully be realised, and the temporary privilege which literature affords such figures is frequently a fleeting one, as it was for Wheatley, who died in poverty and neglect, despite the international acclaim which had followed the publication of her *Poems on Various Subjects: Religious and Moral* in London in 1773.

The authorship and authenticity of Ottobah Cuguano's *Thoughts and Sentiments on the Evil and Wicked Traffic of Slavery* (1787) has been the subject of considerable controversy since it is written in two quite obviously distinctive styles. It has been suggested that only the sections which recount the capture of the young Cuguano were written by him. It has also been suggested that Olaudah Equiano, a close friend of Cuguano, read the text very closely, and may have had a hand in re-writing parts of it. The most likely case is that Cuguano wrote the whole account, and that, like Sancho, when he writes in 'high style', to present his historical and theological case against slavery, he is simply demonstrating his mastery of the appropriate style for such a subject within eighteenth-century conventions of decorum.[9] There is little doubt, though, that it is the more personal sections that a modern reader finds most attractive and informative:

> I was early snatched away from my native country, with about eighteen or twenty more boys and girls, as we were playing in a field. We lived but a few days journey from the coast where we were kidnapped, and as we were decoyed and drove along, we were soon conducted to a factory, and from thence, in the fashionable way of traffic, consigned to Grenada.[10]

He also provides a number of accounts of life in the village from which he had been snatched. The details he gives suggest that he was older than some of the other slaves, and able to recall his early experiences in ways which they do not. For this reason it is to be greatly regretted that the bulk of his work is a long treatise against slavery, and that even the short accounts he offers of his life before capture are prefaced by an apology: 'perhaps it may not be amiss to give a few remarks, as some account of myself, in this transposition of captivity' (48). The primary concern of his anti-slavery patrons was, of course, with his arguments against emancipation. However conventional these were, the very fact that they had been written by an African was itself a proof of the wrongness of the treatment of slaves as not human. Understandable as this is, it is still a matter of regret that the patronage systems which encouraged and published such accounts were not more interested in the recording of the details of African life for their own sake. It is yet another example of the ways in which the goals of patronage shaped and dictated the contents of so much African English writing. What account we do have is both interesting and precise.

> I was born in the city of Agimaque, on the coast of Fantyn; my father was a companion to the chief in that part of the country of Fantee, and when the old king died I was left in his house with his family; soon after I was sent for by his nephew, Ambro Accasa, who succeeded the old king in the chiefdom of that part of Fantee known by the name of Agimaque and Affinee. I lived with his children, enjoying peace and tranquillity, about twenty moons, which, according to their way of reckoning time, is two years. (48)

10

There follows a description of how Cuguano is invited to live with his uncle for a while, and how a group of young men taunt him to accompany them on a trip 'into the woods to gather fruit and catch birds, and such amusements as pleased us' (48). Accosted by Africans searching for strays to sell as slaves, they are captured and taken to another village. After a scene in which it is suggested that he may be sent back to his uncle after the rest of the captives have already gone (presumably sent to the coast), he is sent after them and is sold to the white slavers. The treatment he receives then is recorded in graphic detail:

> After I was ordered out the horrors I soon saw and felt, cannot be well described; I saw many of my miserable countrymen chained two and two, hand-cuffed and some with their hands tied behind. We were conducted along by a guard, and when we arrived at the castle, I asked my guide what I was brought there for, he told me to learn the ways of the *browsow*, that is the white-faced people . . . and then he told me that he must now leave me there, and went off. This made me cry bitterly, but I was soon conducted to a prison, for three days, where I heard the groans and cries of many, and saw some of my fellow captives . . . From the time that I was kid-napped and conducted to a factory, and thence in the brutish, base but fashionable way of traffic, consigned to Grenada, the grievous thoughts which I then felt, still pant in my heart; though my fears and tears have long since subsided. And yet it is still grievous to think that thousands more have suffered in similar and greater distress under the hands of barbarous robbers, and merciless task-masters; and that many even now are suffering in all the extreme bitterness of grief and woe, that no language can describe. (50–1)

Such accounts had considerable force and circulation in the period, designed as they were to drive home the horrors of the slave trade and to help the emancipationist cause. This external project accounts for the much larger part of the work which details and refutes the justifications offered for the slave trade in scriptural authority and in economic and other arguments. Cuguano's text is, in large part, a tract outlining the false evidence of these arguments. It shows its author had a firm grasp of contemporary theological and scriptural scholarship and knew the economic arguments advanced by theorists such as Adam Smith against slavery-based societies. Although the text in these parts reads very ponderously, and without the easy and detailed flow of the accounts of the slavers and his capture, there seems to be no substantive evidence to doubt that Cuguano also wrote these passages. A typical example is the argument Cuguano advances against those who see the darkness of Africans as a sign that they are descendants of those cast out by God, the sons of Ham. His rebuttal of this frequently asserted argument shows that he is aware of the details of the story of Ham's sin in gazing on his father's nakedness. He is aware too that the Bible does not assert that Ham's descendants are punishable for this, except in so far as his descendants, the Canaanites, 'became an exceedingly wicked people, and were visited with many calamities' (64). In fact he turns the tables on those who associate the descendants of Ham with black men by giving his audience a little history lesson:

The Hebrews, chiefly under Moses, Joshua and Barak, as they were directed by God, cut off most of the other Canaanitish kingdoms, and reduced many of them to subjection and vassalage . . . Many of the Canaanites who fled away at the time of Joshua, became mingled with the different nations, and some historians think that some of them came to England, and settled about Cornwall, as far back as that time; so that, for any thing that can be known to the contrary, there may be some of the descendants of that wicked generation still subsisting among the slave-holders in the West Indies. For if the curse of God ever rested upon them, or upon any other men, the only visible mark thereof was always upon those who committed the most outrageous acts of violence and oppression. But colour and complexion has nothing to do with that mark; every wicked man, and the enslavers of others, bear the stamp of their own iniquity, and that mark which was set upon Cain. (64)

Cuguano was freed, though the account gives no details of this, and by the 1780s he was active in London assisting other blacks. Like his friend Equiano, he was involved in Granville Sharpe's scheme to set up a colony for freed slaves in Sierra Leone. The letters written between Cuguano and Equiano show that, even at this early date, Africans had begun to form intellectual and political associations as writing in English gave them a tool for expression and self-assertion.

Despite the limitations placed on their work, many of these diasporic intellectuals of slavery succeed in presenting a powerful and critical picture of the world of the African enslaved, the African 'freed' by manumission, and also, in some cases, the existence of an independent African world outside the knowledge of the European society to which the narratives were addressed. A number of slave narratives include a reference to the African world they knew before their enslavement, representing the only contemporary written accounts by Africans of their own world before European invasion. These include the greatest of the eighteenth-century slave narratives, *The Life of Olaudah Equiano* (1789), which was produced by the Ibo slave Olaudah Equiano, writing under the denigratory soubriquet of 'Gustavus Vassa, the African'. This followed the general practice of giving slaves inflated names, often from great historical or classical figures, as a parodic and ultimately denigratory practice, creating signifying monkeys with a vengeance. Significantly Equiano retained the name Gustavus Vassa to the end of his life, and it appears on the title-page, though equally significantly so does his original Ibo name, Olaudah Equiano.

Olaudah Equiano's *Life* has achieved a deserved pre-eminence in most literary discussions of slave narratives. Equiano, like Cuguano, retained an awareness of the African world from which his enslavement had rudely ripped him. Nevertheless, as with all narratives, we need to be cautious in claiming an authentic or inside vision for these accounts. Many such narratives are, as Curtin reminds us, 'recollections of the distant past'. Many were subject, as we have already noted, to the process of transmission by an amanuensis or editor, whose mark cannot now be effectively discerned or eradicated from our reading of them. Finally, as Curtin notes, even

the Westernised narrators who wrote in English were writing for a European audience, and they took that audience into account in deciding what to tell and what to omit. Thus not only Equiano, but even Crowther and Wright were subject to a kind of self-imposed censorship as they sought to explain themselves and their past to aliens of limited background.[11]

Despite this limitation, by the 1780s writers like Cuguano and Equiano were achieving a degree of direct and free expression, appropriating the patronage structures to their own aims and projects. Unlike Cuguano, whose story remains largely within the genre of an anti-slavery tract, Equiano's narrative appropriated a far more potentially powerful form, the autobiography. This provided the European reader with a generic frame which much more profoundly subverted the common current perception of the African slave as sub-human. The autobiographical form is rooted in the central European social construction, that of the dominance of the individual sensibility, a construction central to post-Renaissance Europe's own self-determination and identity. The identification of an African subject with this frame, implicit in making the African a subject of autobiography, challenged the reader to recognise a kinship even as significant cultural and social difference was dramatised in the stories' detail. Equiano's tale claimed a space in which Africans could begin to describe themselves, using the language of their expropriators as a tool of self-expression and self-assertion. Through the story of his life before, during and after capture, Equiano could lay bare the stages by which European constructions of the African remodelled the African into the reductive mimic man of the slave economy. The considerable literary achievement of Equiano is in appropriating the European genre to this wider and more socially representative purpose.

Equiano's *Life* presented European readers with the first account of society from an African perspective. As well as the more obvious purpose of exposing the inhumanity of the barbarities which accompanied the forcible transportation of so many million Africans, the most interesting section of the narrative was Equiano's representation of his relations with those Europeans with whom he formed a social, if not always an equal, relationship after his admission to the emancipationist circles of eighteenth-century England.

It was also important as a model for later writers. The autobiography, as a form, continued for a long time to provide non-European writers with a tool for appropriating the literary text to the task of recording the moving and personal evidence of the barbaric treatment of Africans and African-Americans. In the process they also appropriated its inherent claim to a fully human subjectivity, framed in the invisible ideologies of individualism and sensibility, to the task of recording their own cultural and social difference. Thus, not only in later diasporic narratives, such as those of Frederick Douglass, Booker T. Washington, W. E. B. Du Bois, Marcus Garvey and the writing of many contemporary African-Americans, from James Baldwin to Mohammed Ali, but also in innumerable examples from contemporary Africa, the autobiography has provided a narrative frame into which many alternative stories could be placed.

Of course, the appropriation of the genre carried dangers too. Frederick Douglass wrote no fewer than three autobiographies, each of which, at different stages of his life, recounts the experience of slavery and the subsequent result of his 'freedom from bondage'. Interestingly, in the last of these, *My Bondage and My Freedom*, written in 1855, he records his disillusionment with the reception and effect of such 'narratives'. He objects to their popularity with an audience of liberals merely seeking a frisson of identification with the oppressed, and also records how the existence and popularity of freedom narratives in the American North did not mean that the North ceased to act repressively towards freed Negroes.[12]

The nature of autobiographical writing also tended to elide the personal and the social, making the recording of personal experience too easily, and sometimes too glibly, able to claim a representative status for total communities, erasing the many differences within such communities. This was a danger also frequently associated later with much anthropological ethnographic writing, both because autobiography provided a model for the recording of such experience and, more insidiously, because the classic anthropological author often engaged in a process of displacement in which his/her people substituted as a form of self-narrative. Nevertheless the 'life' was the principal form by which early Africans, subjected to slavery and transportation, forced their voice into the written text, and it continued to be a significant feature of diasporic African writing in English as well as of the early writing in English to emerge from Africa itself.

Since Equiano's account has received more critical attention than the other examples I have quoted, as well as being readily available for perusal in a number of widely circulated and easily accessible editions, I have not quoted from it extensively. Suffice it to say that it has even more details than earlier work by ex-slaves like Cuguano, and that it gives an extended account of Equiano's capture and of his life in the plantations. It also describes his life as a sailor after he is purchased by a sea-captain, a circumstance which afforded him much more freedom than he would have received in other forms of slavery. The text also describes how he saves for and eventually purchases his freedom; the struggle to maintain that freedom against the multiplicity of conflicting laws which could so easily drag a freed man back to slavery, especially in America, which still had no anti-slave-owning laws; and, in the final sections, the details of his involvement in the various schemes to provide for the liberated slaves in England and elsewhere. It is recommended that anyone wanting to read an account of an eighteenth-century African speaking with a considerable degree of self-assertion, despite the inevitable constraints imposed by the dominant forms and patronage available to him in the period, should read Equiano's *Life*. In addition to its forcefulness, the *Life* shows how, at their best, such early texts are not only valuable as historical documents, but also possess a liveliness of style and a wealth of subtle observation which raise them to the status of literature.

The Letters of Philip Quaque (*c.* 1750–1816), despite their early date, more properly belong in the later chapter dealing with missionary writing, because he was never a transported slave. The dates of his work, however, and the style of his prose, associate him with these early figures of the slave diaspora.

His work also forms a significant link to the work of the nineteenth-century secular and mission writers dealt with in the two following chapters. His letters, sent home to the London-based Society for Promoting Christian Knowledge (SPCK), are precursors of the reports and investigations undertaken on behalf of similar missionary societies by later nineteenth-century African writers such as Samuel Ajayi Crowther. As the son of a powerful local chief and trader, Quaque was a privileged protégé of the missionaries, sent by them to be educated in England. On his return, with an English wife (who quickly succumbed to the climate and died), he assumed what was to be a lifelong position as a chaplain to the English settlement at Cape Coast. Since this was at the time when slavery was still in force, his comments are of unique significance as those of an African caught between two conflicting cultural imperatives. He represents the complex and ambiguous position which European education forced onto this first generation of English-speaking African intellectuals.

The letters demonstrate the fact that Quaque was trapped between two worlds. He had lost his fluency in his own language as the result of his removal to England at a young age, being forced to rely on others to make clear what he tried to teach:

> I went to them again in the evening about four o'clock, where I gave a specimen of what was intended more fully when Mr. Frederick Adoy comes from his kroom [village], the person who assisted Mr. Thompson in his employment. I imitated [*sic*] to explain the necessity and reasonableness of baptism in my own lingo, as well as I was able, to about 25 of them in number and told them that what they have now imperfectly heard from me will be, I hope, more perfectly or clearly laid open to them at his return.[13]

The sad alienation of Quaque is fully encompassed in that phrase 'my own lingo', where Quaque is forced to acknowledge the language as his own and yet to denigrate it in the terms used ('lingo') by the white traders and missionaries to whose discourse he is now in thrall.

His descriptive writings on the social customs and habits of the people around the Cape Coast Castle settlement provide further evidence of the degree to which Quaque's perceptions of the society from which he had been removed at an early age were formed by this alien discourse. They are constructed from the viewpoint of an outsider. If we were not aware that the author was African they could pass for reports from any of his white colleagues:

> The funeral ceremony of the late Cudjo Caboceer, whose death I mentioned in my last account, was pompously exhibited on the 20th day of October last after the blacks' usual custom or manner of burying their deceased . . . The computation of the number of souls that came to perpetuate the memory of their deceased monarch might be upwards of a million. But the manner in which they make their public entrance on these occasions deserves a place in this cursory description, as it is not only laughable but curious withal, in which drama you will find the generality of them equipped with their warlike apparel. Some are covered with a cap of a tiger's skin, others again with deer's, a third the skin of monkeys . . . They likewise paint

themselves, both men and women, some with white chalk, others yellow earth . . . But the most detestable scene in all their actions is the barbarous and inhuman practice of sacrificing innocent lives as attendances to the great folks only in the other world, which diabolical custom and a mistaken vile notion seems to prevail much with them when any of their reputed head[s] dies. (129)

The significance of this account lies partly in the tropes employed, which place Quaque as an outside spectator of a theatre ('public entrance', 'drama', 'scene') in which he can find curiosities and humour. This distancing surveillance of the events described extends to the political claims for its significance: 'On the 15th day of last December the *supposed* heir to the stool *so called* (or in their words, the crown of the late Cudjo Caboceer) was publicly installed by a grand procession' (129–30). Quaque is at pains to insist that the really important recognition is that of the Governor, whose reception of Caboceer's 'oath of allegiance' is the culmination of the ceremonies, and whose nine-gun salute denotes, 'I imagine, the public consent as well as the British Protection and attachment of them' (130). That this is Quaque's interpretation ('I imagine') is significant in so far as Quaque's editor Curtin notes that, at this time (1778), 'it was the British object to limit active protection to the minimum and to steer clear, as far as they could, of direct involvement in African politics' (130). No direct sovereignty was officially claimed, and when Quaque refers to Caboceer as a 'subject of Great Britain', Curtin notes that 'this must be interpreted to mean, rather than political sovereignty, the special type of connection based on trade, not territorial rights, that grew up around a European fort' (130). It might also be interpreted as part of Quaque's desire to assert a link between Britain (his patron) and the indigenous society from which his position alienated him. Yet he remained attached to that indigenous society. Strangely, only by the suppression of the political differences between the two, and a promotion of this unity, could the sense of self-division endemic in the position of figures like Quaque be reconciled, or at least temporarily held in abeyance.

The ideology of this account, which equates the African funereal customs with barbarism and inhumanity, and which offers no ameliorative inside view to understand what motivated such actions within the African belief system, is cognate with the views to be maintained by later missionaries, including the nineteenth-century African re-captive missionaries such as Samuel Crowther, whose writings we will examine in Chapter 3. The stress on human sacrifice as a marker of African barbarity, and as an implicit justification for their suppression and control by the 'civilised' European, is a common one, and akin to the function of cannibalism as a marker of difference in the earlier justifications of the conquest of the Indies.[14] Significantly, though, Quaque, in the same letter, gives indications of how tightly he remains bound to this same society whose practices he declares barbaric. He renews his plea to the Society for additional financial support, a regular feature of the correspondence, based on the ongoing claims which members of his extended family make upon him. At this time, he notes, he is obliged to participate in the family contribution to the funereal ceremonies, as well as to maintain his general support for family members:

The Society may also remember of my hinting to them in my last favour the un-avoidable expense I was likely to be involved in by the death of this great man, which so poor as I am amounts to £127 7s. 6d. I mention this merely to show them the difficulties I frequently labour under through numerous family connections, whose sole dependence rest entirely upon me, exclusive of domestic care, a wife and two children and another shortly expected, by God's blessing. (131)

This brief unvarnished passage is redolent of the divided worlds and cultures between which Quaque was trapped. The language itself is hardly adequate to differentiate for the distant Committee of the SPCK, to whom his plea is addressed, the different social structures ('family connections' / 'domestic care') that Quaque had to reconcile in his daily life.

As the *Letters* also make clear, his white associates could take exception to the contradictions involved in Quaque's own status when they felt provoked or slighted. Thus, as Quaque records, the irascible Richard Brew, with whom he had an exchange of 'trifling words', responded by informing the Governor of the fort at Anomabu 'that he would never come to Cape Coast to be subservient to and sit under the nose of a blackboy to hear him pointing out their faults before them' (121). Brew, an Irish merchant, was a prominent figure in the West African trading community during the second half of the eighteenth century. As Quaque's own letters record, Brew had earlier received Quaque as a guest at his residence in Anomabu, where Quaque 'aboded with him for the space of a week, during which time he behaved in the most polite manner imaginable' (119). Quaque baptised Brew's two mulatto daughters on the same occasion, 'and three others besides, to the universal satisfaction of the whole congregation both black and white then assembled' (119). The tensions beneath the surface of these multi-racial trading communities, in which miscegenation was common, and to which a large number of mulatto children were born, is hardly surprising when one reflects that the specious social structures between black and white they promoted were erected on a founda-tion of trading in African slaves. At this time there would have been no general idea of belonging to a larger pan-African community, and figures like Quaque would not have had a natural sense of kinship with other Africans greater than that they might have forged with the various European trading communities with whom they associated. The later sense of a racial unity based on skin-colour was produced by exactly this kind of generalised slight, to which people like Brew were increasingly subjecting their African associates as slavery gen-erated and institutionalised these racial attitudes. The letters are thus also a fascinating account of the shaping of attitudes and articulations which, viewed with hindsight from the modern period, have too frequently been presented as eternal, natural and fixed rather than as historically specific, socially created and thus politically changeable.

When Quaque sought to revive the educational ventures begun by his pre-decessor, the white chaplain Rev. Thomas Thompson, in the early 1750s, he concentrated on the mulatto children of the traders whom he 'regarded as the more promising material' (118):

17

I was requested by the earnest importunity of Gilbert Petrie, our present Governor, whether I should choose to take the trouble of an arduous task upon me in the education of children . . . I established a seminary, by his order, in my own bed-chamber for the instruction of mulatto children of both sexes, the number of which at present is but ten, who seem to take their learning surprisingly well and some have made a good progress, considering the very short space of time they have been with me. And I do intend shortly, God willing, to take a few of the rougher kind to see what can be really made out of them. (118)

The implications of this passage are interesting. The 'rough' material of the native African can be moulded, perhaps, into something else, that new form which can be 'made of them'. The mulatto child, being already half-moulded thus by nature, is an easier proposition for the desired transformation towards European civilised values and practices. What renders the passage so ironic, and in a sense expressive of the tragic alienation of Quaque from his own self-apprehension, is the fact that he himself was wholly African by birth.

Quaque's letters are usually seen as being of interest primarily as eyewitness accounts of the life of the coastal trading communities of the late eighteenth and early nineteenth centuries. But they are of interest too in the story of the evolution of a local discourse. Expressive as they are of a classic case of Gramscian hegemony, they can be deconstructed to reveal the tensions which the use of the English language, and English cultural expectations, created in this first generation of European-schooled Africans. They were torn between the world from which they came, and to which they still held attachments, and the values of the religion and culture they had embraced. The results of this tension are traceable in the evolution of a local sensibility in the texts in English produced by these hybrid figures, whether they were products of the missionary education system or of the secular colonial institutions.[15] Significantly, as we shall see, for the history of West and East African consciousness, it was from this social group that the early nationalists of the regions were drawn.[16] Quaque stands as an interesting precursor of these figures, writing as he did from *within* the West African world, unlike the majority of the diasporic eighteenth-century Africans using English whom I have considered earlier. But before we move on to examine the later-nineteenth-century and early-twentieth-century writers in English in the region and the texts they produced, I want to glance at one other example of the use of English to produce texts in eighteenth-century West Africa.

It is interesting to compare the accounts of the European-educated slaves of the diaspora with the work of other, less formally educated West Africans, who found a use for the English language through direct contact with the English slavers in this period. *The Diary of Antera Duke* (c. 1785), an eighteenth-century slave-trading chief, is one of the few extant records of this kind.[17] Duke's diary is of interest to literary scholars as an early example of the appropriation and modification of the English language by local speakers and writers. Forde's 1957 edition offers a translation into standard English and then records the original entry as it appears in the diary. A typical original entry runs as follows:

25.1.1785

about 4 am in Eyo Willy Honesty house so wee walk up to see Willy Honesty in yard so his killd 1 Big goat for wee soon after wee walk up to see wee town & Did tak one great guns to putt for canow for two Egbo Young men Bring hom in aqua Landing so wee join to Henshaw Town and com Back ant at 3 clock noon wee Everry Body go com to Deash Eyo Willy Honesty Daught . . . 1496 Rods besides cloth & powder & Iron so wee play all day befor night.

(Translation: 25.1.1785

About 4 a.m. I went to Eyo Willy Honesty's house and we walked up to see Willy Honesty in his yard. So he killed a big goat for us. Soon after we walked up to see our town and took one great gun to put in a canoe for two of Egbo Young's men to bring home to Aqua Landing. So we went together to Henshawe Town and came back; and at 3 o'clock [after]noon we and everybody went to dash Eyo Willy Honesty's daughter . . . 1496 rods besides cloth, gunpowder and iron. So we played all day until night.)

Numbers of slaves, trade goods and items of exchange dominate the entries, since, after all, the primary purpose of this diary was to serve as a sort of *aide mémoire* to a life spent chiefly in trading and exchange. The active, and indeed in many ways reciprocal nature of power in this early period of trade between black Africans and white venturers is captured in the spirited negotiations recorded in the diary. In such exchanges there is no evidence of the barbaric savagery, laziness and ignorance recorded in so many later European accounts of the West African coast. Instead what emerges is a picture of a shrewd, tough, hard-working and early-rising businessman every bit as competent as the Europeans he deals with, if every bit as ruthless, and well able to sustain his end of any social or commercial exchange.

6.3.1785

about 6 am in aqua Landing with fine morning so wee have all Egbo men & Egbo Young go to Henshaw Town for get Egbo moony after 2 clock noon see Duke send his wife for call wee say Captin Loosdam send his mat to till Duk about news ship com so I & Esien go Bord Captin Loosdam to know so wee see news ship mat on bord so wee did ask him way ship be so his say in pointstanbd (?) so wee com ashor and 7 clock night wee have all Egbo men com back the say Henshaw Town putt moony for 19 men Cobhan Town for 5 men one for Guiunea Company Egbo.

7.3.1785

about 6 am in aqua Landing with fine morning so I go down for Landing after 10 clock wee go chop for Egbo Young house Liverpool Hall and after 12 clock Day wee see news ship mat com & com to till his will not com heer Did go Commrown so Duke say berry well may go way plase.

12.3.1785

about 6 am in aqua Landing with great rain morning so I go down for see Duke I & Ewien in his palaver house soon wee have Willy Honesty to meet for Duk with all genllmen for new ship Captin plaver so wee writ to his for com ashor so his say will not com ashor & wee 3 go on bord his for ask him and his answer be say he will not stay for us River soon that wee com ashor and till all genllmen so the say veery well may go way his plase to go.

(Translation: 6.3.1785
About 6 a.m. at Aqua Landing with a fine morning, so we make all the Ekpe men and Egbo Young go to Henshawe Town to get Ekpe money. At two o'clock after-noon Duke sends his wife to call us. She says that Captain Loosdam has sent his mate to find out. So we see the new ship's mate on board and we ask him where the ship is. He says in Parrot Island so we come ashore and at 7 o'clock at night all the Ekpe men come back. They say that Henshaw Town has put money for 19 men, Cobham Town for 5 men, and one for the Guinea Company Ekpe.

                                                                                                          7.3.1785
About 6 a.m. at Aqua Landing with a fine morning so I go down to the landing. After 10 a.m. we go chop (have a meal) at Egbo Young's House 'Liverpool Hall' and after 12 noon the new ship's mate comes to tell us that he will not come here but go to Cameroons. So Duke says, 'Very well, go away please.'

                                                                                                         12.3.1785
About 6 a.m. at Aqua's Landing, and a very rainy morning; so I go down with Esin to see Duke in his palaver house. Then we get Willy Honesty to meet at Duke's house with all the gentlemen to discuss the business of the new ship's captain. So we write to ask him to come ashore, but he says he will not come ashore. Then we three go aboard his ship to ask him and his answer is that he will not stay in our river. So we come ashore and tell all the gentlemen, and they say: 'Very well, he may go away, please go.')

The diary offers scant comfort to modern writers who want to over-idealise the African past, baldly detailing, as it does, the role of these coastal traders in actively promoting the slave trade from the interior.

                                                                                                         21.4.1785
at 5 am in Aqua [*sic*] Landing with fine morning so at 12 clock Day wee 3 go Bord Buowon so wee beg his to Trust slave to carry for pay so he will not come after that wee com back and wee have Eshen Duke com hom from Orroup with 7 slave so I have my fishman com hom with slave and Robin send me 1 girl & my first Boiy com from Curcock with slave and 12 clock night wee go to Savage.

(Translation: 21.4.1785
At 5 a.m. at Aqua Landing with a fine morning; so at 12 o'clock noon we three go aboard the Brown. We beg him to 'trust' for slaves but he will not. After that we come back. Esin Duke comes home from Orroup with seven slaves, and my fishermen came home with slaves and Robin sent me one girl and my first boy came from Curcock with slaves and at midnight we went to Savage's [ship].)

What emerges from the diary is a picture of a world peopled by very human beings, who fight, quarrel and trade, whose wives give birth, and whose children die. It is a world in which the practice of traditional religion and medicine exists alongside the new world of European trade in human beings. It is a world in which the new language is being used actively to record the complex and hybridised realities of late-eighteenth-century coastal West Africa.

11.2.1786

about 5 am in Coqua Town so have Arshbong Desire me to walk up for Commrown with him so I Did and wee pas 3 Little Comrown town for way wee tak walk for 1 clock . . . to get Big Town so the killd goat and Deash 1 iron 2 Rod for me so wee mak long time bob for th to Arshbong good so Did pay Boy slav and the Beg wee to Drink Doctor with them so arshbong mak one his father son nam Ebetim to Drink Doctor with him to the Deash one men cow to be killd & 8 Rod about that th Chap wee us so com Down in 6 clock night

2.3.1786

. . . Captin Potter go way with 284 slaves . . .

17.3.1786

. . . We com ashor and I Did tak one goat for mak Doctor at my god Bason . . .

(Translation: 11.2.1786

About 5 a.m. I was in Coqua Town and Archibong desires me to walk up to Cameroon with him. So I did and we passed 3 little Cameroon towns on the way. We walked until 1 o'clock . . . to get to Big Town. There they killed a goat and dashed me 1 iron and 2 rods. So we had a long discussion with them about Archibong's trading goods. So they paid a boy slave and begged us to drink doctor (medicine) with them. So Archibong made one of his father's sons named Ebetim drink doctor with him. They dash us one male cow to be killed and 8 rods for the chop. We came down at 6 o'clock at night.

2.3.1786

. . . Captain Potter went away with 284 slaves . . .

17.3.1786

. . . We came ashore and I took one goat to make doctor (offering) at my
god-basin (shrine) . . .)

Texts like Antera Duke's *Diary* establish the fact that once English enters the West African scene it becomes available for appropriation to local ends and aims. The struggle to maintain such local ends, and to evade or subvert the controlling influences of the various patronage systems which emerge in the next two hundred years, is one which we will explore more fully in later chapters.

Despite such appropriations in West Africa itself, as well as the examples afforded by the success of earlier writers like Equiano, the process of transcription by and through an amanuensis continued to be the only means by which many black slave voices found expression. Despite the constraints this involved, they remain powerful accounts which cannot be ignored in any story of African diasporic writing. Such controls remain a feature of transcribed accounts purporting to be the stories of Africans as told by themselves until well into the twentieth century, as Chapter 3 will show. A powerful and interesting example of such transcribed accounts is *The History of Mary Prince* (1831), in which the life of this unfortunate woman is recorded as told to a young, white amanuensis, Susannah Moodie, in a structure whose limitations are fixed by boundaries beyond the control of speaker or transcriber. In this account the graphic details of the punishments of slaves are recorded, but the sexual abuse of female slaves is passed over in silence, whether due to the reticence of the young, female white amanuensis to record such matters or the refusal of the distributors of the text to print them. Gillian Whitlock has argued that the narrative has to suppress the sexuality of its central figure to fit with the nonconformist, emancipationist's expectations of what is proper in a narrative of a young female.[18]

Eventually of course the secret had to be let out, and in Harriet Jacobs's *Incidents in the Life of a Slave-Girl* (1861) the sexual harassment and seduction of female slaves is openly made the subject of the text.[19] For a long time it was assumed that this text was transcribed by a white abolitionist, L. Maria Childs, acting as an amanuensis, but it now seems indisputable that Childs's role was only that of an editor and adviser to Jacobs. Jacobs adopted the pseudonym Linda Brent, probably because the audience, even at this late date, would have felt that the open acknowledgement of her sexual abuse reflected badly on the author. In this harrowing account, Jacobs tells of how she escaped the advances of her owner by marrying another white man, by whom she had two children. She succeeded in getting to England, where she worked as a governess, but even then she records that she was in danger of being recaptured and returned to America, where she and her 'mulatto' children would still have been regarded as slaves. This late example shows the complex interrelationships which existed between the roles of author, editor / adviser / amanuensis, publisher and audience in the construction of these slave narratives.

An even more problematic example of a black woman's voice in nineteenth-century Britain was that of Mary Seacole, whose autobiography, *The Wonderful Adventures of Mary Seacole* (1857), enjoyed great success. The daughter of a Scottish soldier and a black Jamaican woman, she was born in Jamaica. She served as a nurse in the Crimea and, although overshadowed in Victorian mythology by Florence Nightingale, she was in her time a famous heroine, with a benefit held for her in 1857 drawing a crowd of forty thousand people. *The Times* reported that 'few names were more familiar to the public during the last war than that of Mrs. Seacole'. The popularity of the autobiography, especially the long sections describing the war, was due in part to the fact that Seacole was an 'out and out' patriot whose descriptions accorded well with the jingoistic spirit of late Victorian England. Although Seacole had herself at times been subjected to public, racial abuse, and elsewhere in her account records this, she emphasised her Scottish ancestry and was often very ambivalent towards her own blackness, speaking of other blacks as 'niggers' and of herself as a 'yellow' or 'brown' woman. In fact the text is filled with such racist references, suggesting how ubiquitous the discourse of race was in late-nineteenth-century England. Her editors comment that, 'Unintentionally her narrative yields a valuable insight into the divided loyalties of colonial people of mixed blood and heritage'.[20]

The emergence of a distinct, independent and proud African voice was arrived at only unevenly and with much struggle and cost. Despite the individual achievements of black people in the period during and immediately after slavery, and in the heyday of colonisation, they were only rarely able fully to appropriate the tools of the master to express themselves. They were always subject to the ongoing dominance of a view of Africans based on pejorative race classification and general prejudice against difference. This general, prejudicial attitude strictly limited their ability to represent themselves in written texts. The struggle for expression occurred on two fronts: externally, against the institutions and patronages by which their voices could be heard; and internally, against the denigratory self-constructions of their condition as black Africans. It is interesting to note that their struggle, and the successes they achieved, did not occur evenly nor in a simple progressive curve. In fact, as we shall see in later chapters, in many ways there was a growth in the prejudicial construction of black and colonised voices, as a more strident imperial vision emerged as the century wore on.

Notes

1. David Dabydeen, *Hogarth's Blacks: Images of Blacks in Eighteenth Century English Art* (Mundelstrup, Denmark: Dangaroo Press, 1985), pp. 21–6.
2. Similarities may be noted to texts in the case of later patronage systems such as those of the missionary presses, which adopted similar processes. See Chapter 3 below.
3. Philip D. Curtin, *Africa Remembered* (Madison: University of Wisconsin Press, 1967), pp. 4–5.
4. Quaque's letters are contained in the Archives of the Society for the Propagation of the Gospel, London, designated as 'C' Manuscripts, West Africa, Letters of Philip Quaque, or Kweku, from Cape Coast Castle, 1765–1811. Ten of the letters in shortened form are reproduced in Curtin, *Africa Remembered*, pp. 113–39.
5. Curtin, *Africa Remembered*, pp. 4–5.
6. *The Collected Works of Phillis Wheatley*, ed. J. E. Shields (New York: Oxford University Press, 1988), p. 74. Further page references are to this source.
7. Ibid., pp. 230–1.
8. Ibid., p. 231.
9. See Paul Edwards and David Dabydeen, *Black Writers in Britain 1760–1890* (Edinburgh: Edinburgh University Press, 1981); also Anne K. Mellor and Richard E. Matlak, *Eighteenth Century British Literature, 1780–1830* (Fort Worth: Harcourt Brace College Publishers, 1996), pp. 51–4.
10. Ottabah Cuguano, *Thoughts and Sentiments on the Evil and Wicked Traffic of Slavery*, in Francis D. Adams and Barry Sanders (eds), *Three Black Writers in Eighteenth Century England* (Belmont, Ca.: Wadsworth Publishing Co., 1971), p. 48. Further page references are to this edition.
11. Curtin, *Africa Remembered*, p. 7.
12. See Introduction to G. P. Rawick, *The American Slave: A Composite Autobiography* (Westport, Conn.: Greenwood, 1972) and Introduction to Frederick Douglass, *My Bondage and My Freedom* (1855; New York: Arno Press, 1968).
13. Quaque's letters reproduced in Curtin, *Africa Remembered*, pp. 122–3. Further page references given in the text are to this source.
14. Peter Hulme, *Colonial Encounters: Europe and the native Caribbean 1492–1792* (London and New York: Methuen, 1986).

15. See Chapters 3 and 4.

16. See Chapter 4.

17. *The Diary of Antera Duke*, in Daryll Forde (ed.), *Efik Traders of Old Calabar* (1902; London: Dawsons, 1968). Further page references are to this edition.

18. Gillian Whitlock, 'Outlaws of the Text: Women's Bodies and the Organisation of Gender in Imperial Space', unpublished paper from the Proceedings of the Australia/Canada: Post-colonization and the Women's Texts Conference, Calgary Institute of the Humanities, 13–16 February 1992. Part of this is reproduced in B. Ashcroft *et al., The Post-Colonial Studies Reader* (London: Routledge, 1995), pp. 349–54.

19. See, for example, Mellor and Matlak, *Eighteenth Century British Literature*, p. 5.

20. Edwards and Dabydeen, *Black Writers in Britain*, p. 185.

Chapter 2

Nineteenth- and Early-Twentieth-Century Histories, Travel Accounts, Political Writing and the Beginnings of Fiction

West Africa

The period from the early nineteenth century to the early twentieth century was one of strong intervention by European cultures into West Africa. It saw the founding of such modern nations as Sierra Leone and Liberia, which were to have a profound effect on the development of intellectual life in the whole of West Africa. The writers and intellectuals they produced were to provide an inspiration and a model for the nationalist movements across Africa in the twentieth century.[1] Both settlements were the result of a mass return of freed slaves to Africa. In the case of Sierra Leone these were mainly from England and the English colonies (especially from Nova Scotia, where many loyalist blacks had settled after the American War of Independence, and from the British West Indies, especially Jamaica). Later, after the abolition of slave trading in the British Empire in 1807, these early returned slaves were joined by others from many parts of West Africa, as the anti-slave patrols of the British navy dropped their freed slaves at the new colony. In the case of Liberia, the new arrivals came mainly from those American states where slavery was not a feature of the economy. Runaway slaves who had fled to these states often found themselves the victims of ongoing prejudice, causing many of them to seek a solution in the return to Africa.

Encouragement and support for this repatriation to Africa had mixed motives. Emancipation of the slaves was applauded in theory, but their integration into a society still profoundly racist in its attitudes was the cause of continuing friction. Both the American and English governments supported the repatriation programmes to solve the problem of what to do with the increasing number of freed slaves in both England and America. Coupled with this was the desire of the freed slaves themselves to achieve economic and social independence and a separate identity. The two motives came together in the development of schemes for the re-location of the expatriate African in 'his own land'. Abolitionists, such as Granville Sharpe in England, organiser of the first expedition of freed slaves to settle in Sierra Leone in 1787, and the American clergymen, businessmen and slave-owners who formed the American Colonisation Society in 1816, were 'inspired by a mixture of religion, economics and politics'.[2] Some leaders of the black community in America opposed such repatriation, arguing that it was a symptom of the failure to address the problem of the ongoing racist attitudes of American society. Others supported the movements from a weary conviction that it would never be possible to obtain social justice for blacks within the American context. Faced with continued segregation, discrimination and oppression, many freed slaves saw in these colonies the opportunity to establish a place of their own, free from prejudice and racism.

The ex-slave colonists were also motivated by the belief that they could raise the 'aboriginals', as the native Africans were usually designated, to the benefits of civilisation and Christianity, though many of the writers of the period incorporated considerable irony into their presentation of the Christian virtues of the European and American civilisations which sponsored them. For example, Olaudah Equiano, whose influential autobiography was discussed in the previous chapter, was involved in the project to set up the colony in Sierra Leone. He was taken on by Granville Sharpe as Commissary to the project, but, his narrative claims, was dismissed because of his opposition to the inadequate provisions and self-serving practices of the expedition's white agent, Irwin.[3] Equiano, although a favoured figure of the religious emancipationists, who supported such expeditions as part of the mission to the pagan African, was himself inclined to regard Christianity as deeply flawed, in practice if not in theory. At one stage in his life he even contemplated moving to Turkey, where he had 'always found the Turks very honest in their dealings', and where he had encountered less overt racism as a Negro. In contrast to this, Equiano had found that as a freed slave in the Americas and in the British West Indies, he was subjected frequently to false dealing, and was not given fair treatment under the law. A comparison with Frederick Douglass's account, almost a century later, of his reception in New Bedford, in the heart of abolitionist New England, demonstrates how persistent this problem was.[4] These ongoing discriminations were a powerful factor in the alienation such men felt from their 'own' societies. The various resettlement movements, from the founding of Sierra Leone and Liberia to Marcus Garvey's 'Back to Africa' movement in the early twentieth century, were all the product of this ongoing sense of alienation and exclusion.

The figures involved in these early resettlements, and their so-called Creole descendants, gave rise to one of the most significant groups of writers in English to emerge in West Africa in the nineteenth and early twentieth centuries. As we might expect, they concentrated their energies on the genres most appropriate to their task, which was to establish an African presence in the professional fields they had entered. This writing ranged from treatises on medicine and ethnography through travel writing, historical accounts, essays on social and cultural theory, and political polemic. The fact that such genres have often been excluded from literary histories has meant that this early body of writing by Africans has been unjustly neglected. Yet a brief glance at many of these emphasises that these genres were often the only means by which Africans of the period could speak of their condition. The texts they produced were inevitably controlled by the circumstances of their production. In the case of the earlier texts, they were directed toward the re-education and re-forming of the prejudices of the non-African audiences on whose support the ventures relied. Later texts concentrated on persuading the colonial author-ities to reconsider their policies with regard to African society and its develop-ment. For this reason, they frequently combined a strong reliance on European genres with a powerful, assertive attitude on issues of race and culture. These writers were forced to placate the authorities, whose power alone allowed them access to a voice in print, even as they asserted their differences from that power. This inevitably involved them in a form of double vision. Yet, despite these constraints, they managed to create accounts of Africa which were more broadly based and more generous in certain respects than those of some later writers.

They were frequently inspired by a vision of Africa as a whole, and the nationalism they favoured was rarely merely local or regional. In this respect they challenged the artificialities of colonial structures, and argued for a mutu-ally supportive development towards independence for the peoples of Africa as a whole. The power and insight of these accounts should not be lightly dismissed, as they too often are in accounts of African writing.[5] Figures like Edward Wilmot Blyden (1832–1912), Alexander Crummell (1821–98), Samuel Ajayi Crowther (18??–91), James (Holy) Johnson (1836–1917), and James Africanus Beale Horton (1835–83) laid the foundations for the modern forces of nationalism in West Africa. They looked forward, too, towards a regional cultural identity which has still to be fully developed. These ideas were taken up in the late nineteenth and early twentieth centuries by a host of others such as the Rev. Attoh Ahuma, John Mensah Sarbah, Mojola Agbebi, Rev. Samuel Johnson, Kobina Sekyi and Joseph Ephraim Casely Hayford. The dominance of male voices in this list reflects the patriarchal nature of the period, though modern scholars are beginning the task of unearthing the testimonies of the women of the period, such as that of J. E. Casely Hayford's wife, Adelaide Smith Casely Hayford. Women's 'memoirs' were usually not published at the time, despite the crucial role their authors played in indigenous educational and independence movements. These unpublished memoirs are now being recovered and published by literary scholars.[6] Historians have also begun the task of recording the crucial role women played in the political and economic life of the African colonies and in the early resistance and independence movements.[7]

J. E. Casely Hayford's *Ethiopia Unbound* (1911) is one of the earliest African literary texts to adopt a fictional form. Until quite recently, this was usually cited as the earliest fictional text written by a native-born African, but this dis-tinction must now be given to the recently re-discovered text of the Liberian (Vai) author Joseph J. Walters, whose *Guanya Pau: The Story of an African Princess* was published in 1891, twenty years before Caseley Hayford's text.[8] Although it is written as a fictional account, *Ethiopia Unbound* is strongly autobiographical. It is clearly meant as a platform for Casely Hayford to express his views on a number of central issues of the period, particularly the right of Africans to control their own affairs. It not only establishes Casely Hayford as one of the most important voices of early modern West African nationalism, but also has a claim to being amongst the most forceful and stylish English-language texts dealing with African experience and opinion. Using the fictional figure Kwamankra to represent himself, Casely Hayford details the education and ideas of an idealistic young Creole intellectual, his ambitions, his politics and his personal life:

> Among the enthusiastic band who canvassed the educational questions was Kwamankra, and none more ardently than he. He was a man of remarkable intelligence, who, receiving the best education the schools of those days could afford, had, by hard work and natural taste for book-learning, so impressed the community with his ability that at the age of nineteen he had been entrusted with the editorship of the national newspaper, and had already come to be regarded as one of the coming leaders of the people.
>
> Upon the opening of the National University, Kwamankra gave up newspaper work and joined the University staff. . . . It was recognised that the best part of the teaching must be done in the people's own language, and soon several text-books of known authority had, with the kind permission of authors and publishers, been translated into Fanti, thereby making the progress of the student rapid and sound.[9]

The importance and influence of his political work has overshadowed Casely Hayford's achievements as a writer, though the detail and the interest in character and incident in passage after passage of *Ethiopia Unbound* indicates why it was, until recently, credited with being the first African English 'novel'.

> At a corner, all by himself, sits a son of Albion, a man of independent character, the butt of the camp, who dares to worship with the black folk on this holy day. It is a motley gathering of all conditions of men in all sorts of costumes from the latest Regent Street cutaway coat to the ample four fathoms of Manchester calico print, gracefully wound round the person. At 10.30 of the clock there mounts the pulpit a black parson who, from that hour till 11.50, reads Psalms and Litanies and hymns to the melody of an inharmonious portable American organ. No wonder half the congregation go to sleep, and the beadles have their work cut out for the rest of the morning. One of their number, aggravated by the extra rise in the thermometer, is a bit aggressive, and no wonder that a distinct unchristian scowl is clear on the face of a Christian gentleman sitting next to the observer. (147–8)

His later work, such as his account of the wandering Grebo (Sierra Leonean) revivalist, *William Waddy Harris: The West African Reformer, the Man and his Message* (1915), had a strong influence on the ideas and leadership style of later nationalists, such as Kwame Nkrumah in the Gold Coast and Jomo Kenyatta in Kenya.

The blanket term 'Creole intellectuals', which is frequently applied to these writers, needs some explanation. It lumps together a number of very different kinds of figures whose filiative and affiliative relations to Africa vary widely. For example, Blyden and Crummell were emigrants (Blyden came to Liberia aged nineteen, in 1851, after being born in the West Indies; Crummell; an African-American, was educated in America and Britain, and after graduating from Cambridge, emigrated to Liberia aged thirty-two, in 1853); Crowther was a 'recaptive', a slave rescued by the British navy and set free at Sierra Leone, in his early teens, in 1822; Horton was born in Sierra Leone of 'recaptive' parents and spent most of his working life as a British army doctor in the settlements of the Gold Coast and The Gambia.[10] The later intellectuals who inherited their mantle, and who looked to them for inspiration, were all African-born. But most of them were members of that same social group (coastal Creoles), who had a long association with the Europeans trading, and later governing, from their coastal enclaves. For such people the effects of Europeanisation were long established and, in a certain sense, indelible. This is especially significant because the burden of the Creole intellectuals' discourse frequently included a disputation as to the nature of race and racial characteristics, and the associated assertion of the value of indigenous cultural practices and institutions. This was often accompanied by defensive justifications, which emphasised how the understanding and study of such indigenous practices was the only way in which the civilising mission of the earlier period, or the more overtly imperialist mission of the latter period, could be effectively accomplished. This has made these texts seem to modern readers overly complicit with the invading cultural forces, and thus lent to the idea of creolisation a negative connotation. But such readings are, arguably, superficial. In a series of associations, confederations and other groupings these creolised intellectuals worked to establish the possibility of an administration by Africans based on a respect for, and accommodation with, traditional social customs, and indigenous political and cultural institutions. Although they were often primarily concerned with the immediate policies of the relatively small areas of the European coastal enclaves (until the end of the century only a very small proportion of the West African land-mass had any direct contact with and settlement by the European powers), they couched these policies in terms of their visions of Africa and Africans as a whole. In this sense, they forged the modern idea of an 'African', an idea which would have been alien to a figure like Quaque. In a real sense, they made the modern African into someone who could conceive of a connectedness above and beyond local structures and allegiances.

Even those Creole intellectuals who saw themselves as loyal British subjects, such as Horton or Crowther, had a powerful sense of their role as 'representative figures' for all black people. Blyden, the most radical of them in this respect, as in many others, was characteristically outspoken in his argument for the future of the Negro race as a whole, and addressed himself, unabashedly, to the freedom and recovery of Negroes and Negro culture everywhere. Later Creole intellectuals such as Samuel Johnson and Casely Hayford constructed powerful defences of traditional practices, and rebutted the garish and denigratory colonial narratives of traditional African societies, which emphasised indiscriminate human sacrifice, mass cannibalism, and other horrors with which the invaders had justified their political and military incursions into the interior of the kingdoms of Ashanti and Benin. Ironically, in so doing these figures have been characterised by some modern historians as 'conservative'. Their stress on the need to preserve the traditional ruling institutions and practices may, however, better be seen as a very modern defence of the distinctive forms and needs of African societies. In fact, the later Creole intellectuals were to find themselves in some conflict with the traditional rulers, as they demanded a greater say in the governance of their region. Nevertheless, they were also mostly, as men of their time, committed to the continuity of the relationship with the European institutions of Church and State. These institutions had provided them with their education and professions, and continued to command their allegiance, if they also sometimes provoked their criticism and scorn.

Of the earlier figures, Blyden was the most outspoken opponent of any compromise with colonial authority, arguing much more forcefully than most of his contemporaries that 'Negro civilisation had something positive to contribute to world culture and did not need to go through the processes of Christian and European acculturation before being able to make this contribution'.[11] Blyden even went so far as to reject Christianity in favour of the idea that Islam might be more suited to African needs and customs in *Christianity, Islam and the Negro Race* (1887):

> The introduction of Islam into Central and West Africa has been the most important, if not the sole, preservative against the desolation of the slave-trade. Mohammedanism furnished a protection to the tribes who embraced it by effectively binding them together in one strong religious fraternity, and enabling them by their united effort to baffle the attempt of powerful Pagan slave-hunters. Enjoying this comparative immunity from sudden hostile incursions, industry was stimulated among them, industry diminished their poverty; and, as they increased in worldly substance, they also increased in desire for knowledge. Gross superstition gradually disappeared from among them.[12]

Blyden's work also asserts the need for Africans to value and preserve their own institutions in a way which is unusual at such an early date:

> we are held in bondage by our indiscriminate and injudicious use of a foreign literature: and we strive to advance by the methods of a foreign race. In this effort we struggle with the odds against us. . . . The African must advance by methods of his own. He must possess a power distinct from that of the European. It has been proved that he knows how to take advantage of European culture, and that he can be benefited by it. This proof was perhaps necessary, but it is not sufficient. We must show that we are able to go alone, to carve out our way.[13]

This more aggressive and assertive tone of Blyden's work makes him sound more modern than many of his contemporaries. We should remember, though, that Blyden worked within the context of Liberia, where 'his own Americo-Liberian immigrant group was supreme . . . [H]aving literally turned his back on America and Europe [he] could face Europe on his own terms and be accepted.'[14] Towards the end of his life, in exile, and after more aggressive imperialist policies were ushered into West Africa by the 'new imperialism', Blyden's tone changed and he welcomed the new involvement advocated by open imperialists such as Joseph Chamberlain, failing, for whatever reason, to see the wider implications of these policies of involvement for his earlier dreams of African independence and self-reliance. Thus, in 1901, in an address to the Liverpool Chamber of Commerce, he welcomes the new policies:

30

when the 'earth hunger' referred to by Lord Ripon the other day began to take possession of certain Continental powers, compelling Bismarck . . . to suggest an international conference to discuss the situation in that vast 'no man's land', as it was called; and when, as a result of that conference, a partition of Africa was made on the map, then England began to realise the mistake of her *laissez faire* policy, and to awake to her rights and duties in connection with West Africa. Within the last few years a great statesman (Joseph Chamberlain) has come to the front at the Colonial Office who, impatient of the slumber of years . . . has brought unaccustomed, we may say abnormal, activity to the 'development of that portion of the estates of the Empire', which has lain fallow for generations, nay for thousands of years.[15]

Despite these later lapses and revisions, Blyden stands out from the other nineteenth-century African spokespeople for his vigorous prosecution of the independent position of Africans.

Yet the contribution of other figures, such as Horton, should not be under-estimated on this account. In British settlements before the last quarter of the nineteenth century, intellectuals, such as Crowther, Horton and others, could look with some degree of hope to a future in which a genuine partnership of European and African might be developed. The official policy of the British governments of the day was to proceed to a self-governing status for the African colonies as rapidly as possible. In this political climate, it was possible for someone like Horton to perceive of himself as a nationalist and a loyal subject of the Queen, at one and the same time. Thus in *West African Countries and Peoples* (1868) he could write:

> The Governor or Administrator of the Gold Coast should be a man of tact, resolution and great independence. Whilst firm in his decision, which should only be arrived at after matured consideration, he should be a man who, by long experience in the manners, customs and habits of the peculiar people of this coast, could form an adequate judgement as to the measures necessary to avert internal disturbance, and to give them a generalised conception of the interest the Home Goverment has always manifested, and will still continue to manifest, towards their advancement.[16]

The fact that in 1872 he was to apply for the Governorship himself may indicate that here he is suggesting that a local, such as himself, might be best suited to supply these particular qualities. This was not out of line with the official policy of the British goverment at the time, though it must be said that the official policy of the government for these settlements was not very strongly enforced. It was, perhaps, as much the product of inertia, and of the costliness of colonial expansion, as of real enlightenment. It was also always opposed on the ground by the more aggressive and predatory interest of the local traders, and even by some sections of the missionary movements. Nevertheless, a collaborative future, such as Horton envisaged, did not seem to people like him in the period either doomed to failure or simply the product of cultural dependence and self-deception. The opening of his last political work, *Letters on the Political Condition of the Gold Coast* (1870), which presents Horton's view that Africans were now travelling the same road that Europeans had once travelled, from barbarism to civilisation, may now seem unpalatable, but at the time it was part of an important and necessary assertion that Africans

31

could come to rule their own lives, and as such it represented a progressive position.

> 'Rome was not built in a day'; the proudest kingdom in Europe was once in a state of barbarism perhaps worse than now exists amongst the tribes chiefly inhabiting the West Coast of Africa, and it is an incontrovertible axiom that what has been done can again be done. If Europe, therefore, has been raised to her present pitch of civilisation by progressive advancement, Africa, too, with a guarantee of the civilisation of the north, will rise into equal importance . . . We may well say that the present state of Western Africa is, in fact, the history of the world repeating itself.[17]

However, the relationship between these Creole intellectuals and the European institutions within which they had received their education, training and advancement deteriorated rapidly after the development in the new imperialist doctrine of the last quarter of the nineteenth century.

Crowther, who lived until 1891, was, by the end of his life, the victim, on numerous occasions, of the arrogance of the new generation of administrators who accompanied and sought to implement the new policies. Horton's tragically early death, in 1883, meant that he was spared the worst disillusionment of this period, though, already, after his clash with the local authorities following the publication of his *Letters on the Political Condition of the Gold Coast* (1870), he had fallen silent on political issues. After failing in his application for the vacant Governorship of the Gold Coast in 1872, he published only medical textbooks, and took early retirement from the Army Medical Service. He returned to Freetown in 1880, where he died three years later. He had taken an active part in the final Ashanti War of 1874, under Sir Garnett Wolseley, a war which clearly marked the end of an era. This war imposed impossible conditions on the Ashanti and created a power vacuum which made the second and decisive intervention in the last years of the century, and the final defeat of the Ashanti kingdom, inevitable. In the earlier period, the Fanti, like other coastal groups, had seen the Europeans as useful allies in resisting the interior nations, such as the Ashanti, in their expansionist moves towards the sea. The Fanti of the coast now had little to fear from conflict with the interior kingdoms. In the period which followed there was a dramatic growth in opposition to colonial rule among the more thoughtful and intellectual members of the Fanti and other coastal groups, who had been the collaborative extras on this particular imperial stage for fifty years or more. However, the Fanti leadership was quickly disillusioned. After the trade-off of coastal forts and enclaves between the British and the Dutch in 1867, the final suppression of the Ashanti in the interior in 1874, and the subsequent establishment of a Crown Colony of the Gold Coast in the same year, the earlier dreams of the Creole intellectuals of a form of collaborative government leading to independence under the Empire, comparable with that of the white dominions, was finally destroyed. As one historian has noted, 'the decisive defeat of the Ashanti in 1874 put them [i.e. the British] in a position to do whatever they liked with Ghana'.[18] What they liked was increasingly to pay only lip-service to the idea of eventual African self-government whilst in practice developing stronger and more rigid policies designed to tie the colonies to the Empire for centuries to come. Especially after the accession of the arch-imperialist Joseph Chamberlain, architect of the so-called 'new imperialism', as Colonial Secretrary, in the last years of the century, its exponents argued that a time-scale of centuries would be necessary to bring Africans to the level of 'civilisation' necessary for self-government. This had certainly not been the view of people like Horton, when he supported a gradualist and developmental path for Africans in his writings in the 1860s. In fact, the writing and public achievements of men such as Blyden, Crummell, Crowther and Horton clearly exposed this view as only a self-serving lie.[19]

Blyden was expelled from Liberia in 1873 and returned to America, a victim of the internal pressures of Liberian politics, and of his own clashes with the leadership of the Republic. Nevertheless, he continued to write on, and interest himself in, Africa. The differences between Blyden and the other Creole intellectuals of this early period lay, principally, in his continued rejection of the 'assimilationist' policies of the missionaries and government agencies, by which even the most enlightened of African intellectuals, such as Crowther, 'Holy' Johnson and Horton, were restrained. Despite their differences, the gap between the two views was not absolute. Blyden reserved his worst condemnation for the missionaries. The pragmatic policy of 'indirect rule', favoured by the new breed of imperial administrator, was a policy designed to make ruling the native easier and less costly. Blyden, however, seems to have detected in this new imperial policy an opportunity for an enlightened intervention, which might slowly move it towards a full restitution of independent native government. As a result, in his later work he did not fully recognise the dangers involved in the shift from the earlier policy of nurturing the colonies to independence, to an overtly imperial policy of long-term economic exploitation and dependency. This may have been partly because, as a resident of the American colony of Liberia, he was not directly affected by this shift in British policy. The other weakness of Blyden's later work lies in his emphasis on race, which also blinded him to the more pressing problem of the new imperialism. In his later work, he embraced a fatalistic view, based on his belief that the demise of the Europeans in Africa was inevitable, given their inability to 'adapt' racially to the climate, and to the diseases of the region. As a result, he failed to see the effects of these crucial changes in colonial policy for the politics of the later period of European intervention in West Africa. For Crowther, on the other hand, who had once seen European acculturation and the Christianisation of the African as a route both to modernity and to self-controlled political and religious salvation, the emergence of this more pragmatic and exploitative late imperial policy was the final betrayal of his early vision of cooperation and mutual growth and benefit.

That the various positions of these early nationalists were not absolutely irreconcilable is further demonstrated in the development of their work by those who followed them at the end of the century. The generation which took up their struggle constructed a synthesis of their views, in which an awareness of the more exploitative aspects of the new imperialism was modified by an increasingly sophisticated grasp of how indirect rule might be used to promote the re-generation of modernised forms of traditional African social structures and political institutions. Casely Hayford, J. M. Sarbah, Mojola Agbebi, and a host of anonymous followers, journalists and pamphleteers, in centres such as Freetown, Accra, Abeokuta and Lagos, wove an intricate and complex web of arguments, which were designed simultaneously to appeal to the self-interest of the ruling Europeans and to generate a revived self-image and self-respect in Africans for their own culture. The role of these figures in promoting a vigorous, uncontrolled press which allowed Africans to speak out on important issues cannot be overestimated. Although there were relatively few strictly literary texts produced by these writers, the body of writing they initiated offered a model for a local patronage free of the kinds of direct external influences which I have traced elsewhere in this account.

In 1897, the 'Creole intellectuals' of the Gold Coast and the traditional rulers had come together to form the Gold Coast Aborigines' Rights Protection Society. The Society became especially important after the introduction of the imperialist doctrine of 'indirect rule' into Ghana in the 1920s which divided the Creole intellectual elite from the traditional rulers, led by figures such as Nana Offori Atta, himself a Western-educated traditional ruler. The statesman-like attitudes of Nana Offori Atta and Casely Hayford temporarily settled these differences, and Nana Offori Atta strongly supported Casely Hayford and the other Creole intellectuals in their drive to Africanise the colonial administration. At the time, as one historian has noted, 'Few Ghanaians wanted chieftaincy abolished but few also approved of the bias in the system against Western-educated men. Rural Ghanaians wanted both their chiefs and their educated men.'[20] It may be the tragedy of later African politics that this moment of juncture between the impulse to modernise and the desire to retain links with the institutions of the African past was lost in the subsequent development of the later independence movements.[21]

Davidson (Abioseh) Nicol has summed up the achievement and difficulties of the early Creole nationalists, such as Blyden, Crowther and Horton, very well:

> It is important for our present era that these men succeeded in the European Victorian context. They had first to prove to the world that it was possible to do so before the particular and unique contribution of the African could be made and readily accepted. They were essential as a bridge to make it possible for their descendants to cross over to the distant side of the river where African political and cultural independence lay. Edward Blyden was before his time in insisting that the total African contribution could then be made at once. But he was necessary to the others as a warning that the situation had a dynamism which carried beyond mere European acculturation.[22]

The complex, and sometimes conflicting views of this first generation were developed in the work of their successors, such as J. E. Casely Hayford and John Mensah Sarbah. Together, they presented Africans with an image of their capacity to contribute in all fields of human endeavour on an equal footing, not least in the mastery of writing and of the language which had come to them in the luggage of slavers, unscrupulous traders, missionaries, administrators and imperial carpetbaggers of all kinds. Well before the end of the nineteenth century, Africans had made a strong and distinctive contribution to the forms of the essay, memoir, travel account, treatise and letter. In these texts, they had already demonstrated their skill in appropriating the language of the invader to the task of self-expression and self-identity. This work laid the foundation for the use of English as a vehicle of indigenous literary expression alongside the African languages. It was the same generation of men who had been instrumental, along with their European missionary colleagues, in making African languages available as a mode of *written* expression, by constructing the first effective orthographies and compiling the first dictionaries and grammars of the various African languages.[23] They had founded, edited and contributed to the many indigenous-language and English-language journals and newspapers published in the region. In fact, rather than the colonial and indigenous languages being in competition as mediums of written expression, they evolved in tandem, with many of the journals and newspapers of the period being bilingual.[24]

> It was characteristic of the time that such men of affairs should also belong to educational, cultural and research institutions in their spare time. For this was a period of writing. The elite newspapers put forth a continuous stream of commentary: social reportage on and by the elite, but also philosophical and political polemics, reviews and critiques of cultural events, and wide-ranging social debates.[25]

As the example of Casely Hayford's text *Ethiopia Unbound* shows, it is not always possible to keep a strict separation between narrative fiction and other genres, such as polemic, history, autobiography or memoir. Nor is it possible to assert that non-fictional forms did not profoundly alter the discourse available to later writers in Africa, sharing as they do such tasks as establishing a written history and a written cultural tradition. It is not even possible to draw a simple chronology of influence, as texts were often written far earlier than their eventual publication date.

Some specific examples can serve to illustrate these general facts, and they happen also to be among the most important texts for a literary history of African English writing. They are the Rev. Samuel Johnson's *The History of the Yorubas*, R. E. Obeng's *Eighteenpence*, and Kobina Sekyi's early play, *The Blinkards*.

Johnson's work was completed in 1897, but it was not published until 1921, when it was edited by his brother Obadiah Johnson, and issued by the Church Missionary Society at Lagos. *The History of the Yorubas* can be said to be both the principal source for much subsequent African historical writing, and also to have been the source on which later literary works drew for many of the basic facts of early Yoruba culture and identity. The Yoruba were not a single people, but a group of related peoples, whose ongoing diasporic impulse is reflected in their long history. Johnson clearly sets out to foster a sense of unity between these disparate peoples, based on the creation of a shared historical past. In so doing, he is motivated by the fact that, only by attaching contemporary European concepts of the nation and nationality to African peoples and cultures, to whom such ideas were alien, can the African claim to 'national' independence be advanced. Johnson's work sought to establish a historical origin for the Yoruba nation in the ancient Oyo kingdom and it is with the story of this kingdom that he begins. In selecting Oyo as the original Yoruba culture, he is in a sense indulging in a fiction, since there is no evidence that Oyo was the earliest or the most dominant of the various Yoruba states. Existing Yoruba oral histories, on which Johnson clearly drew, have a local and specific viewpoint. Johnson weds this tradition of local chronicle to an abstract historical discourse, staking his claim to a Yoruba 'history' in classic European historiographic terms.[26] Nevertheless, for Johnson the writing of history also continued to involve material from a very different range of discourses from those of classic European history. For example, his work continues to reflect the traditional Yoruba mode of *ìtàn*. 'The *ìtàn*, as an oral mode of relaying the traditions, give scope for the inclusion of a wide variety of other oral genres, such as songs, *oríkì* (praise poems and epithets), proverbs and etymologies in the historical framework of their narratives.'[27] In addition, he draws together and correlates many oral sources from the various constituent groups of the modern Yoruba to establish what the Yoruba were at a time when the 'traditional boundaries of a "Yoruba" culture were being formed in the face of wider historical processes that were to integrate it into a larger nation that was to become Nigeria'.[28] Nevertheless, Johnson's work is the source for many later accounts by more conventional historians, who select from it the elements they wish to employ. It is drawn upon heavily, too, by anthropologists, and, more to our purpose, is the source for many modern fictional accounts of 'traditional' culture. In other words, Johnson's text illustrates that the boundaries between orally transmitted tradition and written account are always difficult to determine absolutely, and that the process of interrelationship between the two is crucial. It also indicates that English, as well as the written forms of the indigenous languages, was a vehicle for the transmission of much material from oral, indigenous culture. These indigenous English-language accounts continued to influence oral and written texts in both the indigenous languages and English. For early writers like Johnson, English provided a vehicle to effect that creative and powerful 'brokerage' which de Moraes Farias has identified as the primary characteristic and achievement of the early nationalists, who literally forged the nations they were to champion against the colonisers. In such a process texts like Samuel Johnson's *The History of the Yorubas* were crucial.[29]

Many of these early African nationalists and intellectuals were also Christian ministers and published their work through church or mission presses and journals.[30] The strong interrelationship between Christian education, publishing and the establishing of a national and African discourse in the period needs to be noted. Johnson's ground-breaking work, which historians like Ajayi and literary critics like Quayson argue was a crucial part of the process of bringing into being the identity of the modern Yoruba culture, and the later emergence of a discourse of Nigerian nationalism, was published by the same Church

Missionary Society to which Crowther had delivered his reports a half-century earlier.[31] Nevertheless, the work of Johnson, like that of Crowther, seems to me to be best treated as an enterprise which became increasingly distinct from that of the colonial authorities, secular and sacred, whose language and institutions they employed, as the century wore on. This was particularly so as the biased nature of these authorities became more pronounced towards the end of the century.[32] During the period between and after the two world wars, many other writers and journalists emerged in West Africa who maintained this tradition of intellectual and social critique, such as J. B. Danquah in Ghana (the then Gold Coast Colony). But few turned to fiction to express themselves. Two notable exceptions are both Ghanaian, the work of Kobina Sekyi, particularly his play *The Blinkards*, and one of the earliest 'fictitious prose tales' in English by an African, R. E. Obeng's *Eighteenpence*.

Kobina Sekyi's *The Blinkards* has no date on its manuscript, which announces that it is 'Set in Cape Coast, Time, the Present'. But it was produced in 1915 by members of the Cosmopolitan Club in Cape Coast, the members of which also appear as characters in the play, where their pretentions are satirised. This date makes it one of the earliest of African English literary texts. J. Ayo Langley, who has edited the text, has been unable to find any contemporary reviews or accounts of the production, but speculates that 'the play was well received, particularly as it was spiced with telling Fanti aphorisms'.[33] However, Act 3 Scene 2, which is set in the Cosmopolitan Club, presents a rather unflattering picture of the members, suggesting that they used a very convoluted English intended to impress the 'natives' with their understanding of English culture. Their resolutions at the meeting dramatised here are clearly part of Sekyi's satire of the tendency of such Gold Coast 'intellectuals' to denigrate their own customs and promote European habits. The plot, such as it is, revolves around the desire of the law clerk, Mr Okadu, to marry the daughter of the cocoa-magnate Mr Tsiba. She has been forced by her father to attend lessons with the pretentious Anglophile Mrs Brofusem, to learn to be English and 'civilised'. Okadu, in his turn, seeks employment with the young 'been-to' barrister Mr Onyimdzi, a figure clearly modelled on Sekyi himself, from whom he hopes to acquire the status of a European-educated man to impress Mr Tsiba. The resulting engagement allows the text to explore the ways in which Anglicisation has operated to break down and belittle traditional social customs and practices. Miss Tsiba's grandmother, Nana Katawira, is appalled when she discovers that her granddaughter is to be married without a proper involvement of the family, and without receiving a bride-price. This slim plot is really an excuse for Sekyi to present the consequences of the Coast intellectuals' obsession with Anglicising their society. In Mr Onyimdzi he has a figure who can act as a mouthpiece for his own arguments about the need to retain traditional custom and to resist the idea that everything English is superior. Onyimdzi's arguments succeed in converting the oppressed Mr Brofusem to his viewpoint, and he fights back against his wife's pretensions in the final scenes of the play. Describing the advantages of the traditional engagement processes, Mr Brofusem notes that, 'We of these so-called enlightened days know little or nothing of these grand old customs' (145). The play ends with Brofusem's assertion that:

> Really, Onyimdzi was right all along the line. If only we were national, we should be more rational and infinitely more respectable. Our ways and our things suit our climate. For one thing, our drinks have not the same maddening effect on our people as European drinks have. The people of the old days were wise indeed: if only we would follow the customs they left us a little more, and adopt the ways of other races a little less, we should be at least as healthy as they were. (147–8)

Although, as this suggests, the play is openly polemic, many of the scenes have a genuine comic flair. The satirical portrait of the snobbish Anglophone Mrs Brofusem reaches significant comic heights and has a real theatrical bite. For example, the following scene illustrates her attempts to convince the young Miss Tsiba to adopt English habits, as her status-conscious *nouveau-riche* father wishes.

> Mr Ony.: (*To Mrs Brofusem, filling a wine-glass*) May I?
> Mrs Brof.: Thanks.
> Mr Ony.: (*To Miss Tsiba, filling another wine-glass*) May I?
> Miss Tsi.: No, thank you! If it is port, I do not like it: it smells like Elexir.
> Mrs Brof.: Oh, Erimintrude!
> Mr Ony.: (*Aside*) Good heavens, what a name! I suppose she wanted to say 'Ermyntrude'. (*To Miss Tsiba*) Well I shan't press you; but won't you try a piece of cake or a chocolate, or some *buredzi tutui*?
> Miss Tsi.: I think I will take *buredzi tutui*.
> Mr Ony.: Please do. Here is a finger-bowl for you. (*Raising his voice*) Half-crown! (*Enter Half-crown*) Bring another finger-bowl (*Pointing to the finger-bowl. Exit Half-crown*).
> Mrs Brof.: Do behave, Erimintrude. A cake is more genteel . . . than *buredzi tutui*. Or else take a chocolate. I recommend creamy ones. All young ladies in England chop creamy chocolates.
> Mr Ony.: I am afraid there is none in this tin: they are all more or less hard.
> Miss Tsi.: Never mind. I do not like creamy chocolates. When the thing inside comes for your tongue, it is like eating cock-roaches or beetles. When you walk on them something white co—
> Mrs Brof.: (*Very loudly*) Oh, Erimintrude! (42–3)

Perhaps the most significant achievement of the text is the way in which it weaves into its dramatic effect the pretentions of the Anglophile characters to speak English properly, whilst exposing both their ignorance of this alien culture and their own failure either socially or linguistically to reproduce it effectively.

Mrs Brofusem's admonition to her long-suffering husband not to call her 'my dear' but rather to call her 'duckie' because 'Mrs Gush, my friend at Seabourne, on the East Coast, always addressed her husband as "duckie"' (23) illustrates Sekyi's conviction, expressed elsewhere in his work, that Africans who travelled in England generally found themselves exposed only to the lower classes, and modelled their behaviour on these. Sekyi himself was clearly something of a snob in such matters, and elsewhere comments on his dislike for Christianity having been exacerbated by his attending church meetings in England where he was forced to associate with the 'skivvy' class. However, this class-consciousness provides him with the tool for a social satire which allows him to expose the pretensions and inadequacies of figures like Mrs Brofusem.

The text is unique too in that it weaves English (in various forms from standard English to pidgin) into dramatic interaction with Fanti. Almost a third of the total dialogue is in Fanti, making this text the earliest play to insist on the audience dealing with the multi-linguistic reality of West African culture. The published form offers translations of the Fanti, but in performance the use of both languages on stage would dramatise the ways in which English was always only one element in the language continuum inhabited by these would-be English imitators of the creolised Cape Coast society of the period. For this and other reasons, Sekyi's play offered a significant early model of successful multi-linguistic dialogue, which West African plays were only to return to after many decades.

Sekyi published a number of other books, on law and custom, as well as authoring a substantial body of political journalism. In addition he wrote a number of short stories and plays, only a few of which have survived. A passionate advocate of the need for Africans to respect their own customs and traditions, he remained a faithful member of the Gold Coast Aborigines' Rights Protection Society with its attachment to a traditional model of political action. As his editor J. Ayo Langley has commented: 'This in my view is the clue to Sekyi's inability to emerge as a national leader (assuming he wanted to). He was trapped in Cape Coast by the ideology and organisation of an institution that had long outlived its usefulness. Nevertheless, both the man and his message are of great significance not only for contemporary Ghana but for Africa as a whole.'[34] In essence, Sekyi stood for the need to respect traditional Ghanaian culture and not to denigrate it as unprogressive, as was done by many Ghanaian intellectuals in his youth and later. He was not against modernisation. In fact, his view of the increasingly undemocratic attitudes which the traditional chiefs had been encouraged to adopt by their colonial masters was scathing. He advocated a return to the more open and effective traditional practices of the pre-colonial period. In his play, he satirised the pretensions and self-denigration of the men and women of the Gold Coast cities. In characters such as Mr Okadu, he attacked the mindless Anglocentrism of such people:

'All native ways are silly, repulsive, unrefined,
All customs superstitious, that rule the savage mind.
I like civilisation; and I'd be glad to see
All people that are pagan eschew idolatry.
I reckon high the power of Governors and such;
But our own Kings and Chiefs – why they do not matter much!

And so you see how loyal a Britisher I've grown . . .
I soon shall go to England . . .
And there I'll try my hardest to learn the English life,
And I will try to marry a real English wife!'[35]

39

The Blinkards deserves to be much better known, and it remains one of the most interesting accounts of the struggle in the early part of the twentieth century between the conflicting cultural forces which impinged on West African life. Its use of the dramatic form to record these clashes establishes that the recent emphasis on fiction and poetry has been at the expense of the long tradition of dramatic writing in Africa in English. For this reason, perhaps, it is still less well-known and less frequently commented on than the narrative prose fictions of the early period, such as R. E. Obeng's *Eighteenpence*.

Eighteenpence (145 pages long in the reissued edition) was first published in 1941, but it was probably written earlier, and deals with events set some three decades previously. It is really a series of distinct stories, held together loosely by a central figure, Obeng Akrofi, who appears in most of them. Writing the introduction to it, the Gold Coast scholar and independence fighter J. B. Danquah hailed it as 'an immeasurably important book . . . [which marked] . . . a new epoch in Gold Coast approach to English Literature' (preface to first edition, 1941). It is certainly one of the first books to constitute an opposed and different African written tradition in English. But, although Danquah refers to it as the Gold Coast equivalent of Fielding's *Tom Jones*, that is as a founding novel in a new tradition, he viewed it primarily as an addition to English literature, rather than as the beginning of an alternative African English literature. This is shown clearly in his preface, which praised the book for its success in using 'a mode of the King's English that would live for long years'.

Eighteenpence illustrates the tensions involved in writing an English fictional text in this period. It employs a mixture of Received Standard English and a localised form of Nigerian English, a feature which is well illustrated in the opening sequence:

> In the ancient and salubrious town of Abetifi, in the district of Kwahu, there lived, during the reign of Nana Addo Kese Pambuo, a man whose name was Obeng Akrofi. Obeng, though kind-hearted, was as poor as a church-mouse. He was also so self-conscious that he could not approach any of his friends or relatives for anything. His earthly possessions consisted of a loin-cloth, which was threadbare, and a small dog that followed him everywhere he went. This dog he called 'Poor-No-Friend'. (1)

Whilst Danquah is probably right in noting that the bulk of the narrative is in a slightly modified form of Received Standard English (or King's English, as he terms it), the dialogue is often slanted to include a distinctive local flavour in diction and lexis.

> 'What are you saying, you senseless fellow?' she demanded. 'Are you scolding me? You know that we two are alone here on this farm; do you wish to beat me? If you like, do so, and the police will punish you!'
>
> In a tremulous voice Akrofi ejaculated: 'How would I dare to beat you, my master's wife? I find you are as dangerous as a loaded gun, and your words are poisonous as a snake. I will no longer remain here with you. Farewell.' And he quickly left the farm. But Konaduwa remained there until very late in the evening. (5)

The themes Obeng selects also illustrate the cultural tension within the society. The opening narrative deals on the surface with the conflict between genders. The role of protagonist, occupied by the ostensible hero Obeng Akrofi, is hotly contested by the fiery Konaduwa, wife of the man who loans him the eighteenpence after which the novel is named, and from which trivial-seeming event the whole plot flows. However, the real underlying contest is between the two views of events which the novel dramatises: the view of the Ghanaian world, with its indigenous courts of nobles and elders, and that of the colonial District Commissioner's and local magistrate's courts. In the inability of the view of the one world to mesh in any meaningful way with the other, *Eighteenpence* dramatises the colonial encounter, and asserts an indigenous viewpoint on events long before the more famous accounts of the writers of the late 1950s. In what follows, the point of view veers between descriptions which assert the power and dignity of the local world and its traditions, and those which extol the virtue of the modern ways brought by the colonisers. Long and detailed accounts of the dignity and commonsense exercised by the traditional officials, and sumptuous descriptions of the local rulers, vie with accounts of the success Obeng Akrofi has with his farm when he abjures the traditional planting methods and employs the advice of the Government Agricultural Service. Overall, the traditional world is favoured, and the descriptions of local law and social practice establish, in Achebe's later, memorable phrase, that 'African societies had a dignity and beauty of their own', long before the colonisers introduced their modern changes.

> At two o'clock the drums began to beat, and at half-past two the court was crowded. The Omanhene, bedecked with ornaments, was escorted thither. His arms were laden with gold trinkets from elbow to wrist, and he wore a heavy ring on every finger . . . The agile sword-bearers with their gilded swords ran to and fro in front of him as swiftly as bees seeking their hive. The court-criers were there, with their gold-plated caps, and the 'soul-washers' with their well-polished breast-plates suspended round their necks by woven pineapple fibres, glittering like stars . . . The pandemonium that reigned was beyond description. Amid the din, the Omanhene advanced slowly towards the court. When he came into view, Amenaku, Chief Palanquin-Carrier, shouted thunderously: 'Arise'. The whole assembly, chiefs and everybody, sprang to their feet as one man, and remained standing until His Majesty was seated. (40)

Despite the power of these descriptions, a tension resides in the choice of epithets (pandemonium, din), which conflicts with the overall design of asserting the power and dignity of the traditional African society. It is as if two visions and two voices are competing on the site of a single event. It is worth restating here that, although not published until 1941, the text almost certainly dates from earlier. The setting of Obeng's *Eighteenpence* around 1913 makes it contemporary with the setting of the later novels of colonial encounter by writers such as Achebe to which it is the generic ancestor.[36] But these descriptions, which in some respects look forward to the kind of celebratory view Achebe offers of the assemblies of Umuofia and Umuahia in the novels *Things Fall Apart* (1958) and *Arrow of God* (1964), also reflect a certain ineradicable ambiguity. Looked at now, *Eighteenpence* can be seen as an example of the kind of liminal text which alone could be produced under the colonial process of control, deeply imbued with a local power and vision, but restrained and influenced in innumerable ways by the colonial patronage system which brought it into print. Furthermore, the fact that no extensive local market for this kind of fiction existed at this time meant that, despite the praise of important local figures such as J. B. Danquah, Obeng's short novel was to remain a relatively isolated cultural event. Further development of the novel in English was restricted to popular pamphlets and short fiction, until the new market produced by the boom in post-war education in the colonies generated the demand for a new generation of English-language writers.[37] Nevertheless, despite these reservations, R. E. Obeng's *Eighteenpence* represents a foundational moment for fiction writing in English in Africa.[38]

East Africa

I have concentrated so far on the scene in West Africa because events there unfolded much earlier, and resulted in the production throughout the nineteenth and twentieth centuries of a much larger body of significant writing in English. The principal difference between the two regions was the absence in the coastal enclaves of East Africa of a group comparable with the nineteenth-century Creole communities of West Africa. No equivalent springboard to Sierra Leone or Liberia existed in East Africa to nurture such a group. Although the British navy had been active in suppressing the slave trade in the Indian Ocean, it had done so in a much more restricted way, through a series of accommodations with the local Arab rulers, notably the great Sultan of Oman and Zanzibar, Seyyid Said, and his successors. Those slaves who were 're-captured' from the Arab slavers in the Indian Ocean or on the mainland were brought to the various missions on Zanzibar and Pemba, or to one of the missions in the coastal enclaves still controlled by the Sultan, such as the Catholic mission at Bagamoya. The smaller numbers involved, and the dominance of Muslims in these areas, meant that there was no possibility of these freed slaves forming a distinctive and controlling group in these settlements with the power and influence of their equivalents, the 'recaptives' of West Africa, whose energy and numbers transformed the Creole communities of Liberia and Sierra Leone. Communication and trade with the interior was in the hands of the descendants of those Arabs who had been settled here for several centuries, and this control was not wrested from them until much later by European venturers. The comparatively late date of a really active drive to establish missions in the interior of East Africa also meant that the equivalent role to that played by African Christians such as Crowther and others in the West African hinterland in the 1840s and 1850s was delayed until almost the end of the century. In East Africa, too, equivalent educational institutes to Fourah Bay College, Sierra Leone, which nurtured so many of the West African intellectuals, did not develop until well into the twentieth century. Makerere, in Uganda, was not opened until the 1920s, and it did not achieve university college status until the 1930s. As in West Africa, the interest of the British government in controlling the interior was limited, and indeed largely negative, before the 1890s. Trade was restricted to the islands of Zanzibar and Pemba, and the coastal regions. Even when attempts were made to move into the interior, it was by the indirect method of establishing independent charter companies, as in West Africa. The failure of the attempt of the Imperial British East African Company (IBEAC) to make an economic success of its drive in the Buganda region meant that there was little incentive for the British government to view the East African interior as anything but a financial and political liability. It was the pressure of the competition of the other European countries, as well as that of the downward thrust of Egypt towards the region, which caused the policy to be revised, as part of the so-called 'Scramble for Africa', in the last years of the century.

For the reasons I have outlined, there was no equivalent in East Africa to the body of diverse writing in English produced in the West African region from the mid-nineteenth century onwards. The nearest equivalent group to the nineteenth-century Creole intellectuals of West Africa in the English-speaking areas of East Africa were those local leaders (Ganda, Maasai, and so forth) with whom a special relationship was established by imperialists such as the young Lugard, then a Captain in the forces of the IBEAC. In Buganda, where this policy of working with and through local leaders was most vigorously pursued, it was not really the result of a genuine acceptance of local power and institutions, but rather the product of an attempt to displace from power 'intransigent' traditional rulers, such as the Kabaka Mwanga. The IBEAC policy, initiated by Lugard's concept of indirect rule via the local Bugandan administrative forms, developed a sharper political edge when it was used to foster and support the Christian party within the Muslim–Christian divisions of the local chiefs. An internal struggle between these factions occurred in the Buganda kingdom, especially after 1894, when, following the failure of the IBEAC to establish effective political or economic control, the British officially took control of Buganda as part of the new Ugandan Protectorate.

In 1897, when Kabaka Mwanga of Buganda, and his ally Omukama Kabarega, the *Mukama* of Bunyoro, revolted against British control, the British supported the Christian chiefs, notably the *Katakiro* (chief minister) Apolo (later Sir Apolo) Kagwa, in placing the young boy Daudi Chwa on the throne of Buganda. Kabaka Mwanga's revolt was suppressed in 1899, and he and Kabarega were exiled to the Seychelles. Apolo Kagwa is significant in that his role, and that of his Kabaka, within the modified Bugandan society that developed after British intervention, was, in a number of important respects, the model for the policy of indirect rule which Lugard later transported to and perfected in Nigeria. This policy was later employed extensively as the model for all the British West African colonies other than Sierra Leone. But there was no East African equivalent to the Creole intellectuals who, as we have seen, in the late nineteenth and early twentieth centuries interacted with and modified the position of these traditional rulers. As a result the role of Kagwa and his fellow chiefs was a very different one in the early development of nationalist sentiment in the respective regions.

The East African equivalent of the early West African nationalists and modernisers emerged only after the First World War when, as a result of missionary and government education schemes, a new generation of Africans arose to challenge the position of the traditional chiefs. This challenge was, as one historian has expressed it, 'not a contest between rich and poor but between the best educated and most wealthy Africans in the rural areas. It has been termed a conflict between "competing modernisers".'[39] Perhaps so, and certainly the evidence of the texts of Kagwa and his companion and amanuensis Ham Mukasa, such as their famous account of their visit to Edward VII's Coronation, *Uganda's Katakiro in England, being the official account of his visit to the coronation of His Majesty King Edward VII* (1904),[40] suggest that 'modernisation' and an admiration for and desire to emulate European technical achievement were also motivating forces for the British-sponsored traditional leaders such as Kagwa. But the political model for Kagwa was clearly very different in orientation from that of the generation of nationalists who emerged in the inter-war years, and who were to lead the East African drive for independence.

The modifying and softening influence of figures like Casely Hayford, who, as we have noted above, successfully forged the possibility of an alliance of interests between traditional rulers and modern, secular intellectuals in Ghana in the period after the First World War, did not have an equivalent in East African territories like Uganda. Later leaders, however, like Kenyatta in Kenya, clearly did seek to position themselves between these competing groups of mission-educated intellectuals and traditional elders in their attempt to create a unified sense of nationality amongst peoples such as the Gĩkũyũ from the 1920s onwards.

In addition to these internal differences within the African communities themselves, the presence of a large and increasingly vociferous body of white settlers in Kenya, a presence bolstered by the large number of soldier-settlers who flowed in after 1918, exacerbated the possibilities for conflict. There was also an increasing tendency for British administrations to favour the settlers: for example, in the ongoing debates between those who advocated that the land was to be held in trust for the development of African societies with their own economic base, and those who advocated the development of the land as a 'white man's country' on the Rhodesian and South African models. All this meant that nationalist sentiments had a sharper, more confrontationist path to tread in the years between and after the two world wars. By 1926, British nominees such as Sir Apolo Kagwa were under increasing direct control by British officials in the Uganda Protectorate, even though extensive white settlement was not a factor in Uganda at the time. Sir Apolo Kagwa resigned as *Katakiro* in 1926, after refusing to accept the right of the Provincial Commissioner of Buganda to issue him with direct orders. The conflicts between administrators and chiefs in Uganda concerned the excessive demands being made on Africans by traditional chiefs to fulfil conscripted labour needs and to supply work levies, which rights the British had earlier yielded to the traditional rulers. Under an agreement made in 1900 with the British these traditional rulers had been granted title to most of the arable land within the Uganda Protectorate.

Elsewhere, in Kenya and Tanganyika, the conflicts were more frequently between government administrators and white settlers. The settlers' insatiable need for conscripted labour was forcing the administration to support policies designed to force Africans away from the growing of their own cash crops, and towards the role of paid labourers on European-owned, plantation-style enterprises. In both situations, however, the opposition was led by the new generation of European-educated African intellectuals, who opposed the demands of the British and their clients, the traditional rulers in the case of Uganda, and the settlers in the other East African territories. Both these groups sought to prevent the development of African economies based on cash crops grown by ordinary Africans on their own land.

Sir Apolo Kagwa is of especial interest to literary scholars because of his prolific output as a writer. But it is significant that he wrote his texts, recording the history and customs of the clans and kings of Buganda, in Luganda, not in English. Ham Mukasa, Kagwa's amanuensis on the *Katakiro*'s trip to England, was also a member of the Bugandan nobility; like Kagwa he too had been a 'page' at the court of the reformist, pro-British Kabaka Mutesa, and a Christian convert. He was also one of the earliest Bugandans to learn English, and an indefatigable writer and recorder in both English and Luganda. He was the author not only of an account of his and Kagwa's epic journey to Edward VII's coronation, but also of commentaries on the Gospels, a history of the reign of Kabaka Mutesa, and various newspaper articles on educational, religious and social questions. Taban lo Liyong records how, in 1945, when it was proposed to transfer Makerere College to Kenya, Mukasa authored a spirited article in English in the *Uganda Argus*, defending its retention in Uganda.[41] In some ways, these late-nineteenth- and early-twentieth-century Bugandan intellectuals have more in common with the aristocratic leaders of Hausa-Fulani Nigeria than with the creolised coastal intellectuals who dominated intellectual life in the West African colonial settlements in the same period. In Uganda, Luganda remained a powerful alternative written vehicle to English throughout the colonial period, and it continues to be a language with an active and powerful publishing presence.

Elsewhere in East Africa, for example in Kenya, few texts independent of government or missionary control were published in the period between the two world wars. The only significant example is the first book in English published by a black Kenyan, Parmeneo Gĩthendu Mockerie's *An African Speaks for his People* (1934), published by the Hogarth Press in London. It was the first book in which a black Kenyan presented a view of the British administration without direct or indirect censorship. The book is particularly critical of the standards of mission education. No other book was published in English by a black Kenyan until Jomo Kenyatta, later to be the first President of independent Kenya, published *Facing Mount Kenya* in 1938. There was some writing in indigenous languages such as Gĩkũyũ, published by mission presses, and later by the colonial literature bureaux, but the emphasis was on textbooks rather than fiction. Some independent local writing in these languages did emerge in the period from the mid-1940s onwards, for example in

Gĩkũyũ in the work of the prolific author Gakaara wa Wanjaũ, who established locally controlled writing in the Gĩkũyũ language. Gakaara began to write after returning from military service in 1945, when he tried, unsuccessfully, to establish the first independent cooperative of black Kenyan writers. Known as African Book Writers Limited, this was an organisation which sought to allow black Kenyan writers to publish outside official channels. Despite these early attempts, it is arguably only after Kenyan independence in the 1960s that he, with others, was able to establish regular outlets for the publication of Gĩkũyũ-language writing which was not controlled by colonial or church authorities.[42] Thus, apart from some early political broadsheets, such as the Gĩkũyũ-language newspaper *Muigwithania*, which Kenyatta edited in the late 1920s, vernacular writing did not develop extensively in Kenya until after the Second World War.[43] This relatively late start has prompted Ngũgĩ and others to argue the need to encourage and foster the ongoing use of Gĩkũyũ as a literary language. With the emergence of an armed opposition to colonialism in Kenya in the early 1950s – the Mau Mau movement – government policies which had until then favoured vernacular language education in the lower school now swung sharply against it. Ngũgĩ, amongst others, has recorded the policies initiated then against the use of local languages in schools.[44] Conversely, in the areas which now comprise Tanzania (erstwhile German East Africa, later Tanganyika/Zanzibar), ki-Swahili was far more developed as a lingua franca, a fact which affected the development of writing in English. This relative paucity of English usage was partly the result of the educational policies of the Germans in erstwhile German East Africa (Tanganyika after the First World War), who favoured the use of ki-Swahili. German administrators 'went much further than the British in providing financial aid to the mission schools and in establishing schools themselves. Making wide use of Swahili as the medium of instruction, the German authorities established schools throughout the colony. After World War I these helped to produce a generation of educated young men who would claim to be more effective communicators between Europeans and Africans than official chiefs.'[45] The result was the preservation of ki-Swahili as an effective and widespread alternative to English. It remained the principal medium of written expression during the period when the burgeoning nationalist opposition to colonialism forged links across and between the various territories making up British East Africa. With the development of the *ujaama* philosophy, in post-independence Tanzania, this emphasis on the use of local languages and of ki-Swahili as a lingua franca has meant that much of the significant modern writing in Tanzania has continued to be produced in ki-Swahili rather than in the medium of English.

Notes

1. See P. F. de Moraes Farias and Karin Barber, *Self-Assertion and Brokerage: Early Cultural Nationalism in West Africa* (Birmingham: Centre of West African Studies, University of Birmingham, 1990).

2. J. B. Webster and A. A. Boahen with M. Tidy, *The Revolutionary Years: West Africa Since 1800* (London: Longman, 1980).

3. For a discussion of this 'tangled affair' see Introduction to *The Life of Olaudah Equiano, or Gustavus Vassa the African, written by himself,* ed. Paul Edwards (Harlow: Longman, 1989).

4. Frederick Douglass, *My Bondage and My Freedom* (1855; New York: Arno Press, 1968).

5. Historians have usually given these writers a great deal of attention as documentary sources, but their achievement has been relatively neglected by literary scholars.

6. See Lucilda Hunter, *Memoirs and Poems by Adelaide Casely Hayford and Gladys Casely Hayford* (Freetown: Sierra Leone University Press, 1983) and Adelaide M. Cromwell, *An African Victorian Feminist: The Life and Times of Adelaide Smith Casely Hayford 1868–1960* (London: Frank Cass, 1986).

7. Nina Emma Mba, *Nigerian Women Mobilised: Women's Political Activity in Southern Nigeria 1900–1965* (Berkeley, Ca.: Institute of International Studies, University of California Press, 1982).

8. A discussion of this important text will be found in Chapter 3.

9. J. E. Casely Hayford, *Ethiopia Unbound* (1911; reissued, London: Frank Cass, 1969), pp. 16–17. Further page references are given in the text.

10. The peculiar term 'recaptive' was the one used in the period for West African slaves who had been freed after the vessels in which they were being transported had been intercepted and captured by the British naval patrols set up after the abolition of the slave trade. Such slaves were invariably landed at Sierra Leone. Although slaves were similarly rescued, at a later date, in East Africa, and usually re-settled in missions on Zanzibar, the term does not seem to have been employed there.

11. Davidson (Abioseh) Nicol, *Africanus Horton: The Dawn of Nationalism in Modern Africa* (London: Longman, 1969), p. 9.

12. *Christianity, Islam and the Negro Race* (1871), in Hollis R. Lynch (ed.), *Black Spokesman: Selected Writings of E. W. Blyden* (London: Cass, 1971), pp. 278–9.

13. *The Aims and Methods of a Liberal Education for Africans* (1881), in Lynch (ed.), *Black Spokesman*, p. 236.

14. Nicol, *Africanus Horton*, p. 9.

15. Speech published in *West Africa Before Europe* (1905), in Lynch (ed.), *Black Spokesman*, pp. 323–4.

16. Nicol, *Africanus Horton*, p. 68.

17. Ibid., p. 177.

18. Webster *et al.*, *The Revolutionary Years*, p. 165.

19. Later West African nationalists, such as Danquah and Nkrumah, as well as others in remoter parts of Africa, such as Kenyatta in Kenya, looked to these early figures for inspiration and example in their own struggles to oppose this imperial fiction. See, for example, the introduction by J. B. Danquah in M. J. Sampson's *Gold Coast Men of Affairs* (London: Dawsons, 1937; reissued in the Colonial History Series, ed. D. H. Simpson, 1969).

20. Webster *et al.*, *The Revolutionary Years*, p. 209.

21. See Basil Davidson, *The Black Man's Burden: Africa and the Curse of the Nation State* (London: James Currey, 1992).

22. Nicol, *Africanus Horton*, p. 14.

23. See, for example, J. F. A. Ajayi, *Christian Missions in Nigeria 1841–1891: The Making of a New Elite* (London: Longman, 1965), pp. 127–31.

24. For more detailed accounts of the development of locally owned and produced broadsheets, newspapers etc., see M. J. Echeruo, *Victorian Lagos* (London: Macmillan, 1977); K. A. B. Jones-Quartey, *History, Politics and Press in Early Ghana: The Fictions and The Facts* (Legon, Ghana: School of Journalism and Communication Studies, University of Legon, 1975); F. I. A. Omu, *Press and Politics in Nigeria 1880–1937* (London: Longman, 1978); F. I. A. Omu, 'The Newspaper Press in Southern Nigeria 1800–1900', in B. I. Obichere, *Studies in Southern Nigerian History* (London: Frank Cass, 1982). For a useful general overview of intellectual life in nineteenth- and early-twentieth-century Africa see R. W. July, *The Origins of Modern African Thought* (London: Faber, 1968).

25. De Moraes Farias and Barber, *Self-Assertion and Brokerage*, p. 3.

26. For accounts of local Yoruba histories and their practice see, for example, the works of Toyin Fayola.

27. Ato Quayson, *Strategic Transformations in Nigerian Writing: Orality and History in the Work of Rev. Samuel Johnson, Amos Tutuola, Wọle Ṣoyinka and Ben Okri* (Oxford: James Currey, 1997), p. 20.

28. Ibid., p. 20.

29. Quayson uses a more positive phrase than 'brokerage', referring to this and the other works of the time as 'Nutritive Junctures' of the various oral and written discourses which inform them. It is interesting to look at this claim in relation to Quayson's arguments about the shifting goal of later writing in English. He notes that there are great differences between the nationalist goals of Johnson, whose task was in certain senses to 'broker' a relationship with that culture for the new elite intent on forming a nation, and later writers whose task was to deal with the realities of post-independence conditions in a period of rapid change and adjustment, change in which new ideologies of the individual emerge which clash with the communalist ideals of indigenous cultures. 'This change from a largely positivist paradigm to a discursively eclectic, hybrid and potentially chaotic one may be related to the growth of individualism at the conjuncture of the traumas of post-colonialism. In the late nineteenth century, it was desirable and possible to affirm a coherence for indigenous culture precisely because any potential disillusionment of the individual writer was a function of the Other's oppression. Indigenous culture is posited as coherent in a program of self-definition against the colonising Other. With the attainment of Independence the coherence of indigenous culture is buffeted from various angles. Widespread education weakens the bonds of ethnic identification as does the growth of large urban centres attracting labour from across the country and crossing ethnic identities with the stratifications of class.' Quayson, *Strategic Transformations*, p. 164.

30. Although I have dealt with figures like Samuel Ajayi Crowther and Samuel Johnson in this chapter, this raised the problem of establishing indisputable boundaries between the different kinds of texts and the patronages which enabled them, as I mentioned when discussing Philip Quaque in the chapter on slave diaspora writing rather than the chapter on missionary patronage.

31. It was more like three-quarters of a century by the time that Johnson's work was finally published by the CMS.

32. Compare the ways in which Kenyatta and later nationalists in East Africa employed mission presses in the 1940s in East Africa (Chapter 3 below). I have included these texts there because they were published specifically within mission series, though they employed the generic forms developed by mission presses for their own ends.

33. *The Blinkards*, ed. with an introduction by J Ayo Langley (London: Heinemann, 1974), p. 11. Further page references are given in the text.

34. *The Blinkards*, p. 11.

35. *The Blinkards*, pp. 46–7. The poem, which Mr Okadu speaks in the play, was later published separately under the title *The Sojourners*.

36. See Chapter 6 below for an account of these 'novels of celebration' of the late 1950s and early 1960s.

37. See Chapter 5 for an account of popular writing in English immediately after the Second World War.

38. Though, as Karin Barber has argued, the continuity of indigenous languages as a means of expression meant that oral performance and writing in African languages continued to provide a means of expression throughout the colonial period. See Karin Barber, *Readings in Popular African Culture* (Oxford: James Currey, 1997); and Karin Barber, 'Time, Space and Writing in Three Colonial Yoruba Novels', in *The Yearbook of English Studies, Special Issue: The Politics of Postcolonial Criticism,* ed. Andrew Gurr, 27 (1997), pp. 108–29.

39. R. M. Maxon, *East Africa: An Introductory History* (Morgantown, W. V.: West Virginia University Press, 1986), p. 183. Maxon makes this point specifically about Tanzania, but it has a wider relevance in the region.

40. This important and interesting text is available in a shortened form in a modern edition *Sir Apolo Kagwa Discovers Britain*, ed. Taban lo Liyong (London: Heinemann, 1975).

41. The article is reproduced in Taban lo Liyong's introduction to the Heinemann edition, *Sir Apolo Kagwa Discovers Britain*, pp. x–xi.

42. See Chapter 4 below.

43. See Bruce J. Berman and John M. Lonsdale, 'The Labours of Muigwithangia: Jomo Kenyatta as Author 1928–1945', *Research in African Literatures*, 29, 1 (Spring 1998), pp. 16–41.

44. Ngũgĩ has spoken of the policy to punish and humiliate children who spoke Gĩkũyũ in school, even in the playground. That this policy had long antecedents in imperial educational policy will be well known to those familiar with the notorious mid-nineteenth-century example of the suppression of Welsh in schools in the Principality following the report of three monoglot, English, Anglican Commissioners, Lingenh, Symons and Johnson. They were charged to investigate the quality of education in Wales, and, in particular, whether the largely monoglot and nonconformist Welsh working class was being adequately trained in the use of the English. Their report to the Welsh Education Commission was bound in three blue-covered volumes, which are known unsurprisingly as the Blue Books. They concluded that the education system in Wales was inadequate – which it probably was – but, moreover, that the reason for this was that the Welsh were indolent, filthy, superstitious, corrupt, and intoxicated, and that the principal reason for these personal inadequacies was the combination of Nonconformism and the Welsh language. As in Kenya, the children who spoke Welsh were singled out, punished and humiliated by having placards hung about their neck. The popular reference to this event as 'Brad y Llyfrau Gleision' (the Treason of the Blue Books) is contemporary with the publication of the report, and harks back to the medieval betrayal 'Brad y Cyllyll Hirion' (the treason (night) of the long knives) when Danish mercenaries slaughtered the Welsh at the court of Gwrtheyrn.

45. Maxon, *East Africa*, p. 171.

Chapter 3

Nineteenth- and Twentieth-Century Missionary Writing-Testaments and Writing by Africans Produced under Missionary Auspices and Control

It is impossible entirely to separate the texts in English produced under the patronage of the missionary societies from the writing of the slave diaspora, or the secular writing of the nineteenth century. The slave narratives of the diaspora were often produced with the encouragement of religious, anti-slavery societies in England and America. The same groups were also to found, or revitalise, many of the missionary societies which led the drive to Christianise Africa. Anti-slavery sponsors in both the dissenting churches and the Anglican Church were responsible for publishing the work of writers such as Equiano or Prince. Similar sponsors in America encouraged the publication of the poetry of Wheatley. Members of the same churches and groups later encouraged the development of the Protestant African missions in the period following the abolition of slavery in the British settlements of Africa. This overlap is to be expected, and it continues with regard to the figures considered in the second group of 'Creole intellectuals'. Crowther and James Johnson, for example, were also active Anglican missionaries; indeed both became bishops of the Anglican Church. Later figures among the early nationalists, such as the Rev. Attoh Ahuma and the Rev. Samuel Johnson, were also clergymen.

However, it is necessary to distinguish the kind of control exercised over the work of figures like Blyden, or Horton, and even the later clerical intellectuals, who had access to the pages of the same local, secular journals and news-papers to express their views, from that affecting earlier figures like Crowther.[1] Crowther's early works were printed under the direct control of the missions who sponsored the expeditions in which he took part, and supported his work on African languages. In 1837, the young Crowther completed a narrative letter, addressed to the Rev. William Jowett, detailing his capture as a slave and containing details of his life before that event. This important example of early African writing in English is also a very early example of the 'rescue' narrative form which came to be so important a part of later missionary-controlled publications. Crowther subsequently wrote accounts of the two expeditions he accompanied in 1841 and 1854 to the Niger/Tshadda River system, expeditions which were mounted with a view to establishing the first missions and trading posts there. The first is a supplement to the long account

of the leader of the 1841 expedition, the Rev. J. F. Schön; the second reportage of the 1854 expedition is a longer, independent account of considerable
detail and significance.

The *Journal* Crowther kept of the 1841 expedition is crucially different
from the similar accounts kept by Europeans, though of course it also shares
many of their forms and prejudices. The fact that two journals were kept, by
Schön and Crowther, and published in a single volume in 1842 offers a unique
chance to compare the style and substance of the reports written by European
and African missionaries.[2] Crowther's *1841 Journal* is notable, amongst other
things, for the stress it places on the work of native Africans in the missions,
and on the importance of using Africans who could preach effectively in the
native languages without the use of interpreters, whose inadequacies Crowther
notes he 'knows by experience'. He also stresses the need for 'studying the
language of the people, and translating the Scriptures into it' (267). Most notable, though, is the degree to which Crowther shows an interest in and facility
for observing and recording the details of the lives and customs of the peoples
he encounters. The Rev. Schön's account in the same volume is far more
abstract, and far more concerned with the details of the lives of the Europeans
on board the steamers (almost three-quarters of whom were to perish of fever
on the voyage). As a result, there is an insider feel to Crowther's account,
despite the need he frequently feels to qualify his descriptions with references
to the African scene as a 'heathen world' and its inhabitants as 'benighted
savages'. His lively interest in the details of this benighted world is demonstrated at every turn in descriptions which are far more concrete and circum-
stantial than those of his European superior:

> The natives of Fernando Po, generally called Bubies, are the most singular people
> I have ever met with. They will have nothing to do with clothes. They are quite
> satisfied with their grass leaves, beads, fowls' feathers, and some bits of monkey's
> skin, which they tie about their legs, waists, arms, necks, and other parts of their
> naked bodies. The rich among them have, in addition to these, some lumps of fat
> sewed up, exactly like large sausages, on their necks, and a very large lump of red
> clay fastened to the hair of their heads on the back part; while the whole hair and
> their bodies are rubbed over with the same stuff mixed with palm-oil . . . (341)

Such exactness of observation betrays an interest which belies the common-
place strictures which Crowther makes, from time to time, on the natives'
refusal to dress in a way acceptable to European convention: 'Some had only
dirty bits of cloth about their waists and others about their shoulders; which,
together with their smoky bows and arrows, and their dirty hair plaited in
different forms, gave them a complete appearance of barbarity' (290). Most
striking, though, is the certainty and completeness of Crowther's reportage of
local political events when compared with Schön's. Despite the distance from
the culture imposed on Crowther by his own early removal and by his relative
lack of facility in the local language at this time, his accounts show a far more
detailed grasp of the practices and motives of those they encounter than those
of Schön. Thus, when they have an audience with Rogang, the Chief at the

51

river settlement of Egga, the differing degree of inside knowledge manifested in the two accounts is very noticeable. Crowther, while confirming the basic facts as presented in Schön's account, shows a much more detailed understanding of the local politics and the delicate position of Rogang, as well as a knowledge of the names of those involved in the discussion:

> Rogang, the Chief, was very much pleased to hear this good news; but as he is only a Chief under Sumoh Zakki – properly Sumo Sariki – the Fulatah king of Rabba, he deferred giving me an answer to the principal subjects of my message till he had called me to his courtyard, admitting no more than about five of his friends besides Legamah and Lusah, when he ordered the gate to be shut. He said that he was glad to hear all that the White Men have come to do: and as for his part, he would have very readily and gladly done as they wish, had it been in his power; but that before any thing of this kind could be done, it must be referred to Sumo Sariki at Rabba, as whatever he says is the law. (316)

In his account Crowther also shows himself much more aware of the internal politics, and of Rogang's fear of spies amongst his own court. His work elsewhere, too, shows a detailed knowledge of local affairs, which is for the most part missing from Schön's account. For example:

> Katunga, the capital of Yaruba, was deserted after the death of Abiohdung, the king of Yaruba. Atiba, the heir to the throne, removed the seat of government from Katunga to Aggoh, because the former was too near to Illorrin; while Oluyorle, the commander of the soldiers, or head warrior, took his seat at Kishi, otherwise called Ajanna, in confederacy with Ibariba, a people on the border of Yaruba, nearly speaking the same language. They have since had three battles: one at Igboda, about seven years ago; and another at Oshogbo, about three years ago; in both of which Illorrin, headed by Sitah, a Fulatah, was defeated with great loss. (318)

Nowhere does Schön's *Journal* of the same period and events provide this sort of detail of the past and recent political events within the communities they visited, nor show any interest in doing so. Perhaps Schön showed a better judgement of what the Committee of the expedition's sponsors, the Christian Missionary Society (CMS), was likely to want to hear. It is notable that in his second account, of the 1854 expedition, ten years or more later, Crowther does not provide this kind of detail of local political events to anything like the same extent. In the meantime, no doubt, he had learned that to present the politics of African peoples as the product of competing powers and interests, which should be understood as not dissimilar to European countries and states, was unacceptable to the prevailing mission view of the peoples of the region as a backward and divided group of warring tribes. The complex political alliances and conflicts of the *1841 Journal* are represented in later missionary narratives simply as barbarous inter-tribal skirmishes, motivated by a general native brutality, and meaningful only in so far as they excused the intervention of the civilising European influence. Crowther's *1841 Journal*, by contrast, has all the seriousness of a history, and is, in some respects, a notable precursor of such foundational works of local historiography as Samuel Johnson's late-nineteenth-century *The History of the Yoruba*s (completed in 1897).

The *1841 Journal* shows less tension than the later writings, after Crowther had emerged as a spokesperson for the African community in Sierra Leone and Nigeria (Yorubaland), as a champion of its aspirations in education, and of its claim to an equal partnership in the enterprise of opening up the interior to religious and commercial dealings. In this period he came increasingly to face the prejudice of white missionaries, such as his long-time rival Henry Townsend, who advocated a subordinate role for Africans in these enter-prises. There is little doubt, too, that Crowther's work was subject to increas-ing self-censorship, as he strove to convince, without alienating, the authorities in London with whom he dealt. He was also subject to more direct censorship, with the publication of some of his more positive descriptions and observa-tions of African society and customs. In the last analysis, his voice was under the control of those who owned the presses, which could issue or ignore his memorialisation and his reports, or edit them as they saw fit. As one Nigerian scholar has noted, some of the most significant accounts of traditional practice recorded by Crowther, and sent in reports to the CMS, were not published, and have still 'never been noticed'.[3]

Despite these difficulties, Crowther's *Journal* of the 1854 expedition con-tinued to record the fact that African peoples had values and religious con-cepts of their own which they exercised with as much, if not more, dignity than the Europeans.[4] For example, Crowther notes the failure of the European crew to practice religious observation: 'This morning, as the Krumen were set to cut wood for the furnace, I could not but feel for them, as they went very reluctantly to work. It is a reproach to us, who profess to observe the Lord's day, and teach others to sanctify it, thus to violate it ourselves' (89). By contrast he notes how punctilious the African notables are in this respect: 'He was invited to breakfast, but he would not eat . . . until he had performed some religious ceremony which he called washing . . . However to oblige Dr. Baikie . . . he . . . touched the wine in the glass with his finger, and rubbed it on his head and hands' (171). However limited such portraits of difference may seem from a modern, post-independence viewpoint, in the context of the mid-nineteenth century they were a strong assertion of African cultural values. In fact, such observations were soon to be viewed as a threat – one which, by the end of the century, had made Crowther a thorn in the side of the Church, and which brought him into direct conflict with the secular colonial authorities from the 1880s onwards.

The frequent modern portrayal of this generation of mission-educated Chris-tian intellectuals as simply complicit with the colonial powers, or as tools and dupes of imperialism, and the betrayers of their countrymen, is a view one can only construct with hindsight, and one which does little justice to the real events or people of the period. During the nineteenth century, figures like Crowther acted as a living challenge to the assumptions, which grew as the century progressed and imperial control tightened, that native peoples in Africa, as elsewhere in the Empire, were not yet fit for responsibility, and that their admission to the order of 'civilisation' was likely to be a matter of centuries rather than decades. From the earliest accounts of the expeditions to the Niger/Tshadde, to his innumerable later reports, letters and memorials, Crowther had written into the record a series of positive images of Africans. Although even in his later work he often continued to reflect the common belief of his time, that to be truly 'civilised' Africans needed to evolve towards imported European standards of behaviour, dress and morals, he also gave strong support to the values resident in their local cultures. He celebrated and recorded these values as the foundations upon which an independent and self-governing African society could be raised. In this regard Crowther, despite being contained within the institutions of the Anglican Church, as Horton was within those of the British army, was a figure whose work and writings came to symbolise the inadequacy and falsity of the denigratory European char-acterisation of Africans. His own tragic rejection by the increasingly racist authorities in the later years comments, ironically, on the falseness of his trust in those white men whom he had characterised in his earlier accounts as 'the friends and well-wishers of all mankind' (146).

The single most important contribution of the missions to self-realisation and self-representation for Africans was the introduction of writing and print-ing, technologies which gave Africans the means to present African views, albeit in constrained forms. The development of printing in Africa related to the demand in the mission settlements for printing skills. The great need for on-the-spot prints of religious texts, tracts and so forth, prompted a need to train local personnel. The Presbyterians had led the way by importing their own printing press, which by 1849 had produced hundreds of local copies of Bible lessons, almanacs with the commandments in Efik, catechisms, and edu-cational material such as multiplication tables. The CMS also brought out a hand-press and sought to train several local boys as printers. The American Colonisation Society sent a Jamaican printer, Robert Campbell, to Abeokuta in 1859, where he was instrumental in helping to set up a press. The Yoruba language journal *Iwe-irohin* was founded as a result. It included notices of Church affairs and 'didactic essays on history and politics'.[5] Robert Campbell went on to Lagos in 1862, where he founded the *Anglo-African* with printers trained at the CMS establishment in Abeokuta.

What we see emerging here is a pattern which was to be central to the missionary role as a patron of writing and publishing in and about Africa. From an impulse to proselytise, mixed with a conscious or unconscious idea that writing and literacy were coterminous (as was the notion of brick and stone buildings, and European clothing) with the ideal of 'civilisation', the missionary presses unintentionally created the institutions through which the voices of Africans could find their way into a printed form in their own languages, and in the language of the dominant patronage system. As a result the missionary presses in the later periods were under an increasing tension resulting from the internal contradictions of their roles. In time, as we shall see, they even became the patrons of the first generation of nationalist leaders such as J. B. Danquah and Jomo Kenyatta, whose work they published, though the texts were framed within styles and genres which disguised their rad-ical content. Such subterfuges made this writing acceptable to the liberal, if paternalistic, missionary support for African independent cultural and social identity.

It was the missionary introduction of printing and the training of locals in printing skills in the mid-nineteenth century which led to the development of many local journals, tracts and newspapers. These became the instruments of the local intellectuals who led the struggle to put an 'African' viewpoint before the European communities of the settlements. They offered Africans a platform for the expression of their views, and the formation of their own cultural, social and political identity, in forms increasingly recognisable by the colonial authorities as a challenge to their own views. The missionaries introduced the printed word into Africa for their own ends, but it was an instrument which was amenable to the many other and quite different purposes which were to emerge in the years to come. The complex metaphor of 'The Word' in Wọle Ṣoyinka's play *The Road* (1965), in which Professor, the defrocked catechist, searches for a Word which will liberate the forces which link Life and Death in the Yoruba cosmology, is an example of how powerfully this ambivalent symbol continues to be in modern African writing. For Africa the Word (as written and oral sign) is the ground on which ideas of destruction and modernisation, betrayal and renewal, communication and silencing, meet and mingle in complex and powerful ways. Nowhere is this more apparent or more complex than in the case of texts produced under mission patronage.

Missionary press patronage influenced the production of texts over a considerable period of time, and in a wide variety of different cultural and geographic contexts across Africa. It also created a number of specific literary forms. These forms, although simple in themselves, raise issues about how missionaries saw and represented indigenous life, what they focused on and how they structured it in narrative. In addition the forms were available from the earliest period for elaboration and appropriation to more complex ends. Three of the most common generic forms are: 'release narratives', which tell the story of a slave's rescue and conversion; the exemplary life, in which the story of a successful convert is told; and the informative account of a specific people or group, the ethnographic narrative. These forms overlapped and developed into various hybrid combinations. But, in one form or another, they were the dominant means of representing Africans in English-language texts for a considerable period of time.

Among the earliest narratives published by missionaries are the so-called 'release narratives', which tell the stories of the slaves released from slavery and brought to missions, where their life stories are written down by missionary amanuenses. These stories, especially in the early period, were aimed at the metropolitan congregations, and were intended to encourage financial contributions to the task of the missions, which is represented as a literal and metaphorical 'bringing forth from bondage' of the African peoples. The story entitled *Trapped* establishes a number of classic features for the mission 'release narrative'.[6] It recounts how two young boys go to trade for a fishing hook and are captured by Arab slavers. On their way to Zanzibar the slavers are delayed. An *askari* speaks to the boys and they confide in him. They are freed and are sent to the Universities Mission to Central Africa boys training centre at Kilimani, Zanzibar. The story concludes with their voluntary baptism. 'It was not many years till, at their own desire, they were prepared for and received Baptism at the great Slave-Market Church; and some day, if they pass satisfactorily, through the schools and Training Colleges at the Universities' Mission, they may carry the good news of the Gospel back to their native lands' (10–11). The text is illustrated with a woodcut of a starving child titled 'A shadow of his former self', and another showing slaves in chains. The photographs and the titles are generic rather than narrative-specific: that is, they could be used to illustrate any number of tales of this kind. They do not represent specific characters and events. The genre as a whole is generalised, only rarely showing individualised character. This is in line with its primary purpose, which is to represent Africans as 'children' in need of rescue and succour, and African societies as essentially savage and irredeemable.

Another tale, *Cast Out*, offers a variant introduction, but quickly reverts to the basic pattern. This is the story of a slave-girl, 'Sofi', 'cast out' by her master because she has a sore on her leg, then received at the mission at Mbweni, Zanzibar, where, we are told, 'Sofi was received and tended'. She then 'tells' her tale. Her real name is Ndunde and she is from the Great Lakes region. The story of her enslavement and release is followed by that of her mission reception, and the whole ends in baptism. 'Let us wait six months and look in at Mbweni again – It is the feast of Pentecost – The one who walks last, the child whose happy face and white garments shine in the light of the carefully carried candle, has just been given the name of Barbara. Once she was Sofi, the sad-faced slave. Barbara has the ability to learn. If she is faithful she may one day in her own time teach others' (13). It is significant that her original, pre-enslavement name, Ndunde, is not recalled in this ending, emphasising that the concern of these stories is with the redemption of enslaved Africans, and not the recording or recovery of the identities and values of Africa's indigenous societies, about which we learn nothing.

In place of enslavement, the story entitled *Baby Sefu* offers a significant variant on the reason for the child's arrival in the mission. It is the story of a small child, adopted and nursed by the mission children. The child has been cast out from his 'tribe' as supposedly unlucky, because his top-teeth came first, and he is not killed only because the father was a catechist. Instead, the father sends him to the mission, though he still arrives undernourished, since the father had to hide him in the forest and could not feed him until he was supposed dead or fled by the elders of the tribe. Despite the care given to him at the mission, Baby Sefu dies (but not before he is first baptised). On the grave is written in Swahili 'Sefu', which we are given to understand translates as 'Safe in the Arms of Jesus'.

One of the most elaborate of these early stories is called *Panya*. It is an account, written in December 1901, of the rescue of Panya, a nine-year-old girl, from Arab slavers. What makes the tale especially interesting is the way in which it dramatises the process by which the matter of these tales is transmitted from 'subject' to 'author'. It reveals that in these early tracts the claim to represent the authentic tales of Africans is deeply suspect. Panya's tale is 'as told', we are informed, by herself to one A. F., a female missionary at the Mbweni Training Establishment, Zanzibar, in 1894–95. She had been released from an Arab dhow in April 1893. The story is unusual in that it describes in detail the period between Panya's release and her finding of 'peace' at Mbweni, the act of 'conversion', and the degree to which this conversion is synonymous with the creation of the 'true' narrative of Panya.

The narrative describes an elaborate process, in which what is at issue is the revision of the child's perception and memory by the missionary amanuensis. There is an obvious struggle for control between the teller and the recorder of these events: 'I remembered Panya's story, and I gave her fair warning I should expect it to be ready in a week' (8). Panya has been taught Swahili by A. F., but she has, somewhat disconcertingly to A. F., also picked up English. A. F.'s response to this is revealingly rueful: 'I found if I didn't want the Little Pitcher to enjoy all my talks with the other ladies, she must be sent away before we began' (7). Communication is to be a one-way process, with information flowing from Panya to A. F. but not the other way. She has also, we are informed, slowly been 'trained to tell the truth':

> And now Panya began to tell the truth sometimes. I found she very much disliked having to say afterwards what she ought to have said first, when she had told a lie. At first she only cared a little, but I think each time she cared more, and the last time she lost her temper; in fact, we both did considerably, and she gave me a lot of trouble. But when I came up a long time afterwards, and found her lying with her face pressed down upon the concrete floor, and saw that sympathising friends were met by silence and kicks, if they came too near, I said to myself, 'Good, we have learnt something at last.' And from that day forward she began to try to speak the truth. (6–7)

The alternative possibility, that Panya's anger might have been frustration at having to modify her story to fit the expectations and prejudices of her listener, does not seem to occur to her amanuensis, A. F., or, presumably, to the turn-of-the-century English readers of this tract.

Only after this narrative control has been established is 'Panya's story' able to be told. Even then the story which we are given is not, we are informed, that story of 'misery' which the 'men and women' of the mission have heard from Panya's lips during her illness, but a censored version. What aspect of her story is suppressed, and for what motives? Clearly the elements of brutality are played down, but one might also speculate that the unbowdlerised tale involved the slaver's sexual abuse of these recaptive children, a public acknowledgement of which was unacceptable to the intended readers of these 'tracts'.[7] Significantly though, after this long process of negotiation, the 'true' story which emerges displays all the essential features of the classic 'release narrative', suggesting that, by this time, a single narrative form existed into which all the varied histories of these released slaves had to be fitted. This form reflected the fixed ways in which the mission presses represented Africans and African societies, and also the expectations of their readers that African lives would reflect these stereotypes.

Panya relates how at three years old she goes from Uganda to 'live among the Nyamwezi' (how or why is not related). She is there approached by a man who 'carried me away to the houses of his people, and then that deceiver took me away to another house and sold me'. She is sold on, until she ends at:

> Saadani (*an Arab town on the coast, nearly opposite Zanzibar*)[8] and we stayed there two months (*meaning some little time*). And we went on from Saadani just the same, only we went in a boat. It was a very large boat, so high that I could not climb up into it by myself. And we stayed in the boat, and we slept in it at night; but the man who had bought me loved me and took care of me in the boat, till one day we landed near a town. (10)

At this juncture an Arab steals her and she is smuggled out of the town on another dhow. Since the children screamed they were beaten and Panya's ear is cut off and fed to a dog. At this disturbing point of the narrative they are rescued by an English gun-boat. The rest of the story concerns their reception and settlement 'in great peace and quietness' at Mbweni.

This last phrase suggests none of the tensions between Panya and the rescuing missionaries recorded in A. F.'s long preamble. This text reveals the complex, palimpsestic nature of its construction *vis-à-vis* alternative texts, 'truths' which the tale notes but does not, for various reasons, record in full. The degree of control and intervention involved in the production of this narrative stands revealed. In fact, early texts such as *Panya* are remarkably transparent about this process of control compared with those which succeeded them in the next forty years. Later examples of 'release narratives' show how the form developed as the audience at which it was aimed changed in the different periods of production of these mission texts.

Little Books for Africa was a series issued by the Sheldon Press, London, in the late 1920s and early 1930s. It is typical of the readers produced by missionary presses in the period between the wars. The series differs from the accounts before and immediately after the turn of the century in so far as many of them lay a more explicit claim to 'African' authorship, with titles which claim them as an 'autobiography', or as 'told by himself or herself'. A number of texts are given named African authors, thereby laying a direct claim to be considered as texts produced by Africans. Others claim to be transcribed accounts by Africans, but the process of transmission and transcription continues to be very problematic. They frequently involve translation between as many as three languages, since, if the first transcriber's language is German, the text is a translation of that transcription, itself, of course, initially translated from the original language of the 'teller'. Despite these processes of multiple translation and transcription, we are told, on the title pages, that the subject speaks for him or herself.

These transcribed accounts include, for example, *Ways I Have Trodden*, subtitled *The Experiences of a Teacher in Tanganyika Told by Himself*. The cover page tells us this is 'Translated and abridged by MARGARET BRYAN from the German edition of Frau Elise KOOTZ-KRETSCHMER. Published by kind permission of the Verlag der Missionsbuchhandlung, Herrnhut.' The translation is dated 1932. But the text clearly has a pre-war origin. Such a complicated palimpsest, with its varying levels of excision and control, is fascinating, as is the fact that the transcribers and translators are privileged by the capitalisation of their names. The original African subject is, as one might expect, unnamed.

As with the earlier accounts of pre-Christian and pre-mission Africa, recorded in the early 'release narratives', these tales also emphasise the negative side of African life. Despite the late date of their publication, they continue to suggest an Africa of incessant tribal divisions, with warfare and inter-tribal enslavement as the characteristic and unremitting condition of everyday life.[9] The pattern is often that a war occurs, the protagonist (male or female) is captured, enslaved and then sold to slavers. They escape. They are taken into the mission. They are healed in body. They are baptised. They confirm the view of the African past currently favoured by the mission societies, presenting as they do a picture of brutality and violence from which Christianity can 'rescue' the African peoples.

A paradigmatic example of this from the Sheldon series is the volume entitled *Stories of Old Times: Being the Autobiographies of Two Women of East Africa.* The text consists of two tales, that of Grandmother Narwimba (as she is called in the preface), and that of Chisi-Ndurisiye-Sichayunga. The headings give the narrative structure within which the 'life' of the African subject is shaped: Childhood, Stolen From Home, Slavery, Escape, Marriage, Ill-Treatment, Death of My Husband, I Marry Again, The Sin of Senga, Utengule (the Mission Station), Baptism. This final chapter concludes with the two sentences: 'I was baptised on August 1, 1914. I have finished' (18). The second tale, that of Grandmother Narwimba, has an almost identical narrative spine: Childhood, Marriage, Widowhood, I Marry Mirambo, War, Mirambo becomes Chief, The Inamwanga (the enemy of her husband's people), Slavery, Flight, My Children, My Grandchild, A Quarrel (describing the start of another inter-tribal conflict which causes her to go to the Mission), Utengule (the Mission Station). This text too ends with baptism. 'When I had been taught for some years I was baptised, and given the name Musundjjiriwa – that is, "You are cared for". My granddaughter is a Christian too, and is called Mukumburiwa, "You are thought of" or "Jesus has thought of you and not forgotten you".'

The narrative contains and shapes these lives within a frame of representation in which the African past, presented as violent, arbitrary and brutal, especially in its treatment of women, is redeemed by Christian conversion. African life is defined in these terms and the arrival at the state of conversion is literally the end of life, that is to say the protagonists of these texts are not just born again but literally disappear from narrative possibility. This decisive closure in baptism may be interpreted as their having arrived in a Christian 'H(e)aven' (the Mission is the end of a 'savage' *Pilgrim's Progress*, but also a metaphorical death). Their life after this bears no relation to the past, nor does it usually need a continuity with a subsequent narrative. To all effective purpose baptism ends both narrative and life, since, as we have seen in the case of the earlier 'release narrative' *Panya*, the story is not a mere transcription but a conscious re-construction of the life it relates. The project of these texts is contained within the limits of a 'release narrative' structure whose effective closure is conversion. No indication of how the conversion affects the subjects of these narratives is subsequently aired. Nor is there any discussion of the conflicts with their own society which might be consequent on conversion. This may be because these later texts are literally preaching to the converted. In addition to the original metropolitan audience for the early tracts, the audience now includes the congregations of converted Africans themselves. The choice of subject matter is significant, since, by the time they are printed in English, many of these texts are dealing with matters often at least fifty years in the past. The purpose of this is to present the brutish and savage African *past* from which the *present* congregation, descendants of these early converts, are now separate. The past related in these stories is that benighted savagery from which they have been delivered by the wisdom of their converting ancestors. Although the theme of the text is conversion, its principal project is to confirm the present, already converted audience in its superior status, and in the correctness of its new belief.

Thus, in some of these later narratives, the 'rescue' theme now extends not just to actual enslavement, but, metaphorically, to enslavement in ignorance and heathenism, and the 'release' dramatised is not from literal slavery but from the enslaving demands of their communities, and the heathen 'native customs' to which they may be tempted to return. A good example of this development in the form is the *Tale of Rachel Dangilo*. The burden of its narrative is now a post-conversion one. Although Rachel, the heroine, has her leg saved by the mission doctor after her release from an enslavement during which she has been tortured by her owner, the text stresses that this is not the central miraculous event. What constitutes the real miracle is her conversion, since, although the missionary doctor saves her life, she remains lame and in pain throughout her life. The main narrative now deals with her life after conversion. It consists of an account of a series of temptations to return to the pre-Christian community structure. Rejecting these, Rachel is praised for following the Bible injunction to 'forsake all others and follow me'. Those she forsakes include even her parents. This story of excision from and resistance to 'pagan' life is clearly aimed at an audience of the post-converted. The fact that such rejection also involves a wholly denigratory portrait of traditional and customary practice is, of course, not noticed, or, if it is, is presented as truthful.

The ubiquitous, modern pictures of pre-colonial African life as savage and awful emerge first in the form of the late-nineteenth- and early-twentieth-century 'release narrative', in which the cause of slavery is located not in the greed of the slavers, but in the divisions and savagery of pre-colonial African life itself. Here the text's principal audience is the home one, the source of the mission funds. In the later post-First World War narratives the representation of the past as savage functions as a confirmation to the convert of the wisdom and superiority of their chosen practices, a rhetorical shift consequent on the intended audience being the new African Christian community itself, in addition to the continuing 'funding' audience at home. The gradual extension of the time-frame of the 'release narrative' form to encompass the trials of post-conversion experience reinforces the practice of denigrating the African past, as this has to be contrasted with the correct choice of the convert in the ongoing struggle for his or her allegiance between family group and Christian community.

Many early missionary accounts are identical with late colonial ethnographies in their possessive appropriation of the people they discuss. The titles of these often take the form of 'My/Our People of the . . .'. This new genre is also a development of the earlier 'release narrative' form, in so far as the secondary concern of the 'release narrative' with the limitations of the pre-colonial African world, now becomes the dominant concern of the text. The heathen practices of the past are still presented as a sufficient cause for the choice of the African convert. But now the new converts, in line with the more 'liberal' thinking of the period, are also required to see that past as valid within certain limitations. The world of their ancestors is presented as interesting and vital, if flawed and in need of modernisation and correction by Christian precept and example. This is, of course, an offshoot of the projects of the classic early accounts produced by earlier African Christians, such as Crowther, since these early recaptive writers are also engaged in negotiating a politics of recuperation within a discourse of modernisation.

When these early writers went beyond what the missionary societies deemed appropriate subject matter, the material was simply suppressed. Some of the most specific and detailed accounts of traditional practice recorded by Crowther and sent in his reports to the CMS were never published, and have still 'never been noticed'.[10] These include accounts of such important cultural practices as the Yoruba Egungun masquerades and the Ifa divination texts. Significantly, in his reports, Crowther tries to explain his motives in recording these 'benighted' practices as a mere offshoot of his language work: 'In tracing out words and their various uses, I am now and then led to search at length into some traditions and customs of the Yorubas'.[11] The tension that such justifications hint at is characteristic of these early West African intellectuals. Their position on many customary practices shows a struggle between a desire, and indeed eagerness, to identify with the enlightened and 'civilised' practices of Christianity, and an ongoing attachment to and belief in the importance of the native institutions and societies which could never wholly be shared by their European colleagues.

Accounts by white authors of great Africans who exemplify desired character traits and practices are another dominant and popular mission-sponsored genre. For example, there were many biographies of Samuel Crowther himself, such as *The Life of Bishop Crowther First African Bishop of the Niger*, by the Ven. J. McKay, published in the Sheldon Little Books for Africa series. Of more interest to us, and analogous with the testaments of the released slaves in the earlier period, are those 'exemplary lives' which claim to be direct accounts by their subjects. An example of these in the same series is *The Life of Aaron Kuku of Eweland Born 1860 – Died 1929 Told By Himself*. Although it purports to be a true account, it replicates the narrative structures of the earlier missionary tales of 'release', as witnessed by its sub-headings: Childhood, The Ashanti War 1869–70, The Report of the War to the King, How I Was nearly Killed, Three Months With Pagan Priests, I See My Father, Flight, The Return to the Ewe Country, At Home, The Death of My Wife and How I Revenged Her Death, I See My Mother and Relations Again, I Become a Christian, My Work as Evangelist, How I Teach. The 'exemplary life' genre also shares with the earlier 'release narratives' a view of pre-mission and pre-colonial African life which stresses their disruptive and barbaric nature. Once again, the story usually culminates in a conversion, and the basic evangelical Christian structure of sin and redemption, derived from the earlier narrative forms, is taken over by this later form. These similarities are less surprising when we notice that although these texts are not now overtly acknowledged as transcription (*Told By Himself* is ambiguous), the frontispiece acknowledges that it is again translated and abridged from the German version of Rev. P. Wiegräbe. This is evidence of the same multiple transcription and editing process described in the analysis of the earlier forms. The ambiguous claim to an authentic African authorship disguises this ongoing control.

In these texts, too, slavery is seen primarily as the product of inherent weaknesses within African traditional societies. Africans, it is implied, are responsible for their own enslavement, either directly, when they are sold as captives after inter-tribal wars, or indirectly, when they are separated from their families as a result of the disruptions caused by warfare. Both of these events were the causes of some enslavements, but the almost ritual way in which they are invoked, with no emphasis on the larger causes, nor of the ways in which domestic forms of slavery were replaced by active, commercial forms of chattel slavery, as European or Arab interventions into the local scenes of West and East Africa strengthened, suggests that the mission patrons had a strong interest in emphasising the negative aspects of pre-colonial African culture. By so doing, of course, they could present a conversion to Christianity as an escape from darkness into light, and from an evil past into a healthy future. This simplified version of the past remains a dominant feature of missionary 'historical' accounts such as *The Life of Aaron Kuku of Eweland*, where they are presented as part of an objective account of the African past. In fact we might conclude that the narrative spine and principal thematic features of the 'release narrative' form have, by this later period, become the standardised way of framing any African story published by missions.

It is clear from an examination of these mission-sponsored texts that there is a profound difficulty involved in classifying any of these forms as genuine 'African writing', even though they claim, in many cases, to be 'authored' by Africans. The palimpsestic nature of their transmission, and the discursive and institutional practices which they encode, both militate against an assertion that they are, in any simple sense, African texts. Yet they represented a significant part of the available vehicles of written representation in English for Africans through the nineteenth and early twentieth centuries. They also played an important role in shaping European attitudes towards Africa and African life, since the various tract series in which they appeared were widely distributed and eagerly read. Finally, they had a great effect on African peoples' self-apprehension, as they helped form attitudes towards the past and towards traditional practices within the newly Christianised African communities themselves.

The African text produced under missionary patronage was one of the principal means of expression available to Africans of all political persuasions for a considerable period of time. As a result, in time even these highly controlled missionary genres could be appropriated by African writers with completely different agendas. Wherever Africans mastered writing, they could subvert their patrons' control and wrest the controlling structures to their own purposes. Many examples of this process of 'resistance' exist within the missionary-controlled texts which have survived. Two examples will have to suffice here: J. J. Walters's *Guanya Pau* (1891), now increasingly recognised as the earliest 'novel' written by an African, and the double text *My People of Kikuyu* and *The Life of Chief Wangombe*, by Jomo Kenyatta (1942). Despite their wide separation in time, both are texts which were written under the impulse of 'modernisation'. Both also incorporate elements of the basic narrative spines of the 'release narrative', the 'exemplary life' and the 'ethnographic' descriptive text. The earlier text was published by a commercial press (Lauer and Mattill, of Cleveland, Ohio). It was written while Walters was a student at Oberlin College, where he had been sent by missionaries from St John's Episcopal Mission at Robertsport, Liberia. The mission opened in 1878 and Walters was one of the earliest students. The later text, Kenyatta's *My People of Kikuyu* and *The Life of Chief Wangombe*, was printed in the Africa's Own Library series, numbered No. 1, and issued by the United Society for Christian Literature at the Lutterworth Press in 1942. A second edition appeared in 1945 and the text was re-issued again in 1966 by Oxford University Press, Nairobi, by which time its author had become the first President of independent Kenya.

Let me try to identify the ways in which mission patronage influenced these significant texts from two very different periods and regions, and the ways in which they resisted or dismantled this patronage by foregrounding the tensions between the mission publishing project and the local experience it sought to represent.

Joseph Jeffrey Walters's *Guanya Pau: The Story of an African Princess* runs to 146 pages in the 1891 edition.[12] It has a claim to being the first long fiction by an African, predating J. E. Casely Hayford's *Ethiopia Unbound* (1911) by twenty years. Like this later text, *Guanya Pau* is highly polemic, centring on a defence of reform for the position of women in African societies. The title page notes that Walters is a 'Native of Liberia, West Africa'. By 'native' it is implied that, as a Vai, he belongs to the 'aboriginal' Liberian tribes rather than to the community of freed slaves resettled there from America. *Guanya Pau* is arguably more formally constructed as a fiction than Casely Hayford's text, which is a blend of polemic essay and fictionalised autobiography. Walters's text draws heavily on forms such as the picaresque, with a loosely related series of episodes, each encapsulating a single, illustrative encounter. It is also clearly intertextual with the evangelical form of the *pélegrinage* tradition, pre-eminently represented by Bunyan's *Pilgrim's Progress*. Bunyan, as has been often noted, had a powerful effect as a role model on much English and indigenous language writing in Africa.

For these reasons *Guanya Pau* is a very important text in the history of English writing in Africa. Its scale and complexity mean that a full analysis of its many features cannot be offered here. I want only to note that it incorporates many of the features of the 'release narrative' structure I have already described, whilst simultaneously differing from it in a number of significant ways.

The story concerns a young Vai princess who is required to marry polygamously. She wishes to marry a young man who shares her abhorrence of polygamy, and who has gone to Freetown to earn the money to marry her. In the face of her mother's refusal to entertain her pleas against the arranged marriage, she flees her home with a female companion. At first, she intends only to avoid the marriage, but as the journey continues, and after a number of encounters which confirm her in her view of the subjugated and inhumane position of women in her society, she forms the intention to go to Freetown. There she knows that the missionaries will support her in her desire to avoid the evils of polygamy, and she will be free to marry her lover, Momo. In putting forward her case she develops a strong and surprisingly modern view of women's position:

> The truth is, *men are ever exercising their prerogatives to the letter, and we accept it without a question: but as soon as we assert ours, they brand us with transcending our sphere.* So long has woman been deceived that her condition seems to be *organic*. I may not even now succeed, but Jassah, *the day will come*, THE DAY WILL COME. (123–4)

The main drive of the polemic is clearly in line with the long-standing missionary policy against polygamy, and this is the text's dominant message, as the introduction stresses: 'In short our women must be educated. The infamous system of betrothing girls when three or four years old must be obliterated. *Polygamy must be wiped out of the land*' (6). But the text does not equate this drive to modernise with an attack on all customs, nor with a negative portrayal of African societies in all their aspects as many later 'release narratives' do. In fact Walters is careful to distinguish between the men's (Poro) and women's (Sande) secret associations, discriminating between them in terms of their social effect, as he perceives it, and constructing a history and a genealogy for them which further this discrimination. In the only detailed analysis of the text so far published, J. V. Singler sums this up succinctly: 'From *Guanya Pau* alone, there is ample evidence that Walters was very much his own person, appalled by the abuse of women in Vai society yet fiercely proud of his Vai heritage, thoroughly Christian (and Christianised) yet able to laugh at the missionaries' imperfect adaptation to Africa'.[13]

Walters presents the origin of the Poro, the 'Boy's Gregree Bush' (or secret society), in positive terms as 'founded by a highly respected Vai elder who sought to forge a unity that would enable the Vai to protect themselves from belligerent peoples from the interior'.[14] The Sande, Girl's Bush (or secret society), however, is characterised in the text as founded by 'the old wizard

Pandama-Pluzhaway, the Devil's brother-in-law' (26). Singler comments on this discrimination as follows: 'of the men's and women's society it is only the women's society that Walters sees as a major agent in the continued sub-jugation of women and only the women's society that is incompatible with Christianity. Thus his differing accounts of each society's founding corresponds directly to his divergent view of each society's merits.'[15]

In addition to these internal discriminations, which contrast strongly with the uniform presentation of barbarous African societies in the simpler form of the 'release narrative' described above, *Guanya Pau* also incorporates a number of very positive examples of local culture. For example when the 'trite' song of the owl is recorded:

> Task done or no done, 'tis time to go home, go
>   home;
> I wear the shoe-boots, and chicken-soup, so
>   good, so good,
> Big dinner at my house tomorrow,
> John Bedab, Will Bedab, his wife,
> And the Devil knows who all, who all!

Walters shows a real desire to lay the 'local' voice alongside the accepted forms of the invading culture and language in the contrasting quotations from standard mission verse which the text also serves up. Similarly, although the positive nature of the African world is presented finally within a narrative which privileges ideas of development and modernisation, it has a prideful ring which contrasts strongly with the negative tone of the later 'release narratives':

> The traveller, away out in the forest, if his provision gives out, need not famish. Almost at any time of the year the woods have a liberal supply of fruits and nuts – walnuts, colanuts, hickory-nuts, troves, several kinds of plums, wild plantain, figs, monkey-apple and fruit, persimmon, lady-finger, alligator-pear and pepper, etc.; if no brook is near, from which to quench his thirst, a large vine can frequently be found that has in its hollow abundant supply of cool, sweet water.
>
> The Africans have not yet awakened to a full consciousness of their worth. It needs only the application of the scientific principles to the illimitable resources of that wonderful land which are lying dormant, to make her rival the most affluent of her sister continents. (67)

However, this important and, in some respects, independent text has a narrative spine identical with that of the more controlled and edited later 'release narratives' transcribed by the mission amanuenses, reminding us that, for all its resistant features to the usual stereotypes of Africa, it still had to meet the expectations of its missionary sponsors.[16] But, unlike the totally negative images of the African societies presented in the majority of the later examples of the form, the world from which Guanya Pau flees is depicted as a rich and diverse one, which is marred only by a specific failing, its treatment of women. It is not characterised as a society subject to a general benighted-ness and barbarity. Importantly, too, the objections to this flaw are voiced by figures within this society, since neither Guanya Pau nor her lover Momo, both of whom object to polygamy, are direct products of Christianisation or of missionary influence. Thus the reformist impulse is presented as self-generated from within the society itself. The text does not lay stress on the missionary presence as offering anything but a distant example of an alternative social structure, and when Guanya runs away it is not, initially at least, in order to reach this alternative world. Most significantly, that alternative world is never reached, except in a symbolic way. At the end of the narrative, Guanya and her companion are detected and are being taken by canoe back to her father. They cast themselves into the river and drown. 'After a minute Guanya Pau came to the surface and said pathetically: "This is preferable to being Kai Kundu's headwife." Then she sank to rise again at the last day, when the seas and lakes and rivers shall give up their dead.' Ironically, this ending clearly invokes the closure of the classic 'release narrative' where, as we have seen, baptism (immersion in or anointing by water) is also a form of narrative 'death'.

Guanya Pau shares many other features with the later 'release narratives'. It shows a journey from the pagan world towards a modern, Christian world. It is structured in similar ways, with chapter titles such as 'Caught', 'Escape', and so forth. It presents the mission settlement as a kind of 'H(e)aven' where slavery is overthrown, and where women are treated as individuals and held in respect. However, it employs this form to present a picture of the African past as not just 'redeemable', but also as powerful, complex and valuable in itself. It allows considerable agency to the African in his or her own enlightenment and does not present them simply as the 'object' of redemption. It invokes a future in which the reform of African society is not synonymous with the rejection of its culture and values. It illustrates the way in which the 'release narrative', and the missionary project which brings it into being, can be appropriated to a more specifically local project involving the inscription of African pride and identity as part of a process of modernisation and change.

At the other end of a long process of control by mission presses of African English texts is the way in which twentieth-century nationalists were able to employ the acceptable mission-press genres to generate trends which served their own purposes. A good example of this is Kenyatta's two short works, *My People of Kikuyu* and *The Life of Chief Wangombe* (1942).[17] Again, the form of the 'ethnographic text' and the 'exemplary life', respectively, underpinned these texts. Many ethnographies, some entitled *My People of . . .*, and accounts of exemplary Christian lives, written by Africans, already existed. These represent a first stage in the appropriation of these European mission genres by Africans. By 1942, they were ready for a more radical appropriation by Kenyatta, in a way which gave them a fresh, ironic emphasis, and a very different politics. The older ethnographic forms do not disappear even at this late date, as a further example from the Africa's Own Library series, by Max Garvie, dated 1944 and entitled *Our People of the Sierra Leone Protectorate*, illustrates. This shows that the emergence of the more radical forms of these genres can not be accounted for simply by the liberalisation of the mission patronage structure. In fact, Kenyatta's text illustrates the increasing tension which, by the early 1940s, was part of the internal contradictions within the missionary patronage of the African English text. By this time, the missions are far more aware of the possibility of losing control of the text, as the publisher's disclaimer to the Africa's Own Library series suggests:

This series is designed to stimulate Africans to take an interest in reading of the great tribes and personalities of their continent. Many of the books are written by African authors, who as far as possible are left to express their own views in their own words. The Publishers cannot always guarantee the accuracy of what is written, nor do they necessarily associate themselves with the views expressed. Their desire is to afford a medium whereby Africans of education may give their fellows the benefit of their knowledge and research. They are always ready to consider material, especially from African authors.

Kenyatta's text, No. 1 in the series, announces its liberationist project in its dedication to 'the members of various tribes in Africa who died in the service of African peoples'. The two texts it contains are, seemingly, quite separate, echoing the distinctive forms of the ethnography and the 'exemplary life'. But read as appropriations of these forms to a resistant, nationalist purpose, as they surely must be, they form a single political project.

My People of Kikuyu tells of the Gĩkũyũ creation myth and describes the development of the various Gĩkũyũ sub-groups. A social history of the evolution of Gĩkũyũ communal structures follows, including, for example, a description of the change-over from the early matriarchal and polyandrous social form to the later patriarchal and polygamous one. Here we can see Kenyatta's political strategy of appropriating classic anthropological material and forms for a contemporary nationalist purpose. For example, when he describes how the overthrow of the initial patriarchal monarchy initiated a period of popular rule, the modern political project of the text is abundantly clear. In the account, he stresses the mechanisms by which power was handed on from one generation to the next in a formal ceremony, held every thirty or forty years, with an elder group (Irongo) and a younger group (Mwangi) alternating. As a result, the text claims, non-hereditary chieftainships evolved. In this apparently innocent historical account Kenyatta could describe his own struggle as a younger, educated leader against the more entrenched elements of the traditional elders, who continued to support colonial rule. He could also draw attention to the political implications of this tradition for the evolution of a modern, independent, Kenyan political system:

It has been assumed, especially by Europeans who either do not know much about the Kikuyu system of chieftainship or wish to uphold the British Government's method of appointing salaried chiefs for small localities, that the Kikuyu people never had a chief who could command nation-wide respect. This book, however, shows in some detail how before the coming of the Europeans the Kikuyu had reached the stage of overthrowing a despotic monarchy, had established a democratic system, and afterwards evolved out of it a system of democratic chieftainship, supported by strong units of fighting warriors ready to defend the territory. From time immemorial the Kikuyu have always been great lovers of their country, jealous for its fertile soils and beautiful scenery. For this reason they have defended it vigorously against all invaders. (25)

Again, under the guise of recording a traditional prayer for the preservation of the land, addressed to the Gĩkũyũ deity Mwene-Nyaga, a firm political message is transmitted: 'We pledge to you, O Mwene-Nyaga, that we shall not sit idle and let anyone snatch away what you have promised to our forefathers, to be our children's birthright for ever' (28). Towards the end of the narrative, the political message becomes even more overt, and this may well be the section which provoked the disclaimer by the press in the frontispiece.

> The spirit of independence, love of freedom in thought and action, and hatred of autocratic rule, are ingrained in the minds of the Kikuyu people . . . in their high-lands and mountain homes, the people cherished the system of democratic govern-ment, the principles of which have been passed down from generation to generation. Their love of freedom and manhood has made them defend their country fearlessly. Warriors armed with spears and shields, bows and arrows, have shed blood to defend their freedom, for they said: 'Kindo Kiega gitìumaga hege' (meaning 'The tree of liberty is watered with blood' or 'a good thing is not easy to get'). (29)

The second part of this dual text, *The Life of Chief Wangombe*, is an account of the important early Gĩkũyũ leader Chief Wangombe wa Ihora. It follows the classic mission form of the 'exemplary life'. This account, though, is clearly designed to counter the many missionary narratives which present pre-colonial tribal life as 'short, brutish and nasty'. It emphasises the self-sufficiency of the protagonist, for example when, as a young man, he is shown killing a leopard stealing a goat from his father's herd.

> In its death-agony the beast leapt forward, and had not Wangombe retreated quickly it would have fallen upon him. He ran for help, and when he came back with his comrades they found the leopard lying dead on the spot where he had stood, with a big gash in his throat and the top part of Wangombe's spear protruding from its heart. (54)

The text goes on to describe how the mature Wangombe led a successful war against the Masai, but the war is presented as successful and heroic not brutal and wicked, analogous to European wars whose historic heroes figure as positive role models for nationalist narratives. The defence of the Gĩkũyũ territory, which Wangombe successfully leads, is tempered with mercy when Wangombe realises that one of the Masai enemy was a play-fellow of his:

> He was about to thrust his spear into the enemy's flesh, when suddenly he heard a beseeching cry: 'Ole yoyo, tapala', meaning, 'Brother, stop!' At once he looked intently, but could hardly believe his eyes that he was face to face with an old playmate, who as a young boy had gone to Masailand with his Kikuyu mother who was married to a Masai elder. (54)

Wangombe calls a truce, and from that time onwards trading with the Masai is initiated. When disease attacks the Masai, the group who trade with the Gĩkũyũ are able to survive. The contemporary message of the virtues of inter-tribal unity in the face of an outside threat is clearly implied. Wangombe is also shown to have dealt successfully with the Arabs, whom he initially welcomes. But when Arab traders kidnapped women and children, the portrayal of an inept, brutal and uncaring African pre-colonial culture in the standard missionary 'release narratives' is replaced by a vision of a determined African self-sufficiency.

> He fought against them and captured rifles and ammunition which he quickly learned to use. With this new equipment and the strength of his spearmen he was able to check the mischief which the Arab trade might have brought into the country, and to prevent them from finding in his territory a fertile ground for the slave-trade. (62)

When the 'Athongo' (Europeans) arrive he gives them building sites. But shortly afterwards he dies of a kidney disease which the Europeans cannot cure. The Europeans are presented not as saviours, bringing infallible medicine and a superior system and culture, but as an unknown factor which a sensible people will treat with caution. His dying words emphasise this:

> 'Don't forget that you have a great task in front of you, you may not have to fight with spears, shields or bows and arrows, in the way with which you are familiar. But in the short time I have had contact with the Athongo, I have seen how hard it is to deal with them. . . . Learn their clever way of talking for it is by using your wisdom that you may safeguard your country'. (63)

Kenyatta's text exemplifies this prescription of 'learning' and, indeed, turning to his own use 'the clever way of talking' represented by the written text and the mission press.

At the beginning of the process of missionary patronage Walters's text illustrates the tension resident in the opposed projects of recording the practices of African cultures, and of 'civilising' and 'modernising' African societies. Even writers who had a conscious desire to serve this latter project might still resist the denigratory rhetoric of the standard mission accounts. The resulting tension can be seen to inform the development of the narrative forms which characterise the missionary patronage system for the next seventy years or more. Kenyatta's text, coming at the end of this period, illustrates how the drive to articulate an African viewpoint finally acquired the ability to appropriate and subvert those same controlling forms.

Notes

1. Though, as we have seen, even in the case of a late text such as Samuel Johnson's *A History of the Yoruba* control could still reside in the mission patrons.

2. Reissued in a facsimile edition: *Journals of the Rev. James Frederick Schön and Mr. Samuel Crowther: who, with the sanction of Her Majesty's Government, accompanied the expedition up the Niger in 1841 on behalf of the Church Missionary Society*, ed. with introduction by J. F. A. Ajayi, 2nd edn (London: Cass, 1970). Further page references are incorporated into the text.

3. J. F. A. Ajayi, *Christian Missions in Nigeria 1841–1891: The Making of A New Elite* (London: Longmans, 1965), p. 128.

4. Samuel Crowther, *Journal of an expedition up the Niger and Tshadda rivers, undertaken by Maegregor Laird in connection with the British Government in 1854*, ed. by J. F. A. Ajayi, 2nd edn (London: Cass, 1970). All further page references are incorporated into the text.

5. Ajayi, *Christian Missions in Nigeria*, p. 159.

6. All the examples given in this section are collected in the tract series *Stories of Africa*, Universities Mission to Central Africa, 9, Dartmouth Street, London. British Museum Catalogue no. BM 4766 aa 19, which contains stories originally written between the 1850s and the turn of the century, with most dealing with East Africa from the 1890s onwards; or in the later Little Book for Africa Series, issued in London by the Sheldon Press between 1925 and 1935. The whole of this latter series is also held in the British Library. Page references given in the text are to these sources.

7. For evidence of this kind of suppression in earlier evangelical narratives see Gillian Whitlock's work on the text of *The History of Mary Prince* in 'Outlaws of the Text: Women's Bodies and the Organisation of Gender in Imperial Space', a paper presented at the Australia/Canada: Post-colonization and Women's Texts Conference, Calgary Institute for the Humanities, 13–16 February 1992. Part of this important but, sadly, still unpublished paper is reproduced in B. Ashcroft *et al.*, *The Post-colonial Studies Reader* (London: Routledge, 1995), pp. 349–52.

8. My italics. These internal glosses are interesting both in terms of their stress on the text's intended audience, the 'home' audience which needs to be 'informed', and, even more significantly, as evidence of the intrusive 'voice' of A. F. even within this narrative, itself as we have seen a product of complex control, manipulation and now offered as accurate 'transcription' of Panya's 'own' tale.

9. In fact many of these texts draw on much earlier sources. There is a slippage between the period of production and the period of the events these tracts record. This chronological slippage is a feature of many missionary tracts.

10. See Ajayi, *Christian Missions in Nigeria*, pp. 128ff.

11. Ibid.

12. It is most easily consulted in the recent edition by Oyekan Owomoyela, *Guanya Pau: The Story of an African Princess* (Nebraska: University of Nebraska Press, 1994). All later page references in the text are to this facsimile edition.

13. J. V. Singler, 'The Day Will Come: J. J. Walters and *Guanya Pau*', *Liberian Studies Journal*, 15, 2 (1990), pp. 125–33. Further references are within the text.

14. Ibid., p. 127.

15. Ibid., p. 128.

16. The exact relationship between Walters and his mission sponsors at Oberlin College, and the fact that the work was published by a commercial press, bears further investigation. A full, scholarly edition of this important text is still much needed, since the Owomoyela edition is not properly annotated and has only a very brief introduction.

17. Jomo Kenyatta, *My People of Kikuyu* and *The Life of Chief Wangombe*, Africa's Own Library, No. 1 (London: Lutterworth Press, 1942). Later page references are incorporated into the text.

Chapter 4

Twentieth-Century Secular Patronage: Literature, Education, Control

Missionary-controlled presses continued to be a major form of non-indigenous patronage for African English writing during the period between the two world wars, and immediately after the resumption of peace in 1945. But the same period also saw the growth of an awareness by colonial authorities, and by metropolitan commercial publishers, that the increasing number of literate Africans were creating a local market for textbooks and general books. The missionaries had initiated public education in West and East Africa, but in both regions, in the period following the First World War, the colonial authorities began to establish public education systems which sought to regulate, harness and replace the existing missionary institutions. In addition, in line with the general administrative policies which flowed from the Lugardian theory of indirect rule, the colonial authorities in Anglophone Africa also sought to establish government literature bureaux. At first, these bureaux were designed to encourage the spread of literacy in indigenous African languages. Thus, in 1931 Rupert East set up a Translation Bureau in Northern Nigeria, which, as well as supervising the translation of school-texts from English into Hausa, broadened its scope to publish 'two books dealing with the history and customs of the Hausa and their neighbours. This ampler scope became formalised when the institution was turned into a Literature Bureau [this occurred in 1934], which was situated in Zaria, and which deliberately tried to foster Hausa creative writing in the Roman script.'[1]

As Graham Furniss has shown, East was also instrumental in establishing an important Hausa-language newspaper, *Gaskiya ta fi Kwabo*, which was 'the only Hausa language paper of any note distributed throughout the north since 1938 so that publication in its columns was much sought after'.[2] Furniss's analysis, in the same article, of the kind of control exercised over this publication makes a fascinating case study in the colonial patronage of African writing.

As East himself records in *Overseas Education* 1940[3] the newspaper *Gaskiya* was founded as a successor to the defunct *Northern Provinces news sheet* which had been produced by the Government. East had however gained for the newspaper some independence from Government control, and had appointed a Hausa editor, Abubakar Imam, assisted by an Administrative Officer, L. C. Giles, who could 'provide the raw material for his articles on foreign policy, advise about the selection of local news, deal with printing firms and news agencies, organise the finances'. (438–9)

By controlling the paper in this way, the government hoped to counter the influence of pro-independence propaganda reaching the north from the southern provinces. As Furniss recounts, this suggestion had come from Lord Lugard himself, although by then he was officially in retirement in Surrey. But East was also motivated by a desire to promote literacy and adult education. East's own account of the objects of *Gaskiya*, as quoted by Furniss, are in line with his aims for the Literature Bureau which had developed out of the Translation Bureau in 1934:

> First, to promote literacy by giving the people something which they will find pleasure in reading, and to accustom them to pay, however little, for this pleasure. Secondly, by giving them the truth about matters of internal policy and external affairs, to contradict false rumours which are difficult to check in an almost illiterate community, especially deliberate propaganda of a subversive kind which has filtered in from the outside world in small quantities in recent years . . . Thirdly, when the paper has found its feet and is being widely bought for its own sake, it is hoped to insinuate unobtrusively articles of an educative nature. (439)

When the newspaper became the Gaskiya Publishing Corporation in 1945, the controlling role of the Administrative Officer was abolished, but 'this measure of freedom did not alter the editorial criteria that the Hausa editor [Abubakar] Imam had held for some time and [which] were generally in line with the views of his European colleagues' (440). Furniss reports Imam as saying that his 'independent' policy was to publish poems which had a good message in them, or, as he expressed it, had 'meat and meaning to them':

> These policies account for the publication during the 1939–45 war of poems in praise of Churchill and other war leaders . . . attacks upon the Germans and Japanese . . . praise for the Nigerian troops fighting in East Africa and Burma . . . exhortations to grow more crops, particularly the groundnut cash crop for the war effort . . . After the war and during the adult literacy campaign poems were often published exhorting people to learn to read and to send their children to primary schools. (440)

The task, as seen by people like East, was not just to get the younger, educated Hausa intellectuals to write in a script accessible to and compatible with the systems of the European colonial power, but to persuade them to move away from the traditional conservative forms, and to 'write prose fiction on the western model'. As East saw it, in an account replete with the racial and cultural assumptions of the period, the difficulty was that:

> The influence of Islam, superimposed on the Hamitic strain in the blood of the Northern Nigerian, produces an extremely serious-minded type of person. The art of writing, moreover, being intimately connected in his mind with his religion, is not to be treated lightly. . . . To these people, therefore, the idea of writing a book which was frankly intended neither for edification of the mind, nor the good of the soul, a 'story' book which, however, followed none of the prescribed forms of story-telling, seemed very strange. . . . In short, it was necessary to explain to a very conservative audience a conception which was entirely new, and of doubtful value if not morality.[4]

Organisations with these attitudes clearly had the most profound effect on the values, social function and aesthetic structures of the texts they produced, and these, in their turn, sought to shape and re-shape the society they claimed merely to represent.

More recently, Furniss appears to have revised his earlier opinion of the degree of control exercised by outsiders like East.[5] In an attack on recent post-colonial theories of the 'silencing' of local cultures by colonial discourse, Furniss offers the publication of five novellas by East's bureau as evidence of the independence of local indigenous-language writing from colonialist power, although he again acknowledges that 'there was no pre-existing tradition of imaginative prose-writing in Hausa culture' before the bureau was established. Furniss argues that in these novellas, produced under the bureau's instigation, a local voice emerged. This voice, he claims, was based partly on existing Arabic traditions, and partly on 'the knock-about world of Hausa oral tales in which pomposity was deflated, the powerful outwitted, and stereotypes rein-forced'. Nevertheless Furniss continues to acknowledge the importance of these colonial literature bureaux in acting as the patron of these new forms, but now plays down 'the degree to which East provided positive guidelines', argu-ing that this remains 'unclear' (88). Despite these revisions, Furniss reiterates that East and his organisation actually commissioned these works, and that they were a product of his conscious attempt to encourage Hausas to write in new and alien forms, such as long imaginative prose fiction. It seems, there-fore, that to argue now that such writing was not 'even aware of English and the colonial presence' is to overstate the case. Clearly, the existence of such texts here, as in many other parts of the colonial world, suggests that the degree to which colonialist discourse literally silenced the voice of the people has been exaggerated. It would seem fairer to conclude that texts like these, which drew on local practices, and which articulated local concerns and agendas within the very institutions set up by the colonisers, suggest an ongoing capacity for the appropriation and subversion of these institutions. It is in this appropri-ation that their resistance lies. In this regard, they illustrate a practice similar to that which we observed within other external patronages, such as those of the missionary presses. The existence of such texts clearly demonstrates the continuity of local cultures after colonial domination, but they do not suggest that colonisation did not affect these cultures profoundly. Nor are they proof that the colonised culture was not indelibly changed by the colonial process. Furniss himself argues that, in texts such as these Hausa novellas, we see a displacement of the anguish felt by colonised peoples at the ' "defeat" of [their] society'. He goes on to argue that this was achieved 'through victory in fantasy and through survival and success in spite of suffering'. Indigenous concerns and the interests of the colonisers engaged and struggled on a profoundly ambi-guous and disputed territory. The colonisers and their institutions were often forced to lace their aggressive economic and cultural projects with justificatory ideas of colonisation as a modernising and civilising force, a contradiction obviously at play in the work of figures like East and the colonial literature bureaux. But the colonised, too, were forced to negotiate a space in which profoundly local concerns, issues and responses could be expressed, a space which embraced alien forms such as prose fiction. In fact, what these texts exemplify is the emergence of a post-colonial, counter-discourse of precisely the kind which Furniss seems to want to deny ever existed. They exemplify the ability of colonised peoples to appropriate and subvert even the most alien of forms, and the most disruptive of institutions, to their own ends.[6] The fact that this kind of writing did not engage directly with the theme of colonial onslaught, as the later English-language texts of the late 1950s and 1960s did, does not mean that they were not affected by the colonial process. At the very least, they were dependent upon it for the means of publication, and for the forms they employed. That they were able to appropriate these successfully and use them for their own ends is proof neither of the absence of a dominant colonialist discourse, nor of the unaffected continuation of a local, indigenous culture. It is a proof rather of the ongoing interaction of both these forces in constructing the modern, post-colonial African world.

In 1947, Charles Richards, the manager of the CMS Bookshop in Kenya, was asked by the government to establish an East African Literature Bureau. According to the annual reports this was actually established in 1948. It took as its brief the provision of written material for the whole East African region. Although excellent annual reports for this bureau exist from 1952 onwards, so far little work has been done comparable with the work on the Northern Nigerian Bureau. A perusal of these annual reports from 1952 to 1967 suggests that it may have had similar aims to the earlier Northern Nigerian Bureau. The stated purpose, however, was simply 'to meet the situation arising from the rapidly increasing demand of literate Africans for books of all kinds' (Annual Report 1952). The consolidation of government control over the content of education, until then largely in the hands of missionaries, was an inevitable consequence of increasing government control of the various East African colonies. After the Second World War, with the growth of government schools, they became the principal provider of textbooks and instructional manuals, as well as of general reading materials for the wider population. The Advisory Council, set up in 1949, had a number of missionaries on each of its regional and language boards as listed in the 1952 report, but the various regional directors of education, community development officers and representatives of the secular schools and colleges were also strongly represented. The greater degree of penetration by Christian missionaries in these areas, compared with the predominantly Muslim Hausa region of which East writes, may be noted, though no doubt a very similar situation to that in Northern Nigeria existed in predominantly Muslim regions of East Africa, such as Mombasa and Zanzibar. A good deal of work remains to be done to establish whether or not publishing policies in these different areas were similar, or whether different policies developed in each area.

Charles Richards has indicated that the policy of the bureau was 'to produce a lot of literature that would help the development of the country – books on health and agriculture, and so on. But also on the imaginative side, books to express the African personality – fiction, history, poetry, recording of the past and such things.'[7] In the initial brief, there was a stress on vernacular-language publishing, as there had been in Northern Nigeria. The first four language committees set up were in ki-Swahili, Luganda, Gĩkũyũ and Dholuo. The total of volumes printed in the four years between 1948 and 1952 was 915,949. Swahili accounted for 41 per cent of titles, Luganda for 13 per cent, while 'other Kenya and Uganda Vernaculars' accounted for 17 and 9 per cent respectively. English titles account for only 12 per cent, while English with an accompanying East African language translation accounted for 8 per cent. An analysis of sales in the first four years from 1948 to 1952, provided by the first report in that year, indicates that in percentile terms, 2 per cent of the books issued were biographies, 10 per cent were fiction and poetry, while general education accounted for a further 20 per cent. The predominant categories of agriculture and veterinary and health accounted for 35 per cent of the total output. The intriguing category of civics accounted for 15 per cent, suggesting that the teaching of the colonial version of good citizenship ranked high in the priorities of the bureau. History, tribal lore, customs and traditions accounted for a further 15 per cent. The fiction and poetry components, we are told, were mostly 'contributed by African authors. Most are of the traditional East African type of folk tale, but several authors are experimenting in writing longer tales with a formal plot: some of these are in English, and as schools progress to a greater amount of teaching and use of English these tales should provide useful reading matter for classes.'

This analysis, in the 1952–53 Report, suggests that the role of English texts was seen as a means of modernising Africans, and of introducing them to the benefits of a contemporary education in a manner not dissimilar to the aims of the Northern Nigerian Bureau. There is little doubt that the political crisis of the period also played a role. The Mau Mau rebellion in Kenya began in 1952, and it seems likely that this played a part in the decision to expand the bureau, which could act as a means of combating dissent and disseminating government views, just as East's agency was set up in Northern Nigeria to combat nationalist propaganda from the south (Zikism) in the pre-independence period. The period immediately after the war also saw attempts by Kenyans such as Gakaara wa Wanjaũ to publish uncontrolled material, but these were unsuccessful. Gakaara was later detained under the Emergency Laws after the Mau Mau conflict broke out.[8] It is interesting to note too that the growing educational market drove this process forward in East Africa, just as it had done in West Africa. This suggests that the later commercial publishers, who entered the market for educational texts, already had a model in place, designed by these earlier colonial organisations.

Much more detailed analysis of the work of the East African Literature Bureau remains to be done, but it may be interesting to note that, in the first years of the bureau, the fiction output contained a number of texts translated from English, such as a version of Washington Irving's *Rip Van Winkle* in Ankole, and a version of R. L. Stevenson's *Treasure Island* in Luganda. Other English texts are more clearly concerned with local ideas and characters, such as those in the Eagle Fiction Library series, with titles such as *The Beautiful Nyakiemo* and *The Lonely Village*, both by African authors. The 1956–57 Report offers some illustration of the kind of English texts which the civics list offered. They include a series of tracts with titles such as *How Kenya is Governed?* and *Why Do We Need Government?*, as well as the disingenuously titled *East Africa Owes Much to British Rule* by J. K. Kebaso. A further title, *English Manners and Customs*, suggests that education and the acquisition of European lifestyles were directly equated. A secular version of the earlier mission form of the account of the ideal African convert, entitled *The Ideal African Chief – Chifu Hodari wa Kiafrika*, by J. P. Oyende, is a clear example of how this government-sponsored bureau had taken over the mission-text forms. Of course, as we saw earlier, leading nationalists such as Kenyatta had already appropriated these same forms to their own ends in the early 1940s. In a real sense, a battle of texts was going on here for the hearts and minds of ordinary Africans through the power of writing, especially as general literacy increased.

Although the colonial literature bureaux did not produce a large *volume* of literary texts, they had a profound effect. Their organisers saw the encouragement of writing as part of a larger project, that of the 'civilisation' and 'modernisation' of the people of the region. They also had a residual effect in that they acted to alert later, commercial publishers to the existence of a potential educational market in Africa. If we compare the projects of these varied early patrons, we find that the colonial literature bureaux inherited many of the motives which drove the mission presses, especially the project of 'modernisation' and 'education' in European values and ideas. It is also possible to see links between these earlier forms of patronage and the operational practices of the commercial pressures, which pioneered African English texts in the period after the 1950s.

The colonial literature bureaux established a pattern whereby literature developed as a supplier of the ready-made market for educational texts, according to policies and preoccupations shaped elsewhere. As we shall see, this had an incalculable influence on the development of African writing in English, an influence which arguably continued even when this initial, specialist market broadened from the mid-1960s onwards. For this reason, the first generation of literary texts, aimed at the growing overseas market for African English texts in the late 1960s, was shaped by forces quite different from those affecting the general production of literary texts in the metropolitan societies in the same period. The educational and general books market had a substantial and important overlap, and this continued on into the 1970s and early 1980s. Studies of the popular literary tradition have emphasised the overlap between the audience for fictional narration and instructional manuals and self-help or advice books in the so-called 'market literatures',[9] but it should also be noted that there was a greater overlap of the market for educational texts and literary texts even in the elite literature of the period from 1960 onwards.

Locally controlled occasional printed media also continued to encourage and sponsor English writing. Bernth Lindfors has shown that many English-language writers who published successfully with foreign presses in the late 1950s and early 1960s had previously been nurtured by such local outlets. As early as 1987 in a paper to the African Literatures Association of America he argued that 'Virtually all the major authors in English-speaking Africa got their start in local periodicals with limited circulation'. He linked this to the importance of the 'little magazine' in sustaining and developing both new voices and established writers. At that time Lindfors seemed quite optimistic about the ability of such magazines to renew themselves, arguing that 'What is most significant about these short-lived vehicles is not their hasty demise, but their regular resurrection, their continuity in new guises'.[10]

More recently, in an essay which covers similar ground, he seems less optimistic. He continues to assert the historic importance of school and university publications, literary reviews, popular magazines, pamphlets and newspapers, all of which offered 'regular outlets for short fiction, poetry, drama, essays and reviews', and concludes that 'nearly all young writers in [Nigeria, South Africa, Kenya, Ghana, Zimbabwe, and Malawi] got started by addressing their own countrymen in inexpensive media produced domestically'. He adds that 'When comprehensive histories of modern African literatures come to be written, some attention will have to be given to ephemeral printed media that provided aspiring authors with opportunities to express themselves'.[11] But he seems less optimistic about the capacity of such publications to succeed, and less optimistic about the future of the important 'little magazines' to survive the current African book and publication drought.

Nevertheless, Lindfors's recent work has been vital in drawing attention to the historical importance of such outlets: for example, student magazines like *The Horn*, the literary voice of Ibadan University at the time when Ṣoyinka, Achebe, Okigbo and Clark were all undergraduates there. *Penpoint*, the Makerere publication, which published Ngũgĩ's early work; and *Busara*, the literary journal of Nairobi University, which the young Jared Angira edited, both played a vital role in encouraging new writers to develop their craft. Other journals, such as *Dhana*, published in Nairobi, and which replaced *Penpoint*, received support from the East Africa Literature Bureau. It included contributions by most of the writers who later came to be well-known names in Kenya and Uganda. *Zuka* appeared in 1967, also in Nairobi. It also published work by many writers who later made an important contribution to the development of East African writing. *Asemka: A Bilingual Literary Journal of the University of Cape Coast* was published at the UCC, Ghana. Its editors included writers such as Aidoo, Sutherland and Awonoor. It published work by these and other writers, and thus acted as a channel for the new African writing of the early period. *Okyema* was published quarterly by the Ghana Society of Writers, in Accra. Its founding editorial committee in 1960 consisted of E. A. Winful, G. Adali-Mrotty and Cecile McHardy, and the first issue included work by Efua Sutherland, among others. She also served on the editorial committee in the next issues. Eventually, nearly everyone who had an impact on the development of Ghanaian letters came to pass through its pages. Finally, *Okike: An African Journal of New Writing*, whose founding editor in 1972 was Achebe, was published by Nwamife Publishers. Others who served on the editorial committee, or worked as editorial assistants, advisers, or local representatives in various countries, read like a roll-call of recent African writing and criticism: they include C. Nwankwo, Chinweizu, Isidore Okpewho, Ernest Emenyonu, Jemie, Maduokor and Micere Mūgo. The Australian-born critic C. L. Innes, as well as being an early editor whilst in Amherst, Massachusetts, where the magazine had its home for a while, was its representative in the UK. It had a major role there in promoting the early wave of writers and familiaris- ing wider British literary circles with African writers and texts. These maga- zines are representative of many others whose role was vital in providing a literary patronage not controlled by outside forces. These magazines meant that the tradition of self-controlled outlets for writing first established in West Africa in the late nineteenth century continued to flourish in different forms into the modern period. The majority of writers in West and East Africa got their start in such magazines, and they provided an ongoing outlet for younger writers after the establishment of African English writing by the overseas commercial presses. This continuity of locally controlled patronage is a vital component of the story of African English writing which deserves a closer investigation by scholars.

In addition to the role of the little magazines, the various authors' societies and associations of writers also played a vital role in encouraging new writing, and in providing an outlet for the work of emerging writers. The Association of Nigerian Authors, for example, provided and continues to provide outlets for younger writers to get their work into print, and to receive critical feed- back from more established authors. The prizes associated with these writers' associations provide incentives to younger writers, and also assist them with obtaining funding to get their early work in print. Although I have stressed the role played by external patronages in developing African English writ- ing, it should be noted that local patronages of this kind also played a vital role in encouraging and sustaining writing in English in the various African countries.[12]

Many contemporary African writers continue to publish predominantly in newspapers and magazines, or to self-publish their work. Publication in these forms does not necessarily mean that the work is of low quality, or that it lacks permanent, literary value. Rather, it reflects the relative absence of national and international publishing outlets for English writing in many African countries. Texts published in this way feature in many of the sections below, especially those which discuss areas where English is a minority language of expression such as Ethiopia, Somalia and Cameroon. Before a more com- prehensive general history can be attempted, we will need more specialist area studies of these ephemeral publications, and when these are produced we will be able to cover this material in more detail than I have been able to do here.

Nevertheless, despite these local efforts, the main patronage for the develop- ment of contemporary English writing in East and West Africa clearly came from overseas commercial publishing houses, who were responding to the develop- ment of new markets with the growth of education in the independent countries. The emergence of series such as Heinemann Educational's African Writers series indicates how the newly independent nations of the erstwhile Empire were ripe for development as a market for educational texts.[13] Other firms, including Longman, later sought to enter these markets with the development of cheap format paperback series, such as the Longman Drumbeat series. But Heinemann Educational Books remains the paradigmatic example. In a sense, these modern ventures were only inheriting the mantle of the great colonial publishing networks, established by firms like Macmillan, who had always seen the Empire as a special and valuable market-place. But, unlike the publishing firms of the nineteenth and early twentieth centuries, which concentrated on the export of texts produced in England, the new firms saw that the ex-colonial countries were a developing market for a new, home-grown product. It is arguable that the product was created deliberately to fill this need, and that the aim of series like the Heinemann African Writers series was not so much to publish existing contemporary African English writing, as to create it. That is to say that the themes and forms of texts published in this series were designed to meet market needs. While it is easy and, indeed, has sometimes seemed almost obligatory to emphasise the controlling, hegemonic practices of the missionary presses and of the colonial literature bureaux, it has been less usual to perceive that the publishing policies of the overseas commercial presses in the modern period may have functioned in remarkably similar ways.

Once it became apparent that literary texts in English writen by Africans were needed for this new market, they were quickly found amongst the existing local writers. When this source proved insufficient to meet the growing demand, they were commissioned by proactive development policies on the part of the new publishers. This was not in itself a bad thing, in so far as it encouraged a variety of powerful new voices to speak. But a number of consequences inevitably followed. The disputes as to what constituted a 'genuine' or 'authentic' African English text, between rival publishers in this period, echo the patronising attempts to define 'authentic' African practice in a long colonial discursive archive. Their views affected the choice of which writers were published in these series, and which were left out. They also affected the relative preponderance of genres published. Certain forms were clearly privileged by the needs of the educational market at which they were aimed. Thus, novels and short stories tended to dominate poetry, and even more so plays, since the educational demand for the latter was less developed. For example, of the first twenty-six titles published by Heinemann in their African Writers series, twenty-one were classified as fiction (that is novels and short story collections), three as non-fiction (all autobiographical accounts), and only one as poetry, and one as drama. The single drama example was also unusual in that, although published under the African *nom de plume* Obotunde Ijimere, it was the work of the expatriate Austrian academic Ulli Beier, and consisted of translations by him from the Yoruba.[14] Later texts by Beier in the series were published under his own name. Of the first twenty-six titles only one was by a woman, No. 26 in the series, Flora Nwapa's novel *Efuru*.[15] Writers whose work was nurtured by Heinemann also differed markedly in their output, style and genre choice from those published by independent publishers, who did not boast a major African educational list. For example, Ṣoyinka is pre-eminent amongst those writers who were never recruited by Heinemann,

79

and who thus retained an independence from the patterns which emerged for writing in the series.[16] As I have argued throughout these opening chapters, African English writing was profoundly influenced by the interaction between African writers and the varying patronages which gave them access to print in the last two hundred years. That this was also the case for the first generation of post-independence African writers may seem less surprising in the light of this longer history of intrusive control.

On the positive side, the interest in African writing by these overseas commercial publishers aided the development of a large local and overseas audience for African writing in English. Despite the long history of writing in English, which preceded the overseas publication of Tutuola and Achebe in the mid to late 1950s, the more widespread interest in African writing in English in the US and Europe dates from this period. This coincided with a renewed general awareness of Africa, as the colonial powers began to respond to the 'wind of change', which politicians of the period acknowledged was blowing across Africa. That an interest in African writing abroad coincided with moves towards the granting of independence to African nations is no accident. Africa was suddenly newsworthy, and the new writers were eagerly sought out by rival publishers. African English-language writers had some international success before this, especially writers from South Africa, an interest in whom had been generated overseas by the upsurge in Afro-American studies in the American academy. For example, the work of Peter Abrahams was published in both Britain and the US from the mid-1940s onwards. Some of this work found its way into the Heinemann African Writers series. Abrahams's novel *Mine Boy* was re-issued as No. 6 in the series. Other older writers published in the early days of the series include the Nigerian, Cyprian Ekwensi. The publication of three of his titles in the early series – *Burning Grass* (No. 2), *People of the City* (No. 5) and *Lokotown and Other Stories* (No. 19) – reflected the fact that, at the beginning, publishers had to look to the few established local writers to continue the breakthrough initiated by Achebe's success, while they actively sought out new writers to publish.[17] The new writers who were discovered were more likely to reflect the Achebe model and forms. As a result the mainstays of the early period of the Heinemann African Writers series were mainly 'realist' writers. They often shared specific themes: the impact of modernisation on traditional life, in the early period; and, later, denunciations of post-independence corruption. Writers like John Munonye and T. M. Aluko exemplify this pattern. The Longman Drumbeat series, launched with Festus Iyayi's novel *Violence* in 1979, was far less dependent on an active editorial recruitment policy, since by that time a much larger body of established writers existed, and a contemporary tradition of writing in English was well established in both East and West Africa. In addition, it had a wider agenda, since by then it was a series which published Caribbean as well as African writers, a policy to which Heinemann also moved when it combined its African and Caribbean Writers series into one. For these reasons, Heinemann's role in intervening actively to create the material it published remains unique.

The growth in the overseas and local educational market for texts was accompanied by a growth in interest in African English writing in both Europe and America. To some extent, the two events were symbiotic, and the issue of precedence is probably unresolvable. Certainly, texts which were initially produced for the local educational market rapidly established a wider reputation for African writing. They fuelled interest in the new literatures in English being produced in Africa, first with an academic audience and subsequently with the general reading public. Kirsten Holst-Petersen has recently interviewed many of the main figures involved in the development of the Heinemann African Writers series. All the participants, including the then chairman of Heinemann, Alan Hill, make the point that the series was never aimed exclusively at the educational market, even though it was published by Heinemann Educational Books, the educational subsidiary of the William Heinemann company.[18] But, if these interviews are compared with accounts of the same events recorded earlier, for example in Hill's autobiography *In Pursuit of Publishing* (1988), the story of the venture becomes less clear and more ambiguous. In the interviews, the history of the emergence of this important series is presented as a liberal enterprise by a group of young publishers who were driven by an idealistic desire to publish the new English-language writers from Africa. This is a view which Holst-Petersen gently probes, and seeks to question, but which all the interviewees resolutely defend. To quote Alan Hill's response, 'In 1961 we had just two novels by Achebe, and beyond that we faced the unknown ... complete darkness. . . . Then why Heinemann Educational Books? The reason is simple. We were the only firm with the faith – the passion almost – and the will to do the job' (152).[19]

Later in the same interview, though, Hill does concede that the perception of a new, educational market was also central to the decision to develop the list, and in his autobiography, which is much fuller and franker, the more personal passion of building up the Educational Books offshoot of Heinemann, until it rivalled, and even surpassed, its parent company, is frankly and disarmingly acknowledged. It is also made clear that the market developing in Africa was part of a wider market, perceived by Hill, in other similar, post-colonial locations. Under his leadership, Heinemann Educational Books established publishing enterprises in the West Indies (the Heinemann Caribbean Writers series which eventually merged with the African Writers series to form one entity in the late 1980s), in Singapore/Malaysia, and in Australia, where similar new writers were waiting to be discovered for the burgeoning local and overseas book markets. The company also attempted to establish itself in non-British ex-colonies, with a subsidiary in Indonesia, and a very successful sales campaign in Thailand, which, of course, had never been a European colony.[20] But the linchpin of Heinemann's remarkable success was their English-language lists from Africa, notably Achebe's best-selling works, and, in the early 1960s, those of Ngũgĩ wa Thiongo (or James Ngũgĩ, as he was then known).

In the Holst-Petersen interviews, Hill and the others involved, like James Currey and Keith Sambrook, are unanimous in their assertion that the series was never designed only to publish 'school textbooks':

> We decided in the end to be guided by literary qualities – to publish anything of real merit which came our way, irrespective of its 'category'. In point of fact, the great majority of the first new titles were new fiction, interspersed with poetry and drama. The fact that some of the titles were set for school and university examinations was an incidental, though very welcome, bonus. (152)

Nevertheless, as James Currey insists in the same interviews, the educational developments in the ex-colonies in this period were crucial to the success of the venture:

> The other important factor that happened during the period of decolonisation – and this is the period we're talking about – was the establishment of examination boards in both East and West Africa. These boards were all part of the enthusiastic decolonisation process, and they insisted quite rightly that everything needed to be more African oriented. When it came to literature, initially they were pretty conservative – Shakespeare etc. But there was a great interest in and enthusiasm for things that were African, and fairly rapidly they realised that there were interesting works being produced by young Africans and examination questions could be asked about these works. But as publishers we came up against a general problem: what was appropriate for an educational publisher to publish? Fiction was for a general publisher. William Heinemann had the proud record of being one of the most enterprising London-based fiction publishers. But even they needed their arms twisted a bit to publish these books. Meanwhile there was a demand building up in Africa for 'set' books. As publishers who were interested in literature, as both Keith and I were, we managed to override our colleague's initial scepticism and get away with it because of the sales success of the series as a whole. However, one of the great pleasures of the African Writers Series was all the different books which one published in hope, and publishing in hope is always a risky business. It turned out, however, within the context of the 60s that Heinemann with its growing educational market, with mailings to schools, contact with inspectors and universities, etc. was actually able to get these books into the educational network in Africa. (156)

It seems clear from comments such as this that the development of general fiction in Africa in this period was symbiotic with that of the educational market created by decolonisation. The evidence seems to be that whilst the sales were predominantly overseas until the early 1960s, and limited in large part to a few spectacular successes such as Achebe, whose sales the publishers have claimed supported much of the rest of their publishing programme, by the mid-1960s the series had established itself firmly in Africa. Keith Sambrook comments as follows on Currey's observations:

> However it is still true that initially the African Writers Series attracted more interest outside Africa than it did inside Africa. That was not the intention. Our original intention was to provide books at a price which readers could afford. But they hadn't heard of Achebe in Nigeria, so it took a little while to establish him in his own country. The interesting thing is that it happened in a surprisingly short space of time. It started in 1962 when the first four volumes came out, and by 1965 we were selling quite a large number of the first ten titles in Africa itself. (156–7)

Nevertheless, despite these enthusiastic memories by those involved, the critical response to African English writing outside Africa was uneven, and the majority of texts published before the late 1960s did not receive wide attention. Courses in African English writing in universities were also slow to establish themselves, especially outside the US, where the black writing model enabled an early appearance of a few African English texts on a number of courses across the academic institutions. In Britain the earliest courses involving African writing usually took the form of comparative courses in Commonwealth literature, and even at the time when Heinemann had published its 100th volume in the African Writers series, Achebe's collection of short stories *Girls At War*, only a handful of courses involving African texts were being offered in UK universities. The history of the reception of African writing in the academy is crucial, since it was through this process that the texts were slowly introduced to a general reading public, and it was a long time before African English writing received attention from the wider literary establishment. Even after African writing in English began to receive some overseas critical attention in the late 1960s, it was frequently characterised as an exotic and marginal literature. The theme of cultural recuperation, in writers like Achebe, was often dismissed as a sign of the ingratitude of Africans for the sacrifice and hard work of the imperialists who had struggled to bring them civilisation. Achebe captures and exposes this latter kind of response in his foundational 1974 essay 'Colonialist Criticism'. He quotes from a 1971 review which epitomises this kind of response: 'The peaceful village of their childhood to which they nostalgically look back was one which had been purged of bloodshed and alcoholism by an ague-ridden district officer and a Scottish mission lassie whose years were cut short by every kind of intestinal parasite'.[21] However, as Achebe's own essay bears witness, African critics were themselves beginning to offer spirited critiques of the more excessive and ignorant claims of the Euro-American academy, initiating a vigorous cross-cultural exchange which continues unabated to this day.

By the early 1970s, an established readership for African texts existed outside the African educational market. The intermeshing of the interests and influences of these two markets had a profound effect on the themes and forms of the English-language texts which developed in Africa in this period. In this process, the role of Achebe himself was crucial, going well beyond that usually associated with a single author or editor in other literary contexts. As the first editor of the African Writers series, he was directly involved in finding and selecting many of the writers published in those crucial early years. For example, he was personally responsible for finding Ngũgĩ. As Alan Hill recalls in the Holst-Petersen interview:

> For the first ten years Achebe was the editor of the series and he did all this work for nothing. He did it for the good of African literature. And, you know, this is what the younger generation of critics just don't realise, that he made an enormous contribution to the African Writers Series. His name was the magnet that brought everything in, and his critical judgement was the decisive factor in what we published. And in addition to that, the fantastic sales of his own books selling by the million provided the economic basis for the rest of the series. . . . Keith has already mentioned a very good example of how Chinua attracted a new author. It happened like this: I was

at a board meeting at our offices in Kingswood, in Surrey [in 1962] and I had a telephone call from Van Milne in Makerere. There was a symposium going on in Makerere organised by the Council for Cultural Freedom, a CIA-funded outfit which was a mixture of the British Council and the Pentagon. They were running this thing, and Wọle Ṣoyinka and Chinua Achebe were both there. Anyhow, Van Milne phoned me up and said a young student at Makerere had shown to Achebe an almost finished manuscript of a novel he'd written. Achebe was very impressed with it and he'd shown it at once to Van Milne. Van Milne read it and told me over the telephone: 'I think it's terrific, and I want your agreement to take on this book sight unseen.' And I said, 'You've got it,' and went back to the meeting. The book was Ngũgĩ's *Weep Not, Child*. Now that would never have come to us in that way if the author hadn't taken it and shown it to Achebe. And that is how the African Writers Series was built up. (154)

Dramatic though this story is, and important as Achebe's contribution to the development of writing in West and East Africa clearly was, these enthusiastic memories do not tell the whole tale. They beg a series of questions which need to be addressed. For example, they cast new, and not entirely positive, light on the reason why writing from West and East Africa in this period is so remarkably similar in theme and form, given the vast differences of the societies they record and of the impact colonialism had on them. Ngũgĩ has himself recorded how strong an influence Achebe's published work had been on him prior to this historic meeting. Speaking of his excitement at attending the Conference, he records that 'I was then a student of English at Makerere College, an overseas college of the University of London. The main attraction for me was the certain possibility of meeting Chinua Achebe. I had with me a rough typescript of a novel in progress, *Weep Not Child*, and I wanted him to read it.'[22]

Achebe, the admired and imitated older author, was also the man who selected and gave his imprimatur to the texts to be published by Heinemann, a fact which may have influenced the choice of themes and forms which were presented to the world in the African English text in this early period. It raises the issue of the extent to which these texts, aimed at an overseas and local elite, were formed in a relationship with a specific publishing programme, as strong in its controlling influence as any of the previous patronages of the colonial period which we have examined earlier. This is not, necessarily, to denigrate either this patronage or its products. There is no reason to doubt that Chinua Achebe simply selected the texts he believed had the most literary value; and if these reflected his own tastes, and his own position in the various debates about African writing in the period, this is no more than could be expected. Indeed, a close examination of the earlier patronages I have discussed, even those of such consciously manipulative institutions as the mission presses and the colonial literature bureaux, did not, as I have tried to show, result in a simple or absolute censorship, but provided extensive opportunities for independent and even subversive expression. The liberal project of the publishers of this period clearly did so to a very much greater extent. Their policy of encouraging the involvement of local editors, like Achebe, and local managers, like Aig Higo, who became Nigerian manager of Heinemann in

1965, mean that the texts they published have full claim to being African writing in every meaningful sense of that term. They represent a massive advance on the products of these earlier patronages in terms of both African content and African control. But the structure of interconnectedness they provided between areas very different from one another, and the concentration on some areas rather than others as the result of a network of colonial period relationships and connections, meant that the active encouragement described by Hill and others in their accounts of the period resulted in an ongoing strong influence on the choices of theme and form. It also meant that encouragement for writing in English, whilst strong in some areas of Africa, was noticeably absent in others. For example, the writers published in the period of the 1960s and early 1970s were clustered strongly in Nigeria and Kenya, with lesser representation from Ghana, Uganda and elsewhere, and even fewer writers from areas such as Sierra Leone, Liberia, Ethiopia and Tanzania. This might simply reflect the fact that less writing was being produced there in that period. Or it might indicate that writing in the forms, language and models favoured in the period by the new elite, overseas market developed most extensively in those countries where the new publishers concentrated their local infrastructure. As evidence of this, we may note how profoundly the centres of production of English texts shifted from the dominance of Liberia and Sierra Leone, under the older nineteenth-century forms of patronage, to the relative absence of published writers from these areas, under the new commercial forms of patronage in the twentieth century.[23]

The heavy concentration of texts, especially novels, by Ibo writers in the early publications in the Heinemann series meant that many readers formed the impression that the disruptive effects of colonisation were the dominant theme in all West and East African writing in the period. As we shall see in the chapters which follow, this was not so. In East Africa, for example, a concern with urban–rural conflict before and after independence was just as important in even the earliest post-war publications.[24] Because of the predominant representation of writers from a single region and language group in the Heinemann series, a particular African instance was frequently taken as the general African condition, in ways which a better informed view might question. Seeking to account for the dominance of Ibo novels, and of the theme of 'the confrontation of two civilisations, European and African', in the series, Hill suggests that it is the result of the special nature of colonial disruption on Ibo society: 'Significantly, half of the first twenty English language novels in the African Writers Series were written by Ibos from Eastern Nigeria where the confrontation was most damaging to local culture'.[25] This assertion that Ibos wrote more and better novels because their society suffered most from colonial disruption is simply not borne out by the historical evidence. Nor is it true that all the significant writers of the 1950s and 1960s were concerned with this theme. This is a classic case of an argument after the event. Of course, it might equally be possible to conclude that the privileging in the Heinemann series of novels about colonial disruption might have resulted from an overrepresentation of Ibo writers, who had this as a dominant concern.

The work of Ṣoyinka from the same period – for example, *A Dance of the Forests* (1963), *The Lion and the Jewel* (1963), *The Road* (1965) and *The Interpreters* (1965) – shows a completely different, but equally important, set of concerns. These include: an examination of the external pressures acting on Yoruba society; the continuity of the complex forces which comprised the Yoruba past; and the emerging 'movement towards chaos' in contemporary African politics, which powerful phrase Ṣoyinka used when he addressed the Stockholm Conference on African Writing in 1967. Ṣoyinka's writings from this early period are arguably more, not less, democratic in their politics than those of his Ibo counterparts.[26] In fact, Ṣoyinka later argued that the concentration on a celebratory, recuperative reading of the past by writers like Achebe distracted the African writer during the immediate post-independence years of the early 1960s from 'looking at the obvious symptoms of the niggling, warning, predictable present, from which alone lay the salvation of ideals'.[27] We must be careful, though, not to overstate this case either. Ṣoyinka certainly did present, in plays such as *A Dance of the Forest* (1960), a vision of a clear, present danger of corruption and discord, at the very moment of national euphoria following independence. But recent readings of Achebe's and Amadi's texts as unproblematically celebratory, and as still tinged with a colonialist and Eurocentric bias, are equally overstated.[28] Whilst they point to the real limitations of these texts, notably in their treatment of women, and their uncritical support for dubious traditional practices such as polygamy, Ṣoyinka's own work in this period, for example *The Lion and the Jewel* (1963), displays similar weaknesses.

In conclusion, then, however valuable the publication of texts by these international publishers of African English texts was, it is necessary to bear in mind the political and cultural context within which this came about, and not to over-idealise it. In concentrating on Hill and Heinemann Educational Books, I do not imply that he or they were unique in this regard, only they have been more open in recording the attitudes prevalent at the time. I have little doubt that an investigation of the archives of any of the other major publishers involved in supplying these new and lucrative markets, such as Longman or Oxford University Press, would reveal identical attitudes in place at this time.

Whatever the conclusions we reach about the effect of these international series on the development of the forms of African English writing in the late twentieth century, and they must at this stage be tentative, it at least seems clear that far more work needs to be done on the effect and influence of these kinds of commercial patronages. Nor is this a matter of historical interest only. In a recent article, Bernth Lindfors has discussed the complex situation affecting the commercial publication of African English writing in the 1980s. He drew attention to the effect of the rapid take-overs of early specialist publishers by international conglomerates:

> Heinemann . . . found itself taken over by British Tyre and Rubber and then by other corporate raiders who were more interested in increasing their profits than in promoting a foreign literature; the African Writers Series was not completely jettisoned,

but it was so severely reduced in scope and significance that it ceased to serve as an important outlet for new, experimental writing from Africa. Longman, which had developed its own line of African literature in an attempt to compete with Heinemann, had to scale back its activities and release some of its editors when it couldn't collect millions of pounds in revenue from the Nigerian Central Bank. Most other multi-national publishers rapidly lost enthusiasm for entering an African market where significant returns on investment seemed so improbable.[29]

The conclusion Lindfors draws is a damaging one: 'while the outside world was busy courting Africa's established, literary superstars, the very publishers who had brought those brilliant luminaries to international attention were deliberately turning away from a whole constellation of lesser lights who had emerged in their shadows' (28). The continued dependence of many inter-national educational institutions on series like those of Heinemann and Longman, at a time when the new groups no longer shared even the liberal, paternalistic aims of the early pioneers of international Anglophone African publishing, meant a shrinking list of available new texts.

These younger writers were increasingly dependent on a local audience, and a local publisher, and whilst this was perhaps a good thing in the light of the support this gave for the development of local publishing, and the resistance to the so-called 'Coca-Cola' publishing syndrome, in which international pub-lishers squeezed out the locals, such publishing outlets as subsequently emerged only infrequently provided a viable means of support for local writing. As Lindfors succinctly put it, 'the new generation of African English writers seldom saw silver, let alone gold' (28). This was especially true in those areas where the neglect of the international market had failed to develop a local audience for English-language writing. The positive side of this was in the development of new forms of locally published, popular writing, discussed below.[30] A further consequence of this slowdown in the recruitment of new writers to the exist-ing series was the canonisation of the first generation of African writing stars, whose work was endlessly recycled through educational courses at home and overseas.[31] Deserving as many of these writers are, the inability of these new writers to become part of this new literary canon has had a deleterious effect on the financial viability of being a full-time writer in English in Africa in the 1980s and early 1990s. Apart from the new, successful popular writers, the main exceptions to this are some of those writers whose work has been taken up by the non-specialist, international literary market, writers such as Emecheta and Okri in West Africa, or Mahjoub and Vassanji in East Africa.[32] The older, specialist publishers have played some part in this new development: Mahjoub and Vassanji in East Africa, Emecheta and Laing in West Africa, all having published texts in the Heinemann African Writers series. Clearly, though, the take-over of these series by large conglomerates, interested primarily in gener-ating global sales, may well have influenced the emergence and promotion of these new transcultural texts. For these reasons, the story now may be even more complex than Lindfors suggested in 1993.

The sad fact is that, despite the emergence of many talented new writers, few of these have penetrated that still vital market for African English books, the overseas educational sales market. The figures on this form a table in Lindfors's 1993 article, and indicate that of those texts taught regularly on international syllabuses, some thirty of the forty-one titles listed continue to be published by Heinemann. Significantly, though, the list contains few recent writers. However we may regret it, and however strenuously dedicated individuals struggle against it, by setting up their own publishing companies, or by restricting their publication to local companies, this lack of opportunity for new writers continues to be a fact of publishing from the 1980s onwards. The restrictions of circulation and sales this entails makes it even more difficult for new Anglophone African writers to emerge who are able to function solely as writers.

Notes

1. Albert Gérard, *African Language Literatures: An Introduction to the Literary History of Sub-Saharan Africa* (Harlow: Longman, 1981), p. 62.

2. Graham Furniss, 'Reflexions sur l'Histoire Récente de la Litterature Hausa', *Association de'études linguistiques interculturelles africaine*, 8 (1985). Further page references are included in the text.

3. R. M. East, 'A Hausa Journal', *Overseas Education*, 11, 2 (Jan. 1940), p. 89. See also Rupert East, 'An Experiment in Colonial Journalism', *African Affairs* (April 1946). Furniss, 'Reflexions sur l'Histoire Récente de la Litterature Hausa', also lists two accounts by East of his early work on developing Hausa literature in roman script: 'A First Essay in Imaginative African Literature', *Africa*, 9, 3 (1936), pp. 350–8 and 'Recent Activities of the Literature Bureau, Zaria, Northern Nigeria', *Africa*, 14, 1 (1943), pp. 71–7. Two useful studies of the period and of East's work in the Bureau are A. N. Skinner, 'NORLA: An Experiment in the Production of Vernacular Literature 1954–59', *Revues des langues vivants*, 36, 2 (1970), pp. 166–78 and D. J. Cosentino, 'An Experiment in Inducing the Novel in Hausa', *Research in African Literatures*, 9, 1 (1978), pp. 19–30.

4. East, 'A First Essay in Imaginative African Literature', pp. 350–7. Quoted in Gérard, *African Language Literatures*, p. 63.

5. Graham Furniss, 'Hausa Creative Writing in the 1930s: An Exploration in Postcolonial Theory', *Research in African Literatures*, 29, 1 (Spring 1988), pp. 87–103. Further page references are incorporated in the text.

6. I have considerable sympathy for the projects of critics like Furniss, and other similar arguments based on this kind of evidence. There is little doubt that some earlier accounts of the 'silencing' of the colonised voice have had a negative effect on the acknowledgement of local culture and its continued viability throughout the colonial period. But many of these rebuttals seem to have been based on a very simplistic understanding of what colonialist discourse critics, such as Gayatri Spivak, Jenny Sharpe and Homi Bhabha, were trying to draw attention to in discussions of the 'silencing' of the subaltern voice. They do not, as Furniss seems to believe, imply that colonised cultures did not continue to exist, and even to thrive under colonialism. What they do suggest is that the hierarchy of voices established by colonisation, and the dominance, in the public sphere, of colonialist discourse, meant that subaltern voices could no longer speak or be heard unproblematically, or in isolation from their interaction with invasive colonial practices and institutions. For a much more sophisticated account of this dispute see Robert Young, *Colonial Desire: Hybridity in Theory, Culture and Race* (London: Routledge, 1995), especially Chapter 7, 'Colonialism and the Desiring Machine'.

7. Interview with Charles Richards by Keith Smith, *The African Book Publishing Record* II, 2, (1976), p. 161: quoted in Christiana Pugliese, *Author, Publisher and Gĩkũyũ Nationalist: The Life and Writings of Gakaara wa Wanjaũ* (Bayreuth African Studies No. 37, Bayreuth, in association with the Institute for Research in African Literatures, Nairobi, 1995), p. 34.

8. See Chapter 2 above. See also Pugliese, *Author, Publisher.*

9. Emmanuel Obiechina, *Literature for the Masses: An Analytical Study of Popular Pamphleteering in Nigeria* (Enugu, Nigeria: Nwamife, 1971); Emmanuel Obiechina, *Onitsha Market Literature* (London: Heinemann Educational Books, 1972); Emmanuel Obiechina, *An African Popular Literature: A Study of Onitsha Pamphlets* (Cambridge: Cambridge University Press, 1973).

10. Bernth Lindfors, *Loaded Vehicles: Studies in African Literary Media* (Trenton, N.J.: Africa World Press, 1996), p. 45. Lindfors himself has done much of the hard groundwork necessary to assess this material in his work on the juvenilia of such established writers as Achebe, Ṣoyinka, Okigbo, and so on, in studies such as his *Early Nigerian Literature*, and in the many other collections of critical essays which he has brought out in recent years. See entries in General Bibliography.

11. See also Bernth M. Lindfors, 'African Little Magazines', in Anne V. Adams and Janis A. Mayes (eds), *Mapping Intersections: African Literature and African Development*, (Trenton, N.J.: Africa World Press, 1998).

12. Literary prizes, as I have noted elsewhere, also played an important role both in encouraging writers and drawing attention to their work by publishers and others. As well as the success of African writers in arenas such as the Nobel Prize and the Booker Prize, prizes such as the Noma have been very influential in establishing writers who have won them. Other specialist awards, such as the various Commonwealth Writers Prizes, have also been an important means for new writers to establish themselves, their winners including some of the best-known names in recent African English writing.

13. A product, significantly enough, of the educational subsidiary Heinemann Educational Books and not of the parent company, William Heinemann Ltd., the publisher of the works of such twentieth-century literary figures as Lawrence, Priestley and Maugham.

14. Compare the relative demand by genre in the popular writing discussed in Chapter 5 below.

15. See Chapter 11.

16. As a result, his work is different from the writers nurtured by the Heinemann series in a number of ways, which I will discuss in later chapters. These sociological factors may well have as much to do with his differences from other early major writers such as Achebe, as with the more ideologically based distinctions, put forward by critics like Chinweizu *et al.*, *Towards the Decolonization of African Literature* (Enugu, Nigeria: Fourth Dimension Pub. Co., 1980) and Adewale Maja-Pearce, *A Mask Dancing: Nigerian Novelists of the Eighties* (London and New York: Hans Zell, 1992).

17. Ekwensi, as Chapter 5 below shows, had begun writing and publishing in the 1940s. His earliest work appeared in the Onitsha Market and, some literary historians have suggested, was simultaneously published in Lagos. The use of some existing writers quickly gave way to the generation of 'new' (discovered) writers. Even more significantly, of course, few attempts were made to translate existing indigenous writers for the new market. Of course, educational policy in the higher secondary and tertiary sectors at the time precluded this since the stress was unequivocally on 'English' texts.

18. Anna Rutherford and Kirsten Holst-Petersen (eds), *Chinua Achebe: A Celebration* (Sydney: Dangaroo Press, 1991), pp. 149–59. Further page references are given in the text.

19. The choice of metaphors in this interview may suggest how steeped even these liberal publishers were in the idea of Africa as a dark continent, and how they viewed their

enterprise through the spectacles of generations of explorers and adventurers who had ventured into its 'darkness'. The final sentence also suggests how much this essentially commercial enterprise was viewed as part of a greater, idealistic project, in terms which are, ironically, redolent of those used to justify the colonial enterprises of earlier periods.

20. The Indonesian venture was not a success. See Alan Hill's account of this in his autobiography, *In Pursuit of Publishing* (London: Chatto and Windus, 1988), pp. 285–7, an account which is remarkable for the exposure of the close linkages Hill maintained with figures engaged in the very active destabilising activities of the British Foreign Service in the region during the Sukarno period. However valuable the publication of texts they achieved, it is necessary to bear in mind the political and cultural context within which this publishing drive came about and not to over-idealise it, as Hill's later interviews tend to do.

21. Chinua Achebe, *Hopes and Impediments: Collected Essays 1965–1987* (London: Heinemann, 1988).

22. Ngũgĩ wa Thiong'o, *De-colonising the Mind: The Politics of Language in African Writing* (London and Portsmouth, N.H.: James Currey, 1986), p. 5.

23. In addition, of course, the number of texts translated from indigenous languages in the period were far fewer than might have been the case had different publishing policies been in place. In this respect, though, the publishers were simply echoing wider critical responses at the time. Ngũgĩ has recorded that, at the conference at which he was discovered by Achebe, and which was billed as a conference on 'African Writing', there was no consideration of the work of indigenous-language writers such as Fagunwa, Shabaan or Gakaara. In effect, as he says, at this time African writing meant only African writing in English.

24. See Chapter 6.

25. Hill, *In Pursuit of Publishing*, p. 124.

26. Alan Hill claims that it was the 'democratic' nature of Ibo society as opposed to the 'monarchical' societies of the Yoruba and Hausa which made their writers more profoundly egalitarian, and by implication, better writers. In fact, some more recent critics have argued that Ibo texts of this period were overly concerned with a recuperation of this pre-colonial past, a concern which, paradoxically, led to a more conservative slant in their writing, and prevented it from addressing the abuses of post-independence society. See Maja-Pearce, *A Mask Dancing*, p. 9. See also Chapter 6 for a fuller discussion of this dispute.

27. Wọle Ṣoyinka, 'The Writer in a Modern African State', in *Art, Dialogue and Outrage: Essays on Literature and Culture* (Ibadan, Nigeria: New Horn Press, 1988), p. 18.

28. I am thinking especially of the strictures against Achebe and Amadi made in Maja-Pearce, *A Mask Dancing*, and of his virtually uncritical praise for Ṣoyinka.

29. Bernth Lindfors, 'Desert Gold: Irrigation Schemes for Ending the Book Drought', *Matatu*, 10 (1993), p. 28. Further page references in text.

30. See Chapter 5.

31. Raoul Granqvist, *Canonisation and Teaching of African Literatures* (Amsterdam: Rodopi, 1990).

32. See Chapter 12.

Chapter 5

Self-Help: Indigenous Traditions, Popular Literatures and Twentieth-Century Local Patronages

The opening chapters of this account have focused on the historical importance of external patronages on the development of English writing in Africa.
For this reason it is important also to stress the importance of the recovery in
recent critical accounts of the history of the continuous and interactive practice
of indigenous cultures in Africa throughout and beyond the colonial period,
including their ongoing influence on local writing in English. A number of
recent books and articles stress the important influence on modern writing of
oral cultural practices, which early accounts tended to reify under the category
of the traditional, a category which relegated it to the past or to a static model
of culture. This more recent work emphasises that this view of orality and its
influence is both limited and inaccurate.[1] Although it is arguable that African
writing as a whole has been overvalued as a cultural sign of Africanness and
that material culture has been devalued, it is also possible to argue that in recovering the value of material popular expression in dance, sculpture, ceramics,
weaving, and so forth, the many ongoing and powerful verbal traditions of
oral culture have also been neglected. Work by African and European scholars
in recent times increasingly insists on the ongoing viability and power of verbal
arts in Africa, arts which have a recognised tradition and history of practice in
their own societies and whose practitioner's status is at least as well established
as the recently vaunted status involved in being an African English-language
writer. In addition, of course, there is an increasing recognition that the indigenous languages of Africa continue to function, as they have since the nineteenth century, in a new form, using the appropriated tool of writing to create
a powerful, local, written tradition.[2] Thus, writers like Ngũgĩ recognise that,
in arguing the need to continue to write in African languages like Gĩkũyũ, he
is advocating a practice with powerful historical antecedents and an ongoing
tradition. The continuing viability of this tradition, as well as its influence on
contemporary English writing, can be seen in the importance of contemporary
Tanzanian writers such as Ebrahim N. Hussein, who writes in ki-Swahili rather
than in English, or in the work of writers like D. O. Fagunwa, from Nigeria,
who inherited a vigorous tradition of writing in Yoruba from the nineteenth
century onwards.[3] There are many more examples one might cite across the
continent of such long traditions of writing in indigenous languages. Obviously,
the time and extent to which indigenous languages were used as a written

literary medium differs from region to region, and even from country to country. The contemporary use of ki-Swahili as a literary language, for example, has long historical antecedents in Tanzania, as does the use of Luganda in Uganda. In neighbouring Kenya, the decision to write literary texts in languages such as Gĩkũyũ or Luo has a relatively late and consciously political origin, exemplified in Ngũgĩ's own decision to move to writing in Gĩkũyũ in the late 1970s, after a long and successful career writing in English.

Despite incontrovertible evidence of their ongoing popularity in their own language communities, the fiction writers who have written in African languages have not, so far, been successful in gaining a wider pan-African and international audience, unless their work has been translated into English or some other ex-colonial language. For example, although D. O. Fagunwa is mentioned in many accounts, and was a mainstay of the Yoruba school syllabus for many years, he received scant attention outside the Yoruba-speaking community and the work of foreign Yoruba scholars, until one of his texts was adapted into English by Wọle Ṣoyinka. Similarly, Hussein's work in ki-Swahili is widely influential elsewhere in Africa mainly because of the English translation of his play, *Kinjeketile*. Although there has been an increasing recognition of the importance which indigenous language texts have had in their respective regions, writing in ex-colonial languages continues to be privileged above oral practice and indigenous language texts, at least outside the original language communities involved. This has been exacerbated by the failure to develop inter-language and inter-country literary exchange and influence across Africa in these languages. Individual authors, writing in local languages such as Luganda, Gĩkũyũ, Twi, or Yoruba, have an equal, or even greater, status in their own language communities than Anglophone writers. However, most of this writing remains unknown elsewhere in Africa, unless it has been translated into English or another European language. Translation between the various African languages remains a decisive and important development if these languages are to be made a viable means of continental exchange between Africans.[4]

Drama has provided an especially powerful platform for successful work in indigenous languages in West and East Africa. It has more easily overcome the barriers to popularity imposed on written texts by the prevailing low literacy rates in many African countries, even in the indigenous languages. The popular travelling theatre troupes in Nigeria and their less bruited equivalents elsewhere in West Africa (notably in Ghana and Sierra Leone) developed successful hybrid forms, which wedded local and imported dramaturgies into a new and distinctive whole.[5] These formed an important performance tradition, using indigenous languages. They also created a broad-based, popular audience, something which, for all their good intentions, the later university-based, radical dramatists, writing mainly in English, signally failed to do. The playwrights and performers associated with this tradition, which began after the Second World War, such as Hubert Ogunde and Duro Ladipo, directly inspired later English-language playwrights like Ṣoyinka and Osofisan, who have both used plots previously dramatised by Duro Ladipo in their own work.

The influence is even stronger in the work of playwrights such as Ola Rotimi and Wale Ogunyemi, who write in both Yoruba and English, and whose dramaturgy directly reflected techniques developed by these popular troupes.[6] Similarly, in East Africa, the work of a number of popular troupes working in indigenous languages was used for political ends, and as a tool for social and economic development. The work of Ngũgĩ wa Thiong'o at the Kamiriithu Community Centre in the late 1970s is the best-known example of the use of indigenous-language drama to increase the political and social awareness of the ordinary people; but one might also cite the work of Ugandan playwright Wycliffe Kiyingi and his protégé, Byron Kawadwa, in the 1960s and early 1970s, as earlier examples of successful East African popular, indigenous language theatre.[7] A number of important studies exist of this kind of theatre and its employment as a tool of social development, and of resistance to traditional and contemporary forms of oppression.[8] So far, though, the indigenous and popular material which has had most effect in promoting indigenous culture both outside Africa, and across and between different African cultures, has been popular, mass-media forms such as music and song-lyrics. More recently, the emergence in many parts of Africa of a viable film industry has meant that film, too, has emerged as a powerful aid to pan-African communication, and as a means of reaching an ever-widening, general audience outside Africa.

Recent scholarly work has pointed to the continued importance of contemporary popular oral forms, and the long traditions of writing in indigenous languages in many African societies, practices which they argue are an important, neglected element in contemporary self-expression for the majority of Africans.[9] A further feature of this work has been a critical revision of the relationship between African writing in English and oral and written texts in the indigenous language, in studies such as Ato Quayson's *Strategic Transformations in Nigerian Writing: Orality and History in the Work of Rev. Samuel Johnson, Amos Tutuola, Wole Ṣoyinka and Ben Okri* (1997). This study argues that each of these major African English writers, although writing in very different periods and in very different genres, is directly influenced by the body of indigenous oral and written material. It shows how each of these African English-language writers forges a distinctive, specific and reflexive relationship with the indigenous-language culture. Drawing on recent studies of Yoruba indigenous-language culture by Karin Barber and others, Quayson's account emphasises the ways in which orality established effective contexts for constructing and expressing opposition to domination, throughout and beyond the colonial period. However, Quayson's work also emphasises that these indigenous-language cultures themselves were constructed, in their present form, in a complex, dialogic relationship with external influences. He argues that the imported sign of writing was a major influence on the formation of the modern Yoruba identity, although he also continues to emphasise that the patronage of external forces, which I have highlighted in the preceding chapters, was an important factor in the emergence of a unified Yoruba mythology and history, and a sense of communal unity between the various groups, even within indigenous-language culture itself.

Also significant in the relative stabilisation of what is considered Yoruba Culture was the general movement towards setting down the language in writing, a process which was spearheaded by the clergy. This process was a long one with debates on orthography raging into the middle of the twentieth century. As the language came to acquire a significant status in the formal education system of Western Nigeria, there was a growth of a class of people who could read and write in the local language thus giving them a sense of community beyond their individual tribes.[10]

Quayson is well aware of the danger that fixed models of orality and of indigenous cultures may create and perpetuate essentialist, ethnically determined cultural models: 'The noting of indigenous influences on African literature was part of the project of defining the national status of the emerging literatures, especially after decolonization' (3). He comments on the fact that a number of critics, such as Appiah and Hountondji, have recognised the inherent dangers in these approaches, since they 'have unexamined implications for the evaluation of cultural forms which is problematic'. However, there is a positive side too, in that they 'tend to downplay putative ethnic differences in the constitution of the African nation-state' (3). A further danger, in simply linking indigenous and oral elements with the idea of an originary national culture, especially in literary historiography, is that 'literary activity is never juxtaposed to other discourses that draw on indigenous resources' in such formulations. Quayson concludes that 'Even though writers and critics have in their various ways pursued questions of literary history in African writing, the question of possible paradigmatic shifts in various literary uses of orality and in the face of changing socio-cultural and political realities has only been sporadically formulated' (3–4). Studies of this kind, which investigated such socio-political and cultural realities on a detailed and specific site, would be invaluable, and many more need to be done before the full story of the relationship between the various forms of African English writing and the indigenous languages can be told effectively in a general, introductory account such as this.

The emphasis, in the few existing studies, on an ongoing active relationship between oral popular culture and written indigenous-language cultures is an important one. These studies also draw attention to the development of a popular culture, employing appropriated languages such as English to create new popular written forms. Further work needs to be done on the continuities which exist between these forms, and those of indigenous written literatures and oral practices, to be set alongside their debts to external models.[11] Some recent popular forms employ inter-languages, such as modified pidgin, which reflect the usage of the ordinary African; others are popular by virtue of their themes and ideas, which are aimed at a market of non-elite readers, whose interest is in writing which entertains, diverts, or instructs in some practical way, rather than in a 'high culture' model of literary and aesthetic value. Beyond these, there exists a body of more formal texts which, for political reasons, wish to reach out to a mass, non-elite readership, and seek to embrace popular forms to do so. All these various categories of 'popular' forms include texts which use varieties of English. In many cases the motives and categories overlap. It is increasingly clear that it is in popular culture, including popular literature, that many of the most distinctive, contemporary cultural practices of these societies are located. The pejorative and limiting view of this category which prevailed in earlier periods has broken down as critics have recognised it as a powerful means of supplying African writers with a local patronage, and a voice less controlled by the demands of overseas publishers or audiences.

Popular writing using English, including fiction, existed in West Africa from a relatively early date in the twentieth century. The so-called Onitsha Market Literatures – local, self-published and self-distributed writing – sprang up after the Second World War in one of Nigeria's largest trading centres. This body of writing represented a specially important local development, one which gave voice to the concerns and interests of ordinary Africans in ways which more formal literary texts were less likely to do. Texts with titles such as *The School of Love and How to Attend It, They Died in the Bloom of Love, Agnes the Faithful Lover, Rosemary and the Taxi-Driver, Beauty is a Trouble, Money is Hard to Get But Easy to Spend, Why Harlots Hate Married Men But Love Bachelors, How to Write Business Letters and Applications, How to Know Proverbs and Many Things, How to Get a Lady in Love, About Husband and Wife Who Hate Themselves, Veronica My Daughter, Eddy the Coal-City Boy, Life and Death of John F. Kennedy, Patrice Lumumba, Dr. Nkrumah in the Struggle for Freedom,* and *The Bitterness of Politics and Awolowo's Last Appeal* illustrate the wide range of subjects and forms which the pamphlets embraced. Many of these titles, we may note, emphasise self-help and self-advancement. Their development is part of an extended historical process in which English usage is equated with modernity, self-development and education. The same process, as we have already observed, also helped bring many of the elite texts into being. The titles also show that imported, mass entertainment forms, such as the romance and the crime-thriller, had a ready appeal for local audiences. Thus, these market pamphlets prefigure more recent developments, in both West and East Africa, in which writers have continued to have great success, publishing local versions of these mass forms. The Onitsha authors, as Emmanuel Obiechina has argued, were strongly influenced by imported examples, especially Indian popular pamphlets, which, in turn, were based on the Victorian popular magazine fiction, introduced into India by the colonising troops and traders.[12] These Indian pamphlets were brought back by African soldiers, returning from the Burma and the Far East campaigns after the Second World War, and they inspired the development of the Onitsha Market pamphlet. Onto this basic form was grafted an eclectic mixture of influences, including: Ibo folk-tales, from which plots and stylistic features were frequently borrowed; the English classics studied in schools, especially Shakespeare, Austin and Dickens, from whom the pamphleteers happily derived character types and plot lines, as well as frequent literary allusions; newspaper reports of great men and events, such as President Kennedy, Dr Azikwe and Patrice Lumumba, all popular subjects for the pamphlets; foreign cinema films, which provide the inspiration for the heroes and heroines; and Christian allusions to the Bible and the liturgy. This latter influence also involved the use of a Christianised moral framework of 'temptation, sin, confession, contrition, forgiveness and repentance', a discourse which, Obiechina notes, is ubiquitous in the pamphlets. This Christian, moral dimension provided a contemporary frame on which to hang the traditional oral folk-tales' moral and instructive function, and both influences ensure that the entertainment is almost always combined with some form of instruction or admonishment. In the preface to *Florence in the River of Temptation*, for example, the author John Ngoh writes in what Obiechina characterises as 'a typically Johnsonian vein', when he states that his 'aim in composing this novel is to expose vice and to praise virtue'.

However, although the story often has a moral tone, it is not necessarily a pessimistic one. In fact, most of the stories end with reconciliation, and the triumph of the hero or heroine over their problems or temptations. Popular fiction is generally optimistic and positive, in contrast to much elite writing in English in Africa. Obiechina emphasises that, in other respects too, many of these popular pamphleteers writing in Onitsha in the post-war years had a very different vision from that held by the elite writers who were promoted by the overseas publishing companies aiming at the new educational market. Whereas the elite writers tended to view the acquisition of wealth or the move away from tradition as problematic, popular writers were clear advocates of both. Obiechina suggests that 'In contrast to the more intellectual novelists and dramatists of West Africa, who are deeply sceptical of the contemporary society and its changing values and who use their works to express their scepticism of change, the pamphlet authors identify with change, are enamoured of the possibilities which come with change and use the pamphlet literature for promoting the cause of change' (13). In particular, they embrace the new philosophy of individualism, championing such causes as love marriages against parental choice, and the increase of personal wealth as a sign of success not of moral degeneracy. As Obiechina sums it up:

> The emergent values they espouse are entrenched in individual responsibility. The individual man or woman, the authors assume, has the right of free choice in love and marriage, as in economic pursuits, and should abide by the consequences of this choice. Whether the confidence reposed in modernity and individualism is justified or not does not trouble the writers seriously. As people expressing popular attitudes and aspirations, their task is to reflect accurately on the ideals and values of that section of the community covered by the pamphlet literature. They are interested in helping this section of the community to find happiness, fulfilment and social integration. (18)

In this process, popular writing may not only reflect its audience's needs and wishes, it may also offer a significant challenge to the construction of modern Africa in the elite writing, which has often emphasised disabling discontinuities, cultural fracture and fragmentation, and embraced a pessimistic vision of the past, present and future of Africa. The generally pessimistic tone of much African elite writing in English is challenged by the vigorous positive and optimistic tone of the popular fiction.[13]

Many of the early Onitsha pamphleteers were amateurs, who wrote only one or two pamphlets. They often seem to have been motivated more by the status gained from seeing their work in print than by money. Such writers often produced only one or two works, while continuing their other occupations. Yet, even this early period saw a number of writers emerge who established a significant name as professional, popular writers. These include some writers who went on to publish their works in mainstream presses, such as Cyprian Ekwensi, whose earliest books, *When Love Whispers* and *Ikolo the Wrestler and Other Ibo Tales*, were published in the Onitsha Market in 1947.[14] Obiechina's account also singles out Okenwa Olisa, who died young in 1964, but who had by then written more than a dozen successful best-selling pamphlets. Individual best-sellers, such as Ogali A. Ogali's *Veronica My Daughter*, which Obiechina estimates to have sold 60,000 copies between 1957 and 1972, when it was still selling well, suggest that such writers could make a living from the popular market. This was especially so since many of the writers also acted as publishers, and sold the books direct, often through outlets in the same building as the press. The existence of a local audience for popular English writing also meant that popular writers were able to reflect local audience taste directly, rather than to accommodate an external view of what 'real' African English writing could or should include. Of course, many of the texts published are very obvious copies of Western forms, such as the romance novel or the crime-thriller. Both of these forms were very popular in Nigeria, for example, where dozens of local, usually Lagos-based cop thrillers have been produced since, and where series of romance novelettes, clearly modelled on European series like Mills and Boon, have also sprung into existence. Despite their formulaic and imitative nature, the role of these popular texts has been a very important one, endorsing a sense of local identity. Their familiar setting and characters make the local world and the day-to-day life of its people coexist with the world of writing, familiarising and establishing that world as a legitimate subject of literary representation.

As well as these popular copies of Western genres, more radical and differentiated forms of local popular writing have also emerged. It is significant, for example, that many of the Onitsha pamphlets employ dialogue form in telling their stories. Although clearly never intended to be used as scripts for performance, the pamphlets frequently employ dramatic dialogue rather than discursive prose fiction to tell their stories. This may well be a direct influence from oral practice, reflecting the fact that the mass audience is more comfortable with a form which emphasises people speaking to each other directly. This preference for dramatic dialogue form is in stark contrast with the genre bias in the later, elite literary series, which was discussed earlier. In those, the dominant genres, as was noted, are extended prose fictions or short story collections.

In Kenya, too, in more recent times, the work of David G. Maillu illustrates how a popular, self-published writer can continue to exploit a local taste for literary styles with clear and obvious links to indigenous forms. Maillu is one of a small group of African writers whose marketing model has been the

Western best-selling author. His novels sell at African airports and bookshops, alongside those of writers like Arthur Hailey, Robert Ruark or Wilbur Smith. His frankly entrepreneurial approach to writing and publishing, and the successful life-style this has procured for him, has inspired a number of other writers to develop similar popular forms. Yet Maillu's work is far from being merely a copy of Western styles and genres. In a text like *After 4.30* (1974), he shows that, for East African readers, the long poem form can be successfully used to structure a modern, popular narrative. In employing poetry in an extended fiction Maillu is not making an academic point about African style or culture. He employs the form because it has a direct familiarity and appeal to his readership. *After 4.30*, the story of a woman driven to prostitution in Nairobi, has all the ingredients for popular success: sexually explicit subject matter, and a touching plot which invites sympathy for the woman Emili and castigates the callous behaviour of men, particularly rich men. It maintains the moral and exemplary function of traditional forms alongside its modern concerns.

> I learned that
> to sleep with a man, sometimes
> is not to make love
> but to make enemies
> give yourself away to men fully
> if you want to burn.

> They say it's better to marry
> than to catch flames
> only that they don't say
> whom to marry
> and how not to catch flames
> when there's no man
> to marry you.

> Yet there's no path safe
> for women
> in every street you pass
> in every corner
> in every deal
> there's a man rubbing his hands
> to make your life difficult . . . (28)

The moral element of warning, and the lessons Emili passes on, are part of the popular appeal. A similar warning moral tone, this time against the dangers of drink, occurs in Maillu's other early best-selling success, *My Dear Bottle!* (1973), which is also couched in the form of a long verse narrative. Not all Maillu's work involves the use of obvious local forms, such as verse narrative. Later, successful works such as *The Ayah* (1986) are in prose. But he must be credited with establishing the wide market for such popular work in Kenya and in East Africa as a whole.

The success of this kind of text soon influenced the publishing policies of the more established presses. New popular series rapidly emerged, such as the

Longman (Kenya) Crime Series, with titles such as *The Men From Pretoria* (1975). This is a spy story, starring the hard-bitten crime-reporter 'Scoop' Nelson Naeta, as he falls foul of the infamous BOSS (the South African Security Service) whilst hunting down a scientist who has disappeared in Kenya. Series by these overseas subsidiary companies were produced in a more expensive format than the locally published texts. *The Men From Pretoria*, for example, has the obligatory international paperback thriller cover, showing the automatic gun and the pocket spy camera. Popular texts like this signal the fact that, by the mid-1970s, these established local offshoots of the international commercial publishing companies had identified the popular market as their new target. Other popular successes in East Africa by the local offshoots of the international companies include the novel by John Kiriamiti (the alias for Jack Zollo), *My Life in Crime* (1984), based on the 'true story' of this convicted bank robber, and written by himself whilst in prison. This was published by Spear Books, a subsidiary of Heinemann (Kenya), whose list is aimed at the popular market. The success of this kind of true crime story can be judged by its being followed quickly by a sequel, *My Life with a Criminal: Milly's Story* (1989), which claims to be Kiriamiti's girlfriend's version of the same events. The fact that this sequel is not cast as a novel, but as an autobiography, emphasises the fluidity of these genres in this world of popular writing, since both texts are first-person narratives. Texts like these rely for their success on the audience's belief in their truthfulness, both to convince and to allow them to make the moral points which this popular writing exploits. In fact, as the copyright indicators make clear, Kiriamiti was also the author of this account, even though it begins by having 'Milly', as the narrator, denounce his earlier work for not telling her side of the story accurately and truthfully. The 'true' basis of the story is clearly more a selling device than a serious claim.

The same Spear Books series has titles such as *Sugar Daddy's Lovers, Mystery Smugglers, A Girl Cannot Go On Laughing All the Time*, and *Life and Times of a Bank Robber*, titles which indicate a similar kind of form and audience to the earlier popular literature. But the same popular series has also published texts by established writers, such as Samuel Kahiga's *Lover in the Sky*, Mwangi Gicheru's *The Ivory Merchant*, Laban Erapu's *Queen of Gems*, and Thomas Akare's *Twilight Woman*, emphasising that the categories of popular and elite used here are fluid, and that writers who have made a name as so-called elite authors may publish in these popular series and forms too.

A significant example of this is Kenyan author Charles Mangua. His first novel, *Son of Woman* (1971), was one of the earliest Kenyan texts to be claimed as part of the new 'popular' writing in Africa. The publisher was the government-owned publishing company East African Publishing House (EAPH). It tells the story of Dodge Kiunyu, a crooked son of a father who died in prison, and introduces the reader to the world of Nairobi criminals and corrupt businessmen. It was one of the first novels to show this life from the inside, and in a way which made its protagonist, if not a hero, then at least a sympathetic portrait. Dodge is a figure with whom many ordinary Kenyans sympathise, or, at least, whom they might admire even whilst they condemned his actions. The popular appeal of the novel was in its tone, since it treated the life of the city in terms of a slapstick farce, rather than with the high moral seriousness of the later elite, urban novels of Mwangi, Akara, Kahiga and others. Yet to suggest that this made it somehow an entirely different kind of book is to gloss over its similarities with the concerns and themes of these later authors, who have not been classified as 'popular', though their work, as in the case of Akara, appeared in some of these popular series. The line between the two categories of text is even more blurred in the case of Mangua's second novel, *A Tail in the Mouth*, which was also issued by EAPH in the following year (1972). The publisher's blurb for this second novel does not mention the category of 'popular literature', but speaks instead of the book as 'an astonishing *tour de force* and a major African literary event'. Unlike *Son of Woman*, which eschewed an obvious moral dimension, this second novel engaged with the problems of its hero, Samson Moira, as a symptom of society and its history. In many ways, this second novel seems to echo some of the concerns and ideas of earlier elite writing, such as Ngũgĩ's *A Grain of Wheat* (1967), in its treatment of the Mau Mau years and their consequences. It looks forward also to the later work of writers like Meja Mwangi, in their new and raw treatment of the urban world to which these conflicts gave rise, and the disappointments for the survivors of the liberation struggle in the new post-independence world. In other words, it would be perfectly feasible, on the basis of this novel, to slot Mangua into a narrative of the development of so-called elite writing in Kenya. Yet the very different tone of the hugely successful, best-selling *Son of Woman* is returned to when, more than a decade later, Mangua published a sequel to that novel, *Son of Woman in Mombasa* (1986). But, to make matters even more confusing, there are considerable differences, too, in this sequel. The hero, Dodge Kiunyu, has metamorphosed from a small-time crook to a would-be politician, who admonishes the reader that if they want any more information they can write to him: 'explaining why I should waste any more of my time telling you stuff that is none of your business anyway, care of "Parliament Building, Nairobi" where I expect to be in a few months' (2). The tone remains flippant and aggressive, and reflects Dodge's appeal for the mass audience as a smart, street-wise character; but his involvement in political scams and in corruption suggests that Mangua now wants to alert this audience to a deeper message, one which is more congruent with the aim of his 'serious' novels, such as *A Tail in the Mouth*, than the earlier, popular *Son of Woman*. The next novel, *Kanina and I*, written in 1994, and published by Spear Books, the Heinemann Kenya popular subsidiary, carefully invokes *Son of Woman* and its status as 'an instant success and the beginning of Kenyan popular literature' on its back cover. But the story it contains is a dark one, which tells of Joseph Njeru's life after his parents are killed by a white settler during the Mau Mau uprising. Although the melodramatic qualities of the story are calculated to engage a popular audience, it is a very different kind of 'popular' text from that of the deliberately exaggerated, amoral, 'hip' world invoked in *Son of Woman*.

The development of Mangua's work shows how an individual author may negotiate between the forms and themes of both elite and popular texts, establishing an intertextuality with both writing practices. The Spear Books list confirms that many books and authors, marketed on the back of the wave of interest in 'popular' writing, share identities and themes with the elite tradition. In practice, it would be almost impossible to draw a firm line between the two based on lists of authors, or even on themes and styles. The importance of the emerging critical concept of an African popular literature is less its fixed and agreed boundaries, than the indisputable fact that it reflects the emergence of a broad readership for light fiction within the countries concerned, and recognises that this readership has an eclectic taste which is rapidly evolving.

The influence of these early Kenyan texts quickly spread to neighbouring countries. Tanzania, for example, has produced one of the more prolific authors from the region in Prince Kagwema. There is little doubt that his locally produced texts are aimed at a wide popular market, and that the titles and blurbs are carefully designed to appeal to this broad-based readership. For example, Kagwema's *Married Love is a Plant* (1983) claims to be 'pure entertainment for the bachelors, the unmarried girls, the marrieds and the divorced'. He has followed this up with texts such as *Chausiku's Dozen* (1983) and *Society in the Dock* (1984). In fact, despite being clearly aimed at a popular readership, each of these novels also has a serious theme. For example, *Society in the Dock* deals with how society is responsible for creating crime, whilst *Chausiku's Dozen* criticises society's obsession with female virginity and the unfairness of its demands and double standards. So we can see that these later East African popular forms continue to share many features with the earlier, though far less complex and extended narratives of the West African market pamphleteers of the post-war period, blending popular themes and storylines with moral examples and social concerns.

West African writers have also continued to reach out to the growing readership for popular fiction, with the development of many local series and imprints. Perhaps reflecting the larger populations of the West African countries, many more local publishing houses have appeared. In many cases, individuals or groups of writers have banded together to act as their own publishers. A series like the Nigerian Trumpeters Books may serve as an example. In this case, the publisher is the Writers Fraternity Limited, based in Lagos. Authors, like Ola Omiyale, who has published several titles in the series, function as both writer and co-publisher in these joint ventures. Titles and themes are typical of the forms we have already discussed, and show that writers do not restrict themselves to a special genre, as is more usually the case with Western popular authors. Thus, in 1988, Omiyale published two titles: *Ring Finger*, a romantic melodrama about the love rivalries between women over a man, and *Second Dream*, a fantasy adventure. In *Second Dream* a man seeks to persuade his fellows to act on a dream, which offers them a great opportunity if they will go to the mysterious land of Aja-Ile, where they will learn how to gain knowledge and power. Although it has a modern setting, the plot invokes the traditional practices of magic and divination. Omiyale's *Second Dream* illustrates the continuity of the eclectic tradition of the popular African writer, whose roots are still in the early pamphlet tradition, with its hybrid and complex influences, and its readiness to weave together modern and traditional influences and themes.

The success of these popular writers has influenced writing in general in a number of ways. Writers whose reputation has been made in a less popular market have frequently gone on to write books aimed at the new mass audience, including thrillers, romances or children's books. In a period when many African countries have seen gross inflation and the virtual collapse of local currencies, some writers have turned to this kind of popular text as a means of economic survival. Even well-known elite writers like Sowande, Omotoso, Akare and others have, at various times, written books which seem designed to have a frankly popular appeal and to generate large local sales. They were also, no doubt, motivated by a genuine desire to reach out to a broader, local audience. Popular oral and written styles and forms have become part of the techniques available to elite writers, such as Ngũgĩ, in books which consciously aim at developing and politicising a mass audience, such as *Devil on the Cross* (1980) and *Matigari* (1987). Writers like Meja Mwangi have also employed various popular forms, such as the thriller, to engage with the issues of contemporary Africa, and also to ensure a viable sales base for his work in local and international markets, for example in *Weapon of Hunger* (1989) or *The Bushtrackers* (1989). Critical opinion has often been divided over whether such texts are simply popular novels, aimed at mass sales, or whether they are employing the form to effect a link with a mass readership. In fact, the question is probably irrelevant, since as recent cultural studies have argued, dividing literary modes in this way simply misreads the ways in which all texts act to reflect and engage with ideological and institutional forces. As this opening section has emphasised, literature in English in Africa has frequently been produced within the ideological and political constraints of specific patronages, yet these constraints never managed entirely to prevent their radical appropriation to local ends. The development of the 'popular' text in Africa can also be understood in the light of this wider, ongoing struggle, between outside influences and local appropriations.

A number of elite authors whose reputations were established through international commercial publishing houses, or through local academic presses, have also turned to various forms of local, self-publishing. They have done so to achieve more control of subjects and formats, and to allow prices which will attract, not exclude, local readerships. For example, Ayi Kwei Armah, after a long silence, has issued his latest novel, *Osiris Rising* (1995), through Per Ankh, a press based in Popenguine, Senegal, which is described on the cover as 'an African printing and publishing company founded and managed by friends committed to the emergence of a quality African book industry'. Ken Saro-Wiwa, the Nigerian writer, whose stand on behalf of the Ogoni people of the Niger Delta led to his execution by the military government in 1995, also founded his own publishing company, Saros International Publishers, to publish his own work and that of others. As well as giving him direct control over what was, or was not, published, the press allowed him to develop a policy of differential pricing, allowing him to keep local prices low.

Saro-Wiwa is a classic example of a writer whose work defies classification as either popular or elite, as he worked in virtually every kind of genre. His early successes included radio and television scripts, as well as stage plays. Beginning with the Ibadan University Travelling Theatre, whose work was associated with the attempt by Fẹmi Osofisan and others to reach out to the people,[15] Saro-Wiwa adapted one of his popular stage farces, *The Transistor Radio*, for the radio. This was broadcast on the BBC African Theatre Programme in 1972. Subsequently, it was developed as the pilot script of a television series, *Basi and Company*, which was produced by a television production company which Saro-Wiwa set up, Saros International Productions. This series screened over sixty episodes, and became one of the most popular shows on Nigerian television in the early 1980s, with an estimated audience of thirty million for each episode, that is, almost one in three Nigerians. Reviewers at the time claimed that its 'huge audience cuts across all classes of Nigerian society' and that it 'seems to have struck a chord because it lampoons modern Nigeria's get-rich-quick mentality'. Other more established writers, such as Fẹmi Osofisan, were also seeking to reach a mass audience through television at this time, and this shows again how hard it is in practice to draw any absolute line between those who employed popular forms from the beginning of their career, and those who came to them later as a result of a conscious political programme.[16]

The emergence of a large body of popular writing in English in many parts of East and West Africa announces the latest in a series of ongoing appropriations Africans have made of the publishing practices, as well as the languages and the literary forms of the ex-colonial cultures. The undeniable force of external patronages on the production of African English writing clearly needs to be supplemented with further work, in specialist texts, on the ways in which these forces interacted, and continue to interact, with the many local indigenous writing traditions, with popular publishing ventures, and with the ongoing and important role played by local publications in magazines and newspapers, as well as in locally established presses supported either by individuals or by associations of writers, as discussed in the preceding chapter. In an article published recently, but delivered as a talk more than a decade ago, Nigerian poet Niyi Osundare emphasises that the tradition of publishing literary material in newspapers initiated by the journals and newspapers of the late nineteenth century continues into the present day. He acknowledges that there had always been 'Poet's Corners' in many newspapers in Nigeria and elsewhere in Africa, which were a useful means by which established poets could test out their work and younger poets see their work in print for the first time. Osundare relates how together with the editor of the Lagos based *Sunday Tribune* he decided in 1985 to further 'attempt the popularization of written poetry through the medium of the newspaper' by developing a regular series of newspaper-published poems under the title *Songs of the Season*.[17] Although Osundare clearly saw this as part of the attempt in this period by many younger Nigerian writers to 'reach out to the masses', he is also obviously the direct heir of the great author-editors of the nineteenth century who saw newspapers as the platform of their own uncontrolled expression.[18]

The emergence of presses partly owned by individual writers or groups of writers, which include those established by the late Flora Nwapa and Ken Saro-Wiwa in Nigeria, as well as by Ayi Kwei Armah and others in Senegal, which I discuss in the following chapters, indicate that African writers have been increasingly aware of the need to wrest control of the production of their writing back from these various external patrons. This is a feature not only of the popular literatures discussed here, but of those writers who would see themselves as contributing to the ongoing growth of mainstream literature in English from Africa. Only when this development is fully explored can a complete history and sociology of the English text in Africa be undertaken.

Notes

1. Karin Barber and P. F. de Moraes Farias, *Discourse and its Disguises: The Interpretation of African Oral Texts* (Birmingham: Centre of West African Studies, University of Birmingham, 1989); Isabel Hofmeyr, *We Spend our Years as a Tale that is Told: Oral Historical Narrative in a South African Chiefdom* (London: James Currey, 1994); Ato Quayson, *Strategic Transformations in Nigerian Writing: Orality and History in the Work of Rev. Samuel Johnson, Amos Tutuola, Wọle Ṣoyinka and Ben Okri* (Oxford: James Currey, 1997).

2. See Karin Barber, 'Time, Space and Writing in Three Colonial Yoruba Novels', *Yearbook of English Studies*, 27 (1997), pp. 108–29, for an account of the continuity of writing in Yoruba; and Graham Furniss, 'Hausa Creative Writing in the 1930s: An Exploration in Postcolonial Theory', *Research in African Literatures* 29, 1 (Spring 1988), pp. 87–103, for a similar account of early Hausa fiction.

3. As I noted in the introduction, I have not attempted in this volume a full and effective account of the many influences from indigenous writing on English African literatures. The number of languages in the regions covered by this volume, and the variety of their usages, means that such an account must await further specialist work of the kind cited in this chapter and elsewhere in this volume, before an effective introductory survey of this material can be undertaken for East and West Africa as a whole in a series of this kind.

4. A similar problem exists in India despite the strong efforts made there by the Sahitya Akademi to encourage and sponsor translations between the many Indian language literatures. So far, no such active programme of encouragement has been proposed in the far less unified African situation.

5. See Biodun Jeyifo, *The Yoruba Popular Travelling Theatre of Nigeria* (Ibadan: Nigeria Magazine Publications, 1984) and *The Truthful Lie: Essays in a Sociology of African Drama* (London: New Beacon Books, 1985).

6. Accounts of genuine difference of view as to the use of traditional forms and of the relevance of the experience of the popular troupes to modern dramaturgy can be discerned in the disputes, fanned by zealous supporters, between Rotimi and Ṣoyinka who were both at various times in the 1970s and 1980s directors of Unife (university theatres) at Ile-Ife. See 'Rotimi and Ṣoyinka at Unife: A Newspaper Controversy', in Bernth M. Lindfors, *Loaded Vehicles: Studies in African Literary Media* (Trenton, N.J.: Africa World Press, 1996). Behind the spleen of these disputes a genuine debate emerges about

the use of traditional forms and the relevance of the dramaturgy developed by the popular, indigenous-language troupes to modern theatre in Nigeria.

7. See Chapter 8 for details of these.

8. See, for example, Penina Muhando Mlama, *Culture for Development: The Popular Theatre Approach in Africa* (Uppsala: Nordiska Afrikainstitutet, 1991) and I. Björkman, *Mother Sing for Me: People's Theatre in Kenya* (London and Atlantic Highlands, N.J.: Zed Books). A useful more general recent study is David Kerr, *African Popular Theatre from Pre-Colonial Times to the Present Day* (London and Portsmouth, N.H.: James Currey, Heinemann, 1995).

9. Graham Furniss and Elizabeth Gunner (eds), *Power, Marginality and African Oral Literature* (Cambridge and New York: Cambridge University Press, 1995); Karin Barber, *Readings in African Popular Culture* (Oxford: James Currey, 1997); Raoul Granqvist, *Canonisation and Teaching of African Literatures* (Amsterdam: Rodopi, 1990). See also the section on Orality in the General Bibliography.

10. Quayson, *Strategic Transformations*, p. 11. Later references to this work are in the body of the text. See also Gareth Griffiths, 'Writing, Literacy and History in Africa', in P. Hyland and M. H. Msiska (eds), *Writing in Africa* (London: Longman, 1996), which argues that there are similarities with Arabic influence on African cultures in earlier periods to those which have been noted in accounts of relations with nineteenth-century European invaders, such as these.

11. This is not true only of popular forms. Increasingly, African critics, and others with a knowledge of specific indigenous languages, are seeking to make clear the complex and rich linkages between indigenous-language cultures and the work of 'high culture' African English texts.

12. Emmanuel Obiechina, *Onitsha Market Literature* (London: Heinemann Educational Books, 1972), Introduction. Further quotations from this source are all to the introduction to this anthology.

13. A point made by Ngũgĩ when he drew on popular forms to write *Devil on the Cross* and *Matigari*. See Chapter 8, where these texts are discussed in detail.

14. There is some evidence that these were also published simultaneously in Lagos by small, professional presses there.

15. See Chapter 8.

16. See Chapter 8.

17. Niyi Osundare, 'Bard of the Tabloid Platform', in Anne V. Adams and Janis A. Mayes (eds), *Mapping Intersections: African Literature and Africa's Development* (Trenton, N.J.: Africa World Press, 1999).

18. For an account of this attempt to 'reach out to the people' in Nigeria and elsewhere in this period, see Chapter 8.

Part Two

DOMINANT THEMES AND PATTERNS IN EAST AND WEST AFRICAN ENGLISH WRITING

Alternatives: Contrasting Themes and Patterns in Post-Independence African English Writing

Many accounts of African English writing begin with Achebe, Tutuola, Ngũgĩ and the other writers of the 1950s and 1960s.[1] As the earlier chapters have argued, it is more accurate to see these writers as the culmination of a longer and more continuous tradition. The critical neglect of this earlier writing is, in part, because these earlier writers did not usually write fiction, poetry or drama, but employed forms such as letters, journals, essays, legal prose, histories and ethnographies. Despite such differences, the earlier writers often explored themes and concerns similar to those embraced by the later fiction writers of the post-war and post-independence period. So, for example, the early nationalists we have mentioned, such as J. B. Danquah (Ghana) and Jomo Kenyatta (Kenya), appropriated colonial languages and genres to their independent aims in the period between the two world wars. Even earlier, writers like the great Yoruba historian Samuel Johnson appropriated European historical discourse and the English language to celebrate the complex and rich past of their own people. Johnson's monumental work, *The History of the Yorubas* (1921), which has a strong claim to being one of the most important historical African texts of the late nineteenth and early twentieth centuries, is slowly recovering its deserved place in accounts of the evolution of modern African history. It is important to note, too, that this neglected early writing in English went hand in hand with the rich traditions of writing in African languages, which evolved after written forms for those languages were developed.[2] Both these written traditions also had an active ongoing relationship with the living practices of oral cultures.[3] The late nineteenth and early twentieth centuries, for example, saw many writers who moved easily between African languages and English, as well as many local journals and newspapers which published material in both English and the indigenous languages.

As we have seen, to meet the demands of the new market for educational texts in English, publishers were forced to seek out locally published writers, many of whom had been writing and publishing in English in the period between the wars and afterwards. Such writers had already published occasional prose and poetry in local presses and magazines, or developed scripts with local theatre groups. When series like the Heinemann African Writers were established, some of the earlier work of these writers was recovered and republished. These early literary texts offer interesting examples of the process of patronage in action, and its effect on the material and styles of the writers involved. Two examples of this must suffice, though others could be easily found. In Ghana, two writers, born in 1923 and 1924 respectively, and working principally in poetry and in drama, namely A. W. Kayper-Mensah and J. C. de Graft, illustrate how work which had been produced earlier could be taken up and disseminated in this way. Kayper-Mensah's poems were published originally in a variety of local journals, and found their way into the early anthologies such as *Messages: Poems from Ghana* (1971), title No. 42 in the Heinemann African Writers series. Four years later, in 1975, with more than a hundred titles added to the series in that boom time for African English publishing, Kayper-Mensah's work achieved a single volume, *The Drummer in Our Time* (1975). Even a cursory examination of the poems in this volume quickly reveals attitudes and ideas which seem incongruent with those of the new writing which had emerged in the 1950s and 1960s. This is hardly surprising, given that some of these poems reflect the work and thought of a man born a decade or more earlier than the new writers. This time gap was especially crucial, in that it meant that writers like Kayper-Mensah came to early manhood before it was evident that the colonial period was past, and when the more confident attitudes associated with the later post-independence writers were still only in formation. *The Drummer in Our Time* and *The Dark Wanderer*, which Kayper-Mensah had published in Germany in 1970, although published well after Ghanaian independence include poems which seem to have been written much earlier, and which reflect the attitudes and influences of a much earlier period. This can be easily shown if we compare the poetry in these two early collections with those published a year or so later, for example in *Proverbial Poems* (1976). These later poems have far more localised themes, settings and stylistic influences. They shift dramatically towards a use of local references, and towards much more assertive themes. But in the early collections, published before 1975, we can see the stylistic and thematic constraints on these early African Anglophone poets, struggling to free themselves from colonial educational influences and European aesthetic preoccupations in the decades immediately after the Second World War. For example, in the poem 'Student Days', from *The Drummer in Our Time* (1975), Kayper-Mensah recalls his time at Cambridge three decades earlier. He describes how we 'pushed / Our groping way, In three short years, / Some twenty years ago'. The poem evokes a student's experiences in the last years of the war and after. Even if it was, as the poem itself asserts, written ten or more years later than the events it describes, its tone and ideological assumptions are quite different from the general mood of other texts of the late 1950s and early 1960s. The distinction is even more obvious in another poem from the same collection, 'How I Woke to Nature'. Here the poet speaks of 'Looking up deep in the woods' and of 'the poet of the woods, / Wordsworth, Shakespeare, Shelley, Keats' in a way which makes one momentarily think the poem is set in England, but then continues:

But there was a push quite early
At Mfantsipim one noon.
Reverend Warren picked me up
In his car that afternoon
When the green of the trees was new
In the rainy season sun . . . (25)

making it clear that the setting is Ghana not England, but a Ghana relocated in a very Anglicised natural discourse. In noting the influences on these poems, I do not intend to be ungenerously critical of an important and significant Ghanaian writer, but rather to place Kayper-Mensah's early poetry within the continuum along which the appropriation of English to discourses of the local and indigenous evolves in Ghana, from the earlier world of figures like Horton, to that of later writers such as Aidoo and Awoonor.

Joe de Graft was also educated alongside Kayper-Mensah at Mfantsipim Mission School, and so, presumably, absorbed the same diet of English canonical authors, possibly even taught by the same Reverend Warren. However, his poetry, published by Heinemann in the same year, reflects a different and potentially more radical sensibility, which has absorbed a different set of influences. Its very title, *Beneath the Jazz and Brass* (1975), openly embraces a modernity from which Kayper-Mensah's work seems far removed. The modernist American and Afro-American influences hinted at in the title are confirmed in the collection, which contains poems about Jack Kerouac and about the science of genetics. Shakespearian and other classic references are also present here, though handled rather differently, as witness a poem such as 'Witch':

Here are no cauldrons
Nor assignations on blasted heathland
Stewed in fog and filthy air –
A fevered Shakespeare's fancy. (119)

Here Shakespeare is transmuted to a hot and fevered Ghana, rather than Ghana being greened by the discourse of English poetry, although this in itself may reflect a certain ongoing colonial cringe.

These poems were probably written much closer to the date of publication than those in Kayper-Mensah's early collections, and the sensibility they reflect has been formed after de Graft had completed his earlier work. Most of this early work was in theatre, where de Graft wrote and directed plays which are amongst the earliest in West Africa to present specific local concerns and form. This may have allowed him to avoid having to satisfy the conservative tastes of local editors and poetry publishers, constraints which bore more heavily on the work of the poet Kayper-Mensah. However, in his early plays such as *Visitor From the Past* (1964), *Sons and Daughters* (1968), and *Through a Film Darkly* (1970), which represent the work he had done whilst setting up the Ghana Drama Studio in Accra, de Graft still shows a dependency on European dramaturgy which is in unresolved tension with his desire to reflect local themes and characters, a tension not dissimilar to that manifested in Kayper-Mensah's poetry.[4]

In *Sons and Daughters* (1968), de Graft explores the shifts between the generations in a middle-class Creole family. The self-made father wants his son Aaron to become a professional, a lawyer or engineer. But the son wants to become a painter. The play becomes a pretext for a debate about the values of the newly emerging elite for whom money is valued above culture or service. Despite its radical theme, its form is strictly that of an English drawing-room comedy and the dialogue never really explores the tensions between the father and the newly educated sons at any level beyond the thematic. They speak an identical English, as does the wife, and a differentiation of characters by local language markers is almost entirely absent. *Through a Film Darkly* reflects a drive to innovate theatrically, but remains very dependent on European dramaturgical models. Pirandello's *Six Characters in Search of an Author* (1921) clearly inspires the contrived, false start and the presence of a character whom the 'playwright wouldn't allow to appear in this play' (4). Despite this flirtation with experiment, the bulk of the play is still fairly conventional, though the dialogue shows a pronounced tendency to incorporate local markers, as in the following speech:

> When a lady goes trailing Tokyo Joes after her everywhere she goes, and is known to own ten taxis, at least four of them Mercedes Benzes, and is good-looking fit to make you choke on your beer, and drinks and smokes freely in public, and is to be seen frequently in night-clubs – well, what more do you need to know about a woman to convince you that she could be dangerous. (12)

For all its local elements and concerns, de Graft has clearly been restricted to expressing them through European dramatic conventions, and is pushing to explore themes which, it is increasingly clear, only a revised African dramaturgy can properly explore.[5] For all their limitations, early dramatists and poets like de Graft and Kayper-Mensah have not been given the attention they deserve, reflecting the dominance of the novel form in most criticism of African writing.

Efua Sutherland, in particular, demonstrates how dramatic form could become the vehicle to incorporate indigenous forms into English-language texts in a direct way, with the development of her dramas employing the local Ananse folk-tales and the musical and performance elements associated with these oral forms.[6] Work like Sutherland's shows that poetry and drama allowed Africans a form which was potentially less susceptible to the external patronages which influenced African novels in the 1950s and 1960s. Drama and poetry, despite the dominance of a European model in much of the early work, provided an easier interlink with the rich traditions of local indigenous performance, incorporating, if not always the forms, then at least the rhythms and intonations of local speech, helping to establish crucial differences in African English writing from the English literary tradition. These earlier writers, whose work in drama and poetry did not get much immediate critical attention, form an important and neglected part of the story of the development of English African writing.

Many of the earliest and best-known of the new African English texts to be published in English reflected a burning desire to supplant the biased, colonialist accounts of African societies and the African past. These new writers set out to celebrate and recover the African past on its own terms and from the perspectives of Africans themselves. As we have seen in earlier chapters, they were neither the first writers to celebrate African societies, as has sometimes been suggested, nor the first to deny the superiority of the European viewpoint to that of the African. The process of abrogation of the European viewpoint had suffused African English writing in different ways from its inception, as I have tried to show in earlier chapters. But they approached this task with the new, enthusiastic spirit created by political independence. On the other hand, these new writers, like the older nationalists and freedom fighters who had preceded them, were not entirely free from the influences of what Biodun Jeyifo has characterised recently as 'the central social formations of the world system', which, as he argues, persisted to dominate the criticism and reception of African texts.[7] Thus, as I have argued in the preceding chapters, despite these new aims, powerful external forces continued to influence the selection of the texts published, and even their themes and forms. As a result, African English writers in the period immediately before and after independence still employed European and American literary forms, which, in the words of their contemporary, the Nigerian critic Emmanuel Obiechina, they sought to 'domesticate' to their own uses.

They were also influenced, as recent critiques by feminist historians and critics have shown, by accounts of their own recent and past history which reflected a patriarchal and limited view of the cultures they were recording. In part, this was because the writers of this generation were strenuously and self-consciously engaged in a process of recovering local knowledges from a wide variety of sources, since, for a number of reasons, they themselves had often been distanced from the traditional cultures they sought to celebrate and record. Their daring project, to present the African world much more decisively from an 'insider' standpoint and to represent that world as functional and meaningful in its own terms, and not simply in terms of its engagement with or response to the outside world, was both valid and successful. Yet these writers were, in one sense, 'critical insiders'.[8] They were not writing in any simple sense from within the pre-colonial culture they celebrated, and which they sought to recover as a dignified and meaningful cultural heritage. It has been argued by critics such as JanMohamed that their texts frequently represent in some sense a rewriting of the misrepresentation of the African past in the English-authored colonial texts about Africa which flourished in the inter-war years, and which the new generation of writers had encountered in their own education in the English departments of the colonial universities such as Fourah Bay, Ibadan, and Makerere.[9] Texts such as those of Joyce Cary and Elspeth Huxley form a reflexive background to some of the novels of the first generation of post-war writers using English in Africa. But these young African writers also incorporated into their work their own written traditions and the 'local knowledges' incorporated in the continuing and living oral cultures. However, the writers of this first post-war generation, at least as much a product of their colonial education as of such 'local knowledges', were also often the sons of fathers whose own social identity was invested in a turning away from many of these indigenous practices and values. The resulting tension renders this incorporation of local knowledges more complex and problematic than is sometimes acknowledged.

Chinua Achebe, for example, has written of how difficult it was for a person of his generation, the son of a Christian catechist, to access this oral tradition, given the fact that his village was divided into Christian and non-Christian communities, and that, as a child, his father had refused to allow him to hear the traditional tales. He was only able to listen to those his mother told him when his father was away at church. Naturally, too, the tales told by his mother were women's tales, and, as such, of a different kind to those which would have been told to boys by the men in a 'non-Christian' household. The tales of traditional life and warfare, which Achebe records his father had forbidden, would have incorporated considerable amounts of historical and political information about the Ibo past.[10] Similarly, John Pepper Clark in the introduction to his collection, *A Reed in the Tide* (1965), the first poetry volume to be published internationally by an individual African writer, wrote of himself as:

> that fashionable cultural phenomenon they call 'mulatto' – not in flesh but in mind! Coming of an ancient multiple stock in the Niger Delta area of Nigeria from which I have never quite felt myself severed, and going through the usual educational grind of an English school at its end, I sometimes wonder what in my make-up is 'traditional' and 'native' and what 'derived' and 'modern'.

As a result, first-generation elite writers drew on both the European and African worlds for their ideas and images. Stylistically, they wove together the structures of European fictional narratives and poetic forms, and the oral practices of the African societies they sought to celebrate. Poised as they were at the crossroads of two cultures, as Achebe has expressed it, they discovered in their precarious situation both great potency and great peril. An examination of the provenance and structure of some examples from these texts will allow us to indicate the features of the texts of this period, and to establish in more detail their concerns and stylistic practices.

J. P. Clark's own work takes the form of drama and poetry, and so, like those earlier figures I mentioned, Kayper-Mensah and de Graft, many of his earlier plays and poetry were produced by local school and undergraduate theatre groups, or appeared in magazines such as the very important undergraduate publication *The Horn*, which he helped found at Ibadan University, and which also published many early pieces by writers such as his friend Christopher Okigbo and the young Achebe. His first collection, *Poems* (1962), was published in Ibadan by Mbari, emphasising again how local presses were much more instrumental in publishing poetry than novels in the early period, since novels required a much greater investment in money, personnel and distribution infrastructure than small local presses could readily afford. In 1964 Clark published *Three Plays*, which contained the two plays *Song of a Goat* and *Masquerade*.[11] This latter deals with the consequences for a Niger Delta family of a crime against the gods. The emphasis on inevitable, retributive consequences made many critics speculate on the influence of Greek tragedy on his work. The strong emphasis on European classics in the Ibadan curriculum at the time makes it possible that this influence was present. Clark's friend Okigbo, for example, had studied for a degree in classics at Ibadan, and there were Greek tragedies in translation on the Ibadan English syllabus, which both Clark and Achebe studied. Although, in early interviews, Clark drew attention to the fact that his own Ijaw culture also used a chorus, and that he incorporated many elements from Ijaw burial rituals in the play, he also acknowledged that he owed a debt to Euripides, Sophocles and T. S. Eliot, especially in his ongoing preference for the use of poetic dialogue in the theatre.[12] Like de Graft's work, these early plays by Clark are obviously influenced by European dramaturgical practices, but here this influence is balanced with a much stronger element of traditional Ijaw cultural forms and thematic material. Clark's plays also deal with a far less Europeanised section of the population, the fisher-people of his native Niger Delta. The ongoing influence of Clark's early, ground-breaking work in Nigerian theatre can be seen as late as Femi Osofisan's play *Another Raft* (1988), which reworks Clark's *The Raft* (1964), modifying and developing its allegory of modern Nigeria as the crew and passengers of a raft drifting towards a shrine on the lower Niger. Clark's later work, with his own and his wife's company in Lagos, the PEC Repertory Theatre, made him an ongoing influence on writing and dramaturgy through the 1980s and even into the early 1990s.

His collected poems, *A Decade of Tongues* (1981), consolidated Clark's reputation as one of West Africa's most influential poetic voices, despite the accusations by fellow Easterners that he had served as an apologist for the Federal Forces ('Gowan's praise-singer') in the period of the Nigerian Civil War. He defends his position in that bitter conflict in several powerful poems in the section entitled 'Casualties', directly addressing those who took a different line on the war, such as Chinua Achebe. This set of poems, which is at the heart of the later controversy about Clark's role, constitutes a defence of his decision not to participate actively in the war, unlike his erstwhile friend Okigbo (who was, of course, killed in 1967 on the Nsukka Front, fighting for the Biafran side), or Soyinka (who was imprisoned by Gowan for seizing a radio station and broadcasting anti-war speeches), or even Achebe (whose role as one of what Clark calls the 'emissaries of rift', when he travelled abroad to raise funds for Biafra, is criticised by Clark). Achebe responded by calling the collection 'a terrible book'.[13] Soyinka also implicitly criticised Clark's role, when he spoke against Clark's position in the appendix to his prison notebooks, *The Man Died* (1972).

Despite these controversies, Clark's strength as a poet of natural scenes and a sensitive recorder of traditional practice and custom was never in doubt. His work is especially important and touching when he is celebrating the landscape and practices of his native Niger Delta region. However, in his next collection, *State of the Union* (1985), which he claims was written before 1981, but which was withheld from publication because of conflicts with the government over specific poems, Clark reasserts his claim to be taken seriously as a commentator on contemporary social issues. In a poem like 'One Country' (which was excised from a BBC broadcast by the government), he takes up a stance in defence of local interests against the false centralism of those who 'in the name of one country / To turn waste regions into garden cities' have taken away the lands of 'The aborigines who generations / Ago kept the strangers at bay' (22). Clark's later post-war work continues to be surrounded by controversy. Few modern Nigerian writers produce such a heated response even now, but his place as one of the literary pioneers who sought to celebrate the past and engage with the issues of modern post-independence Africa is surely not in dispute.

Chinua Achebe's *Things Fall Apart* (1958) was one of the first texts to be published by the new wave of publishers in the period immediately before and after independence. Together with Amos Tutola's *The Palm-Wine Drinkard* (1952), it was one of two texts cited in the dispute as to what constituted an 'authentically' African text amongst the new publishing barons who were the overseas patrons of this so-called 'new African writing'. As we have seen in this account, however, there was nothing very new about Africans writing in English or even publishing fictional accounts and poems. To look at this dispute is very instructive, since it illustrates the extent to which there was an external process of legitimisation of certain styles and themes within African English writing, legitimations which shaped the bulk of the material published in English in Africa for a considerable period.

Alan Hill of Heinemann Educational has recounted the clash between rival publishers in the period about the appropriate form for African writing in English in his autobiography, *In Pursuit Of Publishing* (1988):

> *Things Fall Apart* came as a revelation to many of my colleagues in Britain, whose opinion of African writers had been influenced by the works of Amos Tutuola – particularly his quaintly-told allegorical fantasies of Yoruba folk-tales. I remember Fred Warburg telling me that Tutuola's *The Palm-Wine Drinkard* (published by Faber in 1952) was the only sort of African book that he would want on the Secker & Warburg list, as 'it represented the real Africa'. For this very reason, Tutuola's work was anathema to many educated Nigerians – to whom his linguistic virtuosity seemed plain illiteracy.[14]

Achebe's work had the advantage, from Hill's perspective, of sharing many features with the traditional English language 'novel' in ways which Tutuola's work did not, making it easily recognisable and assimilable. That it proved to be at least as different as it was similar to these forms was a fact that dawned only slowly on its early advocates. Its initial reception is marked by a search for Eurocentric identifying markers. Early accounts emphasise the allusion to the English literary tradition in its title, and the way it locates itself within the various discursive regimens of colonial writing, notably the ironic counter-point in the final paragraph to the long tradition of anthropological accounts and memoirs by colonial officials.[15] This was a process of validation of the text in the eyes of those critics who still, consciously or unconsciously, saw European aesthetic values and forms as the principal means of legitimating African written accounts. Thus Alan Hill's very defence of the Achebe model in his autobiography, *vis-à-vis* the 'quaintly-told' tales of Tutuola which Fred Warburg preferred as more authentically African, reveals an equal, if different, set of Eurocentric prejudices as to what features legitimised African English writing. After castigating Warburg's preference for Tutuola, Hill concludes: 'In *Things Fall Apart* we now had something entirely new from Africa: a novel which affirmed permanent human and social values in the context of a traditional tribal society in crisis, and which expressed these values in terms which the Western-educated reader could understand' (121).

The 'many educated Nigerians' in the late 1950s whom Hill, correctly, insisted shared his preference for Achebe over the 'illiterate' Tutuola were, of course, largely the new Western-educated elite who, like Achebe himself, had defined the function of the modern Nigerian text in English as a subversion and rewriting of the forms of the English text to which they had been subjected in their secondary and tertiary studies. That this was an important and meaningful project was undeniable. However, the alternative concern of Tutuola, to preserve a more direct link with local speech patterns, oral forms, and the ongoing body of writing in Yoruba by earlier writers such as I. B. Thomas and D. O. Fagunwa, was to be defended by later Nigerian critics such as Chinweizu.[16]

Achebe himself has said that he was moved initially to write by his distaste for the patronising presentation of the African in the English novels he had studied at Ibadan, such as Joyce Cary's *Mister Johnson*. In presenting his protagonist, Okonkwo, he sought consciously to show that the African condition might generate a truly tragic character, and not a merely bathetic one as in the case of Cary's white colonial text. In fact, the congruency of African texts with such European modes as 'tragedy' was both a part of the project announced by writers such as Achebe and J. P. Clark, and part of the process of legitimisation of these texts by the first generation of European critics. Their very different projects meet incongruously on the site of this single signifier, tragedy. The text was more directly influential than Tutuola's because, by the early 1960s, it was clear that Alan Hill's Heinemann Educational Books had won a decisive victory in the battle for market control in both West and East Africa, as well as establishing a strong hold in the overseas component of the more diverse South African market. Achebe's novel had a more general appeal too, in so far as it represented a rewriting of a familiar theme in colonial fiction, the so-called 'colonial encounter'. But Achebe reversed the prejudicial expectation of colonial discourse, making the intruding European the other to the African Self. His purpose in writing, as he stated in 1964, was to show that 'African peoples did not hear of culture for the first time from Europeans; that their societies were not mindless but frequently had a philosophy of great depth and value and beauty, that they had poetry and, above all, they had dignity'.[17]

Thus Achebe's work was directed towards an end defined as much by social aspirations as by literary purpose. Whether Achebe's success in the new overseas elite market helped to consolidate the form he adopted over that of the more picaresque tradition represented by Tutuola remains a matter of speculation.

The picaresque form was, however, to return powerfully in the 1980s in the work of novelists as diverse as Ben Okri and Syl Cheney-Coker, and, in a different way, in some of the later work of Ngũgĩ, notably in sections of *Devil on the Cross* (1980) and *Matigari* (1987). In the 1960s and 1970s, though, the publishers of the 'new African fiction' were more interested in works which would fit the syllabuses of the new and expanding universities of West and East Africa. This favoured the work of those writers who had this kind of background themselves. Alan Hill is quite explicit about this in his autobiography:

> It was now clear to me that I should visit Africa, in particular West Africa – and for more than one reason. Achebe was not an isolated phenomenon. He was a product of the newly-established University of Ibadan which – soon to be followed by other universities – was creating a new intellectual dimension in the life of West Africa. Then again, our new school books, particularly in science, were selling in large quantities in Nigeria. Something was stirring in that part of the world. (122)

Achebe, as we have already noted, was the first general editor of the Heinemann African Writers series, and it is possible to speculate, as I have already done, that his own taste and interest had a strong influence on the shaping of the list. By the mid-1960s, an unofficial 'template' existed which guided potential young African writers towards certain themes and stylistic choices rather than others, and which favoured some forms, for example prose narrative, and to a lesser extent poetry, over others, such as drama. Whatever may be the effect of that, for good or bad, it is clear that Tutuola, without much of a formal education, and steeped in Yoruba oral and written culture, was atypical of the writers who succeeded with the new overseas and local audience for African writing in English. The new writers who exploited Achebe's breakthrough into overseas publication were typically university graduates, the so-called 'been-to's', who had either been educated overseas or had travelled overseas for other reasons.[18] All were, in various ways, members of the relatively well-off post-independence elite. Tutuola's work, on the other hand, can be seen to be more closely linked to a body of earlier, popular writing in Yoruba, which married the traditions of Yoruba orature to the narrative forms which had emerged as Yoruba speakers encountered English writing, especially in the religious forms popularised in the missionary schools, such as Bunyan's *Pilgrim's Progress* (1678).[19] The new writers in English, however, moved away from the non-sequential, episodic structure which these intertexts encouraged, and which grafted so well onto the thematic material and images of the orature traditions, and worked much more consciously in an adaptation of the Western novel form, which they consciously sought to adapt to their own local ends.

The creation of a self-contained representation of the 'local', or the 'pre-colonial', is a complex and deeply problematic task. Novels like *Things Fall Apart* (1958), or Ngũgĩ's *The River Between* (1964), and even more so perhaps Elechi Amadi's *The Concubine* (1966) or *The Great Ponds* (1969), which seek to present almost entirely self-contained accounts of pre-colonial African societies, can be seen to share in the dilemma Christopher Miller identifies for similar, early Francophone texts such as Camara Laye's *L'Enfant Noir* (1954):

Lévi-Strauss describes ways in which aberrances are merely translations of various 'constants' within a society; the individual difference is still dependent on the collectivity for its meaning and interpretability; the exception proves the rule. But our problem is in deciding, *What is the system?* The traditional Mande world can clearly be considered a total system in Lévi-Strauss's sense. However, the only perspectives we have on this total system are given by representations which are *aberrant to the system itself*: oral traditions that are transcribed and translated, ethnographies written by Europeans or European-trained Africans, a novel that foregrounds its own unreliability. *L'Enfant noir* wants to describe the coherence of the traditional Mande world but keeps tripping over the condition of its own creation: the break with the total system that motivates the nostalgic return.[20]

The act of authorship in such circumstances, and the recovery and celebration it seeks, is involved simultaneously in an inevitable and unwitting complicity with the forces which destroyed the world it seeks to celebrate, and the forms which are intrinsic to that deeply ambiguous (ad)venture.[21] This positioning of the African text in English on what Achebe has referred to as the dangerous but exciting terrain of a cultural cross-roads, means that the production of meaning in such texts will always be a complex, over-determined process.[22] The first generation of novels, such as Achebe's *Things Fall Apart* (1958), strove to dramatise this complex 'moment of contact' and the implications of this for African societies. Or they tried to show the consequences of this moment for the generations which followed, for example in Achebe's *No Longer at Ease* (1960) and *Arrow of God* (1964). These themes were adopted also by the early English-language novels in East Africa, for example Ngũgĩ's *Weep Not, Child* (1964) and *The River Between* (1965).

This striking similarity of theme may have been influenced as much by the pattern established for African writing by the commissioning editors of the major publishing houses, such as Heinemann, as by internal literary intertextual influences. It is hard otherwise to account for such unlikely congruencies between areas whose histories and contemporary 'local conditions' were as different as Nigeria and Kenya. Whereas the production of these texts clearly did involve the recording of local knowledges and of specific conditions in the different African regions, they also show a remarkable consistency of concern and style, considering how greatly different were the societies they recorded and the nature of the imperial intrusions with which West and East Africans had to deal. This similarity is almost certainly attributable to the effect of the shared colonial and neo-colonial literary patronage structures. To deny this effect seems to fly in the face of the evidence, and to deny the success of the authors of this first generation in adapting these patronages to their specific and local needs.

Amongst the most widespread of these early forms was the colonial contact novel. Achebe's *Things Fall Apart* (1958) remains one of the earliest and best of these, and illustrates the form as well as any. It tells the story of an Ibo community already riven with internal tensions. These tensions centre on the psychological and social struggle of the protagonist Okonkwo to compensate for the perceived failure of his father, the economically unsuccessful and impractical musician Unoka. In Okonkwo, Achebe created a figure with whose demise the reader empathises, whilst recognising that his fall was the product of a complex set of factors including Okonkwo's own character, his clash with the values of his society which he embraces with an overzealous and distorting vigour, and the changes within that society brought about by the impinging pressure, as the novel proceeds, of the European colonisers. The result is an examination of the moment of colonial contact in which the African world is seen as a participant in the historical events, and not merely as its victim. It is this preservation of the agency of African society and the African characters of the novel that allows Achebe to create in Okonkwo a figure for whom the term tragic hero seems very apt, despite cultural difference. The inter-cultural nature of the form which emerges is further evidenced, as Okonkwo's story is told in a style which weds the syntax and rhythm of orality to the linear narrative structures of the European novel, creating an effect which goes a long way to illustrate Achebe's claim to have made the English language, and we might add English cultural genres, 'bear the burden of [his] experience'.[23]

The novel is placed within the Ibo community, immediately before the arrival of missionaries and colonial officials. At the outset, the society has heard of the arrival of the white man, but has not been directly affected by it.[24] The initial conflicts which the novel dramatises are those within the society itself, and as the narrative progresses, and with it the influence of the outside forces of colonisation, a complex history of the interconnectedness of the two unfolds. Okonkwo's demise is not produced simply by the entry of the white man into the Ibo world. His own character and history are also part of the cause and effect. For example, his friend Obierika and the elder Ezeudu both warn him against excessive zeal, an especially important warning in the case of Ezeudu who, as an elder, is a repository of communal wisdom, since, in a literal sense, the law of an oral society is in the mouths of the old. When the village oracle declares that Ikemefuna, a tribal hostage placed in the care of Okonkwo's family, and with whom his son Nwoye has become close friends, must be killed, Ezeudu warns: 'Yes, Umuofia has decided to kill him. The Oracle of the Caves and the Hills has pronounced it. They will take him outside Umuofia as is the custom, and kill him there. But I want you to have nothing to do with it. He calls you his father' (51). Characteristically, Okonkwo ignores this admonition against excessive zeal and strikes down Ikemefuna himself since, we are told, 'he was afraid of being thought weak' (55). For this, and other such excesses, the village 'called him the little bird *nza* who so far forgot himself after a heavy meal that he challenged his *chi*' (28). In so challenging his personal spirit (*chi*), Okonkwo is as much in violation of the communal spirit which had held his clan together, as his father had been in his weakness and self-indulgence.

Not that Achebe absolves the white invaders from their share of responsibility for the destruction of the societies they encountered, but he is at pains to show that the society of Umuofia was itself a complex and evolving entity, with its own agendas and internal contradictions, whose interaction with the mysterious new forces of the white man produced a volatile and finally irresistible set of changes. These changes are not shown to be entirely negative. Thus Nwoye's rejection of his father, Okonkwo, and his subsequent decision to join the new Christian sect, is the result of his anguish at Ikemefuna's death, as well as of his increasing alienation from other aspects of the clan's traditional practice, such as the exposure of twins in the 'Evil Bush'. In this, Achebe is stressing the fact that Ibo society was neither perfect nor static, but was itself capable of evolving and undergoing development from tensions and attitudes resident within itself. When Okonkwo is banished to his mother's clan for an offence against the Earth Goddess (the accidental killing of a clan member), he is taken in by his uncle Uchendu, who reminds the young man that the present state of aggression between the various Ibo clans was not always the case: 'Those were good days when a man had friends in distant clans. Your generation does not know that. You stay at home, afraid of your next-door neighbour. Even a man's motherland is strange to him nowadays' (124). Thus, the kind of male, warrior-strength which Okonkwo has shown, and which leads him to demand that he resist the white invader, is not presented as a *sine qua non* of Ibo pre-colonial life. In fact, the emotional and personal rigidity of Okonkwo is, in some ways, a metaphor for the recent rigidity and lack of subtlety in the society itself, which has become self-divided and unable to respond wisely to external threats for that reason.

There is some suggestion that this may have come about because of the changes which had already taken place within Ibo society prior to the arrival of the white man in the region. These changes are only hinted at in the text, though clearly they included the shifting power structure within the larger frame of Ibo society, its changing relations with its neighbouring societies, and demographic factors, such as a rapid population growth, and so forth. These changes must also include the effects historians attribute to the pressure on all societies in West Africa of the coastal settlements of the European and American slavers, and their 'domino' effect on inland communities, even on those like Umuofia, to whom the white man remained 'a rumour'. But the narrative choice not to stress this as the sole or even the primary cause of the tensions between Okonkwo and his community is a significant one.

The same theme of self-division as the precursor of the successful control of the white man features in Achebe's later account of the interaction of Ibo society and the white colonial power in *Arrow of God* (1964), which is set in the 1920s. In this later novel the chief priest of the village of Umuaro, Ezeulu, allows his internal desire to consolidate his power in the clan to overcome his judgement. By withholding the vital Feast of the New Yam, on which crop planting traditionally depended, he opens a door for the white District Commissioner to impose the system of paramount chieftainships on the recalcitrant and strenuously democratic Ibo society.[25] This change of governing practice was a principal issue of contention between the British colonial authorities, with their preferred policy of indirect rule, and traditional Ibo society.

The success of Achebe's novels in dramatising the internal agendas of those who faced the colonial encounter takes on new significance in the light of recent arguments for the continuity of internal agendas within colonial societies.

For example, Aijaz Ahmad has argued that the colonial incursion did not displace local agendas rooted in pre-colonial concerns and practices.[26] Karin Barber has also argued that the pre-colonial interacted with and survived within the colonial period in ways which are often underplayed in many accounts of post-colonial dependency.[27] Achebe is not alone in thus presenting the pre-colonial world, and the world after colonisation, as having an independent functioning agenda. Ngũgĩ offers a similar view in his early novels *Weep Not, Child* and *The River Between*. Soyinka makes the same point in his play *Death and the King's Horseman* (1975). But Achebe's strength as a model resides in the fact that he presents the colonial invader, with great fairness, as a complex mixture of liberal intention and false ideology. Thus negative characters, such as the Commissioner at the end of *Things Fall Apart*, whose view of the complex world of Umuofia is seen through a narrowly distorting colonial anthropological lens, or the uncompromising missionary, the Reverend James Smith, whose zeal, matching Okonkwo's own, provokes the convert Enoch to desecrate one of the *egungun*, the sacred masks of the clan's ancestors, are set against the earlier missionary Mr Brown, who offers a more respectful and subtle approach:

> Mr. Brown came to be respected even by the clan, because he trod softly on its faith. He made friends with some of the great men of the clan and on one of his frequent visits to the neighbouring villages he had been presented with a carved elephant tusk, which was a sign of dignity and rank. (162)

In later texts like *Arrow of God* Achebe presents a more satirical portrait of figures like D. O. Winterbottom, but even then he never descends to mere caricature. The absence in these texts of a polemic stress on the evils of colonialism works to establish their assertion that the colonial world was one in which the dignity, and to a certain extent the self-determination, of the colonised survived even the worst excesses of colonial rule.

Elechi Amadi's texts focus even less on the invader's influence. They seek to recover a picture of the pre-colonial world as complete in itself, able to generate its own narrative struggles and concerns. Although they have attracted less critical attention than Achebe, they offer an equally powerful celebratory view, and one which also presents a sophisticated portrait of a pre-colonial society, riven with its own internal agendas and contradictions.

Amadi's *The Concubine*, for instance, presents the story of Ihuoma, the beautiful but ill-fated wife of Emenike. Emenike has been involved in a fight with Madume, his erstwhile rival for Ihuoma's hand. The quarrel between the two erupts over a dispute about a piece of land, but it is clearly part of the much older struggle which has begun with their rivalry over 'the most desirable girl in Omigwe village' (6). The unfortunate Emenike sustains an injury from which he recovers, but on a visit to the shrine of Amadioha, he has a premonition of his death. Emenike's death is not described, and the next chapter opens with Ihuoma alone and widowed. Amadi's peculiar narrative strength is encapsulated here. Unlike Achebe, there is no attempt to place the premonition of Emenike into some envelope of alternative belief systems. The force of this belief is total and internalised, and the text frequently dramatises this rather than constituting it as a subject of analysis. Of course, like Achebe before him and like others after, Amadi is aware of an external audience for his writing as well as a local one, and the detailed descriptions of the history, ceremonies and practices of the people of the village of Omokachi are couched in a familiar form, explanatory and even ethnographic in parts:

> The nearest village to Omokachi was Omigwe. Igwe, the founder of Omigwe, was forced to leave Omokachi when one of his babies cut his upper teeth first. This was a terrible omen signifying that Igwe had done something very wrong, though no one seemed to remember exactly the nature of the offence. Some whispered that he went to work on Great Eke; others that he accidentally killed a vulture, the sacred bird of Ojukwu. Whatever it was, the sacrifices needed for absolution were too involved and costly. Among other things the medicine man had mentioned seven rams. Igwe could not collect these things and to ward off the wrath of the gods the villagers ejected him from the village. But he prospered (some say he performed the sacrifices later) and founded Omigwe. (18)

The absence of an external threat to this world allows Amadi to concentrate on presenting the world of Omokachi as one which generates its own conflicts, tragedies and joys, and this is Amadi's principal aim in constructing a narrative which is referentially self-contained. After Emenike's death, Ihuoma settles into a joyless but correct widowhood. She reorganises her life with the help of her dead husband's brother Nnadi, who takes on the traditional role as her protector, helping her with such male tasks as the re-thatching of her roof. Ihuoma is presented as a self-sufficient and moderately successful widow. She re-establishes her husband's farm on a more modest scale, since she is now called upon to maintain it herself. She is actively courted by a young man, Ekwueme. Although she likes him, she is not ready to remarry. Indeed, the pressure on her to remarry, from female friends and relatives, is contrasted by her own sense of self-sufficiency and her desire to raise her children in independence. Her reluctance to remarry is not explored openly, but the indications build up that she is aware that there is more unhappiness in store for her if she yields to her inclinations. Having been publicly refused by Ihuoma, Ekwueme agrees to go ahead with the courtship of Ahurole, the woman his family has selected for him. The marriage of Ekwueme and Ahurole takes place, and both Ekwueme and Ihuoma seem reconciled to it. Of Ihuoma we are told: 'Her liking for Ekwueme was not frantic nor was it sudden. It had grown gradually over a long period. Since it did not take her by storm she was able to keep it firmly under control' (165).

This analysis is placed within an ideological framework in which male perspectives dominate. Recent feminist criticism of this text, as of others of this period, correctly exposes the weaknesses in representing the inner workings of a woman's mind within a social and discursive framework which is constructed along strongly patriarchal lines. This ideological bias is clearly exposed in the descriptions of Omokachian social values which surround these moments of decision, moments in which the detached, objective tone of ethnographic discourse in which they are couched masks the ideological constructions which they reflect and sustain.

> Omokachi village life was noted for its tradition, propriety and decorum. Excessive or fanatical feelings over anything were frowned upon and even described as crazy. Anyone who could not control his feelings was regarded as being unduly influenced by his agwu. . . . Even love and sex were put in their proper place. If a woman could not marry one man she could always marry another. A woman deliberately scheming to land a man was unheard of. True, she might encourage him, but this encouragement was a subtle reflex action, a legacy of her prehistoric ancestors. A mature man's love was sincere, deep and stable and therefore easy to reciprocate, difficult to turn down. That was why it was possible for a girl to marry a man without formal courtship. Love was love and never failed. (166)

It is this rather contrived and ideologically conditioned portrait of the traditional past to which feminist critics have objected; and it is this particular 'worlding'[28] which Amadi constructs as the defining boundaries of Ihuoma's choices, without identifying this as either a construction of a specific idealised male modern view of the past, or as operating in forms which are profoundly hegemonic.

It is proper to acknowledge, as recent critiques have done, the limitations of this discourse, but such readings have been less than fair to the complexity of tone involved. Amadi is at pains to note that this world is neither as perfect nor as much in control of its affairs as it might like to think it is. The invocation of the gods is a further echo of the power of fate and the outside forces of supernatural beings to act on human affairs, a note first struck in the tragic death of Emenike, even as ceremonies of thanks for his recovery are underway. Ihuoma is undoubtedly created on a male pattern of ideal wifely behaviour, presented objectively as the ideal of the traditional society the text sets out to celebrate. But we should remember that, as the novel progresses, the power of the supernatural world to overwhelm human aspirations of virtue and ideals of social behaviour is also stressed, leading to a more complex text than some recent feminist readings suggest.

The famous medicine-man, Anyika, becomes aware by divination that Ihuoma is fated to destroy all her husbands, as Emenike was destroyed, since she is a wife of the Sea-King in the spirit realm, from which all humans come and to which all must eventually return. The jealous King has destroyed her first husband, and he will destroy Ekwueme if she marries him. She may live as a man's concubine, if the God is propitiated with the appropriate sacrifices, but she may never marry. Refusing to accept this verdict, the lovers seek another opinion from the *dibia* (or traditional medicine-man) of another village, who agrees to do rites to propitiate the God. The tragic ending, in which Ekwueme is killed by a play arrow of Ihuoma's son, Nwonna, on the very day of their wedding, signifies the power of the Sea-King and the tragic truth of Anyika's prediction.

This construction of Ihuoma as a being fated to be desired by men, but also to be the unwitting cause of their doom, offers itself in two different readings: as a construction which problematises woman, casting her in the traditional role of temptress and source of danger, a role which even the most conscious virtue cannot evade or set aside; and as a tragedy of divine intervention in human affairs, an intervention whose motivation and causes are set outside the social patterns through which they are manifested. Amadi's scrupulous avoidance of anything which breaks the narrative's pre-colonial framework goes a long way to help the tale's project of reconstructing a world in which the interactions of gods and humans are to be taken with the utmost serious-ness, and not as a mere metaphor or image. But it is impossible to read the text without being aware that this construction reflects problematic positions within the present, which is its moment of composition and reading. The objections posed by feminist readings have already been discussed. Some readers have also felt that there is a general limitation in Amadi's stressing that the flaws in this otherwise perfect and idyllic world precede from supernatural, rather than human causes. These secular readings lay bare the ongoing tension between accounts of pre-colonial societies which operate from within the beliefs held by those societies, and the demand of a modern readership that the author expose the limitations of these and their effects from a modern perspective. Yet unless we take these systems of belief with utter seriousness, how can the text claim to represent that world effectively?

Amadi requires us to take the elements of traditional religion as seriously as he does, and not reduce them to metaphor, myth or image. The tragedy of Ihuoma may suggest other meanings to a modern reader, and Amadi is clearly aware of these, but at the level of the tale he demands that we set aside our modern views of motive and cause, and surrender ourselves to the perspectives of a traditional world which is usually rendered, if at all, in a denigratory and pejorative fashion, as superstitious savagery. The novel, as it stands, acts to recuperate this alternative world. It shows how it offered those who lived in it coherent, meaningful ways to order and understand their lives. It shows, also, the tragedies which sometimes characterised them. This project should not be forgotten in our critiques of the novelist's limited and circumscribed view on gender issues, or his failure to analyse the flaws in traditional political and social institutions.

Feminist readings have compared Amadi unfavourably with texts such as Flora Nwapa's *Efuru* (1966). It is perhaps more fruitful to recognise that Amadi's text, like those of Achebe and other first-generation male novelists, is part of a wider male construction of the 'traditional', which emphasises, and helps to construct, the image of the traditional African woman as dutiful and subservient to a male-oriented world. Correctives to this construction are clearly necessary, and the recent critical acclaim for texts like *Efuru*, which, it is argued, present the traditional world from a more feminine perspective, has gone a long way to do this.[29] This earliest Nigerian woman's text shares many of the thematic and structural preoccupations of the early male authors, par-ticularly the concern with celebrating and recording pre-colonial cultures, and the impact on these worlds of colonialism. As in Amadi's *The Great Ponds*, or in Achebe's *Arrow of God*, the white presence is registered in Nwapa's novel. As in these earlier novels, too, Nwapa's text centres its vision within the Ibo society it depicts, and the white presence is presented as a visible and significant but not a dominant element. But *Efuru* also offers a very different reading of the internal values and social practices of the pre-colonial past, one which indicates that the male novelists offer only a specific gendered view of traditional customs.[30]

The Achebe model was also followed in this period, though with less individuality perhaps, in the work of John Munonye. Munonye has sometimes been presented as the archetypal post-Achebe novelist, and certainly in the early novels which deal with the clash of modern and traditional values, such as *The Only Son* (1960) and *Obi* (1969), the influence of Achebe can be clearly seen. In Munonye's work, however, the setting is usually later in time, and the plots stress the modern forms of the inter-cultural clash, rather than the colonial period encounters. His later novel, *A Dancer of Fortune* (1974), deals with the corruption of modern post-independence society with some vigour and edge. Older than some of the other writers of this period, T. M. Aluko is another novelist whose work shows Achebe's direct influence. Aluko, like many other early African writers, had already published stories in journals and newspapers in the 1940s and 1950s. His work focuses on post-independence corruption, and shows the influence of Achebe's later work, especially *A Man of the People*, whose theme is echoed in Aluko's *Chief the Honourable Minister* (1970). Aluko was a powerful satiric voice in this early period, but he fell silent in later years. Together Munonye and Aluko can stand as representative of a number of other lesser writers for whom the realist form and themes of Achebe's work created a precedent and example.

In East Africa a similar impulse of recovery and celebration can be detected in the early 1960s, though a little later, since, as we have seen, some of these texts were generated by the direct influence of Nigerian writers like Achebe. Pre-eminent among these early East African texts were the novels of Ngũgĩ.

In 1965, some seven years after Achebe had published *Things Fall Apart*, Heinemann published Ngũgĩ's *The River Between* as No. 17 in its new African Writers series. Although another novel, *Weep Not, Child*, had been issued the year before as No. 7 in the series, *The River Between* was actually written first. It is also set earlier and deals with the moment of 'contact' with outside colonial forces. This short novel dramatises the encounter between an isolated part of the Gĩkũyũ homeland, the ridges of Kameno and Makuyu, lying either side of the Honia River, and the outside world. This occurs first in the form of missionary influence, and later in the encroaching demands of the settlers' drive to create a plantation labour force from the independent agriculturalist Gĩkũyũ people of the region. Despite this specificity, the text has a generalised, representative quality. The land of the ridges is presented in quasi-allegorical terms in the opening paragraphs: 'The two ridges lay side by side. One was Kameno, the other was Makuyu. Between them was a valley. It was called the valley of life.' The struggle between these two ridges for the domination of the region is also initially presented in these mythical terms: 'they faced each other, like two rivals ready to come to blows in a life and death struggle for the leadership of this isolated region' (1). As the text unfolds, the ridges become identified with the struggle between the forces of tradition and the new influences of mission education and Christianity. The more self-consciously allegorical tone of the text is the principal difference between this 'contact novel' and those of its West African predecessors, especially Achebe. The social contextualisation of the novel is also more overt, a feature which is more strongly developed as Ngũgĩ's later writing unfolds. Nevertheless, it is possible to see even in this early text the lineaments of the style of the later works, such as *Matigari* – a style in which allegory and myth are deployed alongside acutely observed social detail, and in which the novel's events are a microcosm of larger historical and cultural forces.

The River Between offers an account of the development of a modern intelligentsia amongst the Gĩkũyũ, as a result of their exposure to mission education, and dramatises the clash between this class of mission-educated 'readers' (*athomi*) and the traditional elders. For the most part, the text endorses the struggle of the young *athomi*, Waiyaki, to bring the benefits of education to the two ridges. But it clearly exposes the political problems which result, problems of collusion with the intrusive forces of the mission and the settlers who follow them, whose primary interest is in the dispossession of the Gĩkũyũ from their traditional lands, and their conversion from free farmers to landless labourers on the coffee plantations. The analysis of the process in the text is acute, if necessarily partial. Thus, the missionaries are presented, rather simplistically, as active participants in this dispossession, and the text fails to acknowledge the powerful oppositional role missions had played in early Kenya against the policies of the settlers in this dispossession process. This is partly because the text focuses on the crucial rupture which occurred from the 1920s onwards between missionaries and nationalists over Gĩkũyũ circumcision rites. It was this conflict which historians note led the missionaries into opposition to the growing Gĩkũyũ independence movement. This crucial and problematic marker of culture, which functioned in the period in complex ways as a signifier of Gĩkũyũ unity, and of European opposition to Gĩkũyũ independence, is at the heart of one of the two principal narrative lines. The novel links the story of Waiyaki's mission education and his leadership role in bringing schools to the ridges with the story of young Muthoni's desire to be circumcised, despite the opposition of her catechist father, the zealous Christian convert Joshua. For Muthoni, circumcision is a sign of her full participation in Gĩkũyũ life and of her transition to womanhood: 'Look, please, I – I want to be a woman. I want to be a real girl, a real woman, knowing all the ways of the hills and ridges . . . I too have embraced the white man's faith. However, I know it is beautiful, oh so beautiful to be initiated into womanhood' (29–30). The representation of a female view of circumcision by a male novelist must be open to strong question. It is significantly similar to the general defence of circumcision as a crucial signifier of Gĩkũyũ culture by the early male leaders of the nationalist movement, themselves amongst the mission-educated generation portrayed in the novel through Waiyaki. It also echoes the strong defence of circumcision in texts such as Kenyatta's *Facing Mount Kenya*. Ngũgĩ's novel finally takes a very ambivalent stand on the issue of female circumcision.

Muthoni's defence of the practice as culturally empowered is a spirited one, but it leads to her death. Eventually Waiyaki dies, partly because the Kiama can represent his decision to marry Muthoni's uncircumcised sister, Nyambura, as a betrayal of the tribal purity. The text might best be seen as representing the complex, and central, role the disputes over the signification of traditional rites, such as circumcision and oaths, played in the constitution of a contemporary Gĩkũyũ identity. The story of Waiyaki also shows that the zeal for education is useless unless it is accompanied by a struggle for political control. He learns as the novel progresses that knowledge is never free of power, and that by itself education may simply divide and weaken the people, as the ridges split over the demands of the two cultures and the social and economic forces they embody. 'Now he knew what he would preach if he ever got another chance: education for unity. Unity for political freedom' (164).

The novel clearly focuses the loss of opportunity in this failure, and the inability of either Waiyaki or his traditionalist opponent Kabonyi to deal with the threat represented by the invasive forces. Kabonyi's answer, an unyielding conservatism, is exposed as equally inadequate.

> Kabonyi was determined to win or die. . . . Not that Kabonyi knew exactly where he would lead the people. For he too was grappling with forces awakened in the people. How could he understand that the people did not want to move backwards, that the ridges no longer desired their isolation? (165–6)

The narrative seems to suggest that both Waiyaki and Kabonyi need to recognise that some elements in the traditional culture need to be respected, and others need to be questioned and changed. Unquestioned traditionalism on its own will not resist the inevitable changes the society faces. Conversely, modernisation and education without political power cannot lead to liberation but only to further hegemonic domination and control. In this respect Ngũgĩ's text moves the emphasis on the impact of colonial contact in early West African novels, such as those of Achebe or Amadi, towards an analysis of the internal conflicts within Gĩkũyũ society itself, which modernisation and colonialism have exacerbated.

In Uganda and Tanzania, too, early texts also followed a similar pattern. One of the first texts published in English in the modern period in Tanzania, Peter Palangyo's *Dying in the Sun* (1969), deals not with the conflict between the colonial world and traditional African society, but between the rural world and the new forces of urban government following independence. This novel, the first Tanzanian novel published in the very influential Heinemann African Writers series, deals with resistance by the rural world to change. But here the agent of change is the new government of the post-independence state, based in the distant cities, and embodying values which are just as disruptive to the traditional patterns of this rural world as the earlier colonial incursion. Early novels like Palyango's establish the urban–rural conflict as a theme in East African writing as important as the colonial encounter in early West African writing, reflecting perhaps the greater continuity through the colonial period of traditional practices in the East African rural areas.

128

A more light-hearted treatment of the theme of traditional rural values and new administrative demands is also at the heart of one of Uganda's earliest novels, Bonnie Lubega's *The Outcasts* (1971). The story tells of the struggle between the outcast Karekyezi and the wealthy Bugandans for whom he keeps cattle, and from whom he exacts an unofficial tax of their produce. In a sense, though, the novel is less about the clan divisions between Karekyezi and his rich Bugandan masters, than about differences between his earthy and rural vision of reality and the blindness of the more sophisticated vision of the village council, whose basic ideas are already infected by the ideas of the modern, urban world. As a result, the celebration of this traditional, rural world is less politically oriented towards the idea of a recovery and celebration of the values of the pre-colonial world than in the West African novels published at the same time. Since those West African novels had quickly established a sort of template for writing, early criticism tended to ignore these East African texts, as not dealing with the issues African fiction *ought* to handle. Just as the contemporary feminist re-readings refute the early critics' dismissal of texts by writers like Nwapa and Ogot as simplistic, and demonstrate that their concerns are just as complex, if markedly different, so these 'aberrant' texts deserve now to be reconsidered and re-evaluated. Lubega's novel, for example, published in 1971, clearly records the tensions between the Bugandan 'masters', favoured ever since colonial times, and the subaltern ethnic groups in the rural areas. Although the politics of the text are not explicit, it would be foolish to assume that, in the light of the radical changes after the Bugandan King was deposed by Obote's revolution in 1966, the tensions between the poor and the wealthy in Ugandan society, and the very hierarchichal and tribal nature of that society, would not be as important a theme as the struggle between nationalism and the colonial powers. In Uganda, it would be hard to separate colonial power and the rule of these Bugandan 'masters', especially in the rural world which Lubega's novel portrays. For the same reason, since settler rule was far less direct in Uganda, and since independence did not involve an armed liberation struggle on the Kenyan model, the themes of the early writing also reflect these differences.

A significant feature of the texts produced in the early 1960s in East Africa was the interface between the use of indigenous languages and the texts produced in English. In part this seems to have been the result of the role of the East African Publishing House, the post-independence descendant of the East African Literature Bureau.[31] This independent local publishing house was committed to the policy of the East African Colonial Literature Bureau to publish texts in both English and in the many East African languages. Its continuity as a publisher across, and between, the territories and languages of the new post-independence nation-states meant that a viable readership and an effective distribution network for these works could be sustained in the relatively small population nations of East Africa. The new and independent EAPH, which unified work across the previous colonial territories of Uganda, Kenya and Tanganyika/Zanzibar (Tanzania), offered a viable, local alternative for East African writers to overseas publishers such as Heinemann and Longman. It also offered a place for writers from adjoining territories, such as the Sudan or Malawi, to publish their work, further emphasising its importance as a regional unifier. Also the greater willingness to publish work in translation shown by EAPH in comparison with overseas publishers, opened a space for forms which were less dependent on the aesthetic and cultural conceptions of a European publisher and the demands of a European influenced market-place and educational system.[32] Thus even the earliest published texts include examples of long narrative verse texts. For example, Okot p'Bitek, writing in Acoli, and translating his own work into English, provided, in *Song of Lawino* (1966), a powerful portrait of a society changing as the result of the new values brought by European colonisation, and the increasing level of settlement following the First World War.

For p'Bitek this text becomes a means of defining both the tensions resulting from the clash of values brought by white colonisation, and the degree to which these values, internalised by the colonised, have been destructive of the traditional ways. The clash is dramatised in the lament of Lawino, a traditional Acoli wife, for her husband Ocol's migration to European values and, finally, to a new mistress:

> Ocol rejects the old type.
> He is in love with a modern woman,
> He is in love with a beautiful girl
> Who speaks English. (21)

Lawino notes the attempt by the new wife, Clementina, to appear fashionably as a 'white' girl:

> her lips are red-hot
> Like glowing charcoal,
> She resembles the wild-cat
> That has dipped its mouth in blood,
> Her mouth is like raw yaws
> It looks like an open ulcer,
> Like the mouth of a fiend!
> Tina dusts powder on her face
> And it looks so pale;
> She resembles the wizard
> Getting ready for the midnight dance. (22)

In contrast, Lawino celebrates the traditional Acoli forms of beauty:

> When you go to a dance
> You adorn yourself for the dance,
> If your string-skirt
> Is ochre-red
> You do your hair
> With ochre,
> And you smear your body
> With red oil
> And you are beautifully red all over!

If you put on a black string-skirt
You do your hair with *akuku*
Your body shines with simsim oil
And the tattoos on your chest
And on your back
Glitter in the evening sun. (55)

Song of Lawino, followed later by Ocol's 'response' in *The Song of Ocol* (1970), is important in that it represents the possibility for the direct incorporation of Acoli narrative forms into the world of the English written text, despite Okot's cautious warning that in doing so he has 'murdered rhythm and rhyme' in the translation process. The ability to publish a long narrative in verse speaks of a possible continuity with discursive forms which rupture the modern, Eurocentric assumption that long narratives must be in prose. Okot p'Bitek's work opens the space for the employment of verse in later long narratives, such as the popular narratives by writers such as David G. Maillu which were discussed in Chapter 5. Recently, Okot p'Bitek, along with other writers of his generation, has been criticised for uncritically employing woman as a symbol of traditional culture, a trope which feminist critics such as Stratton have identified as extending a masculinist tradition dating back to Senghor and the discourse of négritude.[33] The limitations of his project are clearly identified by such criticism, but, together with the other first-generation texts cited in such accounts, the useful focus of p'Bitek's work in dismantling negative images of traditional culture should not be forgotten in acknowledging the limitations of these early texts with regard to gender representation.

As in West Africa, the East African women writers of this period were strongly critical of this idealisation of the traditional world. Grace Ogot provided a powerful critique of the male perspective involved in these texts in her novel *The Promised Land* (1966). As Florence Stratton has noted, this was published in the same year as Flora Nwapa's *Efuru*, and 'can thus be said to mark the advent of a contemporary female tradition in fiction'.[34] A further dimension of the revisionary effect of these readings of these early texts by women has been to show how the first generation of male novels do not represent an unproblematic 'insider' stance. Not only do they stand revealed as specifically masculinist readings of these traditions, but this fissure in their textual authority opens up our awareness of other ways in which they are problematised as 'authentic' accounts of traditional practices and values.

It is important to remember that none of these modern accounts of the traditional culture are historical records. Not only are they fictional accounts, which need to be read with an awareness of their formal narrative and stylistic modes, they are also reconstructions by a generation of writers whose parents were the very figures (such as Nwoye/Isaac in *Things Fall Apart* or Oduche in *Arrow of God*) who 'betrayed' the traditional clan and received the religion and education of the white invader. Readings of these accounts as a sort of 'true' ethnography, replacing the 'false' ethnography of the Commissioner's text, *The Pacification of the Primitive Tribes of the Lower Niger* at the end of *Things Fall Apart*, are not, of course, wrong.[35] The conscious attempt at a recovery of an 'inside' perspective is part of the textual project of this early period in contemporary African English writing, and was the most striking and important feature of these texts to many of the early readers inside and outside Africa. The danger of such readings is that they represent all of the texts' preconceptions, including their gendered biases, as if what is being described is an objective and unproblematic view. In fact, like all narratives they continue to reflect both their author's and their period's predilections.

A further problem with these early texts is that, because of their widespread distribution and their canonical status on courses in African literature, texts like Achebe's have sometimes been taken by naive readers as definitive patterns for the 'colonial encounter' in the whole of Africa. Such assumptions are dangerous. They fail to note the particular and distinctive nature of the specific African societies these novels portray. For example, to take Ibo colonial contact as typical would be to oversimplify greatly. The relatively late date of Iboland's encounter with colonial invasion compared with the people of the coastal regions or of the Western Yoruba regions, both of whom had a far earlier and more direct contact with both missionaries and traders, makes its use as a generic marker of colonial encounter deeply problematic. Similarly, the tendency to read the encounter of the Gĩkũyũ, as described by Ngũgĩ, as a general account of colonialism and its impact in East Africa, when the Gĩkũyũ for various historical reasons were subject to direct external influence much later than other East African groups, for example those in Uganda, or in the coastal regions of modern Kenya and Tanzania, poses similar problems.

More recent accounts of these texts are beginning to place them within such specific historical frameworks, rather than treat them as somehow generic African texts, as was the case with earlier accounts. Nevertheless, because of the power of these texts as templates for later writing, they constituted the formative texts of a genre of 'contact novels', which became one of the dominant forms of the early post-war novel in English in both West and East Africa. In this sense, they created an intertext which continues to be influential and which did much to shape the form of the modern novel in English in many other parts of Africa.

Despite the dominance of the celebratory project in African English writing in the late 1950s and 1960s, a number of early texts openly or tacitly refused, in their choice of theme or setting, or by their ideological bias, to participate in the assertion of the dignity and self-sufficiency of the pre-colonial past. The overall dissent from this celebratory presentation of the pre-colonial past by women writers has already been mentioned, and it forms an ongoing pattern of female dissent from the stereotypes of male writing, which will be dealt with separately below, to emphasise the importance and continuity of the development of a distinctive tradition of African women's writing.[36] Apart from this strain of dissenting texts by women, a number of other African English texts of this period were not concerned with presenting Africa in terms of a celebratory recovery of the pre-colonial past. Tutuola's work we have already discussed, though inadequately. In Tutuola, the pre-colonial continues in the present, since his world does not acknowledge any such break in the continuity of culture as haunts the texts of Achebe, and acts as a sort of defining penumbra to the texts of Amadi. The importance of his experiment in developing an inter-language to record in English the complex nature of African traditional orature, and the way in which his work melds this with the forms of imported literature, such as the religious parables of Bunyan, points the way to a fruitful interaction of the oral and literary in a relationship of effective mutuality. The linguistic patterns of Tutuola were echoed in the work of the Ijaw writer Gabriel Okara, whose experimental novel, *The Voice* (1964), was an innovative attempt to bend English towards directly accommodating the forms of African indigenous languages, by incorporating into English the lexis and syntax of Ijaw. The result was a memorable rendering of the Ijaw world, emphasising both its difference and its shared humanity in passages which have the force of poetry.

> The engine canoe against the strong water pushed and slowly, slowly it walked along the side river with the tall iroko trees, kapok trees, palm trees, standing on its banks, the sky's eye reaching. Soon the day's eye became bad. It became so bad and black and closed that it could not be looked at. And soon lightning flashed in the day's eye and the thunder sounded like one hundred cannons going off near your ears. (61)

More recent works, too, echo these early attempts to make contemporary African English writing reflect the complex nature of language usage in a modern African society, for example the late Ken Saro-Wiwa's *Sozaboy* (1985). The suggestion, implicit in some early accounts of African English writing, that these were experiments which led nowhere, and that they were only premature trials which fell away when African English texts discovered a more appropriate style in the work of realist novelists such as Achebe, seems itself now to be both premature and false. In fact, the increasing interest in recent African English texts in verbal experimentation, and in producing inter-linguistic forms, echoes the development of a mutually influential relationship between traditional oral forms and literary forms in modern Africa, which suggests that this strain of writing has been very fruitful indeed.[37] In fact, the most influential texts of the 1980s and 1990s seem to have their roots here, rather than in the early realist accounts favoured by the writers who stressed the theme of celebration and recovery.

The poets of this early generation also developed complex forms, which reflected the multiple sources of written and oral culture available in the African context. Christopher Okigbo's 'Path of Thunder' sequence from the *Labyrinths with Path of Thunder* collection (1971), or the early work of Kofi Awoonor, such as the 'Songs of Sorrow' sequence from *Rediscovery and Other Poems* (1964), are early examples of such successful interlinks. Okigbo's poetry is arguably one of the strongest influences on poets in Africa, with writers across the continent acknowledging his example. His earlier poetry employed a dazzling array of Euro-American referents, drawing on sources as diverse as the Greek and Latin texts which he studied in the classics department at Ibadan, through Shakespeare, to Pound and Eliot. This eclectic range of influences drew criticism from those who saw him as unduly influenced by the modernist style of poetry, popular in the syllabus imported from British universities in the 1960s, when metaphysical and modernist poets with a strong imagistic slant were in favour. Yet, even in this early work, Okigbo had blended these influences with a wide range of local referents, as the following extract from the early sequence 'Heavensgate' (1962) shows:

> DARK WATERS of the beginning.
>
> Rays, violet and short, piercing the gloom,
> foreshadow the rain that is dreamed of.
>
> Rainbow on far side, arched like boa bent to kill,
> foreshadows the rain that is dreamed of.
>
> Me to the orangery
> solitude invites
> a wagtail, to tell
> the tangled wood-tale;
> a sunbird, to mourn
> a mother on a spray.
> Rain and sun in single combat;
> on one leg standing,
> in silence at the passage,
> the young bird at the passage. (4)

By the time Okigbo completed his last major sequence, 'Path of Thunder: Poems Prophesying War', first published posthumously in the influential magazine *Black Orpheus* in 1968, the local references are so dense that he is now often hailed as the founder of the movement to take poetry back to its indigenous roots. It is fruitless to speculate whether Okigbo's later work would have continued in the direction of his later poetry. Certainly, though, it is to poems like this that later writers looked for inspiration in seeking a new programme for African poetry:

> WHATEVER happened to the elephant –
> Hurrah for thunder –
>
> The elephant, tetrarch of the jungle:
> With a wave of the hand
> He could pull four trees to the ground:
> His four mortar legs pounded the earth:
> Wherever they treaded,
> The grass was forbidden to be there.
> Alas! the elephant has fallen –
> Hurrah for thunder –
>
> But already the hunters are talking about pumpkins:
> If they share the meat let them remember thunder.
>
> The eye that looks down will surely see the nose;
> The finger that fits should be used to pick the nose.

> Today – for tomorrow, today becomes yesterday;
> How many million promises can ever fill a basket . . .
> If I don't learn to shut my mouth I'll soon go to hell.
> I, Okigbo, town-crier, together with my iron bell. (67)

Ghanaian Kofi Awoonor's work is also a foundational source for this emerging movement towards a stronger local flavour within the discourse of modern African English poetry in the early 1960s, as the sequence 'Songs of Sorrow' makes clear:

> I am on the world's extreme corner
> I am not sitting in the row with the eminent
> But those who are lucky
> Sit in the middle and forget
> I am on the world's extreme corner
> I can only go beyond and forget.
>
> My people, I have been somewhere.
> If I turn here, the rain beats me
> If I turn there the sun burns me
> The firewood of this world
> Is only for those who can take heart
> That is why not all can gather it.
> The world is not good for anybody
> But you are so happy with your fate;
> Alas! the travellers are back
> All covered with debt.[38]

These early poets look forward directly to the work of contemporary poets, such as Niyi Osundare and Kofi Anyidoho, or to the poetic prose of a writer such as Ben Okri, all of whom are influenced by these earlier examples.

Not all those writers whose work presented images of the past were concerned to offer a celebration of that past or its dignity. Even in the writing of this post-1950s generation, texts existed whose view of that past was different in various ways. Some of Wọle Ṣoyinka's work from this period, for example, was pre-eminent in presenting the past in terms of its allegorical and specific message for contemporary political realities. In Ṣoyinka's work the past often offered images through which the present might be given clear warning of the dangers of assuming that independence meant an end to problems and difficulties. His work constituted a different model from the theme of recovery and celebration announced by Achebe. It looked forward more strongly to the more radical tone of the texts which I have characterised as texts of self-criticism and discord, and which tend to dominate the period after the initial phase of recent African English writing in the 1950s and 1960s. Ṣoyinka's early work from this period illustrates how such broad periodisation or thematic groupings fail to deal with the full complexity of the work produced in any decade. Ṣoyinka's work before his return to Nigeria, and that produced during and immediately after the independence celebrations in 1960, show how the past might need to be represented in relation to contemporary realities and fears, and how the task of representing the pre-colonial past needed to go hand in hand with that of confronting the present urban and modern reality of African life.[39]

Another writer of considerable importance, who is often left out of strictly thematic accounts of the development of the modern African text, precisely because he does not fit with the dominant pattern, is Cyprian Ekwensi. The evaluation of Ekwensi's work has been the subject of considerable dispute, in part because Ekwensi has occupied the position of a professional writer in a sense different from that of many of the other writers in this period. Older than most of those who were published with him in the Heinemann African Writers series opening set of texts, he had already authored numerous books, and had published widely and eclectically in fields such as children's stories, popular adventure fiction and so forth. His work questions the extent to which these categories can be held separate in any account of African English writing. Ekwensi is, in a number of significant ways, the cuckoo in the nest of the early writers to be given wide publicity abroad. Yet his work has proved remarkably durable. It has inspired a considerable local following and a body of imitators who have used popular genres to explore contemporary realities. Pre-eminent among the early works as a model for later writing were Ekwensi's first collection of stories of African urban life, *People of the City* (1954), a second collection of short stories dealing with modern Lagos, *Lokotown and Other Stories* (1966), and a novel dealing with the life of a woman in the world of Lagos's 'high life' nightclubs, *Jagua Nana* (1961). These are all texts which, through their considerable narrative power and accessible style, established novels of modern, urban low-life as a popular and enduring form.

In East Africa, even harsher accounts of urban life such as Meja Mwangi's *Kill Me Quick* (1973) provided stylistic models which may well have had an influence later in West Africa, notably in the harshness and abruptness of style of some of the texts dealing with the Nigerian Civil War, and in those texts dealing with domestic and urban violence by writers such as Festus Iyayi in the late 1970s and 1980s. Nkem Nwanko's *Danda* (1964) was a rural version of the same kind of low-life text, presenting, as its paperback version cover put it, a 'vital, entertaining story of a brazen young rebel unashamedly in love with the good life'. For the moment, it is important to note that as early as the late 1960s, forms not concerned with the dominant pattern of celebrating a pre-colonial past were emerging, mainly in ways which suggested the possibility of a developing popular fiction, less ideologically rigid, but active in recording the complex and often brutal realities of modern African societies.

Ernest Emenyonu deserves notice for the forcefulness with which he pursued an advocacy for Ekwensi, which, although sometimes too uncritically accepting of the overall quality of the writing, which is far from even, was nevertheless a salutary correction to the dismissive tone of most critics. Most critics dismissed Ekwensi as a producer of 'pot-boilers', in a low-brow/high-brow model of cultural production which said as much about their own idea of the literary as about the importance of the development of texts of this kind for the future of writing in West and East Africa. The emergence of the work of frankly popular writers, such as David G. Maillu in East Africa at a later date, occurred after this model of high-brow/low-brow culture had been subject to considerable revision in the European and American literary world too, and so was part of a wider and fairer examination of African English writing which gave due emphasis to such material, and did not simply dismiss it pejoratively as populist and ephemeral.

A classic example of this kind of critical dismissal was the reception of Ekwensi's best-known novel, *Jagua Nana*. One of the first attempts at portraying the life of West Africa's new cities, and the lure of the fast-lane set who inhabited the popular 'high-life' bars, it also offered a portrait of the world of catch-as-catch-can violence associated with the local politics in the new Africa. The protagonist, Jagua Nana, is the daughter of a local pastor from Ogabu, who is lured to the city by her desire for a freer and more glamorous life than the rural world can offer. Travelling first to Ghana, where she makes a success of textile trading, she soon becomes an *habitué* of the Tropicana nightclub in Lagos, and a 'sweet-time' girl of the new rich class of senior government bureaucrats and businessmen, growing wealthy on the profitable manipulation of corrupt government contracts. Unable to have children, she takes a young lover, Freddie Namme, the son of a local Chief, and descendant of one of the old coastal trading families from the Niger Delta near Port Harcourt, whom she assists with his ambition to go to England to become a lawyer. Whilst he is away, Jagua meets his family and seduces his rich kinsman Chief Ofubara, who pursues her with offers of marriage which she rejects, since only in Lagos can she find the 'freedom' she craves. On Freddie's return from England, to contest a Lagos seat for a local political party, Jagua discovers he has married her young rival. She herself, in the meantime, has taken up with his rival in the election, the older politician Uncle Taiwo. Freddie is killed by Taiwo's henchmen, but the killing loses Taiwo the election, and he is killed in his turn by his own party. Jagua, learning of her father's death, returns to her village, and there discovers that Taiwo has left her a bag filled with money. Pregnant, at last, from a passing affair, she loses the child after only three days. The novel ends with her reform, and her plan to use part of the money on good works, and part on establishing herself in Onitsha as a market princess, or trading woman.

Whilst it is often prejudicial and unnecessary to compare African texts with European models, it is difficult for anyone familiar with the English literary tradition to read this book without hearing echoes of Defoe. The same uneasy combination of delight in mercantile success and puritanical moral consequence which characterises the world of *Moll Flanders* (1722) is found here. The melodramatic plot and the highly romanticised portrait of Jagua as the classic golden-hearted whore, who nevertheless must be punished for her loose ways, doesn't prevent the book from capturing the seductive power of Lagos nightlife for the young Jagua. Even by the standards of the then prevailing literary model of culture, *Jagua Nana* was a text which offered a great deal. Viewed as a text which sought to reach out to the mass audience of Nigeria, it looks very prophetic of the more recent developments in popular form and writing.[40] Much more to the point than the early criticism of the text's lack of

137

'high seriousness' is the more recent criticism by feminist critics. They condemn its presentation of the heroine as doomed and unable to control her existence, until she reverts to the traditional village setting. Like Defoe, the puritanical condemnations are clearly present. Jagua's would-be husband, Chief Ofubara, has become a local benefactor, and Jagua decides to help his scheme for education and welfare by giving him some of Taiwo's money. But she cannot accept his offer of marriage whilst she is pregnant with another man's child. Despite this act of contrition, Jagua loses her child. Ekwensi's moral view of Jagua is, and remains, a harsh and unforgiving one. It is clearly throughout a man's portrait of a woman's world, and suffers from this limitation. This is only partly redeemed when Ekwensi registers that among the motives for Jagua, Rosa, Ma Nancy and her other city sisters in seeking the bright life is not only the glamour, but also the freedom and power it bestows in contrast to the restrictions of the rural world: 'You think you kin buy me with money? Am a free woman. An' I already sleep wit' you ten night an' give you experience of Lagos woman dat you never dream!' (98). For Jagua, her sexuality buys her a seeming equality with men which the traditional African wives can never achieve.[41] This power, though, is ultimately dependant on the manipulation and control of men, and the text never questions this as the appropriate, indeed the only, source of power for women. The opposed ideal of wealth of the successful trading woman, the Onitsha market princess status to which Jagua aspires at the end, is, as it is for Moll Flanders, not perceived in opposition to this view, but as an extension of it into a different sphere. For this reason, the criticism of the text from a feminist perspective is probably well deserved. But as a vivid record of Lagos low-life it deserves considerable praise. It can certainly stand as one of the earliest and most influential models for the later vigorous portraits of city life which are such a feature of recent popular African writing in English.

In a quite different way, Obi Egbuna's work was also at variance with the general presentation of traditional values, and its relative neglect by critics may serve as an exemplum of the fate of other work which did not conform to this model. Given its own very problematic representation of gender, it may also illustrate that it was not only women writers who suffered exclusion by the narrowness of the defining models of the period. In *Wind Versus Polygamy* (1964), for example, Egbuna tackles the issue of polygamy versus monogamy, an issue which formed the basis for a number of other African works in the 1960s, such as Wọle Ṣoyinka's play *The Lion and the Jewel* (1963). As in the Ṣoyinka play, the struggle is in part an allegory of the struggle between the forces of 'modernisation' in contemporary Africa and the need to maintain traditional African values in the face of cultural neo-colonialism. Significantly, in both these texts the trope used to stand for traditional values is polygamous marriage, that *bête noire* of the nineteenth-century missionary and civiliser.

The central figure is a paramount Chief, the wily and powerful Chief Ozuomba. The heroine, the beautiful Elina, is presented as the victim of the corruption of traditional ways in Nigerian society, ways which have been distorted from their effective purpose by the wind of change (modernisation and Europeanisation). Elina is caught between an inherited debt to the hunter

Okosisi Ojukwu, converted to a bride price by her dead father, and the pressure of her father's brother, Maza Ofodile, to marry the crooked and corrupt Councillor Ogidi. In the conflict which follows, Chief Ozuomba acts as the traditional authority. He appears to resolve the dispute by getting Elina to agree to marry him. The Chief knows that in so doing he is laying himself open to charges under the new anti-polygamy law. The main part of the text is a detailed account of the trial. Although represented by council, the Chief defends the practice of polygamy in a series of polemic speeches. He castigates the societies of the West for hypocrisy in insisting on a practice (monogamy) which they can neither sustain nor justify in terms of the profound negative social effects to which it has given rise. For Chief Ozuomba, what is on trial is the right of African cultures to their own values and social practices. The arguments are often fairly bizarre, ranging from the convincing, 'You want facts? All right, I will give you facts. In the United States of America alone, ten thousand monogamous homes break up every day' (67), to the absurd and grossly sexist, 'an average man is capable of having three thousand children in his lifetime. But the lifetime capacity of the average woman is ten only. . . . From each man according to his ability, distributed among women according to their needs. Sex democracy must prevail' (68). Egbuna fails to distance the reader from Ozuomba's more bizarre views, or even to show a clear intention to do so. However, the reader does not have to accept all the Chief's polemical arguments in order to understand that the text seeks to articulate a general stand against cultural neo-colonialism. Nevertheless the fact that, as we have already noted, a text like J. J. Walters's *Guanya Pau* could as early as 1891 present a much more complex and less sexist criticism of traditional African culture, indicates the limitations of some of these more recent defences of African cultural practices, and their constriction within the bounds of classically patriarchal concepts. It also indicates that such readings were not intrinsic to traditional African cultures, but were produced by the dominant masculinist ideology of the immediate post-independence period.[42]

This neglected text has been discussed in some detail because it exemplifies how strongly the dominant model of realist, celebratory texts by writers like Achebe and Amadi have overshadowed these more idiosyncratic texts of the same period in most accounts. However influential these may have been on the writers who followed them, and on the shape of the critical accounts of the African text which emerged in the late 1960s and 1970s, they should not be permitted wholly to obscure the existence of a range of other concerns in this first period of post-war African writing.

Notes

1. This is true even of the revisionist accounts of recent times, in which, for example, women writers of the period are reclaimed for the record.
2. See Karin Barber, 'Time, Space and Writing in Three Colonial Yoruba Novels', in *The Yearbook of English Studies*, 27 (1997).

3. See Karin Barber, *Readings in African Popular Culture* (Oxford: James Currey, 1997).

4. The scripts and productions are obviously earlier than these publication dates of the scripts. A great deal of work remains to be done in dating the productions and writing of many plays produced in Africa.

5. To be fair to de Graft this is probably true even of the work of younger writers such as Ama Ata Aidoo, born fourteen years later than de Graft, whose play *The Dilemma of a Ghost* (1965) deals with similar themes, and is similarly constrained by a conventional European dramaturgy.

6. See Chapter 11 for a fuller account of Efua Sutherland's work. Sutherland, who was born four years earlier than de Graft, nevertheless managed to develop an effective blend of imported and indigenous dramaturgy in plays like *The Marriage of Anansewa* and *Foriwa*. Her work is only now beginning to receive the attention it deserves.

7. See Biodun Jeyifo, 'Literary Theory and Theories of Decolonisation', in J. Gugler *et al.* (eds), *Literary Theory and African Literature* (Münster/Hamburg: Literature Verlag, 1994), pp. 17–30.

8. This evocative phrase is one which the Indian novelist and critic U. R. Ananthamurthy coined to describe the position of modern Indian intellectuals and writers. Ananthamurthy goes so far as to apply this even to writers who use indigenous languages, as he does, implying that no writer is immune from the influence of the external forms and modes which colonisation brought with it. See B. Ashcroft *et al.*, *The Empire Writes Back: Theory and Practice in Post-colonial Literatures* (London: Routledge, 1989), p. 119.

9. For example, Chinua Achebe cites Joyce Cary's *Mister Johnson* as such a text. In East Africa the work of writers like Elspeth Huxley or Karen Blixen played a similar role. See Abdul JanMohamed, *Manichean Aesthetics: The Politics of Literature in Colonial Africa* (Amherst: University of Mass. Press, 1983); Abdul JanMohamed, 'Humanism and Minority Literature: Towards a Definition of a Counter-Hegemonic Discourse', *Boundary*, 2, 12 (Spring/Fall 1984), pp. 3–13.

10. See the account of this in the essay 'Named for Victoria, Queen of England' in Chinua Achebe, *Hopes and Impediments: Selected Essays 1965–1987* (London: Heinemann, 1988).

11. Again we should note that this publication date is much later than the productions of these plays.

12. See the interview with Lewis Nkosi in Dennis Duerden and Cosmo Pieterse (eds), *African Writers Talking* (London: Heinemann, 1972). This volume also contains a second interview with Clark, conducted by the Jamaican writer Andrew Salkey.

13. For an account of the controversy see Thomas Knipp, 'Militancy and Irony', *Ba Shiru*, 8, 1 (1977), p. 55.

14. Alan Hill, *In Pursuit of Publishing* (London: Chatto and Windus, 1988), pp. 120–1. Further page references are given in the text.

15. See, for example, M. A. G. Leonard, *The Lower Niger and its Tribes* (London: Frank Cass, 1906, reissued in facsimile, 1968). The date of this text would place it at precisely the right time to be an analogue for the imaginary text Achebe invokes.

16. Chinweizu, Jemie Onwuchekwa and Ihechukwa Madabuike, *Towards the Decolonisation of African Literature* (Enugu, Nigeria: Fourth Dimension Pub. Co., 1980).

17. Chinua Achebe, 'The Role of the Writer in a New Nation', *Nigeria Magazine*, 81 (June 1964), pp. 157–60.

18. 'Been-too' refers to those who had 'been-to' foreign places and returned.

19. A text which had a powerful influence on early writing in many African languages, as many scholars of twentieth-century African literature have noted. See Albert Gérard, *Contexts of African Literature* (Amsterdam and Atlanta, Ga.: Rodopi, 1990), p. 49. The publication date given in the text is for Part One; Part Two was published in 1684.

20. C. L. Miller, *Theories of Africans: Francophone Literature and Anthropology in Africa* (Chicago: Chicago University Press, 1990), pp. 160–1.

21. Gareth Griffiths, 'Chinua Achebe: When Did You Last See Your Father?', *World Literature Written in English*, 27, 1 (Spring 1987), pp. 18–26.

22. Chinua Achebe, 'Named for Victoria, Queen of England', *New Letters*, 40, 1 (Autumn 1973), p. 18.

23. Here Achebe is quoting the Afro-American writer James Baldwin. See *Morning Yet on Creation Day: Essays* (London: Heinemann, 1975), p. 62.

24. The lack of a central authority in Ibo culture meant that the colonisers were denied the means to effect a decisive 'defeat' of the Ibo. The process of colonisation of the Ibo territories took more than twenty years to complete from its commencement in the mid-1890s.

25. The success of Achebe's novels in presenting the internal agendas of those who faced the colonial encounter takes on new significance in the light of recent arguments for the continuity of internal agendas within colonial societies. For example, Aijaz Ahmad has argued strongly that the colonial incursion did not entirely displace the continuity of local agendas rooted in pre-colonial concerns and practices. See Aijaz Ahmad, *In Theory: Classes, Nations, Literatures* (London and New York: Verso, 1992). Karin Barber has also argued that the pre-colonial interacted with and survived within the colonial moment in ways which are often underplayed in accounts of post-colonial dependency. See Barber, 'Time, Space and Writing in Three Colonial Yoruba Novels'. It should be noted, though, that other critics like Adewale Maja-Pearce, *A Mask Dancing: Nigerian Novelists of the Eighties* (London and New York: Hans Zell, 1992), argue that Achebe's view of the traditional pre-colonial past is a distorted and partial one and that it does not succeed in creating the ironic reversals of the dominant viewpoint that most critics have argued occur in these texts.

26. Ahmad, *In Theory*.

27. Karin Barber and P. F. de Moraes Farias, *Discourse and its Disguises: The Interpretation of African Oral Texts* (Birmingham: Centre of West African Studies, University of Birmingham, 1989).

28. I employ the term coined by Gayatri Spivak to indicate the hidden ideological construction in the presentation of a locale or time as 'natural' in usages such as 'the Third World'.

29. In fact, as I argue in Chapter 11, *Efuru* is a text which can also be read as a reflection of the same, hegemonic self-policing practices which determine the images of traditional culture constructed within modern patriarchal discourses. The critique of earlier texts by later women writers, such as Buchi Emecheta, whose own work is the subject of considerable and ongoing current debate, is focused as much on a critique of the practices of texts such as *Efuru* as it is on those of the first generation of male novelists who portray women in traditional society, such as Achebe and Amadi.

30. This important early text is discussed in detail in Chapter 11.

31. The joint publishing house is one of the few residual legatees of the short-lived East African Community, set up in 1966, which disintegrated in most other respects in the early 1970s. In this respect, as with the Federation of the West Indies, whose only residual legatee is the West Indian cricket team and the University of the West Indies, it may be hopeful evidence that cultural links may survive political and economic collapse.

32. The policy of Heinemann, with regard to publishing material in translation, can only be determined by an evaluation of the list. Whether because of the focus on the educational market (largely based on an English language syllabus), or for other reasons, the first fifty texts in the African Writers Series contained only four texts not originally written in English or translated from French. One of these is the Arabic writer Tayeb

Salih's *The Wedding of Zein*. The other three are all translations from the Yoruba by the Austrian academic Ulli Beier. These translations tell a fascinating story. The first is published under a Yoruba pen-name (Obotunde Ijimere), the second has Ulli Beier, under his own name, as editor, and the third is a co-authored text with Bakare Gbadamosi. Thus the texts are in various ways mediated by European transcription. Compare the mediation of mission texts discussed in Chapter 3.

33. Florence Stratton, *Contemporary African Literature and the Politics of Gender* (London and New York: Routledge, 1994), pp. 39–55.

34. Ibid., p. 58. See also Chapter 11.

35. See for instance, Leonard, *The Lower Niger and its Tribes*, especially pp. 256–61, where African suicide is discussed in ways which are identical with the attitudes of the fictional Commissioner in Achebe's text.

36. See Chapter 11.

37. See Chantal Zabus, *The African Palimpsest: Indigenisation of Language in the West African Europhone Novel* (Amsterdam and Atlanta, Ga.: Rodopi, 1991).

38. Gerald Moore and Ulli Beier (eds), *Modern Poetry from Africa* (Harmondsworth: Penguin, 1863), p. 98.

39. For this reason, the discussion of these works which date from the same time as the celebratory texts of Amadi and Achebe have been dealt with in Chapter 7.

40. As was noted in Chapter 5, Ekwensi had published several Onitsha pamphlets in the late 1940s. In a sense, he is the earliest writer to bridge the gap between the traditions of popular and elite writing.

41. Compare Emecheta's *The Joys of Motherhood* (1979), pp. 168–9.

42. For a contrastive account see Emma Mba, *Nigerian Women Mobilised: Women's Political Activity in Southern Nigeria, 1900–1965* (Berkeley, Ca.: Institute of International Studies, University of California, 1982).

Chapter 7

Self-Criticism and Post-Independence Disillusion

West Africa

In the mid to late 1960s, a period of what has often been called 'disillusion' set in for a great deal of West African writing, reflecting the sense of dismay with which the writers confronted the corruption and divisions in the new post-independence regimes. Although Achebe's first novel, *Things Fall Apart* (1958), set the agenda for the texts of celebration and recovery, Achebe also produced one of the earliest of the texts of post-independence self-criticism, in his examination of corruption amongst the young Nigerian 'been-to's' in *No Longer at Ease* (1960), and followed this with a strong condemnation of post-independence political culture in *A Man of the People* (1966), exemplifying how the work of a single writer may embrace different agendas at different times.

In *No Longer at Ease*, Achebe presents a vision of a Nigeria in transition to independence, struggling to address the clash of old and new cultural imperatives. The protagonist, Obi Okonkwo, grandson of the protagonist in *Things Fall Apart*, strives, unsuccessfully, like his grandfather, to reconcile the claims of the changes between the modern and traditional worlds. Traditional claims are expressed through the calls for fraternal assistance by the Umuofia Progressive Union, which has helped pay for his education abroad, and which, in return, asks for his help in procuring positions and scholarships for its other members and their families. Such practices, natural and effective in the rural world of the Ibo village, conflict with the modernised, urban world of Lagos. In the eyes of the European administrators, retained during this transitional period to prepare Nigeria for full independence, such practices are nepotistic and corrupt. The portrayal of the administrator of Obi's department, Mr Green, is a fair and even sympathetic one. Nevertheless, his view of Nigeria and Nigerians is shown to be distorted by a prejudice against Africans, whom he regards as essentially child-like, and not mature enough for self-government. He is fully convinced that he must train his young subordinates, such as Obi, to break absolutely with the old values, and embrace the new, as part of the necessary adjustment Africa must make if it is to be accepted as a modern nation. That what he perceives as corruption and a lack of impartiality may, judged by the indigenous value system, be seen as a necessary recompense to the group, and as required communal practice, is dramatised in the story of Obi's decline and final imprisonment. The connection between Obi and his grandfather Okonkwo, the protagonist of *Things Fall Apart*, strengthens the intextual linkage which is an important feature of Achebe's work, creating a historical pattern through which he is able to trace the effects of colonisation on traditional society and its destructive consequences for modern Nigerian life.[1]

In his next novel, *No Longer at Ease* (1960), Achebe still places the weight of blame squarely on the shoulders of colonialism, especially on its inability to recognise and accommodate African differences. But six years later, in *A Man of the People* (1966), a stronger disillusionment with post-independence politics is apparent. In this later novel, Achebe paints an uncompromisingly scathing portrait of the first generation of Nigeria's politicians in the figure of the corrupt Chief Nanga, whose patronage of the young protagonist, Odili Samalu, exposes him to the temptations of post-independence Nigerian political life. The character of Odili has been the subject of a long critical dispute. Some readings of the text view him as a decent young man who is tempted, but who recovers his sense of values and ends up opposing Nanga and his world. This is a view which Achebe seems to share, judging by the comments he has made in interviews.[2] Other readings see Odili as much more problematic, and stress the character's ongoing capacity for self-deception and for an inflated and finally rather crass self-regard. This view sees the text as much more self-ironic and reflexive. Whatever our view of Odili, the novel sends a clear message that the first generation of characters who have taken centre-stage in Nigeria's political life are flawed, and that there is an urgent need for reform. The young anti-corruption activist Max, with whom Odili sides at the end of the novel, is 'accidentally' killed by political thugs hired by Nanga's party boss, Chief Koko. Koko is, in turn, shot by Max's lover, Eunice. Odili reflects bitterly that:

> in the affairs of the nation there was no owner, the laws of the village became powerless. Max was avenged not by the people's collective will but by one solitary woman who loved him. Had his spirit waited for the people to demand redress it would have been waiting still, in the rain and out of the sun. But he was lucky. . . . I say, you died a good death if your life inspired someone to come forward and shoot your murderer in the chest – without being paid. (167)

This ending recapitulates the theme addressed by the earlier novel *No Longer at Ease*: the question of whether the laws of the village may be inappropriate to the needs of an emerging modern nation, or whether Mr Green's view that Obi is guilty of the modern crimes of embezzlement and nepotism is irreconcilable with those of the Umuofia Progressive Union, who see the same actions as a matter of loyalty and clan obligation. In *No Longer at Ease*, the examination of this clash of moral imperatives complicates its condemnation of post-independence corruption. But in *A Man of the People* Achebe is far less compromising in his analysis of where blame lies. Odili may be a portrait of a young man struggling to make choices in an increasingly complicated world, but in Chief Nanga a hitherto uncharacteristic bitterness and disillusionment with post-independence Nigerian society is expressed. After *A Man of the People*, Achebe did not write another major novel for almost twenty years.

This long silence was mainly the result of the outbreak of the Nigerian Civil War in 1966, the same year that *A Man of the People* was published. The war clearly diverted Achebe from his literary task, especially as he spent a good deal of his time in the next few years as a roving ambassador for the Biafran cause, raising funds for the separatist state in Europe, Canada and the US. In the intervening period, until his next novel, *Anthills of the Savannah* (1987), he published only a volume of poems, *Beware, Soul Brother and Other Poems* (1971), a collection of short stories, *Girls At War* (1972), several of which dealt directly with the Nigerian Civil War, and some children's stories. But the silence of twenty years, until the next major novel, also reflects a long period of consideration by Achebe of Nigerian politics, and of the problem of internal corruption which he had addressed in *A Man of the People*. He expressed this concern in a number of political pamphlets and articles published during this time, most notably *The Trouble With Nigeria* (1984), in which it is possible to see, in embryo form, the arguments dramatised in the next novel which he eventually wrote, *Anthills of the Savannah* (1987).

This latest novel deals with the re-emergence of military governments in the modern period. It may be read as a direct comment on the regime of General Ibrahim Babangida, the military successor to General Buhari, who had seized power in a coup in 1983, after declaring that the civilian government of President Shagari was corrupt. Babangida was still in power at the time the novel appeared.[3] Many of the episodes in *Anthills of the Savannah* echo the events of this set of military take-overs. The collusive or oppositional role of writers and intellectuals in recent Nigerian politics is also reflected in figures like Chris, the Minister for Information, and Ikem, the editor of the influential national daily paper. The theme of the corruption of power is expressed in a classic realist narrative, which stands out from much recent African English fiction in this regard. In comparison with recent work by younger writers, and even the work of those closer to his age, such as Ngũgĩ and Armah, Achebe has chosen to remain faithful to a fairly conservative form. The main formal difference from the earlier novels lies in his use of multiple narrators, rather than a single authorial voice. In the new novel Achebe also retains the form or substance of the classic, national liberation narrative. The text is critical of the current leadership and of its values, but does not critique the fundamental nature of the post-independence nation-state, as either a neo-colonial mask or as a hindrance to a wider and more effective pan-African or pan-Negro vision for Africa, as Ngũgĩ's and Armah's recent texts respectively do. To this extent, Achebe's project is a revisionary rather than a revolutionary one, and his recent work extends and consolidates, rather than alters, the direction of his earlier forms and concerns. Having said this, the apparent conservatism of the text may be deceptive. In this new novel Achebe makes the role of narrative itself central to his perception of the creation of power. Power flows not only from the barrel of a gun, but from the control of the pen and the tongue; story, speech and reportage are the means by which reality can be subdued, and by which dictators can repress both their fellow citizens and their own sense of reality. The larger truths by which a vision of the objective world is sustained is, Achebe suggests, the first victim of such self-deceptive story-telling. Achebe captures the almost auto-hypnotic effect of this inner dialogue and story-telling by entering the mind of the characters, especially that of the dictator, His Excellency, exposing the way in which the world is mediated through his selection and his compilation of events from the present and the past.[4]

> The Attorney-General was perched on the edge of his chair, his left elbow on the table, his neck craning forward to catch His Excellency's words which he had chosen to speak with unusual softness as if deliberately to put his hearer at a disadvantage; or on full alert on pain of missing a life and death password. As he watched his victim straining to catch the vital message he felt again that glow of quiet jubilation that had become a frequent companion especially when as now he was disposing with consummate ease of some of those troublesome people he had thought so formidable in his apprentice days in power. It takes a lion to tame a leopard, say our people. How right they are. (21–2)

The way in which the dictator incorporates folk-wisdom and past comment into his present reactions demonstrates how he is himself the product of a self-deceptive story, a story in which power 'speaks' him and takes over the 'simple soldier', whom he continues to believe himself to be.

Simon Gikandi has commented astutely on this presentation of the power of narrative in the novel thus: 'the story by rewriting history (by creating a timeless and autonomous version of events so that they can speak to future generations) contests the constant attempt, by powerful institutions, to repress those collective memories that threaten control, memories that are obliterated when official history is textualised'. This Orwellian project, confirmed by Achebe himself in recent interviews, is also part of a wider and more powerful awareness of narrative and its worldly consequence. As Gikandi asserts:

> [textual] works need commentaries on the way they should be read because their meanings are often censored by the other historical factors that accompany the invention of narratives. In Frederic Jameson's words, metacommentary 'aims at tracing the logic of the censorship itself and of the situations from which it springs: a language that hides what it displays beneath its own reality as language, a glance that denigrates, through the very process of avoiding, the object forbidden.' In a world which has been turned upside down, Achebe believes that reality itself is a forbidden object; thus, narrative must be geared towards the institution of an African hermeneutics that might help us to recover the hidden objects of our own contemporary history.[5]

All the major characters – Chris, the disillusioned political colleague of His Excellency; Ikem, the sceptical and radical newspaper editor; and Beatrice, Chris's girlfriend, who proves to be perhaps the most enduring opponent of the falsity of His Excellency's world, and a symbol of possible successful resistance and change – are deeply involved with the interpretation of reality, and with the 'readings' of it which they are offered in their time. As Beatrice comments, 'I had definitely taken on the challenge of bringing together as many broken pieces of this tragic history as I could lay my hands on' (82).

This challenge is arguably that which Achebe also undertakes in the novel as a whole.

Nevertheless, despite this defence of his latest work by critics like Gikandi, others, such as Adewale Maja-Pearce, have continued to be scornful of Achebe's earlier analysis of post-independence Nigerian politics, arguing that his stress on celebrating and recovering the past created a mode of fiction which failed to engage with the actual problems of post-independence African societies. Maja-Pearce argues that Achebe and his followers, such as Amadi, Munonye and Aluko, whose concern was to free 'the African past from what [they] considered the distortions of the colonising present . . . [failed] to resolve the problems [they] posed'.[6] Soyinka, on the other hand, Maja-Pearce asserts, publicly warned his contemporaries as early as 1967, 'of what he termed the "movement towards chaos" that was beginning to engulf the country'.[7] This indictment is part of an interesting, if overstated, case Maja-Pearce advances, which promotes Soyinka over Achebe as the only writer who really engaged with the intrinsic structural problems facing post-independence West Africa. Maja-Pearce is correct in asserting that for Soyinka the processes of celebration and of self-criticism are not separate, but he is less than fair to the subtlety of Achebe's texts, which also register this complex dialectical process, though in a different form.

It is certainly true that Soyinka's work showed a very early and clear awareness of the neo-colonial structures which were to shape the limitations of 'independence' in post-independence African states like Nigeria. Soyinka's theatre troupe, formed for the occasion, and aptly named the '1960 Masks', performed *A Dance of the Forests* at the independence celebrations in 1960. Read even with the advantage of three and a half decades of hindsight, it is still a startling text, perhaps the most powerful and least self-serving of plays ever to have been offered at such a moment in a nation's history. No politician or civil servant who saw it could ever say, afterwards, that Soyinka had not issued a clear warning to the new rulers of the dangers that lay ahead, and the need to view both the future and the past of Nigeria with a clear and unsentimental eye.

Parallel groups of characters link the world of Nigeria's past and present, as the action moves between the court of the traditional, pre-colonial ruler, Mata Kharibu, and the post-colonial, modern state which is being celebrated. *A Dance of the Forests* offers a strong critique of power and its tendency to corrupt in both times and places, and also offers the artist a special role in the process of exposing such abuse. Demoke, a wood-carver, is called upon to celebrate the new state with a massive carving of an *araba* tree. He is a figure who represents the role of the artist in the state, and a general warning against hubris for artist and politician alike. Soyinka shows in this early play that he is well aware of how the mythologised past can be employed to create a new power base in the modern nation-state. Characters like Demoke also feature as the Court Poet of the traditional ruler Mata Kharibu, as does the prostitute Rola, who is echoed in the King's courtesan, Madame Tortoise. The figures of the local officials, such as Adenebi, the modern Council Orator, and Agboreka, the so-called Elder of Sealed Lips, reappear in similar roles in the traditional

147

court. This paralleling structure undermines the unproblematic official recruitment of the past in the rhetoric of the modern celebration:

> ADENEBI: . . . Have you no sense of history? . . . The accumulated heritage – that is what we are celebrating. Mali, Chaka, Songhai. Glory. Empires. But you cannot feel it, can you?[8]

The reference to Songhai, of course, invokes Fanon's analysis of the dangers of employing such parallels in constructing a nationalist discourse. In his analysis of such an uncritical 'recovery' of the past, Fanon acknowledges the implicit problem of celebrating a glorious past as a confirmation of the present: 'I admit that all the proofs of a wonderful Songhai civilisation will not change the fact that today the Songhais are underfed and illiterate, thrown between sky and water with empty heads and empty eyes'.[9] Like Fanon, Şoyinka is not opposed to the process of celebrating the past *per se*, recognising that it is a vital part of the renewed self-apprehension by which colonised cultures can escape what Fanon had defined as 'that Western culture in which they all risk being swamped'.[10] But he offers a clear-sighted awareness of the danger that this process may be employed by the newly emerged national bourgeoisie simply to consolidate their power and privilege. The figure of Obaneji, who works as a lowly filing clerk in the modern legal system, is used to expose the corruption which has already crept into the new regime. Obaneji is trying to find the name of the official who was bribed to license the use of a dangerous lorry, which burst into flames, killing its passengers. This episode serves to expose the existence of corruption, even in this moment of national euphoria, and to warn of the dangers ahead for the new state, unless it opposes such practices from the beginning. The image of the *abiku*, the spirit-child who returns to plague the living in birth after birth, is invoked in the play's ritual ending to suggest this process of interaction between past and present, and to place the play's perceptions within a Yoruba cultural frame. The future, it is implied, can only be assured when the past is seen as an effective and meaningful part of the present. This is a theme which Şoyinka was to elaborate with great effect in later plays, such as *Death and the King's Horseman* (1975). Here it reinforces the theme of the lessons which the new regimes can learn from the errors of the African past. The play also invokes the natural world and the Yoruba spiritual realm, in a series of episodes involving the gods of the Yoruba pantheon and the spirits of the forest and the bush. It is in this dialogue that the voice of the people is most clearly expressed, and in which a clear warning is given to the new leadership not to imitate the arrogance of the old empires, which forgot the central importance of the ordinary man and woman:

> ANOTHER: We are the dried leaves, impaled
>   On one-eyed brooms.
> ANOTHER: We are the headless bodies when
>   The spade of progress delves.
> ANOTHER: The ones that never looked up when
>   The wind turned suddenly, erupting
>   in our heads.

ANOTHER: Down the axis of the world, from
    The whirlwind to the frozen drifts,
    We are the ever legion of the world,
    Smitten, for – 'the good to come'. (67–8)

Ṣoyinka has been frequently accused by self-proclaimed radical critics of unnecessary obscurantism, and, more specifically, of reifying myth in a manner
which reinforces rather than dispels mystification. Even in this early piece such
criticism seems hard to sustain. The triplets, who ring the Half-Child round in
the final ritual dance, offer a clear message which could have left no doubt in
the mind of the audience at the Nigerian independence celebrations of Ṣoyinka's
political concerns.

> FIRST TRIPLET: (*speaking as he comes in*) Has anyone found the Means? I am the
> End that will justify it.
> (*The Interpreter turns quickly and does a round of 'ampe' with him. Enter Second
> Triplet. An over-blown head, drooling.*)
> SECOND TRIPLET: I am the Greater Cause, standing ever ready, excusing the
> crimes of today for tomorrow's mirage. Hungry I come, hearing there was a feast
> for the dead . . . Am I expected?
> (*The Interpreter and the Second Triplet 'ampe', then the Interpreter with the First,
> and then the two Triplets together.*)
> SECOND TRIPLET: (*stops suddenly. Goes to where Demoke, etc., stand huddled
> together. Sniffs them, turns to the Interpreter.*): But who are these?
> FOREST HEAD: They are the lesser criminals, pursuing the destructive path of
> survival. Weak, pitiable criminals, hiding their cowardice in sudden acts of bluster.
> And you obscenities . . .
> (*Waves his hand towards the Triplets, who shriek and dance in delight.*) You
> perversions are born when they acquire power over one another, and their
> instincts are fulfilled a thousandfold, a hundred thousandfold. But wait, there is
> still the third triplet to come. You have as always decided your own fates. Today
> is no different from your lives. I merely sit and watch.
> (*Enter the Third Triplet, fanged and bloody.*)
> THIRD TRIPLET: I find I am Posterity. Can no one see on what milk I have been
> nourished? (69)

The Half-Child is then claimed by the trickster-god Eshuoro, so the future will
again be still-born.

Five years later, in 1965, the same company performed *Kongi's Harvest*.
This piece gave an even more explicit warning of the way in which the new
regimes had already begun to recruit tradition and myth to serve their present
ends. It also spoke out against the general corruption of the governments in
the newly independent African states. Kongi, President of the African state of
Isma, seeks to persuade the traditional ruler, Oba Danlola, to lend his authority
to the ratification of his oppressive regime. The Council of Elders (*aweri*) have
already been tamed and renamed by Kongi as the Reformed Aweri Fraternity.
Danlola alone has stood out and refused his support, for which he has been
imprisoned. For Kongi, Danlola's public submission is crucial for his plan,
which is to turn the traditional harvest ritual of the eating of the New Yam

into a secular celebration of Kongi's power. He plans to rename this vital, traditional ceremony, Kongi's Harvest.

> FOURTH [AWERI]: I think I see something of the Leader's vision of this harmony. To replace the old superstitious festival by a state ceremony governed by the principle of Enlightened Ritualism. It is therefore essential that Oba Danlola, his bitterest opponent, appear in full antiquated splendour surrounded by his Aweri Conclave of Elders who, beyond the outward trappings of pomp and ceremony and a regular supply of snuff, have no other interest in the running of the state.
>
> SIXTH [AWERI]: Who says?
>
> FOURTH [AWERI]: Kongi says. The period of isolated saws and wisdoms is over, superseded by a more systematic formulation of comprehensive philosophies – *our* function, for the benefit of those who still do not know it.
>
> THIRD [AWERI]: Hear hear.
>
> FOURTH [AWERI]: And Danlola, the retrogressive autocrat, will with his own hands present the Leader with the New Yam, thereby acknowledging the supremacy of the State over his former areas of authority spiritual or secular. From then on, the State will adopt towards him and to all similar institutions the policy of glamorised fossilism. (81)

The novel *Season of Anomy* (1973) had also taken up the theme of disillusion with the policies of the new elite, expressed in *A Dance of the Forests* and *Kongi's Harvest*, but in a form which showed how the new elites were also being used as fronts by large-scale multinational corporations and the forces of global capitalism. It demonstrates Ṣoyinka's clear perception that independence was not in itself a solution to the social problems facing modern Nigeria. It shows that the post-independence economy remained firmly tied to overseas interests, and the new nation still needed a developed and independent middle class, who could initiate productive economic change and resist the temptation to feather their own nests at the expense of the nation.

The sense of confusion and indecision for the overseas-educated generation, which Achebe had represented with Obi Okonkwo in *No Longer at Ease*, had also been the burden of Ṣoyinka's first major novel, *The Interpreters* (1965). Here a group of young men come together to 'interpret' the meaning of the new nation and their roles in it.

In plays such as *The Road* (1965), he had also examined the need to sustain the local cultures, and to preserve what he calls a proper 'self-apprehension' in the face of global acculturative processes, whilst simultaneously recognising that change is inevitable, and, indeed, functions as part of that very self-apprehension. This play uses the accident-prone Nigerian road system as a metaphor for the political and economic system. It centres on the lives of a body of society's rejects, who group themselves around the charismatic figure of the disgraced Christian catechist known as Professor. The owner of a ramshackle spare parts store, he stocks it with the products of car 'accidents', which he deliberately arranges. The play creates a powerful metaphor of a society which preys on itself, and which has lost any real sense of purpose. As the title suggests, the road, on which these figures live out their fragmented and brutalised lives, is one which comes from and goes to nowhere. Professor's search for the Word, symbol of a force which can unite and give meaning back to this world, is subsumed by the ending, in which the 'dead' lorry-driver Murano sweeps Professor off in a ritual *agemo* cult dance – a dance which celebrates the role of the transitional world between spirit and flesh in sustaining the purpose and meaning of the Yoruba cosmos. The meaning of this ending depends upon understanding the importance in Yoruba culture of such rituals of renewal, in which the contact of the spirit world (the past) and that of the present generation is renewed and maintained. This was also the burden of Soyinka's important critical essay 'The Fourth Stage: Through the Mysteries of Ogun to the Origins of Yoruba Tragedy', first published in 1973.[11] It also informed the foundational critical work he published three years later, *Myth, Literature and the African World* (1976).

The same theme is taken up in *Death and the King's Horseman* (1975). This play is based on an actual historical event, which had also inspired an earlier work by the popular, Yoruba-language dramatist Duro Ladipo. In Soyinka's hands, it becomes a fable about the relationship between tradition and change in modern Nigeria. The price of neglecting the past to endorse modern society, or failing to recognise that the future cannot be bought at the cost of severing the links with the past without creating a rootless and valueless society, is brilliantly dramatised. Yoruba people have a social system based on a kingship structure. Each of the ancient Yoruba states, such as Oyo, Ife etc., had a hereditary ruler and a hereditary caste of officials. Elesin Oba is the King's Horseman, a noble administrator, and the King's close friend and adviser. The King's Horseman was both a court favourite and an important political figure. In Yoruba culture the power of the King derived from his role as a mediator between the gods and men. The King, through his divine nature, had one foot in both worlds. Figures like the King's Horseman had an important role to play in maintaining this link. When the King died, they were expected to accompany him on the journey between the worlds to ensure the connection is maintained.

Yoruba cosmology involves a close, but disrupted relationship between the world of the past (ancestors and gods), the present (the world of human beings), and the future (the unborn). In Yoruba cosmology the passage between these worlds is crucial. The purpose of life is to maintain the links between these worlds through the proper maintenance of ritual. In the past, the gods and men were intimate in a way which is no longer possible. But an equilibrium has been struck after the disruption of that idyllic period when gods and men, past, present and future were unified. The purpose of life now is to maintain that balance of forces, lest the actions of people literally 'wrench the world adrift' (17). In fulfilling the obligations of the ritual, Elesin is literally holding the world in his hands. He is the link between past, present and future, a link analogous to the cord which joins mother to child, and through which life flows from one to the other. 'Coiled / To the navel of the world is that endless cord that links us all / To the great origin' (18).

The play is more than the description of a ritual; it is a re-enactment of it. Indeed, this is characteristic of Soyinka's dramaturgy. Soyinka also weaves specific Yoruba rituals into the action of his earlier plays, such as *A Dance of the Forests* and *The Road*. Thus, as we have seen, in *A Dance of the Forests*, an *abiku* ritual, celebrating the casting out of the *abiku*, the child who cannot rest between spirit world and mortal world and so is continually reborn, only to die again, is enacted at the end of the play. Similarly, at the end of *The Road*, the ritual dance of the character Murano, 'killed' in a lorry accident, and trapped between life and death, is enacted in an *agemo* cult dance, in which the realm of dissolution, the transitional zone between death and life, is celebrated. At such moments, the ritual is being acted and, in a sense, re-enacted. In the case of *Death and the King's Horseman*, the basic subject of the play is the ritual of transition, when Elesin is required to follow the King to the spirit world. Pilkings, the white policeman, believes this is a barbaric rite, designed to satisfy the King's ego. But to Elesin and his people it is a role of great honour, essential to maintain the links which allow the present world to continue and the future world to grow from it.

The tragedy at the heart of the play is not the colonial onslaught as such, but the potential disruption to Yoruba society if Elesin fails to complete the link which sustains the world and keeps it on its course. The play explores the interacting forces which bring about this failure, of which Pilkings's action, in interrupting the moment of Elesin's transition from one world to the next, is only one. As important is Elesin's decision to renew his attachment to the things of this world by his marriage to a young girl on the eve of his sacrifice. To attribute Elesin's action to any one of these forces is as simplistic as to try to decide absolutely, from among the many influences working upon them, why Hamlet fails to act or why Macbeth becomes evil. Plays explore complex interactions; they do not merely illustrate simple precepts.

Elesin himself is aware of the effect and importance of the white man's intervention, but he sees it as only one of many desires, temptations and failings, which together have prevented him from fulfilling his role. One of the important points of interpretation we must make, when we read or watch this play, is how far we credit Elesin's belief that he could have shaken off the weight of his renewed attachment to the world if Pilkings's intervention had not occurred. However we decide this, we are forced to recognise that he had a degree of complicity in his own fate, and therefore in the tragic consequences of it for his son Olunde, consequences which, as I shall indicate later, have to do with the future of the society as a whole and not just with Olunde's specific fate.

The treatment of the decision of Elesin to marry a young girl on the day before his death is the first of many moments during the play's action when the complexity of Elesin's motives is explored. Initially, when he asks the market woman, Iyaloja, for her daughter, she suggests that this may be an example of his being tempted to '[eat] and leave nothing on his plate for children' (20) – in other words, to use up more than his allotted time and portion of life. But Elesin strenuously denies this, arguing that he wishes only to leave behind him a final seed to blossom in the world. Although he denies seeking only sexual pleasure, his own description of the girl is profoundly sensual. Most importantly, this set of internal concerns within the Yoruba world frames and overshadows the play's reference to the white world. A self-contained Yoruba world, with its own virtues, rituals, flaws and failings, is fully dramatised before we encounter the white figures of the Pilkings. When we do, they are, ironically enough, dressed in modified *egungun* costumes. As ancestor masks, the *egungun* are representatives of the world of the dead, the world of the past, the world which now lays its claim on the present in the form of the ritual passage by Elesin from one state to the next. The lack of cultural sympathy and understanding shown by the Pilkings in using *egungun* masks as fancy-dress costumes extends to their behaviour *vis-à-vis* their servants, Amusa and Joseph. Their treatment of them (especially Simon Pilkings's) is notable for its complete failure to understand the sensibilities and values of the world they 'rule'. This is in contrast to the presentation, in the scene which follows, of the younger generation of Yoruba characters, who are shown to be able to caricature the whites who rule them with considerable accuracy. In other words, the ruled are shown to possess an understanding of the rulers which the rulers do not possess of their subjects:

– And how do you find the place?
– The natives are alright.
– Friendly?
– Tractable.
– Not a teeny-weeny bit restless?
– Well, a teeny-weeny bit restless. (37)

This scene prepares us for the realisation that the world of Elesin is also a world which is altering under the impact of the colonial invasion, and that the younger generation are preparing to deal with this world by understanding, appropriating and resisting its ideas. They do this not in order to accept the new values, but in order to be able to maintain a flexible but potent link between the traditional past and the developing future. Yoruba society, like any other, is not irrevocably fixed, and it is intrinsically capable of absorbing change and adjusting to new forces. The play is aware of the profound importance for Yoruba culture of the impact of modernisation and colonialism. The essential tragedy of Elesin lies in his failure to unite the worlds of the Yoruba past, present and future through his ritual death. The dominant theme is not the 'clash of cultures', though this theme is also explored. The events Ṣoyinka dramatises are primarily concerned with revealing the consequences of Elesin's failure to fulfil the Yoruba world's demands, not with what they reveal about the impact of colonialism on that world. The priorities of the text are internal to Yoruba cultural concerns.

Olunde's sacrifice is simultaneously necessary and yet wasteful, since he, like the young girls, could have functioned to resist the destructive impact of the coloniser in ways Elesin cannot. As Achebe had said, 'each man must dance the dance of his times'. Olunde's tragedy is that he must sacrifice his own dance to complete the unfinished dance of his father, a dance for which he was not meant. The loss to the community, where there are, as the young girls have shown, many young people who might have responded to his new modern approach, is a principal theme of the text. Soyinka here, as elsewhere in his work, insists that the creation of an effective and meaningful future for societies such as Nigeria can only come about if there is a proper link preserved with the past. But, as is clear from his public dispute with Chinweizu *et al.*, and with what he mockingly called the neo-Tarzanism of their view, Soyinka believes that African society is defined not only by traditional images of iron bells and calabashes, but also by oil-rigs and typewriters. This does not mean that he is opposed to modernisation. Modern Africa needs to have its roots in the continued apprehension of the local and the traditional. It is this vital linkage between past and present in the evolution and transmission of effective change which the play dramatises so successfully.

Writers like Soyinka, and others, increasingly saw that laying the blame for all contemporary ills at the doors of colonialism was over-simplistic. In fact, it was often used as an excuse for the excesses and failings of the new elite. As a result, a strain of self-criticism was emerging in many places, which modified the euphoria of the early texts of celebration. In Ghana, Kofi Awoonor had worked, in his early poetry, towards a powerful integration of traditional Ewe forms with modern English writing, and had produced poetic sequences which blended modern and traditional forms with remarkable success. The impulse behind his early poems, such as the 'Songs of Sorrow' sequence, was to recover Ewe traditional forms and to employ them in an effective new way. In the poem entitled simply 'A Dirge', from the 1971 collection *Night of My Blood*, the impulse to celebrate the traditional is implicit in the very form the poem employs, as well as in its sentiments.[12]

> Tell them, tell it to them
> That we the children of Ashiagbor's house
> Went to hunt; when we returned
> Our guns were pointing to the earth,
> We cannot say it; someone say it for us.
> Our tears cannot fall.
> We have no mouths to say it with.
> We took the canoe, the canoe with the sandload
> They say the hippo cannot overturn.
> Our fathers the hippo has overturned our canoe.
> We come home
> Our guns pointing to the earth.
> Our mother, our dear mother,
> Where are our tears, where are our tears?
> Give us our mouth to say it, our mother.
> We are on our knees to you
> We are still on our knees. (49)

Awoonor also used the forms and references of traditional verse to deal with the most immediate and modern of subjects, as in the prison poem lamenting the death in his cell of the political prisoner Allotey, from the 1978 collection, *The House by the Sea*.

What is this will we claim
in arguments
against pain, silence
or hope?
So our silence will sing
with the daylight gong
a dirge at birth time
that in love we rise
to go to the ferry port
long deserted in dreams.
We place our headloads
on the platform
to await our friend
and ferryman.

Those expecting us
we see them waving.
They make us live,
our love longing for home
is heard
in this river, our river
this valley, our valley
this land, our land.

Where are all the people gone? (183)

Awoonor has a claim to being the most consistently successful poet to employ the traditional forms in an appropriated way in English verse. But even he was aware that such a cultural recovery was often marred by its use as a tool of self-endorsement by an elite whose primary allegiance was not to local culture but to the bribes of multinational capital. As a result, even from the earliest times, his endorsement of traditional cultural recovery was never uncritical, as his satirical juxtaposition of the new institutions for the 'celebration and recovery' of African culture and those of the new culture of greed makes clear, in his powerful poetic novel *This Earth My Brother* (1972):

> He drove past the Institute of Arts and Culture where a crazy group of drummers and artists and their leaders were reviving African culture with a vengeance every day. On his left were the temporary buildings that housed the National Lottery, a monument to the greed of men, erected to satisfy the money lust of the lowly workers of the city. (19)

In *This Earth My Brother*, Awoonor dramatises the growing gap between the new Europeanised elite and the ordinary Ghanaian, despite the promises of the populist, revolutionary rhetoric of Nkrumah's government. His lawyer hero, Amamu, prefigures the disillusioned heroes of fellow Ghanaian Ayi Kwei Armah's fictions.

At about the same time, Ama Ata Aidoo, also a Ghanaian, was creating texts which showed the problems for the new returned elite and their dilemma as what she termed 'ghosts', invisible figures in the social landscape which had

155

given them birth. Aidoo's work was also notable for its early depiction of women and women's roles.[13]

In her play *The Dilemma of a Ghost* (1965), Aidoo offers an account of the clash of cultures which results from the decision of the young Ghanaian 'been-to', Ato Yawson, to marry Eulalie, an Afro-American girl he has met whilst at college in America. The play dramatises the clash which occurs when Ato and Eulalie return home to Ghana, and they confront the fact that the cultural differences between Eulalie's Afro-American culture and Ato's Ghanaian culture are greater than the similarities their shared racial origins led them to expect. The play critiques the idealised expectations of such Afro-American returnees, and their dream that they will 'rediscover' their lost African roots. This is a theme in a number of African English novels, with often quite satirical portraits of the Afro-American seeking his or her lost culture. Aidoo shows a sympathy for Eulalie, who, despite her failure to integrate, is finally accepted into Ghanaian society when she is led into the Clan house by Ato's mother in the final scene. The fault for her failure is, in part, attributable to Ato's selfishness in refusing to allow her to have the child she wants, a child which would confirm her status in the eyes of his female relatives. Her slide into alcoholism is seen to be the result of this refusal by Ato, and her subsequent dismissal by the women of his clan as 'barren'. Later texts by Aidoo develop a more critical examination of some of these themes, especially *Anowa* (1970).[14] However, in this early play, Aidoo does not analyse the implications of these contradictions as fully or as forcefully as she was to do in the later work. Nevertheless, she is more critical of the traditional world and its values than most of the male writers of the period, and she is one of the first writers to dramatise the way in which traditional society interacts with gender to produce specific and different pressures on men and women.

Writers who emerge in the wake of these early figures do not show the same urge to celebrate the past before beginning the task of self-criticism. Notable amongst these was the Ghanaian writer Ayi Kwei Armah, still one of the most controversial and disputed figures to emerge in recent African English writing. Armah's first novel, *The Beautyful Ones Are Not Yet Born* (1968), created an immediate controversy, challenging as it did the then predominant themes of celebration and recovery, and presenting instead a harsh and uncompromising picture of corruption and self-interest in Nkrumahist Ghana. The choice of an anonymous hero reflected the influence on Armah of French existential fiction, an influence which I believe is still present, despite the considerable evidence that Armah's work also has a strong basis in traditional Akan culture.[15]

In *The Beautyful Ones Are Not Yet Born*, Armah deals very explicitly with the theme of corruption, and with the disillusionment which many Ghanaians felt by the late 1960s with the Nkrumah government. The anonymous hero, a clerk in the administration, is suborned by his ambitious wife, and by powerful friends, such as the minister Koomson, to pursue the search for the 'shiny things' which wealth can bring, and to use his position to aid their crooked get-rich schemes. The collapse of the regime sees Koomson fleeing into exile with the help of the protagonist. The novel works through powerful chains of imagery involving human waste. Eating, digestion and excretion are used meta-phorically to represent the process of social corruption and the effect of the new elite's hunger for consumer goods. The ending, when Koomson is forced to escape arrest by squeezing himself through the toilet hole, from which the nightsoil men extract the household waste, creates a vivid and reversed image of birth. This graphic image emphasises the novel's message, that the new world of post-independence Ghana is essentially uncreative, mistaking the pangs of consumption and excretion for the productive labour of creation and birth.

Armah extends this critical vision in his next novel, *Fragments* (1970), to deal with the effect on the newly returned, foreign-educated intellectuals, or 'been-to's', of this universal demand for goods obtained from others and not generated by the society's own efforts. Using the metaphor of the New Guinean 'cargo-cults', he suggests that what the new society seeks is to receive goods from elsewhere, not to make things of its own. The post-independence elite see their role simply as mediators between the owners of these goods and their own people, transmitters of these gifts from the foreign 'gods', not makers in their own right. Faced with these demands, Baako, the hero, gives up his uneven struggle to create critical and meaningful work, and retreats into a catatonic silence. Armah also sees the increased dependence on imported luxuries as a betrayal of the link with the past. This is emphasised by the sympathy which exists between Baako and his grandmother Naana. She, too, is alienated by the modern world, which merely goes through the motions of acknowledging the ancient ways, appropriating their symbols to serve its own projects of self-aggrandisement and wasteful consumption.

In *Why Are We So Blest?* (1972) Armah offers a Fanonesque analysis of revolutionary consciousness, interwoven with an account of the tensions resident in black–white sexual relations. He analyses the relationships between three figures, Solo, Modin and Aimée. Solo is the dominant narrator, who relates the story of Modin, the would-be revolutionary, who has abandoned his American Ivy League school to seek an active role in the African revolution. His white mistress, Aimée, seems to be a satirical portrait of the expatriate white woman, whose motivation is partly sexual, as she voraciously pursues black lovers, and partly political, as she seeks in the third world a solution to her own first-world boredom and disillusion. The narra-tive sections are interspersed with a long series of reflections by Solo. Unfortu-nately, his hyper-sensitivity seems to prevent him from effectually analysing either the action or the inadequacies of the other characters' responses. The novel lacks Armah's usual force, which is dissipated by a structure which offers little narrative cohesion. Clearly determined to avoid the realist form of the dominant African fiction of the period, in this novel Armah struggles to find a way of linking psychological and social concerns, with only moderate success.

In the novels which followed, he turned to a wider and more historical framework. In ways reminiscent of Şoyinka's analysis of the post-independence malaise, Armah argued that the failure of the new elite, and of the young foreign-educated intellectuals, was rooted in a false and idealised representation of the past. This misrepresentation of history allowed the new elite to use colonialism as a convenient stalking horse, and as an excuse for every current ill. In two highly controversial texts, *Two Thousand Seasons* (1973) and *The Healers* (1978), Armah offered radical re-readings of African history, which laid much of the blame for Africa's historical woes at the feet of its own practices. In the first of these, *Two Thousand Seasons*, Armah tells the story of the long and often brutal pre-colonial past. His account of the involvement of Africans in the slave trade, and in internal wars and struggles, caused a good deal of criticism by those who saw this as colluding with Eurocentric, anti-African histories. Like his Francophone counterpart, Yambo Oulogouem, Armah pulls few punches, and these revisionary histories caused so much offence that their importance as a critique of the contemporary uses of cele-bratory 're-constructions' of the African past, and the political consequences of this, were neglected in the outrage occasioned by the more extreme asser-tions of the texts. Unlike the project of the earlier generation of writers, such as Achebe, which attempted to recover 'true' history and social practice from beneath the occlusion of colonial discourse, these texts perceive history as always written in the present. They deliberately pillage it for its effect in a contemporary political debate, rather than as part of a classic revisionist realist account.

The second of these two historical novels, *The Healers*, is less ambitious in scope, dealing as it does with a single specific and crucial moment in Akan history, when the 1874 British expeditionary force under Sir Garnett Wolseley began the destruction of the independent Ashanti nation. Armah uses this event to dramatise the struggle between those who act in collusion with the white invaders to their own benefit, and those who wish to resist. However, this clash is itself seen to be only symptomatic of the emergence in Africa in pre-colonial times of warring factions within larger groups, such as the Akan people. The Akan themselves are seen to be only a fragment of a larger, lost pan-African unity, from which modern African history represents a falling away. There is a utopian dimension to this fiction, with its account of the mystic 'healers', a secret body of people who have striven through time to resist and to heal the wounds imposed on the African people by these divisions. But the analysis of power it offers is clearly meant to suggest that the solution may lie beyond the project of resistance to movements like European colonisation, important though these were, and may need to be sought in the very structures of African culture itself.

After these novels Armah did not publish for a long period. More than any other recent African writer, Armah has reacted strongly against what he sees as the tyranny of Western publishing controls, as well as the dominance of African writing by the forms and themes favoured by foreign critics and editors. He published a scathing attack on the American critic Charles Larson's early study 'The Emergence of African Fiction'[16] in his essay 'Larsony or Fiction as Criticism'.[17] Difficulties with his American publishers over the novel *Why Are We So Blest?* led him to publish the following two novels with the East African Publishing House. That does not seem to have produced the control he felt

African writers should have either. Armah has not spoken directly about the reasons for his long silence, though one may speculate that he felt that none of the options open to African writers produced the financial and artistic control they needed to break away from neo-colonial dominance in publishing. Recently, though, Armah has issued a new novel. As interesting as its content is the decision he has taken not to publish with one of the major international or even African publishers who had handled his earlier fiction. Writing from exile in Senegal, the new novel, *Osiris Rising* (1995), is only obtainable directly from his locally based publisher, Per Ankh. In making this decision, Armah is clearly making a statement about the control still exercised by foreign patronage over the direction and content of African writing. In this respect, this erstwhile foreign-published writer joins others, such as the late Flora Nwapa and Ken Saro-Wiwa, as writers who have set up locally and even personally owned presses to resist the control of foreign publishers. In this respect, these elite writers have built a bridge to the practices of local publishing more often associated with popular writing traditions, from the Onitsha pamphleteers to the works of contemporary writers like the Kenyan David Maillu.[18] Significantly, despite its radical publication form, *Osiris Rising* does not represent a major break from either the concerns or style of Ayi Kwei Armah's earlier work. In fact, in some ways it returns to the themes central to Armah's earliest novels, such as the corruption of contemporary African regimes. It also shares some concerns about the validity and relevance of outsider visions of African culture with *Why Are We So Blest?* The narrator of *Osiris Rising*, a returned African-American woman, comes to Africa to seek a means of connecting with the real values of African culture. She wants to link modern Africa with the cradle of all African civilisations in Ancient Egypt. Her revulsion from the recent neo-colonialist elites who govern Africa reflects her belief that they have trivialised and falsified both the African past and its future potential. But the novel is aware of the dangers involved in creating an idealised, expatriate vision of Africa's past. Juxtaposed with the vision of the protagonist is a rather wry account of a figure which may be based on Alex Haley, the author of *Roots* (1977), and several satirical portraits of would-be Afro-American saviours, bringing millennial fantasies back to Africa.[19] The result is a subtle critique of both the celebratory fictions of an earlier period and the more disillusioned texts which Armah had written earlier. Although this fresh work from such a powerful and important writer has been welcomed by commentators, interest has focused on the radical break with Armah's early practice of publishing abroad. The new Armah has received little detailed critical analysis compared with the volume of international and local writing which greeted Achebe's breaking of a similar long silence with *Anthills of the Savannah*. This may well be a direct result of its place of publication, which means most foreign critics, and even many in other African countries, have found it hard to obtain. This neglect is an ironic confirmation of Armah's assertion that African English writing continues to function and to be valued mainly as a commodity in a Western-controlled market-place.

East Africa

In East Africa, where again similar processes and reactions occur a little later, the development of Ngũgĩ's fiction mirrors that of Achebe. *A Grain of Wheat* (1967) celebrates the freedom fighters of the Mau Mau liberation struggle. But it also records the disillusionment which mars that struggle, even before the Independence (Uhuru) celebrations with which the novel ends. The protagonist, Mugo, has betrayed the freedom fighter Kihika. The story of his hidden guilt and its exposure offers a counterpoint to the public joy of the celebration of Kenyan independence. It emphasises the problematic nature of that freedom, and the burden of the past which must be assuaged before it can be embraced. Mugo's confession inspires others, such as the carpenter Gikonyo, to face their own past and to refrain from idealising it. Gikonyo is haunted by his own confession of the secret oaths when he was tortured in the detention camps. When Mugo confesses he reflects: 'What difference was there between him and Karanja and Mugo and those who had openly betrayed people and worked with the whiteman to save themselves? Mugo had the courage to face his guilt and lose everything' (278). The confession and trial of Mugo shows Ngũgĩ's continuing interest in the theme of the relationship of past and present. It also shows that public institutions, such as the traditional Council of Elders (*Kiama*) and the Party officials of the new post-independence regime, need to be subjected to close scrutiny if they are not to become oppressive and reactionary in their turn. As well as portraying the personal cost to the characters of these traumatic events, there is a growing concern in Ngũgĩ's writing with the politics of corruption. Even in this relatively early text, there is a note of disillusionment with the new freedom, even as it is celebrated and announced. At this stage of his writing, though, the novel ends on an optimistic note, with Gikonyo's carving the stool he makes for Mumbi with an image of a pregnant woman, a wedding gift which emphasises fruitfulness and continuity, especially as Gikonyo and Mumbi echo the names of the founders of the Gĩkũyũ people, Gĩkũyũ and Mumbi.

A decade later, in *Petals of Blood* (1977), the theme of corruption and betrayal in *A Grain of Wheat* has become the dominant theme of Ngũgĩ's work and there are many echoes of this earlier work. Despite the developments in Ngũgĩ's work, it is possible to detect an ongoing unity of theme, if not of method, in all the novels. The concern with the betrayal of the ideals of the freedom movement, and the belief that the future is determined by the past, is a consistent theme from the earliest to the latest novels. In *Petals of Blood*, the setting of the novel is the village of Kamiriithu and the town of Ilmorog, a region which is the focus of all Ngũgĩ's later work. But it has a broader, political context than the earlier texts. The struggle over the conditions at the Theng'eta Brewery is told, characteristically for Ngũgĩ, in flashback, a technique which allows the novelist to bring to the surface of the narrative the hidden roots of personal actions and relate them to the wider realm of politics and social choice. The more explicitly political project in the work of this middle period is still contained within a realist framework. Of course this realism is characterised by a rich and varied use of language, in which appropriated English registers the wide variety of linguistic and cultural frames within which the people struggle to deal with the realities of post-independence life. Thus, for example, the elders of Ilmorog debate the decision to send a delegation to the capital to protest to their MP about the unfair treatment they have received in a region literally sucked dry of both people and resources to serve the growing modern conurbations, in an English which echoes local usages and languages:

> I think we should go. It is our turn to make things happen. There was a time when things happened the way we in Ilmorog wanted them to happen. We had power over the movement of our limbs. We made up our own words and sang them and we danced to them. But there came a time when this power was taken from us. We danced yes, but somebody else called out the words and the song. First the Wazungu. They would send trains here from out there. They ate our forests. What did they give us in return? Then they sent for our young men. They went on swallowing our youth. Ours is only to bear in order for the city to take. In the war against Wazungu we gave our share of blood. A sacrifice. Why? Because we wanted to be able to sing our song, and dance our words in fullness of head and stomach. But what happened? They have continued to entice our youth away. What do they send us in return? Except for these two teachers here, the others would come and go. Then they send us messengers who demand twelve shillings and fifty cents for what? They send others who come every now and then to take taxes: others to buy our produce except when there is drought and famine. The MP also came once and made us give two shillings each for Harambee water. Have we seen him since? Aca! That is why Ilmorog must now go there and see this Ndamathia that only takes but never gives back. We must surround the city and demand back our share. We must sing our tune and dance to it. Those out there can also, for a change, dance to the actions and words of us that sweat, of us that feel the pain of bearing. . . . But Ilmorog must go as one voice. (16)

The generations and the patterns of life which have flowed over Ilmorog are captured in this multi-faceted novel, as the different characters register their experience. There is the young schoolteacher, Munira, the son of a wealthy landowner, whose other children have succumbed to the lure of wealth and the new city life; the sole exception is his sister, whose suicide casts a long shadow forward through the events of the novel. Then there is Wanja, the barmaid and erstwhile prostitute. Her life-story gives the novel an insight into the new world of the corrupt cities, from which she has chosen to return to the rural world of Ilmorog and the obscurity of Abdullah's bar. There is Abdullah himself, the shopkeeper and trader, whose feud with the village over the grass eaten by his donkey, which he uses to pull his produce cart, symbolises the tensions in any rural community between those who farm and those who buy and sell produce. There is Karega, Munira's pupil, who led a strike at the elite school to which he won a place, and who now leads the workers in their struggle against the owners of the Theng'eta Brewery. Finally, there is Karega's brother and Munira's childhood playmate, Nding'uri, who was hanged by the Europeans for his part in the Mau Mau liberation struggle. Together with Munira's dead sister, he symbolises the price paid in the past for a future which has now been sold to greedy businessmen, corrupt politicians and foreign capitalists.

At first, the protest goes well, with Ilmorog's MP, Nderi, bringing 'progress' in the form of the work associated with the new Trans-Africa Highway, which passes through Ilmorog and rapidly transforms it from a rural area into a town. But things rapidly go wrong, and the story of Ilmorog and its development is used by Ngũgĩ to analyse change and development as they have affected modern Kenya.

> Within a month we witnessed even more amazing things. Surveyors pulling clanking chains along the ground came and planted red pegs. Just like the ones who came many years back. But this time they were followed by caterpillars and a cheering team of all nationalities and we crowded round them and listened to their nonsense work songs:
>
> > Brave one of my father, Njamba ya Awa,
> > Work is done by a full stomach, Wira ni Nda,
> > A man cannot be eaten by work, wanorago uu?
> > Except he be carrying an empty stomach . . .
>
> And the machines wallowed and whined and roared in the mud, clearing bush and grass and occasionally huts that stood in the ways of trade and progress.
>
> So we stood and watched as the machines roared towards Mwathi's place.[20] We said: it cannot be. But they still moved towards it. We said: they will be destroyed by Mwathi's fire. Just you wait, just you wait. But the machine uprooted the hedge and then it hit the first hut and it fell and we were all hush-hush, waiting for it to be blown up. Even when the Americans landed on the moon and we thought the earth would tremble or something would happen, we were not as scared as when Mwathi's place was razed to the ground. (264–6)

At first the fears seem foundless:

> The road. Trade. Progress. We saw the new owners of plots bring stones and concrete. We watched the trenches being dug and we were glad that at least two of us from Ilmorog, Wanja and Abdullah, had secured a plot and so would show these outsiders that even Ilmorog had people who could put up stone buildings. Flowers for our land. Long live Nderi wa Riera. We gave him our votes: we waited for flowers to bloom. (268)

Gradually, however, the progress which the road brings begins to sour, and the fear felt at the destruction of the old values, symbolised by Mwathi's hut, is confirmed. Slowly, the farmers are lured into taking out loans with the African Economic Bank, which they are persuaded they can easily afford to repay: 'Not in one lump. Oh no. Paying back would also be spread over a number of years. No steady farmer would ever need to feel the pinch. Only one condition: payment had to be regular. Easy. It was a year of hope . . .' (268). The increase in drinking, deliberately encouraged by the establishment of the Theng'eta Brewery, and the introduction of a potent form of foreign drink, affects many in the community, including the teacher, Munira.

> Theng'eta. Deadly lotus. An only friend. Constant companion. The trouble with drinking was that he felt he needed a little bit more to get back to yesterday's

normality and, in time, to prevent his hands from trembling so that they would remain firm enough to hold another horn. Theng'eta. The spirit. Dreams of love returned. (270–1)

Soon the banks foreclose on the properties, among them that of the old woman Nyakinyua, who had exhorted them to go to the city and seek justice. Munira, sunk now in drink and self-pity at losing Wanja, is unable to answer the queries of people, who cannot understand what is happening to them and who turn to the schoolteacher to explain:

> How could a bank sell their land? A bank was not a government, from whence then its powers? Or maybe it was the government, an invisible government, some others suggested. They turned to Munira. But he could not answer their questions. He only talked about a piece of paper they had all signed . . . But he could not answer, put to sleep, the bitter scepticism in their voices and looks. What kind of monster was this bank that was a power unto itself, that could uproot lives of a thousand years? (275–6)

Wanja, Nyakinyua's daughter, also loses her money in this crisis:

> Wanja was not quite the same after her recent loss. For some time she continued the proud proprietor of the old Theng'eta place. . . . But Wanja's heart was not in it. She started building a huge wooden bungalow at the lower end of the shamba, some distance from the shanty town that was growing up around Abdullah's shop, the lodgings and the meat-roasting centre, almost as a natural component to the more elegant New Ilmorog. (277)

Wanja returns to her life as a high-class prostitute, making Munira, who has waited years for her to return to him, her first client: 'This is New Kenya. You want it, you pay for it, for the bed and the light and my time and the drink that I shall later give you and the breakfast tomorrow. And all for a hundred shillings. For you. Because of old times. For others it will be more expensive.' Munira, as a result of Wanja's betrayal, becomes a born-again Christian and retreats into a private world to seek redemption.

But this is not only a story of individuals and their tragedies. Ngūgī is careful to point to the wider social causes and results of these changes, as the old unified Ilmorog divides into slums and wealthy suburbs:

> There were several Ilmorogs. One was the residential area of the farm managers, County Council officials, public service officers, the managers of Barclays, Standard and African Economic Banks, and other servants of state and money power. This was called Cape Town. The other – called New Jerusalem – was a shanty town of migrant and floating workers, the unemployed, the prostitutes and small traders in tin and scrap metal. Between the New Jerusalem and Cape Town, not far from where Mwathi had once lived guarding the secrets of iron works and native medicine, was All Saints Church, now led by Rev. Jerrod Brown. Also somewhere between the two areas was Wanja's *Sunshine Lodge*, almost as famous as the church. (280–1)

It is this continual and subtle intertwining of the stories of individuals with these wider social changes which gives the novel its power, and which makes it one of Ngūgī's most powerful texts. Karega returns, metamorphosed into a trade union organiser, after he has worked with the radical lawyer who had helped the first Ilmorog delegation to go to the city. His return provokes a final confrontation of the four old friends, Wanja, Munuri, Abdullah and Karega, and also a confrontation with the owners of the Theng'eta gin works. Karega begins to organise the workers in the region and trade unions spring up, to the consternation of the employers. In this final section of the novel, the overtly allegorical style which emerged in Ngũgĩ's later Gĩkũyũ texts begins to develop, especially in the representation of the European capitalists and their hangers on:

> a party [was] thrown at the premises of a new golf club to welcome Sir Swallow Bloodall, the General Manager of the parent Anglo-American Gin Company that had invested money in the Theng'eta project. It had turned out to be one of their most successful ventures in partnership with the locals. There were many dignitaries: European, Asian, African, including the MP, Nderi wa Riera and his KCO henchmen of Fat Stomach and Insect. (313)

But, despite these intimations of Ngũgĩ's later allegorical style, this earlier English-language text remains predominantly realist in tone, with the final sections moving rapidly to and fro between the final events, and the subsequent treatment of Karega and the others after their arrest for the murder of the Theng'eta Brewery owners, Kimeria, Chui and Mzigo. The killing is the result of Munira's twisted desire to save Karega from the corruption of Wanja, leading him to set fire to her hut. Unknown to him, she has lured the owners of the brewery there, in order to confront them with her decision to repudiate them in favour of the poor Abdullah. The final events allow Ngũgĩ to explore the complex web of motives, past and present, which underpin the actions of the four friends. But they also allow him to expatiate on the social problems the novel has uncovered. Thus, the novel ends with Karega being visited in prison by a young girl, who tells him that the workers of Ilmorog want to join him in a new strike. The final section is a revolutionary vision of the future which will result, if only the workers and peasants can unite and rise:

> Tomorrow it would be the workers and the peasants leading the struggle and seizing power to overturn the system and all its crying bloodthirsty gods and gnomic angels, bringing to an end the reign of the few over the many and the era of drinking blood and feasting on human flesh . . . 'Tomorrow . . . tomorrow . . .' he murmured to himself. 'Tomorrow . . .' and he knew he was no longer alone. (344–5)

Petals of Blood marks the shift from Ngũgĩ's early work to the later, more overtly decolonising fictions, which are discussed in the following chapter. It has a claim to being the most successful of his novels, combining the use of the novel as a vehicle for social change with a subtle and complex narrative, and a cast of characters who remain both credible and vibrantly drawn. In the texts which followed, the decision to relinquish English in favour of Gĩkũyũ, and to adopt a more overtly polemic style to politicise the masses, means that it is difficult to compare these texts meaningfully with those which went before. *Petals of Blood* is, in this sense, very much a transitional text between Ngũgĩ's two periods of writing, both the culmination of the techniques of his early novels and a signpost to the concerns of the texts which follow.

In East Africa, from the 1970s onwards, a number of writers employed the classic social realist novel to record the injustices and social disruptions which followed the post-independence drift to the cities. The earliest and most influential of these was Leonard Kibera's *Voices in the Dark* (1970). In this novel, the stories of the dispossessed Kenyan city-dwellers were heard for the first time. Kibera gave urban Kenya a tongue. For all his political force, Ngũgĩ was, and remains, a predominantly rural writer. His world is that of the villages of the ridges, and the episodes set in the towns and cities, whilst having the power one might expect from a writer of his talent, do not speak with the conviction of those writers for whom the city was the natural setting. Kibera's text spoke from within that world and recorded, for the first time, the bitterness felt by those for whom the struggle for Uhuru had brought only disillusion, unemployment and a hand-to-mouth existence on the fringes of the new wealth of the cities. The novel tells the story of the ex-freedom fighters Irungu and Kimura, who lost their hands and their legs respectively in the struggle for independence in the forest. Deserted by their wives, they are now reduced to begging on the streets of Nairobi. Their world is contrasted with that of the young intellectual Gerald Timundu, who is trying to write plays to be staged at the new university, and with the world of the new rich and the power brokers of Etisarap Road, one of the new rich suburbs. The narrative is fairly conventional and the plot is really little more than an excuse on which to hang contrasting portraits of these different worlds. But Kibera's novel is important for its attempt at a realistic description of the contemporary urban world of Nairobi:

And now the night wraps around the back alley like a thick and firm mist that only tantalises and gives no rain. It must be that hour of the night near dawn when the pavement turns into cold metal, when the sun refuses to come, when the night is darkest and when the moon is gone. It must be that hour of the night when the night is most frightening and silent, when beggars long for the old countryside where at least the early birds in the trees called the worm with a song, where at least one heard the donkeys shake their ears and cry for the dawn. It must be that hour of the night too when your thighs iced on the gravel of the broken pavement, you think of the lovers five floors above your head who wake you up with their fights every midnight, only to fall warm into each others arms while you know you cannot get to sleep again and your night is ruined; while you know that you cannot even wrap your rags round you for you have no hands. You think of many things: like the parliament clock over there which, at six o'clock in the morning, will strike loudly and with arrogance to tell you its time to get up when you have been up all night. You think of many things – Freedom before and after. Bedbugs. The health department. Safety pins. Oath number seven. Mosquitoes. The whole world from parasites and cigarette-ends to the House of Representatives. You think of many things: like Kabura your wife who deserted you because you lost both legs; or even a possible fortune waiting for you in one of hundreds of dustbins all over the city . . . (169–70)

Descriptions like these set the tone for the new realistic fiction which followed in the mid-1970s. Influenced by Kibera's example, the early work of

Meja Mwangi presents a scathing indictment of the failure of the new state to provide opportunities for the young, and portrays the awful conditions of the new underclass of displaced urban youth who have drifted to Nairobi from the rural areas. In *Kill Me Quick* (1973), Mwangi dramatises the life of Meja, one of the innumerable young people who moved to Nairobi from the country-side in search of a better life. Quickly learning that his proudly obtained Secondary School Certificate is of no use to him in the dog-eat-dog world of the Nairobi backstreets, he is educated into the reality of street life by his friend Maina:

> The two waited by the ditch behind the supermarket for the city rubbish collectors to come round. Until then they could not sleep without the risk of ending up in the rubbish dump five miles out of the city. Whenever a night watchman or a policeman was sighted they dived into the spacious culvert to avoid having to explain that somebody had not cleaned their house yet and so they could not go home. Time passed swiftly and the dim backstreet lights came on. The night chill started settling in and conversation was discouraged by the chattering of teeth. And at about ten o'clock the cleaners came and cleaned house. The two boys crept out of their hole and watched as the huge truck rumbled down the road emptying more dustbins. Then when the vehicle had gone and there was no policeman in sight they sprinted across the road and hopped into the largest of the supermarket dustbins. They snuggled close to each other for warmth and immediately fell asleep intoxicated by the foul smell of rotten vegetables. (8)

Unable to survive in the city, the boys try to return to the country to work for a white man, but their feud with the foreman leads to their being framed for stealing, and they are forced to return to Nairobi and the streets. Gradually and inevitably, with no chance of employment, the boys are drawn into the world of petty crime. Meja is struck down by a lorry, after running away when accused of stealing two rotten apples. Maina falls in with the street thief Razor and his gang. Meja tries to return to his family, but there is no place now for him in a countryside facing its own problems of poverty and land shortages. Reluctantly, he returns again to the city, where, despite getting a job in a quarry, he falls foul of the system again and ends up with Maina in prison. The narrative reverses the time-sequence of many of these events, for example by placing the arrival of Meja in prison immediately after his unexpected triumph, when he passes the quarry foreman's employment test by hewing nine square feet of rock with wedges and hammer. The story of Meja's subsequent dismissal from the quarry job, and the unsuccessful career in house-breaking which follows, is told after the prison scene, again reversing the traditional cause and effect sequence of classic, realist narrative. Maina, too, tries to return to his village, after an unsuccessful suicide and a quarrel with Meja. Another reversed narrative time-sequence, and the repetitive nature of the fate of the two protagonists, again suggest the inevitability of failure in the world of the city, and the impossibility of retreat to a rural world, itself plagued by famine and drought. In prison once more, Meja relates to his fellow inmates how Maina has killed two people in his village, and has subsequently gone mad. Remembering his early life in the city, he reflects that

Maina and he had been caught up by things they never really understood: '"he would rather eat from dustbins than steal. I knew him well. He would not just kill people". . . . He shook his head painfully and the tears overflowed. He did not dry them. "Why did this have to happen to him? They say it is fate, but is it really? Is it?"' (148). The narrative sequence avoids distancing the events, or providing any external explanatory view. The experience is seen only through the eyes of Meja and Maina, and this is clearly intended to assert the authenticity of the story. The breaking of the normal time-sequence of the story is also designed to convey that the events are the result of unavoidable forces, which the boys do not understand and so cannot relate in any causal way. The story is made all the more effective by the absence of any possibility of understanding by the boys themselves, making resistance or protest impossible. The reader is left to supply the hidden dimension, which suggests that the plight of these young people is the result of the political and social failure of the new society.

Mwangi's next novel, *Going Down River Road* (1976), is also set in the slum areas of modern Nairobi. More conventionally shaped as a narrative, it tells the story of Ben, his ex-prostitute girlfriend Wini, and her son Baby. Like *Kill Me Quick*, the story presents an inside view of life in the slums of River Road and Grogan. When Wini runs off with her white boss, Ben is left to look after Baby alone. Although his initial reaction to Baby had been negative, he now becomes committed to raising the boy and giving him schooling. With his friend Ocholla, whom he meets at a building site, he manages to find a place to raise Baby and a series of portraits of the people and places of River Road provide the background to Ben's new sense of commitment and purpose. A sunnier and often humorous book compared with *Kill Me Quick*, it lacks anger and social focus, though in Ben Mwangi creates an appealing hero.

Mwangi's later novel of city life, *The Cockroach Dance* (1979), seems to me not to have managed to achieve the same focus and intensity as the first novels. However, a recent and comprehensive study of Mwangi's work argues that this later novel offers a different kind of critical analysis of post-independence Kenya.[21] Lars Johansson argues that there is a shift from the earlier Nairobi street-life novels, *Kill Me Quick* and *Going Down River Road*, where 'characters are more "realistically" portrayed in terms of psychological credibility, towards "allegorical" personalities embodying tensions and contradictions in the Kenyan society of the 1970s' (51). Johansson argues that in *The Cockroach Dance*, for example, the image of the cockroach is invoked to represent both the oppressors and the oppressed, and that the cockroach image, like the structure of the novel itself, incorporates a deep level of irony. On the surface, as Johansson admits, the text seems to present a far more ambiguous and less committed picture of the slum-dwellers, unemployed and beggars of modern Nairobi. He contends that this is in line with an emerging tendency in the 'dominant ideological climate in the Kenya of the 1970s'. He argues that 'The narrative is in the latter respect reminiscent of a rhetoric from the backbenches in parliament, where criticism of excessive exploitation in Kenyatta's time was tolerated as a "useful safety valve"'. Nevertheless he contends that:

167

the claim that the novel has been incorporated into a dominant discourse ascribes a very passive role to it where there is little room for opposition or difference. There is, however, a reading which opens up a register of counter-discourse. The resistance to the dominant ideology is to be found in the field of tension between dominator and dominated, in the ambivalences and ambiguities of the dealings with a contemporary situation. (65)

The novel's hero, the suburban water-meter reader Dusman, punishes the *Umbwa Kalis* (or new rich) by increasing their water-bills. He is presented as in opposition to the values of the landlord of the slum tenement in which he lives, the pious but self-serving Tumbo Kubwa, who combines a Christian and capitalist ideology with no apparent tension. Dusman regards the inhabitants of the tenement, and those he meets in the streets, as dirty, ignorant and unable to act without leadership from outside. The tensions Dusman experiences make him seek help and report himself as mad. His madness, which takes the form of an obsession with cockroaches, clearly symbolises the appalling conditions of life he sees around him, and also the parasitical life of the new rich, who are 'cockroaches' of a different kind, living, parasitically, on the poor of the world. Dusman is a figure who allows us to focus the inadequacies of the new rich, and of the whites who, like his psychiatrist Dr Bates, cannot connect his mental problems to the physical conditions of his daily life. However, compared with the earlier novels, the portraiture of the street poor, the collective world of Nairobi's underclass of beggars and unemployed, is ambivalent. There is no inside and sympathetic portrait of the world of the collective poor here, as in Mwangi's earlier novels. Johansson's reading of the novel offers an ingenious explanation for this shift in perspective, and it is certainly one which deserves to be considered. But most readers, I suspect, would find the political and social messages of the later novel far more ambiguous and even, in places, merely confusing.

A further reading of the shifting concerns of the later work of Mwangi is offered by Johansson when he argues that, after *The Cockroach Dance*, Mwangi's fiction moves away from a concern with portraying the Nairobi proletariat to embrace international themes and locales. This shifts concern away from what the author calls 'competing discourses of Kenyan sociopolitical reality' to 'emphasise African cultural values and a concomitant anti-West stance'. For Johansson the new concerns of Mwangi's novels in the 1980s are international resistance and opposition, when he embraced popular forms such as the thriller. Johansson also argues that the novels show the influence of the growing concern with popular fiction in East Africa, and that the changing themes and locales are connected with this shift to embrace popular genres such as the thriller. He continues to claim that these novels, nevertheless, represent an ongoing if more hidden and subtle politics of opposition.

In the meantime, other Kenyan writers, such as Thomas Akare in his 1981 novel *The Slums*, continued to present a vivid and uncompromisingly realist account of the dispossessed urban class. The protagonist, Eddy, lives off the rich women who visit this world to consult local medicine dealers, or to find young lovers, to supplement their wealthy but impotent sugar daddies. There is little sentimentality in the portrait of Nairobi slum life, and a vivid sense of the politics of dispossession and unequal wealth which results from the corruption of modern society.

> I kept on sitting, looking at these people going into the church, others going to their businesses, and some going, where to they didn't know, trying to escape the world's trouble. I thought and wondered to myself, why doesn't the government want us? Why charge us for vagrancy in our country, unemployed or tax-defaulters, while it is not our wish or fault? We don't eat their food or beg. As for education, we have that, but no jobs. What crime is that? And it is all due to corruption and tribalism, nepotism. Why send us back to the land where today is the same as yesterday, and so is every year. Then I found myself having a feeling of hatred watching these people and all their commotion. The feeling was so deep that I felt myself envying them. I looked at them with envious eyes when I thought where they had slept, what food they ate and the way they dressed. The mumbo-jumbo fashions. Suits, minis, maxis, bell-bottoms and flares, slim-fit shirts and all ... To have a bath in the Slums you have to line up on the toilets or else lick the dirt and scratch it off. I looked at my jacket. The patch which I had sewn on there had started to wear out. I cursed this sack thread. It couldn't hold for long ... My last Y-front was almost worn to a thread in the centre and to add to it I saw three lice along the strap. They had started laying the eggs of their young. I thought I would throw it away with the lice, because I didn't kill them when I saw them. They too had to make a living. (3)

Through the story of Eddy and his father, Akare gives us a history of the poor in Kenya through the war years, when they were drafted for service in Burma, and afterwards, when they returned to attempt to educate their children and to face the struggles for independence. There is little glorification of the independence struggle here, as it is woven into a drunken history of white and black oppression of the poor by Eddy's friend Massopo:

> 'IRA, this is the Irish army and I tell you man they are giving the British a hard time there in Ireland. Just like the Vietnamese to the Americans. They don't allow their women to be seduced by the British. If one is found she is shaved quite clean and then decorated with black tar. Hare Krishna, this is a new sect in town here with its followers shaved clean with only a small part left in the centre of their head. Almost like Yul Brynner and that singer from the ghettoes, Isaac Hayes. Mau Mau, oh man these are our fighters in the forest who gave Lord Delamere a time to remember.' (10)

Massopo's tumbling, drunken account of rebellion and violence, which strings together Mafiosi, the Palestinian Liberation Movement, Nkrumah, Martin Luther King and the Biafran war, is a picture of politics from the underside, exposing the pretensions of its exponents, and the urgent need the poor have to cling to any myths of freedom and revenge. Eddy's sardonic reception of Massopo's drunken lecture does not deny it its force as a realistic portrayal of the way the people of the slums view great events, through the wrong end of the telescope of their deprived and embittered lives. The strength of Akare's writing is in its faithfulness to the viewpoint of the slum-dwellers themselves. Although the novel has been criticised for not suggesting solutions, and for ending on a deeply pessimistic note, it is arguable that it is a far more realistic and convincing examination of slum life than the polemic fables of Ngũgĩ, whose mythologising of the slum-dwellers into potential radical proletarians seems sometimes to smack of a programme, rather than of any real observation and credible portrayal of social reality. Akare's world is a brutal one in which morality must attend on survival, and in which there is one law for the new rich and one for the poor:

> the news reached us that two of the slum boys had been picked up. Kokroch was taken at Ngara. He entered a music shop and as if it was his father's shop, tried to walk out with a tape-recorder. The beating they gave him will remain in his bones to be felt in his old age. Odunde was taken at River Road in a Bata shop. He had money, yes, to buy the pair of shoes he wanted. He went into the Bata shop with sandals on his feet. He tried on a pair and, thinking that he was not being watched, he tried to walk out with them on, leaving his sandals behind. When the *Utumishi kwa Wote* arrived, he was half dead. . . . We thought nothing about the picking up of the boys. They were only trying to keep pace with the moving world. Trying to survive the world of hell's pressure. (138)

Akare's novel presents the gap between rich and poor through Zakia, the wife of a minister, who literally slums by visiting the world of River Road. Meeting Eddy she becomes his sugar mammy, buying him new clothes and taking him to discos and bars. Although her interest in him is obviously sexual, she is also clearly fascinated to be introduced to his world, a world from which her privilege bars her, and of which she knows little. Her fascination and ignorance of the realities of life for the majority of Kenya's urban poor dramatises the huge gap which has arisen between classes in the post-independence world of Nairobi, sweeping away sentimental assertions of national identity in the realities of social inequality and economic differentials so great as to make comprehension across the class divide almost impossible.

Notes

1. The publication of the so-called Achebe Trilogy in America, consisting of *Things Fall Apart, Arrow of God* and *No Longer at Ease*, has confused the issue of whether Achebe's novels constitute a sort of family saga. Achebe's early references in various interviews and papers to his intention to produce a 'trilogy' of novels suggests that there should have been a novel covering the generation of Nwoye, the son of Okonkwo in *Things Fall Apart*, and the father of Obi, the protagonist of *No Longer at Ease*. Although *Arrow of God* is set later than *Things Fall Apart* (in the 1920s), it is also a 'contact novel', and does not deal with the generation of converts such as Nwoye. For an account of the reasons for this see Gareth Griffiths, 'Chinua Achebe: When Did You Last See Your Father?', *World Literature Written in English*, 27, 1 (Spring 1987), pp. 18–26.

2. See 'Interview with Chinua Achebe', in Bernth Lindfors (ed.), *Palaver: Interviews with Five African Writers in Texas* (Austin, Texas: African and Afro-American Research Institute, 1972), p. 9.

3. Babangida, it may be recalled, was eventually succeeded, after a democratic election process was set aside, by his one-time subordinate and fellow plotter, the late General Abacha. Abacha was the man responsible for the decision in 1995 to execute the writer Ken Saro-Wiwa, and a number of other pro-democracy protesters, causing a wave of

international protest. It was Abacha, too, who drove Wọle Ṣoyinka from Nigeria, and into an attempt to found a government in exile. His recent death from a heart-attack, and his replacement by a more moderate military leader, General Abubakar, has, fortunately, recently seen elections at which a civilian government was formed, hopefully ending this long period of military dictatorship.

4. For a defence of the novel along these lines see, for example, Simon Gikandi, *Reading Chinua Achebe* (London: James Currey, 1991).

5. Ibid., p. 131.

6. Adewale Maja-Pearce, *A Mask Dancing: Nigerian Novelists of the Eighties* (London and New York: Hans Zell, 1992), p. 10.

7. Ibid., p. 9.

8. *A Dance of the Forests*, in *Wọle Ṣoyinka: Collected Plays*, Vol. 1 (Oxford: Oxford University Press, 1974), p. 11. All further page references are to this edition.

9. Frantz Fanon, *The Wretched of the Earth*, trans. Constance Farrington (London: Penguin, 1967), p. 168.

10. Ibid., p. 168.

11. In D. W. Jeffares (ed.), *The Morality of Art: Essays Presented to G. Wilson Knight* (London: Routledge & Kegan Paul, 1969).

12. All page references to Kofi Awoonor's poems in the text are to the collected edition of his poems, *Until the Morning After – Collected Poems 1963–1985* (London: Heinemann, 1987).

13. Interestingly, she has received less attention from contemporary feminist revisionist accounts of African writing than some other writers, despite her claim to being as provocative in her challenge to the existing modes as any of the later writers. For example, Florence Stratton offers no extended discussion of any of her works, nor does she offer an extended discussion of the work of Efua Sutherland, although Sutherland is arguably the most neglected of Africa's major women writers. We may note that Aidoo, like Sutherland, first published mostly plays. Indeed, Sutherland's whole output was in the form of drama. Does the relative neglect of their work reflect a continuing, unconscious influence on modern critics of the prejudice in favour of prose fiction by the new publishing firms discussed earlier in Chapter 4? The relative difficulty of publishing plays as opposed to novels continues to this day and still biases the discussion of modern African writing.

14. See Chapter 11.

15. See Derek Wright, *Ayi Kwei Armah's Africa: The Sources of His Fiction* (London: Hans Zell, 1989).

16. Charles Larson, *The Emergence of African Fiction* (Bloomington: Indiana University Press, 1971).

17. 'Larsony or Fiction as Criticism', *Asemka*, 4 Sept. 1976, pp. 1–14, reprinted in *New Classic*, 4 Nov. 1977, pp. 33–45.

18. See Chapter 5.

19. The reference to Haley might suggest that the novel had been written earlier. There is some anecdotal evidence that Armah has continued to write in exile in Senegal, but has not chosen to release this material until now. Whether further novels published in the same manner will now appear remains to be seen.

20. Mwathi is the local seer and man of spiritual knowledge, who rules on the difficult issues that face the community.

21. Lars Johansson, *In the Shadows of Neo-Colonialism: Meja Mwangi's Novels 1973–1990* (Umeå, Sweden: Dept. of English, Umeå University, 1992). All page references are given in the text.

Chapter 8

Opposition, Resistance and Decolonisation

Opposition and dissent in African writing in English have been directed out-wardly against the external forces of neo-colonialism, and inwardly against the governments and social processes of the post-independence regimes, many of whom have been accused of acting simply as agents for those external forces. For this last reason, it is impossible to separate absolutely these forms of oppositional texts. I have tried to group the texts into two main positions: political texts which seek to oppose and expose corruption and injustice in modern African life since independence; and texts which directly address the influence of neo-colonial forces on the forms of government and society in post-independence Africa. A shift away from a concern with the impact of colonisation and the historical past towards an examination of current socio-economic problems characterised the writing from the late 1970s.

The writers who addressed these new issues were generally born a decade or so later than the first generation of writers. The shift of concern can be discerned in both regions (West and East Africa) and in most of the genres, suggesting that the disillusionment with the post-independence regimes it reflects was very widespread. The shift of theme and concern can be seen to affect the styles of writing, too, as writers sought to find forms which would appeal to a wider, mass audience, and involve them in the struggle against the corruption, inequalities and privileges of the new elite. Some of the writers in this period continued to employ social realism, in accounts of the life of the new post-colonial underclass. Others sought out new media, reaching out to forms like television, or popular fiction genres, to convey their message to the masses. Still others employed allegorical forms to convey their social message, linking their desire to act as social critics to the traditional role of African oral texts, and drawing on them for inspiration. These choices were often bound up with movements which stressed the negative effect of a continuing Euro-centrism on African society, and which emphasised ongoing cultural domination as one of the features of neo-colonialism. This led to a number of calls from the early 1970s onwards for a return to more 'authentic' African themes and forms, and for the revitalisation of writing in the indigenous languages under the banner of cultural decolonisation.[1] These calls often involved an emphasis on formal changes as well as on suitable subjects, with calls for a return to a simpler, local, African style. As might be expected, others resisted this call, and the suggestion that such a definition of an authentic African subject or style was necessary, or even possible, in the light of modernisation and the rapid change which characterised African society in the twentieth century. The struggle over these issues dominated much critical writing and involved many of the writers in the period through the late 1970s and 1980s.

In Nigeria, especially, a very long public debate on how writers should address these post-independence problems took place. It was characterised by the struggle of a younger generation of writers, such as Bode Sowande, Kole Omotoso, Femi Osofisan and others, to define their views against the pioneer work of the earlier generation, notably Christopher Okigbo, Chinua Achebe and Wole Soyinka, whose influence and paramount importance in shaping the form of modern Nigerian political writing in English they all, to a large extent, acknowledged. It was argued that, although the older generation did engage with the politics of their time, they retained a basic belief in the private role of the artist, and emphasised historic and mythic elements above immediate social issues. The younger generation claimed to embrace a more radical position, emphasising that the artist needed to be in direct contact with the people and to reflect specific struggles at a local level. The impact of the Nigerian Civil War also helped to encourage this movement from a personal, mythopoeic vision of poetry to a more radical and public vision.

The moment of change is sometimes located in the late verse of the Ibo poet Christopher Okigbo. Okigbo's earlier verse had been strongly influenced by his classical training, and by the style and doctrines of European modernism. This early work is essentially private, concerned with the artist as a seer and as a visionary, rather than as an active social agent. However, Okigbo's last poems in the 'Path of Thunder!' series show a remarkable shift towards a local rhythm and diction, as well as a strong commitment to the public role of the poet. These poems influenced many of the younger poets, especially those of the so-called Nsukka school, an influence strengthened by Okigbo's decision to fight as a soldier on the Biafran side in the civil war, leading to his death in action in 1967. In this shift, the writers were joined by a younger generation of critics. In particular, the critical troika of Chinweizu, Jemie and Madubuike rejected what they saw as the politically disabling complexity of much of the writing of the first generation. In particular they attacked Soyinka's writing as unnecessarily complex and too influenced by foreign models. Their work was tied to an agenda which stressed the need for art to return to its 'traditional' role of directly influencing the ethical and social decision-making processes by addressing the ordinary people.[2] They sought to limit African writing to traditional themes and diction and to avoid what they characterised as the difficult, obscurantist style of earlier writers such as Soyinka. The troika strongly promoted the work of Achebe, suggesting that he and Soyinka represented two distinct styles of writing in English, one faithful to the African tradition and one aberrant to that tradition. These attacks led to a notable series of rebuttals by Soyinka himself, which criticised the essentialism of the definitions of Africanness employed by these so-called *bolekaja* critics,[3] accusing them of an over-simple nativist vision of modern Africa which he, with typical bravura, labelled 'neo-Tarzanism'. Much of this extreme criticism of Soyinka focused on his poetry, and failed to acknowledge the high degree of traditional content and form in Ṣoyinka's dramatic output. It was also less than fair to the continuing influence of the work of earlier writers like Ṣoyinka and Okigbo on the themes and styles of many of the younger writers. As a result, the criticism of the new writers themselves, such as Osofisan and Osundare, and of a new generation of academic commentators, such as Biodun Jeyifo, was more subtle. They registered the complex and important contribution of writers like Okigbo and Ṣoyinka to the long process of decolonisation in a much juster fashion. Younger writers, such as Osundare, Ofeimun and Ojaide, have said that Okigbo, especially in the later poetry, exercised a strong influence on their own work; whilst Osofisan and Sowande, despite their criticism of Ṣoyinka's emphasis on myth and the role of the individual heroic figure in social struggles, were always careful to acknowledge his ongoing influence on their own practice.

In fact, things have been less problematic than the public critical dispute suggests, with writers emphasising different projects and styles at different periods or in different texts. Kole Omotoso, for example, is one Nigerian writer whose work straddles these critical divisions. Omotoso is unusual too in that he has moved easily and successfully between drama and fiction, showing a versatility of form others have only rarely attempted, and with only small success. Omotoso's early work followed fairly conventional lines. *The Edifice* (1971) was written when Omotoso was a student in Britain. It is a fairly typical 'been-to' novel,[4] dealing with the failure of the hero to adjust to the cultural clash involved in his experience, a clash exacerbated by his marriages to two white women. For all its flow and pace, it presents a less effective analysis of the issues than older writers like Achebe or Ama Ata Aidoo had brought to bear on similar themes. A series of texts followed of mixed form and weight. The civil war novel, *The Combat* (1972), is dealt with elsewhere in this volume.[5] Less weighty was the thriller *Fella's Choice* (1974), which at least demonstrated Omotoso's skill in keeping a fast-paced narrative running and creating a believable and suspenseful plot. Interestingly, while he was employed in producing this lighter fiction, Omotoso had also produced two strong political dramas in *The Curse* (1976), which castigates the new rulers for their corruption and injustice, and *Shadows in the Horizon* (1977), which has a similar theme. In 1978 he returned to fiction with *To Borrow a Wandering Leaf*, which examines the alienation of the new post-independence administrators, who wandered across the land like leaves blown by the wind and had as little connection with the soil, that is with the people themselves. The criticism of social corruption then became the dominant feature in Omotoso's work, for example in the wryly titled novel *Memories of Our Recent Boom* (1982), and the wide-ranging, historical, documentary novel *Just Before Dawn* (1988). *Memories of Our Recent Boom* is the story of Seven, a village boy who has prospered in the dog-eat-dog world of Nigerian business, a world which has floated itself on the sea of easy money produced by the oil finds of the late 1970s and early 1980s. The resulting economic boom saw vast amounts of money spent on grandiose road schemes, national stadia and other public works, few of which involved any real long-term industrial or agricultural infrastructure development, or effective long-term job-creation. The short-lived boom left behind huge social problems, as the people fled to the shanty complexes in the cities, deserting the land, which had once provided a thriving and efficient subsistence farming economy. The novel combines the popular Nigerian novel of racy urban life, the picaresque form initiated by texts such as Ekwensi's *Jagua Nana* (1961), with gritty, realistic descriptions of Lagos squalor and the immorality and shallow opportunism of the elite class.

Just Before Dawn is one of the more interesting experiments in the novel in recent times, if one can call it a novel. This is a 'historical' account, but it abjures the remote and legendary past and concentrates on the story of Nigeria over the last hundred years. It does not present itself as a conventional novel but mixes the discourses of official written history – 'Constitutional talks about Nigeria began in Nigeria from 1947 onwards. Talks were usually held in the regional capitals of Kaduna, Ibadan and Enugu. The talks were usually characterised by horse-trading with the British colonial officials' (185) – with shifts into direct dialogue and fictionalised reconstructions of the events it portrays:

> Azikwe's statement was vague, full of smooth resounding platitudes and quotes about goodwill, parliamentary democracy, harmony, understanding and equality. He spoke as if his mind was not there.
> 'You know the trouble with him?' Ibrahim Imam asked, leaning over to Balewa.
> 'Tell me.'
> 'The Action group is threatening to sue his papers for libel of a quarter of a million pounds unless he goes along with them during this conference.' (187)

This represents an extreme form of the novel as social document, or of the fictionalisation of social history. The novel did not prove popular, or receive much critical notice. But it is indicative of a wider interest, noted later in this account, in fiction in African writing as a means to present historical material to a broad-based audience. Its relative lack of success outside Nigeria may be an indication of the still limited interest in, and knowledge of, Nigerian history and politics amongst a general, non-Nigerian readership.

Femi Osofisan's work serves as a paradigmatic example of the kind of shifting and developing responses writers have employed in the often hectic debate amongst left-oriented critics and writers in the early 1970s. Osofisan, although critical of Soyinka, stressed that he had acquired many of the techniques employed in his early work, such as the allegorical use of Yoruba historical and legendary material, from such influential early pieces as Soyinka's *A Dance of the Forests* (1963), the piece commissioned for the Nigerian independence celebrations, and the later even more bitter political satire *Kongi's Harvest* (1967). The dramaturgical and thematic influence of these on such early Osofisan plays as *Red is the Freedom Road* (1982) and *Morountodun* (1982) can be seen in the way Osofisan echoes Soyinka's technique. Both writers employ episodes from the legendary Yoruba past to make comments on present situations, and mix realistic dialogue and traditional ritual to construct their stage effects.

175

Nevertheless, in line with other critics, Osofisan stressed the political dangers in what he perceived to be Ṣoyinka's tendency to reify myth, and, in particular, his perception of Ṣoyinka's over-concern with the heroic individual whose heroism and sacrifice can redeem the body politic. For the younger Osofisan, this stress on the politics of the individual needed to be replaced by a politics of community, which emphasised the inability of even the most enlightened leader to effect change, unless he was able to alter the lives of the masses and engage their support. In line with this political shift went a concerted effort to get the drama physically to the audience Osofisan sought, the people of the small towns and village communities. Throughout the late 1960s and 1970s, this was very much the aim of Osofisan's theatre. For example, *Morountodun* reworks the legend of the Yoruba princess Moremi, refocusing the tale's politics. The original legend is employed to confirm authority, but Osofisan uses it for a subversive end, by making its hero Titubi recant from her role of secret agent for the ruler and join the rebels, after she experiences their poverty and oppression at first hand. Thus, the play transforms the original traditional material from a celebration of the rulers into a celebration of their radical opponents. This 'subversion' of traditional themes was a conscious process, as Osofisan indicated in an interview published in 1980: 'I may use myth or ritual, but only from a subversive perspective. I borrow ancient forms specifically to unmask them.'[6] This was accompanied by a wedding of these subverted traditional myths to an open, interrogative performance style. Although this performance style acknowledged a direct debt to Brecht, it was also in line with the traditions of African oral performance, with its invited, and occasionally uninvited, audience interventions. Thus, *Morountodun*, for example, ends with the exhortatory lines: 'the real struggle, the real truth, is out there among you, on the street, in your home, in your daily living and dying'. Elsewhere, Osofisan encourages the audience to comment, or even vote, on issues raised in the plays.

By the early 1980s it is clear that Osofisan had become increasingly disillusioned with the effectiveness of these techniques, and with the ability of intellectuals to effect wider social and political change. The disillusionment of this period can be seen in the bitter portrait (self-portrait?) of the university theatre director in the 1981 produced play *The Oriki of a Grasshopper*. The director's work is seen as an ineffective liberal and artistic *cul de sac,* to which Nigerian middle-class society can retreat for refreshment after the daily cut-throat business of politics and making money. For whatever reason, when radical plays had been toured to local venues they had failed to attract and sustain a large, regular audience. Increasingly, Osofisan's work, like that of the other radical writers of the period, was confined to an audience in the university. Significantly, even when the plays were translated into Yoruba they still failed to attract the kind of popular *mass* audience Osofisan sought. This may have been because the treatment and subjects did not appeal to the kind of mass audience which had been successfully attracted by the Yoruba-language folk operas of Herbert Ogunde and Duro Ladipo, and even by more popular playwrights such as Wale Ogunyemi. It may simply have reflected a general decline in the success of live performance events as a whole. The facts have not been properly investigated, nor has any real evidence been assembled to justify the many assertions which have been, and continue to be, made on these matters. There is an urgent need for more work to be done to establish the facts and supplement the few pieces of sociological analysis which have so far been undertaken.[7] Certainly, the period coincides with the growth of a mass audience for television, and the impact of this on even the established popular writers and their troupes seems clear, though again only in general and indefinite terms. Whether or not this factor was crucial, it did affect Osofisan's development, in so far as the 1980s saw him turn increasingly to television, with varying degrees of success, in search of the elusive popular, mass audience his political programme demanded. Almost forty television plays of varying length followed, only a handful of which are readily available in published form. Again, there is no published audience viewing ratings available to assess the success or failure of this work. Judging from the small body of published scripts alone, the plays themselves vary greatly in style and quality, from the very melodramatic, almost soap-opera style of *Altine's Wrath* (1986; televised in 1983), to what seems to me to be one of the most successful of Osofisan's middle-period plays, the hard-hitting analysis of the confrontation of the powerful women's trading groups with the alliance of traditional patriarchal rulers, and the modern, male political leaders in *Fires Burn, and Die Hard* (1990), televised in 1981, and reworked for the stage in 1989. This judgement, of course, may well reflect my own bias, and it would be interesting to see whether or not the popular response judged by viewing figures echoes mine. It seems more likely that it would reverse it, since anecdotal evidence indicates that Osofisan himself did not rate *Fires Burn, and Die Hard* highly despite what seems to me to be its many excellent qualities as a piece of dramatic writing and as a social analysis. This may be because it did not succeed in effecting the popular response he continued to seek, along with other writers during this period, in the new medium of television. Osofisan was less interested in receiving critical praise than attracting large viewing figures when he wrote these pieces. Significantly, in many of these pieces traditional features occur as part of the dramaturgy, but all the plays which are available for scrutiny in print are set in modern locations. They also often involve an openly polemic treatment of specific modern problems, such as, in the case of *Altine's Wrath*, the neglect and abuse of unwanted 'bush' wives by their socially and politically successful husbands.[8]

With the advantage of hindsight, it is clear that during the period from the late 1960s to the mid-1980s Osofisan, like other radical writers of the period, sought to wed a self-conscious and sophisticated dramaturgy to the politics of popular revolution. The underlying perception that theatre (on the Brechtian model) could get the audience out 'onto the streets' in active revolt, ignored the decisive failure of Brecht's own dramaturgy to effect any such process in his own time. The failure of these radical dramatists was reflected in the general failure of this style of radical theatre world-wide effectively to engage direct social action.[9] In addition, it failed to take account of the degree to

177

which Nigerian politics in this period and afterwards resisted analysis by such a simple model of oppression and resistance, in which a single oppressor or oppressive class could be readily and easily identified with specific social groups or organisations. Thus, for example, the shifts from civil to military governments did not, in themselves, necessarily equate with a shift from honest to corrupt regimes, and the sliding politics of disappointment, which resulted from such a perception, was too slippery for a simple revolutionary mode of redress. It was also becoming more and more obvious that traditional culture had a contradictory dual role, as both the endorser of local power bases and regional differences, and as a source of national signifiers which could be manipulated to form a false linkage between the ruling elite and the Nigerian past. In this it was at one with the politics emerging in a wide variety of post-colonial societies, where a neo-colonial collusion of local rulers and multi-national capital, and a politics frequently based on exclusive categories of ethnic grouping, language, or religion, was endorsed by a specious demand for national unity, designed to hide the continuation of gross discriminations and growing material inequalities and injustices.[10]

The theoretical implications of the drive to decolonise African culture and society often neglected to deal with this more complex effect, an effect in which the practices of local opposition and resistance were themselves homo-genised and presented as an unproblematic national response. The author-itarian rulers in the various societies often recruited these very agendas and their categories to their cause. In this situation, Osofisan's plays struggle, with increasing urgency throughout the early 1980s, to discover a form which will enable the oppressed within the new neo-colonial society to gain a voice. When *Esu and the Vagabond Minstrels* (first produced in 1984) was published in 1991, Osofisan announced in the preface that it was 'the second of my "Magic Boon" plays of which, hopefully, there will eventually be ten'. The first of this sequence, he proclaimed, had been *Once Upon Four Robbers* (1982), produced on stage in 1978. In these plays, the action would revolve around:

> a central dramatic motif borrowed and adapted from the world of folk-lore, namely a group of persons in a moment of desperation (caused by some social or political crisis) suddenly obtains, from some mysterious agent they come across, a magical power capable of altering their circumstances, provided of course that they use the power according to expressed injunctions. The play then is essentially a map of their adventures as they exploit this wonderful boon, teaching us in the process about themselves, their lives and their society.

The 'Magic Boon' formula reflects a conscious attempt to wed the plots common in Yoruba popular narrative to a politically conscious theatrical form. It also echoes the use of the fable form in Brecht's theatre.

For example, *Esu and the Vagabond Minstrels* tells the story of five vaga-bond minstrels, out of favour because of the services they have performed for the previous regime, and now desperate and starving. They are tricked by Esu (the Yoruba trickster God) into accepting a boon, that they can bring a change of fortune to anyone with whom they dance. Most of them select rich people

178

to help, and are denied by these once their fortunes are restored. One of them, however, called Omele, uses his power to assist a woman who has a pregnancy which will not resolve itself. He also cures a pair of lepers, who turn out to be the god Orunmila and his consort Osun. Thus he is tested twice, first by Esu and then by Orunmila. After the first divine testing, the audience is invited to participate in the decision. They are asked whether or not Omele should allow the leper/gods to take back their leprosy. The audience is invited to discuss the issue and vote on it. But at the end of the play this divine fable is replaced by a rejection of this as an acceptable resolution. The actors step out of role and refuse to participate in the action, which they characterise as a 'deceit'. In other words, they reject the magic nature of the fable in favour of social and political resolution. The ending is a series of exhortations: 'Kindness cannot be willed by the waving of a wand'.[11]

Although some elements of this 'Magic Boon' form persist in the later work, the fable element is less central. One can only suppose that Osofisan perceived that, as the ending of *Esu* suggests, the project 'missed the difference between reality and its many mirrors'. If the ultimate purpose of the fable is to recognise that divine intervention is a myth which prevents us from perceiving the social causes of injustice, then the idea of using this reversal of audience expectation in a series of ten plays seems unlikely to succeed in the conditions of performance which Osofisan faced. Since the work was now increasingly being performed in university theatres and other elite venues, with an audience drawn from a fairly self-contained community, the ending would soon become expected and lose its effect. These audiences were also far less likely to respond to the repetitive force of fable, and simply reject it as a recurring device on the grounds of over-familiarity. Paradoxically, of course, if the plays had been touring small, popular venues and playing to the audience of people Osofisan wanted to reach, these objections would have had less force.[12] Osofisan's more recent work – *Another Raft* (produced 1987; published in 1988), *Twingle-Twangle A Twynning Tale* (produced 1988; published in 1992), *Aringindin and the Nightwatchmen* (produced 1989; published in 1992) and *Yungba-Yungba and the Dance Contest* (produced 1990; published in 1992) – offers both a critique of the simplistic politics of the earlier period and a sophisticated analysis of how authoritarian regimes in post-colonial societies maintain their power and their material benefits as a ruling elite. These more recent plays continue to be critical of the traditional institutions, especially when they are employed as a device by the ruling elite to maintain their power. At the same time, they operate in and through the material basis of that traditional culture, employing its forms and concerns to illuminate the problems of contemporary Nigerian society. This renewed outburst of creativity demonstrates that Osofisan continued to take an optimistic view of the future of Nigeria, and of the role of the ordinary Nigerian in resisting corruption and authoritarian solutions to their problems, despite the ongoing series of failed civilian governments and the subsequent military coups.

Since the late 1980s Osofisan seems to have accepted the ineffectiveness of a classic Marxist class struggle to redress the ongoing problems of corruption and continuing authoritarianism. In a series of plays, from 1988 onwards, he analyses the contemporary issues facing Nigeria in more powerful and optimistic forms than the earlier work. The early advocacy of direct class struggle is replaced by a more complex analysis of Nigerian social structures, and the ongoing struggle against authoritarianism in Nigeria, in plays such as *Another Raft* (1988), his rewrite of J. P. Clark's famous allegory of Nigerian society *The Raft* (1964). J. P. Clark's *The Raft* was a classic early play, an allegorical look at the 'state of the nation' in the immediate post-independence period. In using this as the pre-text for his own contemporary political allegory, Osofisan is following his earlier practice of constructing palimpsestic texts which rewrite earlier classic works[13] (a practice inherited from his theatrical mentor, Şoyinka[14]). The most notable change in the long, allegorical play which Osofisan constructs on the framework of Clark's play is that, unlike Clark, Osofisan represents Nigerians as a group of people from a wide set of conflicting social and economic backgrounds. The play also provides a much more detailed account of the penetration of traditional culture by the corrupt values of modern, urban society.

Aringindin and the Nightwatchmen (1989) and *Yungba-Yungba and the Dance Contest* (1990) blend realistic social analysis with the 'heightened' dramatic language and action which Osofisan favours. They examine the problem of how to achieve social security without handing over freedom in the process. Aringindin, the returned soldier, approaches the modern politician, Kansillor (Councillor), with an offer to rid the market of thieves and robbers by initiating a vigilante force of 'nightwatchmen'. Opposed, at first, by the traditional ruler (the Baale), who emphasises the need to retain the links with older social values, his offer is embraced when Kansillor and he set up their own robberies to justify their take-over. Like many politicians before him, Kansillor learns too late that the 'strongarm' men he thinks will bring him to power are likely to overwhelm him, too, in the end. The play powerfully dramatises the dangers of authoritarian rule and the arguments, based on the need for law and order and economic stability, which are used to justify it. In this sense, it allegorises the contemporary politics of Nigeria, but it does so in a realistic, contemporary setting. The struggle for the town market is an effective microcosm of the larger conflict in Nigerian society, yet it also stands on its own as an effective dramatic 'world'.

In a similar vein, *Yungba-Yungba and the Dance Contests* examines the pressures against the successful maintenance of democracy in contemporary Nigeria. The daughters of three extended families or clans compete for the annual dance title of the water-goddess shrine. They discover that the priestess of the shrine now retains her position and power permanently, though traditionally it changed hands each year, passing to the new dance contest winner. The old method ensured that authority remained up-to-date, responsive and reflective of change. When the young dancers demand a return to the traditional system, the priestess, Iyanere, argues that by taking and retaining power she has prevented the internecine warfare that characterised the families' relations in the past. There is a direct analogy here with the justification offered by the military regimes of the period for seizing power, and their reluctance to hand it back to elected, civilian governments. The cynical way in which the strife of the three 'families' (symbols perhaps of the main Yoruba, Ibo and Hausa language groups in Nigeria) is deliberately encouraged by Iyanere dramatises the military government's technique for retaining power.

Another writer who has worked mainly in drama, Bode Sowande, presents a similar set of developments in aims and methods. Like Osofisan, Sowande claimed that theatre could become a 'weapon for the regulation of commercial values, or, conversely, for radical change'.[15] In *The Babylon Trilogy* Sowande offered a direct and immediate theatrical response to real-life events, tracing the experience of a group of young undergraduates, who are involved in the demonstrations which took place on Nigerian campuses after the Nigerian Civil War ended in 1970. The decade of demonstrations and riots which followed saw students in the forefront of the demand for justice and an end to corruption in government, as both civilian and military regimes failed to deal with Nigeria's growing problems. Echoing Jamaican Rastafarian usage, the term Babylon invokes corrupt, authoritarian governments, from which the students Moniran, Onita, Moye, Dabira, Nibidi and Ibilola strive to free themselves and their people. The first of the plays, *The Night Before* (produced 1972), is set on the night before they graduate to face the reality outside the university. It warns of the temptations and dangers which face them when they are called upon to take up leadership roles in the new Nigeria. In the second play, *A Farewell to Babylon* (produced in 1978), Moniran and Onita choose two very different ways to achieve their aim. Moniran opts to work for change from within the power structure. He becomes a member of the government, from which position of power he hopes to exert an influence for good. Drawn into the exercise of power, he is corrupted, and ends up as the head of the Secret Service, whose main task is to repress dissidence. Onita, on the other hand, adopts a classic oppositional stance, as a writer and activist on behalf of the rural poor. When Onita is arrested, Moniran's decision to place him in the same cell as a violent criminal leads to his friend's death. In the final play of the trilogy, *Flamingo* (produced in 1982), Moniran, disillusioned and in exile from his earlier role, has withdrawn from politics.[16] Despite his withdrawal, one of his friends from the first play, Nibidi, and the new emerging military dictator, Kasa, have him killed, as a possible threat to their power. The trilogy attempts to deal with specific modern situations, but fails to provide any really effective social or political analysis of the causes of the crisis in Nigeria. The purpose of the work seems to be to exhort the audience to continue to struggle towards improvement, and not to lose faith in the possibility of a better future. But the overthrow of Kasa by Teriba at the end of *Flamingo* does not offer a real change, only a new generation of coups.

Sowande's work is less exuberantly experimental than Osofisan's. But his range of subjects and settings is greater, embracing industrial relations and class conflict in plays like *Afamoko* (Yoruba for 'Workhorse', produced in 1978), which deals with a strike in a modern factory; corruption and crime in

The Master and the Frauds (produced in 1979); and political ideology and its conflicts in *Circus of Freedom Square* (produced in 1985). Plays like these dramatise the conflicts in modern Nigerian society, and their oppressive effect on the lives of ordinary people. *A Sanctus for Women*, which first appeared in 1976 as *The Angry Bridegroom*, follows the tradition of Ṣoyinka and Osofisan in using traditional legend and myth, in this case the legend of Olorombi, a woman who is forced to sell her only daughter to the god of wealth because of her poverty. Like Osofisan in *Morountodun*, Sowande employs the myth to deal with modern issues. In this case, the god becomes a symbol of systems which exploit people in the name of a higher good, but which in practice use their ignorance and willingness to force them to bow to authority. More recently, Sowande has turned to a more allegorical style in *Tornadoes Full of Dreams* (produced in 1989), and to themes which handle the broader historical reasons for authoritarianism and freedom. *Tornadoes Full of Dreams* is an ambitious play, a sweeping historical drama which covers the whole history of black struggles for freedom over the last three hundred years. It employs the history of slavery to explore contemporary issues, weaving the story of the slave revolts inspired by the French Revolution into an account of the horrors of the Middle Passage, creating from both an allegorical set of images which reflect the contemporary issues of modern Africa. Towards the end of the play, the historical characters metamorphose into contemporary figures, such as bankers and multinational businessmen, illustrating the continuity between roles through the different stages of history, and the causal links between them. This technique, which echoes that of Ṣoyinka in *A Dance of the Forests* (in which the figures of the modern period are counterparts to the figures in the court of the traditional king, Matu Kariba), shows how a line between texts that deal with modern issues and those that have legendary or historical settings can only be drawn tentatively, if at all. It also shows again the continuity of preoccupations, and even forms, from Ṣoyinka to the younger playwrights.

The radical rejection of the first generation's themes and settings, which argued for works which dealt directly with the problems of the modern period, now seem to have been less than adequate as an account either of the concerns of earlier generations, or of the current practice of the younger writers. In fact, when we look back at the texts produced in the late 1970s and 1980s, it is hard to see such a generational gap as simply or as clearly as the critical debate of the early 1970s would suggest. For example, the work of a writer such as Ola Rotimi, very much a part of the earlier generation, since he was born in 1938, illustrates how difficult it is to draw effective lines between the generation born in the 1930s and those born a decade or so later, or between committed and uncommitted writers, or even between writers who can be classified as popular and elite. All such categories reflect a critical desire for neatness and taxonomic clarity, which a detailed examination of the practice of particular writers continually frustrates. For example, Rotimi had written a number of plays, variously employing English, Yoruba and other Nigerian languages and admixtures of all of these, which draw on Yoruba historical material, such as *Kurunmi* (1971), *Ovonramwem Nogbaisi* (1974) and the unpublished, and still incomplete, two-part drama *Akassa youmi*, part one of which was produced in 1977.[17] In all of these plays historical events, such as the Ijaiye wars of the nineteenth century in the case of *Kurunmi*, the British expeditions against Benin City in *Ovonramwen Nogbaisi*, and the Akassa wars in *Akassi Youmi*, are used in various ways to make points which are relevant to the present, just as Ṣoyinka had done. However, as a number of critics have observed, Rotimi fails in these plays to provide the kind of political analysis of these past events which would give them a direct usefulness to the present situation.[18] The plays are primarily designed to recover and celebrate the past which colonialism has obscured, and so belong in many ways to that generation of celebratory writers, such as Achebe and Amadi, discussed in Chapter 6. Unlike other texts of that period, though, they do draw parallels for the audience with contemporary events. Elements in the play *Kurunmi* clearly invoke 'the conflict in the 1960s between the Action Group of Chief Obafemi Awolowo and the rival Nigerian National Democratic Party of his erstwhile deputy leader, Chief Samuel Ladoke Akintola', a breakdown which led indirectly to the outbreak of the Nigerian Civil War.[19] Significantly, the more popular work of Hubert Ogunde, *Yoruba roni* (or Think Yoruba!, 1964), showed a much sharper analysis of the consequences of this split, so much so that Ogunde's troupe was banned from performing this play in the Western region at the time. The fact that Ogunde's popular work in Yoruba had this effect illustrates how false it would be to characterise the work of such popular troupes as merely entertainment, or to set up some kind of inadequate serious/popular division in evaluating the importance of this kind of text. It is true that many of the plays produced in Yoruba by troupe leaders like Ogunde and Duro Ladipo had the kind of direct effect in shaping mass opinion that the university-based radical writers sought in vain and never really attained. Rotimi's work, though, shows, as we noted in the case of other writers, such as Achebe, that to characterise a writer by a single position or form is always dangerous and inadequate.

Rotimi's work in the 1980s shows a much stronger political commitment, and the interactions which clearly occurred between the generations of writers in the late 1970s can be seen to have had their influence on him, as they arguably did on the work of Ṣoyinka in the same period (for example in plays like *Opera Wonyosi*, the 1981 adaptation of Brecht's Beggar's Opera, *Requiem for a Futurologist* (1985), and the satirical *A Play of Giants* (1988), Ṣoyinka's most overt satirical attack on modern African dictatorships and their inflated pretensions). Rotimi's *If: A Tragedy of the Ruled* (1983) and *Hopes of the Living Dead* (1988) also move his work firmly into the present. In *If: A Tragedy of the Ruled*, Rotimi dramatises the interactions between the classes in modern urban Nigeria through the life of a tenement compound. As in many of Rotimi's plays, the characters range across the various linguistic and ethnic groups which make up modern Nigeria, and from the clashes between whom many of the modern conflicts have arisen. As Martin Banham observes, Rotimi's own background, with parents from different ethnic groups, was unusual for his generation, and may well account for the fact that his plays have consistently foregrounded the issue of inter-ethnic relations. *If* suggests that another way is possible than ethnic rivalry, if people would recognise their common condition: 'If . . . the masses, the oppressed masses will use their votes as a tool for their own freedom. IF that fails, then mass-struggle becomes imperative' (16). Despite this apparent revolutionary call to mass popular revolt, the politics of the play veer erratically between Marxist exhortation to mass struggle and a Christian message of individual moral change. In *Hopes of the Living Dead*, Rotimi returns to a historical setting, but this time the theme is not the heroic aspects of the distant past. Instead, it centres on the treatment of lepers, and the struggle of the Nigerian musician Ikoli Harcourt Whyte against leprosy in the recent past. Set in the Port Harcourt General Hospital in 1924, it shows the resistance, led by Harcourt Whyte, to the refusal of the colonial authorities to initiate a proper course of treatment for lepers. Rejecting the bribes offered by the colonial doctors to betray his fellows, Harcourt Whyte unites the lepers, who come from all the different ethnic and language groups of modern Nigeria, into an effective and successful resistance. The play dramatises the importance of self-help and organisation, as well as the need for a unity across the differences of language and culture within modern Nigeria. The play doesn't merely argue this, but shows in practice the need for cooperation, as the patients translate the various languages for each other. The fact that members of the audience need to participate in this awareness of difference, and may even have to cooperate amongst themselves in translating the dialogue for their neighbours, creates a practical dramaturgy for audience sympathy and involvement in the stage action. In his account of the play, Martin Banham has argued that 'These experiments with language are the political heart of the work'. In the same essay he quotes the review of the play by poet Niyi Osundare, in the journal *West Africa*, which says language is

> 'a vehicle for [the play's] dramatic thrust. So many times the stage turns into a cacophony of tribes as each character shouts his desperation in his own language. At such moments, tension takes possession and communal unity receives a savage punch. It is part of the abiding optimism of the play, however, that "though tribe and tongue may differ", a common problem steers the people towards a unified goal.' [20]

It is significant that Osundare should respond so positively to Rotimi's recent work, giving the lie to the simplification that, as a member of the younger and more radical generation, he is necessarily engaged on a different enterprise from that of earlier writers like Rotimi. It also reflects the fact that the recent work of writers like Rotimi and Ṣoyinka shows the influence of the younger generation of writers, and their call for more direct action. For example, Rotimi's character Hamidu, who makes such a call in *If: A Tragedy of the Ruled*, is a young doctor who has chosen to do his national work service in a distant rural area.

There seems little doubt that some of Ṣoyinka's work also modified itself towards a simpler, more directly interventionist style as a result of these leftist criticisms, beginning with the shift to a more direct agit-prop style in the mid-1980s, in *A Play of Giants* (1984) and *Requiem for a Futurologist* (1985). In his more recent work Soyinka, like Rotimi, calls for a more direct involvement of the intellectuals in the struggles of the masses. *The Beatification of Area Boy* (produced in 1996) is set outside one of the new shopping plazas which have sprung up to serve the needs of the Lagos elite, places which quickly accumulate a dependent sub-culture of street traders, and 'area boys', petty criminals who extort money from the wealthy shoppers with minor scams of various sorts. The play shows how this divided society is buttressed by the presence of expatriate companies, interested only in making profits, and by the violent force of the army, which crushes all resistance to the interests of the corrupt regime and its hangers on. As the petty criminals and traders of the Plaza area act out their struggle to survive, they are interrupted by the horrors of the forcible clearance of the Maroko district. This was a shanty town in Lagos, from which a million people were driven in 1991, during which clearance the army bulldozed and burnt the shanties in order, as Soyinka has asserted, to make the desirable, lagoon-side land available for commercial exploitation by the new rich. The historically ineffective and corrupted role of the Nigerian intellectual is dramatised in the figure of Sanda, a university drop-out who runs the street gangs of the area from his position as doorman of the Plaza complex, and in the figure of his ex-girlfriend, Miseyi, who has used her university education only as a stepping stone to enable her to marry the son of a corrupt rich local politician. Their decision to return to Maroko, after Miseyi runs away from her Plaza wedding to her mega-rich, corrupt fiancé, is a call by Soyinka to the young educated classes of Nigeria to resist being compromised either by cynicism or by the economic temptations of the new regime. But this new stance can also be seen to be a development from an older and continuous commitment to direct action by Soyinka, which predates the disputes with the younger radical writers, and which has its roots in his active opposition to the civil war. His recent self-exile, and his outspoken opposition to the military dictatorship of the late General Abacha and his successors, confirms his long and ongoing activist stance.

Odia Ofeimun, who, despite having produced only two collections of poetry, had a disproportionate influence in the debate, also provides an interesting slant on the issue of whether there really has been a 'generational' struggle in West African writing. Ofeimun's influence has probably much to do with the fact that his work became a literary test-case for the disputes between the generations. Ofeimun's first collection, *The Poet Lied and Other Poems* (1980), deliberately echoes the title of Soyinka's famous account of his arrest and imprisonment during the Nigerian Civil War, *The Man Died* (1972). It was the subject of a notorious lawsuit, in which John Pepper Clark sued Ofeimun, accusing him of libelling him in the title poem. In this poem, Ofeimun describes a poet who responds to the crisis of the civil war, not with the kind of potent political action of a Soyinka, but with a self-serving cowardice, justifying itself in terms of the artist's role being above politics and social struggle.

185

He wanted to be left alone
to spin his shallow legends, his shy songs
out of the bastardised living of his kind
out of the spectacle of aged mothers
defiled by maniacs
under the noses of their first-born.

He asked this much; to be left alone
to celebrate what his skin was too thick
to absorb. And for this
this and nothing else
he would write his name on the sands
and dare storms to blot it out. (41–2)

The case resulted in the withdrawal by Longman of the first edition of the collection published in 1980. Reissued in a local imprint in Nigeria in 1989,[21] the new edition had a famous postscript, which took the form of an interview with Ofeimun, conducted by one of the *bolekaja* critics, Onwuchekwa Jemie, for the Lagos-based *Guardian* newspaper. What makes the interview of especial interest is the fact that Odia Ofeimun, for all the reputation he had garnered from the libel case as a spokesman for the new radical and disaffected generation of Nigerian writers, takes a very conciliatory attitude. Jemie's questions make the provocative assumption that distinct opposed generations of writers did exist in Nigeria: 'How many generations do you see in modern Nigerian writing?' he asks. Ofeimun refuses to be drawn by this question. His reply, that little has happened in Nigerian writing since Tutuola, or as he amends, since Ṣoyinka and Achebe, that is new enough or different enough to constitute a new tradition, is predicated on the relative lack of a real alternative political or cultural force in Nigerian society. As he argues it,

> Usually literary schools are follow-ups to political and economic schools. I know writers enjoy making the claim that they have helped make changes in society. But the fact is that literary schools are just part of a socio-economic process. Where a major rupture has taken place in society, it is always very difficult for certain things – even in literature – to happen. May be I am being over-deterministic. The point is that not much has happened in our society for clear departures to be made from what went before.[22]

Ofeimun's point, that the disputes about commitment and radicalism in recent West African writing do not reflect any really decisive shift in the politics of the society, is an important one. He reacts with some scepticism in this interview, which took place in 1983, to the claims, made frequently in the 1970s, that a new generation of writers had emerged, radically different from their predecessors: 'I think that what has happened so far is that people who have read Ṣoyinka and Achebe, or read others who work within the same tradition, have simply joined the mainstream'. Jemie asks him, 'You mean you see no difference between this younger generation and the older one?' Ofeimun replies,

> Enough has not been written to warrant that kind of drawline. Maybe it is better to say that enough has not been published. Festus Iyayi's *Violence* and Ben Okri's

Landscapes Within have joined Kole Omotoso's consistent promise that something new is coming. But it is not yet quite arrived. Bode Sowande's works and especially Fẹmi Osofisan's *Morountodun, Once Upon Four Robbers*, and *Who Is Afraid of Solarin?* are in my view the left hand of a tradition of which Wọle Ṣoyinka is still the mainstream. (149–50)

It is over-simple to collapse the work of Achebe, Ṣoyinka and others of the early writers into a single category and a single consistent position, as I have already argued. In a similar way Ofeimun's analysis shows a rare acuity in refusing to draw a simple line between the new radical generation and the old, in terms of either its style or its politics.

Ofeimun's own poetry deserved more careful consideration than the notoriety over the single poem suggested. A careful, and not a prolific writer (his second volume *A Handle for the Flautist* did not appear until 1986 and his third *Under African Skies* not until 1990), he has been undeservedly neglected. Ofeimun's verse is deceptively simple. A strong and direct polemic is a feature of many poems, such as the early 'We Hurtle Down', subtitled 'for student politicians 1974', in which exhortation against corruption and hypocrisy is the main note. The poem records a hopeful belief that the young may successfully address the issues facing Nigeria:

> We hurtle down
> towards dunghills to bare
> the rancid fodder of our own,
> our father's ineptitudes?
>
> We hurtle down like maladies
> wishing to save and be saved
> from the drought in people's minds
> the drought in people's hearts
> breaking and getting broken on our way
>
> We are searching for answers.[23]

Ofeimun's refusal, a few years later, to draw any absolute line between the generations of writers, doesn't mean that his poetry didn't respond to the shift from imagery which incorporates esoteric and international images and references, to a more localised style and imagery. The poems are usually simple in diction and the imagery is one which draws on the local world, even as it exhorts and castigates the wider political and social failures of African post-independence regimes. The final image of the short, early poem 'Resolve' (1970) illustrates this well:

> We need no mourners in our stride
> no remorse, no tears,
> Only this: Resolve
> that the locust shall never again
> visit our farmsteads. (58)

The poems in the second volume, *A Handle for the Flautist and Other Poems* (1986), employ the same blend of political exhortation and popular, local imagery, though the tone has darkened considerably, as can be seen in the final verse of the poem 'The Drought and Us':

> We cannot beat the drought
> bowed at the feet of the rainmakers
> we cannot beat the drought
> leaving divination to the priests
>
> Let the millions rise (110)

The poems from this later collection show a definite debt to the work of Ṣoyinka and Okigbo, reflected in the more complex rhythms and imagery through which they build their effect. For example, in one of several poems Ofeimun writes to a group of journalists who stood up to the government, 'Beyond Fear', there are clear echoes of the later Okigbo, as Ofeimun blends traditional imagery with an elaborate diction and syntax and a wide range of cultural allusions:

> They were not mere hunters for scoops
> In a world turned schizoid by the dicta
> of death-worship in paper-money
> They pushed the moral handle beyond profit
> Beyond the arrogance of normless dictators
> marketeers of spilt milk, spilt hope, spilt minds
> They pushed the moral handle beyond fear.
>
> They were not hunters for scoops
> quarrying for arty banners in their bloody scare
> of maimed careers, maimed lives and cold deaths
> Happy to be seduced by the joy of being human
> human and alive they gripped the bitter tale
> of other lives within their own. They went
> to god as recklessly as only truth can go
>
> They would not romp after the dead
> like crocodiles in pilate's lake of tears. (114)

Ofeimun's later poems deal with a wide range of subjects, including the detention of Ngũgĩ wa Thiong'o by the Kenyan authorities, the Ghanaian leader Kwame Nkrumah, and the American moon landing. They also include poems which deal with his own time abroad, including one entitled 'The Raising of Lazarus', which is modelled 'after Rainer Maria Rilke'. The range of themes and styles suggests that Ofeimun does not feel bound by any commitment to 'decolonise' his writing in the narrow fashion advocated by the *bolekaja* critics in the 1970s. A poem such as 'Come to Our Rally' is one of his most successful attempts at blending political activism with a profoundly Nigerian sensibility and subject matter. Significantly, it does not eschew allusions to other cultural sources, such as the Bible or Shakespeare, where these are relevant, or where they are clearly part of what a modern literary Nigerian sensibility has appropriated from the cumulative effects of two hundred years of European contact:

Come to our rally
I said to the rain
in every sun
that found a blade of grass
renew the sap
from root to budding wish
dare to sing
of life as terminus
a splash of truth
with greenness as home
in the spurting wildness
of forest flowers

Come to our rally
I said to the rockhills
in every seed that dared
to rise
to the sower's itch
join the sparrows
wheeling out of nests
try the sky
with a festive measure
of flowering tassels
as though the time has come
to let a seachange
claim our faith
[...]
Do, come to our rally
I said to the thunder
in every axeman
that felled a tree, a god.
Arm the sagehood of coins
tossed at us by chaos
Raise dawn, raze down
the armed curse
of warlord and merchant price
in the purity of our birthcry
And where prophecy and parable
miss the bull's eye
be thou the weapon
of the weak:
'Destroy this temple'. (138–40)

The poet Niyi Osundare also belongs to the younger group of writers in Nigeria who argued that the use of elaborate diction and recondite allusions by the older writers had driven a wedge between the traditional and the modern, making poetry an esoteric rather than a popular form. Osundare's own father was a noted, traditional, oral poet. He has spoken feelingly of his father's practice and its influence on him and his verse. Osundare's concerns are less obviously political than Ofeimun's. In the early poem 'Poetry Is', which clearly references the many overt European classical allusions in Okigbo's early verse, and the complex diction of his work and that of the young Ṣoyinka, he sums up his alternative view of poetry's role, which is to be:

> not the esoteric whisper
> of an excluding tongue
> not a claptrap
> for a wondering audience
> not a learned quiz
> entombed in Graecoroman lore
>
> Poetry is
> a lifespring
> which gathers timbre
> the more throats it plucks
> harbinger of action
> the more minds it stirs
>
> Poetry is
> the hawkers' ditty
> the eloquence of the gong
> the lyric of the marketplace
> the luminous ray
> on the grass's morning dew
> [. . .]
> Poetry
> is
> man
> meaning
> to man. (*Songs of the Marketplace*, 1983, 3–4)

The title of this early collection, and that of the collection which followed in 1984, *Village Voices*, seem to reflect the *bolekaja* critics' demand that Nigerian verse return to traditional themes and imagery. But a closer examination of Osundare's verse reveals that it is not averse to using allusions to European texts, nor to employing a diction ('luminous ray', 'lowering eaves') in which debts to English Romantic verse might be legitimately detected. Perhaps the most important element of Osundare's claim to embody traditional usage comes in the rhythm of his verse, rather than its diction or themes. In the later collections, he records the fact that many of his poems are written to the beat of a specific traditional drum or gong. In performance, he insists on the use of the appropriate instrument, which echoes and amplifies the sound and metre of the verse. In the preface to his 1990 collection, *Songs of the Season*, he explicitly claims that 'written poetry has remained . . . an alienated and alienating enterprise in Nigeria – a painful irony in a country where every significant event is celebrated in song, drum and dance' (v–vi).

However, Osundare has also been at pains to emphasise that his return to traditional forms was not merely nostalgic or sentimental. He saw it as part and parcel of a wider political attitude, expressed in the need to restore the traditional, public role of the poet as critic and chastiser of social wrongdoers.

Invoking the example of his father, a traditional songster and poet, he has spoken of the vital role traditional poetry played in the life of the community, castigating and satirising social injustice, and exposing anti-social actions by individuals.[24] The traditional practice of composing songs which obliquely exposed social wrongdoers informs much of Osundare's own work, though his targets are as likely to be agencies or government policies as specific people. Even early collections, such as *Village Voices*, show a political edge in poems such as 'The New Farmer's Bank' and 'The Politician's Two Mouths'. The venality of politicians, and the greed of individuals, are linked in Osundare's work to a deep concern with ecology, and with the need to maintain and protect the natural world to which man is inextricably tied. In fact, Osundare is arguably one of the most explicitly eco-conscious of modern African writers, as is witnessed by poems such as 'Our Earth Will Not Die', from the 1986 collection *The Eye of the Earth*, which ends in the exhortatory lines 'Our earth will not die . . . Our earth will see again / this earth, OUR EARTH' (50–1).

Other poems from this same collection, such as 'The Green Peace', 'Operation Stop the Desert', and 'The Save the Amazon Committee', show clearly that Osundare's respect for the local and the traditional is not in opposition to his wider global and international concerns. His work weds a concern with world-wide issues, such as ecology and the environment, to a specific, African context, giving the lie to the simplistic idea that the local and the global can ever be perceived as ontologically distinct regimes. Osundare's later work has encompassed a wider pan-African framework, with poems dealing with Nelson Mandela and with events such as the Sharpeville Massacre. Nevertheless, despite these wider themes, Osundare's work continues to embrace a programme of stylistic decolonisation, with its emphasis on the local and specific, and its fusion of English verse forms with Yoruba oral and written forms. In many ways, his style echoes the cultural fusions which the earlier Ghanaian writer Kofi Awoonor had developed. His poetry remains populist in the best sense of the word. Although less specifically political than some of his contemporaries, his work always satirises the excesses of the ruling classes and celebrates the life of ordinary people.

The claim that there was a new and radically different school of writing in the 1970s, like most critical claims to new schools, was, as noted earlier, exaggerated, but it served to draw attention to some significant shifts in the themes and styles of West African, especially Nigerian, poetry from the mid-1970s onwards.[25] It sought to identify in this new poetry a greater concern with socio-economic problems and a more local focus in theme and form, emphasising links to traditional material and images. It also claimed the new poetry was less susceptible to the modernist echoes of English and American poets, which, it argues, were characteristic of the work of the first generation of writers. But a careful scrutiny of the poetry does not show, as Ofeimun, Ojaide and others have argued, a simple and absolute division into separate schools along the lines suggested by the early *bolekaja* critics.

A number of prose writers who emerged in the late 1970s and 1980s also addressed the issues facing contemporary Africa from a radical perspective.

Novelists like Festus Iyayi, Isidore Okpewho and others took up the theme of the gaps which had opened up between rich and poor in many parts of post-independence Africa, gaps which could no longer be blamed simply on colonial history but which needed to be sheeted home to the greed of a new elite working hand in hand with international multi-capitalism. Festus Iyayi's novel *Violence* (1979) presents a harsh view of the exploitation of peasant workers by the new rich class. The story of Idemudia and his wife Adisa allows Iyayi to paint a bleak picture of the daily existence of many ordinary Africans, with Idemudia trapped in thrall to the brothel-owner Queen and her contractor husband Obofun. In a series of vignettes, Iyayi sketches the impossible struggle of Idemudia to survive as his labour is exploited by Queen, who refuses even to pay him his meagre wages on time. He shows how Idemudia, his health broken by unremitting labour, accidents and by the weakness resulting from his having had to sell his blood to survive, is hospitalised, and is then trapped in a system which refuses to allow him to leave until his bill is paid. Meanwhile, Obofun exploits the situation by demanding sexual favours from Adisa in return for his help. Queen equally seeks to exploit Idemudia sexually, since Obofun has neglected her in favour of his mistresses. This helps Idemudia to understand the pressures on Adisa, and in the end they are reconciled.

Iyayi's second novel, *The Contract* (1982), shows how the foreign-educated and idealistic Ogie is introduced, on his return, to the corruption which has become endemic in Nigeria. At first, he believes that he can resist the trends and remain honest, but he soon becomes sucked into the world of corrupt business practice. The novel concentrates on the world of the new contractors, and shows how difficult it is for anyone to resist these practices in a society where corruption has become endemic.

Although the theme of corruption has been a particularly strong element in recent writing from Nigeria, examples of the same impulse can also be found elsewhere in Anglophone West Africa – for example in Ghana, where the early social and political criticisms of writers like Kofi Awoonor, Ama Ata Aidoo and Ayi Kwei Armah are picked up and developed, though perhaps with less bitterness, in the work of younger novelists like Kojo Laing, or in the poetry of Kofi Anyidoho.

Kofi Anyidoho's work establishes him as one of the most influential and prolific of the recent Ghanaian writers. A critic, editor and theatre director, he is best known perhaps as a poet. His work has received less critical attention than it deserves, despite the fact that he has produced four book-length collections, as well as innumerable essays, and has co-edited a very useful anthology of recent African poetry, and several important essays, including a powerful pamphlet on 'The Pan-African Ideal in Literatures of the Black World'. His first poetry collection, *Elegy for the Revolution*, published in the USA in 1978, exhibits a concern with the same themes that preoccupy his Nigerian contemporaries: the failure of post-independence regimes to ensure a fair society, and the growing inequalities of wealth and opportunity between rich and poor. The use of traditional images, and a debt to indigenous forms and rhythms, is just as marked here as in the Nigerian work discussed. In fact, perhaps because of the example of the older Ghanaian tradition of Kofi Awoonor, who had already, in the 1960s, successfully blended Ewe oral forms and English poetic structures, Anyidoho's poetry shows an easy mastery of this transcultural style.

For example, in the first of the poems in the 'Suite for Revolutionaries' from his first collection *Elegy for the Revolution*, entitled 'Our Birth-Cord', he blends the traditional image of the birth-cord, a central feature in West African religious ideas of re-birth and social continuity, with the idea of personal and public responsibility. A cumulative series of images, in the style of traditional Ewe oral poetry, drives home the message of the ongoing need for traditional communal values in the modern world of power politics and western 'global' values.

> a piece of meat lost in cabbage stew
>> it will be found   it will be found
>
>> If we must die at birth, pray
>> we return with our birth-cord still uncut
>> our oneness with earth undefiled
>
>> Last night on the village square a man
>> bumped into my conscience and cursed
>> our god. I refused to retort, knowing
>> how hard it is for man to wake a man
>> from false slumber
>> Our conscience would not be hurt
>> by threats of lunatics
>
> a pinch of salt lost in cabbage stew
>> it will be found   the tongue will feel it out. (10)

In the second collection, *A Harvest of Our Dreams* (1984), the influence of Kofi Awoonor's example is even stronger, and the use of a traditional rhythm and syntax more marked. But a distinctive, personal voice is already present too, as the themes of memory, loss and betrayal are woven into images which acknowledge their source in traditional performance verse. The long poem entitled 'Fertility Game' is prefaced with the rubric: *'In a public performance the opening line should be repeated by the audience throughout the entire poem'*. This injunction is reminiscent of the attempt by Anyidoho's Nigerian contemporary, Osundare, to bring traditional performance elements to bear on the public performance of his verse, as when Osundare insists on drum accompaniment for the public reading of his poems. Like Osundare, Anyidoho's Ewe background, which he shares with Kofi Awoonor, is rich in drum tradition and he is himself an accomplished drummer.

> Come back home Agbenoxevi come back home
>
> Agbenoxevi Atsu Agbenoxevi
> I have held my passion in check for you
> holding it fast against storms against thunder
> held it firm against the haunting smiles of gods.
> I have strained my bosom against the sharp edges

of harmattan winds against the rumbling weight
of May rainstorms.
I am the rainbow standing guard across
your path of storms.
Atsu I have died a hundred deaths for you.
Each time each night I wake up again and again
in that house we built upon the shores
with pools of troubled seas

        Come back home Agbenoxevi come back home. (20)

It is important not to assume that these are merely translations, or even adaptations, of existing oral poems. The oral element is employed to shape and focus themes and concerns – in a sense it functions as a signifier of the *cultural difference* which Anyidoho has made the interior theme of poems, whose surface theme may be something quite different. For example, some of the poems allude to staple subjects of traditional verse (wisdom of age versus arrogance of youth, for example) but the form is not strictly that of traditional verse. The oral dimension of a poem like 'Nunya', from the collection *Harvest of Our Dreams*, is contained within a conventional literary form, a dramatic monologue, in which the voice of the speaker inserts orality into the written verse:

Ha ... ha ... ha ... ha ... ooo ... yi!
Let me laugh a small laugh as though
my heart were doing a dance of joy.
Your tongue, our brother, is a dawn breeze
spreading peace upon an orphan's fear for eyes
of day but my mother's husband's youngest son
do not eat salt and give yourself heartburns.
I know you've seen the world through windows
in your school, and they say your view is sharp.
Yet you are only our little darling master.
I saw my moon in many many skies before
your sun first raised his head into our clouds.
Please please do not frown and sneer into my face.
I do not deny that even a child may have wisdom. (14)

Yet, as the poem progresses, the images it employs increasingly invoke the specific diction and lexis of Ewe orature, and the body of traditional Ewe orature, so that we recognise that the form referenced here is not the Western dramatic monologue, but Ewe spoken-verse:

So you see my mother's master child?
There is no absolute knowledge
to the waywardness of life's byways.
These little cassava sticks of mine
have left their mark on several tracks of life.
But the thing I chased exchanged his feet for wings
and I am a hunter come home with a basketful
of wild tales of how it is today that the cooking pot
must sleep mouth-down in a corner of the old kitchen. (15)

194

The issue of what relations now exist between orature and writing in contemporary Africa is a vexed one, and would need a separate volume as large as this to handle it adequately. But verse like Anyidoho's indicates that the influence of oral forms is not always a matter of simple transcription, or borrowing, but a complex series of influences in both directions, whose mutual effect changes the whole linguistic, generic and cultural register involved. In the case of a poem like 'Nunya', it is hard to say whether orality is a part of the form or the theme itself, and in a sense it is clear that it is both. Anyidoho's verse, with its very sophisticated and different embodiments of orality, makes it abundantly clear that the idea of a cultural decolonisation achievable by a return to the forms and images of traditional culture, along the lines of Chinweizu's abjuration, is a gross simplification. Inevitably, writing itself overlays the process of employing oral elements, and indeed, as other critics have noted, orality itself is constantly in flux as it engages with the power of writing both as a direct influence and as a sign of difference and modernity.[26]

Another significant recent West African poet is the Nigerian, Tanure Ojaide. Ojaide's work shows the extent to which this generation's concerns emerge from the older concerns more clearly than most. His first volume of poems, *Children of Iroko* (1973), is very strongly influenced by the work of Christopher Okigbo and is, as the poet acknowledged, often very personal in theme, embracing the idea of the poet as exile from his society and the idea of the poet as myth-maker and special being. His second and subsequent volumes adopted a much more radical and populist approach. Ojaide has contributed a very clear and lucid account of the mutual debts of the different generations in West African writing in his 1989 critical essay 'The Changing Voice of History: Contemporary African Poetry' (1989).[27] He argues that there are discernible differences between the 'new' and 'old' schools of Nigerian poetry, reflecting the degree of influence on the older and younger generations of European and local traditions.[28] However, Ojaide recognises that a poet like Okigbo had already started the shift. More importantly, perhaps, he also recognises that this shift was the result of a two-way influence, in which the preoccupations of the older poets, notably Ṣoyinka, also shifted under the influence of the preoccupations of the new generation, whilst that new generation continued to be influenced by the older models and writers. As Nwachukwu-Agbada and other African commentators have shown, many of these writers used proverbs and riddles as structuring devices in ways which look back to the work of the late Okigbo, and also to the practice of the first generation of novelists, such as Achebe. As Nwachukwu-Agbada argues it: 'The riddle mode is a fairly common feature of Nigerian poetry of the Eighties. By "riddle" one is referring not to the traditional question–response model but to the mode of what Kongas Maranda calls the "hidden term" which is the common ground of all riddle traditions.'[29] He illustrates this with references to poems by Niyi Osundare, Femi Osofisan and Tanure Ojaide, for example in one of Ojaide's poems from the 1986 collection, *Labyrinths of the Delta*:

> They arrive at night with snares
> And trucks to loot her market
> They club her totem pet, spit at her feet
> . . .
> And as if they have been in a furnace,
> They race out with cries of burning winds;
> As if mendicants were their hosts,
> They sing their children obscene songs;
> As if they caravaned the moon
> They speak eloquently of vacant streets. (57)

A further significant stylistic shift in the 1980s was the move to a much more widespread use of pidgin as a vehicle of poetic expression: 'Before the Eighties, most of the poets considered pidgin outside the lofty language of poetry and failed to utilise it. . . . But in 1982 Aig-Imoukhuede returned to pidgin poetry, this time with a bumper harvest, while Mamman Vatsa published a full volume of pidgin poems in 1985.'[30]

An army general as well as a poet, Mamman Vatsa was executed by the military regime in 1986 on charges of planning to overthrow the government. The recent execution of Ken Saro-Wiwa and the other Ogoni activists draws international attention to the fact that many other writers in Nigeria have also suffered the same fate, as have many other opponents of elitist post-colonial African regimes. The use of pidgin is often, but not always, tied to an oppositional stance. As the lingua franca of the urban poor, it is a suitable vehicle for the concerns of both these poets with the life of the ordinary masses. These social concerns are obvious in Aig-Imoukhuede's poem 'Sufferhead', from the double collection *Pidgin Stew and Sufferhead* (1982), though the poem does not reflect as strong a pidgin usage as others in the same volume.

> Suffering and praying
> Hustling and preying
> Scratching and slaving,
> Only reward for poor man;
> grumbling and hard work! (28)

The poems in this collection also directly address the issue of military governments and their oppressive use of force:

> By force no'be likeness
> Rape na rape
> Whether na gun or strong prick. (1)

Other poets also took up the use of pidgin, for example Ezenwa-Ohaeto in the very popular collection, *I Wan Bi President* (1988). The title poem sums up the way in which pidgin could be used to speak for the poor, and also to undermine elite claims to be working on behalf of the 'man in the street', that ubiquitous phrase of Nigerian political rhetoric.

> I never see President hungry
> I never see President thirsty
> President no go worry for road

196

Police no stop am for checking
President no go worry for house
Na government cook dey prepare food
Na government dry cleaner dey wash cloth
Na him make I wan bi President. (34)

Clearly pidgin offered a new form to exploit in the drive to radicalise African English writing, but even in West Africa, where it was most active, it did not replace the continued use of appropriated Standard English.[31] It is, perhaps, not inappropriate to end this brief account of some of the recent attempts to generate new forms in West African English writing with reference to the work of the late Ken Saro-Wiwa. His innovative and powerful novel *Sozaboy* (1985), which employs modified pidgin, which he terms 'rotten English', will be discussed in the section below on the texts dealing with the Nigerian Civil War.[32] He is also one of those writers who have attempted self-publication, to resist the control implicit in African writing being 'owned' by foreign presses.[33] He has also been a successful contributor to both popular radio and television shows in Nigeria. Ironically, Saro-Wiwa's literary work has received wider international attention since the tragedy of his execution, with other Ogoni activists, by the military government of General Sani Abacha in 1995. Saro-Wiwa was born in part of what declared itself as Biafra, though as an Ogoni he was not a member of the dominant Ibo ethnic group in the breakaway republic. At the outbreak of the war, he left his university job at Nsukka and returned to Lagos, since, like a number of other intellectuals from the Eastern regions, he opposed the secession of Biafra.[34] He was appointed Administrator for the River States town of Bonny when it was recaptured by Federal Forces, and later became Federal Commissioner for the River States. This earlier commitment to federalism is ironic, given his later opposition to the discriminatory, centralist policies of the national government towards regional, minority peoples such as the Ogoni, and the characterisation of him by the Nigerian military junta as a treasonable separatist. His early poetry also reflects a pacifism which is hard to reconcile with the violent image of him as a revolutionary, gun-toting activist promoted by the Abacha military regime:

I have sat at the machine all day
Waiting hopefully to find music
To soothe my troubled soul
But there is nothing
Save the monotonous rhythm of rain
The thumping thud of bombs

Over there at the front, young men
Clubber one another to the din
Of mortar shells and rockets
They groan painfully and die
For a cause they barely understand.

Perhaps they must die
So we live for ever.
For this have we told the lie

The famous lie about the sweet and honour
That lie in dying for one's country.
But death is a taskmaster
And only the living can know
That honour and sweet we preach
To them that are to die . . .[35]

A collection of short stories, *A Forest of Flowers*, followed in 1986, in which he varies tales of a rural environment with a second half which has a more urban setting. Although these stories use some pidgin, they are generally written in a standard Nigerian English which does not show the experimental vein of language he was to develop so dramatically in *Sozaboy* the following year. In 1989 Saro-Wiwa published a second collection, *Adaku and Other Stories*, which centres on the plight of Nigerian women. In the late 1980s, the series of 'Jebs Prison' books marks the emergence of Saro-Wiwa as a writer dedicated to exposing the viciousness and corruption of the contemporary ruling elite in Africa. The imaginary Jebs Prison, set up by the Organisation of African States on an imaginary artificial island in the sea off Lagos's notorious Bar Beach, the site of earlier public executions, allows Saro-Wiwa to show his talent for biting satire. The motley crew of dissidents imprisoned here illustrate the paranoia of the contemporary elite, who can imagine that figures like this represent a threat to their security. The prison and its policies allow Saro-Wiwa to develop a fable of contemporary Africa, which targets the role of corrupt politicians, businessmen and intellectuals in buttressing corrupt regimes. The two books, *Prisoners of Jebs* (1988) and *Pita Dumbrok's Prison* (1991), began as a series of articles in the Lagos-based newspaper *Vanguard*, and many of the figures in these *romans-à-clef* were readily identifiable by their local audience.

The author also of a large number of children's books and a collection of folk-tales, in addition to several polemic essays on modern Nigeria, by the time of his execution Ken Saro-Wiwa had earned a reputation as one of Nigeria's most prolific and talented writers. It is a tragedy that his voice was silenced in such a brutal and appalling way. Still only in his mid-fifties, he was clearly destined to become one of the more powerful of the younger voices of modern Africa. It is an irony of the global interest in the dramatic and the media-worthy event, that it took his grotesque and bloody execution to make Saro-Wiwa a globally known figure. Overnight, he became the most recent and most renowned of the many writers in Africa who have fallen victim to the violence of authoritarian regimes and their supporters. It is a tribute to these writers and to the spirit of other African intellectuals that they have always refused to allow these vicious events ever to silence them or lessen their courage.

In East Africa, pidgin forms of English were never well-established, since the older lingua franca, ki-Swahili, was already in use to facilitate inter-linguistic exchange amongst the speakers of the various indigenous languages before the impact of colonialism was felt in many regions. As a result, it has not been a major feature of recent East African writing. The use of highly modified forms of English is usually restricted to the dialogue, and is a notably stronger feature in the popular fiction. As we have already noted, in East Africa there has been a self-conscious drive to return to indigenous languages by writers who had previously worked in English, such as Ngũgĩ and Ogot. This has also been associated with the political task of decolonising the culture. Nevertheless, appropriated English continues to be used by writers with a strong oppositional, political programme. The Kenyan poet Jared Angira, for example, strongly supports political reform in his verse, even though it remains rather literary in its basic forms. Although Angira's verse incorporates many local images and influences, the political messages are framed in poems whose references remain complex and multicultural. In this respect, as in some others, such as his choice of theme and diction, Angira resembles some West African poets, whose influence he acknowledges. Since 1970, Angira has produced six verse collections. In the preface to the first, *Juices* (1970), Angira ironically juxtaposes Shakespeare, Milton and local East African writers like Taban lo Liyong ('Bill and Milton expressed much concern over a man called Taban lo Liyong. They feared for space to store the piles of lists of overwritten, overquoted names that were being given as verdicts') with direct political commentary:

> Anyway the new government . . . the government headed by Monsieur Opportunity . . . has done away with that Ministry and instead introduced the vital Ministry of Speculation and Gambling. Card-houses, casinos and turf-accountants have arrived on the scene with revolutionary speed. Thanks to rapid development skywards. Let's hope the sky will clear tomorrow. (10)

It concludes with a direct statement of his radical intention in writing, which is both to reflect his own time and condition, and to effect changes in them:

> the shadow of Karl Marx seems to give my trembling self some consolation; for how can I talk of the tower of Babel without recording the presence of the ground on which the tower stands? It is this ground I want to understand, it is this much trampled on ground that decides the course, for if the ground is sandy and porous how long can the tower stand? (12)

The tone of the poems in Angira's first collection, *Juices*, varies from the nostalgic and elegiac tone of 'Dusk on my Village':

> Green girls in salad time
> from waterholes and rivers
> proudly climb the gentle slope
> with quiet pots
> as shepherds count
> the beads on their waists (29)

through the understated social critique of the ending of a poem like 'On Market Day at Ugunja':

> It may be peacetime we know
> but under the fig tree
> are clubs and shields
> ropes for our bulls
> axes and jembes for our farms
> and all for
> nationbuilding (21)

199

to the emergence of a much more direct political message in poems like 'One Pot', with its implicit criticism of the self-serving nature of party politics in modern Kenya:

> Politicians
> from the reeds
> from the hills
> from where potatoes thrive
> from where carvers crowd
> from where the palmtree sings
> Great combatants
> come trotting
> to duel for Uhuru
> the old saying
> two cocks never cook
> in one pot
> shall be proven false
>
> tomorrow the new party
> a hostile party
> then the liberators
> each cock crows
> on its village gate. (52)

The collection ends on a strident note with the bitter and powerful poem 'Rape 1', in which the body of the young abused woman seems almost to be a symbol for modern Kenya:

> For there . . .
> she lay nude to the world
> her belly tattooed
> her blood spilt across
> and ere I could inquire
> . . . curfew
> . . . martial law
> and I longed no more to see her nude. (59)[36]

The occasional poeticisms and self-conscious references of this first collection could not hide the fact that in Angira a powerful new voice had emerged in East Africa. In the collections which have followed, the themes have remained the same, but the assurance and skill have deepened. A poem in homage to Chris Okigbo, in the second collection, *Silent Voices* (1972), indicates the conscious debt Angira acknowledges to the Nigerian poet, and illustrates how links and influences continue to act across and between the different generations and the different regions of African English writing. Like Okigbo, Angira refuses to restrict his references to the merely local, but his verse, like that of the later Okigbo, has a confident resonance, rooted both in observation of the African world, and in an acute and powerful analysis of the failure of the politics of post-independence Africa to live up to its promise. The poem 'No Coffin, No Grave' from *Silent Voices* (1972) illustrates both:

He was buried without a coffin
without a grave
the scavengers performed the post-mortem
in the open mortuary
without sterilized knives
in front of the night club

stuttering rifles put up
the gun salute of the day
that was a state burial anyway
the car knelt
the red plate wept, wrapped itself into blood its master's
the diary revealed to the sea
the rain anchored there at last
isn't our flag red, black and white?
so he wrapped himself well

who could signal yellow
when we had to leave politics to the experts
and brood on books
brood on hunger
and schoolgirls
grumble under the black pot

sleep under torn mosquito net
and let lice lick our intestines
the lord of the bar, money speaks madam
woman magnet, money speaks madam
we only cover the stinking darkness
of the cave of our mouths
and ask for our father who is in hell to judge him
the quick and the good

Well, his diary, submarine of the Third World War
showed he wished
to be buried in a gold-laden coffin
like a VIP
under the jacaranda tree beside his palace
a shelter for his grave
and much beer for the funeral party

anyway one noisy pupil suggested we bring
tractors and plough the land. (46–7)

An early poem like this illustrates just how quickly Angira achieved a complex and subtle poetic voice, one which challenged the reader in its aesthetic and political range. We are a long way here from the simplistic world of 'calabashes and iron bells', which Ṣoyinka had suggested was the implication of Chinweizu *et al.*'s 'neo-Tarzanism', yet it would be difficult to claim that this poetry is not rooted in a profoundly African sensibility. What Angira appears to have borrowed from both Okigbo and Ṣoyinka is a wide-ranging referential net, and an acute sense of the multivalent meanings of poetic image and phrase.

A shorter poem from the same collection, 'Mirage', embodies the last quality, wedding a deceptively simple diction to a complex set of effects:

> For all the salt
> it's a fibrous existence here
> they swore
> the sun would never sink
> and now its dusk
>
> It has rained
> and what difference
> has it made to the ocean?
>
> I try to catch
> the footsteps of past
> I fail
> and I ask
> didn't the auditors
> check the accounts?
>
> Peasants
> in cocoons of livelihood
> heave in cinders of hope
> And yet
> the end of the road
> is at the water's edge
>
> behind the wall
> classics shout in dusty shelves
> and cockroaches examine them
> with no symptoms of insanity
> so the owner empties
> bottles at the bar. (78–9)

In the later collections, such as *Soft Corals* (1973), Angira has successfully tackled a number of longer poems, for example, 'singing along the palm-beach road' (9–18) and 'the bats of shimo la tewa' (150–3). But it is in the short lyric that his best work has been done. The simple tone of some of these in the later collections emphasises the fact that Angira's verse never neglects its social role, and although the recent verse seems to have lost some of its more obvious complexity, it still resonates with irony. The lyric 'The Stage', from the 1979 collection, *Cascades*, illustrates my point:

> We have left the stage
> For men of the age.
> The loud-talking Christians,
> The sweet-tongued politicians.
>
> The new moon comes and goes
> Illuminating our shadows on the seas,
> The noonday sun burns and woes
> Drying the little we have on our knees.

Over the platform roar the politicians
A new arrival, packet of lies;
Over the pulpit shout the Christians
A new revival, new version of rites.

And in their race to excel
A loud talking at the park
They lose the battle
Into a new religion:
Fighters at the frontline,
Soldiers at the helm,
Arguments abandoned! (129)

As in West Africa, the political concerns in recent East African writing reach back across the generations. In the later work of the first generation of English-language writers, like Ngũgĩ, a more overtly oppositional politics emerged, as he combined the celebration of pre-colonial cultures with a growing awareness that there had been a betrayal of the national liberation struggle. Onto this concern was grafted an increasing awareness of the need to forge an effective opposition to the corrupt post-independent elite.[37] But, since Ngũgĩ's more radical work, after *Petals of Blood*, has also involved him in a struggle over the politics involved in language choice, and in the broader issues of decolonisation involved in such cultural choices, these texts will be reserved for discussion in a separate section below which looks at these texts in more detail.

Interestingly, in many parts of East Africa novels and plays have been employed by a number of historians and political scientists, who have written one or more fictional works embodying their views on contemporary society. Although this is not unknown in West Africa, as the earlier discussion of Kole Omotoso's *Just Before Dawn* shows, it seems to have been a more frequent phenomenon in East African writing. There are a number of earlier precedents for this excursion into fictionalised social commentary by social scientists and historians from East Africa, beginning in 1971 with Ali Mazrui's controversial allegory *The Trial of Christopher Okigbo*, in which Mazrui imagines the Igbo poet Okigbo summoned to a trial in the heavens. During the trial, he is asked to defend his decision, as an intellectual, to participate as a fighting soldier, and to lose his life in the Biafran cause, during the Nigerian Civil War. Although out of our strict area of geographical concern in this volume, a similar example is Zimbabwean historian Stanlake Samkange's *On Trial for my Country* (1966), in which the Matebele national heroes of old hold an *indaba,* or traditional council, to examine who was responsible for handing over the country to the whites. At about the same time, Gabriel Ruhumbika's *Village in Uhuru* (1969) uses the novel form to present a political case for Ujamaa, the Tanzanian form of socialism initiated by Nyerere's TANU party.[38] More recently, fictional works, such as that of the Ugandan political historian and novelist Grace S. K. Ibingira, are explicit in claiming in their title their political purpose, for example *Bitter Harvest: A Political Novel* (1980). This powerful text is a direct and unvarnished account of the situation in Uganda after independence. Although the country is not named, the details make it quite clear that this is a factual picture of Uganda in the 1960s and early 1970s. It portrays a corrupt regime, obviously that of Obote which suppresses dissent by imprisonment and beatings. The military coup against corruption with which the novel ends offers a temporary relief, but the young officers who lead it do not inspire confidence in their ability to effect any real change in the situation the country faces, a perception all too sadly borne out by real life events, when Idi Amin Dada instituted his dictatorial rule of terror and violence. Francis Deng's Sudanese novel *Seed of Redemption: A Political Novel* (1986) offers a similar example of this direct claim to political comment, though Deng has also since written the less explicitly sub-titled *Cry of the Owl* (1989).

One of the more extreme examples of this wedding of literary genre and political content is Akena Adoko's long epic poem *Uganda Crisis* (1970). It presents a detailed account of the Ugandan revolution of Dr Milton Obote in 1966, against the Bugandan ruling elite, led by Sir Edward Mutesa, the *Kabaka* of Buganda (the playboy 'King Freddy', as he was known, whose social antics were regularly featured in the British popular press in the late 1960s). This fascinating text is not without its historical ironies now, especially the section entitled 'Independence Anniversary: Celebration Plot'. This is illustrated by a photograph of the young Colonel Idi Amin with the caption, 'Was the greatest stumbling block to the liquidation plot'. The section celebrates how Amin saved Obote from assassination by the Bugandan ruler's agents. Obote's later dictatorial and autocratic career also presents an ironic contrast to his idealised portrait here as a dedicated democrat and 'great parliamentarian'. From the point of view of the history of African English writing, the significance of the formal elements of the text are more enduring than these flawed political judgements. The choice of short verse lines to present what is in effect a historical essay on the Ugandan revolution of 1966 is a classic interface of political message and what, in Euro-American terms, we might see as the distinctive and opposed discourses of literature and political history. This emphasises that in African English writing these two discourses have been frequently conjoined. In these texts, the idea of literature as a 'private' realm, opposed to, or set over against, the 'public' discourse of politics, is dissolved. It is also significant that the East African text chooses the long poem rather than the extended prose narrative as its form. This reflects the frequent use of long verse as a narrative form in a wide variety of East African writing, for example in the poems of Okot p'Bitek, and in such popular forms as David Maillu's novels.[39] In comparison, as we saw earlier, the casting of political history into narrative in West African English writing has tended to use long prose forms, as in Omotoso's *Just Before Dawn*, which shares many of the concerns of Adoko's text. In Adoko's case, however, the verse form is often merely a matter of typographical presentation, with the words really being standard discursive prose broken into verse lines:

On the eleventh February
Obote met delegates
'Things in Kampala are bad'
They told him, and then went on,
We have come to advise you
Give away the Government
To our Lieutenant Colonel
Okoya whom you know well. (62)

or even more prosaically in passages such as:

One member then quickly moved
A motion congratulating
All Members of Parliament
Who refused to swear an oath
Under the Constitution
In accordance with the orders
Given by the Lubiiko. (90)

The sections which rise above this pedestrian and prose-like diction and syntax are those which reflect the usages and aims of older, oral forms, such as the praise-song. For example the opening, entitled 'Imperialism, Feudalism and Nationalism', is a dramatisation of the two opposed leaders, the playboy *Kabaka*, 'King Freddy', and the emerging nationalist leader, Obote, the man of the people. The lines describing Obote are redolent with the elements of traditional praise-poetry:

Here then was a ruler who
Was one with those whom he ruled:
Who wanted participation
Of all in the Government,
And represented causes
For which all, with great honour,
May serve or may die for them.
Wherever and whenever
The History of those days
Is written or discussed
One man will always stand out
Like Goliath among gentiles,
Like a giant amongst dwarfs,
Like a cyclops amongst men,
Like Elgon or Ruwenzori
In a big sea of ant-hills.
That man is M. Obote. (17)

It is interesting that the preface to the volume, written by the renowned Malawian poet David Rubadiri, in exile from the dictatorship of Hastings Banda at the time, is also in verse, and as is to be expected perhaps, given Rubadiri's skill as a poet, it offers the most accomplished verse in the volume. What is significant about this text, though, is less its aesthetic value, than the fact that it illustrates the different function verse and versification may have in East African societies. Texts like this demonstrate that, for many readers in East Africa, written material which is cast in a long verse form is more accessible and more attractive, even for complex, political analysis, than prose. They illustrate the importance of seeing the choice of genre and form as a sign of the profound cultural synergy which is an intrinsic part of these East African English-language texts.

Ugandan writer John Nagenda's *The Seasons of Thomas Tebo* (1986) also presents an account of recent political events, though in a much more conventional form. Nagende's novel uses the life of the child Thomas Tebo, the illegitimate son of a young girl seduced by a bar-room wolf, to embody the story of Uganda in the post-independence period. The tale of young Miss Jane's desertion and the birth of her illegitimate child, followed by Thomas's own history, is, the cover claims, a device which allows Nagenda to present an allegorical account of Uganda's modern history. The cover of the Heinemann edition calls the book 'A vivid allegory of modern Uganda'. This makes the novel sound more serious and portentous than it is. The first third or so is a Rabelaisian account of the growing up of the very sexually precocious Thomas. It allows Nagenda to insert a variety of fairly salacious, if sometimes rather unlikely, sex scenes into the narrative, seemingly aimed at increasing popular market appeal. It is possible to read these scenes as allegories of the precocity and incipient self-indulgence of the young Ugandan state. This would seem to be the reading which the publisher's description of the book as an allegory seeks to promote. However, the clichéd imagery suggests a more popular and less committed genre, that of the picaresque sex novel:

> Tom's body was shaking against the quiver of her own, while the storm outside began to wane and the rumble of the thunder was strong in the distance and the lightning was little stronger than candlelight, Baby pulled the boy on top of her and gathered up what there was and directed it where it should go. (28)

The rapid shift of tone and genre from one section of the book to the other is disconcerting for the reader. Part Two, which takes up the story of young Thomas's life as a political activist in exile in London, veers into a tone reminiscent of the modern thriller, with secret meetings, plots and assassinations. The language, too, alters abruptly to a tough, realistic style. The plot involves an attempt to assassinate the President, Maduku, clearly based on Idi Amin, using an ex-mercenary called Jones, who hates blacks because they killed his parents in colonial Kenya. When Jones and Tebo return to Uganda, the novel takes on a more serious tone with descriptions of Maduku's broadcasts, his security clampdowns and the indiscriminate killing and burying of people in forest graves. This section is a graphic and powerful account of what took place in Uganda under Amin's regime, but to suggest that it functions as an allegory seems odd. It is rather a fictionalised, realist account. Its style draws its inspiration, as I have suggested, from popular genres such as the political thriller rather than allegory. This second section ends with Maduku's assassination by Jones, and the subsequent army coup. The final section, set again in

London, once more changes style and tone abruptly to present a picture of the now middle-aged Tebo indulging in a series of casual relationships with various women. The sole link with the central section is that one of Thomas's young lovers is the cousin of the assassin Jones. The failure of that relationship is supposedly meant as a corollary for Tebo's disillusionment and bitterness at the failure of his assassination plot to effect any real change in his home country. I have spent some time on this novel, not because I think it justifies the rather inflated claim for it made on the cover, but because it illustrates again the way in which contemporary writing in the region is increasingly fusing popular forms and styles. Even the most serious themes, such as Amin's horrific excesses, may be handled in these narratives, and may be quite accurate in their reportage of actual events, even when the style embraces the forms of popular fiction. Although the result may not always be successful from a strictly literary viewpoint, it is arguable that these texts make their ideas and the events they describe more accessible to a general readership.

Some of the most important work in the period before the overt dictatorship of Amin in Uganda was done in theatre. As previously mentioned, writing in indigenous languages had and continues to have a strong tradition in Uganda. The work of erstwhile secondary school teacher Wycliffe Kiyingi, who wrote in Luganda, was crucial in establishing contemporary theatre in Uganda, and in developing popular touring theatre in East Africa generally. His theatre produced shows which toured widely in other East African countries. Their work inspired later groups which developed at Makerere University in the mid-1960s, such as the Makerere Free Travelling Theatre. This had considerable success touring the whole East African region with plays in several languages including Luganda, ki-Swahili and English. These popular and university-based groups also formed alliances with companies like Theatre Limited, which was the starting point for the work of Robert Serumaga, who was to emerge in the mid-1960s as East Africa's best-known English-language writer and director. Other writers who were associated with the group include playwrights John Ruganda, Nuwa Sentongo, Elvania Namukwaya Zirimu and Byron Kawadwa. Poet Richard Ntiru and playwright-novelist Laban Erapu were also associated with what Andrew Horn has called 'The Golden Decade of Ugandan Theatre', which began with independence in 1962, survived Obote's 1966 coup against the Bugandan monarchy, and ended after Obote's overthrow and the emergence of Amin's dictatorship in early 1971.[40] It is worth noting that Ngũgĩ's first two novels were written whilst he was an undergraduate at Makerere, and that his play *The Black Hermit* was produced there in 1962. This upsurge of creativity in Uganda in this period, which was so tragically cut off by Amin's brutal regime, was a crucial foundation for much of the English writing which developed in East Africa in the late 1960s and 1970s.

Robert Serumaga remains the most widely publicised of the writers from this period, apart from Ngũgĩ. His dramaturgy blended the influences of such diverse Western sources as Grotowski, Brecht and Beckett with local themes and local forms. His early work embraced such apparently personal themes as insanity, for example *The Play* (1967). This one-actor work is strongly influenced by contemporary European dramatists, especially Beckett and Pinter, whose realistic surface, but unrealistic shifts of character and plot, it clearly echoes. There is very little specifically African in the play in terms of image or reference. Yet, as we read it now, it seems irresistibly to suggest the paranoia, and the ability to transpose events and to reinvent history, that characterised the period in Ugandan life which set the scene for Amin's emergence. Mutimukulu's 'insanity' may, obliquely, suggest the difficulty of telling truth from fiction in an increasingly authoritarian, post-independence Uganda. The killing of the two 'murderers' and the death of Rosa, his wife, indirectly reproduce the random violence which was already overtaking Ugandan society. The play is resolved conventionally when the entry of Martha, the maid, appears to confirm Mutimukulu's insanity, but an attentive audience member would note that it is the mad Mutimukulu who claims that it is 1967 (the year of the play's production), not 1966, as the figures of his 'dream' insist. Who is mad, and who sane, is left in doubt.

In *Majangwa: A Promise of Rains* (1971), Serumaga is more successful in blending his European influences and African elements. The symbolism of the road, on which the action is set, and the two old 'entertainers', whose act has degenerated into public displays of sex, are again reminiscent of Beckett. But Serumaga breaks the austere mode produced by Beckett's influence and introduces a more vital element of mime and action from African performance traditions. As with Soyinka's *The Road*, influences may well be present from both foreign and local practice. The symbolic dimension, which may echo Beckett, also invokes the creation and death myths of traditional story-telling. The old couple and their debauched life, their hope for renewal, and the linking of their endless journey move the sparse events onto a different and more abstract plane, congruent with both absurdist theatre, with which Serumaga is clearly familiar, and with elements of traditional oral performance and ritual. The play is also reminiscent of South African playwright Athol Fugard's *Boesman and Lena* (1969). As in that play, the figures of these two old itinerants and social drop-outs resonate with wider implications for the society, whose empty values and viciousness their stories expose. The explicit linking of this narrative of contemporary alienation with the world of the traditional myths suggests that the hollowness of modern life may well be the result of modern Africa's failure to connect with its older values and traditions.

In *The Elephants* (1971), Serumaga explores the same themes, but uses them in a much more ambitious work. The story tells of David, an African academic and writer, whose parents have been killed and who has subsequently gone mad. Recovered, he befriends a refugee, Maurice. Maurice has a lover, Jenny, a young American Peace Corps volunteer. When they decide to marry, Maurice announces his intention of going home to receive his parents' blessings. David reveals to Jenny that Maurice's parents are dead, and that he has faked letters from them. The disclosure of this drives Maurice to despair, and David back to madness. This tragic story is interwoven with the usual surreal elements of Serumaga's theatre as an old man, seeking entry to the sixth floor of the adjacent hospital, which is reserved for members of the privileged new elite, wanders into David's university flat. The old man is subsequently involved in a hit and run accident, but returns at the end, to be present at the final dénouement. As in the earlier plays, it is hard not to see the play as symbolic, with the privileged life of the academy, the artist and the educated elite (those who are 'entitled' to the sixth floor and its privileges) presented as a screen which hides and denies the violence and tragedy of the lives of the ordinary Africans. The title references a story of how pygmies kill elephants by eating them from the inside out. This is applied to the privileged world of the African elite, whose apparent strength and surety is only a hollow cover for an inner decay and weakness. The collusion of the white expatriate intellectuals and the local elite emphasises the alienation of this world from the day-to-day realities, which break through at the end. In 1972, before Amin's rise to power effectively closed the theatre in Uganda, Serumaga also produced the still unpublished *Renga Moi* (1972), based on a number of Acholi myths and employing four different Ugandan languages. This play, according to Horn's account, was 'an attempt to broaden the ethnic base of *Majangwa* and to reach into the non-verbal expression of African ritual, as perhaps sifted through the techniques of Grotowski and Julian Beck'.[41]

Serumaga also wrote a novel, *Return to the Shadows* (1969), which presents a much more direct and realistic account of Uganda after the 1966 coup which brought Obote to power. The story shows how the country is quickly divided between various self-interested groups, whose commitment to announced ideals is quickly shattered when real political pressures begin. It emphasises that in the novel Serumaga feels able to address directly, and in a much more realistic way, social and political issues which remain symbolic in the plays of the same period. This, no doubt, reflects the censorship involved in his work for the then Ugandan National Theatre.

Other Ugandan playwrights of the period, though less well known abroad than Serumaga, were often more successful in attracting local audiences. Nuwa Sentongo, for example, in *The Invisible Bond* (1972), explores the idea of guilt and the way in which survivors are haunted by the deaths of those they cannot forget, in a play which employs traditional techniques and myths to explore this very contemporary theme. In this grotesque black comedy, the protagonist, Kibaate, rescues the corpse of the dead Damulira from the depredations of the feared 'night dancers', a secret society, which bewitches people, kills them and then disinters them to eat their bodies. The corpse clings to him and refuses to leave him alone. Slowly, it is revealed that Damulira, the corpse in question, was once the lover of Kibaate's wife. He has died because of the curse Kibaate has laid on him. In a bizarre finale, Kibaate's wife is also killed by the night dancers, and she and Damulira are grotesquely, and literally, reunited in death, when both are eaten by the members of the society.

John Ruganda's work, in plays like *The Burden* (1972) and the later *Black Mamba* (1973), although criticised by Peter Nazareth for wordiness and inconsistency, were also an important part of the rapidly emerging repertoire which established an audience for theatre in Uganda.[42]

Perhaps the most neglected figure from the period, though, is Byron Kawadwa, who disappeared with some of his actors after being arrested by Amin's police-thugs at the National Theatre in 1977.[43] A protégé of Wycliffe Kiyingi, he wrote exclusively in Luganda. His most important play, *St Charles Lwanga*, about the Catholic Ugandan martyr, was translated into English and produced at the National Theatre by the Malawian poet David Rubadiri, who was then lecturing at Makerere. Kawadwa's 'musical plays' established a fresh, local dramaturgical model, readily available to others, and only the vast exodus of Ugandan intellectuals, fleeing from Amin, prevented them from becoming an even more important influence on the development of Ugandan and East African theatre.

Since the mid-1970s a number of writers in both West and East Africa have addressed ways in which programmes to decolonise Africa should effect cultural production. This task of 'decolonising the mind', in Ngũgĩ's memorable phrase, has been an important aim of many recent African writers, linking issues of language choice and of literary form with political commitment. In 1994–95 the Institute for Advanced Study and Research in the African Humanities, in New York, organised a seminar entitled 'Powers of Expression and Expression of Power'. The seminar's theme was 'the varied ways in which artistic and scholarly production in Africa contends with claims of power and authority'. A range of writers who participated spoke of the kinds of oppositions which African political repressions have generated. They pointed out that repression often may result from self-censorship, from decisions about audience or language of expression. They also pointed out that the choice of a 'traditional' rather than a 'modern' form as an authentic signifier of Africanness, or as a sign of solidarity with the masses, may not be as simple a matter as is sometimes suggested, since both have been employed in complex ways by dominant elites and leaders, as well as by those who have opposed them on behalf of the 'people'. For example, the Ghanaian poet Kwesi Yankah spoke of the use of what he called 'folk poetry' to enhance the image of Nkrumah, a technique, approved by Nkrumah himself, which turned sour when the same popular forms were employed in 'suggestive songs from radio and public performance' to criticise his decisions:

> the folk poetry which had helped create the image of a powerful leader became a mechanism for weakening the image, destroying the myth. Kwame Nkrumah had requested folk poetry to reinforce mysticism and invincibility, but he had been unaware of the multiple significance of the traditional weapon he wielded.[44]

In a similar vein, fellow Ghanaian author Kofi Anyidoho commented that:

> probably the most powerful weapon employed by oral poets against the greed of kings is the use of metaphor and proverbial language. The poet-seer who foretells of Sundiata's birth and greatness [in Niane's epic *Sundiata*] understands the dangers of 'plain talk', so he weaves the truth into a web of codes, leaving everyone to decode it and thereby share in the responsibility of its public meaning.

Another Ghanaian, Kobena Eyi Acquah, reports that a Gold Coast man, arrested during the Second World War for saying Hitler would win, confounded the British court by asking them: 'If I talk say Hitler go win the war, na my mouth be gun?'. Although the court was adequately silenced by his question, it has been increasingly true in Africa that 'mouth be gun' in a number of significant ways, not least in the process of opposing the power of neo-colonial elite regimes in post-independence African states by appealing directly to the oppressed people. The opposition to such neo-colonialist regimes has been an inextricable part of the wider struggle to 'decolonise' African cultures, that is, to deprivilege the forms, and even the languages, of the colonial period. These forms and languages are now, it is argued, largely the preserve of the new elites, and they need to be replaced with modes of communication and forms of writing more accessible to the general populace. This programme underlies the struggles dealt with earlier in this chapter between the different generations of Nigerian writers, but it also figured largely in projects of decolonisation elsewhere, especially in Kenya.

Ngũgĩ wa Thiong'o has been pre-eminent amongst those recent African writers seeking actively to decolonise African cultures. Ngũgĩ's project involves a decisive shift of language regime, from the ex-colonial languages to indigenous languages, as the principal means of expression. Other writers before and since, such as Anta Diop, Ayi Kwei Armah, Obi Wali, Wọle Ṣoyinka and Taban lo Liyong, have also called for a return to African languages for writing. Wọle Ṣoyinka and Ayi Kwei Armah have both, at times, called for the use of ki-Swahili as an international lingua franca for Africa, echoing similar support for ki-Swahili by the Francophone writer Anta Diop. But, unlike Ngũgĩ, these writers did not wholly reject the use of English, and continued to write their own works in that language. Obi Wala made an impassioned plea for African literature in African languages, at the conference in 1963 in East Africa which, ironically, also saw the 'discovery' of the young Ngũgĩ by Chinua Achebe, the then general editor of the Heinemann African Writers series. Ngũgĩ has now embraced Obi Wala's position, after a long period as one of the most successful African English-language writers.

What makes Ngũgĩ unique is that he has acted by renouncing English in favour of Gĩkũyũ and ki-Swahili, his mother-tongue and the lingua franca of much of the East African region respectively. His recent plays and novels have all been written in Gĩkũyũ, which should preclude them from detailed study in a volume on English writing, but since they have all been translated into English (some by the author himself), and since they have had a wide influence on the practice and criticism of English-language writing across Africa, they will be considered briefly here. For similar reasons, I have considered some Tanzanian texts in ki-Swahili where they have had a significant impact on English writing. If this is inconsistent, then I can only plead that within the limited space of this enterprise many inconsistencies seem inevitable. Here, as elsewhere, I have usually included texts where they are likely to be readily encountered by readers concerned principally with the developments in writing in English, even though I have made no attempt to write a full account of inter-linguistic influences in African writing as a whole.

Significant writing in Gĩkũyũ did exist prior to Ngũgĩ. The earliest Gĩkũyũ texts were produced by writers working through mission presses, texts such as

Stanley Kiamka Gathigira's *Mũkarire ya Agikuyu* (The Customs of the Gĩkũyũ, 1934). In the mid-1940s the CMS Bookshop published Mareka B. Gecaga's *Kariuki na Muthoni* (Kariuki and Muthoni, 1946), and Sospeter Munuhe's *Coro* (The Bugle, 1948). Some writers did attempt to self-publish works, such as Justin Itotia, who in 1944 self-published a collection of Gĩkũyũ proverbs entitled *Thimo cia Ugikuyu Itari Thimure: Gicunji kia Mbere* (Gĩkũyũ Proverbs Without Explanation: Part One). At this time, too, the work of the most significant early Gĩkũyũ writer, Gakaara wa Wanjaũ, began with the publication of *Ũhoro wa Ũgũrani* (Marriage Procedures, 1946). Writers such as Wanjaũ, who has published prolifically in the fifty years or so since then, clearly established a precedent for writing in Gĩkũyũ not under the control of missions or government bodies to which writers like Ngũgĩ could look back for inspiration.[45]

Ngũgĩ's initial decision to write in Gĩkũyũ rather than English was, in part, prompted by his experience with the Community Arts project at Kamiriithu, when, in 1977, Ngũgĩ responded to a call by the Community Centre there to help them produce people's plays. The resulting performance, *Ngaahika Ndeenda* (I Will Marry When I Want), was devised by Ngũgĩ with the performers, and attacked the KANU party and government as an elite, out of touch with the workers and acting on behalf of foreign interests. An open-air theatre was constructed by the people themselves, and it became the centre for a variety of communal activities in the following months. The government response was to arrest and imprison Ngũgĩ. Upon his release, the Kamiriithu collective produced a second play, *Maitu Njugira* (Mother Sing to Me), in 1978, which, although it was set in the past, suggested that the history of the resistance by the various Kenyan nationalities was not unproblematic, and implicitly criticised the role of members of the current government. Not surprisingly, the authorities reacted by closing the Kamiriithu Centre and destroying the open-air theatre in which it had been performed, though they were unable to prevent many other Kenyans seeing the show in further rehearsals at the University of Nairobi.[46] After his release from prison, Ngũgĩ was deported, and has been in exile ever since.

As important, in a different way, as the decision to write in an African language, and so to attempt to reach the masses directly, is the decision Ngũgĩ took to address what he regarded as the increasing pessimism of recent African intellectual workers about the state and future of their countries and region. As has already been noted, elite writing in Africa in recent times has often presented a bitter and disillusioned picture of Africa. In this it has differed from the optimistic tone of some popular fiction. The vision of the continent presented by many writers has been one which reflects the general view of Africa in the Western media as a place of political disarray and social violence. Although it would be hard to deny that Africa has suffered greatly from both, the exclusive emphasis on these negative aspects, particularly where they seem to be detached from any attempt at developing an alternative, has led critics of neo-colonialism, such as Ngũgĩ, to attack the fatalism and pessimism of this vision of Africa. In an account of the growth of the novel in East Africa, published in 1984, the Kenyan critic Simon Gikandi discussed what he calls the crisis 'which began to grip the East African novel as early as the late 1960s, of which Mwangi's novels are a part'.[47] This crisis was expressed, as Gikandi notes, by one of the characters in Ngũgĩ's novel, *Petals of Blood* (1977), who speaks of the problem of the East African novel: 'the authors described the conditions correctly: they seemed able to reflect accurately the contemporary situation of fear, oppression and deprivation: but thereafter they led him down paths of pessimism, obscurity and mysticism: was there no way out except cynicism? Were people helpless victims?' (243). Although Ngũgĩ's decision to turn to writing in either Gĩkũyũ or ki-Swahili was part of the response to this, the initial response begins in the English-language novel *Petals of Blood*, from which this comment is taken.

This novel is a formal attempt, as Gikandi and others have noted, to write in the tradition of the 'political novel'. Gikandi suggests that Ngũgĩ here attempts to write a novel 'concerned with the inner workings of the body politic; its characters experience the impact of political forces in the widest possible sense; the author seeks to create a totality of the social, economic and political experience, and his characters address themselves to the life and experience in both the actual world and that of the novel' (243). Gikandi also compares the novel's scope with that of Zola's project to represent the shifting and changing nature of industrialising nineteenth-century France in novels such as *Germinal* (1885). As was noted in the previous chapter, *Petals of Blood* in some ways registers as significant, if not so obvious, a shift in Ngũgĩ's literary project as that signalled by his change of language with the publication of *Devil on the Cross*, written in Gĩkũyũ whilst he was in detention, and published in 1982.

Devil on the Cross is dedicated 'To all Kenyans struggling against the neo-colonial stage of imperialism'. In effect, this text represents Ngũgĩ's attempt to address the task of decolonising the African mind. It is as much polemic as novel, and it is the first text in which Ngũgĩ implemented his belief that the use of European languages perpetuates the neo-colonialist domination of Africa by consolidating hegemonic cultural power, a case he has argued extensively in critical accounts over the last two decades.[48] The narrative of *Devil on the Cross* is an allegory which blends biblical references and the influence of other Christian works made popular by mission education, such as Bunyan's *Pilgrim's Progress*, with Gĩkũyũ oral texts and popular folklore. This eclectic mixture is unified by its being part of the body of reference actively present in contemporary popular Gĩkũyũ culture, where indigenous and Christian references are continually intertwined in everyday life. This is an extreme example of the degree to which modern African discourse, in both English and indigenous languages, has been saturated with external references through both Christian and Islamic influences, a body of influences which remains largely unexplored.[49] To suggest that contemporary indigenous language discourses do not include these appropriated bodies of reference would be grossly inaccurate, and Ngũgĩ does not make that mistake. The novelist is cast in the role of the traditional Gĩcaandĩ player, or oral, musical story-teller, when he is begged by the heroine Warĩĩnga's mother to 'tell the story of the child I loved so dearly. Cast light upon all that happened, so that each may pass judgement only when he knows the whole truth. Gĩcaandĩ Player, reveal all that is hidden' (7). The popular tone which mixes traditional verse with biblically inspired rhetoric is illustrated in this exhortatory opening section:

> and after seven days had passed, the earth trembled, and lightning scored the sky with its brightness, and I was lifted up and borne up to the rooftop of the house, and I was shown many things, and I heard a voice, like a great clap of thunder, admonishing me: Who has told you that prophecy is yours alone, to keep to yourself? Why are you furnishing yourself with empty excuses? If you do that, you will never be free of tears and pleading cries
>
> . . .
>
> But why am I lingering on the bank of the river?
>
> To bathe is to strip off all clothes.
> To swim is to plunge into the river.
> It is good so . . .
> Come,
> Come, my friend,
> Come and let us reason together.
> Come and let us reason together now.
> Come and let us reason together about
> Jacinta Warĩĩnga before you pass judgement on our children. (9)

The plot of this allegory concerns a meeting of the Devil and his disciples at Ilmorog in Iciciri District. Cast out of her rented shack after refusing her boss's sexual advances, Warĩĩnga decides to return to her parents. In descriptions of Warĩĩnga, Ngũgĩ emphasises her blackness, and the extent to which this militates against the modern ideals of beauty which involve lightness of skin and hair straightening: 'What she hated most was her blackness, so she would disfigure her body with skin-lightening creams like *Ambi* and *Snowfire*, forgetting the saying: "That which is born black will never be white"' (11). Warĩĩnga is a symbol of Africa, subject to exploitation, and unable even to recognise its own worth, which has been overlaid by false ideas of value imported from elsewhere, and even internalised by Africans themselves. The reversal of the Christian imagery, in the idea of the crucifixion of the Devil in the title, also emphasises that in the colonial and neo-colonial context imported ideals like Christianity may be employed as screens for the destruction of the people:

> The Devil had two mouths, one on his forehead and the other at the back of his head. . . . Near the Cross he began to tremble and turned his eyes towards the darkness, as if his eyes were being seared by the light. He moaned, beseeching the people not to crucify him, swearing that he and his followers would never again build Hell for the people on Earth.
>
> But the people cried in unison: 'Now we know the secrets of all the robes that disguise your cunning. You commit murder, then you don your robes of pity and go to wipe the tears of orphans and widows. You steal food from people's stores at midnight, then at dawn you visit the victims wearing your robes of charity and you offer them a calabash filled with the grain that you have stolen.'
>
> . . .
>
> And there and then the people crucified the Devil on the Cross, and they went away singing songs of victory. (13)

214

At the centre of the book is the competition, held at Ilmorog by the Devil's assistants, to see who is the most successful at evil. Employing the devices of contemporary popular oral performance, the characters represent the various forms which neo-colonial power and corruption have taken in modern Kenya.

> The master of ceremonies beckoned to the guards at the door. They ran forward, swinging their clubs in the air . . . Ndaaya wa Kahuria was expelled from the feast. The other thieves and robbers laughed and whistled with pleasure. The master of ceremonies again gestured for silence, and then he spoke.
>
> 'This is a competition for *Thieves and Robbers International, yanni,* thieves and robbers who have attained international status. So we don't want any novices or amateurs to come here and waste our time. *Time is money, and every time is robbing time*'.[50]

The intention of the text is clear: first, to reinforce the claims of Gĩkũyũ as a viable literary language in the modern world; and secondly, to employ its use to reach out to the bulk of the population, who, even if literate, are literate only in their own languages, with a revolutionary call to oppose the current, elite regime as corrupt and self-serving. In this first example of his use of Gĩkũyũ in the novel form, Ngũgĩ clearly has a double intention. The message to the 'masses' is complemented by a second one to the African and international intellectual community, a message which illustrates the arguments in favour of linguistic decolonisation, which Ngũgĩ has passionately espoused since the early 1980s. This double role for the text is illustrated by the fact that Ngũgĩ simultaneously translated the text into English, and issued it in this version in the Heinemann African Writers series only two years after its publication in Gĩkũyũ. Seven years after the Gĩkũyũ text was published, Ngũgĩ published his second Gĩkũyũ language novel, *Matigari* (1987). This novel, too, was translated, but not by Ngũgĩ, and issued in English in the Heinemann African Writers series two years later, in 1989.

Ironically, these two novels have had the widest international circulation of any recent Kenyan writing, and they have been at the centre of the international debate about language choice in Africa. Accounts of how successful they have been in their primary project of addressing the non-elite masses of Kenya vary. Certainly, the kind of direct effect which popular theatre forms such as *I Will Marry When I Want* (1980) had on their audience, seem more difficult for a written text to achieve. Literacy rates, even in African languages such as Gĩkũyũ, remain low in Kenya, especially amongst the poor to whom Ngũgĩ's radical message is primarily addressed. There is, however, anecdotal evidence that both texts were read aloud to groups in Kenya, and spread in this form from the literate to the non-literate. In the Preface to *Matigari*, Ngũgĩ claims that there was one wonderfully bizarre result, after its publication in October 1986: 'By January 1987, intelligence reports had it that peasants in Central Kenya were whispering and talking about a man called Matigari who was roaming the whole country making demands about truth and justice. There were orders for his immediate arrest, but the police discovered that Matigari was only a fictional character in a book of the same name. In February 1987, the police raided all the bookshops and seized every copy of the novel.'

Although more conventional in form than *Devil on the Cross*, *Matigari* shares the earlier novel's debt to both oral compositions, and Christian myths and parables. Ngũgĩ says that the idea of the journey in search of a cure for ills is based on an oral story.[51] He also indicates that the text contains a number of deliberate references to Christ and the second coming. Matigari, he says, is an admixture of the hero figure Ndiiro, from the oral source, and the biblical Christ. In this respect the novel resembles some earlier South African work, such as *Woza Albert* (1980) in which the second coming of Christ (or Morena as he is known in that text) is linked with the resurrection of the great African leader Albert Luthuli, and those who followed him, such as Robert Sobukwe, Lilian Ngoyi and Steve Biko, drawing together the two great popular forces of anti-apartheid resistance and African Christian activism.[52] Ngũgĩ's project suffers in comparison with these texts because of the obvious distaste he has for the fact that African popular movements include Christianity, which he sees as predominantly neo-colonialist. Ngũgĩ offers a more narrowly conceived Marxist vision of revolutionary change than plays like *Woza Albert*, which embrace a more liberal, populist road to change. Ngũgĩ's vision may seem somewhat dated from the viewpoint of the late 1990s, and in the aftermath of the notable failure of a number of African Marxist regimes in Ethiopia, Zimbabwe, Mozambique etc., to effect any great change in the lives of ordinary Africans. Here, as elsewhere in Ngũgĩ's fiction, the desire to create revolutionary protagonists, and to construct a strategy for change based on the classic Marxist alliance of workers and peasants, seems sometimes to be rather simplistically imposed on the characters and political struggles of modern Kenya. Nevertheless, the strength of Ngũgĩ's work rests in his relentless exposure of corruption and authoritarianism, and in his powerful dramatisation of these forces. Ngũgĩ, as has already been noted, seems to be a writer less at ease with the depiction of urban than rural life, a reflection perhaps of his own background. For this reason the sections of these late novels which represent urban life are not as convincing as the work of earlier Kenyan realist writers such as Akare and Mwangi.

The vision of a series of small, worker-controlled industries, which ends *Devil on the Cross*, is clearly Ngũgĩ's recipe for Kenyan self-advancement, and his recommended means to free the masses from the control of the neo-colonial, elite rulers. This message sometimes sits uneasily with the characters who embody it, and perhaps represents more the message Ngũgĩ hopes to convey to the population, rather than their present cast of thought. In this respect the novel is openly and directly polemic in purpose. It is designed to radicalise the rural and urban poor, and to illustrate the ways in which the elite leadership of independent Kenya is still held in thrall by international capital, for which they exercise only a comprador function. Whatever our view of the message as politics or of its likely success, it is clear that novels like these are closer to the exhortatory model of classic Socialist Realism than to any idea of a realistic portrait of modern Kenya. This is the Kenya Ngũgĩ would like to see, rather than the Kenya that is.

For instance, in *Devil on the Cross* the scene when the heroine Warĩĩnga enters a garage in River Road, in the slum district of Nairobi, and wins over the male workers by demonstrating her skill as a car-mechanic, is clearly a political allegory rather than a credible description. Using a piece of wood as a primitive mechanic's stethoscope, she diagnoses that the noise in the engine is 'a loose bolt that joined the control to the crankshaft'.

> The people around started clapping their hands. Others went away, shaking their heads, saying: 'Really, I've yet to see anything to beat that! So our women have acquired that much learning!' The other workers welcomed her as one of them. (221)

The polemic is obvious when Wariinga uses her judo skills to give a beating to a customer who refuses to treat her as a worker and seeks to sexually harass her. Finally, she becomes the leader of a radical programme of urban renewal:

> Wariinga's fame spread to every corner of the city. The respect of the other workers for her increased, and they sang of her diligence, perseverance and courage.
> Wariinga, daughter of the Iregi rebels!
> The fruits of each worker's labour went into his own pocket. But at the end of every month each worker would contribute a fixed sum to a common pool, from which they paid the ground rent for the garage to the Nairobi City Council and their other communal expenses. And if one of the workers had an unexpected problem, he or she was allowed to borrow from the common pool to meet his or her needs. No one in that community lived on the sweat of another. Everyone received according to his ability, his reputation and the quickness of his hands. (222)

Matigari is less overtly polemic in its techniques than this. As a result, its project seems less likely to collide with audience convictions about the likelihood and practicality of its politics. It retains the allegorical framework of the earlier work, with the hero, Matigari ma Njirũũngi (the name literally meaning 'the patriots who survived the bullets'), representing the freedom fighters who defeated the settlers and gained independence for Kenya. Matigari returns from the forest to find a world where the young are forced to live in derelict cars and scramble in rubbish heaps for food, and where virtuous young girls are forced to walk the streets to feed their siblings, orphaned by corrupt police who have arrested the parents for smuggling bullets to the freedom fighters. The deliberate collapse of the time line of the events of recent history brings the idealists of the Emergency period and the forest freedom fighters into the modern world of post-independence corruption. The character His Excellency Ole Excellence represents the contemporary leadership, whose ruthless suppression of any opposition mirrors the increasing intolerance and corruption of the post-independence leadership, their hangers-on in parliament, the armed forces and the police force.[53] Although *Matigari* has a more realistic narrative line than the earlier *Devil on the Cross*, allegory is still persistently present, as for example in the use of Settler Williams's 'house' to represent the disputed land of Kenya. The story of the 'house' is an allegory of how the white settlers stole the land, which has now passed into the hands of the same Africans whom the freedom fighters struggled to educate in the white man's ways, only to find themselves betrayed at their hands:

217

> You see, I built the house with my own hands. But Settler Williams slept in it, and I would sleep outside on the verandah. I tended the estates which spread around the house for miles. But it was Settler Williams who took home the harvest. (21)

The take-over of the land is helped by the collusion of the black servants, represented in the novel by John Boy, and in the present by John Boy's son, who was sent to England to the London School of Economics to be educated, and who has now returned to act as the frontman for the white settler.[54] Informed of John Boy Junior's identity, Matigari queries if he is

> the boy we sent abroad? The boy the cost of whose education we all contributed to, singing with pride. The boy we sent off to study, saying that a child belongs to all, that a nation's beauty was borne in a child, a future patriot. The boy for whom we sang: He shall come back and clean up our cities, our country, and deliver us from slavery. (48)

Matigari is arrested and cast into prison by this new white-black leader. In prison, he meets others who have been arrested, and hears of the hardships faced by the people under the new regimes.

The children, and especially young Mūriūki, whom Matigari saves at the beginning of the narrative, represent the young, whose future is wasted by the new elite. Although their world of endless struggle is accurately portrayed, the text lacks the authentic and convincing detail of Mwangi or Akare's accounts of young Nairobi street kids. Once again, for all its political passion, Ngũgĩ's recent work lacks the force of some other accounts of the underclass of the new Kenya, sacrificing realistic detail to a powerful but generalised level of political allegory. Perhaps such a choice of focus is inevitable, and many critics would find the political edge of Ngũgĩ's analysis of recent Kenyan history ample compensation for the lack of credibility in his descriptions of slum life. Nevertheless, it is hard to credit that the slum children, who stone Matigari in Part One, would feel remorseful when they hear Mūriūki's account of his imprisonment. Or that they would react in the way they do against the news broadcast by the government radio station at the opening of Part Two. The motivation here seems rather stretched, and it does not have much credibility as an account of slum children's likely behaviour:

> One of the boys ran to fetch the radio he had found in the garbage yard. The children had agreed that the radio would be communal property, so they could all listen to the news of the country and the world. They had paid compensation to the boy who had found it. They took the radio everywhere they went.
>
> Now they gathered around to hear anything, any news, about Matigari ma Njirũũngi. (69)

The news which follows is of the arrest of university lecturers, of student protests, and of reports from South Africa, and elsewhere, of freedom fighting. It ends with news of the miraculous escape of prisoners from detention. This news offers them, the narrator says, 'something dramatic, something that livened up their otherwise drab lives' (71). But compared with earlier realist novels like Kibera's *Voices in the Dark,* Akare's *The Slums* and Mwangi's *Kill*

Me Quick, this is hardly a credible psychological portrait of street children.[55] As already noted above, Ngũgĩ's aim, as Gikandi and others have argued, is not in fact to create realistic portraits but to create political allegories which will instruct the masses in a programme of political action and resistance:

> What amazing news! How could prison doors open by themselves? Who was Matigari ma Njirũũngi? The people of Trampville composed a song for Matigari ma Njirũũngi:
>
>> Show me the way to a man
>> Whose name is Matigari ma Njirũũngi,
>> Who stamps his feet to the rhythm of bells.
>> And the bullets jingle.
>> And the bullets jingle. (71)

As the text unfolds, the identification of Matigari with Christ also grows in emphasis, as increasingly miraculous events are associated with him:

> 'The children? Did he reveal himself to them? A child and a king are one and the same thing. But children will always be children!'
> . . .
> 'These modern children. They ought to be ashamed of themselves, throwing stones at an elderly man. Suppose they hit him in the eyes?'
> 'That is the amazing thing. Not even one stone touched him.'
> 'What?'
> 'When the stones reached him they changed into doves.' (73)

The government's campaign to find and destroy Matigari allows Ngũgĩ to illustrate, in parable form, the oppressive systems employed by the government to remain in power. Truth is replaced by the parroting of the government line:

> These gentlemen will be assisted by the Permanent Professor of the History of Parratology, the Editor of the *Daily Parratology*, the Ph.D in Parratology and the hooded informer. Do you know who the hooded justice is? He is the one wearing a white hood here. I know that in the bad colonial days you used to call him The Hood. But now we call him the Hooded Truth and Justice. (117)

This reference to the practice of using hooded informers to betray the Mau Mau freedom fighters links the colonial regime with the current government, and shows how little the practices have changed after independence.

Matigari's example finally spurs the people to insurrection and, led by the street children, they burn down the cars and houses of the new elite. The security forces drive Matigari and his supporters to the river, where the police dogs attack them. Together with Guthera, he falls into the river. The narrative deliberately leaves open whether he is killed or not. 'Everywhere in the country the big question remained: Who was Matigari ma Njirũũngi? Was he dead, or was he alive?' (174). Whatever the answer to these unresolved questions, the narrative ends with the young boy from the refuse tip, Mũriũki, digging up the weapons from the original freedom struggle, which Matigari had hidden at the beginning of the story. The text ends with an exhortation to arms and unity:

suddenly he seemed to hear the workers' voices, the voices of the peasants, the voices of the students and of other patriots of all the different nationalities of the land, singing in harmony:

Victory shall be ours! (175)

These recent Gĩkũyũ-language texts of Ngũgĩ represent one of the most determined attempts to resist the ongoing forces of neo-colonialism, and to construct an alternative decolonising mode for fiction. They belong specifically to the category of what has been called resistance literature,[56] that is, literature dedicated to instructing the masses and calling for their participation in the struggle against oppression. In this respect, they seem to share many features with the work which came out of South Africa during the apartheid years. The high standing of Ngũgĩ's work in South Africa may reflect this similarity of aim and form. The texts have clearly had an impact in Kenya too, judging by the alacrity with which the government banned their circulation, though to what extent they accurately reflect the current politics of resistance within Kenya remains problematic. Ngũgĩ's long exile from the Kenyan scene and the emergence of other forces within Kenyan politics – for example, an Islamic-based resistance in the coastal regions – makes the task of judging the effectiveness of Ngũgĩ's call for a classic Marxist peasants' and workers' struggle a difficult one. On the whole, it is likely that the main effect of the books has been to reinforce the growing distaste of many people in Kenya with the current one-party state, and the basic inability of post-independence governments to deliver on the promises made before independence. This message is that which Ngũgĩ has preached, in one form or another, since the publication of *A Grain of Wheat*. The shift of methodology and language reflects his desire to contact the masses directly, a desire echoing that of writers in West Africa in the same period, such as Osofisan, Omotoso, etc. Like those writers, Ngũgĩ clearly felt that his earlier writing was failing to speak to the audience he wished to address, the mass of ordinary people. There is little doubt that the move to Gĩkũyũ has opened up a wider audience. But the choice of a specific, ethnic language such as Gĩkũyũ means that the audience is restricted to speakers from that language group. Despite his earlier statement, that from now on he would write only in Gĩkũyũ and ki-Swahili, so far Ngũgĩ has chosen to write only in Gĩkũyũ. Even more significantly, the translations he and others have undertaken have been into English, rather than into ki-Swahili, arguably the most common lingua franca in the region for people in the lower socio-economic category. Ngũgĩ's drive to decolonise writing in Africa has been one of the most significant events in recent African writing, but it has been also the subject of considerable dispute and debate, inside and outside Kenya. As I noted earlier, there can be little doubt that other realist accounts have more credibility, but their overall effect, in sustaining a pessimistic and negative vision of African conditions, may make them ineffective as tools of social change. In fact, they may even encourage a refusal to engage with the process of change. The dispute about the value of Ngũgĩ's recent writing is the age-old one of whether it is the function of art merely to record social forces and their effects, or to be a conscious instrument in the process of effecting change.[57]

Notes

1. For example, in West Africa the important intervention of Chinweizu, Jemie Onwuchekwu and Ihechukwa Madabuike in *The West and the Rest of Us* (New York: Random House, 1975). In East Africa, at about the same time in the late 1970s, Ngũgĩ had begun his work with the people of the Kamiriithu Community Centre. The group devised Gĩkũyũ plays dealing with contemporary issues, which led to his detention, and to the development of his later critical work calling for cultural decolonisation.

2. See Chinweizu *et al.*, *The West and the Rest of Us*; also Chinweizu *et al.*, *The Decolonization of African Literature* (Enugu, Nigeria: Fourth Dimension Press, 1980).

3. The term 'bolekaja' (literally 'come down and fight') critics is derived from the cries of the Nigerian mammy-wagon touts vying for customers. It is usually translated as combat critics.

4. That is works which deal with those who have 'been-to' a foreign country, to acquire education or wealth and returned as a member of the new elite.

5. See Chapter 9.

6. Ossie Eneke, 'Interview with Femi Osofisan', *Greenfield Review*, 8, 1 & 2 (Spring 1980).

7. For example, Una Hunwick, 'The Impact of Modern Theatre on the Nigerian Audience', *Nigeria Magazine*, 54, 3 (July–Sept. 1986).

8. The term implies the women married by successful men in their youth, usually girls from rural areas with limited education and little knowledge of or interest in modern, urban fashion and habits. These wives were frequently cast aside for mistresses, drawn from younger, town-bred women, as the men became successful. This social issue is handled in a number of earlier texts in both West and East Africa, for example in Achebe's *A Man of the People* (1966), and in Okot p'Bitek's *Song of Lawino* (1966).

9. For an account of the problems faced by radical theatre in many developing countries in this period, see Eugene van Erwen, *The Playful Revolution: Theatre and Liberation in Asia* (Bloomington: Indiana University Press, 1992).

10. See Simon Gikandi, 'The Politics and Poetics of National Formation: Recent African Writing', in Anna Rutherford (ed.), *From Commonwealth to Post-Colonial* (Sydney: Dangaroo, 1992), pp. 377–89.

11. One should also note the similarity of this device to the endings of some of Brecht's work, notably *The Threepenny Opera*, and even more so, *The Good Person of Szechuan*.

12. Brecht had faced precisely the same problem when his work received recognition and production in mainstream or official theatres. The dramaturgy developed for the 'proletarian', informal theatres of his early and middle period, became increasingly cumbersome and unsuited to the new conditions. Brecht, like Osofisan later, was forced to respond by developing new forms.

13. See, for example, *Who's Afraid of Solarin?* (1978), *No More the Wasted Breed* (1982), and *Midnight Hotel* (1986), which rework plays by Gogol, Soyinka and Feydeau respectively.

14. Examples of this in Soyinka's work include *Death and the King's Horseman*, which reworks one of Duro Ladipo's popular plays, and *Opera Wonyosi*, a re-working of Brecht's own rewrite of Gay's *The Beggars Opera* in *The Threepenny Opera*.

15. Quoted in Kimberley W. Benston, 'The Aesthetics of Modern Black Drama: From Mimesis to Metatext', in Errol Hill (ed.), *The Theatre of Black Americans* (Englewood Cliffs, N.J.: Prentice-Hall, 1980), 63.

16. The plays were not published together. The first two appeared in a collection entitled *A Farewell to Babylon and Other Plays* (Harlow: Longman, 1978), and the final play is in *Flamingo and Other Plays* (Harlow: Longman, 1986).

17. The second part has not yet appeared, though Rotimi has discussed in print what it might deal with. See Martin Banham, 'Ola Rotimi', in C. B. Cox (ed.), *African Writers*, Vol. 2 (New York: Scribners, 1997), pp. 711–12.

18. See Brian Crow, 'Melodrama and the "Political Unconscious" in Two African Plays', *Ariel*, 14 (July 1983), and Chris Dunton, *Make Man Talk True: Nigerian Drama in English Since 1970* (Oxford: Hans Zell, 1992).

19. Banham, 'Ola Rotimi', p. 710.

20. Ibid., pp. 707–20.

21. In an edition which included Ofeimun's second collection of poems, *A Handle for the Flautist*, first published in 1986.

22. Odia Ofeimun, *The Poet Lied* (London: Longman, 1980, second edition, 1989), p. 150. This is from an interview conducted by Jemie Madabuike in 1983, appended to the 1989 reissue of the poems.

23. Ofeimun, *The Poet Lied* (1980), p. 50.

24. Niyi Osundare made this claim in a video-taped interview, which I recorded at Ibadan University in 1991.

25. A well-balanced assessment is presented in Adermi Bamikunle, 'The Stable and the Changing in Nigerian Poetry', *World Literature Written in English*, 32 (1992).

26. See, for example, Isabel Hofmeyr, *We Spend Our Years as a Tale That is Told: Oral, Historical Narrative in a South African Chiefdom* (London: James Currey, 1994).

27. Ojaide has also published a very lucid critical account of Wọle Ṣoyinka's verse, and an overview of recent developments in African poetry. See Tanure Ojaide, *The Poetry of Wọle Ṣoyinka* (Lagos, Nigeria: Malthouse Press, 1994); and Tanure Ojaide, 'New Trends in Modern African Poetry', *Research in African Literatures*, 26, 1 (1995).

28. As early as the mid-1980s, the poet Funso Aiyejina had also identified what he saw as an alternative tradition emerging in recent Nigerian poetry, to which he gave the name 'new traditionalism'. See 'Recent Nigerian Poetry in English: An Alternative Tradition', in Yemi Ogunyemi (ed.), *Perspectives on Nigerian Literature: 1700 to the Present*, Vol. 1 (Lagos: Guardian Books, 1988).

29. J. O. J. Nwachuckwu-Agbada, 'The Eighties and the Return to Oral Cadences in Nigerian Poetry', *Matatu*, 10, Special Issue, *African Literature in the Eighties* (1993).

30. J. O. J. Nwachukwu-Agbada, 'Form and Content in Nigerian Pidgin Poetry: The Pidgin Poetry of Aig-Imoukhuede and Mamman Vatsa', *Chelsea*, 46 (1987), pp. 95–6.

31. Once again the inability of a survey like this to do anything like full justice to the range and variety of writing in any single country or period must be noted and regretted. It is particularly the case in countries like Nigeria, where English writing has been so prolific. Using the example of Nigeria, writers I have been unable to cover who might well have been discussed here include Idzia Ahmed, Catherine Acholonu, Afam Akeh, Funso Aiyejina, Ossie Enekwe, Fẹmi Fatowa, Esiaba Irobi, Molara Ogundipe-Leslie. These, and innumerable others from Ghana, and elsewhere, well deserved to be discussed, if space had allowed.

32. See Chapter 9.

33. See Chapter 5.

34. Elechi Amadi, an Ibo who also opposed Biafra, dramatised the attitudes of Ibos opposed to secession in his novel *Estrangement* (1986).

35. Ken Saro-Wiwa, *Songs in a Time of War* (Port Harcourt: Saros International Publishers, 1985), p. 24.

36. This is an interesting example of the ubiquity in male writers of the trope of Africa as a female body, a trope which has been criticised by recent feminist critics such as Stratton. See Stratton, *African Literature and the Politics of Gender* (London: Routledge, 1994), Chapter 2 'The Mother Africa Trope'. Here the male gaze views Kenya as an abused, female body, setting up a tension which is not intended between the subject and its metaphorical vehicle.

37. See Chapter 7 for a discussion of the development of Ngũgĩ's work.

38. Ruhumbika's later writing includes *Towards Ujamaa: Twenty Years of Tanu Leadership*, ed. G. Ruhumbika (Kampala: East African Literature Bureau, 1974).

39. See Chapter 5.

40. Andrew Horn, '*Uhuru* to Amin: The Golden Decade of Theatre in Uganda', *Literary Half-Yearly*, 19, 1 (January 1978).

41. Ibid., p. 33.

42. Peter Nazareth, 'Africa Under Neo-Colonialism: New East African Writing', *Busara*, 6, 1 (1974), p. 22.

43. Their burned bodies were later found in the bush outside Kampala.

44. The quotes in this section are all taken from the brochure publicising this important seminar, which was held at the Social Science Research Council, in New York.

45. Christina Pugliese, *Author, Publisher and Gĩkũyũ Nationalist: The Life and Writings of Gakaara wa Wanjaũ*, Bayreuth African Studies No. 37 (Bayreuth: Breitinger; Nairobi: IFRA, 1995).

46. See Ingrid Björkmann, *Mother Sing for Me: People's Theatre in Kenya* (London and Atlantic Highlands, N.J.: Zed Books, 1989) for an account of the project.

47. Simon Gikandi, 'The Growth of the East African Novel', in G. D. Killam (ed.), *The Writing of East and Central Africa* (London, Nairobi, Ibadan: Heinemann, 1984), p. 243. Further references are given in the text.

48. *Homecoming: Essays on African and Caribbean Literature, Culture and Politics* (1972); *Writers in Politics: Essays* (1981); *Barrel of a Pen: Resistance to Repression in Neo-Colonial Kenya* (1983); *De-colonising the Mind: The Politics of Language in African Writing* (1986); *Writing against Neocolonialism* (1986); *Moving the Centre: The Struggle for Cultural Freedoms* (1993). Together these constitute the most consistent stand against cultural neo-colonialism and for the use of indigenous languages by any African writer.

49. A recent collection of conference proceedings touches on some aspects of these links, but it covers a very wide field including South America as well as Africa. See Susan van Gallagher (ed.), *Postcolonial Literature and the Biblical Call for Justice* (Mississippi: University of Mississippi Press, 1994). There is some comment on Achebe in Susan Gallagher's essay in the collection, and it includes a useful article on 'Ngũgĩ's Narrative' by Oliver Lonesey.

50. In the original Gĩkũyũ version, non-Gĩkũyũ words (e.g. Latin, English and even Swahili) are italicised.

51. Preface to *Matigari*, p. vii.

52. Since the play toured the world and the text was published in a collection of South African plays entitled *Woza Afrika!* (London: Methuen, 1986), Ngũgĩ may even have known of it.

53. The name probably invokes Kenyatta, who, in the latter part of his life, became increasingly enamoured of titles such as this, e.g. His Excellency, Mzee Jomo Kenyatta. But the politics apply equally to Daniel arap Moi, his successor, who exiled Ngũgĩ.

54. Jomo Kenyatta was, of course, educated at the LSE.

55. There is an obvious dispute here between writers like Ngũgĩ and others like Kibera, Akare and Mwangi. See Chapter 7 above. In particular one wonders if Kibera's rather satirical portrait in *Voices in the Dark* (1970), of Gerald Timundu, who is trying to write plays to be staged at the new university, discussed there, is meant to refer to Ngũgĩ.

56. See Barbara Harlow, *Resistance Literature* (New York: Methuen, 1987), for a discussion of the form and ideology of this widespread mode of contemporary writing.

57. The issue of whether or not radical texts should present positive, if unrealistic, portraits of people to act as examples for change is also an old one. It can be illustrated in the dispute between earlier radical writers, such as Brecht when, after composing *Mother Courage*, he was attacked by fellow Marxist, Friedrich Wolf, for not making the heroine a peasant hero, who learned from the loss of her children that war was basically a capitalist plot. Brecht's answer was that such a portrait would be a falsification of history, since peasants are only very rarely able to step outside their social construction and perceive its causes. See J. Willett, *Brecht on Theatre* (London: Methuen, 1964), pp. 226–30. In essence the dispute is whether an idealised, heightened portrait of workers and peasants is justified, if they present role models for people to emulate and learn from, even though such portraits do not reflect the general condition or consciousness achieved by this class of people at the time of writing. This dispute would seem to have a direct relevance to the various critical evaluations of Ngũgĩ's recent work.

Chapter 9

Internal Discord

The great variety of indigenous cultures across East and West Africa, and even between countries adjacent to one another in these regions, had a profound effect on how English writing developed. The differences which resulted include stylistic and generic choices, such as a greater propensity to adapt verse to long prose forms in East Africa, and language choice, such as the use of ki-Swahili in East African countries like Tanzania, where it has been more frequently employed than English as a literary medium.[1] But many of the crucial differences between East and West African writing in English can also be traced back to the differences between the forms which colonisation took in the two regions. The dominance of a commercial form of colonisation in West Africa, based on trading, meant that the region was never extensively settled by Europeans and the expatriate colonisers were restricted to a relatively few traders and government officials. In contrast, in parts of East Africa, such as Kenya, and to a lesser extent Tanzania, the suitability of the land and climate for European farming meant that large-scale settlement by European expatriates occurred. Particularly after the 1920s, it became clear that, whatever the government policy might be towards the eventual independence of the African majority in these regions, such independence would be strongly resisted by the powerful settler organisations.[2] From the turn of the century, the rebellions and uprisings which characterised the colonial period throughout the East African region, such as the Maji-Maji uprising in German East Africa (as mainland modern-day Tanzania then was), made it clear that the process of indigenous self-assertion in East Africa was likely to result in direct military conflict. Although Zimbabwe is outside the region this volume addresses, the situation is comparable there, with the so-called First Chimurenga in the 1890s, a rebellion against Rhodes and his settlers, led by the famous spirit medium, Mehanda. In West Africa, although the colonial penetration of the interior was accompanied by conflict and violence, notably in the wars against the Ashanti kingdom in the second half of the nineteenth century in what is now modern-day Ghana, and in the punitive expeditions against the kingdom of Benin in the 1890s in modern-day Nigeria, the lack of large-scale European settlement meant that there was less friction over issues such as land possession and usage to fuel such rebellions. A notable exception is the so-called Women's War in Nigeria in the 1920s, which erupted over issues of unfair taxation, a persistent source of friction in the West African region during later colonial times.

As a result of this difference, the various armed independence struggles have been a major topic for literary representation throughout East Africa. In

Tanzania, one of the most influential modern texts is the ki-Swahili play *Kinjeketile* (1963), by Ephraim N. Hussein. This deceptively simple play is one of the most powerful and effective political texts to come out of Africa. It has had a strong influence on playwrights using English in East and West Africa, especially since it was translated into English in 1970. It prefigures many of the concerns which surface later in English writing in the East African region, and in a less specific way elsewhere in Africa. It tells the story of the origins and defeat of the Maji-Maji Rebellion (1905–7) against the German colonial authorities. The rebellion, which began in the southern region of what was then German East Africa (now Tanzania), is shown to begin with a struggle between the different and conflicting local clans, who cannot unite to resist the invader. The unity of the people is achieved when Kinjeketile Ngwala draws the rival clans together, after he has apparently survived immersion in water for twenty-four hours without drowning, a feat attributed to his posses-sion by the water spirit Hongo. Kinjeketile's followers believed that if they swallowed the sacred 'water', blessed by Hongo (Maji is water in Swahili), they would be immune to the German bullets. Although the text reflects the historical events of the period with which it deals, it is also clearly intended to provide a commentary on the problems facing modern Tanzania. The dilemma of leadership, which the play explores, applies not only to the situ-ation of the historical Kinjeketile, but also to the leadership of the modern, post-independence nation. Other aspects of the text also echo contemporary Tanzanian issues: for example, the doubt in Kinjeketile's mind concerning the prophecy he has spoken when possessed, which suggests that the rebellion will only serve to exchange the rule of the Germans for that of the Arab rulers of Zanzibar. The fact that the text postdates the post-independence unification of Zanzibar and Tanganyika in the new joint Tanzanian state, and the tensions between this union and the alternative union, much debated at the time, of predominantly Muslim and Arab Zanzibar with the other Arab communities of the Indian Ocean littoral, is clearly reflected here. As we will see later, in discussing other texts concerned with historical rebellions such as Mau Mau, these 'historical' texts often have such a double focus, reflecting contemporary political issues and attitudes alongside the theme of celebration of the histor-ical past, which is their ostensible subject. Hussein's play ends with a strong defence of the importance of the Maji-Maji rising as an early focus for the emerging, modern national consciousness. As Kinjeketile lies imprisoned and dying, he refuses to avoid execution for himself and his followers by denying the potency of the spells which the sacred 'water' (maji) conveyed. Ironically, these are the very spells which, as the text made clear earlier, he and his fellow leader, Kitunde, had doubted themselves from time to time. In refusing to accept the German offer of leniency, they are acknowledging the potency of these beliefs not as 'facts', but as 'symbols', around which their own consciousness and resistance can crystallise.

The Maji-Maji rebellion also figures as a reference point for resistance and national consciousness in a number of later Tanzanian texts, for example in the work of M. G. Vassanji. The rebellion features as a defining moment of self-assertion in *The Gunny Sack* (1989), which deals with the history of the Shamsi (an Indian Muslim) community in East Africa, and spans several generations from the turn of the century to the present day; and in *The Book of Secrets* (1994), which tells the story of a British colonial official and his involvement with the Shamsi community in the period of the First World War and after. It was frequently invoked, as these novels show, by the later anti-colonial forces during the Zanzibari rebellion of the early 1960s and by the subsequent nationalist movement, led by Julius Nyerere and the TANU party, on the mainland. The fact that, in Vassanji's work, these local movements are viewed from the perspective of the diasporic Indian community does not invalidate their force as a record of these large-scale historical events.

In Kenya, the role and character of the more recent armed liberation struggle, known as Mau Mau, has been an even greater concern of many writers since independence. The treatment of the Mau Mau struggle in recent Kenyan writing registers a peculiar ambivalence. As a result, it is hard to decide where to place many of these texts in any wider schema. It might seem that they should form part of a discussion of the struggle for and celebration of independence, but the strength of the theme of post-independence disillusion in many of them also makes them possible candidates for treatment under the theme of social self-criticism and discord.[3] Locating them here, in a discussion of texts which deal with internal conflicts, emphasises, as many critics inside and outside Kenya have done, that they deal not only with Mau Mau as a movement of anti-colonial liberation, but also with the use of the armed struggle since independence by Kenyan writers to record and analyse the changing ideologies and attitudes of post-independence Kenya. These critics have commented on the fact that the focus of these texts is often less on the events of the armed struggle in and for themselves, as on the conflicts and disputes that have developed within Kenyan self-constructions and internal politics. The various depictions of Mau Mau in the literature have been a vehicle for this kind of direct analysis of present-day Kenyan affairs.[4]

In Ngũgĩ's work, for example, as has already been remarked, the representation of Mau Mau and its leaders is part of his conscious attempt at developing a politics of decolonisation. This is so even in the earliest of the novels which deal with the Mau Mau movement – for example *A Grain of Wheat* (1967), which argues that the sacrifice of the freedom fighters is already being betrayed even before Uhuru (Independence) is achieved.[5] The betrayal of the fighters by their compatriots mirrors the larger betrayal of the ideals of the movement in the period following independence. In this early text, the narrative ends on an image which is one of hope and possible regeneration, the carving of the pregnant woman on the stool by the carpenter Gikonyo, whose name, together with his lover Mumbi, can also be read as signifying the Gĩkũyũ people, as they echo the names of the founding parents in the Gĩkũyũ Creation Myth. But when Ngũgĩ returns to the theme of the rebellion and its aftermath in *Petals of Blood* (1977), the note of disillusion and betrayal is much more strongly developed, as we have argued in the earlier discussion of this novel.[6] Thus although Ngũgĩ sets out to celebrate the freedom fighters and their ideals, they are also used to critique the current regime for its rejection of their goals and their sacrifice. In other words, Ngũgĩ's representation of the Mau Mau conflict is a precursor of his later anti-elitist and anti-neocolonialist stand in texts such as *I Will Marry When I Want* (1980), *Devil On the Cross* (1982) and *Matigari* (1989). This is most noticeable when he returns directly to the theme of the Mau Mau rebellion in the play *The Trial of Dedan Kimathi* (1976).[7] As the preface, by Ngũgĩ and his co-author Micere Githae Mũgo, makes clear, the play is primarily a response to the present situation in Kenya, specifically to the representation of Mau Mau and of Kenyan popular leaders in the period of the late 1960s and early 1970s. 'We agreed that the most important thing was for us to reconstruct imaginatively our history, envisioning the world of the Mau Mau and Kimathi in terms of the peasants' and workers' struggle before and after constitutional independence.'

As the same preface goes on to make clear, the book is no less an 'imaginative reconstruction' and a book with a specific political aim, than those colonial texts it opposes, such as Ian Henderson's *The Hunt for Dedan Kimathi* (1958) and, even more importantly perhaps, those texts by Kenyan authors which 'Our historians, our political scientists, and even some of our literary figures were busily spewing out, elaborating and trying to document the same colonial myths which had it that Kenyan people traditionally wandered aimlessly from place to place engaging in purposeless warfare; that the people readily accommodated themselves to British occupation!' (preface). This text is a conscious polemic against such views, since the authors state that 'We believe that Kenyan Literature – indeed all African Literature and its writers are on trial. We cannot stand on the fence . . . the challenge was to truly depict the masses (symbolised by Kimathi) in the only historically correct perspective: positively, heroically and as the true makers of history.' However we may respond to this kind of declaration, it is clear that the text does not embrace a more narrowly defined 'realistic' account of the trial or the events which led up to it. The preface is just as openly polemic:

> The play is *not* a reproduction of the farcical 'trial' at Nyeri. It is rather an imaginative recreation and interpretation of the collective will of the Kenyan peasants and workers in their refusal to break under sixty years of colonial torture and oppression by the British ruling classes and their continued determination to resist exploitation, oppression and new forms of enslavement.

In trying to understand the position of this mid-1970s text in the politics of representation of the Mau Mau conflict, it is important to realise that the events of Kimathi's death had taken place twenty years earlier in 1956, and that Kenya had been independent since 1965. It is arguable, then, that the real target of this text is not the British ruling classes and their colonial policies, but the continuity between such policies and the 'new forms of enslavement' (preface), which the new neo-colonial elite continued to practice. Certainly this, and the Gĩkũyũ-language plays which developed from the Kamiriithu Community Centre involvement a little later, were what led to Ngũgĩ's arrest, imprisonment and subsequent deportation by the government. Kenya's ruling politicians clearly perceived them less as documents of historical revision than as direct statements about the failure of post-independence Kenyan governments to deliver on their promises and commitments to the Kenyan people, symbolised by Mau Mau and its heroes such as Kimathi.

It is necessary to see this later development in Ngũgĩ's work in the context of the influence of younger writers, who had published between the writing of Ngũgĩ's first books dealing with the independence struggle and the later works in Gĩkũyũ, when Ngũgĩ's opposition to the neo-colonialist politics of the KANU leadership became the clear and overt focus of his writing. In the work of these younger writers, the Mau Mau freedom struggle is presented in ways which reflect the various political attitudes which emerged after the formation of a one-party state, under the leadership of Jomo Kenyatta.

Writers such as the younger Meja Mwangi, in his Mau Mau novels *Carcass for Hounds* (1974) and *Taste of Death* (1975), whilst graphically capturing the violence and savagery of the period of the armed struggle, also reflect the impact of internal Kenyan politics during and after the actual conflict on the fictional representations of Mau Mau. Both these novels were published prior to Ngũgĩ's *The Trial of Dedan Kimathi*. *Taste of Death*, the earliest of Mwangi's novels, though not published until 1975, reflects the politics of the mid to late 1960s, when the various forces operating in the independence struggle were still active, and before an enforced national consensus emerged with the suppression of parties such as the KPU (Kenya Peoples Union), which claimed to speak for the landless and the ex-activists, and certainly attracted much support from these groups. Johannson, in the only full study of Mwangi's work to have emerged so far, argues that the presentation of the Mau Mau armed struggle in the novel is profoundly ambiguous. Whilst the novel stresses the political ideology of recovery of the land as the dominant motivation of the Mau Mau leader, General Kariuki, he is also presented, in stereotypical terms, as a ferocious terrorist, motivated by brutality, bloodshed and personal vengeance, in ways reminiscent of the settler accounts of the Mau Mau fighters and in phrases which often echo these negative sources. This, Johannson argues, is in line with the emerging ideology of 'containment' towards Kenyan history, which later led Kenyatta to characterise the Mau Mau fighters as 'a disease which had been eradicated'.[8]

The later novel, *Carcass for Hounds*, is the account of a group of forest fighters at a crucial point of the armed struggle. Again, the characters have that ambivalence of presentation on which both Maughan-Brown and Johansson have commented. The figure of the Mau Mau leader, Haraka, is portrayed as brutal and violent, even towards his own men. Compared with the relatively sympathetic portrayal of the Mau Mau leaders in Ngũgĩ's *A Grain of Wheat*, and the idealistic portrayal of Kimathi in the play *The Trial of Dedan Kimathi*, Mwangi's portraits of Mau Mau are far more violent and ambivalent. As Maughan-Brown and Johansson have argued, the plot of *Carcass for Hounds* depicts the gradual disintegration of Mau Mau from an idealistic movement to a brutal, revenge-oriented affair, a turn in which the specific operation the book recounts, called Operation Anvil, is crucial.[9]

Johansson further argues that in this later novel the ideological underpinning of the first novel in support of Mau Mau disappears. His argument is that the latter book, though ostensibly about the Mau Mau rebellion, is best read as a response to the political and ideological shifts at the time of the book's production. He argues that its real subject is a defence of the political doctrine of centralised leadership. In Johansson's view, Mwangi's text, for all its revolutionary subject matter, ends up lending support to the new Kenyan elite and the external neo-colonialist forces, who are the direct heirs of the colonial 'settler' forces defeated by Mau Mau. This provocative reading of these texts is backed by the analysis of linguistic features, such as the use of terminology which variously names the Mau Mau as freedom fighters, forest fighters (a more ambiguous term frequently employed even in settler accounts), and even, on one occasion, explicitly as terrorists (in a reference by one leader to his predecessor as 'the little terrorist general'). The stress on personal revenge as the motivation of the fighters also undercuts their presentation as idealistic and ideologically committed freedom fighters.

Whether we accept this reading of the texts or not, what is clear from these recent discussions is that it is not possible to read recent accounts of the freedom struggle without taking into account the disputes and struggles within the post-independence regimes since the late 1960s and 1970s. Later literary accounts of the armed struggle of the Mau Mau fighters are clearly an important site for a variety of different purposes and projects, reflecting the complex nature of post-independence Kenyan political experience.[10]

The tone of these early East African texts differs from that of the more directly celebratory work of the first generation of West African authors, although, as Achebe's and Armah's work illustrates, a general tone of disillusionment had already surfaced, even in West African writing, by the late to mid 1960s. The major difference is that no comparable process of armed struggle accompanied the move to independence in British colonies in West Africa, and there is no direct equivalent to these independence struggle texts there. However, in the period immediately following independence, the discord between various groupings inside the ex-colonies in West Africa led to internal struggles, and to a number of violent civil conflicts, the effects of some of which are still with us.

The best-known of these conflicts, and certainly the one which has generated the most literary accounts, is the Nigerian Civil War of 1967–70. The divisions between the various groups linked in the colonial construction of Nigeria had been a feature of the country since independence, but the friction increased dramatically in the late 1960s, especially between the Hausa in the north, and the Ibo in the south-east. This friction resulted in a military coup, led by easterners, in January 1966. The coup was viewed by many as an Ibo attempt to take over the country, and six months later another successful coup was led by General Yakubu Gowan (a non-Muslim, non-Hausa northerner). Gowan developed twelve new states, to break up the four regions, and to lessen the power of the larger ethnic groups and increase that of the minorities. This increased the feeling of threat felt by Ibos, which had begun after the killing of Ibos in the north in the riots of 1966, many of whom then fled to their traditional homeland in the south-east with tales of Hausa torture and oppression, which fuelled separatist sentiments. In 1967, the Ibos, under the leadership of Colonel Ojukwu, attempted to secede as the Republic of Biafra, an action which led to a bloody civil war. The war, like many civil conflicts, was especially cruel and unforgiving, and resulted in hundreds of thousands of casualties. The conflict lasted until 1970, when the Biafrans were finally defeated. Not surprisingly, such a major conflict has led to a large body of literary representations, which deal with the human and political consequences of this appalling event, as well as a substantial body of criticism evaluating these texts.

In one of these recent studies, Craig McLuckie notes that between 1970 and 1990 more than 'twenty-nine works have been written about the civil war. Moreover ten autobiographies have also been identified.'[11] As well as early texts, such as S. O. Mezu's *Behind the Rising Sun* (1971), Chinua Achebe's *Girls at War* (1972), Kole Omotoso's *The Combat* (1972) and I. N. C. Aniebo's *The Anonymity of Sacrifice* (1974), this large body of writing includes such well-known later texts as Isidore Okpewho's *The Last Duty* (1976), Cyprian Ekwensi's *Survive the Peace* (1976) and *Divided We Stand* (1980), Buchi Emecheta's *Destination Biafra* (1982), Elechi Amadi's *Sunset in Biafra* (1978) and *Estrangement* (1986), Festus Iyayi's *Heroes* (1986), and Wọle Ṣoyinka's *The Man Died* (1979), *Season of Anomy* (1980) and *Madmen and Specialists* (1984). Few events in recent African history have produced such a massive literary response.

As we saw in discussions of politically focused novels in the previous chapter, the war also influenced Ugandan historian and political scientist Ali Mazrui's study of the role and duty of African intellectuals in his controversial fictional work *The Trial of Christopher Okigbo* (1971), which examines and criticises the fatal choice made by the Ibo poet to fight and die as a soldier on the Biafran side. This wider response to the Nigerian tragedy reflects, as Sierra Leonean critic Eldred Jones has argued, the fact that the conflict 'served as a paradigm of the agonising teething problems African countries have to experience in the process of readjustment and in the attempt to resolve their more catastrophic colonial legacies'.[12] It is clearly impossible even to list exhaustively, let alone analyse, such a vast response. A number of texts, though, do suggest the different ways in which this event was approached by the writers, as the effect of the war was absorbed into the consciousness of the shattered post-colonial Nigerian state.

Among the earliest literary responses to the war are a number of texts written about the war from the Biafran side. One of the earliest of these is S. Obechukwu Mezu's novel *Behind the Rising Sun* (1971), whose title indicates its provenance in the eastern breakaway region. Published in the immediate aftermath of the war, it shows the confusions and contradictions within the new Republic. Its preamble claims, disingenuously, that 'this novel is entirely objective. It does not even attempt explanation: it is a witness's perhaps naïve response.' Its characters are stereotypes, representing different interests in the

Biafran community. The very name of the protagonist, Freddy Onuoha, reflects this, as *oha* in Ibo means group or community. Thus Onuoha, as he is called throughout, is an attempt to represent the Ibo community who witnessed and suffered the war. The first half of the text deals with the greed and self-seeking of the Biafran bourgeoisie, who, under the guise of constructing various foreign missions to secure arms and supplies for the cause, line their own pockets and remain luxuriously safe, while ordinary Biafrans are dying on the battlefields and in the bombed and shelled towns. The second half of the text gives a picture of middle-class life in Biafra, as the Federal forces gradually overrun the capital Enugu and other strategic towns, such as Port Harcourt and Owerri.

Chukwuemeka Ike's *Sunset at Dawn: A Novel About Biafra* (1976) is both a less ambitious and in some respects a more successful novel, although it shares with Mezu's novel the limitations of presenting the war exclusively from the viewpoint of the Biafran middle class, from which the majority of its characters are drawn. Significantly, though, the final message of the novel, which is that of reconciliation and the need to embrace national unity rather than conflict and war, is spoken by the uneducated village father of the main protagonist, Dr Kanu. The presentation of this village life, to which Fatima, the Hausa wife of Dr Kanu, is sent for safety, is less sentimentalised than in Mezu's work. The portrait of the suspicion and cruelty shown to the refugees who have been forced to flee there, especially those from Onitsha, which, although technically part of Biafra, is associated with the Benin rather than Ibo cultures, goes some way to mitigate and balance the generally much more negative presentation of the Federal forces, their atrocities and violence. The theme of the final part of the novel, the conversion of Kanu's Hausa wife to a positive pro-Biafran stand, as the result of the horrors she witnesses and her personal tragedies, is mirrored in other stories in the text, such as that of the successful businessman Mr Bassey, whose non-Ibo status also makes his loyalty to Biafra, forged in the horror of the war, another object lesson.

Judged by length alone, Eddie Iroh's frankly popular trilogy of 'thrillers' based on the Biafran war is one of the most extensive literary responses to the conflict. Iroh's trilogy is aimed directly at a mass audience, and he sees himself as a writer for the people. His books show the strong influence on popular writers of international authors in the modern period. Arguably, the best-known account of the Biafran war is the opening section of Frederick Forsyth's international best-selling thriller about mercenaries, *The Dogs of War* (1974). Eddie Iroh's first book in the trilogy, *Forty Eight Guns for the General*, written in 1976, clearly shows the inspiration of Forsyth's popular work, both in its theme of mercenary involvement in African conflicts, and in its attempt at a racy popular format.[13]

Like Iroh, Cyprian Ekwensi also published a popular account of the war in the same year, entitled *Survive the Peace*. These popular works have been among the most successful accounts of the war, at least judged by sales.[14] Cyprian Ekwensi, though an Ibo born in the eastern region, was raised in the north. Despite his allegiance to the Biafran cause, Ekwensi was a novelist noted for an interest in the new mixed ethnicities of the cities, whose life he had already dealt with in novels like *People of the City* (1963) and *Jagua Nana* (1975). His assertion of his Ibo status during the conflict is matched by his equally strong claim, elsewhere, to being a passionate lover of 'his country', Nigeria. McLuckie suggests that Ekwensi is a classic instance of how our sense of community can shrink or expand in different circumstances, moving between what he calls 'root' community (ethnic grouping) and wider visions such as nationality, as political circumstances change. He also proposes that Ekwensi's real community is 'the people', suggesting that his more popular work goes some way to address the concerns raised by the class limitations of the characters in novels like Mezu's. In characters like Pa Ukoha, Ekwensi registers that what matters for ordinary people is not 'who is ruling us today' but their need for roads, schools, hospitals and above all 'peace, no more killing' (57). Later, this concern is modulated into a wider political discourse by other characters, such as the Captain, who remarks that such popular goals can only be reached when the appropriate political structure is in place. The Captain also argues that even though the fight for this may mean the need for conflict and war, 'it will all be a waste of our time if after this there is no peace – if we do not get the government we desire' (74). Nevertheless, despite these ambivalent attitudes in his fiction, Ekwensi, like Mezu, Ike and Iroh, was an active supporter of the Biafran cause, and worked as an information officer for the breakaway regime. Of course, Ekwensi is not alone among the earlier Ibo writers in presenting a less partisan version of events than Mezu, Ike and Iroh. For example, John Munonye's civil war novel, *A Wreath for the Maidens* (1973), whilst it presents the war mainly from the Biafran perspective, also shows that its young protagonists are less than enthusiastic about the Biafran leadership, whom they perceive as almost as self-serving and corrupt as those of the Federal forces they oppose.

It is understandable that the earlier responses to the conflict came mainly from Ibo writers, and largely presented the war from the point of view of the Biafran forces and their supporters. The war was largely fought in and on the territory of the mid-west and east, and in most of the north and west it impacted less directly on the civilian population. Nevertheless, a number of non-Ibo writers also engaged with this conflict and its political and human cost. The work produced by non-Ibo writers has, understandably, been less partisan in its concerns, more involved with presenting the cost for everyone involved, even the soldiers of the Federal forces (those 'vandals', as the earlier pro-Ibo texts had generally characterised them).

Isidore Okpewho's novel *The Last Duty*, written in 1976 and set in a 'border' zone, presents the events from the point of view of those on the Federal side of the line of conflict. It is set in a fictional town until recently occupied by 'rebel' forces, and which is now under the control of the Federal army. The novel's setting is a town in the mid-west region, called Urukpe. The Federal Major, Ali S. Idris, whose name identifies him as a Muslim, and a northerner, is presented quite sympathetically. His severity in executing one of his soldiers for a civilian crime, and his well-developed sense of duty, are coupled to a belief in the justice of his cause. In this regard, he is in strong contrast to the leading citizens of Urukpe. These include Chief Toje, who, intent on seducing the wife of Oshevire, his pre-war rival in the rubber trade, has falsely denounced him to the Federal authorities as a collaborator, on no evidence other than rumour and the fact that his wife, like many others in this border region, is an Ibo. Okpewho's technique of using a multivocal narrative works quite well, and it allows us to see the situation from the many different viewpoints of those involved, including that of Oshevire's wife, struggling to remain faithful in a difficult situation, and even that of his young son, whose child's perspective allows us to see the human cost of the war and the vicious behaviour it encourages even amongst the non-combatants. The effect of the war on this once peaceful community and its innocent citizens is captured, graphically, in the child's nightmare of his father attacking him and his mother with a fire-reddened machete. *The Last Duty* graphically addresses the issue of what the duty of soldiers and of all human beings really is. Major Ali is relieved of his post because of his even-handed treatment of all the citizens of the town. Yet he remains convinced that his decision to try to reconcile military duty and his human conscience is the correct one. Okpewho's complex narrative suggests, though, that an ideal of duty may not be enough, and that Ali fails to see that the brutality of modern warfare cannot be reconciled with a personal, chivalric code. Ali's actions, although motivated by good intentions, have contributed to the situation. Individual moral worth is swept aside in the random and bloody brutality which the war has brought in its wake. The story has the feeling of a classical tragedy, in that in the end it offers no social solutions, only a vision of human courage in the face of events which have all the irresistible force of fate. We are left moved, but little comforted by this bleak and cheerless summary of the conflict.

Later works dealing with the war period have attempted a more direct social and political analysis of the war and its effects with varying success. Festus Iyayi's novel *Heroes* (1986) is also set in the mid-west region at the time of the 1969 Federal attack on Benin City. Thus, the geographical location of this novel is again the precise point at which ethnic and linguistic community boundaries became imprecise, and this is reflected in its characters and concerns. When the novel opens, Benin City is still occupied by the Biafran forces. The protagonist, journalist Osime Iyere, a Beninite who supports the Federal cause, has sent his brother and sister to his family home in Ugbegun, in Federal territory, and awaits the arrival of the Federal troops as liberators.

At first it seems that this might be a Federal equivalent to the early pro-Biafran texts. But in fact, Iyayi's has a different project. He does not set out to write in support of the Federal or the Biafran troops and their 'causes', but to expose the brutality which affects everyone dehumanised by war. The title 'heroes' is, in this case, deeply ironic. Iyere quickly learns that his belief that the Federal troops are more humane than the Biafrans is misplaced. After the troops enter the city, Iyere is forced to confront the fact that they too commit atrocities, killing not only Biafran troops but also Ibo civilians. The fact that Iyere is having an affair with an Ibo girl, the daughter of his landlord, makes

234

this realisation of Federal atrocities even more direct and personal. His disillusionment, which begins when he is mishandled by his 'heroes', is completed when his landlord is brutally murdered. From this point on, Iyere pursues a neutral role, seeking to politicise soldiers on both sides by taking them the message that it is only the leaders who will benefit from the war. Iyere risks his life to tell people like the Federal army sergeant, Kesh Kesh, that the leaders of both sides are equally guilty and disinterested in the welfare of the ordinary people.

Iyayi's left-wing stance, and his commitment to the radical and popular movement in Nigerian literature of the late 1970s and early 1980s, is reflected in this war novel, as in his earlier work which deals with the effects of class inequality in normal civil life. Iyayi's war novel is really aimed at showing that the military ruling class is one face of the elite group, whose greed and lack of concern for the people have led to the gross inequalities and tyrannies of recent Nigerian history. The military leaders he attacks here join the businessmen and corrupt civil politicians he satirised and castigated in *The Contract* (1982). Both are specific attempts at further analysing the causes of the brutal and desensitised lives of ordinary Nigerians, which he had captured in his novel *Violence* (1979). In this regard, Iyeri's war novel, published a decade and a half after the war ended, is like the later accounts of the Mau Mau movement in East Africa, which we discussed earlier. Its focus is the current political situation at the time of writing rather than the historical events of the war *per se*. It strengthens the message of the novel that the reader already knows that Iyere's predictions of the collusion of the leadership turned out to be quite accurate, and that the opposed leaders, Ojukwu and Gowan, were reconciled and indeed became political allies in the internal struggles in Nigeria in the post-war period.

The Yoruba writer Wọle Ṣoyinka was involved in strenuous attempts to prevent the war, engaging in a direct action campaign resulting in his imprisonment by the Federal government of General Gowan, which he describes in his prison diary *The Man Died* (1979) and in the prison poems in *A Shuttle in the Crypt* (1972). His other major literary responses to the war, the novel *Season of Anomy* (1980) and the play *Madmen and Specialists* (1984), show how deeply the war affected him, and how it shaped his response to the claims of the various governments in Nigeria to represent the people and their aspirations. The prison diary, *The Man Died*, is a powerful testament to what happens when regimes believe they have the right to set aside the rule of law and act in arbitrary ways. Similarly, in the poems in the prison collection, *The Shuttle in the Crypt*, Ṣoyinka has captured the alienating experience of being locked away in solitary confinement. He records graphically how he was subjected to a series of subtle, and not so subtle, pressures to incriminate and disclose himself and others, when his only offence was his refusal to accept the right of the rulers to define truth and justice according to their political needs. *Season of Anomy* can also be read as a comment on the underlying motives behind the 'nationalist' rhetoric of the civil war period, and one which suggests that it really covers economic and political forces rather than any profound ideological gap between the two opposed factions. The Cartel which rules the country through its exploitative alliance of businessmen and military, and which has both country-wide and international ramifications, is Ṣoyinka's way of symbolising the deeper and less idealistic causes of a conflict presented by both sides as a noble struggle for national identity. But perhaps Ṣoyinka's most powerful indictment and analysis of the war, and of the impoverished ideas which fuelled it, is the play *Madmen and Specialists*, first performed in 1970 in America, the year the war ended, where Ṣoyinka had sought refuge after his release from prison.

What is important about Ṣoyinka's analysis of the war is that he did not advocate for either side like other intellectuals, such as J. P. Clark on the one side, or Achebe on the other. His opposition to the war was also an opposition to the kind of inadequate ideas of identity and community which were embraced by the partisan supporters of both sides. Nor did he embrace the kind of simplistic, radical solution which mars even so powerful an indictment as Iyayi's novel *Heroes*. Clearly rooted in his own experience, and in the atrocities which characterised the Nigerian civil conflict, *Madmen and Specialists* nevertheless seeks to relate these events to the wider underlying forces, which prompted once decent men to hot brutal madness, or to developing the cold specialism of modern scientific-warfare experiments. The perverted world of the war scientist Dr Bero and his now mad old father, The Old Man, is erected on the corruption of those who have been brutalised by the war, the cripples, beggars and outcasts, who have been recruited by The Old Man to the religion of As. This new creed is the ultimate expression of pragmatic mindless power, in which appearance replaces reality, and whatever is exists only as an aspect of some endlessly malleable and corruptible present. Deliberately echoing and perverting the Christian creed of eternal truth, 'As Is, As Was, As Ever Shall Be', the root of this perverted view of man is in the horror of the civil conflict, itself only a single manifestation of the modern disease of totalitarian power, greed and exploitation. The cripples and beggars, themselves the flotsam and jetsam of the war, have been brutalised and are ready-made tools in the service of the new religion. Dr Bero himself, a specialist rather than a madman like his father, is forced to recognise that his own abominations, which are rooted in a false, scientific rationalism, are part and parcel of this older and more permanent abomination, and that he is indeed his father's son. He uses a false and perverted rationalism to justify the cannibalism which he practiced in the wake of the famine produced by war.

> Bero: . . . Afterwards I said why not? What is one flesh from another? So I tried it again, just to be sure of myself. It was the first step to power, you understand. Power in its purest sense. The end of inhibitions. The conquest of the weakness of your too human flesh with all its sentiment. (36)

Dr Bero's conversion has occurred at a modern version of the Atrean feast served by The Old Man to the specialists of modern warfare, including his own son. The Old Man's 'madness' lies in his acceptance of the price of war in the maimed and dead, and in his view that to consume the dead to alleviate hunger and pain is only a natural extension of what occurs anyway in modern war. As the cause, so the consequence. And yet this logic is, of course, also false. It serves the concept of a total limited purpose by which any action can be justified, a concept which, as we have seen, fascinates the specialists even as it appalls them. Here Soyinka may be thinking of the readiness with which scientists everywhere in the twentieth century have served the ends of their brutal masters – for example, in developing weapons such as the vaunted landmine developed by Biafran scientists and known as Ogbunigwe (literally mass-killer or mass-slaughterer), whose success in destroying the enemy is the subject of enthusiastic accounts in early partisan texts such as Mezu's, or other weapons of indiscriminate destruction, from atomic bombs to cheap, mass-produced anti-personnel mines.

Soyinka's response to the war was, from the very beginning, rooted in a perception of its wider implications for Nigerian society. It reflected his sense of the civil conflict as a symptom of deeper and continuing underlying problems, both in Nigeria and in the modern world of which it was now inevitably a part. The more recent work of writer and activist Ken Saro-Wiwa has also had this same contemporary and topical trajectory. The powerful novel *Sozaboy* (1985) is another late response to the civil war, and one which, like Soyinka's *Season of Anomy* and Iyayi's *Heroes*, can be seen to be as much about contemporary reality as about the historical events through which the writer's view is mediated. Written in what Saro-Wiwa calls 'rotten English', a stylised version of the pidgin English spoken by many illiterate and semi-literate Nigerians when they are communicating across their specific language regimes, it is the only novel successfully to present the experience of war and violence from the viewpoint of the common recruit. The protagonist is an intelligent young man from the small town of Dukana in the eastern portion of Nigeria, who, although intelligent, is forced for economic reasons to leave school and apprentice himself to a lorry driver. At the nearby large town, he meets a woman, Agnes, who has fled from Lagos at the outbreak of war. Both she and he are impressed, in different ways, by the power of the new *sozas* (soldiers), who appear everywhere as the conflict begins. Agnes sees them as a source of power which can protect her and she encourages her young husband to join up. Sozaboy, as he has named himself, is also eager to enter what seems to him to be the glamorous world of uniforms, marching, bands and guns. The story traces his awareness of the actuality and horror of military life and warfare, as we get an ant's eye view of the conflict. The technique of telling the story in the first person, and in the limited language of Sozaboy's 'rotten' (modified pidgin) English, creates a powerful, authentic picture of the life of the ordinary recruit, in which we are not even clear which army he has joined. Nigeria or Biafra are never mentioned. The story is contained within the microcosmic view of his hometown of Dukana and its neighbouring towns. The rhetoric of the leadership is dismantled as we see it through the limited vision of the protagonist Sozaboy. In fact, Sozaboy doesn't realise that the war is a civil war. He thinks of it, when he thinks at all of such large issues, as an extension of the Second World War, which he has heard of from the old returned soldiers who had fought in the Burmese campaign.

In fact, ehn, the man was speaking like that D. O. was speaking in the dream for Dukana. Using big words that I cannot understand. But every time he will be calling that Enemy. I begin to fear this Mr. Enemy you know. Because I am thinking he must be a strong man pass Hitla sef. Otherwise why is everyone talking about him? Even the Chief Commander General is fearing this man. Why? Even sef, why all of us will join hand to kill him? Does he have many heads? What is wrong with him? 'E get stronghead? Or did he call another man's wife? Why does everyone want to kill him? (78)

After his first experience of fighting, Sozaboy learns quickly that war is not glamorous. He runs away and, on his capture, is sentenced to a punishment camp, where he is brutally treated. Escaping again, he encounters refugees, in scenes which show the horrors of the war for civilians.

The ordinary soldier's ignorance of any grand design is pointed up by the fact that Sozaboy is then recruited by the other side. When he returns to his home village, he is actually wearing the 'Enemy's' uniform, though at that point he is a deserter from both armies, seeking only to find his wife and mother. Sozaboy struggles to make sense of a world which has gone mad, reflecting that 'That foolish man Chief Commander General have told lie about enemy and no enemy. But was it not the enemy that saved my life? . . . So all this suffering is totally useless. And to fight war is even more useless' (153). In a final image of the collapse of society, Sozaboy returns to his village, only to discover that his wife and mother have been killed by a bomb. His fellow villagers, believing he was killed in battle, now think he is a ghost, who has returned to seek vengeance for the death of his family, and he is forced to flee from his home town. The novel ends with a bitter reflection on the cost of the war:

> And as I was going, I was just thinking how the war have spoiled my town Dukana, uselessed many people, killed many others, killed my mama and my wife, Agnes, my beautiful young wife with J. J. C. and now it have made me like porson wey get leprosy because I have no town again.
>   And I was thinking how I was prouding before to go to soza and call myself Sozaboy. But now if anybody say anything about war or even fight, I will run and run and run and run and run. Believe me yours sincerely. (181)

Saro-Wiwa's novel was published by his own press in Nigeria. The choice of writing it in 'rotten English' may have been designed to make it more accessible to local readers, yet its effect was to make it of great interest elsewhere, especially to academic readers, as an example of language experiment.[15] It certainly presents by far the most convincing portrait of what the experience of war must have been for the majority of ordinary Nigerians who were caught up in it. Its politics are all the more powerful for being implicit in the material dramatised, rather than merely part of a commentary. Its choice of an ordinary soldier as a protagonist dramatically illustrates how the war aims, and their justifications, are far removed from the daily concerns of the ordinary Nigerian. *Sozaboy* reinforces the message, which has strengthened as the war has been analysed by succeeding writers, that the real conflict is between the leaderships of both sides, isolated from the people by their wealth and privilege, and the ordinary people, who must pay the cost of the struggles between conflicting elite groups for a larger share of 'the national cake'.

As well as texts which deal with actual war and civil conflict, there have been a number of texts in English from East and West Africa that have addressed the conflicts in contemporary society in terms of the evolution or destruction of traditional social structures (of age, sex, race, religion, etc.), and their replacement by new, contemporary forms. This was, of course, a feature of such early texts as Achebe's *No Longer at Ease* (1960), which illustrates how the obligations of village society, and the communal values of their urban representatives, lead to the imprisonment of its young, 'been-to' protagonist, Obi Okonkwo, when he seeks to respond to the demands of his fellow Umuofians to help his 'countrymen' get government jobs. What in the world of the village is a good action becomes, in the new urban environment, the grounds for a criminal charge of nepotism and bribery.

In East Africa the same theme is explored in Mude Dae Mude's novel *The Hills Are Falling* (1979), in which the conflict between traditional demands, based on ideas of communality, put great pressure on the educated 'been-to' Galga, who has returned to face similar demands from his relatives, and from his father-in-law. This accomplished novel has had little critical notice, and yet it is amongst the earliest East African works of fiction to explore this important theme. Through Galga's plight, Mude Dae Mude analyses the social and economic pressures which the transition from a rural communal life to a modern urban one has had on many educated East Africans.

As in the novels by Meja Mwangi, discussed above, a whole genre of East African novels has developed concerned with the effects of urbanisation on domestic life.[16] Although East African societies are generally less urbanised than those of West Africa, the rapid growth of cities in a relatively short time, where little or no tradition of urban life previously existed, notably in large conurbations such as Nairobi and Dar es Salaam, has meant that the clash of traditional values and modern life has been especially important and acute. The rapid development of class divisions, and the persistence into contemporary society of the colonial policy of separating peoples according to race and religion, has also exacerbated these problems.

These texts record the conflict which the clash of traditional forms and modern social demands has created with the institution of marriage and parent/child relations. Some of the most important of these accounts have been by women writers, and they are discussed in Chapter 11. But male writers, too, have addressed the theme of the clash of traditional practices, such as polygamy, with modern life, especially in the new world of the cities, where changing employment patterns and economic structures militate against the successful maintenance of social and cultural traditions.

In East Africa a number of modern texts have dealt with the problems which result from mixed marriages, liaisons between people from different classes, or between people from different cultures and religions. This theme is also present in some West African novels, but in countries like Kenya it has been especially prominent as a theme. Mwangi Gicheru's novel *Across the Bridge* (1979), for example, examines the difficulties of a successful liaison between the rich and the poor. As in other Kenyan novels, such as Thomas Akare's *The Slums* (1981), Gicheru examines the relationship between a rich woman and a poor man, in this case the houseboy with whom the daughter of the house becomes involved.[17] The story of how Chuma and Caroline cross the barrier between rich and poor is a rather sentimentalised one, with a contrived happy ending. Chuma is led into petty crime and then into the world of gangsters in an attempt to get the money he needs to impress Caroline and her parents. The account of the world of these petty criminals is the novel's strongest section, and compensates for the unlikely ending in which Caroline and her parents are reconciled to Chuma on his release from prison. Gicheru's 1984 novel *Two in One* deals with the racket in stolen children in modern Kenya, itself a product of the growing divisions based on wealth in Kenyan society, a racket which touched Gicheru's own family, when his eight-month-old daughter was stolen by a housemaid and never recovered.

East African writers have also explored the conflicts which arise when marriages occur between people of different religious backgrounds, especially between Muslim and non-Muslim partners. Samuel Kahiga's 1979 novel, *When the Stars are Scattered*, for example, deals with the problems which arise when a young engineer meets two Muslim sisters, Sophie and Asha, whilst on a visit to Mombasa. After Ricky, the engineer, has a long and stormy relationship with Sophie, she marries a fellow Muslim. The novel ends when, after some years, Ricky meets Sophie again, and they have a brief but passionate affair.

> We spent well over an hour together and I don't remember feeling guilty about the man we were cheating. After all he had cheated me out of love in the first place. And Sophie looked quite comfortable too, lying by my side. Had she not given them everything they demanded, virginal blood and all? Now she could be true to her own feelings – *provided nobody knew*. She felt she had a right to this and she gave herself to me with no visible sign of guilt in her honest brown eyes. It seemed as if at last we had caught up with the game and were playing it right. (137)

In all these cases, the novels concerned engage with the rapidly growing market for popular fiction, skirting the line between serious writing which addresses contemporary issues, and the market for novels which deal with 'problem' relationships and offer self-help advice on how to deal with them.[18] Tanzanian novelist W. E. Mfukwe's *The Wicked Walk* (1977) also explores the problems of modern urban life in cities like Dar. This story of the struggle of young people deals with the pressures of a changing society, in which school is followed by an exposure to the world of bars and older men, determined to procure young girls. As the cover blurb suggests, it is meant to provoke its local readership, as they keep 'bumping into its characters on the streets or at work, and find yourself thinking more and more about the problems [it] puts before you'. The serious tone of this novel discriminates between it and the more obviously popular texts, but its themes and its characters again suggest the increasing overlap in the concerns of frankly popular and serious fiction in recent East African writing.

In West Africa, the theme of personal and domestic conflict has also been handled by a number of writers. Polygamy and its associated problems is a dominant theme here, appearing more frequently than in East Africa. This theme is again handled with particular subtlety and force by women writers, such as Nwapa and Emecheta, discussed at greater length in Chapter 11. I have also already noted the importance of the theme of polygamy in such early novels as Obi Egbuna's *The Wind Versus Polygamy* and Wọle Ṣoyinka's *The Lion and the Jewel*. In these early texts, the textual project seems to have been the defence of polygamy, as part and parcel of a body of traditional practices which colonial cultures had erroneously dismissed as primitive and uncivilised. From the beginning, of course, this view, predominantly held by male writers, had been questioned by women authors. But the romanticisation of institutions such as polygamy, and its problematic role in a world where economic and social structures were changing rapidly, was also the subject of some early male-authored texts, critical of the effects of this institution. For example, Isidore Okpewho's *The Victims* (1970) presents a picture of the conflict which the practice of polygamy can lead to in contemporary Nigerian society. Okpewho's novel deals with the struggles within a poor, urban family when the husband takes a second wife. It shows the differences between the practice of polygamy in a society where subsistence farming made it possible for families to support additional members by increasing their land, and its practice in modern, urban society where, as in this case, the husband is employed at a very low and insecure wage. The changed circumstances make the conflict between the two women, with which the novel opens, inevitable. The jealousy of the two women centres on the fact that they are forced to provide educational and other advantages for their own children. The husband, Obanua, a weak man to begin with, retreats further and further into the solace of drink, as the demands of his two wives become impossible for him to meet. Losing his job as a lorry driver, he ceases to be a support for his family, and spends his whole time in the palm-wine bar, cadging drinks. The job he manages to get, as a nightwatchman to a Christian mission, pays only enough to service part of his bar debt, and allow him to go on drinking and piling up further debt. Nwabunor, the elder wife, determines to poison the younger wife's soup, and so rid herself of what she sees as the main rival to her happiness and Obanua's recovery as her husband and supporter. Unexpectedly, the two sons, Bomboy, and her own child Ubaka, both eat of the poisoned pot with tragic results. As in most male-authored texts which deal with polygamy, the stress is on the poverty which prevents the successful practice of this traditional system, rather than on the psychological experience of the situation and its effect on the lives of the women involved. However, there is a stress on the failure of the system to function effectively in the modern world, which sets these later male-authored texts apart from the earlier nostalgic defences of the system. Even later texts like these, though, necessarily invite comparison with the more insightful accounts of these practices by women writers such as Nwapa, Aidoo and, most recently, Emecheta.[19]

Notes

1. See I. R. Mbise, 'Writing in English from Tanzania', in G. D. Killam (ed.), *The Writing of East and Central Africa* (London, Nairobi, Ibadan: Heinemann, 1984), p. 55.

2. At various times, government policy was in direct conflict with settler interests. 'Liberal' colonial governments in Britain instituted policies designed to encourage the economic independence of the 'native' populations. These frequently advocated the development of indigenous-owned farming enterprises, and other economic measures aimed at preparing the local populations for eventual independence, the officially stated 'long-term' aim of the colonising power. But even when such policies were advocated, they were often bitterly opposed by settler groups.

3. See Chapter 7.

4. See, for example, David Maughan-Brown, *Land, Freedom and Fiction: History and Ideology in Kenya* (London: Zed Books, 1985) and Maina ma Kinyatta's introduction to *Thunder from the Mountains: Mau Mau Patriotic Songs* (London: Zed Books, 1980).

5. See Chapter 6.

6. See Chapter 7.

7. These are the dates of the English translations. See Individual Bibliography for full details.

8. Johansson, citing Maughan-Brown, *Land, Freedom and Fiction*, p. 194. In fact Johansson's arguments here are strongly modelled on the more general account offered in Maughan-Brown's study of the various literary representations of Mau Mau, which anyone needing a full account of these complex issues would do well to consult.

9. Lars Johansson, *In the Shadow of Neo-Colonialism: Meja Mwangi's Novels 1973–1990* (Umeå, Sweden: Dept. of English, Umeå University, 1992), pp. 24–31.

10. Readers interested in these issues may also want to consult other accounts such as Frank Furedi, *The Mau Mau War in Perspective* (London: James Currey, 1989); and John Lonsdale, 'Mau Maus of the Mind: Making Mau Mau and Remaking Kenya', *Journal of African History*, 31, 3 (1990), p. 393.

11. Craig McLuckie, *Nigerian Civil War Literature: Seeking an Imagined Community* (Lewiston, Queenstown, Lampeter: The Edwin Mellen Press, 1990), p. 9.

12. Editorial, *African Literature Today*, 13 (1983), p. vii, quoted in McLuckie, *Nigerian Civil War*, p. 3.

13. Forsyth had covered the Biafran war as a foreign correspondent, and later wrote a strongly pro-Biafran, non-fictional account of the conflict based on these experiences. The regime, for which the mercenary protagonist of *The Dogs of War* previously worked, is clearly based on Biafra. The novel's protagonist, Shannon, is said to hero-worship its leader, referred to in the book only as 'the Colonel', for his honesty and political vision. He is a thinly disguised portrait of the bearded Biafran President, Ojukwu.

14. McLuckie's account provides some illuminating figures on sales of the various Civil War novels, noting that writers like Omotoso, whose novel *The Combat* seeks to put into practice the specific programme for literary decolonisation suggested by critics like

the *bolekaja* group, Chinweizu, Jemie and Madabuike, did not succeed in reaching the mass audience they sought.

15. Saros International Publishers, Saro-Wiwa's publishing house, had an office in Surrey, and so the book was available abroad even before it was re-issued by Longman in 1994. This fact emphasises that whilst there is and has been for a while a struggle between international publishing outlets and local publishing schemes, the two have also over-lapped in various ways. It is arguable that publishing ventures like Saros International may offer a model for the development of local publishing which still offers an outlet to the international market.

16. See Chapter 7.

17. See Chapter 7.

18. See Chapter 5.

19. See Chapter 11 for a fuller discussion of some of these texts.

Part Three

ALTERNATIVE VOICES IN EAST AND WEST AFRICAN ENGLISH WRITING

Minority Voices: English Writing in Non-Anglophone East and West African Countries

This volume has concentrated so far on those countries within the East and West African regions where English has been a dominant force in contemporary writing in non-indigenous languages. Nevertheless, in many other parts of East and West Africa, where English is a minority language in written expression, a number of significant writers and texts employing the English language have also emerged. In fact, these writers include some of the most accomplished to have emerged in English-language literature from Africa, for example the Somalian novelist Nuruddin Farah, or the Sudanese poet and essayist Taban Lo Liyong. In addition, in countries like the Sudan, where Arabic dominates written communication, or in Cameroon, where French is the principal written language, there are significant minority Anglophone writing and publishing communities who use English despite the existence of a dominant other language ethos. In the southern region of the Sudan, a number of indigenous regional languages exist. In this region, where a substantial number of Sudanese Christians live, English is frequently used in place of Arabic as the lingua franca between these language groups, though it is generally restricted to the elite section of the population, which has received mission education. In Cameroon, the literate elite in the western region of the country continues to employ English rather than French as a lingua franca between the various local languages, since in the colonial period they were part of the then British colony of Nigeria.

By contrast, though, in other areas of Africa more directly influenced by English, relatively few English-language writers have emerged. This is the case, for example, in the ex-British colony of The Gambia. Another very special case is Sierra Leone, the source of some of the most important English writing to come out of Africa in earlier periods, but where the contemporary production of texts has declined, reflecting, partly, the relative lack of interest shown by international publishers and presses in seeking out and fostering writing there.[1] Despite these different local factors, all these various countries have produced significant and valuable contemporary writing in English. The following sections offer a brief sketch of some of the more interesting writing to have emerged from these countries, to illustrate the ongoing use of English as a principal written language in these various national communities.

Sierra Leone

As we noted in the early chapters of this account, the use of English in West Africa as a form of expression by indigenes really began with the descendants of the freed slaves settled at Liberia, The Gambia and Sierra Leone. The story of West African English publications in the nineteenth and early twentieth centuries is inseparable from the story of these people and their Creole descendants. However, the patronage of English-language publishers shifted in the period after the Second World War, as new market-places for locally produced educational material developed in areas such as Ghana and Nigeria. This process produced a skewed concern with writing from these countries and they dominate such series as the Heinemann African Writers series, which was so influential in bringing world attention to African English writing. Nevertheless, from the perspective of the late 1990s, it is important to note the continuing output of work in English throughout the modern period by writers in more neglected countries, such as Sierra Leone.

The Sierra Leonean playwright John Joseph Akar's play *Valley Without Echo* (1954) was one of the first African plays to be performed in Europe. A little later, in 1960, Robert Cole published *Kossoh Town Boy*, a portrait of village life, but he published little afterwards. Two other more accomplished, and longer-lasting, early writers are Raymond Sarif Easmon, whose work includes *Dear Parent and Ogre* (1960) and *The New Patriots* (1965), and the novelist and poet Gaston Bart-Williams, a neglected writer of a number of significant works, and a body of interesting poetry, who, unusually for an English-language writer, lived and worked mainly in Germany. For example, he had his experimental, somewhat Joycean play, *The Drug*, performed there on West German radio in 1972. Abioseh Nicol was among the best-known of Sierra Leonean writers in the 1960s and afterwards. He published a collection of short stories entitled *The Truly Married Woman and Other Stories* in 1965. These clearly echo the project of writers elsewhere in the same period, such as Achebe, to celebrate and recuperate the African past.[2] Mainly set in pre-colonial Africa, the stories, we are told, are designed to show that 'most of those who wrote about us seldom gave any nobility to their African characters unless they were savages or servants or faced impending destruction. I know differently. I saw all around me worthy Africans who lived and worked with varying degrees of success, destruction and happiness. [So] I began to write about them' (preface).

In a second collection, also published in 1965 and entitled *Two African Tales*, Nicol noted that the stories were written 'for my young friends to give them an impression of what happened when we were colonial countries under the rule of Europeans'. In the foreword, he admits, disarmingly, 'that they owe something to European writers like E. M. Forster, Joyce Cary, Grahame Greene and Evelyn Waugh, all of whom I admire and who, themselves, wrote about similar situations. However, being both black and African, I was then on the other side of the fence and perhaps saw things somewhat differently.'

248

More recently, a number of significant new writers have emerged in Sierra Leone. Syl Cheney-Coker is one of the more original and powerful poetic voices of recent years. His novel *The Last Harmattan of Alusine Dunbar* is dealt with in Chapter 12. His poetry collections include *Concerto for an Exile* (1973), which is usually taken to be his first collection, though there was an earlier collection, entitled *The Road to Jamaica*, which I have been unable to obtain. Since then, he has published several more collections, including *The Graveyard Also Has Teeth* (1980), which also included a reissue of the poems first published in *Concerto for an Exile*. In 1990 he edited the influential anthology *Heinemann African Poets*.

The early poems in *Concerto for an Exile* contain very explicit references to the hybridised nature of Cheney-Coker's Creole heritage. In 'Hydropathy', for example, he comments on his 'foul genealogy' and how he '[laughs] at this Creole ancestry / which gave me my negralised head / all my polluted streams'. Even here, though, there is a celebration alongside the anger and pain he expresses about this mixed heritage, a celebration which is more explicit in the title poem of the same collection, for example:

> they dance to our mourning here in Freetown
> I dance with them here in exile
> feet deep in my heart
> all my limbs thrust against the acid wind
> if blade will sharpen that wind
> imagine my alcoholic head at dance
> but from what plantation
> and for what people my rum
> in my country the Creoles drink only
> Black and White with long sorrows
> hanging from their colonial faces! (7–8)

For Cheney-Coker, the difficulty is how to reconcile the complicity of his elite, Creole ancestors with colonialism and the sympathy he feels now for the 'peasants'. In the poem 'Peasants' from this early collection, he enunciates their many 'agonies', and warns of their likely reaction:

> the agony of long miserable nights
> that [*sic*] agony of their thatched houses with too many holes
> the agony of erecting hotels but being barred from them
> the agony of watching the cavalcade of limousines
> the agony of state balls for God knows who
> the agony of those who study meaningless 'isms in incomprehensible languages
> the agony of intolerable fees for schools but with no jobs in sight
> the agony of it all I say the agony of it all
> but above all the damn agony of appealing to their patience
> Africa beware! their patience is running out! (22)

Despite his claims, in this early period, that his poetic influences were more Latin American than African, and despite the specific debts he acknowledges to Rimbaud and Vallejo, the early poems now read very much as a statement of a self-conscious desire to identify with the intellectual experience of black Africa, particularly in its radical and revolutionary modes. In the poem 'Guinea', for example, his identity with the struggle of the people of Guinea-Bissau and their revolutionary leader Amílcar Cabral is very direct.

> Bissau Bissau Bissau
> I am of your image
> in spite of my Creole absurdity
> and six hundred Fulani negroes
> behind the guilt of my country. (37)

But the gap between his Creole heritage and the African peasantry, to whom Cabral's revolution was addressed, is caught in the poem 'Agony of the Dark Child', which, in its theme of obsession with skin colour, highlights the false consciousness and crippling guilt of blackness which the returnees brought back with them from the experience of slavery and exile, and the internalised racial discriminations, bred by the skin-lightening miscegenation of the plantation world.

> I came to my mother
> seeking the warmth of her breasts
> she was frightened
>
> you see I was dark
> too dark my grandmother lamented
>
> from the pharmacy
> medicated bars of soap
> drops of oil, drippings of water
> and ornamented cures
> for the naked body
>
> she was frightened she told me
> I was too dark! (29)

In embracing such themes, African Creole poetry echoes Afro-American or Afro-Caribbean concerns. But the poem 'Guinea' nevertheless concludes with Cheney-Coker's insistence on his oneness with the struggle of the ordinary, unambiguously black, African peasant: 'I am not the vampire / gnawing at your heart / to feed capitalist banks / I am your poet / writing No to the world!' (37).

Another recent notable addition to Sierra Leonean writing in English has been the Sierra Leone Trilogy of Lemuel Johnson. Issued in 1995, there are three volumes in this long, poetic sequence: *Highlife for Caliban*, *Hand on the Navel* and *Carnival of the Old Coast*. Johnson's work is influenced by, and references writing as diverse as, that of the Martinican Aimé Césaire and the Afro-American Ralph Ellison. This dominance of Caribbean and North American influences is not unexpected, since the Creole population of Sierra Leone is descended from both Nova Scotian (freed North American slaves) and Caribbean ancestors. His work shares some structural features with the Arrivants trilogy of the Barbadian poet Edward Kamau Brathwaite, and the long transcultural poetic sequences of the St Lucian Nobel-Prize winner Derek Walcott. Like Brathwaite's and Walcott's work, Johnson's poetry blends images from a variety of cultural sources. Like the Caribbean and Afro-American writers to whom his work responds, Johnson recognises that, as a Sierra Leonean Creole, he has inherited a similarly complex set of influences. For Sierra Leoneans, as for many Caribbean or Afro-American people, the issue of what is their 'originating' culture is at the heart of their sense of identity and their sense of difference. It is the complexity of this issue that Johnson addresses.[3]

An interesting contribution, both to African women's writing and to the story of the Creole minority, is Yéma Lucinda Hunter's wide-ranging historical epic *Road to Freedom*. This novel is the life-story of a Nova Scotian, or descendant of one of the loyalist blacks who fled to Nova Scotia during the War of Independence in America and who were resettled in Africa. It is structured in the form of an oral narrative, 'as told to' the wife of a visiting botanist. It covers the period of Governor Macaulay, the slave revolt and other major events in Sierra Leonean history from the point of view of a black woman. It is heavily derivative of well-known, published historical sources, which it acknowledges, such as the work of Falconbridge, Fyfe, Kup and Walker. It offers an interesting African example of a form which has been central to the recovery of women's subaltern histories in many parts of the African diasporic world – for example, the work of Caribbean women writers such as Jamaica Kincaid and Erna Brodber, or Afro-Americans like Alice Walker. However, unlike these, this fairly simple, straightforward, historical novel seems unconscious of the full possibilities of the generic form it employs. For example, the recording of the story by an amanuensis, and the problematics this involves, is not made an explicit subject of the text.

Not all recent Sierra Leonean English writing is concerned with either the Creole cultural heritage or the past. In this respect, the English writing which has come from those born into indigenous, non-creolised groups is distinctive both in theme and style. Nabie Yayah Swaray's play *Worl' Do For Fraid* (1986), for example, is a powerful and dramatically effective indictment of contemporary political corruption and greed, as well as of such infrequently acknowledged subjects as modern-day ritual murder. Swaray's play reminds us of the gap which has opened up in societies such as Sierra Leone and Liberia, between the descendants of the creolised coastal returnees and the indigenous peoples of the interior, gaps which have fuelled the brutal struggles and civil conflicts that have riven both countries in recent decades. The protagonist, Abass, after training as a doctor, returns to his village in the interior of Sierra Leone. He encounters there things he cannot condone, such as ritual murder and blood-drinking, and finds he is unable to come to terms with his 'homeland'. Swaray is clearly highly critical of modern Sierra Leone, and a reader may be reminded of the early work of Ghanaian novelist Ayi Kwei Armah in the play's emphasis on defilement and dirt, and its tone of bitter disillusion.

Yulisu Amadu Maddy is a prominent modern English-language playwright, whose work includes the collection *Obasai and Other Plays* (1971). Maddy is also the author of *No Past, No Present, No Future* (1973), which deals with young men facing change in Sierra Leone and the conflicts involved when they travel abroad. It is unusual in that it also raises the unfashionable topic of homosexual relations, still largely ignored in most African writing. Countries like Sierra Leone, which did not receive the same attention as Nigeria and Ghana in the search for new African texts by international publishers eager to break into this new and lucrative market, often turned to drama, since the production of play texts involves less infrastructure than the printing of stories and novels, or even the printing of poems (though poetry readings also share with plays a relative freedom of transmission). The prolific Prince Down Palmer's frankly popular novels embrace romance and thriller forms, adapting them to the West African setting. For example, in *The Mocking Stones* (1982), Palmer produced a widely read thriller based on the illicit diamond trade which flourishes in Sierra Leone. Like far too many places in West Africa in the last decade or so, Sierra Leone has been torn by civil strife. The military coup of 1992 in this diamond-rich country by Captain Valentin Strasser has initiated a series of civil conflicts in which mercenary forces have played a major role. The rebel forces of Foday Sankoh and the government troops of Valentin Strasser, both buttressed by foreign arms and mercenaries, have been at strife ever since. It is significant that the most recent literary work from Sierra Leone, such as Lemuel Johnson's, has been published outside a country which is being torn apart. Syl Cheney-Coker's only major novel also predates the coup of 1992.[4]

The Gambia

Like Sierra Leone, The Gambia was important in the early days of English writing in Africa, since it was the residence for a while of James Africanus Horton, who spent part of his career as an army surgeon here. However, it never received the same number of 'recaptives' or freed slaves as Sierra Leone, and although it had a similar colonial Creole culture to that colony, it did not develop on the same scale. However, like Sierra Leone, it has adopted Krio (derived from Creole English) as its official national language.

William Conton's novel *The African*, published in 1960, was one of the earliest of the new wave of African writers using English to emerge with the so-called 'discovery' of English African writing in the late 1950s. Although Conton was born in The Gambia in the early 1920s (published sources give his date of birth variously as 1920 and 1925), he lived from an early age in Sierra Leone and later in Ghana, where he worked as a headmaster. Returning to Sierra Leone, he became an educational administrator. He now lives in Paris. Conton's novel is the account of the experience of the scholarship winner Kisimi Kamara, who goes to England and has a love-affair with a white South African woman. When he realises that racial discrimination means that their relationship can never blossom, he returns to Africa and becomes a leading nationalist. The novel makes an interesting link between the personal anguish of its hero and his drive to power, a link which it explores with considerable psychological skill and insight. It is set in the fictional country of Songhai (*sic*). This could be either Sierra Leone or The Gambia, but is more likely to be the former, since, to all intents and purposes, Conton was Sierra Leonean. Conton published a second novel in 1987, a sort of moral political thriller called *The Flight*. The early date of his writing drew some critical notice, but he never really developed as a major writer.

In the modern period, The Gambia has produced the well-known poet and novelist Lenrie Peters. A doctor, Peters published a novel, *The Second Round* (1965), which dealt with the theme, common in early West African fiction, of the problems facing those who returned from study abroad, and how they found it difficult to fit into their old societies. This was followed by two collections of poems, *Satellites* (1967) and *Katchikali* (1971). Significantly, Peters's first publication, called simply *Poems* (1964), was published by Mbari Press in Ibadan. This fact emphasises that writers like Peters, who published in local presses in the larger markets of Nigeria, Ghana, Kenya and Uganda, although from elsewhere, stood a far better chance of being noticed and promoted by the international companies than writers who published in the small local presses in other countries in the West and East African regions.[5]

Few writers of real significance using English as a medium in this small country have come to wider attention since. Another early text was the play by Ramatoulie Kinteh, *Rebellion* (1968), which dealt with the slave period, and which shows a very sophisticated grasp of dramaturgy and good characterisation given its early publication date. Collections of stories, such as Nana Humasi's *A Krio Engagement and Other Stories* (n.d.), have also emerged from local presses such as Banjul. In the 1980s, a new group of younger writers began to be published. Lenrie Peters had initiated the formation of a Gambian Writers Club in 1971, and he published and edited from there a journal called *Ndaanan*, which encouraged younger writers such as the playwright Gabriel J. Roberts, when it published his play *A Coup is Planned*, in 1972.

Despite these attempts to kick-start local writing, little emerged until the mid-1980s, when Ebou Dibba published his first novel, *Chaff on the Wind* (1986). This novel enacts the process of recovery and restoration of pre-colonial culture, which Achebe and Ngũgĩ had initiated elsewhere twenty or thirty years earlier. Set in the 1930s, it deals with the impact of colonialism, but its real theme is the complex mix of cultures which make up The Gambia, dramatised in the figures of two boys, one pagan and one Muslim, who meet on a boat taking them down river to the capital Bathurst. The novel also includes accounts of minority creolised groups, such as the descendants of early Portuguese immigrants. The rivalry between The Gambia and the larger surrounding territory of Senegal is also touched on. Published by Macmillan in London, it initiated a series of local English texts, including a second novel by Dibba called *Fafa*. Although this is called a 'sequel', the connection with the first novel is pretty tenuous, the second tale being a self-confessed idyll, in which the river takes on a metaphorical life of its own, and the descriptions of the life along its banks dominate the narrative and characters.

Among the other significant writers in English to emerge since the mid-1980s is Tijan M. Sallah. He has published two collections of poems, *Kora Land* (1989) and *Dreams of a Dirty Road* (1993). Significantly, his earlier collection of stories, *Before the New Earth: African Short Stories* (1988), was published in India by the Calcutta-based Writers' Workshop, suggesting once again that writers from these smaller countries have to look elsewhere than the UK or the USA for publication opportunities. Its preface states that the stories address the fact that: 'The Gambia is a country without an original voice. These African stories steeped firmly in the Gambian experience attempt to fill this void. They are the moral tales of a society attempting to find and redefine itself – to retrieve the melodies of the past in order to create a New Dance, a New Earth.'

The similarity of these statements with those made by first-generation writers in countries like Nigeria and Ghana shows how false it is to assume a single line of development or chronology for African English writing. They illustrate how preoccupations and themes recur at different times in different societies, as they develop a specific level of literary culture and awareness. Thus Ebou Dibba's novel, set in the 1930s and published in the late 1980s, is basically a colonial 'contact novel' of the kind produced elsewhere in West Africa in the late 1950s and 1960s. Critics like Stewart Brown, one of the few people to take notice of this new writing, have speculated that the upsurge of writing in The Gambia in the mid-1980s might be in response to the need to defend a distinctive Gambian identity within the Senegambian Confederation initiated after the abortive coup of 1981. This coup, the first since independence in 1965, was foiled by the intervention of Senegalese troops, who restored to power the government of President Jawara. Senegal argued that the coup threatened the safety and property of Senegalese residents in The Gambia. As in the case of the Cameroons discussed below, after this coup the Anglophone community became a minority within a Senegalese Francophone majority, since Senegal literally surrounds The Gambia on three sides and has a much larger population. Sherif Sarr's 1984 novel, *Meet Me in Conakry*, shows the drift of Gambian youth to neighbouring countries like Senegal and Guinea, looking for work and a better life. In this novel, the young Gambians are mocked for their foreign pronunciation and their manners. The Confederation was dissolved again in 1989 and the Jawara government was overthrown in 1994 by a military coup led by a young officer, Lieutenant Yaya Jammeh. After external pressure, elections were held in 1996. Ex-President Jawara was excluded from running by the new Constitution. Jammeh was elected to be President of a new civilian Republic. Lenrie Peters was directly involved in this process as Chairman of the National Committee set up to consult on the return to civil rule, illustrating again the propinquity of literary and political culture, and the special role of intellectuals in the public life of many African countries.

Despite these momentous events, The Gambia is now best known outside Africa as a tourist destination for Afro-Americans and others. Many of these visit The Gambia to examine the village home of the hero of Alex Haley's American blockbuster *Roots*, even though it has been suggested that Haley's research in establishing a 'true' history for his ancestral protagonist was largely the product of his imagination. Tijan Sallah's poetry has addressed the consequences of tourism for the future of The Gambia and its culture, and suggested that, economically important as it is, it may have a long-term deleterious effect on the ability of the country to retain its cultural identity.[6]

Liberia

Liberia, after a significant early start not dissimilar to that of Sierra Leone with a long tradition of polemic, nationalist and mission writing from the 1830s onwards, has not produced a great volume of work in English in more recent times.[7] Writers since the Second World War include figures such as Bai T. Moore, who was one of three writers involved in producing the early post-war collection entitled *Echoes from the Valley. Being Odes and Other Poems by Three Colleagues* (1947). The other contributors to this volume were Roland T. Dempster, who continued to write poetry through the 1950s and 1960s, including a long poem *To Monrovia Old and New* (1959), published in Britain in the late 1950s; and Bai T. Moore, who also continued to write through the same period and his works include poetry collections such as *Ebony Dust* (1962) and fiction such as *Murder in the Cassava Patch* (1968). Moore, a Vai, like the early Liberian writer J. J. Walters (who produced, as we have already noted,[8] one of the earliest novels in English from Africa), has also written numerous accounts of Liberian writing, and a short account of the Vai people. This looks at their problematic role as indigenous people in a Liberia still dominated by Creole descendants of the resettled slaves. This important text is undated, but it was published sometime in the mid-1960s. His aptly entitled collection, *Poems from the Grassroots*, was published in Ghana in 1974. The majority of the writers before this period belonged to the Creole descendants of the resettled American slaves, but Moore as a Vai is an exception to this, as the significant and telling title of a recent tribute to his verse indicates: *A Tribute to Bai T. Moore, Liberia's Foremost Jungle Poet* (1988). The struggle between the descendants of the resettled slaves and the indigenous peoples in both Liberia and Sierra Leone, and the brutal political and military conflicts it has exacerbated in both countries in recent years, is beyond the scope of this brief literary account. But it forms a significant feature of the recent history of both countries. Though it has not yet been represented in the published writing to any great extent, it may well become a significant subject for writers when lasting stability is finally restored, as occurred in Nigeria after the Nigerian Civil War.

Other important literary figures include S. Henry Cordor. A selection of his prolific, if rather uneven work was collected in the anthology *Africa: From People to People* (1979). Cordor was indefatigable in promoting writing, and edited the first major anthology of contemporary Liberian short stories in 1980. The poet A. Doris Banks Henries was also an energetic, if rather conservative editor of poetry, and a collector of folk-tales, who compiled a number of literary anthologies and folk-story collections in the 1960s.

Amongst the more recent writing of note is Wilton Sankawulo's *The Rain and the Night* (1979), a novel celebrating the pre-colonial culture of the hinterland people of the Galaland region. It sets out to record the cultures of the people of the hinterland who were, in a real sense, colonised by the Christianised, returned slaves as well as by the Europeans who accompanied them. To this extent it is congruent with the first body of post-independence writing in other countries in the regions of East and West Africa discussed in earlier chapters, with its theme celebrating the dignity and value of the indigenous world disrupted by the invasions of colonising cultures.

Most recent Liberian work does not show the linguistic and narrative experimentation of the work of Sierra Leonean writers such as Syl Cheney-Coker or Lemuel Johnson, which is surprising given that both these complex, hybridised societies have access to forms of creolised English offering exciting possibilities for recording social and cultural differences. Bai T. Moore's novel *The Money Doubler* (1976) broke with the rather stilted, old-fashioned style of earlier Liberian writing and employed local pidgin in the dialogue, but this mode has not been followed up to any great extent. It is also interesting to note the relative absence of any obvious influence of Afro-American or Caribbean writing on this, the only African country with an American component in terms of its nineteenth-century settlement. Again, there is no real equivalent to the intra-cultural complexity of the work of the Sierra Leonean poet Lemuel Johnson, although an Afro-American influence does occur in the work of younger writers, such as K. Moses Nagbe in the poetry collections *The Real Drum Daddy is Back!* (1989) and *The Road to Romeo* (1992).

The military take-over of 1979–80 by Master Sergeant John Doe was clearly a major turning point in recent history, bringing to an end a long period of rule by President Tubman and his successor President Tolbert. Established writers like Cordor have addressed the issues arising from the coup in a number of pamphlets written at the time. Yet another coup attempt in 1989 by Charles Taylor, an official in Doe's government, failed to wrestle power from Doe. In 1990, a six-nation West African peacekeeping force, ECOMOG, partitioned Liberia into two zones. The first encompassed the capital of Monrovia, and was led by President Amos Sawyer. The other zone was controlled by Taylor and his National Patriotic Front (NPFL), and amounted to about 95 per cent of Liberian territory. Despite the signing of various peace accords, strife has continued and in 1996 the capital Monrovia and its airport were virtually destroyed. In recent years, as in the case of Sierra Leone, the violent civil strife in Liberia has clearly made the production of literature an increasingly hazardous and difficult task.

Sudan

The Sudan, too, has been subject to a period of prolonged and almost uninterrupted civil war since 1973. Sudanese modern writing in English has often reflected this political and civil disturbance, since the war reflects the struggles between the largely Arab-speaking north and the south, where English is a more usual lingua franca between the various language groups. Francis Deng's work literally bridges the gap between literature and direct political commentary. In two major novels, *Seed of Redemption* (1986) and *Cry of the Owl* (1989), Deng analysed the plight of the modern Sudan with its communities divided by a violent and long-lasting civil war between north and south. Deng's work represents one of the most far-reaching attempts to use fiction to address social issues and resolve political conflicts. A diplomat and political scientist, Deng has been an ambassador for the Sudan in a number of countries.

In the first novel, he creates in the figure of Faris Khalifa an embodiment of the complex, multicultural history of the Sudan. Beginning in the period after the abolition of slavery under the pressure of the European power, it traces the ways in which slavery became an intrinsic part of the Arab Sudanese culture's sense of identity, and reinforces the emergence of a politics of difference between Sudanese people, on the basis of their skin-colour and their acceptance of Islam. Faris's father, Rizig, is the son of a Dinka (black, southern, non-Muslim) princess, who has voluntarily enslaved herself to save her brother. Her brother, through this sacrifice, has been able to continue to lead her people. This narrative allows Deng to sketch in the mythical nature of the divisions of race and religion which underpin and help sustain the conflicts in the modern nation. He analyses the historical basis of modern ethnic conflicts, and suggests how they militate against the development of an effective and integrated modern nation. The novel argues that the exacerbation of these divisions in the modern period is partly due to the pressure from outside agencies, during the Cold War period, to take a hard line on communism. This drove Sudanese leaders away from earlier unifying policies towards a renewed suppression of those forces in the south which were labelled radical and subversive, and so supposedly had to be communist-inspired. The once reformist President Munir, who is now committed to supporting the fundamentalist Muslim brotherhood, and Faris, now Minister of Defence, come into conflict when Faris decides he must speak out against the new policies which he believes are simply dividing the country along lines of religion and race, and which are detrimental to the multicultural nature of Sudanese society. Munir claims to accept his analysis and invites Faris's friend Peter Gorkwei, leader of the southern, Christian 'rebels', to form a national alliance. But Gorkwei is rightly suspicious of Munir. In the struggle which follows the final split between the two sides, both indulge in an orgy of killing on racial grounds, killing which, as the novel indicates, is exacerbated by the fact that it is often impossible for the murderers accurately to identify the victims of their prejudice in the racial melting-pot of the modern Sudan. The finale, which follows Munir's deposition, has Faris persuading his fellow Sudanese to accept his vision of the past and future of the Sudan, and the novel ends with the hero looking forward to handing over power to 'whomever national consensus would finally produce'.

Deng's second novel, *Cry of the Owl* (1989), picks up from the finish of the previous one with the overthrow of the military dictatorship of Jabir El-Munir. As a result, it is perhaps less directly concerned to educate the readership in the history of the Sudan and of the immediate political past, and so has an easier and more novelistic feel for the reader. The stress of the opening chapters, which see the young Assemblyman Elias Bol return to his southern homeland to participate in the sacrifices for his dying father, the chief, is directed towards showing the complexity and subtlety of the 'animist' cultures. These cultures are too readily dismissed, Deng suggests, by both the Islamic leadership and the local radical Christian elites, as merely primitive superstitions. In this respect, once again, the novel's project is not dissimilar to that of earlier texts elsewhere in West and East Africa, that is, to recover a sense of the 'beauty' and 'dignity' of the cultural past of the peoples it describes. In this case, though, the project is directed towards an internal revision of attitudes, and not, as in the case of Achebe and Ngũgĩ, for example, towards the correction of distortions generated by European colonisers. However, it can be argued that the prejudices addressed by Deng's text are in part the product of the values associated with the two great religious and cultural incursions, Arab/Muslim and European/Christian, which have occurred in the Sudan. In both novels, Deng wants to show that unity is only possible if these historical prejudices are set aside.

> The one label that brings us together in full unity is our common identity as Sudanese. ... The same can be said of our culture. One does not have to be an expert to realise that there is so much cultural intermingling that it would be hard to know what is from the holy books and what is from the customary ways of our mixed ancestry – African and Arab.[9]

Elias's marriage to the daughter of his patron, the orthodox Muslim girl Fadheela, becomes the vehicle through which Deng can dramatise his support of unity amongst the various people of the Sudan. The more personal element of the novel, and its greater stress on the psychological contradictions which both have to overcome, as well as on the public process of struggle which they and their peoples face, make this novel an especially appealing and effective example of this genre of political narrative.

I have already mentioned Taban Lo Liyong's work in a number of other places, and this reflects not only his importance but also the fact that he was originally presented to the world as a Ugandan writer. He has lived and published in a number of African countries and has only in recent years become formally and publicly associated with his homeland region in the southern Sudan. His work has been published in many different places, including Kenya and Tanzania, as well as Zimbabwe, the UK and USA, reflecting the relative weakness of English publishing in the Sudan. In fact, in recent years Taban Lo Liyong has himself been very active in promoting English-language writing and publishing, with schemes to encourage young writers based in both the south (Juba) and the north (Khartoum). Taban Lo Liyong's work has always had a strong political element, reflecting his belief that the writer exercises a direct responsibility for reflecting, commenting on and reforming his or her society. A noted critic and academic as well as a creative writer, Taban Lo Liyong has been a major influence in the East African region as a whole. His early work is less directly rooted in the issues affecting the modern Sudan, and reflects his dominant concerns at the time with wider African and pan-African issues. In the poetry collections *Eating Chiefs* (1970) and *Frantz Fanon's Uneven Ribs* (1971), for example, Taban Lo Liyong examines the relations between traditional culture and modern concerns. Thus the first collection, *Eating Chiefs*, is subtitled *Lwo Culture from Lolwelto Malkal*, and was in part the result of Taban Lo Liyong's anthropological research undertaken at the University of Nairobi. Whilst teaching there, he was one of the initiators of the drive to Africanise the curriculum, especially in the areas of language and literature. The poetry in this collection bridges the gap between the anthropological treatment of traditional culture and the need to bring this alive as a source of inspiration for modern writers. Taban Lo Liyong has long been an admirer and promoter of the work of the Ugandan Acholi speaker Okot p'Bitek, and, more recently, he has sought to do the same kind of work in bridging the culture gap for his own people. Taban Lo Liyong was born in the southern region of the Sudan, but he was brought up in the Acholi-speaking region of northern Uganda, to which his policeman father fled after being accused of helping some relatives of his, who had fled persecution in Ethiopia and entered the Sudan as illegal refugees. Taban's personal history thus illustrates the fluidity of the colonial boundaries in this as in many other regions of Africa, boundaries which determined the geography of the new post-independence nations, and which often divided communities and language groups.

In the collection of essays *Culture is Rutan* (1991), he presents a powerful argument for the need to localise culture and to break down the false barriers between writing in introduced languages and that in the local languages. This work has not received the degree of attention accorded to Ngũgĩ's essays on similar subjects. This may be the result of Taban's more complex and balanced assessment of the complex cultural heritage of modern Africa, notably his continued willingness to employ all the languages which are available to modern Africans as a means of expression. Such a view has less appeal than the simple call to decolonise culture by reverting to African languages which makes Ngũgĩ so popular with those who prefer simple answers to complex issues. In the light of this relative neglect, it is worth bearing in mind that Taban was the first East African to publish a collection of critical essays on issues of culture and literature with his 1969 collection *The Last Word*. In this early set of essays, Taban argued for a careful evaluation of the many influences on modern East African culture, rejecting the simplicities of négritudinist thought in a manner reminiscent of the Nigerian writer Ṣoyinka. Like Ṣoyinka, too, Taban clearly establishes in this early work his commitment to the sources of his own cultural identity, and the need to preserve this, whilst acknowledging the ways it has been modified by the effects of centuries of Arab and European influence on African life in the region. More recently, Taban has continued to write in all the languages which he inherited, including English, whilst also championing the revival of local-language writing.

What makes Taban Lo Liyong's critical work so important is that this cultural theorist and critic is also a poet of great originality and power, able to

259

demonstrate in his own work the kind of integration which he argues for in his criticism. In *Frantz Fanon's Uneven Ribs*, the use of the long poetic monologue form, in a style reminiscent of Okot p'Bitek, is wedded to a sophisticated attempt to turn the tables on European cultural 'instruction', as Taban indicates why missionary opposition to 'polygamy' has been a destructive force for the traditions and values of his own people. In the poem 'Taban woos Beccie', he creates a long defence of African polygamous marriage, as he seeks to persuade his German girlfriend to join him in a polygamous marriage which will maintain his family's tradition. He recalls his father's admonishment:

> You see the tradition
> In this great family
> Is for caring, for human beings.
> I am sure you'll prove your father's son
> And top the record of the family
> With many wives and cows
> And children
> Whoever can care for many
> Has proved a leader of men.
> For what is leadership
> If not the ability to care? (96)

Taban's work never turns its back on public commitment, but weds this to a sense of the personal which allows his work a wry and pointed edge. In the poem 'Student's Lament', from the same 1971 collection, he warns would-be politicians and public spokesmen of the need to keep their sense of their roots:

> If you aspire to public fame
> Stick fast to the umbilical cord:
> For you were never born
> In the market place
> A full blown statue. (135–6)

Recently, Taban Lo Liyong has turned more and more to the problem also addressed by other Sudanese English-language writers, such as Francis Mading Deng: how to reconcile the divided forces within the Sudanese nation. As a southerner, he shares with Deng a concern for the preservation of the local culture and a belief that it can be made to work side by side with the wider forces represented in the Sudan by colonialism, and more recently by an aggressive northern drive for Islamicisation and Arabisation. In the collection *The Cows of Shambat*, which Taban published in Zimbabwe in 1992, he addresses the government abuses of recent times and draws some hopes for the future. The title poem contains an oblique reference to the prevalence of torture by government agencies in the recent civil conflict:

> There are contortions of limbs, sizzling of flesh,
> Loud explosions and blinding flying sparks.
> Then there is utter blankness.
> Bedazzled by the results of their exertions
> – like the proverbial bull in a china shop –

They emerge
Sweating
groping
hobbling
down
the
      stairs
On three legs. (2)

The same collection also contains the long satirical poem, 'The Tongue-twister', with its bitter indictment of the civil war, as the peasants try to understand the military advice of the 'black whiteman, master of war' who advises them to build trenches to shelter in since he has 'no tik tak . . . for shooting down flying missiles', concluding his useless advice with the rhetorical: 'Any more questions?' (69). This poem records the exchange between the visiting 'black-whiteman' and the village elders in council, as it is modified by the local translator who turns his words into Acholi. Its form reflects the proverbial, oral and intimate tone of this world into which the military jargon is a discursive invasion from a realm of totally different and destructive values. The fact that this world is that of the army who claim they are trying to 'defend' these particular people only makes the irony more acute.

My master, the black whiteman who knows the inside
of big fights thanks you from the bottom of his stomach.
He wishes you long life. Also to your wives.
And children.
Greet the old men. And old women. Greet the wives.
And the children. Tell them all things I have said. About holes, sorry, I mean
    kandaks. (69)

Taban Lo Liyong has a much franker and stronger political agenda than earlier Acholi writers like Okot p'Bitek, but he continues to acknowledge a debt to these precursors, as poems like 'See Me Lakayana-Again' make clear. This poem, also from the 1992 collection *The Cows of Shambat*, traces the dismissal of the junior official Lakayana for bringing a charge of corruption against his government office supervisor. Lakayana returns to his village, and the poem, which collapses together protagonist and poet in the final stanza, concludes

So,
See me Lakayana
With my spear
The spear which the smith gave me
The smith who had broken my knife
The knife which the old woman gave me
The old woman who had eaten my pumpkin
The pumpkin that I found in the old homestead of
Okot p'Bitek's Lawino! (62)

This poem sums up Taban's vision of art, as both the extender of the values of the past and their champion as the means of resisting the worst elements of modernisation, political graft, violence and self-interest.

Despite this aggressive stance towards the corrupt practices of the northern Arab and Muslim dominated government and its abuses of the southern Sudanese minority cultures, a short poem to Francis Deng in *The Cows of Shambat* collection seems to indicate Taban's agreement with the novelist's project of inter-cultural national reconciliation when he notes that:

> The seed of redemption[10]
> Needs good soil
> watering
> shading
> By the gardener
> For sprouting chance (24)

Even here, though, one detects the wryer and more world-weary note of Taban, who is, characteristically perhaps, less sure than Deng of a solution at political levels to the human problems of cultural reconciliation facing the Sudan after decades of civil strife and bloodshed.

His response to the problem of language choice, a central concern in much East African writing and the subject of several of the essays in his book *Culture is Rutan*, is equally and disarmingly honest. In the poem 'Messed up by English' in the 1991 collection *The Cows of Shambat*, he reflects on how English is 'not [his] tongue' but has 'messed me up'. He adds

> I couldn't love you more than Wole Ṣoyinka
> Plodding through the Advanced Oxford Dictionary
> (un-abridged)
> To amass the words that frightened Renage Lohiya's
> Papuan son in Waigani[11]
> Whilst maintaining my inherited place amongst the Acholi
> and Bari-speakers. (38)

Yet, as I noted, Taban has not called for the abandonment of English nor himself entirely abandoned it in his own work. He continues to exercise his right to all the languages of his inheritance, though, as recent work shows, he is increasingly drawn towards the need to maintain and nourish the local roots of this international legacy. The fact that he has in recent years worked in South Africa suggests that his interests will still continue to reach out from the local base to the wider issues posed by international racial and political situations.

Ethiopia

Ethiopia is unique in sub-Saharan Africa as having the only extended written tradition predating both the Arabic and European incursions into the continent, first employing the ancient Geez language and then languages such as Amharic, which is still one of the dominant languages of modern Ethiopia. Amharic has a literary tradition more than a millennium old, and it continues to provide a flourishing medium for modern writing. This long history continues to inspire contemporary writers using English and a number of works dealing with the historical past have emerged, notably Sahle Sellassie's *Warrior King* (1974) and plays such as Tsegaye Gabre-Mehdin's *Collision of Altars* (1977) based on the fall of the then third greatest power in the world, Emperor Kaleb's Axumite Ethiopia of the sixth century.

Warrior King is a historical novel written in English. It deals with the unification of the disparate provinces of nineteenth-century Ethiopia under the rule of the great warrior Kassa Hailu, who became Emperor Teowodros II. Told by a peasant boy narrator, who joins the unifying forces of Kassa Hailu, the novel clearly had a message for a contemporary Ethiopia still torn by internal divisions when the novel was written in 1974.

Sahle Sellassie had also written an earlier novel in English, *The Afersata* (1969), which dealt with a traditional Ethiopian method of detecting crime, the Afersata society, and its use to determine who was responsible for burning down the hut of the villager Namaga. The story allows Sahle Sellassie to present a portrait of how village society worked. It celebrates the common-sense of village life and the viability of traditional institutions to deal with social problems and crises. However, significantly, and as is often the case with writers who operate in cultures where English is a minority written-language, as well as these texts in English, Sahle Sellassie has also written short stories and novels in Amharic, and a novel in Chaha, *Shinega's Village* (1964), which has been translated into English.

The use of historical settings to deal with contemporary issues continues to be a feature of Ethiopian English writing, as is witnessed by Bereket Habte Selassie's *Riding the Whirlwind* (1993), which deals with the deposition of the last Ethiopian Emperor, Haile Selassie. Similarly, Abbie Gubegna's novel *Defiance* (1975) is set in 1937 and deals with the Italian occupation. It is a story of the old patriot Abesha, his daughter Aster and the freedom fighters who resisted the Italian invasion. As such, it bears some resemblance to the anti-colonial texts published elsewhere in East Africa.

Daniachew Worku is best known for his writing in Amharic, but has also written an English-language novel. This early novel, *The Thirteenth Sun* (1973), remains one of the most accomplished and ambitious Ethiopian English-language novels. Set in the fairly recent past, it reflects the complex internal struggles within modern Ethiopian culture between the cultural traditions of Ethiopian Coptic Christianity, one of the oldest Christian cultures in the world, and the even older and persistent animist religious traditions of the villages and the illiterate peasantry. It traces the final pilgrimage of the wealthy old merchant, the Fitawrary Woldu, with his son Goytim, his 'daughter-to-be' Woytinu and their servants. The Fitawrary is seeking a cure for a debilitating illness, and in pursuit of this he makes a pilgrimage to one of the many Ethiopian Christian monasteries. Goytim, his heir, doubts the efficacy of the whole charade. He wants to embrace a modern world in which Ethiopia can become a place of justice, and realise its economic future as a 'potential tourist paradise'. Woynitu, the Fitawrary's 'daughter-to-be', also looks forward to a modern life as a translator or an air hostess. As the old man's palanquin traverses the landscape of Ethiopia, Worku paints a picture of the contradictions and complexities of this ancient land with its many traditional practices, and dramatises the strains of its emergence into a modern era. The Fitawrary's conflict of values with his heir Goytim is made clear:

> '. . . half of my property shall go to those who uphold the cause of church building throughout Ethiopia,' he says, 'and the other half to all the people who shall take part in the prayer for my salvation.'
> 'I wouldn't have minded if it were for the building of schools,' I say.
> 'You know well enough that I don't go for that kind of rubbish,' he says. (4)

The novel also dramatises the conflict between the rich absentee land-owning classes and the peasants in the attitudes of the poor farmer and his wife in whose hut the pilgrims seek a night's shelter:

> '. . . if the Fitawrary died, I might be forced to perform the lamentation and the funerary dances free of charge.'
> 'I think you're right. I should have asked him about it before taking him in.'
> 'Where did he say he lived, anyway?'
> 'In Addis, where else?' (21–2)

The Fitawrary undertakes a long and fruitless series of 'cures' by Coptic Christian monks, who make him imbibe holy water and incense ash, which make him vomit, and which are prescribed together with prayers. To make doubly sure, he also engages the sacrifices of the local animist conjure woman and allows her to smear him with blood from a slaughtered sheep. In the Fitawrary's cures the complex, multi-layered practices of Ethiopian society are dramatised. Despite all these curative practices, the Fitawrary eventually dies and the pilgrimage resumes back to the plains with his corpse. The body, already stinking, must be carried, according to his dying wish, back to the designated burial place. The servants revolt against carrying the corpse and Goytim has to resort to bribery to get them to continue. The final descent with the stinking corpse, which is already attracting vultures, is a powerful image of the decay of traditional customs and the past and their clash with the younger generation's visions of a modern Ethiopia. But Worku seems to see this modern alternative, too, as just another set of superstitions, slogans and meaningless rituals, dedicated not to the past but to an equally mindless pursuit of modernity and fashion, a pursuit in which little has changed:

> . . . innumerable hailstones. Slapping our faces. Drumming on the body of my father. Drumming on Woynitu. Drumming on me. Making spring-boards of us all. On the rebound. And we too were drumming on Zekwala – on the rebound. And yet like the Ethiopians we were, slowly and respectfully we trudged down. Respectful of the deceased. Respectful of the thorn-covered bushes and paths. Respectful of the churned and muddy road ahead of us.
> And then the stopping of the rain just as unexpectedly. The momentary fading away of the bad smell. And the moment's silence.
> In the distance, the morning train to Dire-Dawa. Rumbling and roaring and emitting vigorous chuffs of steam. Attaining pitch and tone. Wending its way, following the telegraph poles. Following the electric poles. Following the bill-boards: 'Smoke

Nyala', 'Smoke Elleni', 'Smoke Axum-Filter American Blend', 'Fly Ethiopian Airlines – thirteen months of sunshine . . .' (172)

This thirteenth month of sunshine does not seem to offer a particularly credible or desirable vision of the future, and the novel ends on this bleak and pessimistic note.

The recent revolution against the Mengistu regime and its bloody aftermath has not yet received much treatment in English, though there are a number of Ethiopian texts in the other literary languages of the region which have sought to come to grips with the issues confronting modern Ethiopia. English texts which deal with the Mengistu years include Gebra Selasie Tesfay's *The Company of My Shadow* (1993), which is an account of the author's fifteen years as a fighter in the EPRDF faction's struggle against the centralist Mengistu regime. Although this is more a blend of autobiographical account and political tract than a novel or a fiction, it does offer a sustained narrative of recent Ethiopian experience, and is filled with personal and family details which flesh out its polemic aims. Gebru Astaw's *Dung' Hill* (1992) is a play which rather frenetically dramatises its thesis that Ethiopia's recent problems are all really caused by white civilisation acting out its fantasies in Africa, and includes a symbolic rape by the very woodenly conceived character Dr Wagner (*sic*), as its dramatic centrepiece. Yemani Deneke's *In the Mirror of Love* (n.d.), although far less politically focused, as demonstrated by the fact that it was given official censors' approval in 1994, shows a rural family forced to the city by poverty, and the effects on their lives of the internal power struggles which have swept across Ethiopia in recent times. The author graphically portrays the horrors of his time in the army, when he was conscripted to defend Ethiopia against the Somalian 'invasion' in 1977, and encountered civilian atrocities and massacres committed by both sides. When he is captured, he escapes in an unlikely piece of heroic action, accompanied by rather unlikely outbursts of patriotic fervor: 'Traitors and expansionists have no room and freedom to stroll in my country' (117–19). Perhaps it was these elements which persuaded the official censors to approve the text, despite its 'warts and all' picture of the Ethiopian army and its behaviour during the Somalian campaign. This odd text is a strange mixture of truthful, personal reportage and rather obvious propaganda.

A far more sophisticated and complex literary response to recent Ethiopian experiences is contained in Hama Tuma's collection of short stories *The Case of the Socialist Witchdoctor* (1993). Tuma presents a series of indictments of the vicious oppression and corruption of the then recently deposed Mengistu regime. His work takes a much more direct and vigorous political stand on the malpractices of the Mengistu regime than previous Ethiopian work in English. The first section, a series of fictionalised court cases from the corrupt show trials of the so-called revolutionary courts, combines a grotesque black humour with chillingly realistic details of the regime's propensity to employ torture and summary execution as a weapon of terror and control. Despite a disclaimer that the characters and events are not real, what makes these bizarre narratives so

265

chilling is the horrid apprehension that they reflect actual practices and events in recent Ethiopian history. The opening story, entitled 'The Case of the Illiterate Saboteur', tells of an illiterate peasant who is accused of treason for urinating against the wall of a building belonging to the State Security Police. The ironic defence of the peasant includes the fact that, since he is illiterate, he could not read the signs stating that public urination is forbidden, or that the building was a police headquarters. In a series of Kafkaesque distortions the court construes these defences as part of the crime itself:

> The judge turned to the accused. 'You stand here accused of very many serious crimes. You say you are illiterate but that is also criminal. At least your public admission of it can have clear counter-revolutionary implications. Beasts of burden are ignorant too, but you beat them when they refuse to obey. Socialism needs a beautiful city, yet you have dirtied the capital. Socialism as we know it means obedience to the State but you have not only urinated on a government institution you have refused to confess and to make a rigorous self-criticism.' (19)

'The Case of the Valiant Torturer' is an indictment of the regime's virtually open defence of torture. It presents torture as an instrument designed to consolidate the state by supplying a steady stream of confessions of treason. Such confessions serve to divert the people's attention from the failure of the government to address the real issues. Comparing the new Mengistu regime with that of the old imperial government of Haile Selassie, whom he also served as a torturer, the accused is loud in his praise of the successes of the new order, as he complains about the quality and quantity of victims under the old imperial government:

> 'And after the Revolution?' Lt. Ararso probed . . .
> 'Things changed. The State became the kind to fill the eyes of a professional torturer with tears of pride. Enemies of all sorts, big and small, young and old, male, female, city dweller and raw peasants – enemies from all classes and walks of life. . . . We had our hands full and it was in this exacting period that some of the real professionals like me shone with the required firm brutality. To practise socialist competition we instituted the quota system and yearly prize. . . . During this historic period I slept at the station and did not go to my house for months.' (28)

The ironic punishment given by the court is to have his quota of victims reduced and that of his rival for the yearly prize increased. Outraged, the professional torturer begs for death, rather than such public humiliation.

One of the most effective stories, 'The Case of the Criminal Thought', deals with a poor woman, whose smile, during a Security Police political education session, is automatically interpreted as a sign that she is thinking thoughts against the regime:

> 'The collective spirit, even in sharing poverty, is noble. So, from all the indications, you have nothing to smile at?'
> 'Why not? Are the poor forbidden to smile?'
> 'They have no reason to. Their smile comes after socialism. Till then they are grim, a grimness and commitment and hatred for capital. A beautiful subject for artists.'
> 'You can say what you like. But poor as I am, I laugh and smile a lot of the time.'

'Precisely. Why is the question? If you were not laughing at the cadre and if your miserable life, noble though poverty is, militates against smiles and laughter then why were you smiling if not due to criminal thoughts?' (60)

Tuma's stories offer a powerful indictment of the way in which the rhetoric of the revolutionary left, as much as that of the dictatorships of the military right, can be employed to justify the suppression of all basic human rights and decencies.

Somalia

Most studies of Somali literature emphasise how rich the tradition of Somali oral literature is and how important this has been to the formation of a Somali identity. Somalia is an ethnically and linguistically homogenous country, though one which has a long history of violent inter-clan conflict and disputes which persist into the present. Somalia was formed in 1960 by the amalgamation of the previous colonies of British Somaliland and Italian Somaliland. After eight years of civilian rule, marked by inter-clan conflict and problems relating to the attempts to unify the Somali peoples and their relatives across the borders of Ethiopia and Kenya (leading to a war with Ethiopia in the 1970s), Mohammed Syad Barre seized power in a military coup in 1968. He remained in power until his overthrow in January 1991, though the last years of his increasingly dictatorial regime were marked by a series of rebellions, which were brutally suppressed. In 1991 a separate northern Somaliland Republic, centred on the old region of British Somaliland, separated from the southern regions, which remained as Somalia. Since Barre's demise the clan conflicts have continued and, despite a costly, ill-judged and inefficient attempt at direct intervention by UN and American forces, little effective diminution of the power of the warring clans has resulted.

The history of written literature in Somalia is necessarily short, since the orthography which allowed the Somali language to be written was only developed in 1972. In fact, this is one of the few benefits remaining from the programme of modernisation and development announced by Syad Barre when he took power. As a result, there is no equivalent to the long written traditions of Ethiopia.[12] Since then, writing has developed and a number of authors have emerged, though few translations have yet been made. One of the few novels in Somali to get a wide circulation outside Somalia is the English translation of Faarax Maxamed Jaamac's *Ignorance is the Enemy of Love* (1982). On the other hand, Somali oral literature remains very active within the country and permeates every aspect of Somali life, including politics and political allegiances.[13] Within the ubiquitous clan system, the poet plays a vital role in creating cohesion within the clan and in negotiating relationships between sub-groups, as well as between the various conflicting internal factions. The persistence of the oral tradition, and its vital, living grip on every aspect of Somali life, is reflected in the new writing to have emerged in Somalia, and also, indirectly, in the work of the few writers who have chosen to work in English.[14]

A number of translations from Somali have assisted non-Somali scholars in recognising the range and power as well as the widespread influence of these oral traditions. The Canadian novelist and critic Margaret Laurence was a great enthusiast for Somali oral poetry and translated a number of the poems in her volume *A Tree for Poverty: Somali Poetry and Prose* (1954). The scholar B. W. Andrzejewski also translated a number of the oral compositions, as well as translating some of the recent writing in the new Somali script, such as *Leopard Among the Women. Shabeelnaagood. A Somali Play* (1974). Similarly, French scholars translated work in both Somali and Afar from Djibouti, the erstwhile French Somaliland, which did not join with the new Somali Republic, but which shares some of its linguistic and cultural traditions.[15]

A few writers have emerged who have chosen to use English. The American-born Omar Eby published a number of books in English in the early 1970s, including the collection of short stories *The Sons of Adam: Stories of Somalia* (1970). More recently, as in the case of Ethiopia, a number of fictionalised, personal accounts of the recent civil struggles and wars have appeared. These include Ahmed Omar Askar's *Sharks and Soldiers* (1992), a collection of documentary stories which deal with the events leading up to the overthrow of the Barre regime in 1991 and the civil war which followed. Ahmed Artan Hanghe's *The Sons of Somal* (1993) also mixes fact and fiction, interspersing accounts of his domestic life with that of the political developments in the country at large.

The work of Nuruddin Farah, however, towers above other Somali writing in English. His novel *From a Crooked Rib* (1970) was the first Somali novel to be published in English. Since then, he has published seven more novels and has authored a number of plays, none of which have been printed. The range and quality of his work place him in the first rank of African novelists in English. This is especially significant given the relative absence, until recently, of other writers in English in Somalia. Farah's mother was a well-known poet in the Somali oral tradition. This tradition has had an influence on Farah's own style.[16] The fact that Farah has chosen to write in English reflects the fact that, despite his early welcome for the idealistic programme of social justice and national construction proposed by the revolution of Syad Barre, he quickly ran foul of that increasingly clan-based dictator. As a result, he has lived most of his life in exile in Europe, America and in a range of other African states. His work includes an extract from a novel he had begun in Somali in 1973 to celebrate the availability of a Somali written script. This novel, called *Tolow Waa Talee Ma*, was never published. After the first chapters were serialised in the *Somali News*, it quickly fell foul of the new government's censors. Farah, who was out of the country at the time, was advised that he had better remain abroad, since the government would 'silence' him if he returned. Since then, he has lived in exile, except for a brief visit in 1996 to a Somalia still torn by civil war, and has published exclusively in English. Two distinct but related themes mark all of Farah's work: consistent opposition to Syad Barre's regime and to the violence and oppression of the recent Somali rulers; and the oppressed and powerless position of women in Somali society. In work after work,

Farah has explored what he perceives to be the connection between these two oppressions, illustrating how Barre's public dictatorial practice is buttressed by the patriarchal practices of Somali domestic life, and how this, in its turn, is perpetuated by the public values espoused by the dictatorship.

Although the theme becomes more articulate as the novels develop, it is implicit even in Farah's first novel, *From a Crooked Rib* (1970), which is a sensitive and strong account of a Somali peasant girl who comes to the city and is exploited by Somali men in the name of their religion and their social system. Its heroine, Ebla, is a well-drawn portrait of an intelligent, though uneducated woman, who is abandoned by her husband almost immediately after their marriage, when he leaves to study abroad. The novel traces her growth to an independent consciousness and a sense of her own worth, a growth which leads her to abandon her marriage and to struggle against the definitions of woman's position in her society. The style is simple and direct, markedly different from the more involved and poetic style of the later novels.

Farah's second novel, *A Naked Needle* (1976), deals with the early period of the revolution. Initially, many Somali intellectuals applauded the new military government's programme to create a unified national identity, to overcome the traditional power of the clan lineages and to institute economic and cultural reforms. The movement to develop the national system for writing Somali is one of the few enduring legacies of this programme. It quickly became clear, though, that Syad Barre's own clan was still being favoured by the new government, and that the new policies were, in practice, old-style local nepotism and large-scale modern corruption knit into a fresh unholy alliance. *A Naked Needle* is the only one of Farah's novels which is out of print, and Farah has not sought to reissue it, probably because of its relatively favourable treatment of the Barre regime.

Sardines (1981) is the second novel in the so-called 'dictatorship trilogy'. Here Farah presents a much more unambiguous opposition to the by now clearly corrupt regime of Syad Barre. All three of these 'dictatorship' novels trace the violent course of Syad Barre's oppressive regime. They are also, though, deeply concerned with the ways in which Somali personal relations reflect the traditions of that society, traditions which, for all their richness and value, Farah sees as being essentially oppressive, particularly to women and the young. In these novels, old men dominate and control their families, and old women acquiesce and assist in this dominance, as they draw their own bitter power from its fringes. In many ways, Farah's approach to these issues is closer to that of African women writers such as Ama Ata Aidoo, Flora Nwapa, Buchi Emecheta, Grace Ogot and others, who have also explored the links between patriarchal rule and the enforcement of a biased masculine version of 'tradition'. Some of these women writers, too, have explored the link between these domestic and intellectual tyrannies and the dictatorial attitudes of modern African regimes. But not even these women writers have made that subject more thoroughly or consistently their own than Farah. This is specially notable since Farah was born in 1945 and so, whilst not quite of the generation of Achebe or Ngũgĩ, is certainly in the older group of African writers, most of whom have not shown the sensitivity to women's suffering and social oppression which Farah does in all his writing.

In *Sweet and Sour Milk* (1979), the first novel of the 'dictatorship trilogy', Farah makes his most direct and open attack on the regime, as he traces the arbitrary arrests and imprisonments with which Syad Barre suppressed all opposition. The novel opens with the death (probably by poisoning) of the government's economic adviser, Soyaan Keynaan. The regime constructs him as a martyr and hero, but gradually the story of his hidden opposition emerges as his diaries and secret notes are found. Again, these records can be seen to create an opposition to the role of orality, which here has an oppressive face in the form of the network known as 'Dionysius's Ear', a body of illiterate informers whom the regime uses to infiltrate workers' groups, and even families. Soyaan's policeman father, Keynaan, is prepared to allow this fiction to persist for the gain it brings his 'family'. Soyaan is himself betrayed by an old family 'friend', Dr Ahmed-Wellie. A nightmare world of intrigue and betrayal is built up in this powerful novel, one which forces us to realise how deeply the tyranny of the government is enmeshed with the traditional structures and practices of everyday Somali life, using them, in a perverted way, to control the people.

The second novel of the dictatorship trilogy, *Sardines* (1981), centres on the relationship between the feisty anti-government female intellectual Medina, who is sacked as editor of the national newspaper by the new regime, and her husband, Samater, who remains in the government as a minister, lured by the hope that he can influence the regime from within. The relationship between Samater and Medina reflects the issue of control and rebellion within a traditional household, which in turn reflects the issue of control in the society at large. The plot turns on Medina's fear that her daughter Ubax will be forced to submit to forced circumcision, a rite which she views as an attack on women, and a principal instrument of male control of women's sexuality. Medina's opposition to the regime is transmuted into the domestic struggle for Ubax's education and her growth to a freer life. For this, some commentators have criticised Farah, arguing that Medina's decision to opt out of public protest renders her attacks on the government ineffective. These critics argue that although the regime's decision to execute the opposition figures, Dulman and Nasser, sees Medina reflect on how to act, whether she succeeds in anything but a relatively closeted middle-class intellectual revolt remains doubtful.

It is often hard with Farah, as here, to know to what extent he distances himself from his characters. The explanation may lie in the fact that Farah, like Achebe, for whose work he has expressed a great admiration, never offers only a single viewpoint. In fact, he often presents, without direct comment, the points of view of characters with whom he is unlikely to be in much sympathy. In this respect, he is a novelist who lets his characters and events express the full complexity of the situations he explores and avoids any simple polemic line. However, one is left in no doubt of the passion with which he opposes the negative treatment of all classes of women in Somali society.

The final novel of the trilogy, *Close Sesame* (1983), presents a more favourable picture of traditional authority and of the elderly in the figure of Deeriye.

A family patriarch, Deeriye is an advocate of authority, but it is an authority based on a generous reading of religious and social practice. As a national hero of the colonial resistance, Deeriye has a certain immunity from the new regime. Unlike the other figures who oppose the regime, he is a reluctant opponent, his own political activism being a thing of the past. But, galvanised by the death of his son, who has been drawn into a conspiracy against the regime, Deeriye makes an attempt on the General's life and is gunned down by his bodyguard. The characters who link the three novels are part of a single, unfolding examination in all three texts of the theme of developing opposition. The books move from dramatising tacit opposition, through symbolic gestures of dissent, to active revolt, even though the attempted assassination at the end of *Close Sesame* is ineffective. Whether this failure is meant to express Farah's cynicism about political activism in general, or a realism about its likely effectiveness in the current situation in Somalia, is never fully resolved.

After completing the so-called 'dictatorship trilogy', Farah announced that his next novel, *Maps* (1986), was the starting point of a new trilogy. But with the publication of the second of the novels, entitled *Gifts* (1992; first published in a Swedish translation in 1990), the form of the second trilogy seems fairly loose, if it can be called a trilogy at all. It does not have characters who migrate from one novel to the next, as is the case with the earlier 'dictatorship' trilogy, nor does it even seem to have a similar unified theme. *Maps*, for example, deals with the aftermath of the war with Ethiopia over the disputed Ogaden border region. The novel explores the confused struggle of Askar, who has moved from the Ogaden to Mogadishu to escape the war, to discover his identity. It examines his sense of loss, as he has to separate himself off from his female Ethiopian friend Misra, when the adult Askar identifies himself with the struggle to liberate the Ogaden region from Ethiopian control. This struggle comes to a head when Misra is suspected of betraying the Somalian Liberation Movement freedom fighters, whose cause Askar has espoused. This leads to her murder. In the end, the novel seems to show that Misra, like Askar, is a symbol of the failure of any borders to delineate culture or person accurately and absolutely. Misra is herself an orphan, an ex-slave, who has been abused by her Somali owners. Other figures such as Askar's 'uncles', who are Oromo, members of a small language group, have also been marginalised and downtrodden by the dominant Amharic speakers of Ethiopia. Oppressors in this text are often themselves oppressed in their turn, suggesting an endless chain of cause and effect from which people struggle to break free. As in the novels of the earlier 'dictatorship trilogy', these political and social issues are linked through the figure of Misra to the question of gender, and the link between the treatment of groups discriminated and defined by the abstractions of gender and those equally generalised by abstractions such as nationality is made clear. Farah, though, recognises that the world of modern Somalia is one in which these abstractions continue to have powerful effects, and the novelist's task is to articulate them and to show how they produce the brutalisation of those who are subject to their constrictions.

271

That Farah's next novel, *Gifts*, first appeared in a Swedish translation in 1990 emphasises the international and peripatetic life Farah has led since leaving the Sudan. It is set in the period after Barre's fall, but before the recent renewal of civil conflict between rival clan groups, which led to the intervention of the UN. The famine and the destruction of cities like Mogadishu, which came from the ensuing clashes between the rival groups, is still in the future. *Gifts* looks at the cost for African countries of being on the receiving end of various 'gifts', such as cultural and social aid. Like all of Farah's novels, it does not make the politics the central event. Instead, it focuses on a love-story, and on the life of Duniya, a woman who, like other Farah heroines, is struggling to find a place for herself, independent of the men whose demands have so far defined her life. Married off to a husband much older than her, she then becomes the property of her landlord, who marries her, but who is a drunkard. After the divorce from him, she ends up in a series of further dependent relations on other male relatives, including her half-brother Shiriye and her brother Qaasim. Her other brother, Abshir, is in America, and he sends her the 'gift' of $3,000, which allows her to establish herself in a flat of her own. Much of this echoes the themes of earlier novels, such as *Sardines*. The text weaves a complex pattern of links between the various kinds of gifts and dependencies to which Duniya is subjected, and the controls exercised over countries like Somalia by foreign aid and other fiscal controls. Critics like Wright have suggested that the book reflects the changing conditions of Somalian society after Barre, in so far as it is deliberately written in a more popular, less esoteric style than the earlier novels. Wright also suggests that the theme of *Gifts* has been overtaken somewhat by the events of 1992–93. He argues that the relatively comfortable, middle-class intellectual milieu of the book seems irrelevant in the face of the mass hunger, death and destruction which have followed those events. Nevertheless, *Gifts* remains one of the few recent African novels to address the whole fraught issue of international aid, and its hidden price for modern Africa.

The publication of Farah's most recent novel, *Secrets*, in May 1998, indicates that he continues to be an active force in contemporary Somalian writing in English. Farah was able to return to Somalia in 1996 for the first time since he began his exile twenty years before, though he continues to live abroad, most recently in Kaduna, Northern Nigeria. The novel reflects his thoughts on the recent Somalian civil war and is set in Mogadishu in the week before the war begins. Once again, despite the very public theme, it is focused through private relationships, especially those between men and women, as the protagonist Kalaman is confronted by his childhood sweetheart, who returns to Somalia and so initiates in him a memory of the history of his family and his nation. Through this device Farah is able to reveal again his disquiet at the great divisions in Somalian society resulting from clan loyalties, from the patriarchal nature of Somali society, and from the ways these have interacted with the recent corruption and authoritarianism of the dictatorship period. In the theme of the inescapability of the past and its ongoing effect on the present, Farah suggests the need to understand the current situation in its full historical depth. Although the novel has a powerful political message, it never fails to realise this through specific and beautifully drawn characters and situations, refusing to collapse specificity into mere abstraction. Arguably the most powerful and most clearly written of Farah's recent novels, it ends with a strong plea for replacing the idea of a clan loyalty with a sense of personal value and responsibility, as Nonno Kalaman's dying grandfather reflects that ' "I am a person, a clan is a mob. Talk to me, sell things to me, I am reasonable. Clans are not". I wish many of the fighters visiting havoc on people's lives had been born with luck to hear him. "If we had many like him, there would be no civil strife," Talaado said earlier that day' (297). Such affirmations of the fact that the recent sad history of Somalia is neither inevitable nor irreversible makes the text an affirmative one, despite its frank recounting of the violence and hopelessness of recent events. Farah's most recent novel, for which he received the prestigious Neustadt International Prize for Literature in 1998, consolidates his claim to being one of the three or four most important African writers of recent times.

A more recent novel by Abdirazak Y. Osman, *In the Name of Our Fathers* (1996), is an impressive début novel. It deals more directly than Farah's work with the civil conflict which led to the fall of the Mengistu dictatorship in 1991. A deeply personal and individualised portrait of a young man coming to terms with his society, and with his family, it is the story of the struggle between Ali and his father, who has helped form an opposition faction in the civil war. The young man grows increasingly disillusioned with the tribalist basis for the politics of both government and opposition. *In the Name of Our Fathers* is both a convincing portrait of a Somalian family and an insightful analysis of the flaws in recent Somali political life. Like Farah, Osman shows a sophisticated grasp of the relationships between the political and personal levels of Somali culture, but he has established his own voice, through a more direct and less elaborate style, and an eye for telling and dramatic detail.

> Our bathroom, like everybody else's, was not covered. I don't know. A flock of white birds appeared suddenly in the sky. It was noticeable the freedom these creatures were enjoying. They flew up and down at will. I wished I were a bird, then suddenly I changed my mind and thanked God I was a human being. I don't know what exactly made me change my mind, but one of the reasons was that I once heard that birds had a very small brain compared to other creatures. (68)

Osman's work is an invigorating sign that even after the recent horrors of civil collapse, inter-clan warfare and foreign intervention, Somalis may still be able to find a renewed use for literature to examine the recent past and its messages for the future. It is also a sign that English may still be used to complement the ongoing rich tradition of writing in Somali which continues to flourish.

A further significant recent development has been the emergence of a number of Somali women writers using English. Two Somalian autobiographical works, *Aman* by Aman and *Desert Flower* by Waris Dirie, have appeared recently. Both works are written with the aid of a Western amanuensis, so they cannot be said to constitute original texts in the full sense of the term. *Aman* traces the life-story of a young Somalian girl, Aman, including an account of her excision and infibulation, against a background of rapid social change in Somalia during the 1950s and 1960s, ending with her flight to Tanzania at the age of seventeen due to the military take-over in her country. *Desert Flower* recounts the story of a young Somalian woman, a top model, wife and mother and recently appointed 'goodwill ambassador' to the United Nations. She tells the story of her life from her earliest memories living as a nomad in the Somalian desert, up to her UN appointment. This latter appointment is to help the UN in its campaign to eradicate excision and, as she describes in her autobiography, she is a fervent advocate of this, having experienced excision and infibulation herself at the age of five. The problematic nature of these texts in terms of their having been partly 'ghost-written' and the well-publicised role they have played in the international campaign against female excision and infibulation makes it difficult to evaluate them as Somalian literary texts. Nevertheless, they are a sign of the emerging possibility that Somalian women will soon find a new voice in written forms to complement their long and distinguished role in the oral tradition.

Cameroons

Anglophone Cameroonian writing offers one of the most fascinating and complex examples of how ex-colonial languages like English have been appropriated to a variety of local usages in the post-independence period. The erstwhile territory of the German Cameroons was divided between Britain and France in the aftermath of the First World War. The territories of the north-west and south-west regions of the present République des Camerounes formed part of what was then designated the British Southern Cameroons. This was administered, along with the British Northern Cameroons, as part of the territory of the colony of Nigeria. With the formation of the modern state of independent Cameroon, and following a plebiscite in 1961, the area of the British Southern Cameroons became part of the now predominantly French-speaking state of Cameroon, known thereafter for a while as the United Republic of Cameroon, whilst the erstwhile British Northern Cameroons remained part of Nigeria. As a result, the predominantly French-speaking new state had a substantial minority of Anglophone speakers, grouped on its western border with Nigeria. The use of terms like predominantly French-speaking itself raises the first of many interesting questions, since clearly what this means is that the official language of public affairs in the Cameroons tends to be that of the dominant ex-colonial power, in this case France. However, although the term Anglophone has been commonly applied to the people of the Northwest and Southwest Provinces of the present Cameroon Republic, in practice the region has a number of different language groups, with at least four major African language groups operating in the region. Nevertheless for political reasons the ex-colonial language, in this case English, forms a linguistic unity between these peoples, which differentiates them from the majority of Cameroonians, whose language of public affairs is French. So we can see that the colonial language in this case is not simply a residual legacy of the ex-colonial domination, but acts, too, as a means of distinguishing a number of minority peoples who wish to assert a different cultural and social identity from that of the dominant post-independence majority. In fact, as a result of the discrimination against English in the new national state, these various peoples are forming a new, collective identity based on their adherence to English as a common language. The debate elsewhere in Africa about the need to move away from the ex-colonial language, as part of a decolonising strategy, is replaced here by an embracing of this ex-colonial language as a sign of difference from what one recent Cameroonian Anglophone writer has described as 'horizontal colonialism' by the dominant Francophone state.

The situation is similar in some ways to the role of English in the southern regions of the Sudan, where its use acts to distinguish the region and its cultural differences from the predominantly Arabic-speaking north.[17] Similarly, it has been argued that, for the writers of the region, the designation of their work as Cameroonian Anglophonic literature is a significant part of their struggle to maintain their cultural and linguistic difference from the majority of the people of the Republic. In a recent paper, presented at the first colloquium on Anglophonic Cameroonian writing, the writer Buma Kor notes a growing perception of Anglophonic Cameroonian writing as a distinct literature, by a people who feel increasingly marginalised within the predominantly Francophone state. He comments that:

> If we are talking about Anglophone writing, it is because we now realise that there exists a whole field of writings in present-day Cameroon which we can identify as 'Anglophone', writings by Anglophone Cameroonians treating issues peculiar to Anglophones in Cameroon. This to me is a shift and an important one, from what prevailed in 1977 when the University of Yaounde organised the Colloquium on Cameroon Writers and Critics. At that time there was no distinction made between writings by Anglophone and Francophone Cameroonians. I do not think this shift is just to signal the fact that in Cameroon there exists writings by Anglophones and Francophones.
>
> I see the distinction we are making today as the necessary step towards defining and understanding a people's heritage, the Anglo-Saxon heritage, within a bilingual English/French Cameroon Republic.[18]

Such a comment implies that the Anglophone minority within the Cameroons is in a situation analogous to linguistic minorities elsewhere, for example the Francophonic Quebecois in Canada, whose writings are also recognisably distinct within the matrix of contemporary Canadian literature. In fact, as Kor implies, one of the best-known early Anglophone writers from the Cameroons, the novelist Mbella Sonne Dipoko, whose novels *A Few Days and Nights* (1966) and *Because of Women* (1968) and whose poetry collection *Black and White in Love* (1972) were all published in the Heinemann African Writers series, is clearly not concerned with these issues of minority identity and survival which more recent writers such as Bate Besong, Victor Epie' Ngome and Ba'bila Mutia have addressed. Dipoko's novels, published in the 1960s, reflect his personal experience. Although raised in the Western Provinces and Nigeria and the child of English speakers, Dipoko was educated partly in France and his novels deal with such general issues as the experience of expatriation and the inadequate treatment of women in modern Africa. His first major novel is set in metropolitan France. In Dipoko's case, then, the choice of language does not dictate the themes in the way Kor suggested has become the case for more recent Cameroonian Anglophonic writing, confirming Kor's assertion that this sense of being the writing of a distinctive minority has emerged only since the 1970s. Nevertheless Dipoko's work, although not part of the emergence of a distinctive, self-conscious Cameroonian Anglophonic literature, offers a powerful introduction to the general issues facing young Cameroonians in the period immediately before and after independence. His work has been neglected, perhaps because it has been overshadowed by more widely acclaimed Francophone Cameroonian writers of the period, such as Ferdinand Oyono and Mongo Beti. Dipoko's first novel, *A Few Nights and Days*, although written in English, is set in Paris and reflects a predominantly French-speaking society, with the characters clearly speaking to each other exclusively in French. It is a well-written if conventional contribution to the novels of expatriation, tracing the life of an African student in Paris in the early 1960s. It shares many of its techniques with a whole generation of such autobiographical fictions in both English and French. The student, Doume, is having a love affair with a French girl which involves the usual complexity and cultural contradictions. Pressed by the girl Thérèse to meet her mother, he meets her in a café and the mother arrives with Bibi, the girlfriend of a French friend, with whom Doume has also had an affair.

> Thérèse and her mother arrived and Bibi was with them. Thérèse's mother must have brought her to serve as a cover. Should an acquaintance of her husband's see us she would say that Bibi was my fiancée, if she was asked by her husband to explain her presence with her daughter in a café that afternoon in the company of an African. (39)

Like other early African novels of this kind, there are a number of oversimplified explanations of what is typically African as opposed to European: 'I am attached to my parents, very much. I am even attached to my ancestors whom I never knew. So I can't understand people being discourteous about their parents. In Africa the situation is a bit better; positively better. But in Europe it is catastrophic' (51). From time to time the text reads like a translation, strewn with untranslated French expressions such as 'Et alors', 'Tu parles!', and so forth, which may be the result of the fact that Dipoko is translating conversations in his mind, or trying to capture the syntax of French speech in English. Or it may be that the text is really a surrogate French text written in English. The similarity of the themes and the treatment to other Francophone West African writing of the early 1960s makes this latter possibility not unlikely. The inevitable failure of the relationship with Thérèse brings this interesting but slight narrative to a close. There is nothing in Dipoko's work to suggest that he feels alienated from Cameroonian society, or that he feels that his choice of English as a mode of expression has any political or social significance.

The same comments can be applied to both the poems in *Black and White in Love*, and to the second novel, *Because of Women*, both of which are centred on the exploration of individual and personal sensibilities and show little or no concern with the politics or social situation of the wider Anglophonic community in the Cameroon. Dipoko's work is part of the general themes and trends in early West African writing, trends which are shared by both Anglophonic and Francophonic writers concerning inter-racial sexual relations by expatriate Africans and the unfair treatment of women in modern African societies. Although both are good examples of their respective genres, they cannot be seen as initiating any specific direction in modern Anglophonic Cameroonian writing.

A number of other Anglophone works concerned with themes echoing those elsewhere in West and East Africa have also emerged in the Cameroons, such as those which deal with the clash of traditional and modern values – for example, Kenjo Jumbam's *The White Man of God* (1980), which uses the figure of a Christian catechist to illustrate the complex nature of the effect of white values on African societies. These explorations of classic themes are also present in later novels such as Linus T. Asong's *The Crown of Thorns* (1990), which also deals with the clash of modern and traditional ideas. These, and other works, continue to echo themes which are widespread in West African writing and are not distinctly Anglophonic Cameroonian as such, in the sense defined by Kor above. Since most of these Anglophone writers look to the English writers of their immediate neighbour, Nigeria, for inspiration, and occasionally even publish there in search of a wider, sympathetic audience, there is an obvious influence on these texts from Nigerian writers such as Achebe. Thus Asong's story of the way in which a white nominee is forced into accepting a traditional chieftainship has echoes of Achebe's *Arrows of God*, though its psychology is far less convincing and its portrayal of the white District Officer lays far more stress on the direct intervention of the white man and far less on the way in which this functions in interaction with the local forces than Achebe's more subtle historical fable. Asong's target, here as elsewhere in his work, seems to be the failure of those who would combine modern power with traditional roles. Nevertheless, even writers like Asong continue to register very strongly the disillusionment of Anglophone Cameroonians with the new state and its administrators.

One of the earliest writers to address the clash of old and new values is the playwright Sankie Maimo, whose play *I Am Vindicated* (1959) is one of the earliest and most successful of Anglophone Cameroon texts. Maimo addresses the issue through the conflict of modern science and traditional medicine, dramatised in the conflict of the brilliant school student Bola and the old village fetish priest Baba Kasim, a conflict in which the young student is triumphant.

In 1968 Maimo wrote *Sov Mbang, the Soothsayer* (1969), which again addressed the issue of the old versus the new and which reversed the verdict of the earlier play. Here the traditional is seen as a symbol of an Africanness which is losing ground to a superficial Eurocentricity. In *The Mask* (1980),

Maimo also attacks the corruption of modern society, which he paints as increasingly self-serving and valueless. The law student Baye seeks answers to his searching questions about truth and justice, only to be met by a wall of disinterest and silence, a 'mask' of social hypocrisy and fear. This play, which reflects some of the techniques and language of the European existential texts of the period, nevertheless looks forward to the more politically motivated texts of the later Anglophone writers. For this reason Maimo is an important initiator of serious Anglophone play writing in Cameroon.

As Kor and others have argued, though, the discrimination in Cameroonian society against the Anglophonic minority forms an increasingly dominant theme of much Anglophone writing. The tone of this later writing has been far more polemic and bitter, as the titles of some of this work indicate. Drama has been a particularly favoured form for Anglophone writers, perhaps because the publishing industry based in Yaounde is predominantly oriented towards a Francophone market and plays can be more easily performed than novels can be published. Although English-language presses have sprung up from time to time in Yaounde and English works have been published by presses such as CEPER and SOPECAM which have government funding, or by missionary presses such as Editions CLE, many of the more politically stringent recent Anglophone works, such as the plays of Besong, have been published outside the Cameroons in adjoining Anglophone countries such as Nigeria, or in Europe or America. A number of distinctly Anglophone publishing ventures have been established regionally in centres like Limbe (the erstwhile Victoria). Presses with names which reflect local Anglophonic African ethnic groups (such as Bamende) have also developed to publish these minority language texts.[19] Bate Besong's play *Beasts of No Nation* (1980) is a powerful work from one of the strictest and most uncompromising critics of contemporary Cameroonian society. Besong's play attacks the corrupt rulers of Ednouay (an anagram of Yaounde), in which neither 'anglos' nor 'frogs' (to use the respective local derogatory terms) are spared, but there is a strong emphasis on the inferior role assigned to the 'anglos', who are clearly designated as the rubbish carriers and night-soil removers of the new society, dramatising the inferior position assigned to Anglophones in the new state.

Other writers have been less direct in expressing their problems and dissatisfactions with the new state. For example, the prolific playwright Bole Butake's play *Lake God* (1986) tells of a mysterious explosion at a Cameroonian lake, an explosion which caused many locals to suggest that the government had allowed foreign powers to use the site to experiment with new weapons. Despite the political potential of the theme, Butake defuses its message by resolving the action through traditional mythology, rather than through a contemporary political reading of the events. The active and vigorous censorship operated by the Cameroonian government in recent years may have had some influence on this decision. Significantly, this and other plays by Butake were published by government-supported presses in Yaounde. To be fair to Butake, however, in *Lake God* he shares some of the more metaphysical concerns expressed in the work of earlier writers such as Maimo (for example *The Mask*, 1980), and in the play which followed, *The Survivors* (1989), Butake addressed this same disaster in a more openly political way. In this later play, he shows how the local officials exploited the situation, using their power to profit from this human tragedy by stealing the international aid delivered to the victims. Other recent Anglophone works are more openly anti-government in tone, and directly address the discrimination against the Anglophone community in the new Cameroon. These include Victor Epie'Ngome's play *What God Has Put Asunder* (1992) and Hansel Ndumbe Eyoh's *The Inheritance* (1993). Epie'Ngome's play brings the social conflicts of the language division to light, portraying them in an allegorical form through the marriage of the young girl Weca (West Cameroons) to Emeka (Nigeria) and then Garba (East Cameroons). Although distancing itself through this device from a direct commentary, perhaps in an attempt to avoid censorship, the play is a clear indictment of the unfair treatment of the minority Anglophone community in the modern nation and chronicles their painful recent history. Hansel Ndumbe Eyoh's *The Inheritance* (1992) is a more subtle attempt to deal with the issue of political conflict in modern Cameroon. It concerns the return of a modern politician, a former ambassador, to accept a traditional chieftainship. The hero faces a series of choices, which illustrate how power politics infuse every situation. The play also problematises any simple idea that the traditional leadership is innocent and the modern politicians corrupt, as both are shown to compromise justice and truth. In some respects, it resembles the recent work of the Nigerian Femi Osofisan, though without his force and dramatic subtlety, and it is certainly the case that contemporary Cameroonian writers in English are still very aware of and influenced by what is going on in that neighbouring Anglophone country, to which their region was once attached.

Writers like these, and many others, suggest that, despite international neglect, the Anglophone writers of the Cameroon Republic are actively pursuing a distinctive and systematic goal, to keep alive the traditions of writing in English and to use them to differentiate their local cultures from that of the dominant Francophone state.

Notes

1. In addition, all these countries which have a significant Creole population descended from freed slaves have, to a lesser or greater extent, developed writing in creolised forms of English. These forms have become established enough to constitute effective alternative literary languages. For example, Krio is the joint national language, with English, of Sierra Leone and there are a number of writers employing it.

2. See Chapter 6.

3. Lemuel Johnson's trilogy is discussed at greater length in Chapter 12.

4. See Chapter 12.

5. Once again, it is important to note that these generalisations apply to English-language texts and publishing only. The situation in local languages such as Yoruba, Krio or ki-Swahili, or in other non-indigenous but longer established languages, such as Arabic, have very different histories which this text does not set out to address.

6. I am indebted for many of the facts in this account to Stewart Brown and Samuel Baity Garren's essays in *Wasafiri*, 15 (Spring 1992) which offer some of the few accounts of recent Gambian writing to be produced. Brown's paper was originally offered at a multi-disciplinary conference on The Gambia held at the Centre of West African Studies, Birmingham, in 1990. These papers are published as Arnold Hughes (ed.), *The Gambia: Studies in Society and Politics* (Birmingham: CWAS, 1991).

7. A number of bibliographies of Liberian writing exist and can be consulted for a comprehensive list of authors and texts. These include S. M. H. Condor, *A Guide to the Study of Liberian Literature etc.* (Monrovia: Liberian Literature Studies Programme, 1971) and more recently Moses K. Nagbe, *Books on Liberia by Nationals and Foreign Nationals* (Monrovia: n.p., 1992).

8. See Chapter 3.

9. Francis Mading Deng, *Cry of the Owl* (New York: L. Barber Press, 1989), p. 293.

10. This first line echoes the title of Deng's novel *Seed of Redemption*.

11. Taban Lo Liyong taught literature for a number of years at the University of Papua New Guinea, in Port Moresby, hence this reference.

12. Though access to some of these literatures was possible for a number of Somalis, especially those from the Ogaden region on the Ethiopian border. For instance, Nuruddin Farah, who is from the Ogaden region, is able to read Amharic script, as well as having a knowledge of Arabic and English. He also, of course, spoke Somali, as well as writing the secret, nationalist Somali script called Cusmanniya.

13. Said S. Samater, *Oral Poetry and Somali Nationalism: The Case of Sayyid Mahammad Abdille Hasan* (Cambridge: Cambridge University Press, 1982).

14. Interestingly, although Somali texts in English remain relatively scarce, Somalia was, in the past, a favourite African setting for expatriate stories, notably the many books set there by Gerald Hanley, such as *The Consul at Sunset* (1951). The historian Margery Perham also wrote novels set in Somalia, as well as translating texts from Somali. Her novels set in Somalia include *Major Dane's Garden*, written in 1922 after she spent a year in Somalia.

15. See Didier Morin, with Ibrahim Ahmed Dini, *Contes de Djibouti: textes en somali, Hassan Shekh Mumin textes en afar, Hamad La'de* (Paris: EDICEF, 1980).

16. See Derek Wright, *The Novels of Nuruddin Farah*, Bayreuth African Studies No. 32 (Bayreuth: Eckhardt Breitinger, 1994).

17. See the essays in N. Lyova, Eckhardt Breitinger and Bole Butaka (eds), *Anglophone Cameroon Writing*, Bayreuth African Studies No. 30 (Bayreuth: Eckhardt Breitinger, 1993).

18. Ibid., p. 60.

19. See the bibliography in ibid. for examples of these.

Chapter 11

Women's Voices: Gendered Pasts, Liberated Futures

Women have made a significant and distinctive contribution to the development of English writing in East and West Africa, though early critical accounts often overlooked their work, or misread it with a masculinist bias. Women writers have dealt with virtually all the issues we have raised elsewhere in this volume, and their presence is ubiquitous in all forms of writing in English. For this reason, references to women's texts have featured throughout most of the earlier chapters. However, the number of leading writers whose artistic project is rooted in their analysis of women's experience makes it increasingly important to deal in detail with some of these texts, and to emphasise that their concerns and practices constitute a distinctive tradition within East and West African writing in English.[1]

Flora Nwapa and Grace Ogot were pivotal writers in the 1960s, when the positive representation of the pre-colonial past was so dominant a theme in African English writing, and male authors celebrated pre-colonial traditional customs and practices. Texts such as Nwapa's *Efuru* (1966) and Ogot's *The Promised Land* (1966) offer a clearly contrastive model to the writing of male authors such as Achebe, Amadi and Ngũgĩ in this respect. It is possible to see in texts like these, as some recent feminist critics have done, a whole alternative development. They reflect very different concerns and interpretations of traditional, pre-colonial life. They also construct a single intertext, both amongst themselves, and in opposition to the texts of the dominant male literary establishment.

Flora Nwapa's *Efuru* (1966), as we noted in the earlier chapters, presents a very different view of the pre-colonial and colonial past from that of its male counterparts. This is the result of the action being presented through the eyes of the female protagonist. For example, the destructive impact of the colonial world, a *sine qua non* of the earlier male accounts, is far more ambivalently handled in this novel, with its benefits as well as its costs being emphasised. It is even treated positively, as when the advantage of modern medicine over traditional practice is acknowledged. Thus, for example, Efuru's second marriage breaks down because of her illness. The society and her husband attribute her illness to 'adultery'. The only evidence for this crime is the divination of the traditional, male *dibia* (diviner). In fact, the illness is quickly cured with modern medical treatment by her friend, the European-trained doctor Difu. In such sections the gendered bias of traditional practices is exposed.

Elsewhere, though, the overall negative effects of the European invasion are also recorded, especially in the many scathing references in the text to the effects of the practices of the church-goers on local custom:

> What are we going to do about the thieves in our town? The world is bad. In my youth there was no stealing. If you stole you were sold as a slave. If your property was stolen, you simply went to one of the idols and prayed him to visit the thief. Before two or three days, you recovered your property. These Church-goers have spoilt everything. They tell us our gods have no power, so our people continue to steal. (231)

Unfortunately, the effect of the church-going is not even or complete, so that what the text suggests is that, despite isolated advantages such as modern medicine, the effect of the transculturation of this society has been largely negative.

Efuru's second husband, Eneberi (known to nearly all except Efuru by his mission name of Gilbert), is a product of this transculturation. But his reaction to the crisis provoked by Efuru's illness shows him to be still influenced by the traditional beliefs, particularly when they coincide with his prejudices and interests as a male. His personal knowledge of Efuru's honest character is set aside in favour of an acceptance of this unlikely divination. His acceptance of the *dibia*'s view is influenced by the fact that Gilbert has already shown a declining interest in the marriage. Efuru discovers that he has had a relationship with another woman, by whom he has had a child. His excuse for this is Efuru's failure to produce children, an event which causes a slow estrangement between them. So the divination is a convenient one for Gilbert, providing him with the excuse he needs for his lack of interest in Efuru.

For Efuru, this is the moment when she questions the system within which she is contained, and acts to challenge its conclusions. She confronts the traditional system and puts it to the test in its own terms, challenging the gods to punish her if her testimony that she is not guilty of adultery is untrue. By this action she both acknowledges the traditional culture and demonstrates that, like any system, it is open to interpretation and abuse. Despite its superficial similarities with the early male novels of celebration, *Efuru* contains a distinctive, critical strain in describing the relationship between Efuru, her society and its values. As one might expect in such an early novel (it is frequently cited as the first novel by a Nigerian woman writer), it does not have so openly critical a social project as later women's texts. Nevertheless, it makes it clear that the forces which act to interpellate Efuru as a subject are those of a dominant patriarchy ('distinguished men'), and a self-policing world of women, who construct and perpetuate hegemonic discourses of femininity which value women only in terms of their productivity as child-bearers and as helpmates to men. This latter group are shown to be the principal means by which the dominant male codes are perpetuated. Their presentation is a superb example of how hegemony works to support dominant discourses, by persuading the subjected group that the values which oppress them are coterminous with their identity as women.

Figures like Omirima, the old gossip who leads the cabal of women in the village, are always at hand to criticise other women who do not conform to the pattern of marriage and child-bearing. Omirima uses the traditional proverbs which value children over money, not as figures of the wisdom of preferring family over wealth, but as evidence of the inability of a woman to achieve any value at all, unless she fulfils her primary roles as child-bearer and perpetuator of her husband's lineage:

One day they went to the stream, and while they were swimming the people in the stream began to gossip.

'Husband and wife, they are swimming together,' one woman began.

'They come to the stream every day', another said.

'Nonsense, why should they swim together? Are they the only happy couple in the town? I see them every time I come to the stream. It is disgusting. Can't anybody talk to them?'

'They are simply showing off. I bet they are not as happy as they look. You give them two years, and we shall see what will happen.'

'Seeing them together is not the important thing', another said. 'The important thing is that nothing has happened since the happy marriage. We are not going to eat happy marriage. Marriage must be fruitful. Of what use is it if your husband licks your body, worships you and buys everything in the market for you and you are not productive?'.... When they finished swimming, they came out, Gilbert greeted the women.

'Oh Eneberi did you come to the stream with your wife?' asked one of the women.

'Yes.'

'Are you well? Is your mother well?'

'My mother is well.' Gilbert and Efuru changed and went home.

'Did you look at her body when she was changing?' one of the women asked.

'So you looked at her body. I watched her too. Nothing has happened. You can be sure of that, nothing has happened. And I am afraid, because Eneberi is the only son of his mother. His mother would love to take care of her grandchildren. Nonsense, I must see Eneberi's mother. A woman, a wife for that matter, should not look glamorous all the time, and not fulfil the important function she is made to fulfil'. (172)

The subtext of this conversation, with its hints of envy amongst the women, and of the pressure which they can exert on Efuru and Gilbert through his mother, is clear. It is against this pressure, which defines women according to their primary role as mother, that the text operates a subtle questioning. That this cultural expectation is deeply internalised is shown when we see Efuru reflecting on her barren condition and the sad loss of her dead child Ogonim, whose birth at least confirms her as capable of having children. Of course, the discourse within which barrenness is constructed, as in the case of the illness which causes the disruption between her and Gilbert at the end of the novel, is couched entirely in terms of 'her' failure. The presence of the alternative discourse of Western medicine, however, represented in the novel by the Western-educated Difu, may cause the reader to reflect that the evidence would seem to point to Eneberi's (Gilbert's) low fertility rather than to Efuru's barrenness. But the text is faithful to the internalised perspective of the characters by not permitting this culturally alien interpretation of events to be part of the novel's overt telling. These subtle narrative choices were largely ignored in readings by early critics of the text, whose analysis seems to assume that the choices of narrator and of narrative structure are not carefully controlled to produce exactly these powerful sub-textual disruptions in what only seems to be a simple internalised portrait of the society the text examines:[2]

> Efuru went home that night with a heavy heart. It was not the thought of another wife for Gilbert that made her heart so heavy. It was the fact that she was considered barren. It was a curse not to have children. Her people did not just take it as one of the numerous accidents of nature. It was regarded as a failure.
>   'But thank God my womb carried a baby for nine months. Thank God I had this baby and she was a normal baby. It would have been dreadful if I had been denied the joy of motherhood. And now when mothers talk about their experiences in childbirth, I can share their happiness with them, though Ogonim is no more.' (207)

The text shows that there is a process of educative awareness under way for Efuru, and that she and other women are not absolutely defined by this pervasive discourse. The text acknowledges that discourses are permeable, and that change, although difficult, does come about. The male *dibia* who denounces her is, significantly, one who 'specialised on women and their problems' (273). The *dibia*'s pronouncement of her 'adultery' as the cause of her illness thus leads her to realise that male interpretations of the world are flawed. She is supported energetically by her friend Ajanupe, the aunt of her first husband Adizua. She has continued to befriend Efuru because of her awareness of how worthless her nephew was. She recognises that his treatment of Efuru, whom he deserted, reflects that of his own father, who had treated Ajanupe's sister in the same way. A critique of 'learned' male ill-treatment of women, handed down from father to son, emerges. Ajanupe's total refusal to accept Gilbert's assertion of Efuru's adultery provokes her to a vigorous defence, which leaves him worsted. She strikes a blow for women, in a literal sense: 'Gilbert gave Ajanupe a slap which made her fall down. She got up quickly for she was a strong woman, got hold of a mortar pestle and broke it on Gilbert's head. Blood filled Gilbert's eyes' (276). The ironies of this final chapter are multiple and complex. Telling her tale to her friend Difu, the Western-trained doctor, Ajanupe reintroduces the idea of the relativity of systems, including that of the traditional world, and the corrigibility of all cultural traditions. Traditional divination, like Western medicine, can be influenced by social forces other than the strictly religious or medical. The criticism of the divination of the *dibia*, who 'specialised in women's problems', reflects the critique, which Western feminists have developed, of male doctors who once devised such controlling 'scientific' discourses as women's 'hysteria', or who still insist on male, interventionist gynaecological procedures such as induction replacing the more patient procedures of traditional midwifery.

Nwapa's novel clearly shows where the traditional system was flawed, notably in its treatment of women. But she still offers a strong and celebratory affirmation of its many positive values. Her heroine Efuru never rejects her world, and solves her problems in its terms. She continues to be proud of her father's lineage, and of her mother's virtues, conceived in traditional terms. 'Then a rumour went round that I, Efuru, the daughter of Nwashike Ogene was guilty of adultery. My mother was not an adulterous woman, neither was her mother, why should I be different? Was it possible to learn to be left-handed in old age?' (179). As she says, she has 'ended where I began – in my father's house. The difference is that now my father is dead' (280). Efuru has learnt both to live within tradition and to recognise that it is a force subject to manipulation and to false choice. This is made clear in the sub-text of the novel, in which the dominant patriarchy of 'distinguished families', and of proud male lineage, is itself shown to be a partial historical construction. Here, for example, is the account of the death of Efuru's distinguished father, Nwashike Ogene:

> It was the death of a great man. No poor man could afford to fire seven rounds of a cannon in a day. . . . The white slave dealers gave the people their cannons in exchange for slaves. . . . The white slave dealers gave them the cannons, the guns and the hot drinks. The hot drinks did what the Indian hemp is doing in politics today. The only difference is that the hot drinks were legal and the Indian hemp illegal, but both performed the same function.
>
> The cannons were owned by very distinguished families who themselves took part actively in slave dealing. They were distinguished because they were privileged to have had contact with slave dealers. Nwosu and the fisherman could not recollect what havoc the cannons and the guns and the hot drinks did for their people. All that happened, happened when they were children. Now the shooting of the cannon did not only announce the death of a great man, but also announced that the great man's ancestors had dealings with the white men, who dealt in slaves. (255)

This obviously ironic undercutting of the claims of such distinguished families by the final sentence is placed in the consciousness of the minor narrators, the fishermen. It would be inappropriate as a response from Efuru, whose perceptions could not, with any psychological credibility, be expected to extend to this level of awareness of the flaws in her own patrilineage and her own claims to belong to a distinguished family. But it casts more light on the other flaws, for example that such families, even in older times, were defined as those who had been blessed with sons to help them gain wealth.

The family of the *dibia* who accuses Efuru of adultery, and who later defines Efuru's special relation with the lake goddess Uhamiri, is now poor, though he is the descendant of a family which had been 'large and prosperous years before the Europeans came' (190). The basis of their wealth relates to the values of the traditional world. 'The men in that family were blessed with male children. Every year their wives had boys, they rarely had girls. Women liked to marry into the family because there were many men there' (190). This emphasises the changed economic basis for the wealth acquired since the Europeans came. The *dibia* is now poor, since male children are no longer a simple guarantee of wealth, as they were in a traditional economy based on subsistence farming and barter trading. It also illustrates the ongoing persistence of the belief in the importance of male children, despite the changing nature of the conditions which initially caused this belief to flourish, and to be socially useful. For once important but declined families, like the *dibia*'s, the fixed and unchanging adherence to traditional values is part of their own self-worth. They have a vested interest in the defence of the traditions, whether they are now useful or not.

Efuru's problem in bearing further children is 'divined' as being the result of her special relationship with the lake goddess Uhamiri. This is very similar to the explanation offered in Elechi Amadi's novel *The Concubine* for Ihuoma's tragic life and demise. Unlike Amadi, however, Nwapa critically unpicks this 'explanation'. Her criticism is not as an attack on the traditional system, but a further example of its failure when it functions blindly, and fails to adapt to new circumstances. In fact, the novel, far from rejecting the power of the goddess Uhamiri, transforms her into a symbol of feminine power. Her service, the price of which is the barrenness dreaded in the traditional, patriarchal system, becomes a symbol of the possibilities for an independent female life, meaningful in its own terms, and not a mere adjunct to male needs. The *dibia*'s announcement draws attention to this, when it indicates that the women who have been chosen by Uhamiri have become successful and powerful women in their own right, largely because they have not been subjected to the continual pressures of the 'joys of motherhood':

> You are a great woman. Nwashike Ogene, your daughter is a great woman. The goddess of the lake has chosen her to be one of her worshippers. It is a great honour. She is going to protect you and shower riches on you. But you must keep her laws. Look round this town, nearly all the storey buildings you find are built by women who one time or another have been worshippers of Uhamiri. (191–2)

Significantly, one of the primary taboos associated with Uhamiri involves the withholding of sexual favours from husbands on the day Orie, one of the weekdays of the Ibo calendar, honouring the idea of independent action and choice which the goddess, a symbol of wealth and beauty not tied to a male consort, represents. Her adherents represent an alternative perception of female power to that of the group led by Omirima, and the limiting vision for women which she actively seeks to press onto the next generation. This hegemonic female embodiment of the male view is opposed by the vision of the goddess with which the text ends. Rejecting Difu's advice to 'consider going back to her husband' (281), Efuru dreams of an alternative ideal of independent womanhood, focused through the symbol of Uhamiri:

> Efuru slept soundly that night. She dreamt of the woman of the lake, her beauty, her long hair and her riches. She had lived for ages at the bottom of the lake. She was as old as the lake itself. She was happy, she was wealthy. She was beautiful. She gave women beauty and wealth but no child. She had never experienced the joys of motherhood. Why then did the women worship her? (281)

This wonderfully evocative final question opens up a rift in the entire social discourse which seeks to contain Efuru, a rift which forces us to re-read the novel in a new and illuminating way. It reveals a text profoundly critical of the identification of the traditional with the patriarchal, as was too frequently the case in the masculine texts of the same period.

286

That the text was published in the same year as Amadi's *The Concubine*, and was the adjacent text in the Heinemann African Writers series, suggests that any simple idea that the text was a conscious rebuttal of Amadi is unlikely. The intertextuality now clearly focuses critical response to the two novels. But it is fruitless to seek to rank them in a hierarchy of aesthetic value and social authenticity. They do, however, offer very different perceptions of the pre-colonial traditions, and their continuing usefulness in the modern world. They reflect contesting discourses in the modern period, whose partiality is defined by their own speaking positions, and by the gendered practices involved in constructing these conflicting narratives of the traditional past. The comparison of these conflicting and contrastive texts by male and female writers of the mid-1960s makes it very clear that the traditional is always defined by and through the needs of the present.

Nwapa followed *Efuru* with the novel *Idu*, which was published four years later, in 1970. Significantly, Nwapa did not publish another major novel until 1981. The often negative criticism her work suffered at the hands of early male critics may have had some influence on this long silence; though, like Achebe, whose work also entered a long period of silence after the mid-1960s, her intimate involvement in the Biafran cause may also have been a contributory factor. It is significant that her next book, *Never Again* (1975), is a personal account of her involvement in the war. *One is Enough*, which is also set during and immediately after the Biafran war, appeared in 1981, though it was not published outside Nigeria until 1992. In this novel, Nwapa directly tackles the problem of how women deal with the demands of children and marriage, and their conflicting need for personal independence. The main character, Amaka, is the daughter of a woman of the older generation, who has also had a strong drive towards independence. Amaka's mother has been married to a man she dislikes, and yet by whom she has had seven children. Her solution to the problem has been to work within the traditional system, marrying her husband to a second younger wife, and refusing his sexual advances thereafter, concentrating her energies instead on educating her children and running a business from which she finances this goal. She advises her daughter to follow a similar path. But although Amaka shares her belief that children are central to a woman's fulfilment, she also wants a marriage based on love and respect. Her marriage is a failure, since she is unable to have a child by her husband. With the acquiescence of his mother, and even of Amaka's own mother, he decides to marry a second wife. Determined not to accept this unwelcome and unfair decision, she leaves him and goes to Lagos. Amaka has inherited her mother's business acumen and drive, as well as her desire for children, and the opportunities presented by the Biafran war enable her to develop a successful trading business there. Disillusioned by her first marriage with men, she has relations only with those who can help her in business, or towards whom she feels a sexual but not emotional attraction. She is determined to maintain her independence and not to become a man's chattel, and so refuses to contemplate re-marriage. One of her lovers, Father McLaid, is a priest, a fact which makes Amaka feel secure in sleeping with him. She has twin children by the priest, but she never reveals who the father is, even to her close family. Her close friend, Adaobi, is married, but, through Amaka's example, she decides that she too needs her independence. When her husband loses his government position, in the coup against General Gowan, she too leaves home to set up as an independent businesswoman like Amaka. Amaka is under pressure from her family to marry Father McLaid, who has left the Church, and now calls himself Izu Amaka. She seems almost to be on the point of yielding, when she learns that he has returned to the priesthood, after being forgiven for his sexual 'peccadilloes' by the bishop. Her family are angry, but Amaka sees this as the final confirmation of the rightness of her decision not to rely on men, but to make her own way. Even then, though, she is clear that she shares the traditional view that woman are primarily fulfilled by the bearing of children. She simply does not see this as meaning that women must be subject to men in order to fulfil this need. The final message seems to be that women can be both mothers and independent women, and men can serve their purpose without women having to pay the traditional price of an oppressive marriage.

'Tell Izu,' [Amaka] said, 'that I would like to see him and thank him for this noble decision, and that I was the first to know that there would be no marriage. And finally, that I shall forever remain grateful to him for proving to the world that I am a mother as well as a woman.' (154)

It is interesting to compare this text with the more radical rejection of the idea of woman's role as mother and wife in later texts by younger writers such as Buchi Emecheta. It offers an example of how this later view built upon and developed ideas which had evolved within the practice of a number of generations of African women. It also confirms Nwapa's position as one of the most innovative and influential women writers to have emerged in the post-war period. Her latest novel, *Women Are Different*, was published in Nigeria in 1986, but was not published in the US until 1992. Both re-publications evidence the rediscovery and re-evaluation of this foundational African woman writer outside Africa in the wake of recent attention to her classic early texts. But it also reflects the fact that Nwapa is one of a number of African writers who have sought to address the waxing and waning of overseas interests in publishing new African writing by establishing her own local press, which she set up in the late 1970s. She has also sought actively to provide reading based on local material for children, a task which has been prioritised by a number of other women writers.

Recent stress on texts which address problematic issues for women, such as female excision, have drawn attention to Nwapa's relatively early if only mildly critical evaluation of the impact of such practices on women in the novel *Efuru*. Her use in the novel of such euphemistic expressions as 'bath' for female excision procedures has been criticised by some recent commentators. Nevertheless, she shows how women themselves played a role in perpetuating the pressures on their gender to undergo such practices, a point made more forcefully in later more critical accounts of female excision and infibulation.

The description of Efuru's circumcision plays only a small part in the story, and its relative downplaying should not be allowed to overwhelm the presentation in the novel of Efuru as an independent spirited woman, who resists male wishes in a number of significant ways. In fact, it might be fairer simply to note that Nwapa addressed this issue so early, and thus prefigured its concern in the work of a number of more recent writers, in both the Anglophone and Francophone African traditions. Another early example of a novel by a woman which handles this theme is the Kenyan writer Muthoni Likmani's 1974 study *They Shall be Chastised*. This has been generally ignored in most recent accounts of women's writing.[3] This powerful novel explores the links between the role of the missionaries, the educational process and the social pressure for and against male and female circumcision in Kenya in the inter-war years. Likmani shows an awareness of the ways in which circumcision was intimately involved in political discourses of the period, a fact reflected in the work of such early nationalist supporters of the practice as Jomo Kenyatta in *Facing Mount Kenya*.[4] Likmani's novel offers a complex, internalised view of female excision, which, although it does not reject the practice entirely, emphasises its problematic nature. This largely forgotten text is a useful text to lay alongside the better-known male fictional account of female circumcision in this period provided by Ngũgĩ in *The River Between*, as well as that offered by non-fiction writers such as Kenyatta in *Facing Mount Kenya*. Unlike in Ngũgĩ's account, in Muthoni's text the Christian women are presented as more independent, and not merely submissive to their father's wishes.

The Kenyan novelist Grace Ogot has not been a prolific writer. She has published a collection of short stories, *Land Without Thunder* (1968), a short novella, *The Graduate* (1980), which focuses on the popular theme of the effects of cultural demands on a young Kenyan who returns from study abroad, and a second collection of stories, *The Island of Tears* (1980), published in the same year. This collection includes the title story which deals with the cultural and political discrimination against the Luo people, and the fate of their best-known independence leader, Tom Mboya, whom many claim was murdered by political opponents in the period after independence and during the consolidation of the one-party state of Jomo Kenyatta. Other stories present Ogot's belief in the viability of Christianity as a corollary to traditional African values, and as a support for women in the new Africa. Yet others concern the trauma often felt by Africans in their encounter with the prejudice and alien values of European and American cultures when they travel abroad.

She remains best known, however, for her powerful critique of the male perspective involved in earlier male-authored texts, in her novel *The Promised Land* (1966). This work tells the story of the ambitious young Luo man Ochola, and his wife Nyapol. In her portrayal of Ochola, Ogot clearly has in mind the model of Okonkwo, Achebe's masculinist protagonist in *Things Fall Apart*. In this respect, like other early works by African women, there is a conscious correction of the attitudes and perspectives of the first generation of male writers in the depiction of characters and the choice of plot:

The sufferings of an orphan child had taught Ochola how to work hard. The long hours he had spent in the fields as a boy, taught him that he could only eat by sweat and toil. Ochola's ambition in life was to be rich. Richer than those whom he had known in his youth. He wanted to be rich like Polo, his step-grandfather, who had countless heads of cattle. (86)

Significantly, this response is caused by the early death of his mother, unlike Okonkwo, whose excessive ambition and emotional imbalance stem from his reaction to the weakness and subsequent disgraced death of his father. As a result, whereas Okonkwo's 'defeat' can be presented as a tragedy, even though the weakness of his masculinist over-reactive nature is clearly recognised by Achebe, in Ogot's text the criticism of this kind of world-view is much more fundamental. Ochola's response is presented not just as excessive, but as fundamentally misguided. He can never hope to replace a mother, whose emotional solace and personal love he missed, with a security based on wealth and social standing, not on personal relationships and mutual care. Ogot's text shows this when Nyabula's values, which are concerned with family and personal links, not with success and the accumulation of wealth, are dismissed by Ochola as irrelevant. Her initial reaction to Ochola's proposal emphasises that her opposition to his plan to migrate to Tanganyika is to do with her greater attachment to these values:

> 'I've been thinking we might migrate there. I would work very hard, become rich and make you happy.'
> Nyapol pushed Ochola's hands off her hair and sat upright in bed.
> 'You must be talking in your sleep!' she cried. 'How can you think of such a thing! Leave Nyanza! Leave our old parents to go and live in some foreign land because some unbalanced men with no love of their families have told you so?' (21)

Nevertheless, Ochola decides to follow many of his countrymen and emigrate across the lake to Tanganyika, where 'unoccupied' land is available, and where the soil is less exploited than in his home region. At first, Nyapol is unconvinced, and the male projects of migration and the pursuit of wealth, to which Ochola subscribes, are pitted against Nyapol's female desire for stability and the comfort of the caring community of the family. Significantly, her opposition to the move is supported by Owiti, Ochola's father, who recognises that Nyapol supplies the 'new life' which Ochola seeks in a different sense, replacing as she does the tenderness and care of which his mother's early death had deprived him:

> 'Son, don't go away, don't leave an old man alone,' he began. 'You brought this girl here to feed me. She's kind like your mother and her presence has given us all a new life. Let her stay with us, son. I ask you this favour.'
> 'But I must go father. I'll be more useful to you if I go,' argued Ochola. 'I'll be rich and all the money troubles we've had for so many years will vanish. Whatever I earn I'll share with the whole family.'
> 'You are my eldest son – this land is yours. Our fathers died fighting for this land so that you might inherit it. It is the more precious because your grandfathers bought it with their own blood. Why go to a strange country to buy land? I'll soon lie in my grave. The land we have is more than enough for you, my son. You're married now, stay near me here. If you go away, who will bury me when I die?' (35)

In passages like this, Nyapol's female voice is not employed merely as an abstract symbolic representation of the traditional claim of land and culture, in the way critics like Stratton have argued is the case in male-authored texts, such as Okot p'Bitek's *Song of Lawino*. Here, on the contrary, tradition is allied with a specific body of lived values, personal and communal, and set over against other values, those of abstract wealth and social position. What is contested are two views of current social value, not a simple opposition of tradition and modernity, or of failure and success. Some of Nyapol's arguments eventually strike home with Ochola. He recalls her arguments as they travel across the lake to their 'Promised Land', and he remembers them again later, when his initial success collapses: 'There was no need to show Nyapol that he, a man who had taken her as his wife, did not like his own motherland. Already some of Nyapol's remarks had made him feel as though he was a shallow-minded person without roots' (46).

Amongst other things, Nyapol has warned him that he will be a stranger in the new land, and will be regarded by those there as an interloper and a person of no standing, just as he now regards the Umuri people, who had come into his own land, in this same light. When Ochola is driven away from the new land, at the height of his economic 'success', these warnings are shown to be prophetic and just. Unlike in p'Bitek's text, too, Nyapol is not presented as a figure resistant to change. In fact, after the successful journey, and after Ochola establishes himself, she adjusts with considerable success to the new situation. However, she remains aware that the purpose of these adjustments is the mutual support of the family. She never loses sight of her real values.

Florence Stratton has offered a very convincing revisionist reading of this text.[5] Her reading goes a long way towards justifying her recuperation of Ogot as a writer of great significance, despite her relatively small output. It does so by demonstrating that those features which earlier male critics had read as formally unsatisfying are, in fact, part of a very effective rhetorical dismantling of the ideology and practice of the masculinist African text. The eventual ineffectiveness and weakness of the central figure of Ochola is not necessarily the result of Ogot's failure to construct an effective 'tragic' hero, nor is the long account of his decline necessarily produced by a failure of thematic concentration, as earlier male critics had suggested. Stratton's reading effectively demonstrates that the text interrogates the assumptions of the earlier male texts in the African literary tradition. In her view, it opens up a space within that tradition for an alternative, gendered representation, one which male critics have ignored, to the detriment of a proper analysis of the complexities and richness of African writing in this early period.

Writing critically of Gerald Moore's dismissal of the text in his early review of the novel, and referring to the text's strong evocation of Achebe's foundational 'contact novel', *Things Fall Apart*, Stratton argues that:

Ochola is also not, which is Moore's complaint, a 'tragic figure'. In his greed, he becomes like Tekayo – a man who consumes his own children. For by refusing to leave Tanganyika, he endangers not only his own life but the lives of his children.

Ultimately, he emerges as a pathetic, if not a patently ridiculous figure. Intertextual echoes are, in this context, quite revealing. For while Okonkwo's tragedy is, in the words of Obierika, that he, 'one of the greatest men in Umuofia . . . will be buried like a dog' (187), Ochola's story ends with him looking forward to being united in death with a mad dog. But contrary to Moore's claim, Ogot's story does not lose its 'force and point' as a result of Ochola's diminished status. Rather it is from it that the novel acquires much of its meaning.[6]

Stratton's re-reading of this text concludes that in the novel 'Ogot creates new narrative space for the representation of women' and that Nyapol's 'values prevail over [Ochola's] and her voice is granted authority' (72).

The Ghanaian writer Ama Ata Aidoo is one of the most influential and enduring of the early women writers. Her work helped open up a separate and distinctive discursive space in which women's voices could be heard. Her extremely influential early play, *The Dilemma of a Ghost* (1965), has already been discussed briefly.[7] That play shows the inability of the modern Ghanaian husband, Ato Yawson, to reconcile and deal with the pressures of tradition in the modern world. It depicts the clash between his family's ideas of appropriate behaviour for a middle-class African woman, and the demands of his liberated, self-consciously modern and increasingly alienated Afro-American wife, Eulalie. Eulalie discovers that the 'roots' of tradition are many, varied and open to radically different interpretation depending on the persons who control them. This early play already emphasises that it is the contemporary interpretation of history that controls the way in which traditions function, positively and negatively, in the modern world. In her second play, *Anowa* (1970), Aidoo goes back to that historical past which, she believes, holds the key to this crucial issue. The action of this wide-ranging play centres on the history of the Fanti people in the late nineteenth century, and the crisis which occurs in both the Fanti and Ashanti communities at that time. This crisis is related to the long history of European contact from the fifteenth century to the present day. In the story of Anowa, Aidoo develops a model of the inter-relationship of social and personal forces, and emphasises that imperialism and sexual oppression are often directly linked as aspects of a single ideology. The play involves the use of a traditional form, which had already underpinned the first play, the so-called 'dilemma' tale. In this case, too, the story of Anowa, the disobedient daughter, is one frequently employed in Ghanaian oral tradition, though in these oral examples of the form the moral of necessary obedience by women to men and elders is, usually, unproblematically endorsed. Aidoo takes this oral form and employs it to deconstruct the very ideologies and practices which underpin its traditional usage. The use of two choruses, one of Old Men and one of Old Women, in which the latter speaks for the conservative position, echoes Nwapa's perception that hegemonic forces often make women the most scrupulous guardians of the very traditions which hold them in thrall. This same perception surfaces again in the work of younger writers such as Buchi Emecheta.

Aidoo has proved to be one of the most prolific and long-lasting of the older African women writers. She has written in most forms – drama, poetry and short story, as well as the novel.[8] Her story collection, *No Sweetness Here* (1970), offers an analysis of the class and gender struggles within contemporary Ghanaian society. Her first novel, *Our Sister Killjoy* (1977), is the account of an African woman student in Europe. Most recently, in *Changes* (1991), the title reflects the book's theme of change in the life of the heroine, and in the wider society of modern Ghana. Here she addresses the issue of relations between the sexes in what she has termed 'A Love Story'. In the preface, she recalls once saying that writing about love and romance in Africa was a waste of time 'because there are more important things to write about', and notes that she has had to swallow her own words. It is hard to say whether or not Aidoo's change of view has been influenced by the powerful texts in French dealing with the wider social implications of the personal life of women, which have emerged in the interim period. Certainly, there are many things in common between this book and those of Francophone women writers such as Mariama Bâ and Calixthe Beyala. They share a concern about the ongoing patriarchal biases of many African societies, and the problems for women who seek to develop an independent status, without rejecting the value of or need for heterosexual love. These ideas inform an account of a modern Ghana in which divorce and separation are a reality, and in which the sexuality of women constitutes an important subject of struggle and debate. Aidoo's preface contains a disclaimer that the book 'is not meant to be a contribution to any debate, however current'. But, as one of the more uncompromising wielders of polemic criticism herself, Aidoo could hardly expect that her book would not be judged against the agendas established by such recent Francophone women writers. What all these texts have in common is the perception that social change can only be effective if it also involves a change in the basis of personal relationships, most notably those between men and women.

The *Changes* referred to in the title are changes from traditional to modern practices, especially as they affect women. The central concerns addressed by writers such as Nwapa, in her later work, and by more recent writers such as Emecheta, are also at the heart of this text: issues of the relevance or irrelevance in urban, modern societies of practices such as polygamy; the use of these practices to control women who fail to meet the unfair expectations of their husbands or their husbands' families; and the pressure on women to conform to the demand that they find their primary fulfilment in motherhood. Esu, the main character, is a woman who wants a career, and this is the basic cause of the strife in her marriage. Her husband, Oku, feels neglected as she demands the time and freedom to develop as a person, and to carve out a public role for herself. Aidoo's text presents this conflict from the perspective of both partners, and shows how hard it is for Oku to deal with these changes too. The marriage collapses when Esu wants to spend her week time in Accra, returning home only at weekends. She feels that, given the predominant prejudice against women, unless she works this hard, she will not be taken seriously in her job. As a result of this decision, her marriage to Oku collapses. When she later marries her lover, Ali, she refuses to have more children with him. He already has a wife, Fusema, who has sacrificed her own ambitions to his career. Fusema feels threatened by Esu, who is educated, and so displaces her not only as wife, but also represents the kind of person Fusema herself once aspired to be. Okopuya, Esu's friend, is also locked into a marriage in which the struggle for status and independence brings her into conflict with her husband.

For all these women, the changes and roles which modern society offer are fraught with conflict and difficulty. These changes are placed into a wider historical context when Esu's grandmother tries to tell her that the relations of men and women have always been fraught with problems. As with Amaka's mother in Nwapa's's novel *One is Enough*, the grandmother's solution is to separate off love and marriage, and to see the relationship with men simply as the price which women must pay for their fulfilment as mothers. Unlike Amaka, though, who seems in the end to accept a kind of modern version of this bitter prescription, Esu rejects this 'solution', demanding instead the right to be able to have a relationship with men which incorporates personal emotions as well as functional roles. Her relationship with Ali is infused with romantic love, and the novel presents him frankly as an object of sexual desire: 'He wore kohl around his eyes, moved like a panther, and was very good-looking' (22). Despite her passionate infatuation with Ali, as we have seen, Esu continues to insist on her right to an independent life. *Changes* is notable for the fact that it insists on the woman's right to a sexuality of her own, and to an independence which is not gained at the expense of this, or of her legitimate demand for romantic and sexual fulfilment. Romantic passion, however, never overrides Esu's perception of the fickleness of men's emotions, and of the need for women to protect themselves by not yielding up all their power and independence when they fall in love. At the same time, Aidoo shows that she is clearly aware of how difficult it is to attain such a goal. The problem is that her ideal flies in the face of many deeply entrenched attitudes in African societies such as Ghana, attitudes which are the product both of local traditional practices and of the patriarchal forces introduced by colonialism. When the relationship with Ali begins to break down after three years of marriage, Esu demands a separation but does not annul the marriage:

> Esi never went back to Oko. As far as she was concerned that was not an option. She never had a baby with Ali either. That relationship stopped being a marriage. They became just good friends who found it convenient once in a while to fall into bed and make love.
> She never bothered to look for an annulment of the marriage. (164)

In part, this is because she does not want to be subjected to the scrutiny of a society which would demand an 'explanation from her as to why she would want to "destroy" that marriage too. . . . So the marriage stayed but radically changed' (165). Esu accepts that Ali will go with other women. She even accepts that his insistence that he still loves her was 'true; that he loved her in his own fashion', but she is also insistent that 'his fashion of loving had become inadequate for her' (165). But she is left with the as yet unanswerable question: 'So what fashion of loving was she ever going to consider adequate?'

(166). Is the solution the compromise with unsatisfactory relations, as advocated by generations of past women, or the radical modern solution of the rejection of marriage all together? Esu has no answer, but it is clear that she will no longer settle for the former, and the novel ends with her hope that perhaps the future may provide an answer to the difficulties the changes of modern life have posed for her and other women like her.

Fellow Ghanaian writer Efua Sutherland worked mainly as a theatre director and playwright. She was founder of women's theatre in Africa, as well as a leading exponent of the need to integrate European and African dramaturgies, and her plays represent one of the most important bodies of drama in modern African English writing. Her recuperation as a leading figure is long overdue. Sutherland wrote almost exclusively for the stage. Her other major concern was to provide more effective writing for children in Africa, writing which reflected local issues and needs. To this end, she wrote a children's book, *Playtime in Africa*. She also produced a number of plays designed specifically for young audiences, including *Vulture! Vulture!* and *Tahinta*, which were performed and published in 1968. Sutherland was instrumental in founding the Ghana Experimental Theatre (later renamed the Ghana Drama Studio) in 1958. In 1963 this became the basis for the University of Ghana School of Music, Dance and Drama, and Sutherland joined the staff of that institute. This very early involvement in theatre and theatre training, which predates the founding of the early companies in Nigeria, such as Ṣoyinka's 1960 Masks, has been overlooked in many accounts of theatre in the region.[9]

Her early work, such as the play *Foriwa* (1967), presented a critical but sympathetic look at the need to adapt custom to change, both as the effects of modernisation occur and as the role of women in society changes. The play deals with the struggle between the old, conservative nobleman Sintim and the Queen Mother, who has been placed on the royal stool (the Ashanti throne) much to the old man's disgust. It centres on her hope that her daughter Foriwa may find a new role for herself in the emerging society. It offers a powerful critique of the male-determined social past:

> SINTIM: Up, up! Rise up! Call the townsmen together. Convene them in the Chief Linguist's house. Tell them to come and listen with their own ears. Since our ancestor's days, custom has always been fulfilled in the proper way. They say today. . . . It is the Queen Mother who says . . . If you want to hear, come and listen . . . I told you when you insisted on putting a woman on the stool. I told you, didn't I? A woman who can read. All right come and listen. (24)

For the Queen Mother, the fight with Sintim is inevitable. She notes that, 'For a long time, I've been trying to find a way to make the people of Kyerefaso see; to see at least that for our ancestors, custom was the fruit they picked from the living branches of life. The lesson is long overdue. Come, I must prepare to meet them' (25).

In early plays like *Foriwa*, the form remains basically European, with only the addition of some occasional songs to what is basically a foreign dramatic structure. Yet, by the late 1960s, in her children's plays, Sutherland had begun to experiment with a more radical use of song to structure a whole dramatic performance. In the work with the Ghana Drama Studio, Sutherland was a firm supporter of the need to integrate local performance elements into an African dramaturgy, and this is the basis for her most successful play, *The Marriage of Anansewa* (1975). In this, she takes the local Akan version of the Ananse 'trickster' story-telling tradition (*Anansesem*) and develops the traditional form into a new theatrical form she calls *Anansegoro*. In the introduction to the play, she traces the elements of this story-telling tradition and suggests how she has employed it to construct a unique dramatic form which blends the concerns and devices of the traditional trickster-story with a modern setting and characters.

The play uses elements from the traditional performance style, such as the *Mbogua* dance/song, as a narrative structuring device to link and organise the story sections, and blends them with a narrative of modern Ghana, in which the modern Ananse (George Kweku Ananse) uses his trickster skills to procure gifts from four chiefs, whom he persuades to court his daughter, Anansewa. The daughter at first resists the idea of being married off as 'some parcel to a customer' (11), but quickly becomes reconciled to the plot when Ananse promises her she will be married to the young and handsome Chief-Who-Is-Chief, and not to some old chief with fifty wives. The plot involves the typical Ananse story, in which a seemingly inextricable tangle of promises is made to each of the four suitors, all of whom send Ananse gifts which transform him from a poor to a rich man. By dint of a pretended death and a final 'miracle', in which love apparently brings her back to life, Ananse tricks each of the suitors and allows his daughter to marry the one (Chief-Who-Is-Chief) whom she favours. He even manages to get several final rounds of funeral gifts from the suitors. Sutherland's work has been criticised by some feminist critics for lacking a specific programme of reform in these adaptations. But although Sutherland makes no attempt to force any strong social or political level into the story, there is an implicit criticism of the continuing inequality of society in the modern period, in which the poor Ananse tricking the rich men is clearly designed to appeal to a popular audience.

The strength of Sutherland's later work, though, is less in its radical themes than in the way it prefigures the effective integration of traditional elements of dramaturgy (song, dance and chant), and elements of classic Akan folklore, with a comic representation of contemporary life. The use of a Storyteller is, as Sutherland insists in the preface, a device which allows the play to be a skeleton onto which the teller can graft new flesh:

> refreshing and updating his story by spontaneous improvisation as he tells it. And it is to this artistry in the narration that the audience look for the aesthetic experience they seek. Thus, stories in the tradition are under constant revision for renewal and redevelopment. Also contemporary interest inspires the composition of completely new stories to replenish the repertory. (vi)

Although there is no direct suggestion that this readjustment can be used to make specific social or political points, the form of the *Anansegoro*, as Sutherland develops it, provides a theatrical example of how a traditional form can be employed, and examples from other such amended traditions suggest that figures like the Storyteller can easily be employed to incorporate direct comment on contemporary characters or events which provoke responses in the specific audience addressed. They may also make indirect references to real people or specific events, thus tying the general form to a particular setting.[10]

The implicit possibility of this form for social criticism, though not immediately apparent from the bare, published text, is an important part of Sutherland's radical contribution to contemporary African dramaturgy. Sutherland's notes to the play also suggest her use of a number of devices to facilitate direct audience response, such as the use of audience address (inviting response), and a pool of players who merge with and re-emerge from the audience, thus breaking down these as distinct and separate groups. In much criticism and commentary on later West African plays, these kind of devices are often labelled Brechtian. Although there is little doubt that in some cases a direct Brechtian influence was a factor, it is also clear that local performance traditions, such as *Anansesem*, already possessed all the devices necessary to facilitate these effects in the hands of a modern writer and producer such as Sutherland.

It is true that the issues of social change and the role of women in plays like *Foriwa* were not developed to any great extent in the new form which she evolved in later work such as *The Marriage of Anansewa*. Nevertheless, she was a pioneer amongst West African women theatre workers, and her work offered interesting models for a younger generation to develop.

The emphasis by early publishers on fiction has had a negative effect on the availability of drama texts, as I have noted elsewhere. This in turn has meant that they have received less critical attention. The example of Efua Sutherland and, to a lesser extent, because she worked across genres, of Ama Ata Aidoo, shows that this neglect extends to women writers. Even the recent spate of feminist studies of women writers has tended to neglect those who worked in drama and, to a lesser extent, in poetry.[11] Two Nigerian examples must suffice to show this in practice. A notable example of another early woman writer who has suffered almost total critical neglect is Zulu Sofola. Her work, like Efua Sutherland's, is almost exclusively in drama. Perhaps her plays have also been neglected, in part, by recent feminist accounts because they have, like Sutherland's, been seen to occupy a relatively conservative position in the range of responses by women to oppressive traditional practices. Or at least they have been seen to suggest that the more radical attacks on patriarchal values as inherent in traditional culture, made by other writers such as Emecheta, may be overstated. Sofola's plays, which include *Wedlock of the Gods* (1972) and *The Sweet Trap* (1977), nevertheless do incorporate a strong criticism of the way in which both traditional and modern discourses avoid dealing with the actual conditions women face in Nigerian society. A pragmatic streak, and a dramaturgical interest in employing physical rather than literary elements from traditional theatre, have also militated against her being drawn into the recent discussion of women's writing, which has been very text-centred. Although her work has been criticised for being conservative in its treatment of traditional practices, the themes it embraces, such as women achieving a sense of freedom and personal identity after the death of their husband has liberated them from a loveless traditional marriage (*Wedlock of the Gods*), may suggest that this view is disputable. The neglect of Sofola's work indicates that we need to be careful about the emergence of new unofficial canons, even in areas which seem to constitute a challenge to canonicity *per se*, such as women's writing. It also emphasises the need to be careful, here as elsewhere, about the construction of accounts which privilege forms such as fiction above others such as poetry and drama.

Sofola's fellow Nigerian, Tess Onwueme, shows the persistence of this neglect of the dramatists amongst women writers into more recent times. Twenty years younger than Sofola, Onwueme has received relatively little critical attention, even though plays such as *A Hen Too Soon* (1983) and *The Broken Calabash* (1984) offer very acute analyses of domestic problems in modern African society, analogous with those examined by novelists such as Aidoo and Emecheta, writing at the same time. Onwueme's later work, especially *Cattle Egret Versus Nama* (1989), a prison cell play which rivals such better known African works as Fugard's *The Island* in its dramatic force and intensity, has suffered equal neglect. Onwueme now lives in the USA. Her recent work includes *Tell it to Women: An Epic Drama for Women* (1997). First published in Nigeria in 1995, it has been reissued in the USA in 1997, with a preface by Ngũgĩ. An ideologically and politically powerful work, *Tell it to Women* is a mammoth epic drama of more than two hundred pages. It is critical of the too casual use in Africa of a Western feminist critical discourse, and questions its relevance as a tool for understanding an African traditional perspective. But it is equally dismissive of attempts to set traditional practice apart from contemporary inequalities, as the new leaders have consolidated a class position in which women suffer along with other disadvantaged social groups. In the play, the women leaders of the drive to address the disadvantages of rural poor women, Daisy and Ruth, are forced to recognise that their middle-class problems and prescriptions may not be relevant to the needs of the poor women they seek to help. The play suggests that only through self-help and self-organisation can the needs of Africa's disadvantaged be effectively addressed. The text is courageous, too, in addressing issues such as same-sex relations, which have only rarely been dealt with in African texts. The two women, Ruth and Daisy, have a lesbian relationship.[12] Unlike her earlier work, the play's length and its more than a dozen characters, as well as its many settings, suggest that it may be difficult to stage. Although, from time to time, the considerable dramatic flair of her earlier work remains in evidence, there is a more ponderous narrative element, and the lengthy and over-elaborate development of the ideas seems occasionally to get in the way of a successful dramatisation of the events. There is no evidence in the published text that a staging has occurred, though it may well have done. Hopefully, the fact that Onwueme now resides in America will not cut her off from the performance practice which was such a feature of her earlier work. On the other hand, of course, that this long dramatic narrative exists as a text may well be taken as a further sign of the cross-fertilisation of prose fiction, poetry and drama which, as we noted elsewhere, has been part of the modern African English text's refusal to be contained within the traditional boundaries of European genre categories.

Outside Africa, at least, the best-known recent West or East African woman writer currently using English is Buchi Emecheta. The extended critical and popular attention she has received in America and Europe implies that her writing shares many features with those transcultural writers discussed in the following chapter, and the discussion of her work could well have been located there too, illustrating again how disputable and arbitrary any critical taxonomy must be in this complex field.

The attention paid to Emecheta's work, especially by European and American feminists and by Afro-American women critics and writers, has led to a controversial reading of her work as 'feminist', a reading which has led to her denying that her concerns are congruent with those of Western feminists. A similar rejection of this label has been a feature of Ama Ata Aidoo's recent response to overseas reception of African women's writing. In effect, these African women are loathe to see their work as similar to that of white, middle-class feminists. They argue that to lump together women's experience in this way across cultures is to reconstitute a colonialising discourse which erases cultural difference.

Nevertheless, despite these protestations, it is difficult not to feel that Emecheta's early work, at least, is openly supportive of such a linkage. In her first books, she deals with her experiences as a single parent of five children, following the split between her and her husband after they had gone to Britain to study. She began her career by writing articles for a British newspaper about the plight of women like herself. In *In the Ditch* (1972), her collection of these early pieces, she writes that, 'My experiences were not, I feel, much affected by the fact that I came from another country and was black. They might well have been (indeed they *were*) shared by many women, white and black, living in an over-industrialised society' (ix).

In post-Thatcher Britain, the shared experience of deprivation and marginalisation, based on class and gender, and of the resulting poverty, linked these women beyond their racial difference. This was a powerful subject, and Emecheta's remains one of the most potent voices of migrant poor women in contemporary British writing. In the novel which followed, *Second Class Citizen* (1974), which tells the story of Adah, of her traditional arranged marriage and her subsequent desertion with her children in Britain, the title clearly reflects the fact that the negative treatment she received was both because she was black and because she was a woman. She is a second-class citizen on *both* counts, and the theme of the novel is clearly the intersection of these two forms of discrimination in many modern societies. In the many novels, stories and collections which have followed, Emecheta has continued to explore this theme as it affects modern women, both abroad and at home in Nigeria. Like Sutherland, Emecheta has also recently produced texts designed specifically for children (such as *The Wrestling Match* (1983) and *The Moonlight Bride*

(1983)), which indicates her belief, shared with other women writers, that children are a specifically neglected audience.[13] She has also reached back, like earlier writers such as Aidoo and Sutherland, to the historical past in novels like *The Slave Girl* (1977) and *The Bride Price* (1976), where she sets up an alternative vision of the traditional past, one in which the gender prejudice of traditional practices is exposed. Although most of this later fiction is set in Nigeria, in a more recent text, *The Family* (1994), Emecheta returns to the theme of being black and female in modern Britain, extending her scope by making her heroine Jamaican, and exploring the attitudes to women in both the West Indian British diasporic society, and amongst the whites with whom they interact. Her recent autobiography, *Head Above Water* (1986), confirms both the autobiographical roots of much of the early writing, and also the skill with which this has been transformed into fiction. Her work also includes *The Rape of Shavi* (1983), in which she attempts a more allegorical style, and deals with the theme of colonial conflict and culture clash in an imaginary land invaded by albinos who drop from the skies. This fascinating novel explores the issue of what precisely defines power and identity in cross-cultural encounters, and is an allegory both of colonisation and of the evolution of modern African cultures from a variety of distinctive sources. Throughout her varied output, Emecheta's work is inflected with a specific and corrective gender bias which presents these events from a womanist perspective.

Not surprisingly, perhaps, Emecheta's work has received a mixed reception from male Nigerian critics, with some seeing its presentation of the decline of traditional practices in the modern world as an iconoclastic attack on African tradition, and a kind of betrayal.[14] This reaction was perhaps only to be expected, but it is itself ironic in the light of the long tradition of critical examination of such traditions, especially when they are displaced into urban life, in male-authored African novels from Achebe's *No Longer at Ease* onwards, none of which attracted such adverse comment. There is little doubt that it is Emecheta's uncompromising exposure of the oppressive, patriarchal nature of such traditions which accounts for the virulence of some of these reactions, a point made strongly by many of Emecheta's female defenders.[15] The enthusiastic reception of Emecheta's work by European and American feminist critics might also account for this backlash to some extent. As noted already, Emecheta herself has denied on a number of occasions that her texts are feminist in intent. But perhaps this is best seen in light of this wider cultural politics, since she is at pains to insist that her specifically Nigerian and African perspective needs to be taken into account, to ensure that her work is not simply subsumed into some general discourse of international feminism. In fact, as her best-known text, *The Joys of Motherhood* (1979), shows clearly, Emecheta's work is profoundly rooted in the traditions of African women's writing. Like other earlier African women writers, her texts re-write earlier male texts. They also establish an intertextuality with these earlier women's texts, creating and adding to the distinctive tradition of African women's writing by direct allusion, and by extending and developing the radical new modes of representation these earlier texts embodied.

The Joys of Motherhood (1979) is a classic site of the critical struggles over the definition of modern African women's writing, drawing together as it does the issues of the representation of African culture, and its reading through varied womanist writing practices. It deals with the shift from traditional to modern practice by examining three generations of Ibo women. The first generation is represented by Ona, the independent and feisty daughter of Obi Umunn, a chief. She becomes the mistress of Nwokocha Agbadi, a powerful and wealthy man, who bears quite a deal of resemblance to Achebe's Okonkwo. This is not unexpected, perhaps, since *The Joys of Motherhood* is another revisionist reworking of the textual inscription of women in early masculinist Nigerian fiction, a tradition which began with Flora Nwapa's alternative view of the pre-colonial past in *Efuru*, from the final words of which Emecheta's novel takes its title. The heroine of *Efuru*, the as yet only awakening Efuru, questions why women should worship a goddess who has not known the 'joys of motherhood'. Emecheta's novel sets out to explore the further ironies of this definition of female fulfilment in a modern society in which patriarchal practice persists long after even the traditional structures which gave it form have disappeared. Even the name of Emecheta's female protagonist reflects these processes of control, Ona (jewel in Ibo) being the pet name given to her by her possessive father. Her father also wishes her children to bear his name, and so is content for her to live with Agbadi as mistress rather than wife. Although this gives Ona a limited control of her fate, resident in her relatively free status as a mistress, she is still defined in every way by the patriarchal structures of the society in which she finds herself. The relations of men and women in this society are presented as an unremitting struggle for dominance and control. Although 'people said that Nwokocha Agbadi spent all his life on earth courting Ona' (11), in fact her sexuality, whilst being a source of power, is also a source of her defeat, as Emecheta records when Agbadi, following a near mortal illness, regains his strength and asserts his renewed sexual dominance over her:

> Her struggling and kickening lessened. She started to moan and groan instead, like a woman in labour. He kept on, and would not let go, so masterful was he in this art. He knew he had reduced her to longing and craving for him. He knew he had won. He wanted her completely humiliated in her burning desire. (20)

The death of Agbadi's senior wife is accompanied by the ritual killing of a female slave, who also struggles against her fate. Agbadi's son strikes her down. Agbadi intervenes, but only to prevent her being abused by him, not to prevent her death, which quickly follows. In her dying words, she promises to return to his household as a legitimate daughter, in gratitude for his support. Here the traditional world is presented as one which singles out women for its victims, though the whole episode also clearly echoes the ritual killing of the slave boy, Ikemefuna, in Achebe's *Things Fall Apart*. When Ona's daughter, Nnu Ego, is born, she is recognised as the spirit of this slave girl returned, a recognition which becomes profoundly ironic when, as the text of her life unfolds, she is slowly shown to be a sacrificial victim of a different kind herself.

The main part of the story concerns Nnu Ego's life, and the novel opens with her attempted suicide. The story of Ona, although chronologically earlier, is inserted after this opening, in the form of a flashback. The reasons for Nnu Ego's suicidal impulse are then traced, as we watch her marriages, first to the handsome Amatokwu, who puts her aside when she fails to produce a son for him, and then to Naaife, a fellow villager, who now lives in Lagos. Sent off to marry this man, whom she has never seen, Nnu Ego quickly finds that he is weak and ugly and his work, as a washerman for a white family, repels her. This is the first indication that Nnu Ego is a victim not only of the practices and prejudices of her society, but of her own hegemonically constructed idea of what is appropriate to men and women. She compares him unfavourably with her previous husband, the strong and muscular Amatokwu, forgetting that this strength was used to beat his wives and to accuse them of a barrenness of which he was the cause:

> She was used to tall, wiry farmers, with rough, blackened hands from farming, long lean legs and very dark skin. This one was short, the flesh of his upper arm danced as he moved about among his jubilant friends, and that protruding belly? Why did he not cover it? She despised him on that first night . . . (43–4)

Nnu Ego quickly discovers that the move to the urban world of Lagos has effectively dislocated the values of the traditional society. In Lagos, women have become economic providers too, since, in this urban world, cash rather than crops is the basis of the domestic economy. Women are forced to become petty traders, using the money they make to educate their children, while the men spend their wages on beer and tobacco. Nevertheless, the status of children, especially male children, remains intact. Men still insist on women's fertility to prove their own 'immortality', and the bulk of the money the women earn is set aside to educate the male children. Women like Nnu Ego remain willing participants in this inequitable system, since they continue to perceive the bearing of male children as their principal role as women, as well as their economic prop in old age. Even those who have achieved a degree of economic autonomy, such as Mama Abby, participate in this hegemonic practice. Mama Abby, who has become well off through trading with the money her son's European father sends her, still sees her principal role in life as being the mother of her male child. As was customary, she continues to take her name from that child, and looks to him as her main long-term economic prop and security: 'The wise woman saved all her money to use for her son's education . . . for that would secure her a happy old age' (107–8). Despite the shifts in socio-economic patterns, the male community still insist on maintaining their controlling role, fining the women when they transgress its rules. Again, Emecheta shows that this is only possible because the women acquiesce in their oppression, demonstrating again that it is their actions which permit the perpetuation of this control. When Naaife decides to take a second wife, Nnu Ego concurs, even though he cannot afford to maintain her alone. Also, she is now further trapped by the obligations incumbent on a traditional senior wife, whose duties she must assume, even though she has secured none of the traditional benefits and privileges. At moments like this, Nnu Ego seems almost to become conscious of her predicament, and to see her plight from outside the controlling discourse of tradition:

> On her way back to her room, it occurred to Nnu Ego that she was a prisoner, imprisoned by her love for her children, imprisoned in her role as the senior wife. She was not even expected to demand more money for her family; that was considered below the standard expected of a woman in her position. It was not fair, she felt, the way men cleverly used a woman's sense of responsibility to actually enslave her. They knew that a traditional wife would never dream of leaving her children.... At home in Ibuza she would have had her own hut and would at least have been treated as befitting her position, but here in Lagos ... [it] seemed that all she had inherited from her agrarian background was the responsibility and none of the booty. (137)

But, despite such moments of growing consciousness, she always lapses back. When Naaife is drafted into the army, the economic pressure is even greater on Nnu Ego, but far from finding the traditional elders of the community a support, she discovers they are only a further oppression. They fine her, according to traditional custom, for a supposed breach of her duties of hospitality as the traditional elder wife. Ironically, the fine is of palm wine and tobacco, which the elders, no doubt, later consume. On the other hand, Adaka, Naaife's younger second wife, who is considered a failure because she has had only girl children, uses his absence to break away, becoming a prostitute. Ironically, by selling her body to strangers, she is able to achieve an independence she cannot find within the traditional social framework. Significantly, she also makes the decision to use her money to break with tradition and educate her daughters, rather than as Nnu Ego continues to do, to sacrifice her daughters to provide money to educate her son: 'I will spend the money I have in giving my girls a good start in life. They shall stop going to the market with me. I shall see they get enrolled in a good school' (168).

The text's implicit ironies now become more consciously exploited, as Adaku informs Nnu Ego of her decision:

> Nnu Ego sighed sadly. 'I think you are making a mistake, Adaku. Besides you could have a son when our husband returns.'
>
> 'Maybe you're right again, my senior. Yet the more I think about it the more I realise that we women set impossible standards for ourselves. That we make life intolerable for one another. I cannot live up to your standards, senior wife. So I have to set out on my own.'
>
> 'May your *chi* be your guide, Adaku,' Nnu Ego whispered almost inaudibly as she crawled further into the urine-stained mats on her bug-ridden bed, enjoying the knowledge of her motherhood. (169)

After Naaife returns, things do not improve. Nnu Ego struggles to hold on to her growing perception of the forces which have condemned her to this unfair existence. But although she comes close to understanding her plight, she is never able to break free. Her conditioning and the force of her past are too strong:

The arrival of her twin daughters had a subduing effect upon Nnu Ego. She felt more inadequate than ever. Men – all they were interested in were male babies to keep their names going. But did not a woman have to bear the woman-child who would later bear the sons? 'God, when will you create a woman who will be fulfilled in herself, a full human being, not anybody's appendage?' she prayed desperately. (186)

Perhaps Nnu Ego's perceptions are rather in advance of the character, at moments like this, with the novel's polemic purpose showing too obviously. But, in justification, one might note that it is the inability of Nnu Ego to act on this half-formed alternative vision which Emecheta stresses. She dramatises this through the contrastive choices and actions of Adaku, who does indeed manage to escape these forces, emphasising the possibility of doing so. Adaku's daughters attend school, and she wants them to go on to college, while Nnu Ego has taken her girls out of school to help her trade to obtain their bride price, as she sees only the possibility for her girls of '[getting] good husbands' (189). Nnu Ego invests all her hopes in her son, Oshia, for whom she scrimps and saves, sending him to school, college and then abroad to be educated. Oshia leaves for America, leaving Nnu Ego to face another round of crises in which Naaife is arrested and imprisoned when he attacks his daughter's fiancé who is a Yoruba not an Ibo, a fact which offends Naaife's tribal loyalties. Naaife's trial gives Emecheta the opportunity to show how increasingly irrelevant the traditional male attitudes and roles are to the realities of modern Lagos, as the judge probes Naaife's motives and actions in attacking the family of his daughter's Yoruba suitor. With Naaife in jail, Nnu Ego is increasingly unable to find the money for the schooling of her second son, Adim. Oshia ignores the problem, and refuses to respond to her pleas to return home to help. The final pages pile irony on irony, as the inadequacy and irrelevance of the traditional values to these situations are exposed. Nnu Ego marries her daughter Taiwo to her Yoruba lover Magnus, partly to raise the money for Adim's school fees. But she tells him that he is to 'trust tested friends not relatives' (220), effectively endorsing the new values and denying the validity of the old communal world in the changing circumstances of modern Nigeria. Nnu Ego returns to Ibuza, leaving her younger daughter Obiageli to be raised by Taiwo and Magnus, who promise to give her an education. Nnu Ego, though perhaps not fully liberated into consciousness of her world, is at least now able to act in small ways to secure some future for her daughters. But even now, when complimented by the passenger-lorry driver on her daughters she is quick to point out that: 'I haven't just got daughters, I have a son'. 'A son in America?' responds the driver. 'Goodness you must be full of joy, madam!' (223). The final section is profoundly ironic as on her return to Ibuza she is 'branded . . . a bad woman' (223). Her death is presented with a bitter ironic tone:

Nnu Ego laid down by the roadside, thinking that she had arrived home. She died quietly there, with no child to hold her hand and no friend to talk to her. She had never really made many friends, so busy had she been building up her joys as a mother. (224)

Her son Oshia, who has married a white woman in America, comes home on hearing of her death, though he had ignored her earlier pleas to return, in order to give her the 'most costly burial Ibuza had ever seen' and so 'show the world what a good son he was' (224). Her children set up a shrine for her, to which women who are barren pray, but people say her wickedness is confirmed by the fact that these prayers are never answered:

> Stories afterwards, however, said that Nnu Ego was a wicked woman even in death because however many people appealed to her to make women fertile, she never did. . . . It took Oshia three years to pay off the money he had borrowed to show the world what a good son he was. That was why people failed to understand why she did not answer their prayers, for what else could a woman want but to have sons who would give her a decent burial?
> Nnu Ego had it all, yet still did not answer prayers for children. (224)

This last sentence ironically echoes the ending of Flora Nwapa's *Efuru*, bringing the intertextual linkages of the two texts full circle, and commenting on the need for a more radical reading of these patriarchal controls within Nigerian society.

A number of recent anthologies of African women writers in English offer a broad overview of the range of other women writers, including those who have recently emerged.[16] The number of new writers in these and other anthologies suggests that we can do only scant justice here to the range and variety of recent African English women's writing.[17] A significant feature of these anthologies is the way in which they cross the boundaries of region, including many writers from North Africa as well as from all the regions of sub-Saharan Africa. The implicit and, perhaps, not indisputable claim of this construction is that their shared concerns with womanist issues override their regional and cultural differences. This implies that to compare women's writing between these regions as sharing aspects of a single womanist discourse and specific goals and aims is valid, but it does not imply that these diverse texts do not also have many local variations and influences. The likelihood that the pioneering work of the early writers will be consolidated in a new body of writing is now certain, as so many younger women writers emerge and as their work is increasingly paid critical attention.[18] But a word of caution is, perhaps, in order. Women writers, like other new African writers, are also subject to the constraint of the relative decline in wider publishing opportunities for African writing. However, if internationally based feminist presses and critics have shown a special interest in their work, allowing them to escape some of these constraints, and to enjoy a notably high profile in recent times, this may well be only a just compensation for the earlier period of neglect by male editors and critics.

Notes

1. I have chosen to deal in some detail with selected specific texts to show the range and power of work produced by women writers rather than simply to list their texts in a superficial way. The bibliography will, it is hoped, encourage people to follow up

individual writers in more detail than I can hope to provide here. Throughout this volume I have been aware, too, of how the constraints of space have forced me to neglect writers who deserve mention. This is nowhere more the case than in this section. Writers I might also have discussed include Mabel Segun, Adaora Lily, Catherine Acholunu, Zaynab Alkali, Simi Bedford and Phanuel Egejura (Nigeria), Abena Busia (Ghana), Jane Tapsubei, Charity Waciuma and Miriam Were (Kenya), and many others who must remain unnamed if not unnoticed.

2. See Florence Stratton, *Contemporary African Writing and the Politics of Gender* (London: Routledge, 1994), p. 80 *et passim*.

3. I am grateful here, as elsewhere in this chapter, to acknowledge the role played by my graduate student, Jill Eagling, in drawing my attention to the existence of some of these texts, as well as stimulating my readings of them by her perceptive comments. Her thesis will shortly be completed and will then be available for consultation through the University of Western Australia library. It presents a full account of this text and compares it with male texts of the period.

4. For a study of the role of circumcision in Kenyatta's political strategy and rhetoric see John Lonsdale and Barry Berman's study of Kenyatta, which is due to be published shortly, some of the material of which they have presented at various international conferences in recent years, and some of which John Lonsdale has kindly allowed me to see in ms form.

5. Stratton, *Contemporary African Writing*, pp. 69–72.

6. Ibid., p. 71.

7. See Chapter 7.

8. Perhaps for this reason, she does not feature as a separate writer in the influential feminist account of African writing by Stratton, who, as some reviewers have noted, seems to see the novel and African writing as coterminous. For the same reason, perhaps, Stratton does not deal at all with Efua Sutherland, arguably the most distinguished African woman playwright. Sutherland continues to be neglected but Aidoo's work is now the subject of a number of studies including a recent book-length study: Vincent Odamtten, *The Art of Ama Ata Aidoo: Polylectics and Reading Against Colonialism* (Gainesville: University of Florida Press, 1994).

9. For useful and informative exceptions to this see the entry on Sutherland in Martin Banham *et al.*, *Cambridge Guide to African and West Indian Theatre* (Cambridge: Cambridge University Press, 1994), and James Gibbs, 'Efua Sutherland', in C. B. Cox (ed.), *African Writers*, Vol. 2 (New York: Scribners, 1997), pp. 833–50.

10. See, for example, James L. Peacock, *Rites of Modernization: Symbolic and Social Aspects of Indonesian Proletarian Drama* (Chicago: University of Chicago Press, 1968). See also the account of other interfaces of traditional and modern practice in B. Ashcroft *et al.*, *The Empire Writes Back: Theory and Practice in Post-colonial Literatures* (London: Routledge, 1989), pp. 181–5, especially the account of the contemporary elements in modern productions of traditional Indian theatre.

11. Poetry also continues to be neglected in comparison with fiction but at least some of the work of these writers comes to wider attention in the form of anthologies, appearing on educational curricula and so receiving critical notice from time to time.

12. Ngũgĩ's comment on this in his preface reflects the rather ambivalent attitude that even radical male Africans still display to this phenomenon: 'What is negative [*sic*] about Ruth and Daisy is not so much their lesbian liaison but rather their ideological class position' (9).

13. These are the dates of the American edition. Both were published in Nigeria *c*. 1980. I have not been able to find copies of these editions to verify these dates. Some bibliographies and lists of 'other works' in her books also list other children's texts I have not been able to consult, such as *Titch the Cat* and *Nowhere to Play*. It would be unfair

to suggest that only women writers have addressed this problem. For example, both Achebe and Ngũgĩ have written stories for children, as have Sowande and others. But it is fair to say that the provision of local children's writing has been a special concern of many women writers.

14. For example, Eneogu Afam, 'Enter the Iconoclast: Buchi Emecheta and the Igbo Culture', *Commonwealth Essays and Studies*, 7, 2 (1985), pp. 83–94.

15. Kirsten Holst-Petersen, 'Unpopular Opinions: Some African Women Writers', *Kunapipi*, 7, 2–3 (1985).

16. Margaret Busby (ed.), *Daughters of Africa: An International Anthology of Words and Writing by Women of African Descent from the Ancient Egyptians to the Present Times* (London: Vintage, 1993) and Charlotte H. Brunner, *The Heinemann Book of African Women's Writing* (London: Heinemann, 1993).

17. For example, we may note how many women writers have addressed the needs of children, writing books, plays and stories designed for them. The Ugandan writer Barbara Kimenye, for example, has produced more than twenty novels and short story collections for children. Again, only space precludes me from having a separate chapter on this important area of modern African writing.

18. As the general bibliography shows, in the last ten years the growing body of women's writing in Africa has also been served by a large number of monographs examining these texts and the tradition of women's writing.

Chapter 12

New Transcultural Voices in East and West African Writing

In the opening chapters of this volume I have suggested that the forms East and West African writing in English took in earlier periods can be related, in part, to the influence of the various dominant patronages for English writing. In more recent times, the emergence of a market for local popular writing and publishing involves an important and notable breakaway from this form of hegemonic control. But an opposite development to this growth in local control has also emerged recently. Certain African writers have been taken up or promoted by the international publishing scene, not to cater for a local market, but as writers who are judged to have a wide general appeal to a global audience. Writers seen to embrace transcultural themes or forms with an international appeal are favoured by this new market. Such writers have increasingly attracted more notice overseas than those concerned with specific and local issues, who employ local forms and styles. I say 'seen to' advisedly, since a careful look at some of these successful transcultural writers would suggest that they do not employ techniques or forms radically different from some earlier African English writers, again suggesting the change may be as much in the form of patronage which discovers and promotes them as in the form of the writing itself. The new writers who have sometimes, though not always, been singled out for large-scale international promotion in recent times often reflect influences from earlier phases of African writing, influences which are neglected or not mentioned in the international critical notices they receive. Nor is the kind of cross-cultural influences they show really anything that new in African writing, as the body of this study has hopefully illustrated time and time again. The work of earlier writers as diverse as Wọle Ṣoyinka, Ama Ata Aidoo, Nuruddin Farah, Taban Lo Liyong, Christopher Okigbo, Kofi Awoonor or John Pepper Clark, to select only a few major names, showed a similar ability to move with ease between the diverse cultural sources which are available to an African writer using English as a medium of expression. Nevertheless, a number of the more recent writers, whilst retaining an identification with African themes, have more self-consciously embraced forms which reflect recent international trends, notably, though not exclusively, in fiction. Some examples of these may illustrate how this recent writing in English complements and contradicts the equal and opposite recent impulse we have discussed, to return to a more local and specific vision, or to employ local forms to modify the European genres.

It is possible to argue, as some critics have done, that these more recently acclaimed and published writers share influences and concerns with a new generation of such transcultural writers elsewhere. These critics stress the way in which these writers often embrace in their own person, and in the themes and subjects they address, the complex issues of contemporary post-colonial identity. Their texts, it is argued, question the idea of stable and fixed national or even cultural boundaries, and focus on the liminalities which define much modern experience in an increasingly dislocated and diasporic world. Although there have been fewer such writers in Africa than in India, or Sri Lanka, or in the erstwhile settler colonies such as Canada and Australia, they have formed an increasingly important element in recent writing in English from both West and East Africa. The Tanzanian-born writer and critic Abdulrazak Gurnah, himself one of the most distinguished of these new writers, has written recently of how these international influences have been 'naturalised' (the term, reflecting a modern discourse of borders, customs, immigration procedures and passports, is his) to African writing. Writing of Nigerian novelist Ben Okri, as an exemplar of those whose use of English recaptures and remoulds the ex-colonial languages to new uses, arriving at 'something new and hybrid', he notes that, 'descriptions of his work as "magic realism" – and therefore derivative of South-American writing in Spanish – miss the extent to which this style of writing fiction has been naturalized as an English-novel form'.[1]

Gurnah is aware of, and supportive in these essays of the politics behind the many 'urgent attempt[s] to engage with Europe's representations of Africa', from négritude, with its ground-breaking assertion of African values, to Ngũgĩ's powerful advocacy of the need to decolonise culture and reinvigorate indigenous language usage.[2] The implication of Gurnah's argument is that many of the stylistic and linguistic choices of more recent writers seem, as he says, less 'daring now that critics of African writing have stopped speaking with such high-handed assurance about African aesthetics, identity, and so on'.[3] What these texts open up is a renewed sense of the complexity of forces which have always operated to produce English texts in Africa, and they embody a series of challenges to the idea that African writing in English can, or even perhaps should, ever remain fixed or closed off to international as well as local influences. The following examples from East and West Africa respectively may help to illustrate some of the quality, range and variety of the projects and forms of these recent transcultural writings.

East Africa

Jamal Mahjoub was born in London to an English mother and a Sudanese father. Mahjoub's first novel, *Navigation of a Rainmaker* (1989), is an interesting extension of his own situation. The main character, Tanner, like Mahjoub himself, is half British, half Sudanese. Tanner returns to the Sudan to seek his origins. He finds there the brutality of a society riven by corruption, by war and by the machinations of various local and foreign commercial interests. Attached to an oil-exploration company (Mahjoub himself is a trained geologist), Tanner makes a long journey to the south, accompanying the American oil expert Gilmour. The journey is, ostensibly, to check on the field work of the company, which has hired Tanner as a general rouseabout and trouble-shooter. Gradually it becomes apparent that Gilmour has other concerns. He reveals that his real mission is to exacerbate the conflict between the various rebel forces and the government, so that the multinational 'interests' he represents can retain their control over the country's resources, whichever side wins. In a moment of desperate action, after he discovers Gilmour's real mission Tanner attacks and kills him. He is also wounded by Gilmour and later dies himself. The narrative explores the growth in Tanner of an urge to act, after his initial disillusion with the country he refused to discover.

The novel differs from novels by local writers, such as Francis Mading Deng, in that much of it is told from an outsider's viewpoint, as Tanner seeks to understand the confusion, chaos and corruption which the Sudan initially represents for him. In this, it shares the mood of other expatriate novels, stressing the heat, dust and moral chaos of modern Africa, and contradicts the more involved vision of local writers. Despite his initial alienation, Tanner is finally forced to take sides, suggesting that Mahjoub advocates involvement, even if it means direct action and violence. As a relative outsider, his grasp of the historical, social and political framework of the modern Sudan remains far less complex than in novels such as Deng's *The Cry of the Owl*.[4] The short, lyric sections, which are interspersed with this main narrative, range from elegiac descriptions of traditional Sudanese desert life, to graphic pictures of the street-children of modern Khartoum, and of the effects on both of the long, drawn-out civil war. Tanner's existential struggle is placed against these events, as he slowly comes to terms with the fact that his personal existence, and that of the social chaos of the modern Sudan, are inextricably linked.

Mahjoub's second novel, *Wings of Dust* (1994), is set mainly in Europe, where the narrator is in exile from the Sudan. It is a novel far more concerned with the whole issue of being expatriate, and the effects of this on cultural identity and personal stability. The narrator, Sharif, is living in a small, run-down hotel near Bordeaux, which he had frequented when, as a younger man, he had an affair with the mysterious jazz singer known as the Contessa. The bulk of the novel concerns the early experiences of the narrator in London, and later in Paris. He falls into the role of protector to the Contessa, who is helped by a Rumanian patron of the arts. After helping to run the small hotel at which the Contessa sings, Sharif becomes involved with a number of expatriate Arabs in the Paris community. This section of the novel captures the shifting life of the expatriates and the racial prejudice endemic in French society at the time. It offers some moving vignettes, as for example when the depressed and slightly drunken narrator seeks information on how his body might be returned to his homeland were he to die:

'Do you like biscuits, Ms'ieu?'
'Biscuits?'
'Biscuits, preferably the expensive kind from England. You buy a big tin.' He made the rough size with his hands to demonstrate. 'Then you need a friend, someone who

can be trusted. You must be cremated of course. For a small fee I can arrange that if it is to be here that you will end your days.'

'What happens then?'

'The ashes are transferred to the biscuit tin, which you have kept with you at all times and then the tin is sent to a friend or relative in your home town. Use the public postal system.' He shrugged his shoulders. 'Some biscuits for a friend back home, is not so strange. There is a very good chance that they go straight through the customs without problems. At least you can be sure they will arrive in the country of your choice for a very small investment.'

. . .

I stumbled back up the hill to the silent dark hallways and the restless swaying of the trees. I bolted the door pushing tables and chairs against it to keep the night at bay. I vomited in the bidet and tossed and turned all night groaning and moaning in terror and pity. I imagined myself flying through the world in a tin box from Bangalore to Buenos Aires and back again never finding rest. (119–20)

This surreal vision of the fate of the exiled Sharif is the culmination of a study of the drifting population of people who have been thrown up by colonisation and its dismantlement in the aftermath of two world wars. When Sharif, disillusioned with this world, decides to return to the Sudan where there is 'so much to be done', he discovers that he is as alienated from this world as from that of his expatriate friends in Europe. Classic colonialist images of the climate ('heat and dust') reinforce an expatriate view of a world from which Sharif is excluded by his past and by his lack of identity and direction.

For myself I began an inevitable gravitation towards slothful lassitude and old habits – in particular the card-playing circles of the men's quarters. Long nights in the sleepless smoke of that room shuffling worn packs of playing cards with the idle conversation of five or six fellows from the nearby streets where the goats slept and the women snored in exhaustion after the day's washing and cooking and carrying vegetables from the market. The men treated me with a kind of reverence, they wanted to hear stories of Europe, its hidden cities of beautiful women and shiny automobiles.

It was after one of these particularly gruelling sessions that I woke the following afternoon with a throbbing head and blurred vision as a result of the amount of *Araqui* spirit that I had consumed to find the yard filled with the raging fury of a dust-storm. The dust had entered my room through the gaps in the shutters, under the gap in the door, through the walls which appeared to melt into their source, filling my nose and mouth, pouring in through my ears so that I jerked from sleep with the terror of a man drowning. I stumbled into the yard to meet my mother who stood like a stone figure in the centre of this swirling chaos . . . (142–3)

Despite this unpromising and alienating start, Sharif, with his expatriate education, is recruited by the new government as a senior regional administrator. He meets some of his old London friends, such as the poet Shibshib, now teaching at the university. Shibshib tells him of his vision, that he might 'drag the Department of Literature into . . . the future as he saw it, into the present' (154). Shibshib dreams of

nothing less than an expansion of the consciousness of a generation through the innovation of which he was an integral catalyst, taking the old myths, the superstitions, tales of strange beasts and phenomena, the heroism and betrayal that beat like

311

a mystical drum wandering through his pulse, the stories which had been passed down through the umbilical cord of ages that brought together the separate strands of a group of peoples whose fate as a common mass had been drawn together within the cigar smoke and brandy atmospheres of ancient European capitals when theirs was the hand that traced the lines. (154)

Shibshib's vision, like Sharif's, disappears in the disillusion which follows his exposure to the politics and corruption of the new regime, and he ends in social disgrace and finally madness. As Sharif comments, 'We were thrown into madness or exile if we were lucky, into the grave if not' (155).

The story is told in flashback. This means that the reader is never allowed to forget that Sharif's initial administrative successes – for example, bringing electricity to the villages, and developing new cash crops in his region – are only temporary triumphs in a story which is already clearly identified for the reader as a tale of ultimate failure. As a result, the novel has a fatalistic and tragic tone. Unlike the work of other recent Sudanese novelists such as Francis Deng, whose work suggests that the future of the country may still be in the hands of its people, the cumulative effect of these images of despair and disillusion is to reinforce the stereotypical idea that Africa is a benighted place into which energy is poured in vain. For all its skill, poetic imagery and subtlety, Mahjoub's work seems finally to share this view, and this makes it congruent, in some ways, with earlier European visions of Africa, rather than with the more positive visions of local writers.

Mahjoub's next work, *In the Hour of Signs* (1996), offers an account of the most famous encounter in British–Sudanese history, when the forces of the Mahdi besieged that archetypal Victorian imperial hero, 'Chinese' Gordon, in Khartoum. A fairly straightforward historical novel, it manages to present a balanced account of the motivations of those involved on both sides. At the end of the novel, Hawi, a survivor of the Battle of Omdurman, in which Gordon was avenged and the Sudanese forces defeated, calls on the people of the villages to recognise that they are all involved in a process of change, and that faith can be used to destroy as well as to sustain. This ending embodies the essentially complex, transcultural position of Mahjoub's fictional project.

What did he speak about? Many asked this question afterwards and few could remember with any clarity. He spoke to them of religion and of the world. Of the way in which religion could be used by men who sought only power and that this was the worst betrayal of all, and that what had happened once could easily happen again. He told them that the only defence anyone has against such a betrayal of their faith is to understand their faith, to arm themselves with knowledge. He noticed that children began to pay more attention. First the older ones and then the younger ones, keen to imitate. By the end of seven days he had a regular crowd which assembled every morning at his feet, none of them being older than thirteen. The parents looked on suspiciously when he moved his lessons to a more comfortable spot beneath a large neem tree where the breeze from the river came and lifted their spirits. He told them to look amongst themselves to see how different they all were; how their names contained the names of their father's father, and his father before him, and so back into time, and that each of those names contained a story and very often a journey was connected with that story. That there was a place where all of their stories met and crossed and that this was a place that had to be shared. (244)

This appeal to a broader and less fundamentalist view of truth and religion falls on deaf ears, and the novel ends with Hawi, strapped to a donkey, being driven forth into the desert.

The Tanzanian novelist and critic Abdulrazak Gurnah was born in Zanzibar, but has lived and worked as an academic in the UK for many years. His novel *Paradise* was short-listed for the Booker Prize in 1994.[5] *Paradise* offers one of the most convincing and detailed accounts of traditional coastal East African society at the turn of the century and in the years leading up to the First World War. It tells the story of the young slave boy Yusuf, and looks at the world of domestic slavery from the inside. It contextualises the more unsavoury and brutal accounts of slavery, recorded by missionaries and others in earlier times, without denying the essentially dehumanising nature of this unhappy form of human trafficking. The novel shows an insider view of the involvement of Arab coastal-dwellers and the peoples of the inland tribes in the slave trade. It portrays the form of slavery in which a young boy (or girl) is pledged in payment of a family's debts, in a relationship in which the slave is, and is not, part of the family of the slave-trader. These young bonded slaves are drawn into their master's family and its world, in a relationship of acceptance, as well as of obligation and dependence. Despite this emotional involvement, they always remain fundamentally dependent on their owner and his goodwill. The novel opens up for our understanding a complex social practice which shaped the history of the whole East African littoral for centuries, and which continued well into the twentieth century, despite all efforts at eradication. Yusuf, the young narrator, is pledged in payment for his father's debt to his 'Uncle' Aziz, the Arab trader who supplies his father's small shop with goods.

Yusuf's journey, from the paradisal innocence of childhood to a dawning awareness of his real relationship with 'Uncle' Aziz, frames a narrative in which the various dreams by which men and women live collide with reality, as the dreams of paradise crumble for each of the characters. The central image of *Paradise* is the enclosed garden of Aziz's house, a garden to which Yusuf is admitted from the domain of the shop, in which he helps Aziz's older slave Khalil. Aziz's wife, who suffers from an unknown and disfiguring skin disease, is confined to the house, but she is drawn into the garden by her attraction to the boy Yusuf. At first, she justifies her attraction to Yusuf by her insistence to Khalil that he alone can cure her of her disease by placing his hands on her. Since she only speaks Arabic, and Yusuf only speaks ki-Swahili, the language of the local peoples, Khalil must translate her words for him:

> The Mistress spoke heatedly after Khalil stopped, and for a few minutes they exchanged angry remarks which Khalil did not bother to translate. 'She says it is not your knowledge but your gift that will cure her. She wants you to say a prayer and . . . and . . . touch her there. Don't do it! Whatever she says don't do it! Say a prayer if you know one but don't go near. She says she wants you to touch her heart and heal the wound in it. Just say a prayer and then we go. Pretend if you don't know one.' (210)

As her desire for him is more openly expressed, it inevitably becomes known to Yusuf's master, Aziz. But, in the meantime, Yusuf also comes to have increasingly adult insights, into the world of his master, Aziz, into the psychology of his mistress, and into his own condition as a slave. Aziz is the mistress's second husband. The mistress's first husband was much older than her. When he died, she inherited his house and garden, along with his slaves, including the old man Mzee Hamdani, who sits in the garden in old age singing *qasidas* (Sufi devotional poems). It is the old gardener Mzee Hamdani who gives Yusuf a first glimpse of the more complex issues which the status of master and slave obscure. Mzee Hamdani has refused his mistress's offer of freedom. As he explains to Yusuf, who asks him why he had refused his freedom:

> 'Don't you know anything?' . . . 'They offered me freedom as a gift. She did. Who told her she had it to offer? I know the freedom you are talking about. I had that freedom the moment I was born. When these people say you belong to me, I own you, it is like the passing of the rain, or the setting of the sun at the end of the day. The following morning the sun will rise again whether they like it or not. The same with freedom. They can lock you up, put you in chains, abuse all your small longings, but freedom is not something they can take away. When they have finished with you, they are still as far away from owning you as they were on the day you were born. Do you understand me?' (224)

Drawn into the world of the garden, Yusuf meets the mistress's co-wife, Amina. Amina is Khalil's sister, but, as she explains, she is not related to him. Khalil's father rescued her from kidnappers, intending to sell her as a slave, and brought her up. Yusuf falls in love with her, and Amina warns him of the dangers of her mistress's obsession with him. Khalil tells Yusuf the story of how his father rescued Amina, and how he was forced later to sell her to Aziz in part payment of a debt. Khalil himself is also held as a *rehani* (or bonded man), until his sister is old enough to marry the Seyyid (Master) Aziz. After the wedding, although technically free, Khalil stays on to protect Amina, and also because he is bound by what he perceives to be his honour. This final section of the novel explores the complex of traditions, customs and loyalties with which the practice of bondage slavery is shot through. Waylaid by his mistress, Yusuf rejects her advances, and she cries rape and attack on him. When the Seyyid Aziz returns, he questions Yusuf, recognises his essential innocence in the matter, and then discovers his affection for Amina. In a subtle ending, the Seyyid draws Yusuf into his world by accepting his explanations for his 'dishonourable behaviour', thus binding him even tighter to him. Revealing to him that his parents are dead, he proposes to marry him and Khalil off, and use them to continue his business. The descriptions of the mixed anger and gratitude which Yusuf feels towards the Seyyid Aziz bring us into a fuller understanding of how the bondage of slavery really works in this complex society:

> In the long silence Yusuf could not make himself say the words that were burning in him. *I want to take her away. It was wrong of you to marry her. To abuse her as if she has nothing which belongs to her. To own people the way you own us.* In the

end Uncle Aziz rose to his feet and offered Yusuf his hand to kiss. As Yusuf bent forward into the clouds of perfume, he felt Uncle Aziz's other hand rest on the back of his head for a second and then give him a sharp pat.

'We'll discuss the plans later, to see what work you can best do for me,' Uncle Aziz said pleasantly. 'I'm getting tired of all this travelling. You can do some of that for me.' (242)

Yusuf is aware that he is now expected to remain bound to slavery by Aziz's forbearance and by his stayed anger. Khalil's reaction shows him what is expected. Khalil is overjoyed that the Seyyid Aziz is willing to forgive them for their 'offence' against his wives, and to continue to have them in his service. But for Yusuf the indignity of slavery, although unable to find open expression, continues to rankle, and when the askaris of the German colonial army arrive, he flees 'paradise' and runs after them:

He saw again his cowardice glimmering in its afterbirth in the moonlight and remembered how he had seen it breathing. That was the birth of the first terror of his abandonment. Now as he watched the obliviously degraded hunger of the dogs, he thought he knew what it would grow into. The marching column was still visible when he heard a noise like the bolting of doors behind him in the garden. He glanced round quickly and then ran after the column with smarting eyes. (247)

As this image suggests, this escape is also a form of expulsion, into a real world which is far from perfect. Is slavery a Paradise in comparison with the world into which Yusuf flees at the end of the novel? It is clear that the condition of the captured Africans whom the Germans recruit for the First World War, which has just broken out with the British on the northern border, is at least as enslaving to them as the traditional relations with the older Arab invaders:

Most of the men brought in looked frightened as they were herded into the middle, silently looking around them as if they were in unfamiliar surroundings. Some others appeared happy enough, talking among themselves and shouting friendly abuse at the askaris, who did not seem very amused. They waited for a few minutes before walking among the clowning men, silencing them with sharp blows and wiping the grins off their faces.

When all the askaris had returned, and all the captives were gathered unsmiling in the middle, the sergeant marched up to the terrace to receive his order. The German officer nodded and the sergeant barked with satisfaction before turning back to the men. The captives were formed into two, silent lines, and in the gathering darkness were marched off in the direction of the town. The German officer marched at the head of the shuffling column, his body upright and his movements precisely understated. His white uniform glowed in the fading light. (246–7)

The fact that Yusuf enters this world with the sound of the gate of Paradise closing behind him may imply that the new slavery of the colonising whites will prove as bad, or worse, than that of the Arabs, whose mastery is at least mitigated by an involvement in the lives of their subjects and an emotional link with them, however manipulatively this is employed. On the other hand, there is no simple sense in this complex novel of the pre-colonial past or the world of slavery as idyllic, and as the kidnapping of Amina suggests, the brutality and violence recorded by the anti-slavery texts of earlier times was not without its truth.[6]

This subtle, evocative and poetic novel manages to present a picture of the traditional relations of Arab coastal peoples and the people of the mainland, and of the institutions of religion, custom and tradition which enmesh them, with an insider's view which is unmatched in recent East African writing. Eschewing a general narrative overview for the limited, but highly dramatic, perspective of the mind of the child Yusuf, the result is a brilliant, poetic evocation of this traditional society, at the very moment it is poised to meet the new conditions of the twentieth century. Instead of employing the social realist and anthropological perspective of earlier African texts which record the life of pre-colonial cultures, Gurnah uses a series of discrete scenes, linked by a network of recurring images, which gradually allows the reader to enter into an understanding of these very different forms of social relationship and the emotions they engender. What are we to make, though, of the fact that the British critics on the back of the Penguin edition liken the novel to Conrad? Despite its profoundly insider view, one can perhaps see the reasons for these comparisons with the older colonialist text, in so far as Gurnah's prose has a very Conradian evanescent and slightly mystifying air. The detail of the description is viewed through a distorting, shimmering prose style, strong on suggestive imagery and weak on wider social contextualisation, which lays emphasis on the individual, psychological states of the characters, rather than on the fact of cultural difference.

But the resemblance critics have noted with Conrad also overlooks the strong similarity *Paradise* has to earlier African classic texts such as Achebe's *Things Fall Apart*. Despite the great differences of style, the novel is structured similarly to *Things Fall Apart*, in that its insider view is framed by a shift in the final chapter to a wider, colonial perspective. This shift emphasises in both texts that, until then, we have seen the events from inside their own cultural frame. Unlike Achebe, though, Gurnah's novel weaves a more self-consciously universal thread into the matrix of the specific cultural references, in the imagery of paradise, for example. The Mohammedan paradise of the 'scented garden' and the Christian vision of the garden of Eden are related visions by these different 'peoples of the book'. Their similarities allow Gurnah to create a series of linkages, which invite the European, Christian reader into the world of the other through a series of more familiar concepts. Unlike Mahjoub, whose transcultural stance is evident in the theme and the narrator's viewpoint, Gurnah's work is transcultural less in its themes, or even its narrative structure, than in the way in which it embraces the indirect and oblique style of some recent British and American postmodernist prose. As with these familiar recent texts, it creates a direct link between image and inner mood, directly evoking the mind-set of its characters and their responses to their worlds.

Gurnah's later novel, *Admiring Silence* (1996), is as richly ambiguous as its title. If *Paradise* was very much a novel from an 'insider' narrative viewpoint, *Admiring Silence* dramatises the tangled issue of whether any narrative can ever be more than a partial and shifting body of fictions. It sets out to show this truth as it applies to identities based on such self-constructing modern fictions as race and nation. The anonymous narrator is an expatriate Zanzibarian who has settled in England. He lives with an English woman, by whom he has a daughter, and works as a teacher in a tough, grindingly hard South London secondary school. The complex and uneasy relationship between him, his partner and her family allows Gurnah to explore an inter-cultural relationship without sentimentality or stridency. The gradual emergence of the mix of motives which has led Emma to live with the narrator allows Gurnah to have some fun with her much more assured ability to negotiate the idea that everything is just a narrative. As a postgraduate student of poststructuralist narrative theory, she can resolve their failed eighteen-year relationship and her betrayal with a sharp twist of a theoretical tongue:

> We were a bit drunk when we went to bed, just nice for a jolly romp, but Emma said she was too tired to make love. After a moment I asked her if there was anyone else, and she said yes, there was. Then as we lay there in the dark she began to talk about him and about all the things that had been happening to her over the last several months. She told me her life was a narrative which had refused closure, that she was now at the beginning of another story, one which she was choosing for herself, not a tale she had stumbled into and then could not find a way out of. Clever Emma. I wish I could unhear what she said, so that my silences are not filled with her words and her voice. (210)

This revelation comes immediately after the narrator's return from a visit home, his first in twenty years – twenty years in which he has woven a series of fictional stories about his past for his partner and her family. These stories include typically 'colonial' stories of the ineptitude and squalor of post-independence Africa. These his father-in-law laps up as proof that they should never have left those poor ignorant people to struggle through on their own. In other stories, his father, who fled Zanzibar leaving wife and child, is suppressed and substituted by his mother's second husband, the pious merchant Hashim. The fictions spun by the narrator have replaced his sense of his own real identity. When he finally returns home the narrator is unable to deal with either the personal realities of his past or the social demands of a society which he sees as entirely dependant on overseas aid and funding. The Prime Minister, an old school acquaintance, seeks half-heartedly to persuade him to stay and help in the national task of modernisation and renewal. But the narrator sees this as more a ritual act of self-reassurance by the local authorities than a real and positive chance to participate in building a post-colonial reality.

> 'I have been watching you on TV the last few nights,' I said, wondering if I was about to do something crass and foolhardy, something that would result in a bumpy flight from my homeland. I am not sure, but I think his eyes began to move sideways before he stopped them, as if he was expecting someone over his shoulder to be listening to our conversation. 'They have been inspiring performances. Will you be doing another one tonight? The funding prospects look good.'
> He waved the subject away genially, but his eyes were hard and watchful. I was not surprised. I would have been ranting at the impertinence if I were him, and I knew he could rant. (201)

But this is not a text whose purpose is simply to record the ineptitude of post-independence African regimes. If there is a strongly disillusioned tone, it is one which embraces both sides of the equation. The descriptions of the ramshackle regimes of the post-independence elites, who can see no future that does not continue to depend on handouts or some new external fix-all such as tourism, are matched by those of the ex-colonisers. Cynicism and historical arrogance prevent the ex-colonial power of England from seeing that it, too, has become a left-over fragment of its own imperial past, a decayed small nation whose power is vested only in a few cynically rich groups in a sea of poor schools and increasingly inadequate social services. At the end of the novel, the narrator starts to learn plumbing, as a symbol of a practical force that can both restore the literally unplugged sewerage of his native island, and the clogged social system and inequalities of his adopted one. This cloacal imagery is tied in to the references to early English colonisation in the figures of James I (Jimbo Stuart, as the narrator calls him), John Smith and Pocahontas, with which the narrative opens. At the beginning, he implies, for all its violence and 'murky, free-booting history', England was also inventive and innovative, but that is long gone:

> The ruins are one of the many things which make England a nation, along with a certain over-confident, hedonist cynicism which passes for sophistication and street-wisdom. Because the England of those ruins does not exist any more. Not that one, ask anybody. Not the England which was luminous in the dark, and which gave the world the steam railway and the Greenwich Meridian and penicillin, all invented by Scots in exile. (5)

But the narrator is also cynical about the modern tendency to use these old murky colonial excesses to excuse the recent pillaging of the new post-colonial rulers, in an endless narrative of self-excusing victimage. He explores the idea that perhaps the self-sacrifice of Pocahontas should be accepted as just that, an ideal of humanity, not simply as a 'cunning metaphor' for an attempt to turn people into self-hating 'savages' in an imperial schema. This complex analysis of the Pocahontas narrative becomes, as the story develops, a metaphor for the narrator's own desperate struggle to find a place where he can be neither victim nor victimiser. He wants to avoid being obliged to subscribe either to his wife's father's fantasies of a benign colonial past, or his erstwhile schoolmate's new visions of a place which can solve its problems by regular, self-serving television broadcasts, appealing for national self-sacrifice, while the exhortatory speakers indulge themselves in a minority luxury, and jet off to conferences in Copenhagen and the United States. He questions both self-serving narratives, that of the colonial past, and that of the still dependent post-colonial decolonisers:

> History turns out to be a bundle of lies that covers up centuries of murderous rampage around the globe – and guess who the barbarians are supposed to be. The most gentle of stories are interpreted as cunning metaphors that turn them into beasts and sub-humans, miserable creatures and slaves. Even their evident brutalities against each other can always be blamed on something else: slavery, colonialism,

Christianity, a European education, anything but their own, unmasterable greed, or their unregulated violence, or their artful dodges to escape the burden of having to do anything about anything. (7)

This far from simple, and often quite scathing and uncomfortable novel is not, however, without hope. Nor does it embrace the idea that this post-colonial malaise is a feature only of the colonised world, as is implied in the earlier and more embittered vision of a writer like V. S. Naipaul. For Gurnah, it seems, the problem is one which is shared by coloniser and colonised. The English, as he records, may have invented the water closet, but as the novel has made clear, their own system is itself long overdue for a good flushing out. He decides at the end of the novel, tongue in cheek, that he might go and offer the Prime Minister of Zanzibar his newly acquired expertise to help 'sort out those blocked toilets'. He also recognises, in a wry set of images, that such modernisation is only a confirmation of the ongoing fiction of the present post-colonial rulers, that tourism in a 'renovated colonial hotel' will solve the nation's problems. The irony is further strengthened when he notes that the Prime Minister, despite his brilliant evening television performances, is deposed when he is observed 'wearing [the national] flag as a loin-cloth, and so, despite his wiliness and his ranting displays, off to the jakes with him' (215). But the world of the coloniser itself offers little hope either. When his daughter leaves

> . . . she told me how contemptible I was, how much I disgusted her, and that she was going to move in with a friend in Camberwell. It was the old Amelia, not the excited daughter who had wanted to be taken to the dark corners of the world because she belonged there through her father, not that romantic interlude in her life, but the hard, metropolitan creature who could take everything in her stride, and who despised my blunderings through life with genuine hatred. (217)

At the end, the narrator leaves a crack in the darkness through which a personal future might be glimpsed. He wonders if he should ring the expatriate Indian woman, herself deserted by an English husband, with whom he has flown back from East Africa, but decides not to, as he is 'so afraid of disturbing this fragile silence' (217). However we respond to the much more bitter tone of this recent novel, it suggests that the widespread and numerous diasporic communities of Africans spread across the world are themselves becoming the subject and source of much of the most interesting recent African English writing.

M. G. Vassanji is one of a number of writers from East Africa's Indian communities, and his work embraces the specific world and experience of these expatriate minorities, whose lives have now become so intimately woven for several generations into the African social scene. Now a permanent resident of Canada, Vassanji's work explores the world of the Indian diaspora of East Africa and the ways in which membership of that group involves its inhabitants in complex issues of self-definition and cultural identity. In *The Gunny Sack* (1989), he traces the history of an Indian Muslim, East African family as Tanzanian independence unfolds. The novel shows how the Shamsi community established itself alongside the other races in East Africa, as it traces the migrations of generations of the family from India, to Zanzibar to Mombasa to Dar es Salaam and finally to the West. The novel is structured as a classic family chronicle, covering four generations of Govindis from 1885 to the 1970s. There is, however, also a deliberate construction of the individuals in a larger than life style, which is reminiscent in places of the work of earlier 'magical realist' writers such as Marquez, as the following extract shows.

> My grandfather Mitha Diwano, Mad Mitha, was a deeply religious man of the unusual kind: one who practises simply and consistently what the rest profess. Often he would take his blanket and steal away into the night to spend the rest of it in the bosom of his true mistress. With great reverence he would emerge from the mosque walking backwards, so as not to show his back to it, taking twelve steps, white head stuck forwards. His white suit crumpled, he would stride home, bobbing up and down and muttering a prayer or singing a bhajan. At this time no emergency – no robber, policeman or fire – could have drawn a word from his mouth, until he had reached home and deposited his acquired merits on the household. (61)

The central symbol of a gunny sack, willed to the narrator and imbued with a name and a consciousness by him as 'Sherbanoo', invokes the long Indian tradition of oral story, as the sack becomes the recipient and regurgitator of countless anecdotes and stories from each generation. It is a symbol of continuity and disruption, as the isolated, expatriate Salim, alone in his Toronto flat, becomes the residual legatee of the tales spun by the gunny sack's long history. There are moments, despite the differences, when Vassanji's text clearly does embrace an intertextuality with Rushdie's earlier work, notably *Midnight's Children* (1982).[7] Like Rushdie, Vassanji is conscious of narration as a slippery act, and the narrator's reliability, like that of Rushdie's narrator Saleem Salih, can never simply be taken for granted. As in the case of Rushdie, these fictions, distortions and lies, riddled through with the contradictions and erasures which inevitably constitute a family history of this kind, become a powerful symbol, not only of narrative fiction but of the problem of community, identity and personal and social history. This is a problem which, although universal, has an especial force and poignancy for communities which have been forced by circumstance to exist as a minority in societies within which they feel always marginal, and even excluded. Vassanji's work focuses the plight of minority communities in East Africa, a plight also recorded by other East African minority writers, such as Gurnah in *Admiring Silences*, with its account of the brutalities following the overthrow of the short-lived Arab revolt on Zanzibar by the Tanzanian national forces. Vassanji's Indian (mhindhi) community is the outsider within the newly formed state. When Vassanji states in interviews that he is setting out to record the history of a community whose history has never been recorded, he does so within a vision of story and history far removed from the assured, one-layered version of either the official histories of the colonial past, or the more recent official histories of the post-independence regimes.

> 'This flag,' roared the commissioner, 'it has the colours of Africa! This black and green and yellow flag – what does the black signify, eh jamani?' He held up his arm

and pinched his black skin for all to see. 'This. And the green is the beautiful land of Africa. Eh? And what is this yellow stripe in the middle? Eh?'
'The Indians! The Mhindis!' shouts an unknown voice.
Uproar. Laughter. Gleeful self-congratulation. (162–3)

In his second novel, *The Book of Secrets* (1994), Vassanji paints an even larger and more diverse canvas, using the story of an old expatriate Goanese teacher's discovery of the diary of a colonial British administrator to explore the complex inheritances which make up modern Tanzania. The narrative illustrates that, both genealogically and culturally, it is impossible for any one group of people to claim an unadulterated or authentic Tanzanian identity. This powerful and complex novel begins with the story of a white District Officer, whose whole life is spent in colonial Kenya and Tanganyika, and whose diary locks away not only the personal secrets of the mixed race background of the protagonist's ancestors, but also the secrets of the imperial powers, which manipulated the African scene and the resistances of those who opposed them. For the people ruled by Alfred Corbin, the white District Officer, the diary, which he writes up each evening, becomes what Homi Bhabha has called 'a sign of wonder', a symbol of the power and mastery with which imperialism vested the magical art of writing, itself a symbol of power and authority:

> They called it the book of secrets, kitabu cha siri zetu. Of its writer they said: He steals our souls and locks them away; it is a magic bottle, this book, full of captured spirits, see how he keeps his eyes skinned, this mzungu, observing everything we do; look how meticulously this magician with the hat writes in it, attending to it more regularly than he does to nature, with more passion than he expends on a woman. He takes it with him into forest and on mountain, in war and peace, hunting a lion or sitting in judgement, and when he sleeps he places one eye upon it, shuts the other. Yes, we should steal this book, if we could, take back our souls, our secrets from him. But the punishment for stealing such a book is harsh – ai! – we have seen it.
> They were only partly right, after all, those wazees – the ancients – who voiced wonder-filled suspicion and mistrust at the book and its writer, the all-powerful European whiteman administrator who had appeared in their midst to govern. They could not know that this mzungu first and foremost captured himself in his bottle-book; and long after it left his side – taking part of him with it – it continued to capture other souls and their secrets, and to dictate its will upon them. Even now it makes protagonists of those who would decide its fate.
> Because it has no end, this book, it ingests us and carries us with it, and so it grows. (1–2)

So this modern Prospero's book becomes the device through which Vassanji creates his own narrative, a narrative which demonstrates how story, tale and written account emblematise the struggle for identity and power, as generations and cultures succeed one another in the history of East Africa. Corbin's diary traces his life as a young District Officer on the Kenya–Tanganyika border. He ends up as the Governor of Uganda, and the novel links this early account of a lonely and puzzled encounter with another country with the fate of both Corbin and those with whom his life became entangled:

This is how I have come to picture him: seventy-five years ago, in 1913, the only white man in an African village, sits at a rough, crooked wooden table in his rough wooden house. Above him, from a beam, hangs a pressure lamp. Outside pitch darkness interspersed with a few lamps and candles. The man at the table puts down the glass he's sipped from, picks up his fountain pen, and writes in his diary. By the writing he begins to weave the thread that will connect him to me. (7)

The retired Goanese teacher, Mr Pius Fernandes, himself an immigrant product of a colonial past in which teachers and their colonial curriculum were granted a high status, now lives on the charity of an old pupil of his, who has emerged as a success in the cut-throat business world of post-independence Dar. As Mr Fernandes explores the diary, he is drawn into exploring the lives and histories of the locals recorded there. He is drawn, too, into the lives of their modern descendants, as he seeks to follow up the clues the diary offers. As these more recent secrets open up, the inescapable ways in which the present is interwoven into the past are dramatised. At the same time, the superficiality of the more obvious kinds of restricted definitions of Tanzanian national identity and national history are exposed. The unwilling involvement of the locals in the colonial struggles on the borders of what was then the Kenyan Protectorate and German East Africa is mirrored in the way post-independence Kenyan and Tanzanian national allegiances are traduced by histories in which people have migrated across all these fictional shadow-lines of cultural and national boundaries. The final secret is that even the coloniser Corbin's blood flows on into modern Tanzania, through his secret liaison with the Shamsi girl Mariamu, whom he rescued from being whipped by the *maalim* to drive out the spirit with which she is accused of being possessed. This complex novel is told in a direct and simple style which abjures the more obvious stylistic complexities of the earlier *The Gunny Sack*, but it manages to produce a many-layered vision of the East African community, which puts to flight any simplistic attempt to define what constitutes an authentic identity. For Vassanji, the complex of racial, religious and cultural encounters, which his novel records, is the very stuff out of which East Africa's multicultural reality has grown, and with which it must come to terms if it is to survive and prosper.

But as Neloufer De Mel has noted, in a very useful analysis of Vassanji's work, the figure of the immigrant community representative is a complex one. Even where the community has been rooted in a region or country for several generations, there remains a potential sense of alienation, an alienation upon which, paradoxically, the identity and distinctiveness of the community's sense of self depends. As De Mel says, if the refusal of categories of resolution or of absolute genealogies reflects

a conscious effort on Vassanji's part not to romanticise his land of birth, it is also possible to read them as symptomatic of the ambivalence that informs the migrant writer's narrativisation of his/her native land. At the matrix of this ambivalence is the writer's own alienation from the landscape and its people, a distancing produced by factors of class, cultural conditioning and migrancy itself, which almost always precludes a complete integration with the new homeland. Under these circumstances the land is strange and terrifying and is often framed, rather in keeping with Orientalist paradigms, as eternally violent, dark and irrational.[8]

In confirmation of this, De Mel quotes the description of a night in Dar from *The Gunny Sack*: 'Outside was a thick darkness, a black, menacing universe, with faces occasionally illuminated by moving kerosene lamps, and eerie, momentary shadows, gigantic, cast by passing cars against building walls: a darkness that rang with shouts and cackles and squeals of laughter' (87). Vassanji's next novel, *No New Land* (1992), shows how this tension can still be felt after several generations of settlement in a new land. It deals with those members of the East African Shamsi community who have settled in places like Canada, where their sense of alienation and their problems of integration become even more acute. The story of the migration to Toronto of Nurdin Lalani and his family centres on the profound alienation they feel, especially Zara, Nurdin's wife. Their children seem to be embracing a world with which they have little or no connection. The arrival in Canada of the head of the Shamsi sect, known as Master or Missionary, brings comfort to Zara but it only further alienates Nurdin. This dominating authority is precisely what Nurdin had sought to escape, a claustrophobic, patriarchal authority, also represented in the text by the portrait of his pious father Haji Lalani. Vassanji's work raises the troubled issue of when writers, by their choice of theme or setting, or by their own long-term resettlement, cease to be effectively classifiable as African. Or rather, perhaps, it raises the issue of whether such classifications can ever be more than partial and limited. Objections which have been raised to classifying Vassanji as an African writer have sought variously to re-classify him as an Indian writer, a 'migrant' writer, or as a Canadian multicultural writer. His position is that of an increasing number of writers in the modern world, as writers cross and recross the shadow-lines of national boundaries. The works of the writers we have looked at so far all indicate that a broader and more flexible definition of African writing will need to emerge, in order to accommodate the kinds of texts which we have discussed here, and to acknowledge the various and diverse writing which has an ongoing concern with Africa, its societies and its various peoples.

West Africa

In West Africa Ben Okri's work has done more than almost any other recent writer, with the possible exception of Buchi Emecheta, to gain a new international audience for West African English writing. Like his equally famous female compatriot, Okri was born in Nigeria, but has lived for extensive periods overseas in recent years. His first novel, *Flowers and Shadows* (1980), written at the age of nineteen, is, on the surface, another example of the self-critical texts which emerged in the late 1970s and early 1980s in West and East Africa.[9] Like many of these, it addresses the issue of corruption and of the emergence of an elite divorced from the people and from any goals other than their own advancement. In a foreword to the reissue of the novel in the

Longman's African Classics series, Adewale Maja-Pearce links it with texts such as Festus Iyayi's *Violence* (1979), Kole Omotoso's *Memories of our Recent Boom* (1982), Ifeoma Okoye's *Men Without Ears* (1984), Lekan Oyegoke's *Cowrie Tears* (1982) and Bode Sowande's *Our Man the President* (1981), some of which have already been discussed. The same theme of corruption is also the main focus of the second of Okri's novels, *The Landscape Within* (1981). These early novels, like other novels of that period, employ realist conventions of character, incident and diction. However, even in this early work, it is possible to detect a poetic tone which hints at the more radical use of imagery as a structuring device in the later novels. In *Flowers and Shadows*, for instance, which concerns the relationship between the protagonist, the young Jeffia, and his rich and corrupt father, Jonan, the alienation of Jeffia and his mother from the values of the father, as Maja-Pearce has argued, is expressed through the attitudes they adopt towards flowers. Mother and son value flowers as symbols of the potency of a beauty which seems to have no purchase in Jonan's world, a world where everything has its price, a price based solely on power and the capacity to exploit or be exploited. The invocation of aesthetic values as a correlative for moral vision and truthfulness is expressed in passages which already show a marked poetic suggestiveness, albeit one wedded to a fairly simplistic and occasionally intrusive allegory.

> He walked past the gate into the compound. For once he didn't stop to chat with the watchday, who looked at him expectantly. Jeffia stumbled past, staring at the ground before him, engrossed in his thoughts.
>
> He didn't even go into the house, but walked to the backyard. He stood under the mango-tree. The garden was nothing special to look at. But it was tended by his mother with loving care. The soil, parched with the intensity of the sun's heat, always needed watering. The roses that looked so promising when they were first bought by his mother had turned pale. Their petals had curved inwards and were covered in speckles of yellow and brown. Only the hibiscus did well. They were tall, proud, red. It looked strange to see the two flowers side by side, one set dying, the other thriving. Spaced some distance from them were exotic plants of many exciting colours, that smelt like wild grass. (128)

A similar realist tone also predominates in *The Landscapes Within*, a novel in which Okri explores the tension between the individual artistic project and his increasing sense of disillusionment with the corruption of modern Nigerian society. These themes had been explored by many older writers, such as Soyinka in *The Interpreters* and Armah in *Fragments*, as well as by the following generation of writers, such as Osofisan in *Oriki of a Grasshopper*. Okri's artist-narrator, Omovo, has much in common with the protagonists of these earlier works.

These early Okri novels do not display the characteristic stylistic exuberance of his later work. In the collections of short stories which followed, *Incidents at the Shrine* (1986) and *Stars of the New Curfew* (1988), Okri evolved the distinctive style of the later novels. Although they remain dominantly realist in form, these stories begin to embrace a wider range of social types, and to engage directly with the presentation of the inner worlds of people from a wide variety of social classes. Individual stories begin to explore themes which clearly push the realist mode to its limits, and which suggest that Okri is beginning to perceive that other styles may be needed to explore the full complexity of contemporary West African experience. For example, in the long title story of the 1988 collection *Stars of the New Curfew*, the world of the protagonist, a traditional medicine salesman, is invoked. The story shows a figure who has a foot in two worlds, that of modern commercial Lagos, and that of traditional belief and practice. Fragments of this latter world invade his urbanised life in the form of recurring dreams and night-mares. He is employed by one of the many Lagos-based 'drug' companies, which sprang up to supply the new urban poor with dubious medical cure-alls for the myriad diseases with which they have to contend. The story traces the effects on the salesman of the moral and physical side-effects of the unlicensed medicines he sells, and which he is forced by his employer to sample. These medicines frequently contain such bizarre and dangerous combinations as 'mari-juana, oil, chloroform, and alcohol' (142). Fleeing the effects of his drugs on the driver of a lorry who, maddened by their effects, overturns his passengers into the lagoon, killing seven people, the salesman returns to his home town of W., in the delta region of Eastern Nigeria. The nightmares and psychosis which the drugs have induced pursue him there, and, through his eyes, we see the effects of corrupt and criminally obtained wealth on the society. In par-ticular, he details the insane excesses spawned by the rivalries of the two rich families of his classmates Odeh and Assi, who try to outdo each other in extravagant displays of ostentatious wealth:

> The helicopters hovered over us. Then a door opened and bags of coins were emptied over us. No one moved for a while. It rained coins through the silence. We watched the silvery fall, bright in the coloured spotlights trained on the helicopter. The coins poured out on us, an amazing event. The silvery sparkles floated down through the air like tangible stars. (138)

We are never entirely sure where the descriptions of real events end, and the drug-induced nightmares of the protagonist take over. The effect is to drive home the bizarre and unreal condition of modern Nigerian life, in which the gap between the real and the fantastic has shrunk, as people respond to a world in which all values have been wrenched awry in the mad scramble for status and wealth. The manufacturers of the cure-all drugs are symbolic of the whole leadership of the new society, since they are all 'manufacturers of real-ity' (124), aided by 'salesmen of nightmares' (96). Despite its social satire and its pointedly modern themes and images, the story is reminiscent of earlier fiction, notably the work of Tutuola, whose peregrinatory narratives are cap-tured in some of the sub-headings, such as the section called 'Escape to the Town of Scandals'. The title of this account of the protagonist fleeing to the town of W. seems to echo Tutuola's perambulatory narratives in *The Palm-Wine Drinkard* and *My Life in the Bush of Ghosts*. In his recent study of the influences of Yoruba oral and written practice on Nigerian English writing, Ato Quayson suggests that Okri, like Tutuola and others, has a distinctive and

specific linkage with the common body of Yoruba story and narrative technique on which each draws to meet the specific demands of his artistic project
and its evolving historical context.[10] Such similarities invite us to speculate
on whether or not Okri's success in the international market is the result of
a persistent preference overseas for that kind of 'grisly, thronged tale', to
employ the phrase used of Tutuola by Dylan Thomas, over the more realistic
fictional modes which dominated in the period of the 1960s and early 1970s,
when the principal market was a local educational one.

Several major works have followed in quick succession, demonstrating Okri's
prolixity as a writer: *The Famished Road* (winner of the 1991 Booker Prize),
An African Elegy (1992), *Songs of Enchantment* (1993), *Astonishing the Gods*
(1995), *Birds of Heaven* (1996), *Dangerous Love* (1996) and *Infinite Riches*
(1999). Of these, the earlier works, such as *The Famished Road* and *Songs
of Enchantment*, established Okri's rise to a global level of recognition,
especially after the first of these won the Booker Prize. They went further than
the stories in embracing and developing a narrative mode in which realistic
description mingles with mythical figures and magical explanations. In these
novels of the early 1990s, the metaphysical and religious aspects of African
cultural practice are given a dominant status, becoming the metanarrative
within which the realist world is contained, and to which it is subordinated.
The cultural politics of such a reversal is clear. It rejects the subaltern status
of African modes of knowledge, and reinstates an African ontology and epis-
temology in place of the dominant Euro-American conceptual frame. What is
fascinating about this is that this reversal of the dominant modes of knowledge has resulted in Okri being perhaps the most successful African English
writer of his generation in international sales and perhaps even, with the
possible exceptions of Ṣoyinka, Ngũgĩ and Achebe, the most successful ever.
The appetite for novels which can be interpreted by the overseas reader as
exotic and magical may be one of the reasons for this success. But is it a fair
assessment of Okri's project and the mode he chooses to identify it as exoticising
Nigerian reality, and as aimed deliberately at the international taste for the
'grisly and thronged'? This criticism has certainly been made of Okri's work
by some Nigerian critics, especially those who position themselves on the radical
side of politics, and who demand a narrow local allegiance from Nigerian
writers. The issue is reminiscent of the earlier debates over Ṣoyinka's use of
mythical material and his complex poetic structures in the 1960s and 1970s.[11]
In fact, a fair assessment of Okri's novels would have to acknowledge that
there is a degree of self-consciousness in the employment of the more esoteric
elements of Nigerian traditions and practices, but that this is no more so than
in the work of earlier writers such as Tutuola, or even Ṣoyinka. In fact, the use
of the *abiku* figure in *The Famished Road* self-consciously echoes Ṣoyinka's
use of this same figure in *A Dance of the Forests*, an intertextuality acknowledged in the use of a quote from Ṣoyinka to form the title.[12] *The Famished
Road* explores the essential links, in African thought, between the worlds of
the living and the spirits, a theme which is echoed again in *Songs of Enchantment* in the figure of Azaro, also an *abiku* (or spirit child). However, the

crucial issue is what function these figures perform, and whether they function simply as exotic referents or to make a comment on the issues and problems facing contemporary Nigeria.

In the later novels, Okri returned to a more realistic style, reminiscent of the earlier work, as if he recognises that the 'magical realist' label, which European and American critics were all too happy to hang on this complex individual style, did less than justice either to its commitment to local issues or to its antecedents within Yoruba writing. Ato Quayson's reassessment of Okri within the history of this tradition goes a long way to restoring our sense of the specificity and allegiance of Okri's work:

> There is a growing critical consensus that Okri's work operates within the same tradition of writing as Tutuola's and Ṣoyinka's. *The Famished Road* operates in this tradition of writing in an even fuller and more suggestive way than the short stories. In this work Okri produces what might be termed new mythopoeic discourse with the invocation of myths, folklore and other aspects of indigenous beliefs.[13]

The writers I have dealt with so far have received considerable notice from the international community. Interestingly, other writers whose work is equally innovative and transcultural have not received so much international attention and acclaim. An examination of some of the more recent innovative English writing from Africa which has not received such notice may help to redress this imbalance and to suggest that the development of new forms is not restricted to the few international superstars of African English writing.

I have already discussed the poetic work of the Sierra Leonean writer Syl Cheney-Coker.[14] His long novel *The Last Harmattan of Alusine Dunbar* (1990) clearly embraces some of the themes and concerns of the recent transcultural mode in African writing. As I noted earlier, Cheney-Coker has always acknowledged the influence of Latin American writing on his poetic work. The influence of this writing is very marked in his only novel. Employing a metahistorical narrative and the style of the so-called 'magical realist' mode of much recent Latin American writing, Cheney-Coker's novel tells the story of the evolution of Sierra Leonean society. It begins with its inception as a colony for freed slaves and ends with its recent history of civil war and military coups. The narrative form dissolves conventional historical explanation, interweaving actual historical events with an indigenous narrative which frames these events within the magical vision of the mystic and seer Sulaiman the Nubian, whose magic glass foresees the events of history, dissolving the barriers between past, present and future, and between the living and the dead. This technique dismantles the claims of the grand narratives of European historians to exclusive truth, claims which are not resisted in more conventional 'historical novels', such as that of Yéma Lucinda Hunter's *Road to Freedom*, with which a useful comparison might be made.[15] Unlike Hunter's reliance on and dramatisation of existing conventional historical sources, Cheney-Coker's novel embraces an alternative world-view, accepting the validity of local myth and imaginative story. As a result, it helps to regenerate an alternative, subaltern history. In this alternative history, the refusal of Colonel Tambo to compromise his ideals by supporting the corrupt regime, and his subsequent arrest and execution, frame a narrative whose seeming digressions and meanderings draw into a single multivocal skein the multifarious meanings which constitute Sierra Leonean 'history'. The text refuses to reduce the narrative of the country to a single voice (the voice of 'official' history). Its oppositional politics are expressed through its heteroglossic vision, and through the multiple narratives which make up this dissenting metahistory.

One of the most powerful recent transcultural poetic voices to emerge is also that of a Sierra Leonean, Lemuel Johnson. Johnson's three long poetic sequences, known collectively as the Sierra Leone Trilogy, were published in 1995. They have received only cursory international critical notice, as is the case with the work of Syl Cheney-Coker or Kojo Laing, whose novels are discussed below. This suggests that it is less the transcultural content that determines the notice African texts do or do not receive, especially overseas, than the publishing context, and the degree to which this promotes the text as one with a global appeal. In other words, it may be perceived commercial viability of form, not a preference for certain themes and forms alone, which determines which recent African writers are given the imprimatur by foreign publishers and reviewers.[16] Once again, as one might expect, novels are given preference over other genres, although, as the Cheney-Coker and Laing examples show, this is not an inviolable rule. Early critical notices overseas (e.g. Emecheta) or the winning of a major, international literary prize (e.g. Okri) may be the factor needed to place the writer into the well-oiled machine of international promotion and advertisement. The Sierra Leone Trilogy embraces the diverse heritage of Sierra Leonean Creole society. It uses the multiplicity of cultural referents within that society to produce a transnational discourse, which moves easily from one set of cultural references to another. These various cultural traditions, which form the Creole culture, create a distinctively Sierra Leonean perspective. Thus, for example, the many Latin quotations and references are illuminated by comments which place them within the cultural framework of the creolised Sierra Leonean tradition. In the poem 'Exorcism' from *High Life for Caliban*, the Latin references are shown to be rooted in the specific cultural practices of Sierra Leonean Creole educational institutions, when the following

set upon
I grope
and plough teeth
back into roots

cum Lazaro,
ad adsum!*
set so upon
the voice
that cleaves
the maggot marrow
of the brain

to let this head
altogether gone,
yet be, and be
beaten again
upon grinding stones (52–3)

is glossed as follows: '*from the protocol, in latin, at the Sierra Leone Grammar School: "*salve magister* (greetings Master); *salvete pueri* (greetings, o boys); *ad sum* (I am present); *ab est* (he is absent); *sedete, pueri* (be seated, boys)".'

The poems of the sequence contain a dazzling blend of cultural references, from allusions to English poetry, most frequently to Shakespeare and T. S. Eliot, including scholarly indirect references (e.g. the poem 'Letter to My Tailor', subtitled 'Henrietta St., London', offers an esoteric reference to Eliot's London address when he worked as a Lloyd's Bank clerk), to many references to the Greek and Roman classics, to the Creed and Catholic theology, and to famous European locations from Venice to Elsinore. But interwoven with these are also allusions to the work of Amos Tutuola, to 'Witchdoctors', to Robben Island and many other distinctly African places, people and events. Not since Okigbo has an African poet moved so freely from one cultural realm to another, in open defiance of the prescription that African intellectuals should function only through African modes. Johnson profoundly subverts such narrow definitions. Poems such as 'Al Mukhlit', in the section called 'Viaticum', for example, exist within a profoundly local African referential schema, but nevertheless embrace the Arab influences on African cultures as naturally as other poems embrace European referents. Significantly, as a footnote makes clear, the poem celebrates this cultural hybridity and its subversive possibilities in its very title, ' "Al-Mukhlit": (arabic)–"the mixers;" (heretical mixing of, say Islamic and non-islamic practices':

here Djenne smells like a drowned lake
there are dead fishes among the roots of the bamboo trees
the red eyes of hungry lepers search among broken pots
for the cooked necks of partridges

there are no deltas left on the plains
but leeches reach the head waters;
ochre-colored lithams dry out the heads of the mixers
where the muezzin's voice leans against dead stone.

in december the harmattan blows cold sand
our grey fingers keep warm inside the grey bellies of fish
there are small scales floating to the deltas
on the thin red entrails of the dead. (76)

Johnson has provided his own elegant and accurate summing up of the purpose and form of this ambitious work in the foreword to the second volume, *Hand on the Navel*, where he notes that:

my concern in the poetry trilogy was to . . . recover the years from the 1500s to the 1960s; and to do so by way of a strategic deployment of contexts in my Sierra Leone

Krio heritage. I decided then that I would focus on the remarkably elastic features of this culture's peculiar history of scatteration and re-grouping. In brief, the volumes . . . would ride out and into the various filiations and languages of Sierra Leone's creolization. The sequence would thus negotiate its way, traffic and trade, if necessary, into a complex cultural genealogy; a genealogy which is as much Yoruba as it is Afro-Brazilian Portuguese; as much Liverpool and Hull as Nova Scotia and Jamaican Maroon. (x)

It is arguable that few recent writers have gone so far towards creating a genuine synergy of cultures as Johnson achieves in poems like 'Calypso for Caliban', from the volume *Hand on the Navel*:

> papa prospero
> jig me mama
> an' jig she mama
> papa prospero jig
> jig me mama
> to born the beast
>
> prospero
> atibo legba
> is him goin to make
> all and thee
> prosperous so;
> to make the beast
> is him goin to kiss
> in his own true-true name
> the whores
> until the red part white
> more so than black can
> white in she certain parts
>
> Mary Miranda and mother
> and holy virgin,
> so come to us
> so pray for us
> in all your own
> true-true-name that the will
> be done too for dem mamas with
> the derelict vaginas,
> though defunct; that they be
> holy maid and ready
> now to make the beast
> with atibo prospero
> even till the kingdom
> come, keep the air
> out of Sycorax hole (57–8)

The poem creates such a unity from the disparate modes of calypso and Shake-spearian blank-verse, and from the 'high' art of Shakespeare and the popular culture of Caribbean life, that to quote only a fragment of it here is just to hint at the powerful and complex effects Johnson achieves. One of the more interesting structural effects in the trilogy is that Johnson chooses to repeat a number of the poems, including 'Calypso for Caliban', 'Al-Mukhlit', and 'Short Visit to Auschwitz' more than once as the sequence evolves, each time the context returning a new and deeper meaning to the verses, as the whole sequence accumulates resonances. One may speculate whether this is a way of bringing the often densely literary referents of this trilogy into contact with the popular, oral and traditional forms it also evokes, such as Caribbean Calypso and West African Highlife Music. Repetition of significant images and of whole sections is a marked feature of much oral and performance composition. There can be little doubt, though, however we read this fascinating and complex body of verse, that it deserves far more detailed analysis than it has so far received.

Amongst the less-known but attention-deserving writers to have emerged in recent times is the Nigerian Biyi Bandele-Thomas. His novel *The Man Who Came in from the Back of Beyond* (1991) employs the device of a story within a story. This allows the representation of popular Nigerian life to be contained within a structure and a narrative frame which draws attention to its larger significance, and so eschews the limiting restraints of the realistic accounts of slum life discussed in earlier chapters. Much more accessible in form than Okri's elaborate middle-period fiction, it tells the story of a street-thief turned teacher. This story is used to frame an internal narrative, which is the teacher's own attempt to write a fictional story of Nigerian street-life. Eschewing extreme linguistic experimentation, and employing a modified form of standard Nigerian English, Bandele-Thomas captures the tragic circumstances of the life of young Bozo (David), whose family is the victim of a bizarre murder, in which his mother kills his father and sister, after discovering their incestuous affair. This essentially tragic and often brutal story is told with an absolute lack of sentiment or emotional elaboration. Its strength lies in the way in which Bandele-Thomas manages to ensure that the grotesque details are embedded in a completely convincing socio-political frame. Bozo's friend, Maria (one of fourteen children born to a poor odd-job man), is the product of an equally grotesque and brutal set of events, in which her brothers commit suicide to escape the government taxmen and her father dies of overwork and tuberculosis. At his funeral we are told:

No one cried, because crying was taboo in the Odum family. Crying was reserved for times of joy (which were so rare they could be counted on the fingers of one hand) when everybody could rock with laughter until tears welled in their eyes.

But although there were no tears shed, the loss of father and husband was greatly felt. The family decided that the least they could do was to give him a decent burial, but burials (whether decent or otherwise) are costly and when the Odum family sent a delegation to the local government cemetery to ask for burial-space, they were shocked when the grave-digger demanded a bribe before he would condescend to direct them to the right person. . . . Fifty pounds? Did he think that money fell like manna from heaven? In the dead of night, two of Maria's brothers resolved to smuggle their father's corpse to a nearby hospital mortuary, dump it there and leave the government to carry out the burial. But unluckily for them, they were confronted on the way by a gang of youths who were coming from the movies. The gang demanded to be shown what the two young men were carrying at dead of night. A *mêlée* arose and in the furore that ensued the two boys were battered to death. (82)

Ghanaian author Kojo Laing is another recent writer whose work shows a similar, complex blend of local and transnational influences, and yet whose work has not been as widely noticed overseas as Okri's. Laing's first novel, *Search Sweet Country* (1986), is a sprawling, poetic account of contemporary Accra. Although its characters are often larger than life, and represent a blend of the real and the deliberately exaggerated, the effect of this first novel is to capture the particularity and intensity of modern West African city life. The hero, Kofi Loww, is a kind of everyman, whose disrupted family life and chequered personal history bring him into contact with the varied aspects of Accra life. The story of his life is a device on which Laing can hang observations of everyday events, social comment, political observation, and sharp social satire:

> brightly and oddly Accra sloped backwards down the heads of the four men. . . . 'Look at the people.' Sergeant Kwami said, 'look at them, they sell everything except God! And if he sleeps just for a minute, He'll find himself on a tray in Makola, being sold above the controlled price!' Four men laughing was no joke, for it was difficult for the laughter to move at different heights. . . . When the four men reached the cathedral grounds, the old neem trees had already trapped the sea breeze and were sharing it in a miserly way among strangers in the compound. (152)

In this scene, where the corrupt Dr Boadi tries to bribe Kofi into pretending he hasn't witnessed one of his money-making scams, Laing blends a serious theme with a light humorous style, which makes the underlying point all the more telling. When it seems Kofi has acquiesced in his invitation to take a bribe, we are told that, 'Boadi felt a fine levitation that, after all, Kofi Loww was a good Ghanaian: full of greed and ready to please this greed!' (156). When Loww turns them down, Boadi and the sergeant and their accomplice become angry and threatening. The strength of the novel lies in its powerful and original use of metaphor and image, as in descriptions like this, of the setting of this encounter between venality and innocence: 'Barclays Bank stood like a loaf unsliced, calm and freshly whitened; but all their shadows, dancing up the wall as they went to the road, were like ants eating out the loaf, the white calm did not stretch to the core' (157).

Women of the Aeroplanes (1988), Laing's second novel, is a far more complex narrative, involving the relationship between a Ghanaian and a Scottish town (Laing was educated in Scotland). It includes a durbar in which bagpipes and drums compete in a hysterical blend of culture and competitiveness, and Ghanaian traditional magic and Scottish science engage to create a horrific image of misguided modernity in their invention of a 'stupidity machine'. Through these bizarre events, the novel explores the ways in which modernity has seeped into and perverted the traditional philosophic base of Ghanaian thought, and the route that needs to be followed if Africa is to recover its sense of itself, and if Europe is to discover what it can learn from African ways of experiencing and thinking. Laing is, as critics and reviewers have already noted, a novelist whose vision of Africa is far more positive than many other contemporary African writers, and his novels, despite their acknowledgment of corruption, greed and political ineptitude, concentrate on the positive rather than the negative aspects of modern African life. In this respect, they echo some of the concerns of the earlier African texts of the négritude years, though without the solemn tone of some of these. Laing's work answers those who say that much contemporary African English writing is far too concerned to paint a destructive and pessimistic picture of modern Africa. His novel *Major Gentl and the Achimoto Wars* (1992), despite its potentially bleak theme of a future involving civil conflicts and military dictatorships across much of West Africa, has a positive ending, suggesting that the people can resist these conflicts between the self-appointed leaders of men. The freedom which Laing achieves by inventing an imaginary Ghana, and so taking the contemporary conflict onto an abstract and futuristic level in a text bordering on fantasy and science fiction, allows him to defuse the more depressing elements of recent texts dealing with Africa's bitter modern experience.

The fact that a number of recent writers, who employ an imagistic, allusive, non-referential mode of writing, have been influenced by wider, transcultural models, does not mean that they and their work are not also rooted in local sources and traditions. To begin with, as I have argued already, their work often echoes and reflects the practices of earlier writers. There is, if you like, an alternative tradition of writing to the realist mode initiated by Achebe and Ngũgĩ in the late 1950s and 1960s to which these more recent writers are heir. This alternative mode often draws upon a local idiom, and reflects appropriations from oral composition in technique and theme. However, this is not to suggest that these texts are somehow in any simple way part of a separate 'oral' tradition from which more realist texts are excluded. To suggest that these different traditions of oral composition and writing are hermetically sealed is far too simple. In practice, individual writers move from one mode to another, as we have seen, at different stages of their careers. Indeed, it would be impossible to find any African text, however realist, which did not reflect in some ways the practices of an oral culture. Achebe's extensive use of proverbs is a case in point. Also, the idea that orature and literature are somehow discrete, or exist in a simple teleological relationship of traditional and modern, flies in the face of the evidence.[17] The existence of a body of writing which provides fixed textual forms for oral forms inevitably introduces a reflexive relationship between contemporary oral and written practices, influences which flow both ways. It is impossible, especially in an introductory text of this kind, to investigate fully these complex relationships. It is possible, however, to observe that in the work of modern writers like Kojo Laing or Biyi Bandele-Thomas, the element which one might ascribe to 'traditional' or 'oral' influence is also part of a body of literary practice in African writing to which these younger writers are heir. How they integrate the various strands of their cultural heritage is not to be addressed simply as a mix of discrete literary and oral influences. In practice, the two modes are now so inextricably interwoven that they constitute a cultural mode for which terms such as 'oral' or 'written', 'traditional' or 'contemporary', seem increasingly inadequate as anything but tags of convenience. The oral influence is often from a contemporary mode of orality, which permeates, and is in turn permeated by, modern influences from the print and electronic media. Indeed, it is arguable that this is so for all the post-war writing from these regions. One might recall the figure of Tutuola's 'Television-handed ghostess' from *My Life in the Bush of Ghosts*, who showed the hero the future (a traditional divining function) through pictures on a television screen, which appeared in the palm of his hand. The new written forms incorporate the influences of a society in which orality is still an active and evolving force in everyday communication at all levels of society.

Texts like these illustrate again how difficult it is to characterise recent experimental writing in English in Africa as more or less influenced by oral practice. The disrupted narrative, the fractured and non-linear time sequences, the multiple characters and polyphonic narrative mode can all be traced to oral practice, but they are equally part of much international post-modern writing. It is certainly difficult to determine whether the complex form in which Laing casts these various elements is one which is likely to have a popular readership. For all their similarities with traditional oral form, the dense imagistic structure and the complex narrative form make it likely that these texts would find more favour with the international audience for complex post-modern texts than with a local mass audience created by recent popular, local publishing.

It is impossible to guess what the future for English in Africa may be. It is likely that there will be an increasing demand for a recognition and promotion of culture in indigenous African languages, and this is to be welcomed. The world-wide audience for African English writing shows no sign of disappearing, though there does seem to be an increasing separation between those writers whose work is either aimed at or promoted by the international publishing networks, and those who seek to address a local audience and to promote a viable local publishing industry. But for the moment, at least, the variety and quality of African English literatures show no sign of abatement, and they continue to attract audiences within their own countries and in the world at large.

Notes

1. Abdulrazak Gurnah (ed.), *Essays on African Writing*, 2 Vols, Vol. 1, *A Re-evaluation* (London: Heinemann, 1993), p. ix.

2. Abdulrazak Gurnah (ed.), *Essays on African Writing*, 2 Vols, Vol. 2, *Contemporary Literature* (London: Heinemann, 1995), p. vii.

3. Ibid., p. vi.

4. See Chapter 10.

5. Gurnah had written three novels prior to the Booker listing of *Paradise*. The importance of literary prizes, such as the Booker and the Nobel, in establishing and defining the nature of metropolitan response to English writing from its erstwhile colonies, is a fascinating subject, and one which has still received only cursory attention.

6. It is instructive to compare the account of slavery in this novel, with the accounts of the European missionaries and those of the slaves whose stories they 'recorded', discussed in Chapter 3.

7. The cover of the novel calls it Africa's 'Midnight's Children', deliberately invoking a comparison with the work of Rushdie.

8. Neloufer De Mel, 'Mediating Origins: Moyez Vassanji and the Discursivities of Migrant Identity', in Gurnah (ed.), *Essays on African Writing*, Vol. 2, *Contemporary Literature*, p. 170.

9. See Chapter 7.

10. Ato Quayson, *Strategic Transformations in Nigerian Writing: Orality and History in the work of Rev. Samuel Johnson, Amos Tutuola, Wọle Ṣoyinka and Ben Okri* (Oxford: James Currey, 1997).

11. See Chapter 7.

12. Though again we should note that as Ato Quayson has argued all these writers have a common heritage of such Yoruba cultural forms and practices on which they draw. See Quayson, *Strategic Transformations*.

13. Ibid., p. 121.

14. See Chapter 10.

15. This novel is dealt with in Chapter 10, in the section on Sierra Leone.

16. Once again, international prizes seem to play a hand in this. Winners of major foreign prizes then often seem to be launched on promotional bandwagons.

17. I. Hofmeyr, *We Spend Our Years as a Tale That is Told: Oral Historical Narrative in a South African Chiefdom* (London: James Currey, 1994).

Part Four

FURTHER REFERENCES

Chronology of Literary and Historical/Cultural Events

The following abbreviations have been used:
For literary genre: Drama = D; Novel = N; Poetry = P; Essays = E; Short Story Collections = S; Anthologies or Collections = A.

For countries: Ethiopia = E; Cameroons = C; Ghana = G; Kenya = K; Nigeria = N; Liberia = L; Uganda = U; Sierra Leone = SL; Somalia = S; The Gambia = The G; The Sudan = Su.; Tanzanya = T.

DATE	LITERATURE	HISTORICAL/CULTURAL EVENTS
1688	Aphra Behn's *Oroonoko*.	
1770	Approximate date of Philip Quaque's beginning to compose his letters.	
1773	*Poetry and Prose of Phyllis Wheatley.*	
1780	Briton Hammon's *Narrative of the Uncommon Sufferings and Surprising Deliverance of Briton Hammon, A Negro Man.* Approximate date of the beginning of the composition of the *Diary of Antera Duke*.	
1782	*The Letters of Ignatius Sancho.*	
1787	Ottobah Cuguano's *Thoughts on the Evil and Wicked Traffic of Slavery.*	Sierra Leone is bought by a British anti-slavery league. Granville Sharpe organises first expedition of freed slaves.
1789	Olaudah Equiano's *Life*.	
1807		Britain bans the slave trade in its Empire.
1808		Sierra Leone becomes a colony of Britain.
1815		Britain acquires Mauritius.
1816		American Colonisation Society formed to return slaves to Africa (Liberia).
1824		Governor McCarthy of the Gold Coast invades Ashanti to aid the Fanti Confederation. He is killed on the expedition. Osei Bonsu, the great Ashanti ruler, dies in the same year. The Ashanti are defeated in a second campaign.
1826		Another British campaign against the Ashanti. Ashanti defeated at the Battle of Dodowah.

DATE	LITERATURE	HISTORICAL/CULTURAL EVENTS
1831	*The History of Mary Prince* appears in London.	Treaty imposed on the defeated Ashanti.
1833		Abolition of slavery within the British Empire.
1837	Samuel Crowther's autobiographical account in the letter to Rev. William Jowett.	
1841	Crowther's *Journal of the 1841 Niger Expedition.*	
1848		J. J. Roberts elected first President of Liberia.
1849		Presbyterians import the first printing press into West Africa.
1854	Crowther's *Journal of the 1854 Niger Expedition.*	
1855	Frederick Douglass's *My Bondage and My Freedom.*	
1857	*The Wonderful Adventures of Mary Seacole.*	
1859		Robert Campbell, a Jamaican-born printer, arrives in Abeokuta, Yorubaland (Nigeria).
1860	Yoruba-language mission journal *Iwe-irohin* founded.	
1861	Harriet Jacobs's *Incidents in the Life of a Slavegirl.*	
1862	Robert Campbell founds the journal *Anglo-African* in Lagos.	
1863		Ashanti War of 1863 ends indecisively
1868	James Beale Africanus Horton's *West African Countries and Peoples.*	
1870	James Beale Africanus Horton's *Letters on the Political Condition of the Gold Coast.*	
1871		Revolution in Liberia.
1873	Blyden expelled from Liberia.	British declare war on Ashanti again. J. B. Africanus Horton accompanies the British expedition as a surgeon.
1874		Ashanti defeated by Sir Garnet Wolseley, who imposes the punitive Treaty of Fomona. The Gold Coast and the Fanti Confederation lands are declared a British Crown Colony but Ashanti itself is not formally annexed.
1884		Berlin Conference called by Bismarck to determine the future of Africa. Great Britain takes control of Northern Somalia. Harry Johnson begins survey of East Africa for Britain.

DATE	LITERATURE	HISTORICAL/CULTURAL EVENTS
1885		Carl Peters begins to sign treaties with various East African chiefs on behalf of the German government. Fall of Khartoum, death of General Gordon.
1887	E. W. Blyden's *Christianity, Islam and the Negro Race.*	Jaja, the ruler of Opobo, Niger Delta, arrested as part of a plan to control the Niger Delta. He is deported.
1888		Imperial British East Africa Company formed.
1889		Italy occupies the remaining area, the larger part of Somalia. Ethiopia begins its 'modern' period, under the leadership of Menelik II.
1890		German East Africa comes into being.
1891	J. J. Walters's *Guanya Pau*, the earliest African fictional narrative in English.	
1892		British war against the Ijebu in Western Nigeria.
1894		Nana, ruler of Itsekiri, Western Niger Delta, is attacked and his capital of Ebrohimi is burned. Nana is deported. Uganda invaded by a British force under Lugard and becomes a British Protectorate.
1895		Kitchener begins the reinvasion of the Sudan against the forces of the Mahdi. British East African Protectorate declared.
1896		The Governor of Sierra Leone extends a Protectorate over the hinterland of the country. Ashanti finally annexed as part of the Gold Coast Protectorate after the British and Fanti allies invade. Baden-Powell heads the reconnoitre force. Agyeman Prempeh, the Ashanti ruler, is exiled to the Seychelles.
1897	Samuel Johnson's *The History of the Yorubas* completed (not published until 1921).	Britain invades Benin, burns the city and loots 2,500 of its famous bronze treasures. Benin's ruler, Ovonramwen, is deported. Gold Coast Aborigines' Protection Society formed by Nana Ofori Atah. Revolt of Kabaka Mwanga of Buganda. British place boy-king Daudi Chwa on the Bugandan throne.
1898		British begin the slow process of invading the small states of the Ibo people of Eastern Nigeria in a process not completed until 1917.

DATE	LITERATURE	HISTORICAL/CULTURAL EVENTS
		The Temne-Menmde war in Sierra Leone, in which the Poro (men's society) played a major role. (See J. J. Walters, *Guanya Pau.*)
		The Mahdi defeated by Kitchener at the Battle of Omdurman in the Sudan. British begin a policy of Christianising and isolating the southern Sudan.
1900		The British Labour Party founded.
1902		After the defeat of the Boers at the hands of the British army, South Africa moves closer to becoming a British colony.
		Coronation of Edward VII, attended by Sir Apolo Kagwa.
1903		The British under Lugard invade the Northern Nigerian caliphates.
1904	Ham Mutesa's *Sir Apolo Kagwa Visits Britain.*	
1905		Maja-Maja Uprising in German East Africa.
1910		Union of South Africa formed from four separate states under British rule.
1911	Casely Hayford's *Ethiopia Unbound.*	
1918		Great Flu Epidemic.
1919		Britain claims a mandate to administer the former German territories of German East Africa (Tanganyika and Zanzibar). Mandate confirmed by League of Nations a year later.
1920		East African Protectorate becomes Kenya Colony
1921		Harry Thuku forms YKA (Young Kikuyu Association) in Kenya.
1922		Harry Thuku arrested, detained until 1930.
1925		Kenyatta forms Kikuyu Central Association from YKA.
		Sir Apolo Kagwa of Buganda resigns in protest at British interference.
1929		Breach between Kikuyu nationalists and missionaries over female circumcision.
		Women's War in Nigeria, against taxation.
		Nana Atta and Casely Hayford unite the forces of the chiefs and the Creole elite in the Gold Coast.
		Tanganyika African Association formed.

DATE	LITERATURE	HISTORICAL/CULTURAL EVENTS
1930		Ras Tafari Makanen crowns himself Emperor of Ethiopia, Haile Selassie I.
1931		Rupert East sets up a Translation Bureau in Northern Nigeria.
1934		East's Translation Bureau becomes the Government Literature Bureau.
1935		Haile Selassie I unable to defend his country from Italian occupation.
1941	Obeng's *Eighteenpence*.	Britain takes over Italian-occupied Somalia. End of Italian occupation of Ethiopia.
1942	Kenyatta's *My People of Kikuyu and the Life of Chief Wangombe*.	
1944	Justin Itotia's *Thimo cia Ugikuyu Itari Thimure: Gicunji kia Mbere* (Gĩkũyũ Proverbs Without Explanation: Part One) (K, A).	Nnamdi Azikwe forms National Council of Nigeria and the Cameroons
1945	Onitsha Market pamphlets begin to appear.	
1946	Returning African soldiers form Kenya Land and Freedom Army, forerunner of 'Mau Mau'. Gakaara wa Wanjaũ's *Ũhoro wa Ũgũrani* (Marriage Procedures) (N, K). Mareka B. Gecaga's *Kariuki na Muthoni* (Kariuki and Muthoni) (N, K).	Kenya African Union (KAU) formed.
1947		Kenyatta becomes President of KAU. Nkrumah becomes General Secretary of the Gold Coast Convention, led by J. B. Danquah.
1948	Sospeter Munuhe's *Coro* (The Bugle) (N, K).	East African Literature Bureau founded.
1951	Hanley's *The Consul at Sunset* (one of many texts by English writers set in Somalia).	
1952	Tutuola's *The Palm-Wine Drinkard* (N, N).	In Kenya the Mau Mau liberation struggle begins. King Farouk of Egypt deposed. Talks begin on the future of the Sudan. Egypt claims a plebiscite calls for maintaining links with Egypt.
1953		Julius Nyerere becomes President of Tanganyika African Association. Jomo Kenyatta is imprisoned, accused of being behind the Mau Mau disturbances.
1954		Nyerere forms Tanganyika African National Union (TANU).

343

DATE	LITERATURE	HISTORICAL/CULTURAL EVENTS
		Pro-Egyptian government elected in the Sudan under al Azhari.
1955		Civil War erupts between the Arab-dominated Muslim north and mutinous, separatist forces in the south of the Sudan.
1956	Tutuola's *My Life in the Bush of Gods* (N, N).	Dedan Kimathi and General 'China', Mau Mau leaders, captured. Azhari reverses his pro-Egypt policy and Sudan attains independence.
1957		Ghana becomes the first sub-Saharan African colony to gain independence.
1958	Achebe's *Things Fall Apart* (N, N).	In the Sudan the dictatorship of General I. Abdoud begins; will end in 1964. Guinea-Conakri becomes independent under Sékou Touré (in power until 1984). Ivory Coast now an independent republic, under Houphouët-Boigny. Kwame Nkrumah, leader of Ghana since 1951, declares himself a pan-Africanist, fighting for the independence of all African colonies.
1959	Maimo's *I Am Vindicated* (D, C).	
1960	Soyinka's *A Dance of the Forests* (staged at Nigerian Independence Celebrations) (D, N). Achebe's *No Longer at Ease* (N, N).	Nigeria becomes independent. Cameroon becomes independent. The 'two' Somalias gain independence, although without Ogaden and Djibouti. Léopold Senghor elected President of an independent Senegal.
1961	Fanon's *The Wretched of the Earth* (E, Martinique/Algeria). Ekwensi's *Jagua Nana* (N, N). Easmon's *Dear Parent and Ogre* (D, SL).	Formal independence of Sierra Leone from UK. In Ethiopia, Eritrea declares secessionist intentions and war breaks out. Kenya gains the status of an autonomous entity. Tanganyika becomes independent.
1962	Bai. T. Moore's *Ebony Dust* (N, SL). Clark-Bederekemo's *Poems* (P, N). Ekwensi's *Burning Grass* (N, N). Okigbo's *Heavensgate* (P, N).	Tanganyika becomes a republic with Nyerere as President. Kenyatta as Prime Minister of an autonomous Kenya. Uganda becomes independent with Milton Obote as President. Nigeria becomes a Federation.
1963	Soyinka's *A Dance of the Forests* (D, N). Soyinka's *The Lion and the Jewel* (D, N). Ephraim N. Hussein's *Kinjeketile* (D, T).	Kenya formally independent. The Organisation of African Unity Charter signed, comprising all independent African states, excluding South Africa. Zanzibar becomes independent.

DATE	LITERATURE	HISTORICAL/CULTURAL EVENTS
1964	Ngũgĩ's *Weep Not, Child* (N, K). Awonoor's *Rediscovery and Other Poems* (P, G). Clark-Bederekemo's *Three Plays* (D, N). Conton's *The African* (N, SL). Nwanko's *Danda* (N, N). Peters's *Poems* (P, The G).	Zanzibar Revolution replaces Sultan with an African Revolutionary Council. Zanzibar and Tanganyika join as Tanzania. Kenyatta now President of an independent Kenya, declares a republic. Martin Luther King awarded the Nobel Peace Prize. Sudan returns to civilian rule.
1965	Aidoo's *Dilemma of a Ghost* (D, G). Ngũgĩ's *The River Between* (N, K). Peters's *The Second Round* (N, The G). Soyinka's *The Road* (D, N), *The Interpreters* (N, N).	Kenyatta declares Kenya a one-party state under KANU, suppresses KADU opposition. The Gambia gains independence. Sadiq al Mahdi elected in the Sudan.
1966	Achebe's *A Man of the People* (N, N). Flora Nwapa's *Efuru* (N, N). Ogot's *The Promised Land* (N, K). Okot p'Bitek's *Song of Lawino* (P, U).	Kabaka Mutesa of Buganda ('King Freddy') flees to Britain. In Ghana the army takes over, Nkrumah goes into exile in Guinea. Break-up of the Nigerian Federation. Declaration of a unitary Nigerian state.
1967	Peters's *Satellites* (P, The G). Ngũgĩ's *A Grain of Wheat* (N, K). Serumaga's *The Play* (D, U). Sutherland's *Foriwa* (D, G).	East African Community declared, lasted only until mid-1970s. Uganda becomes a republic with Obote as President. Biafra secedes and the Nigerian Civil War begins (lasts until 1970). Soyinka imprisoned for opposing the war by taking over the Ibadan radio station.
1968	Armah's *The Beautyful Ones are Not Yet Born* (N, G). Ogot's *Land without Thunder* (N, K).	Uganda becomes a one-party state under Obote.
1969	Dipoko's *Because of Women* (N, C). Selassié's *The Aftersata* (N, E). Palyango's *Dying in the Sun* (N, T). Ruhumbika's *Village in Uhuru* (N, T).	In Somalia, General Siyad Barre seizes power. Ghana returns to civilian rule under President Busia. In the Sudan, Colonel Jaafar el-Nimeiry seizes power (in power until 1985).
1970	Adoko's *Uganda Crisis* (N, U). Aidoo's *No Sweetness Here* (D, G) and *Anowa* (D, G). Armah's *Fragments* (N, G). Nwapa's *Idu* (N, N). Kibera's *Voices in the Dark* (N, K). Angira's *Juices* (P, K).	Nigerian Civil War ends.
1971	Mangua's *Son of Woman* (N, K). Awonoor's *Night of My Blood* (P, G). Lo Liyong's *Frantz Fanon's Uneven Ribs* (U). Mezu's *Behind the Rising Sun* (N, N).	In Uganda, a military coup led by Idi Amin Dada overthrows Obote's government. In Sierra Leone, power is in the hands of the army. A republic is declared.

345

DATE	LITERATURE	HISTORICAL/CULTURAL EVENTS
	Omotoso's *The Edifice* (D, N). Rotimi's *Kurunmi* (D, N). Okigbo Collected Poems issued under the title *Labyrinths (with Path to Thunder)*. Serumaga's *Mjangwa: A Promise of Rains* (D, U) and *The Elephants* (N, U).	
1972	Mangua's *A Tail in the Mouth: A Novel* (N, K). Ngũgĩ's *Homecoming: Essays on African and Caribbean Literature* (E, K). Omotoso's *The Combat* (D, N). Awonoor's *This Earth My Brother* (N, G). Armah's *Why Are We So Blest?* (N, G). Sofola's *Wedlock of the Gods* (D, N).	In Ghana, Busia is overthrown by a military coup. Beginning of a truce in the civil war between the government and the southern rebels in the Sudan which lasts until 1983.
1973	Armah's *Two Thousand Seasons* (N, G). Cheyney-Coker's *Concerto for an Exile* (P, SL). Kofi Awonoor's *Ride Me, Memory* (P, G). Mwangi's *Kill Me Quick* (N, K). Soyinka's *Season of Anomy* (D, N). Worku's *The Thirteenth Sun* (N, N). Maillu's *My Dear Bottle* (N, K). Angira's *Soft Corals* (P, K).	
1974	Armah's *Fragments* (N, G). Omotoso's *Sacrifice* (D, N). Selassié's *Warrior King* (N, E). Maillu's *After 4.30* (N, K).	In Ethiopia the army takes over. Haile Selassié I is exiled in September, and a republic is declared. Col. H. Mengistu leads the country through a period of great upheaval.
1975	M. Mwangi's *Taste of Death* (N, K). Nwapa's *Never Again* (N, N). Nwanko's *My Mercedes is Bigger than Yours* (N, N). Osofisan's *Kolera Kolej* (N, N). Soyinka's *Death and the King's Horseman* (D, N). Sutherland's *The Marriage of Anansewa* (D, G).	Mozambique and Angola become independent. In Nigeria a *coup d'état* led by General Mohammed overthrows General Gowan, in power since 1966.
1976	Iroh's *Forty Eight Guns for the General* (N, N). Okpewho's *The Last Duty* (N, N). Omotoso's *The Scales* (D, N).	In Nigeria General Mohammed is assassinated and General Obasanjo takes over.
1977	Aidoo's *Our Sister Killjoy* (D, G). Ngũgĩ's *Petals of Blood* (N, K). Rotimi's *Our Husband has Gone Mad Again* (N, N).	Shortly after launching an attack on Ethiopia over the Ogaden region, Somalia breaks off with the USSR. Djibouti becomes independent.

DATE	LITERATURE	HISTORICAL/CULTURAL EVENTS
	Ngũgĩ's *Ngaahika Ndeenda* (I Will Marry When I Want) (K, D). Sofola's *The Sweet Trap* (D, N). W. E. Mfukwa's *The Wicked Walk* (N, T).	Steve Biko dies in custody in South Africa.
1978	Anyidoho's *Elegy for the Revolution* (D, N). Armah's *The Healers* (N, G). Awonoor's *The House by the Sea* (P, G). Osofisan's *Who's Afraid of Solarin* (D, N). Sowande's *A Farewell to Babylon* (D, N). Ngũgĩ's *Maitu Njugira* (Mother Sing to Me) (D, K).	Somalia is defeated by the Ethiopean army, which received support from both the USSR and Cuba. In Kenya Jomo Kenyatta is replaced by Daniel A. Moi. Ngũgĩ is imprisoned and subsequently deported.
1979	Gicheru's *Across the Bridge* (N, K). Iroh's *Toads of War* (N, N). Nuruddin's *Sweet and Sour Milk* (N, E). Iyayi's *Violence* (N, N). Kahiga's *When the Stars are Scattered* (N, K). Mude's *The Hills are Falling* (N, K). Mwangi's *The Cockroach Dance* (N, K).	In Nigeria Obasanjo devolves power to a civilian government. Shagari elected President. In Uganda, Amin is overthrown by forces, helped by Tanzania, putting an end to Idi Amin's reign of terror. In Ghana a Military Council headed by Ft. Lt. Jerry Rawlings overthrows the government. Both former presidents are executed. After elections, Dr H. Limann forms a civilian government.
1980	Ibingira's *Bitter Harvest* (N, U). Ogot's *The Island of Tears* (S, K).	Zimbabwe gains independence. Master Sergeant John Doe seizes power in Liberia. In Uganda Binaisa is ousted and Obote becomes President for the second time.
1981	Nuruddin's *Sardines* (N, E). Okri's *The Landscapes Within* (N, N). Peters's *Selected Poetry* (P, The G). L. Sowande's *Our Man the President* (N, N). Soyinka's *Opera Wonyosi* (O, N). Osofisan's *Oriki of a Grasshopper* (D, N).	In Ghana, Rawlings and the military allege a deterioration of the political and social situations to regain control of the country. In Senegal S. Senghor resigns, and Abdou Diouf is elected President. After an abortive coup in The Gambia is suppressed with Senegalese help, the Senegambian Federation is formed.
1982	Iroh's *The Siren in the* Night (N, N). Iyayi's *The Contract* (N, N). Sowande's *Without a Home* (N, N). Osofisan's *Morountodun* (D, N). Omotoso's *Memories of Our Recent Boom* (N, N). Sowande's *Flamingo* (D, N). Ngũgĩ's *Devil on the Cross* (N, K)	Daniel A. Moi survives a *coup d'état* in Kenya.
1983	Nurudin's *Close Sesame* (N, E). Osundare's *Songs of the Marketplace* (P, N).	The army once again returns to power in Nigeria under General Buhari. 1,500,000 refugees are expelled.

347

DATE	LITERATURE	HISTORICAL/CULTURAL EVENTS
	Rotimi's *If: A Tragedy of the Ruled* (D, N). Nuruddin's *Close Sesame* (N, E). Onwueme's *A Hen Too Soon* (D, N).	In South Africa whites approve a new constitution. In the Sudan, General Nimeiry's decision to divide the country into three regions, and the imposition of an Islamic code of law, set off a prolonged and destructive conflict. Breakdown of truce in the Sudan and renewal of civil conflict.
1984	Achebe's *The Trouble with Nigeria* (E, N). Anyidoho's *A Harvest of Our Dreams* (N, N). Ṣoyinka's *A Play of Giants* (D, N). Onwueme's *The Broken Calabash* (D, N).	In Uganda Obote is forced out of power by forces loyal to General Basilio Ikello. General Babangida takes over from Buhari in Nigeria, promising economic reform.
1985	Aidoo's *Someone Talking to Sometime* (P, G). Clark-Bederekemo's *State of the Union* (P, N). Saro-Wiwa's *Sozaboy* (N, N).	Overthrow of the dictatorship of Nimeiry in Sudan, power assumed there by General Abdul R. Siwar adh Dhahab.
1986	Deng's *Seeds of Redemption* (N, S). Ekwensi's *Jagua Nana's Daughter* (N, G). Nurudidin's *Maps* (N, E). Ojaide's *Labyrinths of the Delta* (P, N). Nagenda's *The Seasons of Thomas Tebo* (N, U).	In Uganda, the populist-oriented National Resistance Movement, led by Yowri Museweni, take over in Kampala. Wọle Ṣoyinka (Nigeria) is awarded the Nobel Prize for Literature. Sadiq al Mahdi forms his second civilian government in Sudan.
1987	Achebe's *Anthills in the Savannah* (N, N). Gurnah's *Memory of Departure* (T, N). Mwangi's *Bread of Sorrow* (N, K). Ngũgĩ's *Matigari* (N, K). Osofisan's *Another Raft* (D, N).	In Burundi a military coup overthrows Jean-Baptiste Bagaza.
1988	Aidoo's *Birds and Other Poems* (P, G). Gurnah's *Pilgrim's Way* (T, N). Rotimi's *Hopes of the Living Dead* (D, N). Ezenwa-Ohaeto's *I Wan Be President* (P, N). Saro-Wiwa's *Prisoner of Jebs* (N, N). Ṣoyinka's *Mandela's Earth and Other Poems* (P, N).	Peace signed officially between Somalia and Ethiopia. Najib Mahfuz (Egypt) awarded the Nobel Prize for Literature.
1989	Deng's *The Cry of The Owl* (N, S). Mahjoub's *Navigation of a Rainmaker* (N, S). Mwangi's *Weapon of Hunger* (N, K). Mwangi's *The Return of Shaka* (N, K). Nagbe's *The Real Drum Daddy is Back* (N, L). Vassanji's *The Gunny Sack*.	In Liberia war breaks out between forces loyal to Charles Taylor and those of Samuel Doe. The Senegambian Confederation is dissolved. Overthrow of the long shaky civilian regime in Sudan by Colonel Ahmad al Bashir.

DATE	LITERATURE	HISTORICAL/CULTURAL EVENTS
1990	Asong's *The Crown of Thorns* (N, N). Butake's *And Palm Wine Will Flow* (N, C). Cheyney-Coker's *The Last Harmattan of Alasine Dunbar* (N, N). Gurnah's *Dottie* (T, N). Mwangi's *Striving for the Wind* (N, K). Yeoh's *Munyenge* (N, C).	In Kenya, pro-democracy forces demonstrate. In Algeria the political situation deteriorates. Civil war breaks out in Rwanda. Liberia is partitioned under the control of ECOMOG forces. The civil war continues. In South Africa Mandela is freed in the run-up to the first free elections.
1991	Aidoo's *Changes* (P, G). Besong's *Requiem for the Last Kaiser* (N, N). Lo Liyong's *Culture is Rutan* (E, Su). Ojaide's *The Blood of Peace* (P, N). Okri's *The Famished Road* (N, N; awarded the Booker Prize). Osofisan's *Once Upon Four Robbers* (D, N). Saro-Wiwa's *Pita Dumbrok's Prison* (N, N). Vassanji's *Uhuru Street* (N, T).	Nadine Gordimer (RSA) receives the Nobel Prize for Literature, the third African writer in less than a decade to be so honoured. Siyad Barre deposed by the United Somali Congress.
1992	Aidoo's *An Angry Letter in January* (P, G). Epie'Ngome's *What God Has Put Asunder* (N, C). Nagbe's *The Road to Romeo* (N, L). Nwapa's *One is Enough* (N, N). Osofisan's *Twingle-Twangle, a TwynningTayle* (D, N). Osofisan's *Yungba-Yungba* (D, N).	US forces arrive in Somalia. A military coup in Sierra Leone led by Valentin Strasser. In Nigeria, President Babangida begins the run-up to the promised return to civilian rule. Ghana holds first election since J. Rawlings staged coup in 1981.
1993	Mwangi's *The Hunter's Dream* (N, K). Okri's *Songs of Enchantment* (N, N). Sallah's *Dreams of Dirty Roads* (N, E). Selassié's *Riding the Whirlwind* (N, E).	In Burundi, civil war breaks out. Eritrea becomes the latest independent state in Africa. In Nigeria, Babangida refuses to ratify the election results in which M. K. O. Abiola secured a majority of the votes. Power is devolved to General Sani Abacha.
1994	A. Gurnah's *Paradise* (N, T). Mahjoub's *Wings of Dust* (N, Su). Mangua's *Kanina and I* (N, K).	Following the death of the presidents of Burundi and Rwanda, in a plane crash, the region witnesses one of the worst massacres in modern times. A military coup in The Gambia against Senegalese-backed President Jawara by Lt. Yaya Jammal.
1995	Johnson's *Highlife for Caliban* (P, SL). Okri's *Astonishing the Gods* (N, N). Onwueme's *Tell it to Women: An Epic Drama for Women* (D, N).	Ken Saro-Wiwa is executed with other Ogoni activists. Nigeria is expelled from the Commonwealth. In Liberia and Somalia the civil wars continue.
1996	Angira's *Tides of Time* (P, K). Gurnah's *Admiring Silence* (N, T).	In Niger, the government is thrown out of power.

DATE	LITERATURE	HISTORICAL/CULTURAL EVENTS
	Okri's *Dangerous Love* (N, N). Osman's *In the Name of Our Fathers* (N, S). Vassanji's *The Book of Secrets* (N, T).	*Coup d'état* in Burundi. Elections in The Gambia return Yaya Jammah to power as a civilian president. Two Sudanese Peace Charters are signed, but the conflict is not fully resolved.
1997	Okri's *A Way of Being Free* (E, N).	Sudanese conflict continues on the southern border with Uganda.
1998	Mahjoub's *The Carrier* (N, S). Farah's *Secrets* (N, S).	Nigerian troops, acting on behalf of the Organisation of West African States, go into war-torn Sierra Leone. Elections are promised. Death of Nigerian President Sani Abacha, whose place is taken by General Abdulsalam Abubakar. Death of M. K. O. Abiola.
1999	Okri's *Invisible Riches* (N, N).	Election of ex-General Olesegun Obasanjo as third Nigerian civil President in elections held in May.

General Bibliography

Bibliographies, anthologies, general reference works

Adams, F. D. (1971) *Three Black Writers in Eighteenth Century England*, Belmont, Ca.: Wadsworth Publishing Co. (Useful general comment and extracts from Equiano, Cuguano and Sancho.)

Anon. (1970) *The Writers of the West African Republic of Liberia: A List of Liberian Authors and Aspiring Writers Arranged in Historical Order of the Republic of Liberia from 1820 to 1971*, Monrovia: Liberian Literature Studies Programme.

Anon. (n.d.) *Stories of Africa*, London: Universities Mission to Central Africa. (Informally bound collection of early missionary tracts in British Library.)

Cox, C. B. (ed.) (1997) *African Writers*, 2 vols, New York: Scribners.

Brunton, Charlotte H. (1993) *The Heinemann Book of African Women's Writing*, London: Heinemann. (Includes examples of recent, less-well-known writers.)

Busby, Margaret (ed.) (1993) *Daughters of Africa: An International Anthology of Words and Writings by Women of African Descent from the Ancient Egyptian to the Present*, London: Vintage. (Good general overview.)

Condor, S.-M. H. (1971) *A Guide to the Study of Liberian Literature etc.*, Monrovia: Liberian Literature Studies Programme.

Harrow, Kenneth W. (1994) *Thresholds of Change in African Literature: The Emergence of a Tradition*, Portsmouth, N.H.: Heinemann; London: Currey. (Involves English and French texts, though French are dominant. Provides ideas on new links across these traditions and between West and South African texts.)

Himberger, P. E. (1973) *Highland Mosaic: A Critical Anthology of Ethiopian Literature in English*, Athens, Ohio: Ohio Centre for Literary Studies, Africa Program.

Jack, Belinda Elizabeth (1996) *Negritude and Literary Criticism: The History and Theory of 'Negro-African' Literature in French*, Westport, Conn.: Greenwood Press. (Good introduction to this influential early movement in African writing.)

Laurence, Margaret (1976) *A Tree for Poverty: Somali Poetry and Prose*, Hamilton, Canada: McMaster University Press; Shannon, Ireland: Irish University Press.

Limb, Peter and Jean-Marie Volet (1996) *Bibliography of African Literatures*, Lanham, Md.: Scarecrow Press.

Lindfors, Bernth (1979) *Black African Literature in English: A Guide to Information Sources*, Detroit: Gale Research Co.

Lindfors, Bernth (1986) *Black African Literature in English, 1977–1981 Supplement*, New York: Africana Pub. Co.

Lindfors, Bernth (1989) *Black African Literature in English, 1982–1986*, London and New York: Hans Zell.

Lindfors, Bernth (1995) *Black African Literature in English, 1987–1991*, London and Melbourne: Hans Zell.

Collectively, the above four volumes by Lindfors constitute the most authoritative and full bibliography of criticism on African writing to date.

Lindfors, Bernth (ed.) (1980) *Mazungumzo: Interviews with East African Writers, Publishers, Editors, and Scholars*, Athens: Ohio University, Center for International Studies. (Includes interviews with popular writers and publishers in East Africa.)

Lindfors, Bernth and Reinhard Sander (eds) (1992) *Twentieth-Century Caribbean and Black African Writers*, 1st series, Dictionary of Literary Biography, Vol. 117, Detroit: Gale Research.

Lindfors, Bernth and Reinhard Sander (eds) (1992) *Twentieth-Century Caribbean and Black African Writers*, 2nd Series, Dictionary of Literary Biography, Vol. 125, Detroit: Gale Research.

Lindfors, Bernth and Reinhard Sander (eds) (1996) *Twentieth-Century Caribbean and Black African Writers*, 3rd Series, Dictionary of Literary Biography, Vol. 157, Detroit: Gale Research.

Moore, Gerald and Ulli Beier (eds) (1963) *Modern Poetry from Africa*, Harmondsworth: Penguin. (One of the earliest anthologies of African English poetry.)

Nagbe, Moses K. (1992) *Books on Liberia by Nationals and Foreign Nationals*, Monrovia: n.p.

Potkay, A. (1995) *Black Atlantic Writers of the Eighteenth Century*, London: St Martin's Press. (Survey of early black writing by slaves and ex-slaves.)

Westley, David (1990) *Choice of Language and African Literature: A Bibliographic Essay*, Boston, Mass.: African Studies Center, Boston University.

Wilkinson, Jane (ed.) (1992) *Talking with African Writers: Interviews with African Poets, Playwrights & Novelists*, London: J. Currey; Portsmouth, N.H.: Heinemann.

Zell, Hans M. (ed.) (1993) *African Books in Print: An Index by Author, Title and Subject/ Livres Africains Disponibles*, 4th edn, Melbourne and London: Hans Zell.

Zell, Hans M., Carol Bundy and Virginia Coulon (1983) *A New Reader's Guide to African Literature*, New York: Africana Publishing Company.

Zell, Hans M. and Cecile Lomer (1997) *The African Studies Companion: A Resource Guide & Directory*, 2nd revised and expanded edn, London and New Providence, N.J.: Hans Zell.

Historical background

Ajayi, J. F. A. (1965) *Christian Missions in Nigeria 1841–1891: The Making of A New Elite*, London: Longmans.

Berman, B. and J. Lonsdale (1992) *Unhappy Valley: Conflict in Kenya and Africa*, London: James Currey. (African and white settler conflict, especially in Kenya.)

Curtin, P. D. (1967) *Africa Remembered*, Madison: University of Wisconsin Press. (Annotated extracts from many African writers of the eighteenth and nineteenth centuries, e.g. Equiano, Quaque, Cuguano etc.)

Dabydeen, D. (1985) *Hogarth's Blacks: Images of Blacks in Eighteenth Century English Art*, Mundelstrup, Denmark: Dangaroo Press. (The representation and iconography of Africans in eighteenth-century painting.)

Davidson, B. (1992) *The Black Man's Burden: Africa and the Curse of the Nation-State*, London: James Currey. (Controversial critique of the origins and development of the modern African nation-state.)

Echeruo, M. J. C. (1977) *Victorian Lagos*, London: Macmillan. (The intellectual and social life of nineteenth-century Lagos.)

Edwards, Paul and David Dabydeen (1981) *Black Writers in Britain 1760–1890*, Edinburgh: Edinburgh University Press. (Very comprehensive and covers all the writers mentioned in this volume.)

Farias, P. F. de Moraes and Karin Barber (1990) *Self-Assertion and Brokerage: Early Cultural Nationalism in West Africa*, Birmingham: Centre of West African Studies, University of Birmingham. (The role of early nationalists and the relationship in their thought of African and European systems and values.)

Furedi, F. (1989) *The Mau Mau War in Perspective*, London: James Currey. (Modern, radical account of the Mau Mau freedom struggle in Kenya.)

Fyfe, C. (1962) *A History of Sierra Leone*, London: Oxford University Press.

Henderson, I. (1958) *The Hunt for Kimathi*, London: Hamish Hamilton. (An account by the colonial policeman who captured Dedan Kimathi, the Mau Mau leader.)

Irwin, G. W. (1977) *Africans Abroad: A Documentary History of the Black Diaspora in Asia, Latin America and the Caribbean During the Age of Slavery*, New York: Columbia University Press.

Jones-Quartey, K. A. B. (1975) *History, Politics and Early Press in Ghana: The Fictions and the Facts*, Legon, Ghana: School of Journalism and Communication Studies, University of Legon. (Colonial and African newspapers in Ghana in the nineteenth and early twentieth centuries – material on Horton, Casely Hayford, Danquah etc.)

July, R. W. (1968) *The Origins of Modern African Thought*, London: Faber. (Foundational study of nineteenth-century West African intellectuals, e.g. Blyden, Crowther, Horton, Casely Hayford *et al.*)

Kup, A. P. (1961) *A History of Sierra Leone 1400–1787*, Cambridge: Cambridge University Press.

Leonard, M. A. G. (1906) *The Lower Niger and its Tribes*, London: Macmillan; reissued London: Frank Cass, 1968 (A colonial-period ethnography, possibly the one referred to at the end of Achebe's *Things Fall Apart*.)

Lonsdale, J. (1990) 'Mau Maus of the Mind: Making Mau Mau and Remaking Kenya', *Journal of African History*, 31, 3: 393. (The creation of historical myths about Mau Mau.)

Maughan-Brown, D. (1985) *Land, Freedom and Fiction: History and Ideology in Kenya*, London: Zed Books. (The representation of Kenyan history in social and literary texts.)

Maxon, R. M. (1986) *East Africa: An Introductory History*, Morgantown, W.V.: West Virginia University Press.

Mba, Emma (1982) *Nigerian Women Mobilised: Women's Political Activity in Southern Nigeria 1900–1965*, Berkeley, Ca.: Institute of International Studies, University of California. (Feminist account, revising classic histories of women's roles.)

Nicol, D. (1969) *Africanus Horton: The Dawn of Nationalism in Modern Africa*, London: Longman. (Biography by a modern Sierra Leonean scholar.)

Okullu, H. (1974) *Church and Politics in East Africa*, Nairobi: Uzima. (Particularly good on the complex relations between the missions, settlers and government.)

Oliver, R. (1952) *The Missionary Factor in East Africa*, London: Longmans, Green and Co. Ltd. (Standard historical account.)

Omu, F. I. A. (1978) *Press and Politics in Nigeria 1880–1937*, London: Longman. (Standard account of the early press in Nigeria.)

Omu, F. I. A. (1982) 'The Newspaper Press in Southern Nigeria, 1800–1900', in B. I. Obichere (ed.), *Studies in Southern Nigerian History*, London: Frank Cass: 102–26.

Priebe, Richard K. (1988) *Myth, Realism, and the West African Writer*, Trenton, N.J.: Africa World Press. (Examines the use of myth and ritual elements in modern West African writing, with material on Armah, Achebe, Awoonor, Ṣoyinka etc.)

Pugliese, Christiana (1995) *Author, Publisher and Gĩkũyũ Nationalist: The Life and Writings of Gakaara wa Wanjaũ*, Bayreuth African Studies No. 37, Bayreuth: Breitinger; Nairobi: IFRA. (First study of this early Gĩkũyũ language writer.)

Rawick, G. P. (1972) *The American Slave: A Composite Autobiography*, Westport, Conn.: Greenwood. (Transcriptions of ex-slave narratives, undertaken as part of the Federal Writers Project in the 1930s.)

Sampson, M. J. (1937; 1969) *Gold Coast Men of Affairs*, London: Dawsons Colonial Library. (Biographies of early Ghanaian intellectuals, such as Casely Hayford, Danquah etc.)

Strayer, R. W. (1978) *The Making of Mission Communities in East Africa: Anglicans and Africans in Colonial Kenya, 1875–1935*, London: Heinemann; Albany, N.Y.: University of New York Press.

Walker, J. W. S. G. (1976) *The Black Loyalists: The Search for a Promised Land in Nova Scotia and Sierra Leone, 1783–1870*, New York: Africana Pub. Co.

Webster, J. B. and A. A. Boahen with M. Tidy (1980) *The Revolutionary Years: West Africa Since 1800*, London: Longman.

Wilson, G. H. (1936) *The History of the Universities' Mission to Central Africa*, London: Universities Mission to Central Africa. (Account of the Anglican mission based on Zanzibar from the late nineteenth century, whose tracts are discussed in Chapter 3.)

General criticism

Adams, Anne V. (ed.) (1997) *African Literature and African Development: Mapping Intersections*, Trenton, N.J.: Africa World Press. (On the implications for development studies of recent African writing.)

Amuta, C. (1989) *The Theory of African Literature: Implications for Practical Criticism*, London: Zed Books. (An influential Marxist account of recent African writing.)

Appiah, A. (1992) *In My Father's House: Africa in the Philosophy of Culture*, Oxford: Oxford University Press. (A controversial account of African intellectual traditions, arguing that these were often trapped within the very racist ideologies they sought to dismantle.)

Chapman, M. (1996) *Southern African Literatures*, London: Longman. (The most recent and most comprehensive history of writing in the Southern African region.)

Chinweizu, with Jemie Onwuchekwa and Ihechukwu Madubuike (1975) *The West and the Rest of Us*, New York: Random House. (Analyses the ongoing neo-colonialist bias of Western institutions and practices as they act on the rest of the world.)

Chinweizu, with Jemie Onwuchekwa and Ihechukwu Madubuike (1980) *Towards the Decolonisation of African Literature*, Enugu, Nigeria: Fourth Dimension Pub. Co. (A very influential if controversial text, which attacked writers like Ṣoyinka for having failed to write within the aesthetic and cultural traditions of African culture.)

Gérard, Albert (1981) *African Language Literatures: An Introduction to the Literary History of Sub-Saharan Africa*, Harlow: Longman. (Classic, and still unsurpassed, comparative account of African literatures in a number of indigenous languages.)

Graebner, Werner (ed.) (1992) *Sokomoko: Popular Culture in East Africa*, Matatu No. 9, Atlanta, Ga. and Amsterdam: Rodopi. (Essays by various people on popular culture in the region.)

Granqvist, Raoul (1990) *Canonization and Teaching of African literatures*, Matatu No. 7, Atlanta, Ga. and Amsterdam: Rodopi. (Argues that only certain African texts have been accepted and that a new and limiting canon has been constructed in educational curricula.)

Griffiths, G. (1978) *A Double Exile: African and West Indian Writing Between Two Cultures*, London: Marion Boyars. (An early, comparative account of African and West Indian texts in English with material on Achebe, Armah, Awoonor, Ṣoyinka, Ngũgĩ.)

Griffiths, G. (2000) 'Writing African: Post-Colonial Patronage and Control, The Case of the Missionary Text', in Gerhardt Stulz (ed) *Colonies, Missions, Cultures in the English-*

Speaking World, Tuebingen, Stauffenburg Verlag. (An account of the development of controls in missionary texts and of the internal resistances these generated in some African writing.)

Griffiths, G. (1996) 'Writing, Literacy and History in Africa', in Paul Hyland and Mpalive-Hangson Msiska (eds), *Writing and Africa*, London: Longman. (A comparison of the use of writing as a tool of power in both the medieval Arab and nineteenth-century European invasions of Africa.)

Gugler, Josef with Hans-Jürgen Lusebrink and Jürgen Martini (1994) *Literary Theory and African Literature*, Münster. Revised papers presented at the Colloquium 'Theoretical Approaches to African Literature' held at Bayreuth University, 15–16 June 1990. (A useful collection with essays by foundational critics in the field such as Jeyifo, Barber, Bjornson, Julian, Mouralis, Kasse and Maughan-Brown.)

Gurnah, A. (ed.) (1993–5) *Essays on African Writing Vol. 1: A Re-evaluation* (1993) *Vol. 2: Contemporary Literature* (1995), London: Heinemann. (A collection of contemporary essays on a wide range of African texts with material on Achebe, Farah, Armah, Ngũgĩ, Şoyinka, Aidoo, Okri, and Vassanji.)

Hountondji, Paulin J. (1983) *African Philosophy: Myth and Reality*, London: Hutchinson. (An excellent introduction to the distinctive nature of African philosophy and thought.)

Irele, Abiola (1981) *The African Experience in Literature and Ideology*, London: Heinemann. (Classic study of the underlying systems and ideas which produced modern African literary texts.)

JanMohamed, Abdul (1983) *Manichean Aesthetics: The Politics of Literature in Colonial Africa*, Amherst, Mass.: University of Massachusetts Press. (A study of the intertextuality between colonial period fiction about Africa and modern African novels).

JanMohamed, Abdul (1984) 'Humanism and minority literature: towards a definition of a counter-hegemonic discourse', *Boundary*, 2, 12, Spring/Fall: 3–13.

Killam, G. D. (ed.) (1984) *The Writing of East and Central Africa*, London, Nairobi, Ibadan: Heinemann. (A foundational collection of essays including survey articles on Ugandan, Kenyan and Tanzanian writing, and articles on Ngũgĩ, p'Bitek, Taban lo Liyong, Mwangi, and Farah.)

Lazarus, Neil (1990) *Resistance in Postcolonial African Fiction*, New Haven, Conn.: Yale University Press. (Examines recent writing which seeks to decolonise African culture.)

Lindfors, Bernth (1982) *Early Nigerian Literature*, New York: Africana Pub. Co. (Useful source material on Tutuola and Fagunwa, as well as accounts of the juvenilia of later writers like Achebe, Şoyinka etc. Establishes the importance of informal local publishing in school and college journals for these early post-war writers.)

Lindfors, Bernth (1993) 'Desert Gold: Irrigation Schemes for Ending the Book Drought', *Matatu*, 10 (African Literature in the Eighties). (Analyses the effect on African English-language writing of recent shifts in international publishing companies and their market focus.)

Lindfors, Bernth (1996) *Loaded Vehicles: Studies in African Literary Media*. Trenton, N.J.: Africa World Press. (Useful and varied collection of essays on modern African writing.)

Lindfors, Bernth (1997) *African Textualities: Texts, Pre-texts, and Contexts of African Literature*, Trenton, N.J.: Africa World Press. (Another recent collection of essays on a variety of useful topics.)

Lyova, N. with Eckhardt Breitinger and Bole Butaka (eds) (1993) *Anglophone Cameroon Writing*, Bayreuth African Studies Series No. 30, Bayreuth: Breitinger. (Only study so far of this material.)

Makward, Edris (ed.) (1998) *The Growth of African Literature*, Trenton, N.J.: Africa World Press. (Useful general essay collection.)

355

Maja-Pearce, Adewale (1991) *Who's Afraid of Wọle Ṣoyinka? Essays on Censorship*, Oxford and Portsmouth, N.H.: Heinemann. (The social role of the writer in opposing political corruption and authoritarianism in modern Africa.)

Mbise, I. R. (1984) 'Writing in English From Tanzania', in G. D. Killam (ed.), *The Writing of East and Central Africa*, London, Nairobi, Ibadan: Heinemann.

McLuckie, C. (1990) *Nigerian Civil War Literature: Seeking an Imagined Community*, Lewiston, Queenstown, Lampeter: The Edwin Mellen Press. (A useful though very selective account of the writing about the civil war.)

Miller, C. L. (1985) *Blank Darkness: Africanist Discourse in French*, Chicago: Chicago University Press. (The construction of black Africans in Francophone texts.)

Miller, C. L. (1990) *Theories of Africans: Francophone Literature and Anthropology in Africa*, Chicago: Chicago University Press. (Employs anthropological sources to authorise and effect local readings of a number of Francophone African writers.)

Moore, Gerald (1980) *Twelve African Writers*, London: Hutchinson. (Updated and expanded version of one of the earliest studies of African writing; covers both Anglophone and Francophone writing.)

Nazareth, P. (1974) 'Africa Under Neo-Colonialism: New East African Writing', *Busara*, 6, 1. (Influential account of the effects of neo-colonialism on writing in the region.)

Obiechina, E. (1971) *Literature for the Masses: An Analytical Study of Popular Pamphleteering in Nigeria*, Enugu: Nwamife. (The first full-length study of an African popular literature.)

Obiechina, E. (1972) *Onitsha Market Literature*, London: Heinemann Educational Books. (Anthology of extracts from this literature, original editions of which are now difficult to find.)

Obiechina, E. (1973) *An African Popular Literature: A Study of Onitsha Pamphlets*, Cambridge: Cambridge University Press. (A critical study of the Onitsha texts.)

Obiechina, E. (1975) *Culture, Tradition and Society in the West African Novel*, Cambridge: Cambridge University Press. (Contextualises the work of a number of the early writers.)

Obiechina, E. (1990) *Language and Theme: Essays on African Literature*. Washington: Howard University Press.

Ogunyemi, Yemi (1988) *Perspectives on Nigerian Literature: 1700 to the Present*, 2 vols, Lagos: Guardian Publications. (Collection of essays by Nigerian critics.)

Owomoyela, Oyekan (ed.) (1993) *A History of Twentieth-Century African Literatures*, Lincoln: University of Nebraska Press. (Not a comprehensive history, but a collection of essays on recent African writing in a number of ex-colonial and indigenous African languages.)

Riemenschneider, Dieter (ed.) (1993) *African Literatures in the Eighties*, Matatu No. 8, Atlanta, Ga. and Amsterdam: Rodopi.

Schipper-De Leeuw, Mineke (1989) *Beyond the Boundaries: African Literature and Literary Theory*, London: W.H. Allen. (Relates African literature to wider developments in modern literary theory.)

Schmied, Josef J. (1991) *English in Africa: An Introduction*, Harlow: Longman. (Account of English usage and influence in Africa.)

Taiwo, Oladele (1967) *An Introduction to West African Literature*, London: Thomas Nelson. (Early but still useful attempt to survey and contextualise African writing.)

Taylor, R. (1985) 'The Question of Ethnic Traditions Within a National Literature', in *Towards African Authenticity: Language and Literary Form*, Bayreuth: Bayreuth University, Breitinger: 31–47.

Ukadike, N. F. (1994) *Black African Cinema*, Berkeley, Ca.: University of California Press.

Wanjala, C. (1978) *The Season of Harvest: A Literary Discussion*, Nairobi: Kenya Literature Bureau. (Criticism of East African writing by a leading Kenyan scholar.)

Wren, Robert M. (1991) *Those Magical Years: The Making of Nigerian Literature at Ibadan*, Washington: Three Continents. (The formative influence of Ibadan University and its literary life on Nigerian writers such as Achebe, Clark and Okigbo.)

Zabus, Chantal (1991) *The African Palimpsest: Indigenisation of Language in the West African Europhone Novel*, Atlanta, Ga. and Amsterdam: Rodopi. (Provides a theoretical model for dealing with African interlinguistic texts. Useful on many writers such as Okigbo, Okara, Ṣoyinka, Achebe etc.)

Zirimu, Pio and Andrew Gurr (1973) *Black Aesthetics*, Nairobi: East African Literature Bureau. (Early essays on whether a special African aesthetic exists and if so in what it consists. Focuses on East Africa.)

Orality and oral/written relations

Adeeko, Adeleke (1998) *Proverbs, Textuality and Nativism in African Literature*, Gainesville, Fla.: Florida University Press. (Study of the use of oral forms in recent writing.)

Austen, Ralph A. (1990) *Africans Speak, Colonialism Writes: The Transcription and Translation of Oral Literature before World War II*, Boston, Mass.: African Studies Center, Boston University. (Problems involved in the transcription and recording of oral 'texts'.)

Barber, K. (1997) *Readings in African Popular Culture*, Oxford: James Currey. (Analyses contemporary practices in popular, oral African culture.)

Barber, K. and P. F. de Moraes Farias (1989) *Discourse and its Disguises: The Interpretation of African Oral Texts*, Birmingham: Centre of West African Studies, University of Birmingham. (Argues that orality is a living and continuous feature of all African societies.)

Barber, K. with John Collins and Alain Ricard (1997) *West African Popular Theatre*, Oxford: James Currey. (Focuses on the performative elements in contemporary indigenous oral popular culture.)

Furniss, G. (1996) *Poetry, Prose and Popular Culture in Hausa*, Edinburgh: Edinburgh University Press, for the International African Institute. (The development of elite and popular written forms in Hausa.)

Furniss, G. and E. Gunner (eds) (1995) *Power, Marginality and African Oral Literature*, Cambridge and New York: Cambridge University Press. (Debating the role and ongoing power of orality in contemporary African societies.)

Hofmeyr, I. (1994) *We Spend Our Years as a Tale That Is Told: Oral Historical Narrative in a South African Chiefdom*, London: James Currey. (A foundational study of the interactions between oral and written practices.)

Julien, Eileen (1992) *African Novels and the Question of Orality*, Bloomington: Indiana University Press. (The interactions between oral texts and the practice of contemporary novelists.)

Miruka, O. (1994) *Encounter with Oral Literature*. Nairobi: East African Publishing House. (Orality and literature in the region.)

Okpewho, Isidore (1992) *African Oral Literature: Backgrounds, Character, and Continuity*, Bloomington: Indiana University Press. (Account of oral literature from one of Africa's leading scholars of oral culture, also a major novelist.)

Quayson, A. (1997) *Strategic Transformations in Nigerian Writing: Orality and History in the Work of Rev. Samuel Johnson, Amos Tutuola, Wọle Ṣoyinka and Ben Okri*, Oxford: James Currey. (How Yoruba-language culture was intertextual with English-language texts from 1921 to the present day. Model for potential future work of this kind in other African contexts.)

357

Samatar, S. S. (1982) *Oral Poetry and Somali Nationalism: The Case of Sayyid Mahammad Abdille Hasan*, Cambridge and New York: Cambridge University Press. (On the inseparability of poetry and Somali culture.)

Drama

Adowiwe, M. P. (1993) *Excursions in Drama and Literature: Interviews with Femi Osofisan*, Ibadan, Nigeria: Kraft Books.

Banham, Martin, with Errol Hill and George Woodyard (eds) (1994) *Cambridge Guide to African and West Indian Theatre*, Cambridge: Cambridge University Press. (Useful short articles with good bibliographies).

Bjorkman, I. (1989) *Mother, Sing for Me: People's Theatre in Kenya*, London and Atlantic Highlands, N.J.: Zed Books. (Provides useful material on Ngũgĩ's theatrical work.)

Dunton, C. (1992) *Make Man Talk True: Nigerian Drama in English Since 1970*, Oxford: Hans Zell. (Recent Nigerian theatre, with material on all the major figures discussed in this volume.)

Fuchs, Anne (1999) *New Theatre in Francophone and Anglophone Africa*, Matatu No. 20, Amsterdam and Atlanta, Ga.: Rodopi. (A wide-ranging recent collection of essays, some illustrated with interesting production photographs.)

Gbilekaa, Saint (1997) *Radical Theatre in Nigeria*, Nigeria: Caltop Publications. (A recent account of the development of alternative and oppositional theatre in Nigeria.)

Ibitokun, Benedict M. (1995) *African Drama and the Yoruba World-View*, Ibadan: Ibadan University Press. (Explicates the underlying ideas of the African culture which produced dramatists such as Ṣoyinka, Osofisan, Omotoso, Sowande.)

Jeyifo, Biodun (1984) *The Yoruba Popular Travelling Theatre of Nigeria*, Lagos: Nigeria Magazine Publications.

Jeyifo, B. (1985) *The Truthful Lie: Essays in a Sociology of African Drama*, London: New Beacon Books. (Stresses that there is a continuity of practice across and between the popular and literary traditions.)

Ogunba, Oyin and Abiola Irele (1978) *Theatre in Africa*, Ibadan: Ibadan University Press. (A useful introductory survey of theatre in Africa.)

Ricard, A. (1983) *Theatre and Nationalism: Wọle Ṣoyinka and LeRoi Jones*, Ile-Ife, Nigeria: University of Ile-Ife Press. (On the cross-influences between African-American and African drama.)

Fiction

Asein, Samuel Omo and Albert Olu Ashaolu (eds) (1986) *Studies in the African Novel*, Ibadan: Ibadan University Press. (Mainly West Africa.)

Barber, Karin (1997) 'Time, Space and Writing in Three Colonial Yoruba Novels', *The Yearbook of Colonial Studies*, 27. (Argues that the long, continuous tradition of writing Nigerian fiction in indigenous languages has been overlooked in recent critical accounts.)

Bolland, John M. (1996) *Language and the Quest for Political and Social Identity in the African Novel*, Accra: Woeli; Oxford: African Books Collective. (Focuses on the social aspects of Iyayi, Achebe etc.)

Gakwandi, S. A. (1977) *The Novel and Contemporary Experience in Africa*, London: Heinemann. (Addresses the social, cultural and political context of African novels.)

Gikandi, S. (1984) 'The Growth of the East African Novel', in G. D. Killam (ed.), *The Writing of East and Central Africa*, London, Nairobi, Ibadan: Heinemann.

Griffiths, G. (1987) 'Chinua Achebe: When Did You Last See Your Father?', *World Literature Written in English*, 27, 1, Spring. (The cultural and political context of the different generations of Africans in Achebe's work.)

Ker, David I. (1997) *The African Novel and the Modernist Tradition*, New York: P. Lang. (Reflects the recent critical interest in the links between Modernism and various postcolonial cultures, for example Simon Gikandi, *Writing in Limbo: Modernism and Caribbean Literature*, Ithaca: Cornell University Press, 1992.)

Maja-Pearce, Adewale (1992) *A Mask Dancing: Nigerian Novelists of the Eighties*, London and New York: Hans Zell. (An interesting if rather biased account of recent Nigerian fiction.)

Nnolim, C. (1992) *Approaches to the African Novel: Essays in Analysis*, Epsom, Nigeria: Saros International. (Recent African critical essays on a number of writers.)

Palmer, E. (1971) *Introduction to the African Novel*, London: Heinemann. (Early influential survey of African fiction.)

Palmer, E. (1979) 'Ngũgĩ's *Petals of Blood* (Review Article)', *African Literature Today* 10: 153–66. (Influential review article discussed in this text.)

Wright, Derek (1997) *Contemporary African Fiction*, Bayreuth African Studies No. 42, Bayreuth: Breitinger. (Excellent general survey of recent writing.)

Poetry

Aiyejina, F. (1988) 'Recent Nigerian Poetry in English: An Alter-Native Tradition', in Y. Ogunyemi (ed.), *Perspectives on Nigerian Literature: 1700 to the Present*, 2 vols, Lagos, Nigeria: Guardian Books, Vol. 1. (A survey of some of the more interesting younger poets to emerge in Nigeria in the late 1970s and 1980s.)

Egudu, Romanus N. (1978) *African Poetry and the African Predicament*, London: Macmillan. (Places African poetry within the tradition of social criticism and offers a reading of its value in this regard.)

Fraser, Robert (1986) *West African Poetry: A Critical History*, Cambridge: Cambridge University Press. (Comprehensive account of West African poetry, with sections on all the major figures, and with a good general background to the emergence of various traditions and forms.)

Goodwin, Ken (1982) *Understanding African Poetry: A Study of Ten Poets*, London: Heinemann. (Detailed accounts of the work of ten major poets.)

Nwachuckwu-Agbada, J. O. J. (1993) 'The Eighties and the Return to Oral Cadences in Nigerian Poetry' in *Matatu* 10 (African Literature in the Eighties). (Argues that the 1980s saw a move from literary to oral influences and also a reaching out towards a more popular audience.)

Ojaide, T. (1995) 'New Trends in Modern African Poetry', *Research in African Literatures*, 26, 1. (A survey article which seeks to analyse recent shifts in modern African poetry.)

Woman and African writing

Brown, Lloyd W. (1981) *Women Writers in Black Africa*, Westport, Conn.: Greenwood Press. (An early male-authored book but one of the first to argue that women's writing from Africa constituted a distinct tradition with its own concerns and styles.)

Davies, Carole Boyce (1986) *Ngambika: Studies of Women in African Literature*, Trenton, N.J.: Africa World Press. (Comparative study of the emerging discourse and tradition of women's writing in Africa.)

James, Adeola (1990) *In Their Own Voices: African Women Writers Talk*, London: J. Currey; Portsmouth N.H.: Heinemann. (Interviews.)

Mezu, Rose Uregbulam (1994) *Women in Chains: Abandonment in Love Relationships in the Fiction of Selected West African Writers*, Randallstown, Md.: Black Academy Press. (A thesis on the treatment of women in fiction stressing their continuing oppression in recent representations.)

Mojola, Yemi I. (1989) *Nigerian Female Writers: A Critical Perspective*, Lagos: Malthouse Press. (The development of Nigerian women's writing from Nwapa to Emecheta.)

Nasta, Susheila (1992) *Motherlands: Women's Writings from Africa, the Caribbean, and South Asia*. New Brunswick, N.J.: Rutgers University Press. (Essays suggesting similarities in the problems and solutions facing women writers in various parts of the developing world.)

Newell, Stephanie (ed.) (1997) *Writing African Women: Gender, Popular Culture and Literature in West Africa*, London and Atlantic Highlands, N.J.: Zed Books.

Nfah-Abbenyi, Juliana Makuchi (1997) *Gender in African Women's Writing: Identity, Sexuality, and Difference*, Bloomington: Indiana University Press. (Current debates on gender theory and cultural formation.)

Nnaemeka, Obioma (ed.) (1996) *The Politics of (M)othering: Womanhood, Identity, and Resistance in African Literature*, London and New York: Routledge. (On women's writing and literary and feminist theory in Africa.)

Ogundipe-Leslie, Molara (1994) *Re-creating Ourselves: African Women & Critical Transformations*, Trenton, N.J.: Africa World Press. (Recent African women's theory and writing.)

Ogunyemi, Chikwenye Okonjo (1996) *Africa Wo/man Palava: The Nigerian Novel by Women*, Chicago: University of Chicago Press.

Schipper, M. (1991) *Source of All Evil: African Proverbs and Sayings on Women*, Chicago: Ivan R. Dee. (The construction of African writing in traditional and modern discourse.)

Stratton, Florence (1994) *Contemporary African Literature and the Politics of Gender*, London and New York: Routledge. (Argues for a separate and distinctive African female literary tradition.)

Wilentz, Gay (1992) *Binding Cultures: Black Women Writers in Africa and the Diaspora*, Bloomington: Indiana University Press. (Argues that black women everywhere share conditions and issues which link them across their cultural differences.)

Miscellaneous references cited in text

Adejare, O. (1994) *Language and Style in Ṣoyinka: A Systemic Textlinguistic Study of a Literary Ideolect*, Ibadan: Heinemann.

Ashcroft, Bill, with Gareth Griffiths and Helen Tiffin (1989) *The Empire Writes Back: Theory and Practice in Post-Colonial Literatures*, London: Routledge.

Griffiths, G. (1997) 'Islands of Community: Autobiographical Accounts of Indian Displaced Communities: Subject, Community and Nation', in Marc Delrez and Bénédicte Ledent (eds), *The Contact and the Culture*, Liège Language and Literature Series, English Department, Liège University.

Hill, S. A. (1988) *In Pursuit of Publishing*, London: Jonathan Cape.

Pratt, M. L. (1992) *Imperial Eyes: Travel Writing and Transculturation*, London: Routledge.

Rollins, J. D. (1983) *A History of Swahili Prose*, Leiden: E. J. Brill.

Whitlock, G. (1992) 'Outlaws of the Text: Women's Bodies and the Organisation of Gender in Imperial space', Australia/Canada: Post-colonization and Women's Texts Conference, 13–16 Feb. 1992, Calgary Institute for the Humanities. (Unpublished conference paper, partly reproduced in Bill Ashcroft *et al.*, *The Post-Colonial Studies Reader*, London: Routledge, 1995: 349–54.)

Willett, John (ed.) (1964) *Brecht on Theatre*, London: Methuen.

Periodicals

There are a number of journals devoted almost entirely to the subject of African literatures. They include: *African Literature Today; Black Orpheus; Busara; Matatu; Okike; Présence Africaine; Research in African Literatures; Transition; Wasafiri;* and *Zuka.*

Numerous other general periodicals regularly publish material on African writing. They include: *Africa Today; Commonwealth: Essays and Studies; Journal of African Studies; Journal of Commonwealth Literature; Kunapipi, Nigeria Magazine; New African; New Literatures Review, West Africa; World Literature Written in English; Mots Pluriels, Jouvert.*

The many journals with a main focus on African-American Studies such as *Callalloo* and/or African-Caribbean Studies such as the *Journal of Caribbean Literatures* and the *Journal of Caribbean Studies* also publish material on African writing regularly, and can often be consulted with profit.

An excellent internet journal is *Mots Pluriel* edited by Jean-Marie Volet, accessible at www.arts.uwa.edu.au/MotsPluriels/. It covers anglophone/francophone texts.

Individual Authors: Notes on Biography, Important Works and Criticism

In the case of a few writers whose work I have cited in the text, bibliographical information is either limited or wholly unavailable, either because this was never recorded or does not appear in their works or in standard reference works. In these cases, I have used the form (n.a.) for information not available. The bibliographical sources on African writing are still incomplete and many of the standard reference texts are now out of date. For example, the once indispensable Zell Guide was last updated in 1983. Bernth M. Lindfors, that doyen of bibliographers of African literature, has continued to produce his monumental multi-volume bibliography, and anyone who wants to do in-depth work on any of these writers would do well to consult this foundational source. Without Lindfors's indefatigable labours it would have been impossible for much scholarly work on African English texts to have been undertaken in the last decades. But, even in these valuable reference sources, many writers, particularly those from countries where English is a minority language, or where publishing has been disrupted because of civil conflicts, such as Liberia, Sierra Leone, The Gambia, Ethiopia, Somalia etc., do not figure or have only incomplete entries. As a result, gaps remain. I have had no choice but to include an incomplete reference for these. I should be grateful if anyone with further information on any of these texts and writers could send it to me or the publishers so that I can include it in any future edition that might appear. A recent useful bibliographical source is C. B. Cox (ed.), *African Writers*, 2 vols, (New York: Scribners, 1997). There are bio-critical essays in this on many of the major writers covered in this volume. Each essay also has a useful current bibliography of primary and secondary sources.

In the entries below the following abbreviations are employed: A (Accra, Ghana), C (Cambridge, UK), Ca (Cambridge, Mass. USA), D (Dar es Salaam, Tanzania), L (London), E (Enugu, Nigeria), I (Ibadan, Nigeria), K (Kampala, Uganda), La (Lagos, Nigeria), N (Nairobi, Kenya), Ns (Nsukka, Nigeria), NY (New York), O (Oxford), W (Washington D.C.), Y (Yaoundé, Cameroons), *RAL* (*Research in African Literatures*), *ALT* (*African Literature Today*), *JCL* (*Journal of Commonwealth Literature*), *WLWE* (*World Literature Written in English*).

ACHEBE, Chinua (1930–) Born Albert Chinualumogu Achebe in Ogidi in Eastern Nigeria, where his father was a Christian catechist. Achebe was educated at Government College, Umuahia, a premier Nigerian secondary school, and at Ibadan University. Achebe is one of the best known African authors working in English. All his novels are set in Nigeria (although *Anthills of the Savannah* is set in a fictionalised country called Kangan, which bears an uncanny resemblance to Nigeria). Despite this strong local commitment, they have had a strong influence on writing in English across the continent, as well as making him a world-wide reputation. In many ways, his work set the models for the writing which emerged in the modern period in West and East Africa in forms such as the 'colonial contact' novel in *Things Fall Apart* (L, 1958) and *Arrow of God* (L, 1964); the novel about the problems facing returned educated Africans ('been-to's') *No Longer at Ease* (L, 1960); and in the novel of disillusionment with the new independence regimes *A Man of the People* (L, 1966). After leaving university, he worked for the Nigerian Broadcasting Corporation in various capacities, until the outbreak of the Nigerian Civil War in 1966. He was also the first editor of the influential Heinemann African Writers series, in which most of his work and all of his novels have appeared. The series became the single most important patron of new African English writing. When the Nigerian Civil War broke out in 1966, Achebe became a strong supporter of the breakaway Biafran state. During the war, he travelled abroad, raising money for the Biafran cause. After the war he lived in exile for a number of years, before returning to Nigeria and teaching at the University of Nigeria, at Nsukka in 1976. Currently Achebe teaches at Bard College, in the USA, where he is Charles P. Stevenson Jr. Professor of Languages and Literature. His most recent novel is *Anthills of the Savannah* (L, 1987). His other works include: *Beware Soul-brother, and Other Poems* (E, 1971), *Girls At War and Other Stories* (L, 1972) and *The Trouble With Nigeria* (L, 1984). Achebe has also published two collections of essays: *Morning Yet on Creation Day: Essays* (L, 1975) and *Hopes and Impediments: Selected Essays, 1965–1987* (L, 1988).

See: G. D. Killam, *The Novels of Chinua Achebe*, (L: Heinemann, 1969); David Carroll, *Chinua Achebe* (NY: Twayne, 1970); Robert M. Wren, *Achebe's World: The Historical and Cultural Context of the Novels of Chinua Achebe* (W: Three Continents, 1981); Bernth Lindfors (ed.), *Perspectives on Chinua Achebe* (W: Three Continents, 1978); G. Griffiths, 'Chinua Achebe: When Did You Last See Your Father?', *WLWE*, 27, 1 (Spring 1987); C. L. Innes, *Chinua Achebe* (C: Cambridge University Press, 1990); Simon Gikandi, *Reading Chinua Achebe* (L: James Currey, 1991); Kirsten Holst-Petersen, *Chinua Achebe: A Celebration* (Sydney: Dangaroo Press, 1991); Umelo Ojinmah, *Chinua Achebe: New Perspectives* (I: Spectrum Books, 1991); Ezenwa-Ohaeto, *Chinua Achebe: A Biography* (O: James Currey, 1997).

ADOKO, Akena (1931–) Born in Uganda, Adoko trained as a lawyer in the UK, before completing a degree in Anthropology in the USA. He worked as a public servant and as a lawyer, and was for a while President of the Law Society of Uganda. He has written several political studies, including *Coups and Corruption in Africa* (K, 1984) and *From Obote to Obote* (New Delhi, 1983). Like other African political scientists, Adoko turned to literary forms in *Uganda Crisis* (K, 1970). This example of the long poetic narratives which have emerged in East Africa is unusual in having the political history of Uganda as its subject.

AIDOO, Ama Ata (1942–) Born in Abeadzi Kyiako, in south-central Ghana, Ama Ata Aidoo attended Wesley Girls High School, and the University of Ghana, before beginning to work in early Ghanaian theatre with a fellow woman dramatist, Efua Sutherland. She graduated with a degree in English in 1964, and later was awarded a fellowship in creative writing at Stanford University, in the USA. After her return to Ghana in 1969, Aidoo worked for a while as an academic, and in 1982 held for a brief period of time the post of Minister of Education. In 1983 she left Ghana after quarrelling publicly with the policies of the government, settling in Harare, where she continues to teach and write. *The Dilemma of a Ghost* (L, 1965), *No Sweetness Here* (Harlow, 1970), *Anowa* (Harlow, 1970), *Our Sister Killjoy* (L, 1977), *Someone Talking to Sometime* (Harare, 1985), *The Eagle and the Chickens and Other Stories* (E, 1986), *Birds and Other Poems* (Harare, 1988), *Changes* (L, 1991; NY, 1993) and *An Angry Letter in January* (Coventry, 1992).

See: Vincent Odamtten, *The Art of Ama Ata Aidoo: Polylectics and Reading Against Colonialism* (Gainesville: University of Florida Press, 1994); Maryse Condé, 'Three Female Writers in Modern Africa: Flora Nwapa, Ama Ata Aidoo and Grace Ogot', *Présence Africaine*, 82 (1972): 132–44; Dapo Adelugba, 'Language and Drama: Ama Ata Aidoo', *ALT*, 8 (1976): 72–84.

AIG-IMOUKHUEDE, Frank (1935–) A Nigerian poet who writes mainly in pidgin. He belongs to the group of Nigerian writers who have sought to use pidgin as a vehicle to reach a mass audience. His work, although popular, also has a strong political message, and speaks out on behalf of ordinary Nigerians. *Pidgin Stew and Sufferhead* (I, 1982).

See: J. O. J Nwachukwu-Agbade, 'Form and Content in Nigerian Pidgin Poetry: The Pidgin Poetry of Aig-Imoukhuede and Mamman Vatsa', *Chelsea*, 46 (1987): 95–6.

AKAR, John (1927–) Sierra Leonean playwright, author of *Valley Without Echo* (L, 1954), the first African play to be performed in Britain.

AKARE, Thomas (1950–) Kenyan author of *The Slums* (L, N, 1981), one of the most graphic and uncompromising accounts of Nairobi slum life. He has also published *Twilight Woman* (N, 1988) which deals with prostitution in the new Kenya, and which was published in the popular Spear Books imprint.

ALUKO, T. M. (1918–) Aluko had published short stories in journals since the 1940s and his first novel, *One Man, One Wife* (L, 1959), was one of the first Nigerian novels to be published in Nigeria itself. His work was very much in the realist model which the new overseas publishers were seeking, and Heinemann quickly acquired him as one of its earliest regular writers. He published a further four novels with the Heinemann African Writers series: *One Man, One Matchet* (L, 1964), *Kinsman and Foreman* (L, 1966), *Chief the Honourable Minister* (L, 1970) and *His Worshipful Majesty* (L, 1973). They also reissued his first novel in 1967. His most recent novel is *Conduct Unbecoming* (I, 1993). An engineer by training, Aluko's novels detail the problems of post-independence Nigeria, stressing the clash of old and new values. However, they have only a very limited social or political project, their satire exposing the problems but offering no real insight into how they have come about. Nevertheless Aluko's work was very important in reinforcing the models and themes which dominated the early African English novel after Achebe.

AMADI, Elechi (1934–) Born in Aluu near Port Harcourt, in the Eastern coastal region of Nigeria, Amadi gained a degree in physics and mathematics from University College, Ibadan. His first work, *The Concubine* (L, 1966), was followed by *The Great Ponds* (L, 1969). His early work offers an even more rigorous attempt than Achebe's to portray pre-colonial life and recover it from the misrepresentation of the colonial period. He was detained twice during the civil war, and his *Sunset in Biafra* (L, 1973) details his experiences during the war. Amadi has also written a number of plays: *Isiburu* (L, 1973), *Peppersoup* and *The Road to Ibadan* (a combined volume, L, 1977) and *Dancer of Johannesburg* (L, 1978), and another novel, *Estrangement* (L, Portsmouth, USA, 1986), which again deals with the experience of being an Ibo who supported the Federal side during the civil war. In recent years, Amadi's work has suffered critical neglect, but it marks an important stage in the development of post-war African English writing.

See: Alastair Niven, 'The Achievement of Elechi Amadi', in Anna Rutherford, (ed.), *Commonwealth* (Aarhus, Denmark: Akademisk Boghandel, 1971); 'As Grasshoppers to Wanton Boys: The Role of the Gods in the Novels of Elechi Amadi', *African Literature Today*, 11 (1980): 97–109; Naana Banyiwa-Horne, 'African Womanhood: The Contrasting Perspectives of Flora Nwapa's *Efuru* and Elechi Amadi's *The Concubine*', in Carole Boyce Davies (ed.), *Ngambike: Studies of Women in African Literature* (Trenton, N.J.: Africa World Press, 1986); Wole Ogundele, 'Chance and Deterministic Irony in the Novels of Elechi Amadi', *WLWE*, 28 (1988): 189–203; Alfred Kiema, 'The Fantastic Narrative in Elechi Amadi's Works: Narrating and Narrator', *Commonwealth: Essays and Studies* 12, 2 (1990): 86–90; Ebele Eko, *Elechi Amadi: The Man and His Work* (Lagos: Kraft, 1990).

ANDRZEJEWSKI, B. W. (n.a.) A critic and translator who translated *Leopard Among the Women. Shabeelnaagood. A Somali Play* (L, NY, 1974). He has published a number of anthologies of Somali poetry, and texts on Somali language. He also translated the novel *Ignorance is the Enemy of Love*, by Faarax M. J. Cawl (see Cawl).

ANGIRA, Jared (1947–) One of the most distinguished and prolific of modern Kenyan poets, Angira has published several collections of poetry. He was educated at the University of Nairobi, where he edited the well-known literary magazine *Busara*. He was the founder of the Writers' Association of Kenya. His verse, though often lyrical and complex, also has a sharp political focus. His collections include: *Juices* (N, 1970), *Silent Voices* (L, I, N, 1972), *Soft Corals* (N, 1973), *Cascades* (Harlow, 1979), *The Years Go By: Poems* (N, 1980) and *Tides of Time: Selected Poems* (N, 1996).

See: Ezenwa-Ohaeto, 'Conscious Craft: Verbal Irony in the Poetry of Jared Angira', *RAL*, 27, 2 (1996).

ANYIDOHO, Kofi (1947–) Born in Ghana, Anyidoho is the author of several collections of poetry, including *Elegy for the Revolution* (NY, 1978), *A Harvest of our Dreams* (with a reissue of *Elegy for the Revolution* 1978) (L, I, N, 1984), *Earthchild with Brain Surgery* (1985) and *Ancestral Logic and Caribbean Blues* (1993). He has also edited several collections of essays and poetry anthologies, including *The Fate of Vultures*: *New Poetry of Africa*, with Musaemura Zimunya and Peter Porter, which anthologised the entries from the BBB Arts and Africa Poetry Award. He is a well-known academic critic, and he is also a theatre director who has produced many local and international plays at the theatres in Accra and at the University of Ghana, Legon. Anyidoho has been an active contributor to social debate in Ghana, writing frequently in journals and newspapers on controversial issues of the day.

See: Ezenwa-Ohaeto, 'Survival Strategies in Nigerian and Ghanaian Poetry: Osundare's *Waiting Laughters* and Anyidoho's *Earthchild*', *RAL*, 27, 2 (1996): 70–82.

ARMAH, Ayi Kwei (1939–) Born in Takoradi, Ghana, Armah was educated at Achimoto School and then went to Harvard in 1959, where he first studied literature and then sociology, before returning to Africa in 1963. He worked for a while in Algeria, but after a period of hospitalisation as the result of a nervous breakdown, Armah returned to Ghana. Few African writers have met with so much controversy. His early work was greeted by praise and abuse in almost equal proportions, and led to accusations by African critics that he had betrayed his culture by writing with disgust and disdain about its present condition. He was also accused of being a writer who had turned his back on African literary forms and themes and of being a copyist of modern European writers and forms. His later work was said to have been overly concerned with the self-inflicted horrors of the African past as opposed to the effects of outside influence on the development of historical movements such as slavery. To add fuel to the fire, he was even accused of reverse racism in his account of whites, especially his portrait of white women in his bitter and very violent novel *Why Are We So Blest?* (N, 1972; L, 1974). Armah has been strongly defended by others against all these various charges, including a rebuttal of the charge that his novels are Eurocentric in Derek Wright's book-length study, which details the local influences in Armah's work, and the defence of his work against charges of reverse racism by no less a figure than Ṣoyinka. Despite these persistent controversies, no one can deny the power and influence of his writing, nor that despite his long silence after the late 1970s, he has remained one of the giants of recent African English writing. His recently published novel, *Osiris Rising* (Popenguine, Senegal, 1995), breaks almost two decades of silence. A controversial and outspoken social critic, whose opinions forced him into political exile from Ghana, he has published a great deal of journalism and numerous short stories as well as his many novels. He is now living in Senegal, where he has begun working with a group of people involved in publishing African writing in Africa in the hope of regaining control of publishing networks in Africa. His other major novels are *The Beautiful Ones Are Not Yet Born* (NY, 1968; 1969; Oxford, 1988), *Fragments* (N, 1970; L, 1974), *Two Thousand Seasons* (N, 1973; L, 1979) and *The Healers: An Historical Novel* (N, 1978; L, 1979).

See: Derek Wright, *Ayi Kwei Armah's Africa: The Sources of His Fiction* (L: Zell, 1989); Derek Wright (ed.), *Critical Perspectives on Ayi Kwei Armah* (W: Three Continents Press, 1992).

ASFAW, Gebru (n.a.) Born in Ethiopia. His *Dung Hill* (Addis Ababa, 1992) is an example of the locally produced works to emerge after the civil war and the overthrow of the Mengistu regime in Ethiopia.

ASKAR, Ahmed Omar (1952–) Born in Somalia. His *Sharks and Soldiers* (private edn, pub. Finland 1992) is another example of the recent, self-published texts about the civil war in Somalia.

ASONG, Linus Tongwo (1947–) An Anglophone writer born in Cameroon. His works include *The Crown of Thorns* (Limbe, 1990), *Laughing Store* (Bamenda, 1993), *A Legend of the Dead* (Bamende, 1993) and *No Way to Die* (Bamende, 1993).

See: N. Lyova, Eckhardt Breitinger and Bole Butake (eds), *Anglophone Cameroon Writing*, Bayreuth African Studies No. 30 (Bayreuth: Breitinger, 1993).

AWOONOR, Kofi (aka George Awoonor-Williams) (1935–) Born in Wheta, Ghana, Awoonor is one of Africa's foremost poets, although his output is considerable in other areas, too, such as fiction, journalism and critical writing. His work in creating interlinguistic forms between traditional Ewe and modern poetry in English, has been an influential force on the work of many younger African writers. He was educated at UC Gold Coast (Legon), at London University and at SUNY at Stony Brook in the USA, and has held a number of academic posts, including numerous visiting professorships. An outspoken political activist, Awoonor was arrested in 1975, spending eight months in solitary confinement. In the 1980s, he continued to be a strong supporter of the revolutionary military government of Jerry Rawlings. He served the government in a number of domestic posts, as well as being appointed Ghanaian ambassador to Brazil, to Cuba and to the UN. His works include: *Rediscovery and other Poems* (I, 1964), *Night of My Blood* (NY, 1971), *Messages: Poems from Ghana* (L, 1971), *Raid Me, Memory* (NY, 1973), *Guardians of the Sacred Word: Ewe Poetry* (NY, 1974), *The House by the Sea* (NY, 1978), *Until the Morning After–Collected Poems 1963–85* (NY, L, A, 1987) and *The Latin America and Caribbean Notebook* (Trenton, N.J., 1992).

See: Kofi Awoonor, 'Voyager and the Earth', *New Letters*, 40, 1 (Autumn 1973); Kofi Anyidoho, 'Kofi Awoonor and the Ewe Tradition of Songs of Abuse (Halo)', in Richard Priebe (ed.), *Ghanaian Literatures* (Westport, Conn.: Greenwood Press, 1988).

BANDELE-THOMAS, Biyi (1967–) This recent young Nigerian author has had great success there and overseas, with *The Man Who Came in from the Back of Beyond* (O, 1992; originally pub. L, 1991), *The Sympathetic Undertaker and other Dreams* (O, 1991), *Marching for Fausa* (O, 1993) and *Resurrections in the Season of the Longest Drought* (L, 1994). His work combines traditional features with a post-modern sensibility which gives it both a local and an international appeal. He has also published poems in a number of literary magazines and anthologies. Although he has not yet received the international attention of a writer like Ben Okri, he shares with him a powerful way of combining Nigerian themes and culture, with a style which has a wider international appeal. Significantly, all his work so far has been published in the UK.

BESONG, Bate (1954–) A noted Cameroonian Anglophone writer, he has published several volumes of poetry and a number of plays while working as a teacher. *Polyphemous Detainee and Other Skulls* (Uyo, Nigeria, 1980), *Beasts of No Nation* (Limbe, 1980), *The Most Cruel Death of the Talkative Zombie* (Limbe, 1986), *Requiem for the Last Kaiser* (Calabar, 1991), *Obasinjom Warrior: With Poems After Detention* (Limbe, 1991?) and *The Banquet* (Makurdi, Nigeria, 1994).

See: N. Lyova, Eckhardt Breitinger and Bole Butake (eds), *Anglophone Cameroon Writing*, Bayreuth African Studies No. 30 (Bayreuth: Breitinger, 1993).

BLYDEN, E. W. (1832–1912) Perhaps the most outspoken and radical of the West African Creole intellectuals of the nineteenth century, Blyden was born in the West Indies but settled in Sierra Leone. He was expelled from there when he quarrelled with the colonial authorities and their conservative Creole supporters. Blyden was one of the first African intellectuals to assert the role of Islam as a signifier of opposition to European colonial power. He was also a precursor of the twentieth-century idea of négritude in his passionate espousal of the qualities and distinctiveness of Negro culture and people. *Christianity, Islam and the Negro Race* (1887; Edinburgh, 1967); *Black Spokesman: Selected Published Writings of Edward Wilmot Blyden*, ed. Hollis R. Lynch (L: Cass, 1971).

See: R. W. July, *The Origins of Modern African Thought: Its Development in West Africa During the Nineteenth and Twentieth Centuries* (L: Faber, 1968).

BUTAKE, Bole (1960–) An Anglophone Cameroonian playwright and theatre director, he teaches African Literature and Theatre in the Department of Literature of the University of Yaoundé. *Betrothal Without Libation* (Y: 1981), *The Rape of Michelle* (Y, 1984), *Lake God* (Y, 1986), *The Survivors* (Y, 1989) and *And Palm-Wine Will Flow* (Y, 1990).

See: N. Lyonga, Eckhardt Breitinger and Bole Butake (eds), *Anglophone Cameroon Writing*, Bayreuth African Studies No. 30 (Bayreuth: Breitinger, 1993).

CASELY HAYFORD, Adelaide (1868–1960) The wife of J. E. Caseley Hayford, she was a leading advocate of women's rights and of schooling for girls in West Africa, establishing a school for girls which she ran herself. Although she outlived her husband by more than thirty years and was a well-known and much respected figure in Freetown, her poems were not collected in her lifetime and have only recently been issued, together with a memoir in L. Hunter (ed.), *Mother and Daughter: Memoirs and Poems by Adelaide Casely Hayford and Gladys Casely Hayford* (Freetown, 1983). Casely Hayford's daughter, Gladys May, had already published poems in English and Krio in *Take 'um so* (Freetown: New Era Press, 1948).

See: A. M. Cromwell, *An African Victorian Feminist: The Life and Times of Adelaide Smith Casely Hayford 1868–1960* (L: Cass, 1986).

CASELY HAYFORD, Joseph Ephraim (1866–1930). The author of *Ethiopia Unbound* (L, 1911), one of the earliest long fictional West African narratives in English, J. E. Casely Hayford was also a lawyer, scholar, novelist, and formidable statesman. He published widely in the fields of jurisprudence, history and political science. He was a leading contributor to many of the journals and newspapers which sprang up in West Africa in the late nineteenth century, and the editor of the influential *Western Echo*. He was a moving figure in the creation of a unified national opposition to the colonisation of his native Gold Coast and a convenor of the first meeting of the Congress of British West Africa in 1920 (see Danquah). Elected to the Ghana Legislative Council in 1927. His decision to pursue a gradualist, compromise position, on key issues such as the Native Administration Ordinance legislation, lost him many followers, but he continued to write in journals until his death in 1930. His wife Adelaide was one of the earliest and most influential advocates for women's rights and for women's education in Africa. Together, they had an incalculable effect on the shaping of modern African thought. *Gold Coast Native Institutions with Thoughts Upon a Healthy Imperial Policy for the Gold Coast and Ashanti* (L, 1903; reissued L: Cass, 1970), *Ethiopia Unbound: Studies in Race Emancipation* (L, 1911; reissued L: Cass, 1969), *The Truth about the West African Land Question* (L, 1913; reissued L: Cass, 1971), *William Waddy Harris, the West African Reformer: the Man and His Message* (L, 1915), *United West Africa* (L, 1919) and *The Disabilities of Black Folk and Their Treatment, with an Appeal to the Labour Party* (L, 1929).

See: R. W. July, *The Origins of Modern African Thought: Its Development in West Africa during the Nineteenth and Twentieth Centuries* (L: Faber, 1968); Magnus J. Sampson, *Gold Coast Men of Affairs* (1937; reissued L: Dowson, 1969).

CAWL, Faarax Maxamed Jaamac(1937–) Somali novelist born in Sanag, he trained in London as an engineer and later became a colonel in the Somali police force. Cawl writes in Somali using the new script established in 1972 which allowed the language to be written for the first time. His novel *Ignorance is the Enemy of Love* (*Aqoondarro waa u nacab jacayl*) (L, 1982) has been widely disseminated in an English translation. His novel had a phenomenal success in Somalia, selling 10,000 copies in six months. He has published several other books in Somali including non-fictional works such as *The Shackles of Colonialism* (Paris: UNESCO, 1978). His novel is notably free of the internal criticisms of the society which characterise the work of English-language Somali writers like Farah and Osman. It concentrates on a personal love story with little or no problematic social contextualisation. In many ways the work resembles the early 'celebrating the culture' texts from West and East Africa of the 1950s and early 1960s.

CHEYNEY-COKER, Syl (1945–) Born in Freetown, the capital of Sierra Leone, Cheyney-Coker has worked as a teacher, journalist and radio producer. Educated in Liberia and the USA, he taught for many years at Maiduguri in Nigeria. His poetry has appeared in numerous American journals. He has published also the following poetry collections: *Concerto for an Exile* (L, 1973), *The Graveyard also has Teeth* with *Concerto for an Exile* (L, 1980), and *The Blood in the Desert's Eyes*, as well as the long poetic novel *The Last Harmattan of Alusine Dunbar* (L, 1990) which won the African Commonwealth Writers Prize. In the early 1990s he started the fortnightly newspaper *The Vanguard* in Sierra Leone but the coup of 1991 and the following civil strife makes it difficult to find details of this venture.

See: 'The Poetry of Syl Cheney-Coker: The Blood in the Desert's Eyes', *ALT*, 20, (1996): 151–7.

CLARK-BEKEDEREMO, John Pepper (1935–) Born in Kiagbodo in the Ijo region of the Niger Delta in Nigeria, John Pepper Clark or Clark-Bekederemo, as he is known now, is one of Africa's most influential poets, dramatists and literary critics. He edited the very important student journal *The Horn* at Ibadan University in 1957–58, at a time when many of the most important later figures in Nigerian literature were undergraduates there. After attending Ibadan University, he did postgraduate work in America. He then taught at the University of Lagos, where he was Head of the Department of English until his retirement in 1980. Clark-Bekederemo's poetry and plays include: *Poems* (I, 1962), *Three Plays: Song of a Goat, The Masquerade, The Raft* (L, 1964), *A Reed in the Tide* (L, 1965) and *Ozidi* (L, 1966). *A Reed in the Tide* was the first volume of poetry to be published abroad by a single African poet. He later published an influential translation of the traditional saga, *The Ozidi Saga* (I, 1977), which had a great influence on the modern revaluation of oral Nigerian culture. He has also written an early autobiography detailing his student years in America: *America, their America* (L, 1964). His pro-Federal stance during the civil war led to an active criticism in the years which followed, which centred on his defence of his views in the poetry he wrote at the time. More recent poetry collections include: *State of the Union* (Harlow, 1985) and *Mandela and Other Poems* (Ikeja, Nigeria, 1988). He has also been an active theatre practitioner in Lagos for many years.

See: Robert M. Wren, *J. P. Clark* (Boston: G. K. Hall, 1984); Nyong J. Udeoyop, *Three Nigerian Poets: A Critical Study of Ṣoyinka, Clark and Okigbo* (I: Ibadan U.P., 1973); Kirsten Holst-Petersen, 'A Critical View of J. P. Clark's *A Decade of Tongues: Selected Poems 1958–1968*', *Nexus Critical Views* (L: Collins/The British Council, 1981); Dan Izevbaye, 'J. P. Clark-Bekederemo and the Ijo Literary Tradition', *RAL*, 25, 1 (Spring 1994): 1–21.

COLE, Robert (1907?–) Author of an early Sierra Leonean novel, *Kossah Town Boy* (C, 1960), which portrays village life.

CONTON, William (1925?–) Born in The Gambia in the early 1920s (sources give his birth date variously as 1920 or 1925), Conton has lived for most of his life elsewhere, first in

Accra, Ghana, where he was a headmaster, and then in Sierra Leone, where he also worked as an educationalist. He now lives in Paris. His contribution to African literature consists mainly of *The African* (L, 1960), one of the earliest African novels, and, more recently, *The Flights* (I, 1987). He has also written short stories.

CROWTHER, Samuel Ajayi (or Samwel Adjai) (1806?–1891) Crowther was one of the first graduates of Fourah Bay College, Sierra Leone, and went on to have a distinguished career as an Anglican churchman, ending up as the first African Anglican bishop. He, and other members of his family, founded the first Anglican missions in Nigeria at Abeokuta and elsewhere. He wrote many grammars and primers of West African languages for use by missionaries. He also translated the New Testament and the Book of Common Prayer into Yoruba. Although in the early part of his life he showed a certain zealousness, for example in destroying African religious idols and sacred sites, he also displayed a keen interest in and awareness of the importance and meaningfulness of local custom. He often found himself at odds with powerful local white missionaries such as Henry Townsend. As a result of the increasing alienation he felt from the attitude of the Church and the colonial authorities, he became a supporter of African independence in Church matters and by implication in matters of secular self-governance. After a series of quarrels with Anglican Church authorities, Crowther helped found a separate diocese in what is now Nigeria. His accounts of his early mission travels along the Niger–Tshadde River complex are amongst the most important examples of early African English writing. His works include: *Journals of the Rev. James Frederick Schon and Mr. Samuel Crowther: who, with the sanction of Her Majesty's Government, accompanied the expedition up the Niger in 1841 on behalf of the Church Missionary Society*, 2nd edn. with a new introduction by J. F. Ade Ajayi (L, 1970); Crowther, Samuel Adjai and John Christopher Taylor (1806–1891), *Journal of an Expedition up the Niger and Tshadda Rivers Undertaken by Macgregor Laird in conjunction with the British Government in 1854* (1855; reissued L, 1970 ed. with an introd. by J. F. Ade Adjai), *The Gospel on the Banks of the Niger: Journals and Notices of the Native Missionaries Accompanying the Niger Expedition of 1857–1859* (1859; reissued L, 1968).

See: David Sweetman, *Bishop Crowther* (London: Longman, 1981); John Milsome, *From Slave Boy to Bishop: The Story of Samuel Adjai Crowther* (Cambridge: Lutterworth, 1987); Adrian Hastings, *The Church in Africa: 1450–1950* (Oxford: Clarendon Press; New York: Oxford University Press, 1994).

CRUMMELL, Alexander (1819–1898) Born a free man in New York in 1819, he took orders in the Episcopal Church. A formative member in the Negro Convention Movement, at its National Convention in 1847 he endorsed 'moral persuasion' as 'the best means to abolish slavery'. In 1948, he went to England to raise funds for the abolitionist cause, and went to Cambridge University to study. Initially, like other black leaders, he opposed the Liberian venture, but in 1852 he migrated there as a teacher. He founded an African church in Liberia and became a noted educationalist in the settlement. Internal conflicts led to a split with his friend and colleague Edward Blyden, and after the revolution of 1871, he left Liberia. Collections of sermons, such as *The Greatness of Christ* (NY, 1882), and of occasional talks, such as *Africa and America* (Springfield, 1891), made Crummell one of the most widely read Afro-American authors of his day.

See: Gregory U. Rigsby, *Alexander Crummell: Pioneer in Nineteenth-Century Pan-African Thought* (NY: Greenwood Press, 1987); J. R. Oldfield, *Alexander Crummell and the Creation of an African-American Church in Liberia* (Lampeter: Edwin Mellen Press, 1990), *Civilization and Black Progress: Selected Writings of Alexander Crummell on the South*, ed. J. R. Oldfield (Charlottesville, Va.: University Press of Virginia, 1995).

CUGUANO, Ottobah (1757?–not recorded) Probably born in Adjimoko in Fanti territory *c.* 1757, in what is now Ghana. Cuguano, after being freed from slavery, published in London a tract against the slave trade which includes an account of his capture, *Thoughts and Sentiments on the Evil and Wicked Traffic of Slavery 1787*. The text has been controversial, with some scholars arguing that it is the work of two distinct writers. Others have suggested that Olaudah Equiano may have had a hand in its composition as he was a friend of Cuguano. (See entry on Equiano.)

DANQUAH, J. B. (Joseph Boakye) (1895–1965) Ghanaian nationalist leader and author. Born into a chieftainly family, Danquah was educated in London as a lawyer. He wrote several of the earliest studies of local African law, such as *Akan Laws* (L, 1928). A prominent early Gold Coast politician, he founded, with Casely Hayford, the first National Congress of British West Africa in 1920. In 1929, through organisations such as the Gold Coast Youth Conference, he and Casely Hayford forged links with the traditional chiefs which averted a split in nationalist ranks. He was also a well-known journalist, editing the influential *Times of West Africa* in the early 1930s. In the run up to independence, Danquah argued for a gradualist approach, opposing the confrontationist, mass action politics of Nkrumah. He remained Nkrumah's principal opponent after independence, leading the opposition party. Arrested after an attempt against Nkrumah's life, in which the government claimed his party was implicated, Danquah died in jail in 1964, allegedly from a deliberate lack of suitable treatment for his chronic medical condition. As well as his early legal texts, he published a foundational study of African ideas and culture, in *The Akan Doctine of God* (L, 1944). He also wrote several plays. In Twi, he published *Nyankonsem* (A, 1941), and, in English, *The Third Woman* (L, 1943), another example of how early nationalists could appropriate existing patronages since this latter play was published by a missionary press.

See: L. H. Ofosu-Appiah, *The Life and Times of Dr. J. B. Danquah* (Accra: Waterville Publishing House, 1974).

DE GRAFT, J. C. (1924–1978) Born in the Gold Coast, De Graft combined his work as a teacher with his passion for theatre and performance, establishing himself as a profoundly influential founding figure in the performing arts in Ghana. He also wrote poetry. His published work includes *Sons and Daughters* (L, A, 1964), *Visitor From the Past* (A, 1968), *Through a Film Darkly* (L, I, A, 1970), *Beneath the Jazz and Brass* (L, 1975) and *Muntu* (L, N, 1977). A number of his plays were produced but not published. These include *Village Investment* (1962), *Ananse and the Gum Man* (1965) (which he also adapted to a film in 1965 under the title *No Tears for Ananse)* and *Mambo* (an adaptation of *Macbeth*) (1978). He also made a film version of *Hamlet*, adapted to Ghana and called *Hamile* (1965).

DEMPSTER, Roland Tombekai (1910–1965) Born in Tosoh, Liberia. After being educated at mission schools, he became editor of the *Liberian Age* in 1948–54. He later worked as a civil servant, and in 1948–60 was Professor of History, Literature and Creative Writing at the University of Liberia. Much of Dempster's work is characterised by a strongly patriotic tone, supporting the Creole establishment and the government of long-time President Tubman, for example *To Monrovia Old and New* (L, 1958) and the collection he published for the inauguration of President Tolbert, the short-lived successor to President Tubman, *A Song Out of Midnight* (M, 1960).

DENEKE, Yemani (n.a.) *In the Mirror of Love* (Addis Ababa, self-published, n.d.) is an example of the many self-published texts in English which have appeared from time to time in Ethiopia, where English has remained a minority language of expression.

DENG, Francis Mading (1938–) Born in the Sudan, Deng has had a distinguished career as a political scientist and as a diplomat, representing his country in various ambassadorial positions. He has also written two novels: *Seed of Redemption: A Political Novel* (NY, 1986) and *Cry of the Owl* (NY, 1989). More recently, in collaboration with Abdullahi Ahmed An-Naim, Deng edited a collection of essays addressing cross-cultural issues, *Human Rights in Africa: Cross-Cultural Perspectives* (W: The Brookings Institution, *c.* 1990).

DIBBA, Ebou (1943–) Born in The Gambia. One of the new group of writers to emerge in this country in the 1980s, and perhaps the most accomplished. Dibba was first encouraged to write by Lenrie Peters. His first novel was *Chaff on the Wind* (L, 1986). He has published a sequel entitled *Fafa: An Idyll on the Banks of a River* (Basingstoke, 1989), and a third novel *Alhaji* (Basingstoke, 1992).

See: Stewart Brown, 'Gambian Fictions', *Wasafiri*, (Spring 1992).

DIOP, David (1927–1960). Born in France of Cameroonian and Senegalese parents. Diop's early death meant that only a small collection of poetry was published in his lifetime: *Coups de Pilon* (Paris, 1956).

DIPOKO, Mbella Sonne (1936–) Born in the Cameroons, his work includes: *A Few Nights and Days* (L, 1966), *Because of Women* (L, 1968; African Writers series 1970) and *Black and White in Love* (L, 1972). Although he wrote in English he has never really been part of the recent emerged group of politically active Anglophone writers. His work reflects more the themes and styles of the Francophone Cameroonian writers of the early period.

See: Richard Bjornson, *The African Quest for Freedom and Identity: Cameroonian Writing and the National Experience* (Bloomington: Indiana University Press, 1991).

DOUGLASS, Frederick (1817–1895) Born into slavery, Douglass escaped in 1838. Thereafter he devoted his life to the abolitionist movement. A scholar, autobiographer, editor and author of novellas, he is considered one of the foundational nineteenth-century black American writers. He wrote several autobiographical works at different stages of his life, and also many polemic articles and speeches in favour of abolition. *My Bondage and My Freedom* (1855; NY, 1968).

See: *Frederick Douglass: Selections from his Writings*, ed. Philip S. Foner (NY: International Publishers, 1945); Philip S. Foner, *The Life and Writings of Frederick Douglass* (NY: International Publishers, 1950–55).

DU BOIS, W. E. B. (1868–1963) Influential black American leader. He founded Niagara, the first black protest movement, in 1905 and also helped found the National Association for the Advancement of Coloured People in 1909. He edited *Crisis*, the Association's influential magazine, which exposed the brutal treatment of blacks by whites in the American South. He wrote a number of fictional works, but he is best known as a polemicist and as an author of numerous historical and sociological studies of black culture. These include the influential essay collection, *The Souls of Black Folks* (Chicago, 1903). A gradualist, who supported negotiated integration, he was, to some extent, left behind in the early 1920s by the more extreme wing of the Black Movement, led by Marcus Garvey. This quiet, scholarly and moderate man was, at the end of his life, hounded from America by the McCarthyite, anti-Communist witchhunt and died in Ghana, after renouncing his American citizenship.

DUKE, Antera (n.a.) *Efik Traders of Old Calabar*, ed. Daryll Forde, (1902; reissued L, 1956). One of the earliest examples of English usage in West Africa in a modern edition.

EASMON, R. Sarif (1913–) Born in Sierra Leone of Creole and Susu descent, Easmon trained as a medical doctor in the UK. Upon his return to Sierra Leone, where he practiced medicine in Freetown, he became a prominent public figure, active in politics and the arts. His play *Dear Parent and Ogre* (L, 1994) was directed by Wọle Ṣoyinka in Ibadan in 1961, and it was followed by another play *The New Patriots* (L, 1965). He has also written a collection of short stories called *The Feud* (Harlow, 1981) and a novel entitled *A Burnt Out Marriage* (L, 1967).

EBY, Omar (1935–) Eby was born in Maryland in the USA and graduated from Syracuse University and the University of Virginia. He taught for several years in Africa in Somalia, in Tanzania and in Zambia. Most of Eby's work has been in non-fiction or in the translation of Somalian tales. He published *The Sons of Adam: Stories of Somalia* (Scottdale, USA, 1970). His other books include a biography of a Somali Muslim martyr *A Whisper in a Dry Land* (Scottdale, 1968), *Sense and Incense* (Scottdale, 1965), *A Long Dry Season*, and *How Full the River* (Scottdale, 1972). He teaches writing and literature in Virginia.

EGBUNA, Obi (1938–) Nigerian-born writer and political activist, his work has been the focus of much controversy. A prolific writer of short stories, plays and many polemic pieces, his work includes *Wind Versus Polygamy* (L, 1964); *Daughters of the Sun and Other Stories* (L, NY, 1970) and *The Madness of Didi* (L, 1980).

EKWENSI, Cyprian (1921–) Although both his parents were Ibos from the Eastern region of Nigeria, Ekwensi was born in Minna, Northern Nigeria. He trained as a forestry officer, working first in that capacity and later as a teacher. Since 1957, he has worked as a radio journalist for the Nigerian Broadcasting Corporation. His first written work was published in the Onitsha Market in the late 1940s, when popular pamphleteering and fiction was developed in the post-war period. A prolific author, who has never lost his sense of writing for the 'ordinary people', Ekwensi has written novels, short stories and children's books, a combined output few other African authors can match. His work often received mixed reviews, however, and the early critical perception of Ekwensi's work as being too close to a populist aesthetics may be said to account for this. In recent years, his work has been given far more attention and his place as one of the earliest proponents of a popular writing, as well as the founder of the modern city novel in Africa, has received its proper due. His huge output of works includes: *Ikolo the Wrestler and Other Ibo Tales* (L, NY, 1947), *When Love Whispers* (Onitsha, Nigeria, 1948), *People of the City* (L, 1954), *Jagua Nana* (L, 1961), *Burning Grass* (L, 1962), *Beautiful Feathers* (L, 1963), *Lokotown and Other Stories* (L, 1966), *Iska* (L, 1966), *Survive the Peace* (L, 1976), *Divided We Stand* (Enugu, Nigeria, 1980), *For a Roll of Parchment* (I, 1986) and *Jagua Nana's Daughter* (I, 1986). In addition, he wrote a host of children's stories, folklore collections and short story collections, as well as innumerable articles and reviews. In many ways he is the *doyen* of African professional writers, turning his hand to any and every opportunity that came his way for a half-century or more, including working as a journalist and editor on a number of newspapers. In 1981 he was appointed Managing Director of a new paper, *The Weekly Eagle*, in Imo state. The important role he played in breaking down the false barriers between so-called popular and elite writing is now being slowly appreciated.

See: Ernest Emenyonu, *Cyprian Ekwensi* (L: Evans Bros., 1974); Loretta A. Hawkins, 'The Free Spirit of Ekwensi's Jagua Nana', *ALT*, 10 (1979): 202–6; Ernest Emenyonu (ed.), *The Essential Ekwensi* (I: Heinemann Nigeria, 1987).

EMECHETA, Buchi (1944–) Nigerian novelist, who began her writing career publishing articles in London newspapers. Emecheta has produced a huge amount of work in a relatively short time. Despite her international acclaim, her tendency to alternate more serious works with potboilers has led to critical disputes about her importance. It is arguable, however, that few writers have dealt with the experience of Nigerian/migrant women in Britain as well as she has. It is also arguable that with *The Joys of Motherhood* she put the capstone on the argument constructed by women's writing from Nwapu's early work onwards, and made it impossible for critics any longer to deny the power and difference of African women's writing. Her reception was contentious, with critics arguing about the merit of her work and about its truthfulness to African experience. Opinions were often sharply divided according to the gender of the participants. Supported by many Western feminist critics, Emecheta's work has also figured large in the more recent debates about whether the aims and forms of African women's writing are congruent or not with the aims and forms of the international feminist movement. Her books include: *In the Ditch* (L, 1972), *Second Class Citizen* (L, 1974; reissued O, 1994), *The Bride Price* (NY, 1976), *The Slave Girl* (L, 1977), *The Joys of Motherhood* (L, 1979), *Our Own Freedom* with Maggie Murray (L, 1981), *Destination Biafra: A Novel* (L, NY, 1982), *Naira Power*

(L, 1982), *Double Yoke* (L, Ibuza, Nigeria, 1983), *The Rape of Shavi* (L, 1983; NY, 1985), *A Kind of Marriage* (L, 1986), *Double Yolk* (L, 1989), *Gwendolen* (L, 1989; retitled and reissued as *The Family* NY, 1990), *Kehinde* (L, 1994), and her autobiography *Head Above Water* (L, 1988; reissued O, 1994). Her children's books include *Titch the Cat* (L, 1979), *Nowhere to Play* (L, 1980), *The Moonlight Bride* (O, 1980; NY, 1983) and *The Wrestling Match* (O, 1980; NY, 1983).

See: Donna Haraway, 'Reading Buchi Emecheta: Contests for Women's Experience in Women's Studies', *Women: A Cultural Review*, 1, 3 (Winter 1990); Eustace Palmer, 'The Feminine Point of View: Buchi Emecheta's *The Joys of Motherhood*' *ALT*, 13 (1983); Fẹmi Ojo-Ade, 'Female Writers, Male Critics', *ALT*, 13 (1983); Eneogu Afam, 'Enter the Iconoclast: Buchi Emecheta and the Igbo Culture' *Commonwealth Essays and Studies*, 7, 2 (1985): 83–94; Kirsten Holst-Petersen, 'Unpopular Opinions: Some African Women Writers', *Kunapipi*, 7, 2–3 (1985); Christina Davis, 'Mother and Writer: Means of Empowerment in the Work of Buchi Emecheta', *Commonwealth Essays and Studies*, 13, 1 (1990): 13–21; Rose Ure Mezu, 'Buchi Emecheta's "The Bride Price" and "The Slave Girl": A Schizoanalytic Perspective', *Ariel*, 28, 1 (1997); Marie Umeh (ed.), *Emerging Perspectives on Buchi Emecheta* (Trenton, N.J.: Africa World Press, 1996); Katherine Fishburn, *Reading Buchi Emecheta: Cross-Cultural Conversations* (Westport, Conn.: Greenwood Press, 1995).

EPIE'NGOME, Victor (1947–) *What God Has Put Asunder* (Y, 1992). Another of the many Anglophone Cameroonian writers whose work seeks to defend the distinctiveness of Anglophonic culture.

See: N. Lyonga, Eckhardt Breitinger and Bole Butake (eds), *Anglophone Cameroon Writing*, Bayreuth African Studies No. 30 (Bayreuth: Breitinger, 1993).

EQUIANO, Olaudah (aka Gustavus Vassa the African) (1745?–1797) Probably born in Isseke, modern-day Essaka, near Onitsha. The most famous written text by an ex-slave is *The Interesting Narrative of Olaudah Equiano, or Gustavus Vassa the African, Written by Himself* published in two volumes in London in 1789. The late Paul Edwards, who devoted many years to the study of Equiano's work, called it 'the most authentic of several slave narratives published in the late eighteenth century'. Equiano was, as his name suggests, an Ibo. After being captured and sold in the West Indies, he was sold as a slave in America, and after a struggle to obtain and keep his letters of manumission he settled in England. He was a well-known figure in late eighteenth-century London, and after the publication of the *Life* he was something of a celebrity and a spokesman for the black community in eighteenth-century Britain. He was involved with Granville Sharpe in the Sierra Leone project, being appointed commissary for stores, but he withdrew from the enterprise after a dispute about the propriety of its management. His life, published in 1789, was a great success and Equiano was much in demand as a speaker by anti-slavery groups.

See: Paul Edwards, 'Equiano's Round Unvarnished Tale', *African Literature Today*, 5 (1971): 12–20; Paul Edwards, 'Black Writers of the Eighteenth Century', in David Dabydeen (ed.), *The Black Presence in English Literature* (Manchester: Manchester U.P., 1985): 50–67; Catherine Obianuju Acholonu, *The Igbo Roots of Olaudah Equiano* (Owerri, Nigeria: AFA, 1989).

EYOH, Hansel Ndumbe (n.a.) Anglophone Cameroonian writer and academic, teaches at the University of Yaoundé. *Munyenge* (Y, 1990) and *The Inheritance* (Y, 1993).

See: N. Lyonga, Eckhardt Breitinger and Bole Butake (eds), *Anglophone Cameroon Writing*, Bayreuth African Studies No. 30 (Bayreuth: Breitinger, 1993).

EZENWA-OHAETO (n.a.) An Ibo poet and critic from the Eastern region of Nigeria. The author of the collection of poetry in pidgin *I Wan Bi President* (Enugu, Nigeria, 1988) and several other collections, such as *The Voice of the Night Masquerade: Poems* (I, 1996). An influential critic, who teaches at Alvan Ikoku College of Education in Owerri, Ezenwa-Ohaeto has championed the use of pidgin in modern Nigerian verse and seen it as a language which can speak for ordinary Nigerians against corruption and the politics of elites. He also edited the essay collection *Making Books Available and Affordable* (1995). Also the author of the influential essay *Contemporary Nigerian Poetry and the Poetics of Orality* (Bayreuth, 1997). He has just published an authorised biography of Achebe, *Chinua Achebe: A Biography* (O: James Currey, 1997).

See: J. O. J., Nwachukwu-Agbada, 'The Eighties and the Return to Oral Cadences in Nigerian Poetry', *Matatu*, 10 (African Literature in the Eighties) (1993).

FAGUNWA, D. O. (1910–1963) Prolific Nigerian writer who wrote in Yoruba. Part of one of his major novels (*Ògbójú Ode Nínú Igbó Irúnmálè* or The Skilful Hunter in the Forest of Four Hundred Spirits) has been translated into English by Wọle Ṣoyinka as *The Forest of a Thousand Daemons* (L, 1968; New Jersey, 1969), and in this form it has reached a wide audience outside Nigeria. Fagunwa wrote some ten novels in Yoruba as well as numerous short stories. Most of his Yoruba texts were published by Nelson, Edinburgh, or by Oxford University Press; they include his most popular work in Nigeria entitled *Igbó Olúdùmarè* (Forest of the Lord), the second part of *Ògbójú: Àdììtú Olúdùmarè* (God's Secret); and *Ìrìnkèrindó Nínú Igbó Elégbèje* (Adventures in the Forest of Elegbeje). He died in a car accident in 1963 aged only 53.

See: Ayo Bamgbose, *The Novels of D. O. Fagunwa* (Benin City, Nigeria: Ethiope, 1974); Karin Barber, 'Time, Space and Writing in Three Colonial Yoruba Novels', *The Yearbook of English Studies*, 27 (1997): 1089–129; Ato Quayson, *Strategic Transformations in Nigerian Writing: Orality and History in the work of Rev. Samuel Johnson, Amos Tutuola, Wọle Ṣoyinka and Ben Okri* (Oxford: James Currey, 1997); Olakunle George, 'Compound of Spells: the Predicament of D. O. Fagunwa (1903–1963)', *RAL* Special Issue: The Oral-Written Interface, 28, 1 (Spring 1997): 78–97.

FANON, Frantz (1925–1961) Born in Martinique, the short span of his life belies the influence his work has had over a generation of post-colonial writers from all over the world. His major works are: *Peau Noire, Masques Blancs* (Paris, 1952) (tr. as *Black Skin, White Masks* (L, 1968)), *Les Damnes de la Terre* (Paris, 1961) (tr. as *The Wretched of the Earth* (L, 1963)). These remain crucial and often discussed analyses of the predicament of the colonised subject. Other important works include: *Sociologie d'une Revolution: L'An Cinq de la Revolution Algerienne* (Paris, 1952) (tr. as *A Dying Colonialism* (Harmondsworth, 1970)). A collection of his essays has also been translated: *Towards the African Revolution: Political Essays*, tr. Haakon Chevalier (NY: Grove Press, 1967).

See: David Caute, *Fanon* (L: Fontana, 1970); L. Adele Jinadu, *Fanon: In Search of the African Revolution* (L: Kegan Paul Int., 1986); B. Marie Perinbam, *Holy Violence: The Revolutionary Thought of Frantz Fanon: An Intellectual Biography* (W: Three Continents Press, 1982); Hussein Abdilahi Bulhan, *Frantz Fanon and the Psychology of Oppression* (NY: Plenum Press, *c.* 1985); Jock McCulloch, *Colonial Psychiatry and 'the African mind'* (C, NY: Cambridge University Press, 1995).

FARAH, Nuruddin (1945–) Farah is amongst the best-known and most powerful of English African writers, despite the relative paucity of Somali writing in the language. The first Somali author to be published in English, Farah is by far the best-known and most prolific Somali working in that language today. Born in Baidoa in the Ogaden region, Farah studied in Somalia, and then read philosophy at Chandigarh University in India. He then attended Essex and London Universities. Whilst in India, he married an Indian woman and wrote his first novel, *From A Crooked Rib*. Farah has lived in exile in Europe and in various African countries since shortly after the emergence of Siyad Barre's regime. This long enforced absence and the repressive and violent history of Somalia in recent decades has meant that he did not have the direct influence on English writing there which he might otherwise have done. His work is clearly better known and more influential elsewhere in Africa than at home. The linked themes which predominate in his work are a consistent opposition to Barre's dictatorial regime, and to the violence and oppression he sees as characterising modern Somali society; and a concern with the powerless position of women in Somali culture. His major works are: *From a Crooked Rib* (L, 1970), *A Naked Needle* (L, 1976), *Sweet and Sour Milk* (L, 1979), *Sardines* (L, 1981), *Close Sesame: A Novel* (L, NY, 1983), *Maps* (L, 1986). *Gifts* appeared first in Swedish (Stockholm, 1990) and then in English (L, 1992). Farah's latest novel, *Secrets* (NY, 1998), was awarded the Neustadt Prize.

See: Derek Wright, *The Novels of Nuruddin Farah*, Bayreuth African Studies No. 32 (Bayreuth: Breitinger, 1994). This contains an extensive bibliography. Francis Ngaboli-Smart, 'Dimensions of Gift Giving in Nuruddin Farah's *Gifts*', RAL, 27, 4 (Winter 1996).

FIKRÉ, Tolossa (1955–) An Ethiopian playwright and short story writer educated at the University of Addis Ababa. He has lived in Russia and Germany and speaks Russian. His plays are broadly comic, but hide a powerful message beneath their humour, and he has had considerable popular success in Ethiopia. *The Coffin-Dealer and the Gravedigger / A Foot of Land: 2 Plays* (Bremen, 1982).

GARVEY, Marcus (1887–1940) A self-educated, working-class Jamaican, Garvey began life as an apprentice printer. He founded a newspaper in Jamaica and, influenced by the work of Booker T. Washington, he tried to establish a Tuskegee type training school in Jamaica. (See entry on Washington.) When these ventures failed, Garvey moved to America, where he established the influential periodical *Negro World*. A charismatic and theatrical figure, in 1920 he was elected 'provisional president of Africa' by the Universal Negro Improvement Association, which he had founded the previous year. He was an effective popular orator and quickly moved to the forefront of the radical wing of the Black Movement, opposing W. E. B. Du Bois's moderate integrationist line with a call for direct action. He advocated a separation of black people from white society and the repatriation of American and Caribbean black people to Africa, to which end he founded the Black Star Shipping Line to carry his people 'home'. He also developed a pan-Africanist philosophy which influenced a number of African leaders such as Nkrumah and Kenyatta, and which he outlined in his major work, *The Philosophy and Opinions of Marcus Garvey; or Africa for the Africans*, 2 vols, (NY, 1923–25). Apart from several volumes of occasional lectures, addresses and journalistic pieces, his other major work was his poetry. In 1927 he published *The Tragedy of White Justice*, a collection of poems. These were influential on some of the writers in the Harlem Renaissance of the 1920s and 1930s.

GABRE-MEHDIN, Tsegaye (1935–) (Some sources give birthdate as 1936) Ethiopian poet, playwright and novelist. Educated in the US, where he studied law, and then in London, where he was attached to the Royal Court Theatre. On his return to Ethiopia, he became director of the Haile Selassie 1 Theatre in Addis Ababa. His first English-language play, *Tewodros*, was produced there in 1963. He has also published poetry in magazines and anthologies. He is best known internationally for *The Oda-Oak Oracle* (L, 1965), and for *Collision of Altars: A Conflict of the Ancient Red Sea Gods* (L, 1977). Like many other Ethiopian writers he works in both English and Amharic.

GAKAARA WA WANJAŪ, (1921–) Born at Gakansuini village, Nyeri district, Kenya, Gakaara is one of the most prolific writers in Gĩkũyũ. His work has not received much attention outside Kenya, though it clearly forms an important part of the writing in Gĩkũyũ which gave later writers like Ngũgĩ the readership base on which to build when he decided to work in Gĩkũyũ. Gakaara published his first political pamphlets in the late 1940s and his writing was an active part of the independence movement. After independence, he remained a strong supporter of Kenyatta and worked briefly for the KANU party newspaper *Sauti ya*

KANU. In 1961 he established the Gakaara Publishing Service in Nairobi to promote writing in Gĩkũyũ. His fictional work consists mainly of short stories and narratives, beginning with *Ũhoro wa Ũgũrani* (Marriage Procedures) (N, 1946). In the mid-1960s, he began to publish the influential Atiriri series of stories and pamphlets. The series included *Nĩ Nĩĩ Ndĩna Nyarwimbo* (N, 1966) and *Ũngĩ tuĩka Mũkristo no Tũhikanie* (If you become a Christian we'll get married) (N, 1967). In 1972 he founded the monthly Gĩkũyũ newspaper *Gĩkũyũ na Mũmbi*. Imprisoned by the Moi regime, he published his prison diary *Mwandĩki wa Mau Mau Ithamĩrio-inĩ* (Mau Mau Author in Detention) in 1984. His prolific output also includes political writing, poetry, collections of political songs, collections of Gĩkũyũ legends and textbooks on the Gĩkũyũ language.

See: Christiana Pugliese, *Author, Publisher and Gĩkũyũ Nationalist: The Life and Writings of Gakaara wa Wanjaũ*, Bayreuth African Studies No. 37 (Bayreuth: Breitinger; Nairobi: IFRA, 1995). Gakaara wa Wanjaũ, *A Kenyan Market Literature: Gakaara wa Wanjaũ and the Atiriri Series*, trans. Patrick B. Bennett (Madison, Wis.: Ba Shiru, 1983).

GICHERU, Mwangi (n.a.) A popular Kenyan novelist, author of *The Ivory Merchant* (N, 1976), *Across the Bridge* (N, 1979), *The Double Cross* (N, 1983), *Two in One* (N, 1984) and *The Mixers* (N, 1991).

GRONNIOSAW, James Albert Ukawsaw (n.a.) *A Narrative of the Most Remarkable Particulars in the Life of James Albert Ukawsaw Gronniosaw* (Bath *c*. 1770; reissued Kraus Reprints, Nedeln, 1972). An early slave narrative which is an example of an African life transcribed by a white amanuensis; in this case, we are told, by 'a young lady of the town of Leominster'.

GUBEGNA, Abbie (1934–) Born in Ethiopia, works as a playwright, in both English and Amharic. *The Savage Girl* (Addis Ababa, 1964) and *Defiance* (Addis Ababa, N, L, 1975).

GURNAH, Abdulrazak (1948–) Born in Zanzibar, Tanzania, Gurnah has lived in the UK for a long time. He teaches Sociology and Literature at the University of Kent. *Paradise* (L, 1994) was short-listed for the Booker Prize, and since then Gurnah's work has attracted increasingly greater attention. His work includes three earlier novels: *Memory of Departure* (L, 1987), *Pilgrims Way* (L, 1988) and *Dottie* (L, 1990). He has also edited an important collection of critical essays, *Essays on African Writing*, 2 vols (O, 1993). His latest novel is *Admiring Silence* (L, 1996).

HAMMON, Briton (n.a.) *Narrative of the Uncommon Sufferings and Surprising Deliverance of Briton Hammon, A Negro Man* (Boston, 1870; reissued Kraus Reprints, Nedeln, 1972) is an example of the many transcribed accounts of slaves and ex-slaves which are clearly influenced by the amanuensis who has 'taken them down'. The tone of the work makes it very suspect as a true narrative and it is useful in this respect as a comparison with the work of later writers such as Equiano.

HANGHE, Ahmed Artan (or Xaange, Axmed Cartan) (n.a.) Somali author of a novel in English set in the 1960s, *The Sons of Somal* (Cologne, Germany, 1993). Another of the few recent Somali writers to use English. He has also edited several collections of Somali folktales in Somali and English.

HENRIES, A. Doris Banks (1936–) Liberian poet, editor and folklorist. *Poems of Liberia 1836–1961* (L, 1963), *Liberian Folklore: A Compilation of Ninety-Nine Folktales with Some Proverbs* (L, 1966).

HORTON, James Beale Africanus (1835–1883) A leading member of the nineteenth-century Sierra Leonean Creole community, Horton was a medical doctor, pamphleteer and statesman. He rose to the rank of surgeon-major in the British Army in West Africa and served in various colonies there. His works include: *West African Countries and Peoples* (1868; reissued L, 1969) and *Letters on the Political Condition of the Gold Coast* (1870; reissued L, 1970).

HUMASI, Nana (or Nana Grey-Johnson) (1951–) Born in Bathurst, The Gambia, he wrote *A Krio Engagement & Other Stories* (The Gambia, 1987) and *Children of the Spyglass* (The Gambia, 1991) published under the name Nana Grey-Johnson.

HUSSEIN, Ebrahim N. (1943–) Very influential Tanzanian writer who writes in Swahili. His works include *Kinjeketile* (D, 1963; English translation, 1970), *Mashetani* (D, 1971) and *Wakati ukuta / imetungwa na Ebrahim N. Hussein; na kuhaririwa na Farouk Topan* (D, 1971).

IBINGIRA, Grace S. K. (1932–) Born in Uganda, Ibingira is a historian and political scientist and the author of several political studies, including *African Upheavals Since Independence* (Boulder, Co., 1980). One of a number of writers, like the Sudanese Francis Mading Deng, Nigerian Kole Omotoso and fellow Ugandan Akena Adoko, who have employed fiction or long poetry to record the political history of Africa in recent times. *Bitter Harvest: A Political Novel* (N, 1980).

IKE, Chukwuemeka (1931–) Ibo novelist. Author of *Toads for Supper* (L, 1965), *The Naked Gods* (L, 1970), *The Potter's Wheel* (L, 1973), *Sunset at Dawn: A Novel About Biafra* (L, 1976) and *To My Husband from Iowa* (La, 1996).

See: Alex C. Johnson 'Sunset at Dawn: A Biafran on the Nigerian Civil War', *ALT*, 11 (1980), 149–60; K. Ugbade, 'The Child Figure in Chukwuemeka Ike's The Potter's Wheel', *Okike*, 27 & 28 (1988): 67–73.

IROH, Eddie (n.a.) Igbo popular novelist. Iroh's works, modelled on Western war thrillers, have been very successful. He presents a fairly simple view of the Nigerian Civil War from the Biafran side. *Forty Eight Guns for the General* (L, 1976), *Toads of War* (L, 1979), *The Siren in the Night* (L, 1982) and *Without a Silver Spoon* (I, 1991).

IYAYI, Festus (1947–) Born in Benin, Nigeria, Iyayi is an economist by training. Whilst holding various academic posts he was an active supporter of trade unionism in Nigeria and, as the president of the radical academic trade union, Iyayi was detained in 1988. After his release, he worked as a management consultant. Iyayi belongs to the group of younger Nigerian writers whose work sought to offer an uncompromising challenge to the political and social situations in modern Nigeria. His novels include: *Violence* (La, 1979), and *The Contract* (La, 1982). In these early novels he deals with urban poverty and corruption. *Heroes* (L, 1986) examines the effects of the Nigerian Civil War on the lives of the ordinary people. His prose is taut and sparse and his work inaugurated a new sense of social relevance in Nigerian writing. His latest book is *Awaiting Court Martial* (La, 1991), in which he criticises the military governments of recent years in Nigeria.

JOHNSON, Lemuel (1941–) Born in Maidugari, Northern Nigeria, of Sierra Leonean parents, Johnson was educated in Sierra Leone and the US, where he studied Modern Languages at Oberlin College and then gained a PhD in Comparative Literature from the University of Michigan. He has taught at universities in Sierra Leone, Austria and in the USA. He is currently Professor in English at the University of Michigan. A poet, novelist and an acclaimed scholar, his creative works include the poetic trilogy: *The Sierra Leone Trilogy: Highlife for Caliban; Hand on the Navel; Carnival of the Old Coast* (Trenton, N.J., 1995). He has published a number of scholarly works and translations. His most recent scholarly book is *Shakespeare in Africa and Other Venues: Import and the Appropriation of Culture* (Trenton, N.J.: Africa World Press, 1998).

JOHNSON, Rev. Samuel (?–1901) A leading Nigerian churchman and advocate of African rights. His work is the source for much later historiography and for accounts of traditional culture. In many ways it is the precursor of the movement to celebrate and recover the African past from under the shroud of colonialist discourse which was the burden of much of the writing in the 1950s and 1960s. *The History of the Yorubas: From the Earliest Times to the Beginnings of the British Protectorate* (L: Routledge, 1921).

See: Toyin Fayola (ed.), *Samuel Johnson and the Yoruba People: Pioneer, Patriot and Patriarchy* (Madison: University of Wisconsin Press, 1994); also Ato Quayson, *Strategic Transformations in Nigerian Writing* (O: OUP, 1997).

JUMBAM, Kenjo (n.a.) Cameroonian Anglophone writer. He is the author of a novel, *The White Man of God* (L, 1980), a play *Lynda* (Cameroon, 1990), and several collections of children's stories.

See: Wilson Atem Ebot, 'Language and Action in Kenjo Jumbam's Prose Narratives', *RAL*, 29, 2 (Summer 1998): 43–56.

KAHIGA, Samuel (1940–) Kenyan novelist and short story writer. His early collection of stories with his brother, Leonard Kibera, was one of the first attempts at a realistic portrait of life among the urban poor. His later work veers between the serious and the frankly popular. *Potent Ash* (with Leonard Kibera) (N, 1968), *The Girl from Abroad* (L, 1974), *Lover in the Sky* (N, 1975), *When the Stars are Scattered* (Nairobi, 1979), *Flight to Juba* (N, 1979), *Dedan Kimathi, the Real Story, a Novel* (N, 1990) and *Paradise Farm* (N, 1993).

KAYPER-MENSAH, A. W. (1923–1980) Ghanaian poet and author. Educated at Achimota College, Ghana, and later at Cambridge, where he read natural science, and London University, where he studied for a teaching diploma. He taught for many years at Wesley College, Ghana, before he joined the Ghanaian Foreign Service. His works include *The Dark Wanderer* (Tübingen, 1970), *The Drummer in our Time* (L, 1975), *Akwaaba* (A, 1976), *Sankofa: Adinkra Poems* (A, 1976) and *Proverb Poems* (A, 1978).

KELUELJANG, Anai (n.a.) *The Myth of Freedom* (L, 1975) is a collection of poems by a Sudanese poet who was jailed in 1976 for his opposition to the government. Radical in tone, it suggests that the situation in the Sudan is still fuelled by neo-imperialism and international interests.

KENYATTA, Jomo (1893–1978) Born in Ichaweri and died in Mombasa. Kenyan writer and anthropological scholar, and first President of independent Kenya, remaining in power until his retirement in 1978. Arrested by the British in 1952, accused of instigating the Mau Mau revolt, Kenyatta was freed in 1961. *My People of Kikuyu and The Life of Chief Wangombe* (L, 1942), *Facing Mount Kenya: The Tribal Life of the Gĩkũyũ* (L, 1961; repr. 1968).

KIBERA, Leonard (1940–) Born in Kenya, Kibera wrote *Voices in the Dark* (N, 1970). He also co-authored the influential short story collection *Potent Ash* (N, 1968) with his brother, Samuel Kahiga, a collection which initiated Kenyan realist urban fiction.

KINTEH, Ramatoulie (n.a.) The Gambia. *Rebellion: A Play in Three Acts* (NY, 1968). One of the few writers to produce English texts in The Gambia.

LADIPO, Duro (1931–1978) Born in Oshogbo, in Western Nigeria, he was a founder of one of the best-known Yoruba Travelling Theatres. His work includes *Oba Moro* (I, 1964) and *Obo Koso* (La, 1964). In this latter play, Ladipo appeared as Shango (the Yoruba God of Thunder), a figure with whom he became almost mystically associated by his admirers in later years. His other plays include *Oba Waja* (which deals with the same historical event which Ṣoyinka later dramatised in *Death and the King's Horseman*). He also developed several adaptations, notably of the morality play *Everyman*, which he turned into Yoruba as *Eda*. Like other leaders of the Travelling Theatres he turned to television in later years and developed several successful television series, based on the style and themes of his earlier work.

See: Biodun Jeyifo, *The Yoruba Popular Travelling Theatre of Nigeria* (La: Nigeria Magazine Publications, 1984).

LAING, Kojo (1946–) Born in Ghana, Laing has been one of the most prolific of the younger Ghanaian writers. Educated in Ghana and Scotland, he has developed a powerful, individual style which defies easy classification. Although he has written one collection of poems, *Godhorse* (O, 1989), he is best known for his novels, such as his first book *Search Sweet Country* (L, 1986). His later novels include complex transcultural settings and themes, as in *Woman of the Aeroplanes* (L, 1988), or else invoke forms not often employed by African English writers, such as science fiction, in *Major Gentl and the Achimoto Wars* (L, 1992). Despite this internationalist flavour, his novels remain strongly rooted in a Ghanaian cultural context.

See: Pietro Deandrea, 'New Worlds, New Wholes: Kojo Laing's Narrative Quest for a Social Renewal', *ALT*, 20 (1996): 158–78.

LEMMA, Menghistu (1925–) Ethiopian playwright. *The Marriage of Unequals* (L, 1970).

LIYONG, Taban lo (1939–) Born in the Sudan, Taban was taken to Uganda as a young boy. Entering the US on an educational scholarship as a Ugandan, he has in recent years reclaimed his Sudanese heritage, resettling his family in Juba in the Southern Sudan, where he taught for a while at the University and even stood as a parliamentary candidate. Taban lo Liyong has led a truly peripatetic life, moving between Africa, the UK, the USA and a number of other places. He has most recently worked in Japan, in Australia and in South Africa, but he retains his home in the Sudan where his family resides. A prolific writer and critic, he has been an important and influential East African writer, ranking alongside Ngũgĩ and Okot p'Bitek. An eclectic writer who has always refused to be pigeon-holed, the variety of his work has sometimes led to his achievement receiving less recognition than it otherwise might have done from critics who like to attach fixed labels to authors and their work. But few African writers have so consistently produced such a variety of powerful work in every genre. Taban shows no sign of slowing his production, with a recent collection of poems based on his experiences teaching in Japan, *Words That Melt a Mountain* (N, 1996). His other works include: *Fixions, and Other Stories* (L, 1969), *The Last Word: Cultural Synthesism* (N, 1969), *Eating Chiefs* (L, 1970), *Meditations in Limbo* (N, 1970), *Frantz Fanon's Uneven Ribs* (L, 1971), *The Uniformed Man* (N, 1971), *Another Nigger Dead* (L, 1972), *Popular Culture of East Africa: Oral Literature* (N, 1972), *Thirteen Offences Against Our Enemies* (N, 1973), *Sir Apolo Kagwa Discovers Britain*: by Ham Mukasa; edited by Taban lo Liyong (L, 1975), *Ballads of Underdevelopment* (K, 1976), *Meditations of Taban lo Liyong* (L, 1978), *Another Last Word* (N, 1990), *Culture is Rutan* (Nairobi, 1991) and *The Cows of Shambat: Sudanese Poems* (Harare, 1992).

MADDY, Y. A. (Pat) (1936–) Born in Freetown, Sierra Leone, Maddy left for France at the age of 22 to study literature and drama. He moved on to London some time later, and began to write and produce his own plays. In London, he became Director of Drama at the Keskidee Centre. He also worked in radio there and moved to Denmark, also to work in radio, in the mid-1960s. He returned to Sierra Leone in 1968, to head the Drama Department at Radio Sierra Leone. After a spell in Zambia, Maddy began teaching at the Universities of Ibadan and Ilorin, Nigeria. His major works are: *Obasai and Other Plays* (L, 1971), *No Past, No Present* (L, 1973), and, in collaboration with the Ethiopian writer Alem Mezgebe, *Pulse*, a play which received the first prize at the Edinburgh International Festival.

MAILLU, David G. (1939–) This Kenyan-born writer is the most successful popular novelist in East Africa. Maillu single-handedly opened up a market for frankly popular texts by self-publishing his own work and ghosting that of many others. His books are often sensational, but they also embody serious moral warnings against the social dangers of promiscuity, drink etc. His success meant that he could choose whether to self-publish his own later work, or publish it with established local presses. His many books include those published by others, assisted by or with the guidance of Maillu. In this respect his output resembles such earlier 'literary factories' as that of the Dumas father and sons. Many of these books were published under his own Comb Press imprint in Nairobi, a press which really established the local market for popular writing in East Africa. Although his books are mostly written in English, in some cases, such as *Hit of Love* (N, 1980), they were published in both English and a local language (in this case in Kikamba). His large output of works include *My Dear Bottle* (N, 1973), *After 4.30* (N, 1974), *The Flesh* (N, 1975), *Kommon Man* (N, 1975), *Dear Daughter* (N, 1976), *Benni Kamba 009 in the Equatorial Assignment* (L, 1980), *The Ayah* (N, 1986), *Our Kind of Polygamy* (N, 1988), *Kisalu and his Fruit Garden and Other Stories* (N, 1989), *The Black Adam and Eve* (N, 1989), *Without Kiinua Mgongo* (N, 1989), *PO Box I Love You* (N, 1991), and *Sasa and Sisi* (N, 1994). These titles give an idea of the variety of output from Maillu's 'pen' in these years and the wide range of styles and genres his work encompassed.

MAIMO, Sankie (1940–) Anglophone Cameroonian poet and playwright. *I Am Vindicated* (I, 1959), *Sov-Mbang the Soothsayer* (Y, 1969) and *The Mask* (Y, 1980).

See: N. Lyonga, Eckhardt Breitinger and Bole Butake (eds), *Anglophone Cameroon Writing*, Bayreuth African Studies No. 30 (Bayreuth: Breitinger, 1993).

MAHJOUB, Jamal (1960–) Born in London to an English mother and a Sudanese father, in his work Mahjoub has used this background of cross-cultural experience to great effect. After growing up in Liverpool, his family moved back to the Sudan where he finished school. He later studied geology at Sheffield University in the UK. His first novel, *Navigation of a Rainmaker* (L, 1989), is an interesting extension of his situation, as the main character, Tanner, is also half-British, half-Sudanese. He then published *Wings of Dust* (L, 1994), which also deals with the issue of diasporic people and their return to Sudan. *In the Hour of Signs* (O, 1996) is a historical novel set in nineteenth-century Sudan during and after the Siege of Khartoum His most recent novel is *The Carrier* (L, 1998). He now lives in Denmark.

MANGUA, Charles (1939–) Kenyan writer. Mangua straddles the divide of popular and serious fiction. His early work was amongst the first of the recent best-selling popular texts in Kenya and helped establish the market there for popular fiction. Never quite the retailer of salacious detail that David G. Maillu was, his later work shows an increasing concern with the issues of urban poverty and oppression. This gives his work a powerful edge over the more frankly popular work of his contemporaries. *Son of Woman* (N, 1971), *A Tail in the Mouth: A Novel* (N, 1972), *Son of Woman in Mombasa* (N, 1986) and *Kanina and I* (N, 1994).

See: Kathleen Greenfield, 'Self and Nation in Kenya: Charles Mangua's *Son of Woman*', *Journal of Modern African Studies*, 33, 4 (1995).

MAZRUI, Ali (1933–) One of East Africa's most prominent historians and political scientists and the author of innumerable books on African politics and culture. His intervention in the debate on the role of intellectuals in the Nigerian Civil War, and specifically on Okigbo's decision to fight in the army of Biafra, forms the basis for his fictionalised study of these issues, *The Trial of Christopher Okigbo* (L, 1971).

MEZU, S. Okechukwu (1929–) Born in Eastern Nigeria, in his first novel Mezu deals with the issue of the Biafran war, writing from a Biafran perspective. *Behind the Rising Sun* (L, 1971).

See: Craig McLuckie, *Nigerian Civil War Literature: Seeking an Imagined Community* (Lewiston, Queenstown, Lampeter: The Edwin Mellen Press, 1990).

MFUKWE, W. E. (n.a.) Tanzanian author of *The Wicked Walk* (D, 1977). A realistic story of street life in Dar es Salaam.

MOORE, Bai T. (1916–) Liberian poet. Educated in the US, he completed his schooling in Virginia before attending the Virginia Union University, and Howard University. As a member of the Vai group, to whom the important early Liberian writer J. J. Walters also belonged, Moore's work represents the indigenous African Liberian tradition, as opposed to the Creole community with its much stronger Euro-American links, represented by writers like Roland Dempster and Doris Banks Henries (see entries above). As an older member of the Liberian intelligentsia, of course, Moore was deeply involved in that Creole world and published and worked within its auspices. He was educated in agricultural science in the US. Returning to Monrovia in 1941, he worked as a civil servant, becoming Under-Secretary for Cultural Affairs. His many works over more than fifty years include: *Echoes from the Valley: Being Odes and Other Poems by Three Colleagues* (Robertsport, Liberia, 1947?) (with R. T. Dempster, and H. C. Thomas), *Ebony Dust* (Privately Published, Monrovia, 1962), *Murder in the Cassava Patch* (Privately Published, The Hague, 1968), *Voices from the Grassroots* (n.p., 1974) and *The Money Doubler* (La, 1976). His community's position in the wider politics of Liberia was a subject that increasingly preoccupied Moore in recent times, as conflicts between the various communities surfaced in Liberia. His work on this includes the essay *Problems of Vai Identity in Terms of My Own Experience* (n.d.) which he published in the mid-1960s.

MUDE, Dae Mude (1943–) Born in Kenya, educated at the University of Nairobi, Mude received a BA Hons in French and History. He worked for a time for the Ministry of Foreign Affairs, and later as a newspaper editor. *The Hills are Falling* (N, 1979).

MUHANDO, Penina (or Penina Muhando Mlama) (1948–) Born in Berega, Morogoro region, Tanzania. Educated at the University of Dar es Salaam where she studied drama, education and languages, and wrote her MA thesis on Tanzanian traditional theatre. Novelist, playwright and academic. Her work includes *Hatia* (N, 1972), *Pamba* (N, 1975) and *There is a Cure for Rot: A Novel* (D, 1991). She is also the author of numerous critical studies including *Culture for Development: The Popular Theatre Approach in Africa* (Uppsala, Sweden: Nordiska Afrikainstitutet, 1991).

MUKASA, Ham (1868–1956) Born in Buganda, in what is now Uganda. A Luganda-language scholar, as well as one of the first Bugandans to write in English, Mukasa accompanied the Bugandan politician, Sir Apolo Kagwa, on his visit to Britain for the Coronation of King Edward, and his travelogue has come to be seen as a valuable document for the study of African and British relations in the period. *Uganda's Katakiro in England, being the official account of his visit to the coronation of His Majesty King Edward VII. Translated and edited by Ernest Millar; with an introduction by Sir. H. H. Johnson* (1904). This was reissued as *Sir Apolo Kagwa Discovers Britain*, ed. with an introduction by Taban lo Liyong (L, 1975).

MUNONYE, John (1929–) An Ibo from Eastern Nigeria, Munonye early expressed a great admiration for Achebe and, many critics felt, modelled his own work very closely on Achebe's, to the detriment of his own voice and style. Like Aluko, he was recruited early to the African Writers Series, which published all his work, including *The Only Son* (L, 1966), *Obi* (L, 1969) and *The Oil Man of Obange* (L, 1971). In *A Wreath for the Maidens* (L, 1973) he dealt with the civil war. In *A Dance of Fortune* (L, 1974) he analysed the corruption of Nigerian society in recent years. These later works displayed a more political edge than the earlier novels. His latest novel, *Bridge to a Wedding* (L, 1978), completes the trilogy begun with the first two. Together they examine the impact on village and traditional life of change in the modern period in Nigeria.

MWANGI, Meja (1948–) Born in Nanyuki, Kenya, he spent his childhood in a colonial confinement camp, designed to enforce a lack of contact with the Mau Mau freedom fighters, an experience which may have influenced his later work on that period. He later studied science at Kenyatta College, but worked principally for the British Council and for French television in Nairobi, until his books achieved success. This important younger Kenyan novelist has explored two main themes: the Mau Mau revolt and its effects on the life of Kenyans, and the social and political conditions in post-independence Kenyan cities, which he describes with brutal honesty. The later work reaches out to embrace more international settings and themes. The political and social relevance of this later work has been the subject of critical dispute. Meja Mwangi consolidated the exploration of the Mau Mau liberation struggle and the effects of independence on the urban life of Kenya in texts like *Kill Me Quick* (L, N, 1973), *Carcass For Hounds* (N, 1974), *Taste of Death* (N, 1975), *Going Down River Road* (N, 1976), *The Cockroach Dance* (N, 1979), *Bread of Sorrow* (N, 1987) and *Weapon of Hunger* (N, 1989). Later texts such as *The Bushtrackers* (N, 1989), *The Return of Shaka* (N, 1989) and *Striving for the Wind* (N, 1990) show the influence of popular genre development in modern Kenyan writing. More recent work includes *Adventures with Little White Man (Kariuki: aventures avec le petit homme blanc) traduit de l'anglais par Olivier Barlet* (Paris, 1992) and *The Hunter's Dream* (L, 1993).

See: Lars Johansson, *In the Shadow of Neocolonialism: Meja Mwangi's Novels 1973–1990*, Umeå Studies in the Humanities 110 (Umeå Sweden: Dept. of English, Umeå University, 1992); Angus Calder, 'Meja Mwangi's Novels', in G. D. Killam (ed.), *The Writing of East and Central Africa* (L: Heinemann, 1984); Elizabeth Knight, 'Mirror of Reality: The Novels of Meja Mwangi', *ALT*, 13 (1983): 146–57.

NAGBE, Moses K. (n.a.) Recent Liberian writer. In the 1990s Nagbe has emerged as a writer with an original voice in a country whose English writing has tended to be rather conservative and to be tied to a fairly old-fashioned set of themes, and a conservative style. *The Real Drum Daddy is Back!* (Monrovia, 1989) and *The Road to Romeo* (M, 1992) represent a break from this tradition. It remains to be seen whether Nagbe's work will initiate new developments in Liberian English poetry where, as in many other parts of Africa, civil disturbances and conflict have inhibited literary production in recent years. He is also an active promoter of writing and has published an important bibliography of Liberian writing, *Books on Liberia by Nationals and Foreign Nationals* (n.p., 1992). His work has still received very little critical attention and does not feature in any of the standard bibliographical sources. Little or no information is available on his life in published sources. Nevertheless he is clearly a name to watch for any future development of English writing in Liberia.

NAGENDA, John (1938–) Born in Uganda, Nagenda worked for a while for Oxford University Press in Uganda. *Mukasa* (NY, 1973) and *The Seasons of Thomas Tebo* (N, 1986).

NAZARETH, Peter (1940–) A Ugandan-born critic, poet and short story writer of Goanese descent, Nazareth was one of the many intellectuals of Asian descent forced to flee Uganda in the wake of Amin's take-over. He has lived mainly in the USA since then. His many important creative and critical works include *In a Brown Mantle* (N, 1972), *Literature and Society in Modern Africa* (N, 1972), *Two Radio Plays* (N, 1976), and a recent novel *The General is Up* (Calcutta, 1984).

NGŨGĨ WA THIONG'O (1938–) Born at Kamiriithu village near Limuru. The son of a peasant father with a large family (four wives and twenty-eight children) his family was dispossessed of their land by a greedy landowner, a theme which has taken root in Ngũgĩ's later work. Undoubtedly the most famous Kenyan writer, Ngũgĩ attended East Africa's first tertiary institution, Makerere University in Uganda. He published his early fiction under his mission school name of James Ngũgĩ. His early work appeared in *Penpoint*, Makerere's literary magazine in 1960, and a number of short plays were performed by the University drama group in the early 1960s. He was appointed to the staff at the University of Nairobi in 1967, and became the first black African member of the then English Department. In later years with others, such as Taban lo Liyong, he was to lead the call for the Africanisation of the syllabus in literature and in other departments at the University. After initiating drama work with a community group at the Community Centre in his home village he helped produce and script plays in Gĩkũyũ critical of the regime such as *Ngaahika Ndeenda* (I Will Marry When I Want). He was thrown into prison in 1978 and then deported. He has since lived abroad. His academic career has taken him to the UK, to other African countries, and in the 1980s he was appointed Visiting Professor at Yale University. He is currently a professor at New York University. Although *Weep Not, Child* (L, 1964) was his first published novel, it was written after *The River Between* (L, 1965). Ngũgĩ has carved for himself a place as one of the most prolific and controversial writers in modern African literature, a position which his imprisonment at the hands of Jomo Kenyatta set almost in stone. As important as his contribution to the novel in Africa, has been his critical and cultural writings, which have kept him at the forefront of international attention. In text after text, he has developed an argument for the use of indigenous languages to 'decolonise the mind' of Africans. His project to return Africans to writing in indigenous languages culminated in his decision, in the late 1970s, to write only in African languages. He has continued to translate his work, or allow his work to be translated, into English, ensuring that he continues to have an international audience. His many works include: *Weep Not, Child* (L, 1964), *The River Between* (L, 1965), *A Grain of Wheat* (L, 1967), *The Black Hermit* (L, 1968), *This Time Tomorrow*, also contains *The Rebels* and *The Wound in the Heart* (N, 1970), *Homecoming: Essays on African and Caribbean Literature, Culture and Politics* (L, 1972), *Secret Lives and Other Stories* (L, Westport, Conn., 1975), *The Trial of Dedan Kimathi* (Nairobi, 1976), *Petals of Blood* (L, 1977), *Ngaahika ndeenda: ithaako ria ngerekano / riandikiitwo ni* (I Will Marry When I Want) (with Ngũgĩ wa Mirii) (Nairobi, 1980), *Detained: A Writer's Prison Diary* (L, 1981), *Caitaani Mũtharaba-ini* (N, 1980), *Devil on the Cross* (English translation L, 1982), *Writers in Politics: Essays* (L, Exeter, USA, 1981), *Barrel of a Pen: Resistance to Repression in Neo-colonial Kenya* (L, 1983), *Bathitoora ya Njamba Nene* (N, 1983; English translation *Njamba Nene's Pistol* N, 1986) (children's story), *Writing Against Neocolonialism* (Wembley, UK, 1986), *Njamba Nene na Mbaathi i Mathagu* (N, 1982, English translation *Njamba Nene and the Flying Bus*, N, 1986) (children's story), *Decolonising the Mind: The Politics of Language in African Writing* (L; Portsmouth, USA, 1986); *Njamba Nene na chibu king'ang'i* (N, 1986; English translation *Njamba Nene and the Cruel Chief* N, 1988) (children's story); *Matigari ma Njirũũngi* (N, 1987; English translation *Matigari* O and N, 1989), *We Should Increasingly Exploit the Resources of Our Own Languages: An Interview with Kenyan Writer Ngũgĩ wa Thiong'o*, Pierrette Herzberger-Fofana, Erlangen (Stuttgart, Germany, 1988), *Moving the Centre: The Struggle for Cultural Freedoms* (L, Portsmouth, USA, 1993), *Penpoints, Gunpoints and Dreams* (O, 1997). Like Achebe, Ngũgĩ has been the subject of a vast body of critical writing.

See: Carol Sicherman, *Ngũgĩ wa Thiong'o: A Bibliography of Primary and Secondary Sources 1957–1987* (NY: Hans Zell, 1989). Also Carol Sichermann, *Ngũgĩ wa Thiong'o, the Making of a Rebel: A Sourcebook in Kenyan Literature and Resistance* (NY: Hans Zell, 1990); G. D. Killam (ed.), *Critical Perspectives on Ngũgĩ wa Thiong'o* (W: Three Continents Press, 1984); Simon Gikandi, 'The Growth of the East African Novel', in G. D. Killam (ed.), *The Writing of East and Central Africa* (L: Heinemann, 1984); Ingrid Björkman, *Mother Sing for Me: People's Theatre in Kenya* (L: Zed Books, 1989); David Cook and Michael Okenimpke, *Ngũgĩ wa Thiong'o: An Explanation of his Writing* (L: Heinemann, 1983); G. D. Killam, *An Introduction to the Writing of Ngũgĩ* (L: Heinemann, 1980); Bayo Ogunjimi, 'Language, Oral Tradition and Social Vision in Ngũgĩ's *Devil on the Cross*', *Ufahuma* 14, 1 (1984); *RAL*, 23, 1 (Spring 1992); Simon Gikandi, 'Ngũgĩ's Conversion: Writing and the Politics of Language', *RAL*, 23, 1 (Spring 1992).

NICOL, Davidson (Abioseh) (1924–) A well-known Sierra Leonean author, poet and literary historian, Davidson Nicol trained as a biochemist after being educated in Nigeria and Sierra Leone. He is the author of an important study of Africanus Horton: *Africanus Horton: The Dawn of Nationalism in Modern Africa* (L, 1969). He also wrote fiction under his African name, Abioseh Nicol, and published short stories including *The Truly Married Woman* and *Two African Tales* (L, 1965).

NWANKWO, Nkem W. (1936–) Born in Nigeria, Nwankwo taught at Ibadan Grammar School, before seeking employment with the Nigerian Broadcasting Corporation. In 1973 he was Writer in Residence at the African Studies Centre at Michigan State University. He is the author of the early Nigerian picaresque novel *Danda* (L, 1964) and a collection of stories *Tales Out of School* (L, 1964). These were followed by *My Mercedes is Bigger Than Yours* (Enugu, 1975) and *The Scapegoat* (Enugu, 1984).

NWAPA, Flora (1931–1993) Born in Oguta, Eastern Nigeria, Flora Nwanzuruaha died recently at the age of 62. Nwapa was educated at Ibadan and Edinburgh Universities. She then worked as a teacher in Calabar and Enugu. She was the first Nigerian woman to have a novel published, and the first African woman to publish in London. Her first work of fiction, *Efuru* (L, 1966), dealt with the oppression of women in Nigerian society. While working in a variety of posts in the public service, Nwapa went on to write *Idu* (L, 1970), *This is Lagos and Other Stories* (1971), *Wives at War and Other Stories* (E, 1980), *Never Again* (E, 1975; repr. 1986), *Cassava Song and Rice Song* (Enugu, 1986), *One is Enough* (Enugu, 1981; Trenton, N.J., 1992) and *Women Are Different* (Enugu, 1986; Trenton N.J., 1992). She also wrote several books for children. In 1974, because of her dissatisfaction with Heinemann's distribution and publicity, Nwapa founded the Tana Press and in 1977 she set up the Flora Nwapa Publishing Company. These published her own work and those of others. The rediscovery of Nwapa and indeed of early African women writers in general in recent years may account for the interestingly long gap between the publication of her more recent work in Nigeria and the delay of almost a decade before it was reissued by presses in America.

See: Maryse Condé, 'Three Female Writers in Modern Africa: Flora Nwapa, Ama Ata Aidoo, and Grace Ogot', *Présence Africaine*, 82 (1972): 132–44; Ernest N. Emenyonu, 'Who Does Flora Nwapa Write For?', *African Literature Today*, 1 (1975): 27–33; Susan Z. Andrade, 'Rewriting History, Motherhood and Rebellion: Naming an African Woman's Literary Tradition', *RAL*, 21, 1 (1990): 91–111; Chidi Ikonne, 'The Society and Women's Quest for Selfhood in Flora Nwapa's Early Novels', *Kunapipi*, 6 (1984): 68–78; Maggi Phillips, 'Engaging Dreams: Alternative Perspectives on Flora Nwapa, Buchi Emecheta etc.', *RAL*, 25, 4 (1994): 89–103; Virginia Coulon, 'Women at War: Nigerian Women Writers and the Civil War', *Commonwealth: Essays and Studies*, 13, 1 (1990): 1–12; Marie Umeh, 'Finale: Signifyin' The Griottes: Flora Nwapa's Legacy of (Re) Vision and Voice', *RAL*, 26, 2 (1995); Marie Umeh, 'The Poetics of Economic Independence for Female Empowerment: An Interview with Flora Nwapa', *RAL*, 26, 2 (1995); Theodora A. Ezeigbo, 'Traditional Women's Institutions in Igbo Society: Implications for the Igbo Female Writer', *African Languages and Cultures*, 3 (1990): 149–65; Marie Umeh (ed.), *Emerging Perspectives on Flora Nwapa: Critical and Theoretical Essays* (Trenton, N.J.: Red Sea Press, 1998).

OBENG, R. E. (1868–1951) Born in Abetefi, Ghana, Obeng trained as a teacher-catechist. After service as an army teacher, he founded the Juaso Government Mixed School, where he remained as Head until his retirement in 1936. *Eighteenpence* (A, 1941; reissued A, 1971) was one the earliest African novels in English.

OCULI, Okello (1942–) Ugandan author, trained as a political scientist and has taught in this area in Nigeria at Ahmadu Bello University. Oculi has also written several comparative studies of food, health and malnutrition problems in East and West Africa, e.g. *Health Problems in Rural and Urban Africa: A Nigerian Political Economy Health Science* (Zaria, Nigeria, 1981) and *Food and Revolution in Africa* (Zaria, Nigeria, 1986). He has also written a number of fictional books, including *Kanta Rita* (K, 1973), *Kookolem* (N, 1978) and *Malak: An African Political Poem* (N, 1976), making him yet another example of the East African practice of combining social and political writing with fiction. His novels examine social issues in a direct and powerful way. The novel, *Prostitute* (N, 1968), blends prose and verse in a long, fictional narrative. In *Orphan* (N, 1968) Oculi uses verse to create what he terms 'a village opera'. The debt to Okot p'Bitek is clear. These texts again demonstrate the frequent use of verse to create long narratives in modern East African writing.

OFEIMUN, Odia (1950–) Born in Nigeria. *The Poet Lied and Other Poems* (L, 1989: includes *The Poet Lied*, first published in London by Longman in 1980, and *A Handle for the Flautist*, first published in Lagos by Update Communications also in 1980), *Under African Skies* (O, 1990). Although he is best known for the role played by his poems in the early 1980s in provoking the controversy over J. P. Clark's role in the Nigerian Civil War years, he is also a poet of considerable skill and range whose work deserves more notice for its intrinsic merit than it has so far received.

OGOT, Grace (1930–) A Luo, born in Kenya's Central Nyanza district, Ogot trained as a nurse both in Uganda and England. She has worked for the BBC Overseas Service, for the Air India Corporation of East Africa, for the BBC Overseas Service and has held various ambassadorial posts. She was a founder member of the Writers' Association of Kenya. She may well be the first published female African writer in English, in that two of her short stories were published in 1962 and 1964. Her first novel, The *Promised Land* (N, 1966), was published in the same year as Flora Nwapa's *Efuru* and deals with the subject of a family's migration from Kenya to Tanzania. Her second novel, *The Graduate* (N, 1980), relates the story of a male protagonist who, after studying in America, returns to find his place in his own culture hard to regain. Ogot has also published three volumes of short stories in English, *The Island of Tears* (N, 1980), *Land Without Thunder* (N, 1968), *The Other Woman and Other Stories* (N, 1992), as well as a novel in the Dholuo language, *The Strange Bride*, tr. Okoth Okombo (N, 1989), which has been translated into English, mirroring Ngũgĩ's procedures. She has also broadcast a regular radio programme in Dholuo.

See: Bernth Lindfors, 'Interview with Grace Ogot', *WLWE* 18, 1 (1979): 58–68; Marion Kilson, 'Women and African Literature', *Journal of African Studies*, 4, 2 (1977): 161–6; Maryse Condé, 'Three Female Writers in Modern Africa: Flora Nwapa, Ama Ata Aidoo and Grace Ogot', *Présence Africaine*, 82 (1972): 132–44; Ify Achufusi, 'Problems of Nationhood in Grace Ogot's Fiction', *JCL*, 26, 1 (1991): 178–87.

OGUNDIPE-LESLIE, Molara (1949–) A Yoruba Nigerian, Ogundipe-Leslie began writing as a child, initially producing comics and short stories, then poetry. She received a BA Hons in English from Ibadan's University College in 1977. A well-known critic, she has taught both in Nigeria and in the United States. Ogundipe-Leslie is perhaps still best known for her academic writing, authoring a crucial contribution to the revisioning of African women's writing in many early essays and in her book *Re-creating Ourselves: African Women and Critical Transformations* (Trenton, N.J., 1994). Her poetry publications include *Sew the Old Days and Other Poems* (I, 1985).

OGUNDE, Hurbert (1916–1990) One of the earliest and most popular leaders of the Yoruba Travelling Theatre movement. He began writing and performing plays in the 1940s, when his plays *Tiger's Empire* (1946), *Strike and Hunger* (1946) and *Bread and Bullet* (1950) were an integral part of the popular movement against the colonial power. His play *Song of Unity* (1960) was commissioned by the new government for the independence celebrations, but by 1964 his powerful play *Yoruba Roni!* (Yoruba Awake), which warned Nigerians of the dangers as the civil war approached, resulted in his troupe being banned. He reacted to the ban in a typically aggressive way by producing the play *Otitto Koro* (Truth is Bitter), which satirised his censors. In later life, he turned to cinema with all the entrepreneurial skills which had made him one of the founders of the Travelling Theatres, and produced a number of films, including *Aiye* (1980) and *Jaiyesimi* (1981). Partly because of his example, the Travelling Theatres found a new home in the cinema, and in the many television series based on their style and material which developed in Nigeria in the 1980s.

See: Ebun Clark, *Herbert Ogunde: The Making of Nigerian Theatre* (O, NY: OUP, 1979); Biodun Jeyifo, *The Yoruba Popular Travelling Theatre of Nigeria* (Lagos: Nigeria Magazine Publications, 1984).

OGUNYEMI, Wale (1939–) Yoruba and English language playwright, director and actor born in Igbajo, Osun State. Ogunyemi was a member of Ṣoyinka's Orisun Theatre. A prolific playwright, he has written a large number of plays in both Yoruba and English. His work is characterised by his use of all the devices of theatre: music, dance, song and spectacle. In this respect, his work reflects the practice of the popular troupes of Ogunde and Ladipo. Ogunyemi's use of mythic and traditional themes to make pertinent modern points, a technique he may have learned from his work with Ṣoyinka (who also directed some of his earlier plays), looks forward to the work of younger writers such as Osofisan and Sowande, who also worked in Ibadan. His many plays include *Business Headache* (I, 1960), *The Scheme* (I, 1967), *Obaluaye* (I, 1968), *Are Akogun* (I, 1969), *Ijaiye War* (I, 1970), *Kiriji* (I, 1976), *Eshu Elegbara* (I, 1976), *The Divorce* (I, 1977) and *Langbodo* (I, 1980), a drama based on D. O. Fagunwa's Yoruba-language novel, *Ogboju Ode*.

See: Dapo Adelugba (ed.), *Chief Wale Ogunyemi at Fifty: Essays in Honour of a Nigerian Actor-Dramatist* (Ibadan: End-Time Publishing House Ltd., 1993).

OJAIDE, Tanure (1948–) Born in Okpara, in the Western Region of Nigeria, Ojaide attended university in the USA, where he gained a Master of Arts degree in creative writing and a doctorate in English. Since then he has taught African literature and creative writing at the University of Maiduguri, in Nigeria, and in the US. *Children of Iroko* (NY, 1973), was his first collection of poetry, followed thirteen years later by *Labyrinths of the Delta* (NY, 1986), which won the Commonwealth poetry competition for the African region in 1987. *The Eagle's Vision* (Detroit, USA, 1987) received the All-Africa Okigbo Prize for Poetry in 1988. Other works include *The Endless Song* (La, 1989), *The Fate of Vultures and Other Poems* (La, 1990), which won the Association of Nigerian Authors poetry prize in 1988, and *The Blood of Peace* (O, 1991). His critical work has also been acclaimed and includes 'The Changing Voice of History: Contemporary African Poetry' (1989), 'New Trends in Modern African Poetry' (1995), and *The Poetry of Wọle Ṣoyinka* (La, Malthouse Press, 1994), which traces the early writer's influence on later Nigerian poetry.

See: Funso Aiyejina, 'Recent Nigerian Poetry in English: An Alter/Native Tradition', in Yemi Ogunyemi (ed.), *Perspectives on Nigerian Literature* Vol. 1 (Lagos: Guardian Books, 1988); Tijan M. Sallah, 'The Eagle's Vision: The Poetry of Tanure Ojaide', *RAL*, 26, 4 (1995): 24–29; 'Poetry and Repression in Contemporary Nigeria: Tanure Ojaide's Labyrinths of the Delta', *ALT*, 20 (1996): 62–72.

OKARA, Gabriel (1921–) An Ijaw, born at Bumoundi in the Niger Delta region of South-East Nigeria. He was one of the many early Nigerian writers, including Achebe and Okigbo, to be educated at the prestigious Government College of Umuahia, and for a while at Yaba Higher College. The outbreak of World War Two, and the ten years or so difference in their ages, meant that he did not go to the Ibadan University, as the later generation of writers who graduated from that College did. Critics have speculated that this lack of tertiary English literary education which later writers received may explain the early predominance of local allusions in his poetry. After the end of World War Two, which he spent partly in Gambia working for BOAC, he became a journalist and bookbinder and started to write occasionally. He became a part-time lecturer at the University of Nigeria in Enugu in 1964. Okara spent the Nigerian Civil War years working for the Biafran Ministry of Information. After the war, he worked for government agencies in his home region of Rivers State, and was active in establishing radio broadcasting there. A critically very important, though not prolific writer, Okara's poetry features in such influential early collections as Moore and Beier's *Modern Poetry From Africa* (L, 1963). His only solo collection is *The Fisherman's Invocation* (L, Benin City, Nigeria, 1978), which was a joint winner of the Commonwealth Poetry Prize in 1978. He later published acclaimed, short poetry sequences in literary journals: 'Three Poems' in *Okike*, 22 (1982), and 'Ten Poems' in *Black Orpheus*, 5, 1 (1983). He also wrote a few short stories and several children's books. He produced only one novel, *The Voice* (L, 1964). However, its powerful experimental form, which blended English and Ijaw usage, made it a classic source of reference for studies of African interlanguages.

See: Bernth Lindfors, 'Gabriel Okara: The Poet as Novelist', *Pan-African Journal* 4 (Fall 1971); Romanus N. Egudu, 'A Study of Five of Gabriel Okara's Poema', *Okike*, 13 (1978); Obi Maduakor, 'Gabriel Okara: Poet of the Mystical Inside', *WLWE*, 61 (Winter 1987); Ayo Mamudu, 'Okara's Poetic Landscape', *Commonwealth: Essays and Studies*, 10 (Fall 1987); Patrick Scott, 'Gabriel Okara's *The Voice*: the non-Ijo Reader and the Pragmatics of Translingualism', *RAL*, 21 (Fall 1990).

OKIGBO, Christopher (1932–1967) Born in Ojoto, near Onitsha, Eastern Nigeria, Okigbo, like Achebe and Okara, was a graduate of the prestigious Government College, Umuahia, and went on to Ibadan University, where he was two years junior to Achebe. After studying medicine, Okigbo switched to classics, and graduated as a classicist. A contemporary also of Şoyinka and Chukwuemeka Ike, he belonged to a dazzlingly successful group of graduates from Ibadan, who made their mark in every sphere of post-independence Nigerian life. Okigbo worked as a teacher and as a university librarian, as well as in various government and business positions. In the early 1960s, after winning renown as a poet, he became the West African representative for Cambridge University Press. After a brief failed marriage to a Northerner, which produced a daughter, he joined the Biafran army at the outbreak of the Nigerian Civil War. He was killed in August 1967 as an infantry Major, in an early battle defending the town of Nsukka, where he had been the University Acting Librarian and where he had written many of his poems, including *Heavensgate* (I, 1962), *Limits* (I, 1964), and *Labyrinths: With Path of Thunder* (NY, 1971). Although separate editions of these were published in Africa and in the UK, they can be most conveniently found now in the *Collected Poems*. A mass of criticism exists on Okigbo who, despite his early death, continues to be a powerful influence on young writers in both West and East Africa.

See: *Christopher Okigbo: Collected Poems* (London: Heinemann 1986), preface by Paul Theroux and introduction by Adewale Maja-Pearce; *Critical Perspectives on Christopher Okigbo*, ed. Donatus I. Nwoga (W: Three Continents Press, 1984); Charles A. Bodunde, 'Oral Traditions and Modern Poetry: Okot p'Bitek's Song of Lawino and Okigbo's Labyrinths', *ALT*, 18 (1992): 24–34.

OKPEWHO, Isidore (1942–) Nigerian novelist and scholar. *The Victims* (Harlow, 1970), *The Last Duty* (L, 1976). Okpewho has also written several of the standard accounts of orality: *The Epic in Africa: Towards a Poetics of Oral Performance* (NY, 1979), *Myth in Africa: A Study of its Aesthetic and Cultural Relevance* (C, NY 1983) and *African Oral Literature: Backgrounds, Character, and Continuity* (Bloomington, 1992). His novels do not however reflect this interest stylistically, being for the most part powerful realist accounts of contemporary social problems in the tradition of novelists like Iyayi and playwrights like Osofisan, who are his contemporaries. His latest novel, *Tides* (1993), won the Commonwealth Writers Prize for the African Region. One of the very few African novels to employ the epistolary form, and the only one I know in English. A *roman-à-clef*, *Tides* deals with the oil boom and its deleterious effects in regions such as the Niger Delta and the resistance offered to this.

See: Eustace Palmer, 'Isidore Okpewho's *The Last Duty*', *International Fiction Review*, 20, 1 (1993); V. U. Ola, 'Identity Crisis in the Tragic Novels of Isidore Okpewho', *ALT*, 13 (1983): 56–68. There is also an extended review of *Tides* by Derek Wright in *Journal of African Studies*, 33, 1 (1995): 322–34.

OKRI, Ben (1959–) Born in Minna, in Nigeria, Okri has lived for long periods of time overseas, mainly in the UK. His first novel, *Flowers and Shadows* (L, 1980; rep. in 1989 with an introduction by Adewale Maja-Pearce) was written at the age of nineteen, while Okri was an undergraduate student at the University of Essex. Since then, Okri has published extensively, including a recent collection of essays, *A Way of Being Free* (L, 1997). He won the prestigious Booker Prize for *The Famished Road* (L, 1991). Other works include: *Songs of Enchantment* (L, 1993), *The Landscapes Within* (L, 1981), *Incidents at the Shrine* (L, 1986), *Stars of the New Curfew* (L, 1988), *An African Elegy* (L, 1992), *Birds of Heaven* (L, 1994), *Astonishing the Gods* (L, 1995), *Dangerous Love* (L, 1996) and *Infinite Riches* (L, 1999).

See: Ato Quayson, *Strategic Transformations in Nigerian Literature* (L: James Currey, 1987); Biyi Bandele-Thomas, 'Ben Okri: A Literary Giant in his own Right', *Nigeria Home News*, 26 April–2 May 1990; T. J. Cribb, 'Transformations in the Fiction of Ben Okri', in Anna Rutherford (ed.), *From Commonwealth to Post-Colonial* (Sydney: Dangaroo, 1992); Adewale Maja-Pearce, *A Mask Dancing: Nigerian Novelists of the Eighties* (L: Hans Zell, 1992).

OMOTOSO, Kole (1943–) Born in Akure, in Western Nigeria, Omotoso was, from an early age, extremely active in the Nigerian literary scene, both as a writer and as the literary editor for the monthly magazine *Afriscope*. In 1992, as a result of an uneasy relationship with the military government in power, Omotoso left for post-apartheid South Africa. He now teaches at the University of the Western Cape. *The Edifice* (L, 1971), *The Combat* (L, 1972), *Miracles and Other Stories* (I, 1973), *Fella's Choice* (Benin City, Nigeria, 1974), *Sacrifice* (I, 1974, 1978), *The Scales* (I, 1976), *The Curse* (I, 1976), *Shadows in the Horizon: A Play About the Combustibility of Private Property* (I, 1977), *To Borrow a Wandering Leaf* (Akure, Nigeria, Fagbamigbe, 1978), *Memories of Our Recent Boom* (Harlow, UK, 1982), *All This Must be Seen* (Moscow, 1986) and *Just Before Dawn* (I, 1988). His most recent work, titled *Season of Migration to the South: Africa's Crises Reconsidered* (Cape Town, 1994), has not been made available in Nigeria.

See: Cheryl M. L. Dash, 'An Introduction to the Prose Fiction of Kole Omotoso', *WLWE*, 16 (1977); F. Odun Balogun, 'Populist Fiction: Omotoso's Novels', *ALT*, 13 (1983).

ONWUEME, Tess (1955–) Nigerian playwright, born in Ogwashi-Uke, Bendel State. Her plays include *The Children's Way* (Owerri, Nigeria, 1982), *A Hen Too Soon* (Owerri, Nigeria, 1983), *The Broken Calabash* (Owerri, Nigeria, 1984) and *The Desert Encroaches* (Owerri, Nigeria, 1985), which are realist dramatisations of domestic and traditional confrontations. In *Ban Empty Barn* (Owerri, Nigeria, 1986), she produced an Orwellian animal fable on corruption and authoritarian rule in modern Nigeria. Her later work, *The Reign of Wazobia* (I, 1988), *Cattle Egret versus Nama* (I, 1989) and *Legacies* (I, 1989), maintains this strong political concern. The last two deal with women's politics and the influence of Afro-American discourses on modern African women. The later work is more experimental, and breaks with the realist form of her early work. Onwueme is now resident in the USA. In 1994 she published, in Nigeria, an epic drama for women *Tell it to Women* (reissued Trenton, NJ 1997) which further explored the themes of feminism and its relevance to modern Africa. In 1996 she published *Riot in Heaven: Musical Drama for the Voices of Colour* (NY, 1996).

OSMAN, Abdirazak Y. (n.a.) One of the few young Somali writers to use English in recent times. *In the Name of Our Fathers* (L, 1996) is his first novel.

OSOFISAN, Femi (1946–) Born and raised in the Yoruba districts of Ilesha and Ile-Ife and Erunwhon, Western Nigeria, Osofisan has been a successful academic, journalist and playwright, and is certainly one of the most prolific and influential of the new generation of African writers working in English. The bulk of his creative work has been done in the theatre, and the range and dynamism of his many texts establish a claim to his being the most important West African playwright since Soyinka. Among his works are: *Kolera Kolej: A Novel* (I, 1975), *A Restless Run of Locusts* (I, 1975), *The Chattering and the Song* (I, 1976), *Who's Afraid of Solarin?* (I, 1978), *Morountodun and Other Plays* (includes *Morountodun, No More the Wasted Breed, Red is the Freedom Road*) (I, 1982), *Six Plays* (L, 1984), *The Oriki of a Grasshopper* (I, 1986; reprinted W, 1995), *The Orality of Prose: A Comparative Study of Rabelais, Joyce and Tutuola* (Ife-Ife, Nigeria, 1986), *Two One Act Plays* (includes *Altine's Wrath* and *The Oriki of a Grasshopper*) (I, 1986), *Beyond Translation: Tragic Paradigms and the Dramaturgy of Ola Rotimi and Wole Soyinka* (Ife-Ife, Nigeria, 1986), *Farewell to a Cannibal Rage* (I, 1986), *Midnight Hotel* (I, 1986), *Another Raft* (La, 1988), *Birthdays Are Not For Dying and Other Plays* (includes *Fires Burn and Die Hard, The Inspector and the Hero*) (La, 1990), *Cordelia* (La, 1990), *Proceedings of the International Symposium on African Literatures* (La, 1991), *Esu and the Vagabond Minstrels: A Fertility Rite for the Modern Stage* (I, 1991), *Once Upon Four Robbers* (I, 1982, 1991), *Aringindin and the Night Watchmen* (I, 1991), *Twingle-Twangle, a Twynning Tayle* (La, 1992), *Yungba-Yungba and the Dance Contest: A Parable for Our Time* (I, 1992), *The Album of the Midnight Blackout* (I, 1994) and *The Engagement* (I, 1995).

See: Chris Dunton, *Make Man Talk True: Nigerian Drama in English Since 1970* (L: Hans Zell, 1992); Biodun Jeyifo, *The Truthful Lie: Essays in a Sociology of African Drama* (L: New Beacon Books, 1985); Sandra L. Richards, *Ancient Songs Set Ablaze: The Theatre of Femi Osofisan* (W: Howard University Press, 1996).

OSUNDARE, Niyi (1947–) A Yoruba poet, born in Ondo State. His father was a traditional singer and oral poet. He was educated in the UK and Canada, receiving a doctorate in English from the University of York, Ontario in 1979. Since then, he has taught extensively in both Nigeria and the USA, and is now based at the University of Ibadan, where he teaches Creative Arts. An influential poet and critic, Osundare struggles in his verse to bridge the false gap between a populist-oriented approach and the idea of a serious literature. Hence the stress in his verse on African oral traditions, and the attention it pays to the 'performance' nature of all Nigerian verbal arts. After *Songs of the Marketplace* (I, 1983), his first volume of poetry, Osundare went on to publish a number of other works: *Village Voices* (I, 1984), *The Eye of the Earth* (I, 1986), *A Nib in the Pond* (Ife, 1986), *The Writer as Righter* (Ife, 1986), *Moonsongs* (I, 1988), *Waiting Laughters, A Song in Many Voices* (La, 1990), *Songs of the Seasons* (I, 1990), *Selected Poems* (O, 1992) and *Midlife* (I, 1993). He also wrote a critical study, *African Literature and the Crisis of Post-structuralist Theorising* (I, 1993). He has shared the Commonwealth Writers Prize for Poetry.

See: Biodun Jeyifo, 'Niyi Osundare', in Yemi Ogunbiyi (ed.), *Perspectives on Nigerian Literature*, Vol. 2 (Lagos: Guardian Books, 1988); Stephen Arnold, 'The Praxis of Niyi Osundare, Popular Scholar-Poet', *WLWE*, 29 (1989); Aderemi Bamikunle, 'Niyi Osundare's Poetry and the Yoruba Oral Artistic Tradition', ALT, 18 (1992): 49–61.

PALANGYO, Peter (1939–1993) Born in Arusha, N. E. Tanzania, and educated in Uganda and the US as a biologist. In 1972, he returned to Tanzania to teach at the University of Dar es Salaam. Palangyo's only novel, *Dying in the Sun* (L, N, 1969), was the first to be published by a Tanzanian in the Heinemann African Writers series. He died in a car accident in 1993.

p'BITEK, Okot (1931–1982) Born in Uganda, he went to England in 1958 to undertake university studies, and later began teaching at Makerere University College. He has published extensively, both as a writer and as an academic. p'Bitek published his first long satirical poem in the Acholi language *Lak tar* (1953) (trans. into English as White Teeth, N, 1989). Much of his later work was also written and published first in Acholi, and then translated into English. His works include *Song of Lawino* (Wer pa Lawino) (N, 1966), *Song of Ocol* (Wer pa Ocol) (N, 1970), *African Religions in Western Scholarship* (Kampala, 1970; Totowa, USA, 1972), *Song of a Prisoner* and *Song of Malaya* (NY, 1971), *Horn of My Love* (N, 1974) and *Artist the Ruler: Essays on Art, Culture and Values* (N, 1986). Okot's influence has been incalculable. He remains amongst the most important of modern East African writers, having established a powerful link between writing in the local language and the poetic traditions available to him, and initiating the practice of self-translation between his own language and English, both of which had a strong influence on the practice and ideas of younger writers such as Ngũgĩ wa Thiong'o, Grace Ogot and Taban lo Liyong.

See: George Heron, *The Poetry of Okot p'Bitek* (L: Heinemann, 1976); Bernth Lindfors, 'The Songs of Okot p'Bitek', in G. D. Killam (ed.), *The Writing of East and Central Africa* (L: Heinemann, 1984); Ogo A. Ofuami, 'The Traditional and Modern Influence in Okot p'Bitek's Poetry', *African Studies Review*, 28 (December 1985); Charles A. Bodunde, 'Oral Traditions and Modern Poetry: Okot p'Bitek's *Song of Lawino* and Okigbo's *Labyrinths*', *ALT*, 18 (1992): 24–34; Charles Okumu, 'The Form of Okot p'Bitek's Poetry: Literary Borrowing from Acoli Oral Traditions', *RAL*, 23, 3 (Fall 1992): 53–66.

PETERS, Lenrie (1932–) Born in Bathurst, The Gambia, Peters trained as a doctor at Trinity College, Cambridge, where he became President of the African Students Union. After receiving his medical degree in 1959, Peters went on to specialise in surgery. On his return to The Gambia, he set up his own private practice. His works include: *Poems* (I, 1964), *The Second Round* (L, 1965), *Katchikali*, (L, 1971), *Satellites* (L, 1967) and *Selected Poetry* (L, 1981). Although he has continued to write and publish poetry, his major contribution in recent years was founding The Gambia Writers' Club in 1971 and editing the literary journal *Ndaanan*.

PRINCE, Mary (1788–not recorded) *The History of Mary Prince, A West Indian Slave, Related By Herself, With A Supplement by the Editor, to Which is Added the Narrative of Asa-Asa, A Captured African* (1831; reprinted L, 1986) is the story of a woman slave, as told to her emancipationist friend and mistress Susannah Moodie.

See: Gillian Whitlock, 'Outlaws of the Text: Women's Bodies and the Organisation of Gender in Imperial Space', paper from Australia/Canada: Post-colonization and the Women's Texts Research Seminar, Calgary, Calgary Institute for the Humanities, 1992.

QUAQUE (Kweku), Philip (1741–1816) The first African to be ordained as an Anglican priest, Quaque's letters give a unique early insight into life in these slaving settlements. After being educated in England, Quaque returned to Cape Coast as a Chaplain. He opened the earliest schools in the colony where he served for fifty years. Many of the descendants of the students in his schools became the dominant families of the Creole community in Ghana from which the early nationalists and intellectuals of the later nineteenth century were drawn. His letters are contained in the Archives of the Society for the Propagation of the Gospel, London. Ten of the letters, in shortened form, are reproduced in Philip Curtin, *Africa Remembered* (Madison: University of Wisconsin Press, 1967).

ROBERTS, Gabriel J. (n.a.) Author of a play *A Coup is Planned*, published in the journal *Ndaanan* 2, 1 (March 1972), dealing with the political struggle to retain independence for The Gambia under mounting Senegalese pressure and its effects on local politics.

ROBERTS, Shabaan (1909–1962) Born in Vibambani, Roberts is the best-known Tanzanian writer using Swahili. His work illustrates the continuity of writing in African languages in East Africa, to which recent supporters of the revival of writing in indigenous languages such as Ngũgĩ have drawn attention. A prolific and popular writer, he shows that writing in indigenous languages remained a viable option, despite colonial educational policies which insisted on the use of English. He wrote throughout the colonial period using Swahili. His work at this time included several important anti-colonial novels. The first two, *Kufikirika* (N, 1946) and *Kusadikika* (N, 1951), are both named after imaginary countries, allowing him to satirise the colonial authorities and call for opposition. In a later novel, *Utabara mkulima* (Utubura the Farmer) (N, 1968), he explores the effect of colonisation on ordinary Tanganyikans. In 1967 he published *Utenzi wa vita viya uhuru 1939 hata 1945* (N), a work, literally, on a global scale, in which he analyses the Second World War and its effects from a colonial perspective. Significantly, his work reflects many influences from English literature as well as from Swahili culture. References to Shakespeare, Bunyan, Swift and Dickens are frequent. He also predates the work of more recent popular writers in self-publishing his work, establishing his own publishing house in 1934 to overcome the unwillingness of colonial publishing patrons to publish such outspokenly nationalist work. Tragically, this project failed and he died of tuberculosis, leaving many works unpublished at his death. These are being issued in a multi-volume collected works entitled *Diwani na Shabaan* which began publication in 1954 (Dar es Salaam). He also wrote traditional songs, poems etc. and some of these can be read in translation in such anthologies as Ali Jahadhmay, *An Anthology of Swahili Poetry* (L: Heinemann, 1977).

ROTIMI, Ola (1938–) Born in Sapele, in Delta State, Nigeria. A playwright, his work is characterised by a focus on its unifying appeal to traditions from across Nigeria. *If: A Tragedy of the Ruled* (Ibadan, 1983) marked a departure with his previous writing, although all of it has been highly politicised. At times Rotimi has found himself on the wrong side of the politics of the day, partly a consequence of his strong advocacy of social and political change in Nigerian society. Like some other Nigerian writers, e.g. Wale Ogunyemi and Zulu Sofola, Rotimi has written in both Yoruba and English. In this respect they are similar to the writers who took this route in East Africa, though they did not follow the practice of translating their work, preferring usually to keep the two sets of texts discrete and complementary. Some of his other works are: *The Gods Are Not To Blame* (L, 1971), *Kurunmi* (I, 1971), *Ovonramwen Nogbaisi* (Benin City, Ibadan, Nigeria 1974, *Our Husband Has Gone Mad Again* (I, 1977) and *Hopes of the Living Dead* (I, 1988).

See: Dapo Adelugba, 'Wale, Ogunyemi, Zulu Sofola and Ola Rotimi: Three Dramatists in Search of a Language', in Oyin Ogunba and Abiola Irele (eds), *Theatre in Africa*, Vol. I (Nigeria: Univ. of Ibadan Press, 1978); Chris Dunton, *Make Man Talk True: Nigerian Drama in English Since 1970* (O: Zell, 1992).

RUGANDA, John (1941–) Ugandan playwright. His work includes *The Burden* (N, 1972), *Black Mamba* (N, 1973), *The Floods* (N, 1980), *Music Without Tears* (N, 1982) and *Echoes of Silence* (N, 1986).

RUHUMBIKA, G. (1938–) Born in Tanzania, attended university at Makerere, and in 1969 received a degree from the Sorbonne University in Paris. Author of the documentary novel *Village in Uhuru* (Harlow, 1969), also edited *Towards Ujamaa: Twenty Years of Tanu Leadership* (K, 1974).

SALIH, Tayeb (1929–) A northern Sudanese writer who uses Arabic. Because two of his works were amongst the few works in translation published in the Heinemann African Writers series, he was widely read abroad in English-speaking countries when few other writers from the Arab North African countries were. The short story collection, *The Wedding of Zein* and the novel *Season of Migration to the North*, were often spoken and written about by critics and commentators on the new African English writing, when other Arabic writers from these regions were ignored. Despite this, his work seems to have had little direct influence on other African English writers. Salih's work though has helped to draw the attention of English readers to the existence of Arabic-language literature in North Africa.

See: John E. Davidson, 'In Search of a Middle Point: The Origins of Oppression in Tayeb Salih's *Season of Migration to the North*', *RAL*, 20 (Fall 1989); Kenneth W. Harrow, 'The Power and the Word: *L'Aventure ambiguè* and *The Wedding of Zein*', *African Studies Review* 30, 1 (March 1987); *Tayeb Salih's Season of Migration to the North: A Casebook*, ed. Mona Takiekkine Amyuni (Beirut: American University of Beirut, 1985); Patricia Geesey, 'Cultural Hybridity and Contamination in Tayeb Salih's Mawsim al-hijra ila al-Shamal (*Season of Migration to the North*)', *RAL*, 28, 3 (1998).

SALLAH, Tijan M. (1958–) Gambian English poet and short story writer, an important member of the group of new young Gambian writers to emerge in the 1980s. *When Africa Was a Young Woman* (Calcutta, 1980), *Before the New Earth: African Short Stories* (Calcutta, 1988), *Kora Land* (W, 1989) and *Dreams of Dirty Roads* (W, 1993).

See: Samuel Baity Garren, 'Exile and Return: The Poetry and Fiction of Tijan Sallah', *Wasafiri*, 15 (Spring 1992).

SAMKANGE, Stanlake J. T. (1922–) Zimbabwean novelist and historian, Samkange was educated in the then Rhodesia, South Africa and the USA. He taught at Fisk and Harvard Universities before becoming Professor of African History at Northeastern University. He returned to Zimbabwe after independence and established Harare Publishers. Apart from many academic historical works, he has written a number of books with a more literary form, among which are *On Trial For My Country* (L, 1966), *Among the Yanks* (Harare, 1985) and *On Trial for that UDI: A Novel* (Harare, 1986). His work may well have influenced other East and West African writers to use fictional forms to explore political and historical issues and for this reason he has been discussed in this volume.

SANCHO, Ignatius (1729–1780) Born on a slave ship bound for South America, Sancho found his way to England, where he worked for the Duke of Montagu. He later owned his own grocery shop, as well as becoming a prolific letter-writer, a poet and a playwright. *The Letters of the late Ignatius Sancho (Facsimile reprint of the 5th edition (1803)) with an introduction by P. Edwards* (first published in 1802; L, 1968); *The Letters of Ignatius Sancho*, ed. Paul Edwards and Polly Rewt (Edinburgh: Edinburgh University Press, 1994).

SARO-WIWA, Ken (1941–1995). Nigerian writer, academic and political activist, Saro-Wiwa spent much of the latter part of his life fighting for the rights of the Ogoni people. In 1995, following a period of detention at the hands of the military dictatorship in Nigeria, he was brought before a military tribunal, accused of treason, sentenced to death and executed, along with other Ogoni leaders. *Sozaboy: A Novel in Rotten English* (Port Harcourt, Nigeria, 1985) established him as a serious novelist, although he had previously written plays, poetry, short stories, satirical novels, children's literature and a vastly popular TV comedy series, four selected scripts from which were published as *Basi and Company* (Port Harcourt, 1983). This series was based on his earlier stage and radio play, *The Transistor Radio* (I, 1971). His many other works include: *Letters to Ogoni Youth* (Port Harcourt, 1983), *Songs in a Time of War* (Port Harcourt, 1985), *A Forest of Flowers* (Port Harcourt, 1986), *Prisoners of Jebs* (L, 1988), *Adaku and Other Stories* (L, 1989), *Four Farcical Plays* (L, 1989), *On a Darkling Plain: An Account of the Nigerian Civil War* (L, 1989), *The Singing Anthill, Ogoni Folktales* (L, 1991), *Pitta Dumbrok's Prison* (L, 1991), *Genocide in Nigeria: The Ogoni Tragedy* (L, 1992), *Ogoni: Moment of Truth* (Port Harcourt 1994) and *A Month and A Day: Detention Diary* (L, 1995).

See: Bernth Lindfors, 'Ken Saro-Wiwa: in short, a Giant' in *African Textualities: Texts, Pretexts and Contexts of African Literature* (Trenton, N.J.: Africa World Press, 1997),

199–202; N. F. Inyama, 'Ken Saro-Wiwa: Maverick Iconoclast of the Nigerian Literary Scene', *ALT*, 20 (1996), 35–49.

SARR, Sheriff (1951–) Born in Serekunda, Gambia. Sarr is another of the new generation of Gambian writers to emerge in the 1980s. His novel *Meet Me in Conakry* (Basingstoke, 1884) addresses the dominance of The Gambia by its surrounding Senegalese neighbours, and the flight of Gambian youth to neighbouring countries such as Senegal and Guinea.

See: Stewart Brown, 'Gambian Fictions', *Wasafiri*, 15 (Spring 1992).

SEKYI, Kobina (William Esuman-Gwiri Sekyi) (1892–1956) Born at Cape Coast, Ghana, Sekyi wrote the important early play, *The Blinkards* (reissued L, 1974). Kobina Sekyi was a leading figure in the intellectual life of Ghana between the wars and in the lead-up to independence. A lawyer and philosopher, he wrote a number of important studies of Akan law and custom including *A Comparison of Gold Coast, English and Akan-Fanti Laws in Relation to the Absolute Right of the Individual* (L, 1937). He was also the author of an important unpublished polemic text, *The Meaning of the Expression 'Thinking in English'* (L, 1937). A passionate advocate of the need for West African intellectuals to endorse the values of their own cultures, he advocated retention of traditional customs and political institutions. In *The Blinkards*, he satirised the new Anglicised intellectuals who turned their back on and despised their own ways. The play was reissued with a critical introduction by J. Ayo Langley as No. 136 in the Heinemann African Writers series in 1974. Much of his other literary work was not published, or has been lost, including several plays and collections of short stories.

See: K. A. B. Jones-Quartey, 'Kobina Sekyi: A Fragment of Biography', *Research Review* (University of Ghana), 4 (1968). J. Ayo Langley 'Modernisation and its Malcontents: Kobina Sekyi of Ghana and the Restatement of African Political Theory', *Research Review* (University of Ghana), 6 (1970).

SELASSIE, Bereket Habte (n.a.) *Riding the Whirlwind* (Trenton, N.J., 1993). Ethiopian English-language novelist. He is also the author of a number of political and historical studies of modern Ethiopia.

SELLASSIE, Sahle (1936–) Studied in France at Aix-en-Provence and at UCLA in Los Angeles, USA. Ethiopian novelist, journalist, and public servant, Sellassie is the first person to write in the Chaha dialect of Amharic. He also writes in English. His works include *Shinega's Village: Scenes of Ethiopian Life* (Berkeley, Ca., 1964), *The Afersata* (L, 1969) and *Warrior King* (L, 1974).

SERUMUGA, Robert (1939–1980) Born in Uganda, Serumaga combined a passion for drama with a background in business to become one of Africa's best-known playwrights and directors. He died in exile in 1980. Among his works are: *The Elephants* (N, NY, 1971) and *Majangwa: A Promise of Rains* with *A Play* (N, 1974). His unpublished plays include *Renga Moi* (produced Kampala 1972). He also wrote a novel entitled *Return to the Shadows* (L, 1969).

See: Andrew Horn, 'Uhuru to Amin: The Golden Decade of Ugandan Theatre', *Literary Half Yearly*, 19, 1 (1978): 22–49.

SMITH, Venture (n.a.) *Life of Venture Smith* (1798; reprinted Kraus, Nedeln, 1971). This is almost certainly one of the many texts which owe as much to the amanuensis who wrote it as to the ex-slave whose true story it purports to be.

SOFOLA, Zulu (1935–) Well-established though critically neglected Nigerian playwright and director. She was born at Isele-Uku in Bendel State. Educated at Catholic University, Virginia and Ibadan, she became head of theatre studies at Ilorin University. Her plays include *The Disturbed Peace of Christmas* (I, 1971), *Wedlock of the Gods* (L, 1972), *King Emene* (L, 1974), *The Wizard of Law – Adapted from a Mediaeval French Play* (L, 1975), *The Sweet Trap* (I, 1977), *Old Wines Are Tasty* (I, 1981), *Memories in the Moonlight* (I, 1986), *Song of A Maiden* (I, 1991) and *The Operators* (unpublished).

SOWANDE, Bode (1948–) Born in Kaduna, Nigeria, Sowande gained a degree in French from the University of Ife in 1971, and later was educated at the University of Sheffield, UK, where he completed a doctorate in dramatic literature. He taught in the Drama Department at Ibadan University for many years and was an active theatre practitioner, directing and acting, as well as writing plays performed on and off campus. With his wife, he founded Odu Themes Bookshop and Publishers in Ibadan in 1972, finally retiring from academic life in the early 1990s in order to focus solely on the company's work. Although he has published an important political novel, *Our Man the President* (I, 1981), and also written novels and short stories for children, he is best known as a dramatist. In recent years, like other Nigerian writers, he has worked frequently abroad. His plays include *The Babylon Trilogy* [published as *A Farewell to Arms and Other Plays* (Harlow, 1972), it includes *The Night Before, A Farewell to Babylon*, and *A Sanctus for Women*] and *Flamingo and Other Plays* (Harlow, 1986, which contains *Flamingo, Afamako, The Master and the Frauds* and *Circus of Freedom Square*), and *Tornadoes Full of Dreams* (Lagos, Nigeria, 1990). His own commentary on this last is useful: 'History as an Imp: A Playwright's Notes on the Employment of His Most Recent Play, *Tornadoes Full of Dreams*', in *Nigerian Stage*, 1 (March 1990). Sowande has also published a number of novels. These include: *Our Man the President* (I, 1981), *Without a Home* (Harlow, 1982) and *The Missing Bridesmaid* (I, 1988).

See: Chris Dunton, *Make Man Talk True: Nigerian Drama in English Since 1970* (L: Hans Zell, 1992); Eustace Palmer, 'Bode Sowande's *Farewell to Babylon*', *African Literature Today*, 12 (1982).

ṢOYINKA, Wọle (1934–) A Yoruba, born in Ijebu-Isara, near Abeokuta, in Western Nigeria, where he grew up, and where his father was the headmaster of the local grammar school. He was educated at his father's school, and then at Ibadan University, where he studied alongside Achebe, J. P. Clark-Bekederemo, Okigbo and others. He went to the United Kingdom to undertake postgraduate study at the University of Leeds. After completing his masters degree, he spent eighteen months as a play reader at the Royal Court Theatre in London, returning to Nigeria in 1960. He founded a number of theatre companies, including the 1960 Masks and the Orisun Theatre. He was a Professor of Drama at Ile-Ife for a number of years and has held many senior academic posts abroad. Dramatist, poet, critic, editor and translator, with an international reputation, Ṣoyinka was awarded the Nobel Prize in 1986, the first sub-Saharan African writer to be so honoured. His plays have been produced in many countries outside Africa, including the US, the UK, Canada and Australia. He has held a number of important non-academic posts, both in Nigeria and abroad. Arrested by the Nigerian federal government for his role in the Biafran war, Ṣoyinka spent twenty-six months in detention, some of which was in solitary confinement. From this period a number of works emerged, and the event may be said to have strengthened his political convictions. Since then, as indeed long before, Ṣoyinka has never shied away from confrontation on behalf of the dispossessed and downtrodden. Placed under arrest again in 1994 for his opposition to the policies of the regime of General Abache, Ṣoyinka escaped, first to Ghana and eventually to London, where he lives and continues to work. *A Dance of the Forests* (L, 1963), *The Lion and the Jewel* (L, 1963), *Three Short Plays*: contains *The Swamp Dwellers, The Trials of Brother Jero* and *The Strong Breed* (I, 1963; L, NY, 1969), *The Road* (L, 1965), *The Interpreters* (NY, 1965; L, 1970), *Kongi's Harvest* (L, 1967), *Idanre and Other Poems* (NY, 1967; L, 1968), *The Forest of a Thousand Daemons (Ògbójú Ode Nínú Igbó Irúnmalè)*, trans. from the Yoruba of D. O. Fagunwa (L, 1968; N, J, 1969) *The Trials of Brother Jero* (I, 1969), *The Strong Breed* (I, 1970), *Before the Blackout* (I, 1971), *Madmen and Specialists* (L, 1971), *A Shuttle in the Crypt* (L, NY, 1972), *The Man Died, Prison Notes of Wọle Ṣoyinka* (L, NY, 1972), *Season of Anomy* (L, 1973), 'The

Fourth Stage' (L, 1969; section in *The Morality of Art: Essays Presented to G. Wilson Knight*, ed. by D. W. Jeffares), *The Jero Plays* (L, 1973), *Camwood on the Leaves* (L, 1973), *The Bacchae of Euripides* (L, NY, 1973; 1974), *Collected Plays Vol. 1* contains: *A Dance of the Forests, The Swamp Dwellers, The Strong Breed, The Road, The Bacchae of Euripides* (O, 1974), *Collected Plays Vol. 2* contains: *The Lion and the Jewel, Kongi's Harvest, The Trials of Brother Jero, Jero's Metamorphosis* and *Madmen and the Specialists* (L, 1974), *Death and the King's Horsemen* (L, NY, 1975), *Myth, Literature and the African World* (C, 1976), *Ogun Abibiman* (L, 1976), *Opera Wonyosi* (L, Bloomington, USA, 1981), *Aké: The Years of Childhood* (L, 1981; NY, 1982), 'The Critic and Society: Barthes, Leftocracy and Other Mythologies', in *Black Literature and Literary Theory*, ed. Henry Louis Gates Jr. (L, NY, 1984), *A Play of Giants* (L, 1984; Portsmouth, 1988), *Requiem for a Futurologist* (L, 1985), *Childe International* (I, 1987), *Mandela's Earth and Other Poems* (NY, L, 1988; 1989), *Art, Dialogue and Outrage: Essays on Literature and Culture* (I, 1988), *Isara: A Voyage Around 'Essay'* (NY, 1989; L, 1990), *The Credo of Being and Nothingness* (I, 1991), *From Zia, with Love; and A Scourge of Hyacinths* (L, 1992), *Ibadan, the Penkelemes Years: A Memoir 1946–65* (L, 1994), *The Beatification of Area Boy* (L, 1995) and *The Open Sore of a Continent: A Personal Narrative of the Nigerian Crisis* (NY, 1996). As in the case of Achebe there is a mass of criticism on Ṣoyinka's work.

See: Eldred Jones, *The Writing of Wọle Ṣoyinka* (L: Heinemann, 1973); James Gibbs, *Wọle Ṣoyinka* (L: Macmillan, 1986); James Gibbs (ed.), *Critical Perspectives on Wọle Ṣoyinka* (W: Three Continents Press, 1980); Ketu H. Katrak, *Wọle Ṣoyinka and Modern Tragedy: A Study of Dramatic Theory and Practice* (Westport, Conn.: Greenwood Press, 1986); Obi Maduakor, *Wọle Ṣoyinka: An Introduction to his Writing* (NY: Garland Press, 1986); Adelugba Dapo (ed.), *Before Our Very Eyes: Tribute to Wọle Ṣoyinka* (I: Spectrum, 1987); Tanure Ojaide, *The Poetry of Wọle Ṣoyinka* (La: Malthouse Press, 1994); Derek Wright, *Wọle Ṣoyinka Revisited* (NY: Twayne, 1993); Adewale Maja-Pearce, *Wọle Ṣoyinka: An Appraisal* (O: Heinemann, 1994).

SUTHERLAND, Efua Theodora (1924–1996) Born in Ghana, Efua Sutherland trained as a teacher before beginning work as a dramatist, writing and directing in a variety of venues. One of Africa's most influential theatre practitioners, Efua Sutherland also wrote short stories and essays and completed a number of translations. Her works include: *Playtime in Africa*, with Willis E. Bell (L, 1960), *The Roadmakers*, with Willis E. Bell (A, L, 1961), *You Swore an Oath*, in *Présence Africaine*, 22 (Summer 1964), *Foriwa: A Play* (A, 1967), *Edufa*, (L, 1967), *Odasani* (A, 1967), *Vulture! Vulture!: Two Rhythm Plays* (A, 1968), *The Original Bob: The Story of Bob Johnson, Ghana's Ace Comedian*, (A, 1970), and *The Marriage of Anansewa: A Storytelling Drama* (L, 1975).

See: Michael Etherton, *The Development of African Drama* (L: Hutchison University Library for Africa, 1982); Chinyere Okafor, 'Parallelism Versus Influence in African Literature: The Case of Efua Sutherland's *Efuru*', *Kiabara*, 3, 1 (1980).

SWARAY, Nabie Yayah (1953–). Sierra Leonean playwright who writes about the people of the interior rather than the coastal Creole descendants of the resettled slaves. His work is critical of the policy of governments based in Freetown towards the peoples of the rural interior. *Worl' do for fraid: A Play in Three Acts, with Music* (W, 1986).

TESFAY, G. S. (n.a.) Ethiopian author of *The Company of My Shadow* (Addis Ababa, 1993).

TUMA, Hama (n.a.) Ethiopian author of one of the most critical collections of stories about life under the Mengistu dictatorship. *The Case of the Socialist Witchdoctor and other stories* (O, 1993).

TUTUOLA, Amos (1920–1997) One of the most important and influential African writers. Born in Nigeria, Tutuola's first novel, *The Palm-Wine Drinkard* (L, 1952), was acclaimed as an extraordinary work by Western critics, but received little praise in Nigeria. Since then, however, fellow Nigerian writers like Achebe and Ṣoyinka have done much to remedy this situation, and Tutuola's work now enjoys considerable acclaim at home. He is one of the earliest writers to use the whole range of practices available to modern Nigerian authors and is increasingly seen as the precursor of the recent forms of writers such as Ben Okri. Some of his most important works include: *My Life in the Bush of Ghosts* (L, 1954), *Simbi and the Satyr of the Dark Jungle* (L, 1955), *The Brave African Huntress* (L, 1958) and *Feather of the Jungle* (L, 1962).

See: Bernth Lindfors (ed.), *Critical Perspectives on Amos Tutuola* (W: Three Continents Press, 1980); Eustace Palmer, 'Twenty-five Years of Amos Tutuola', *International Fiction Review*, 5 (1978); Ato Quayson, *Strategic Transformations in Nigerian Literature* (L: James Currey, 1997).

VASSANJI, M. G. (1950–) Born in Kenya of Indian parents, and raised in Tanzania, Vassanji studied at MIT in Massachusetts and the University of Pennsylvania. In 1978 he settled in Canada. His novel *The Book of Secrets* (NY, 1995) won the Giller Prize and the Harbourfront Prize. Other works include: *The Gunny Sack* (O, 1989) and *Uhuru Street: Short Stories* (O, Portsmouth, USA, 1991). His latest novel, *No New Land* (Toronto, 1992), is set in Canada and deals with the disaporic community there. Vassanji is typical of those recent writers the genealogy of whose life and work challenges simple constructions of what constitutes an African text or an African writer.

See: H. G. Kirchhoff, 'Figuring that Words are the Way to Go', *Toronto Globe and Mail*, 4 May 1991; Stephen Smith, 'Stories Not Yet Told', *Books in Canada*, 21, 5 (Summer 1992); John Clement Ball, 'Interview with M. G. Vassanji', *Paragraph: the Canadian Fiction Review*, 15, 3 & 4 (Winter 1993–Spring 1994).

WALTERS, Joseph J. (186?–1894) *Guanya Pau: A Story of an African Princess* (Cleveland, 1891; reissued, Nebraska, 1994, with a foreword by Oyekan Owomoyela). This earliest example of an African long fiction was published in America, where Walters had been sent by his missionary sponsors to study at Oberlin College. A Vai, Walters was educated in Sierra Leone and his story was written both to publicise the plight of Vai women and to raise money to promote their education. The text is strongly opposed to the customary practice of polygamy and arranged marriage, but is also positive in its treatment of many aspects of the Vai culture. We owe our knowledge of this earliest African English fictional text to its discovery in the early 1990s by the American linguist J. V. Singler.

See: J. V. Singler, 'The Day Will Come: J. J. Walters and Guanya Pau', *Liberian Studies Journal*, 15, 2 (1990): 125–33.

WANGUSA, Timothy (1942–) Ugandan poet and novelist, educated at Makerere and Leeds Universities, Wangusa was appointed Professor of Literature at Makerere in 1981. A poet, his first collection was *Salutations: Poems 1965–75* (U, 1977). *Upon this Mountain* (L, 1989) was his first novel. His collected poetry to date is now available in *A Pattern of Dust: Selected Poems, 1965–1990* (U, 1994).

WASHINGTON, Booker T. (Taliaferro) (1856–1915) A very controversial but important figure in the history of the Black Movement in America, Washington came to prominence in 1895, when in Atlanta he delivered a speech which emphasised that black and white Americans should work together to achieve economic progress. This remained his public position for the rest of his life. The speech was hailed by conservative whites as a sign of reconciliation in the upheavals which characterised black–white relations in the 1890s. It was condemned by radical black leaders, and was repudiated even by moderates such as Du Bois for its absolute rejection of political agitation as a tool of change. Nevertheless, his account of his life, *Up from Slavery* (Boston, 1901), influenced many later black leaders, including the fiery Marcus Garvey. Believing that economic independence was the best route to the improvement of the condition of African-Americans, Washington set up a training school at Tuskagee, Alabama. The school emphasised industrial and farming skills for boys and housekeeping skills for girls. The religious element and stress on character and morals in the programme was also strong. In many ways, Tuskagee echoes the programme of mission education advocated by African missions in the same period. In recent years his role in the political struggles of the time has been reassesssed, and the public face of accommodation which he presented has been modified by revelations that, in private, he often supported and sustained direct challenges to racial injustice.

WHEATLEY, Phillis (1753?–1784) It is believed that Wheatley was born in either what is now Senegal or The Gambia. Taken from Africa as a slave at a very young age, her African name and history was lost forever. Purchased in 1761 as a maid-servant by the wife of a liberal Boston merchant, Wheatley was taught to read and write, mastering not only English but also French, Latin and Greek. She published her first poem in 1770. *The Collected Works of Phyllis Wheatley (includes a facsimile of Poems on Various Subjects, Religious and Moral, Bell, London 1793), Letters and variants, as well as extant poems not included in the 1793 volume,* reissued with an introduction by H. L. Gates (NY, O, 1988) was the first volume of poems by a single author to appear in America.

See: J. E. Shields, *The Collected Works of Phillis Wheatley* (NY: Oxford University Press, 1988).

WORKU, Daniachew (1936–) Ethiopian writer. Educated in Ethiopia, he is best known abroad for the novel *The Thirteenth Sun* (L, 1973). This early Ethiopian novel in English was suppressed at home but finally came out in Ethiopia late in 1974, after Haile Selassie was deposed. He has also written a number of plays.

Index

Abacha, General Sani 197
Abrahams, Peter 80
academy
  history of reception of African writing in the 83
Achebe, Chinua 41, 82, 86, 117, 133, 153, 270, 277
  Anthills of the Savannah 145–7, 159
  Arrow of God 41, 119, 121, 122, 125, 131, 277
  biography and important works 362–3
  and *bolekaja* critics 173
  'Colonialist Criticism' (essay) 83
  criticism of analysis of post-independence Nigerian politics 147
  difficulty in accessing oral tradition 114
  editor of Heinemann African Writers series 83–4, 118, 211
  extensive use of proverbs 333
  Girls at War 83, 145
  at Ibadan University 77, 117
  influence on other writers 126
  A Man of the People 126, 143, 144, 145
  and Nigerian Civil War 115, 145, 236
  No Longer at Ease 119, 143–4, 150, 239, 300
  presentation of colonial invader 122
  purpose of writing 117
  silence for twenty year 144–5
  Things Fall Apart see *Things Fall Apart*
Acquah, Kobena Eyi 210–11
Across the Bridge (Gicheru) 240
Adaku and Other Stories (Saro-Wiwa) 198
Adali-Mrotty, G. 77
Admiring Silence (Gurnah) 316–19, 320
Adoko, Akena 204–5, 363
Advisory Council 74
Afamoko (Sowande) 181
Afersata, The (Sellassie) 263
Africa: From People to People (Cordor) 255
African Book Writers Limited 46
African Literatures Association of America 76–7
African Speaks for his People, An (Mockerie) 45
African, The (Conton) 252–3

African Writers series *see* Heinemann African Writers series
Africa's Own Library series 66, 67
Afro-American writers 156, 251
After 4.30 (Maillu) 98
Agbebi, Mojola 27, 34
'Agony of the Dark Child' (Cheney-Coker) 250
Ahmad, Aijaz 122
Ahuma, Rev. Attoh 27, 50
Aidoo, Ama Ata 155–6, 269, 292–5
  Anowa 156, 292
  biography and important works 363
  Changes 293–5
  The Dilemma of a Ghost 156, 292
  rejection of feminist label 299
Aig-Imoukhuede, Frank 196, 363–4
Akar, John Joseph 248, 364
Akare, Thomas 102
  biography and important works 364
  The Slums 168–70, 240
  Twilight Woman 99
Akassi Youmi (Rotimi) 183
Akintola, Chief Samue Ladoke 183
'Al Mukhlit' (Johnson) 329
Altine's Wrath (Osofisan) 177
Aluko, T. M. 80, 126, 364
Amadi, Elechi 86, 122–5
  biography and important works 364
  The Concubine 118, 122–5, 286, 287
  The Great Ponds 118, 125
Aman (Aman) 273–4
America 14, 25–6
American Colonisation Society 25, 54
Amharic 262
Amin, Idi 204, 207
Anansegoro 296–7
Anansesem 296, 297
Andrzejewski, B. W. 268, 364
Angira, Jared 199–203
  biography and important works 364–5
  Cascades 202–3
  editing of *Busara* 77
  Juices 199–200
  Silent Voices 200–2
  Soft Corals 202
Anglo-African (journal) 54
Angry Bridegroom, The (Sowande) 182

Another Raft (Osofisan) 115, 179, 180
Anowa (Aidoo) 156, 292
Anthills of the Savannah (Achebe) 145–7,
    159
anthropological writing 14
anti-slavery movement 8, 50
Anyidoho, Kofi 135, 192–5, 210
    biography and important works 365
    Elegy for the Revolution 192–3
    A Harvest of Our Dreams 193–4
Appiah 94
Aringindin and the Nightwatchmen
    (Osofisan) 179, 180
Armah, Ayi Kwei 104, 156–9, 251
    The Beautyful Ones Are Not Yet Born
    156–7
    biography and important works 365
    criticism of Western publishing controls
    158–9
    Fragments 157, 324
    The Healers 158
    and ki-Swahili 211
    Osiris Rising 102, 159
    Why Are We So Blest? 157, 158, 159
Arrow of God (Achebe) 41, 119, 121, 122,
    125, 131, 277
Asemka: A Bilingual Literary Journal of
    the University of *Cape Coast* 77
Asfaw, Gebru 366
Ashanti 32, 158
Ashanti War (1874) 32, 225
Askar, Ahmed Omar 268, 366
Asong, Linus Tongwo 277, 366
Association of Nigerian Authors 78
Astaw, Gebru 265
Atta, Nana Offori 34
authors' societies 78
autobiography genre 13–14
Awolowo, Chief Obafemi 183
Awoonor, Kofi 191, 193
    biography and important works 366
    'A Dirge' 154
    The House by the Sea 154–5
    'Songs of Sorrow' 133, 135, 154
    This Earth My Brother 155
Ayah, The (Maillu) 98

Bâ, Mariama 293
Babangida, General Ibrahim 145
Baby Sefu 56
Babylon Trilogy, The (Sowande) 181
Bamende 278
Bandele-Thomas, Biyi 331–2, 366
Banham, Martin 183–4
Barber, Karin 93, 122

Bare, Mohammed Syad 267, 268, 269
Bart-Williams, Gaston 248
Basi and Company (tv series) 103
Beasts of No Nation (Besong) 278
Beautification of Area Boy, The (Soyinka)
    185
Beautiful Nyakiemo, The 75
Beautiful Ones Are Not Yet Born, The
    (Armah) 156–7
Because of Women (Dipoko) 277
Beckett 208
*Before the New Earth: African Short
    Stories* (Sallah) 254
Behind the Rising Sun (Mezu) 231–2
Behn, Aphra 8
Beier, Ulli 79
Beneath the Jazz and Brass (de Graft) 111
Besong, Bate 275, 278, 366
Beti, Mongo 276
Beware, Soul Brother and Other Poems
    (Achebe) 145
Beyala, Calixthe 293
'Beyond Fear' (Ofeimun) 188
Bitter Harvest: A Political Novel (Ibingira)
    203–4
Black Hermit, The (Ngũgĩ) 207
Black Mamba (Ruganda) 209
Black Orpheus (magazine) 134
Black and White in Love (Dipoko) 277
Blinkards, The (Sekyi) 35, 37–9, 39–40
Blyden, Edward Wilmot 27, 28, 30–1, 33,
    34
    biography and important works 367
    expelled from Liberia 33
    and Negro issues 29, 30
Boesman and Lena (Fugard) 208
bolekaja critics 173, 188, 190, 191
Book of Secrets, The (Vassanji) 227, 321–3
Booker Prize
    (1991) 326
    (1994) 313
Brathwaite, Edward Kamau 250
Brecht 176, 177
Brew, Richard 17
Bride Price, The (Emecheta) 300
Britain
    and Buganda 43
    policy towards Africa 31
Brodber, Erna 251
Broken Calabash, The (Onwueme) 298
Brown, Stewart 254
Buganda 43, 45, 129
Bunyan 63–4, 118, 133, 213
Burden, The (Ruganda) 209
Burning Grass (Ekwensi) 80

Busara (journal) 77
Bushtrackers, The (Mwangi) 102
Butake, Boke 278–9, 367

Cabral, Amílcar 250
'Calypso for Caliban' (Johnson) 330
Cameroons 78, 247
  political history 274
  writing from 274–9
Campbell, Robert 54
Canada 275
Carcass for Hounds (Mwangi) 229–30
Caribbean writers 251
Cary, Joyce 113, 117
Cascades (Angira) 202–3
Case of the Socialist Witchdoctor, The
  (Tuma) 265–7
Casely Hayford, Adelaide Smith 27, 367
Casely Hayford, Joseph Ephraim 27, 29,
  34, 44, 367
  biography and important works 367
  Ethiopia Unbound 27–8, 35, 63
Cast Out 56
Cattle Egret Versus Nama (Onwueme) 298
Cawl, Faarax Maxamed Jaamac 368
Césaire, Aimé 250
Chaff on the Wind (Dibba) 253, 254
Chamberlain, Joseph 30, 33
Changes (Aidoo) 293–5
'Changing Voice of History: Contemporary
  African Poetry, The' (Ojaide) 195
Chausiku's Dozen (Kagwema) 101
Cheney-Coker, Syl 118, 249–50, 252
  biography and important works 368
  The Last Harmattan of Alusine Dunbar
    249, 327–8
  poetry 249–50
Chief the Honourable Minister (Aluko) 126
Children of Iroko (Ojaide) 195
Childs, L. Maria 22
Chinweizu 78, 117, 173
Chinweizu *et al* 201
Christian Missionary Society *see* CMS
Christianity 26
Christianity, Islam and the Negro Race
  (Blyden) 30
Church Missionary Society (Lagos) 35,
  36–7
Chwa, Davdi 43
circumcision, female 127–8, 274, 288, 289
Circus of Freedom Square (Sowande) 182
Clark-Bekederemo, John Pepper 114–16,
  117, 236
  biography and important works 368
  suing of Ofeimun 185

classic social realist novel 165
Close Sesame (Farah) 270–1
CMS (Church Missionary Society) 52, 54,
  61, 212
'Coca-Cola' publishing syndrome 87
Cockroach Dance, The (Mwangi) 167–8
Cole, Robert 248, 368
Collision of Altars (Gabre-Mehdin) 263
colonial contact novels 117, 119–21, 126,
  127, 128, 132, 254
colonial literature bureaux *see* Literature
  Bureax
'Colonialist Criticism' (Achebe) 83
Combat, The (Omotoso) 174, 231
'Come to Our Rally' (Ofeimun) 188–9
Company of My Shadow, The (Tesfay) 265
Concerto for an Exile (Cheney-Coker) 249
Concubine, The (Amadi) 118, 122–5, 286,
  287
Conrad 316
contact novels *see* colonial contact novels
Conton, William 252–3, 368–9
Contract, The (Iyayi) 192, 235
conversion, Christian 59, 60, 62
Cordor, S. Henry 255, 256
corruption, theme of 192
Cosmopolitan Club (Cape Coast) 37
Council for Cultural Freedom 84
Coup is Planned, A (Roberts) 253
Cows of Shambat, The (Liyong) 260–2
Creole intellectuals 28–32, 33, 34, 43 *see*
  also individual names
Crown of Thorns, The (Asong) 277
Crowther, Samuel Ajayi 15, 16, 27, 33,
  50–4
  accounts of (1841) and (1854)
    expeditions 50–3
  background 28
  biographies of 61
  biography and important works 369
  censorship of accounts produced by
    CMS 61
  conflict with colonial authorities 32, 53
  gives positive image of African culture
    54
Crummell, Alexander 27, 28, 369
Cry of the Owl (Deng) 204, 257–8, 310
Cuguano, Ottobah 12, 13
  biography and important works 369–70
  *Thoughts and Sentiments on the Evil
    and Wicked Traffic of Slavery* 10–12
Culture is Rutan (Liyong) 259, 262
Currey, James 81, 82
Curse, The (Omotoso) 174
Curtin, Philip D. 8, 12–13, 16

Dabydeen, David 7
Dance of the Forests, A (Soyinka) 86,
147–8, 150, 152, 175, 182, 326
Dancer of Fortune, A (Munonye) 126
Danda (Nwanko) 136
Danquah, J. B. 37, 42, 54, 109
 biography and important works 370
 on *Eighteenpence* 40
Dark Wanderer, The (Kayper-Mensah) 110
de Graft, J. C. 110, 111–12
 biography and important works 370
 plays 111–12
 poetry 111
De Mel, Neloufer 322–3
de Moraes Farias 36
Dear Parent and Ogre (Easmon) 248
Death and the King's Horseman (Soyinka)
122, 148–9, 151–4
Decade of Tongues, A (Clark) 115
Defiance (Gubegna) 263
Defoe 137
Dempster, Roland Tombekai 255, 370
Deneke, Yemani 265, 370
Deng, Francis Mading 257–8, 260, 262,
312
 biography and important works 370
 Cry of the Owl 204, 257–8, 310
 Seed of Redemption: A Political Novel
204, 257
Desert Flower (Dirie) 273, 274
Devil on the Cross (Ngũgĩ) 102, 118,
213–15, 216–17, 228
Dhana (journal) 77
Dholuo 75
Diary of Antera Duke, The 18–21
Dibba, Ebou 253, 254, 371
Dilemma of a Ghost, The (Aidoo) 156,
292
Diop, David 371
Dipoko, Mbella Sonne 275–7, 371
'Dirge, A' (Awoonor) 154
Dirie, Waris 273, 274
disillusion, post-independence 143–70, 230
 and East African writing 160–70
 and West African writing 143–59
Doe, John 256
Dogs of War, The (Forsyth) 232
Doran, Captain 8
Douglass, Frederick 13–14, 26, 371
drama *see* theatre
Dreams of a Dirty Road (Sallah) 254
'Drought and Us, The' (Ofeimun) 188
Drug, The (Bart-Williams) 248
Drummer in Our Time, The (Kayper-
Mensah) 110–11

Du Bois, W. E. B. 13, 371
Duke, Antera 18–21, 371
Dung' Hill (Astaw) 265
'Dusk on my Village' (Angira) 199
Dying in the Sun (Palyango) 128

Eagle Fiction Library series 75
EAPH (East African Publishing House) 99,
100, 129–30, 158
Easmon, Raymond Sarif 248, 371
East African writing
 and colonisation 225
 concern with urban- rural conflict 85,
128–9, 239
 'crisis' in 212–13
 differences with West African writing
225
 early writings 42–6
 fictional works written by historians and
political scientists 203–6
 novels on post-independence
disillusionment 160–70
 political concerns in recent 203
 texts dealing with relationship problems
239–40
 transcultural writers 309–23
 use of indigenous languages 129, 198–9
 use of long prose forms 204, 206, 225
 see also individual countries
East Africa Owes Much to British Rule
(Kebaso) 76
East African Literature Bureau 74–6, 77,
129
East African Publishing House *see* EAPH
East, Rupert 71, 72, 73
Eating Chiefs (Liyong) 259
Ebony Dust (Moore) 255
Eby, Omar 268, 371–2
Echoes from the Valley 255
educational texts 76, 81
Efuru (Nwapa) 79, 125–6, 131, 281–7,
288–9, 301, 305
Egbuna, Obi 138–9, 241, 372
Eighteenpence (Obeng) 37, 40–2
Ekwensi, Cyprian 97, 136
 biography and important works 372
 Jagua Nana 136, 137–8, 175, 233
 Lokotown and other Stories 80, 136
 People of the City 80, 136, 233
 publishing for Heinemann African
Writers series 80, 136
 Survive the Peace 232–3
Elegy for the Revolution (Anyidoho)
192–3
Elephants, The (Serumaga) 208–9

elite writers 96, 97, 99, 114, 212
  and popular writing 101, 102, 241
Ellison, Ralph 250
Emecheta, Buchi 87, 269, 288, 292,
    299–305, 323
  autobiography 300
  biography and important works 372–3
  In the Ditch 299
  The Joys of Motherhood 300–5
  The Rape of Shavi 300
  reception of work 300
  rejection of feminist label 299, 300
  Second Class Citizen 299
  theme of being second- class citizen 299
  writing for children 299–300
Emenyonu, Ernest 78, 136
Enfant Noir, L' (Laye) 118–19
English (language)
  modification of by local writers 18, 21
  tensions when using 18
  vehicle for transmission of material from
    oral to written 36
English Manners and Customs 76
Epie'Ngome, Victor 275, 279, 373
Equiano, Olaudah
  biography and important works 373
  and Cuguano 10
  involved in Sierra Leone project 26
  The Life of Olaudah Equiano 7–8, 12,
    13, 14
Erapu, Laban 99, 207
Esu and the Vagabond Minstrels (Osofisan)
    178
Ethiopia
  writing from 78, 85, 262–7
Ethiopia Unbound (Casely Hayford) 27–8,
    35, 63
ethnographic narratives 14, 26, 55, 61, 63,
    66
examination boards
  establishment of 82
excision, female *see* female circumcision
exemplary life narratives 55, 62–3, 66, 68
'Exorcism' (Johnson) 328–9
Eye of the Earth, The (Osundare) 191
Eyoh, Hansel Ndumbe 279, 372
Ezenwa-Ohaeto 196–7, 373–4

Facing Mount Kenya (Kenyatta) 45, 127,
    289
Fafa (Dibba) 253
Fagunwa, D. O. 91, 92, 374
Family, The (Emecheta) 300
Famished Road, The (Okri) 326, 327
Fanon, Frantz 148, 374

Fanti (language) 32, 39
Farah, Nuruddin 247, 268–73
  biography and important works 374–5
  'dictatorship trilogy' 269–71
  From a Crooked Rib 268, 269
  Gifts 271, 272
  Maps 271
  A Naked Needle 269
  Secrets 272–3
  themes in work 268–9
Farewell to Babylon, A (Sowande) 181
Fella's Choice (Omotoso) 174
'Fertility Game' (Anyidoho) 193
Few Nights and Days, A (Dipoko) 276
Fielding 40
Fikré, Tolossa 375
film industry 93
Fires Burn, and Die Hard (Osofisan) 177
Flamingo (Sowande) 181
Flight, The (Conton) 253
Florence in the River of Temptation
    (Ngoh) 96
Flowers and Shadows (Okri) 323–4
folk poetry 210
Forest of Flowers, A (Saro-Wiwa) 198
Foriwa (Sutherland) 295, 297
Forsyth, Frederick 232
Forty Eight Guns for the General (Iroh)
    232
Fourah Bay College (Sierra Leone) 42
'Fourth Stage, The' (Soyinka) 151
Fragments (Armah) 157, 324
Frantz Fanon's Uneven Ribs (Liyong) 259,
    260
From a Crooked Rib (Farah) 268, 269
Fugard, Athol 208
Furniss, Graham 71, 72, 73

Gabre-Mehdin, Tsegaye 263, 375
Gakarra wa Wanjaũ
  aubiography and important works
    375–6
  and Gĩkũyũ-language writing 46
  imprisonment 75
Gambia, The
  political history 254
  writing from 247, 252–5
Gambian Writers Club 253
Garvey, Marcus 13, 26, 375
Garvie, Max 66
Gaskiya Publishing Corporation 72
Gaskiya ta fi Kwabo (newspaper) 71–2
Gathigira, Stanley Kiamka 212
Gecaga, Mareka B. 212
Germany 46

Germinal (Zola) 213
Ghana 85, 248
  and Ashanti war 32, 225
  books on post-independence
    disillusionment 155–7
  themes of corruption and opposition
    192–5
  women writers 292–7
  see also individual writers
Ghana Drama Studio 111, 295, 296
Ghana Society of Writers 77
Gicheru, Mwangi 99, 240
  Across the Bridge 240
  biography and important works 376
Gifts (Farah) 271, 272
Gikandi, Simon 146, 212–13
Gĩkũyũ 127, 132
Gĩkũyũ-language writing 45–6, 75
  early texts 211–12
  and Ngũgĩ 46, 91, 92, 211, 212, 215,
    220
Girls at War (Achebe) 83, 145
Going Down River Road (Mwangi) 167
Gokeye 44
Gold Coast Aborigines' Rights Protection
  Society 34, 39
Gowan, General Yakubu 230
Graduate, The (Ogot) 289
Grain of Wheat, A (Ngũgĩ) 100, 160, 227,
  229
Graveyard Also Has Teeth, The (Cheney-
  Coker) 249
Great Ponds, The (Amadi) 118, 125
Gronniosaw, James 8, 376
*Guanya Pau: The Story of an African
  Princess* (Walters) 27, 63–6, 69, 139
Gubegna, Abbie 263, 376
'Guinea' (Cheney-Coker) 250
Gunny Sack, The (Vassanji) 227, 319–21,
  322, 323
Gurnah, Abdulrazak 309, 313–19
  Admiring Silence 316–19, 320
  biography and important works 376
  on Okri 309
  Paradise 313–16

Haley, Alex 159, 254–5
Hammon, Briton 8, 376
*Handle for the Flautist and Other Poems,
  A* (Ofeimun) 187–8
Hanghe, Ahmed Artan 268, 376
Harvest of our Dreams, A (Anyidoho)
  193–4
Hausa 71, 73, 74, 230, 231
Head Above Water (Emecheta) 300

Healers, The (Armah) 158
'Heavensgate' (Okigbo) 134
Heinemann African Poets 249
Heinemann African Writers series 109–10,
  248
  Achebe as editor 83–4, 118, 211
  aim 79, 81–2
  books published 79–80, 85, 126, 128,
    215, 275, 287
  emergence 78–9, 81
  reduction in scope due to take-overs of
    Heinemann 86–7
  theme of colonial disruption 85
Heinemann Caribbean Writers series 81
Heinemann Educational Books 79, 81, 86,
  117
Hen Too Soon, A (Onwueme) 298
Henderson, Ian 228
Henries, A. Doris Banks 255, 376
Heroes (Iyayi) 234–5, 236
Higo, Aig 84–5
Hill, Alan 81, 83–4, 85, 86, 116–17, 118
Hills are Falling, The (Mude) 239
historical accounts 26, 35–6, 62, 175, 236
History of Mary Prince, The 21–2
History of the Yorubas, The (Johnson)
  35–7, 52, 109
Holst-Petersen, Kirsten 81
homosexuality 252
Hopes of the Living Dead (Rotimi) 183, 184
Horn, Andrew 207, 209
Horn, The (magazine) 77, 114
Horton, James Africanus 27, 31–2, 33, 252
  background 28–9
  biography and important works 376–7
  *Letters on the Political Condition of the
    Gold Coast* 31–2
  West African Countries and Peoples 31
Hountondji 94
House by the Sea, The (Awoonor) 154–5
'How I Woke to Nature' (Kayper-Mensah)
  110–11
Humasi, Nana 253, 377
Hunt for Dedan Kimathi, The (Henderson)
  228
Hunter, Yéma Lucinda 251
Hussein, Ebrahim N. 91
  biography and important works 377
  Kinjeketile 92, 226
Huxley, Elspeth 113
'Hydropathy' (Cheney-Coker) 249

I Am Vindicated (Maimo) 277
I Wan Bi President (Ezenwa-Ohaeto)
  196–7

I Will Marry When I Want (Ngũgĩ) 212, 215, 228
Ibadan University 77, 114, 118
Ibadan University Travelling Theatre 103
IBEAC (Imperial British East African Company) 43
Ibingira, Grace S. K. 203–4, 377
Ibos 85, 121, 132, 230–1
Ideal African Chief - Chief Hodari wa Kiafrika, The (Oyende) 76
Idu (Nwapa) 287
If: A Tragedy of the Ruled (Rotimi) 183–4
Ignorance is the Enemy of Love (Jaamac) 267
Ijaw 133
Ike, Chukwuemeka 232, 377
Ikolo the Wrestler and Other Ibo Tales (Ekwensi) 97
Imam, Abubakar 71, 72
Imperial British East African Company (IBEAC) 43
In the Ditch (Emecheta) 299
In the Hour of Signs (Mahjoub) 312–13
In the Mirror of Love (Deneke) 265
In the Name of Our Fathers (Osman) 273
In Pursuit of Publishing (Hill) 81, 116–17, 118
Incidents at the Shrine (Okri) 324
Incidents in the Life of a Slave- Girl (Jacob) 22
independence struggles 225–6
Indian popular pamphlets 95
indigenous languages 91–4, 109
  call for revitalisation of writing in 91, 172, 334
  and East African writing 129, 199
  evolvement in tandem with colonial language 35
  and Ngũgĩ 199, 211–12, 213, 309
  and poetry 118
  relationship with African English writing 93–4
  relationship between oral popular culture and written 94
  and theatre 92–3, 112
  writing in Uganda 207
  see also Gĩkũyũ; ki-Swahili
indirect rule, policy of 43, 71
infibulation, female 274, 288
Inheritance, The (Eyoh) 279
Innes, C. L. 78
Institute for Advanced Study and Research in the African Humanities (New York) 210
Interpreters, The (Soyinka) 86, 150, 324

Invisible Bond, The (Sentongo) 209
Iroh, Eddie 232, 377
Irwin 26
Islam 30, 72
Island of Tears, The (Ogot) 289
ìtàn 36
Itotia, Justin 212
Ivory Merchant, The (Gicheru) 99
Iwe-irohin (journal) 54
Iyayi, Festus 136, 234–5
  biography and important works 377
  The Contract 192, 235
  Heroes 234–5, 236
  Violence 80, 186, 192, 235

Jaamac, Faarax Maxamed 267
Jacob, Harriet 22
Jagua Nana (Ekwensi) 136, 137–8, 175, 233
Jameson, Frederic 146
Jammeh, Lieutenant Yaya 254
Jawara, President 254
'Jebs Prison' books (Saro-Wiwa) 198
Jemie, Onwuchekwa 78, 173, 186
Jeyifo, Biodun 113, 174
Johansson, Lars 167–8, 229, 230
Johnson, James (Holy) 27, 33, 50
Johnson, Lemuel 250–1, 252, 256, 328–31
  biography and important works 377
  Sierra Leone Trilogy 250–1, 328–31
Johnson, Obadiah 35
Johnson, Rev. Samuel 27, 29, 50
  biography and important works 378
  The History of the Yorubas 35–7, 52, 109
Jones, Eldred 231
journals 77
Jowett, Rev. William 50
Joys of Motherhood, The (Emecheta) 300–5
Juices (Angira) 199–200
Jumbam, Kenjo 277, 378
Just Before Dawn (Omotoso) 174, 175, 203, 204

Kabaka Mutesa 45
Kabaka Mwanga 43
Kabarega, Omukama 43
Kagwa, Sir Apolo 43, 44, 45
Kagwema, Prince 101
Kahiga, Samuel 99, 240, 378
Kamiriithu Community Centre 93, 212, 228
Kanina and I (Mangua) 100
Kariuki, General 229

Katchikali (Peters) 253
Kawadwa, Byron 93, 207, 210
Kayper-Mensah, A. W. 110–11, 112, 378
Kebaso, J. K. 76
Kelueljang, Anai 378
Kenya 85, 97, 220
  early writing 45–6
  literacy rates 215
  Mau Mau movement and rebellion 75,
    227
  mixed relationships theme in texts 240
  popular writing 97–101
  post-independence disillusionment in
    writing 165–70
  settlers in 44
  see also individual writers
Kenya Peoples Union (KPU) 229
Kenyatta, Jomo 28, 44, 54, 76, 109, 229
  biography and important works 378
  editing of *Muigwithania* 46
  Facing Mount Kenya 45, 127, 289
  The Life of Chief Wangombe 63, 66,
    68–9
  My People of Kikuyu 63, 66, 67–8
ki-Swahili 46, 75, 91, 92, 198, 211, 220,
  225
Kibera, Leonard 165, 378
Kill Me Quick (Mwangi) 136, 166–7
Kimathi, Dedan 228
Kincaid, Jamaica 251
Kinjeketile (Hussein) 92, 226
Kinteh, Ramatoulie 253, 378
Kiriamiti, John (Jack Zollo) 99
Kiyingi, Wycliffe 93, 207
Kongi's Harvest (Soyinka) 149–50, 175
Kor, Buma 275
Kora Land (Sallah) 254
Kossah Town Boy (Cole) 248
Krio Engagement and Other Stories, A
  (Humasi) 253
Kurunmi (Rotimi) 183

Labyrinths of the Delta (Ojaide) 195–6
Labyrinths with Path of Thunder (Okigbo)
  133
Ladipo, Duro 92, 151, 176, 183, 378–9
Laing, Kojo 87, 192, 328, 332–3, 334
  biography and important works 379
  Major Gentl and the Achimoto Wars
    333
  Search Sweet Country 332
  Women of the Aeroplanes 332–3
Lake God (Butake) 278
Land Without Thunder (Ogot) 289
Landscapes Within, The (Okri) 187, 324

Langley, J. Ayo 37, 39
Larson, Charles 158
Last Duty, The (Okpewho) 233–4
Last Harmattan of Alusine Dunbar, The
  (Cheney-Coker) 249, 327–8
Last Word, The (Liyong) 259
Laurence, Margaret 268
Laye, Camara 118–19
Lemma, Menghistu 379
Leopard Among the Women.
  Shabeelnaagood. A Somali Play 268
lesbian relationships 298
Letters of Ignatius Sancho, The (Sancho)
  8–9
Letters of Philip Quaque, The 14–18
*Letters on the Political Condition of the
  Gold Coast* (Horton) 31–2
Lévi-Strauss 119
Liberia 25, 42, 85, 255–6
Life of Aaron Kuku of Eweland, The
  61–2
*Life of Bishop Crowther First African
  Bishop of the Niger, The* (McKay) 61
Life of Chief Wangombe, The (Kenyatta)
  63, 66, 68–9
Life of Olaudah Equiano, The (Equiano)
  7–8, 12, 13, 14
Likmani, Muthoni 289
Lindfors, Bernth 76–7, 86–7, 88
Lion and the Jewel, The (Soyinka) 86, 138,
  241
Literature Bureaux 71, 72, 73, 76, 79, 84
  see also East African Literature
    Bureau; Northern Nigerian Bureau
Little Books for Africa 58–60, 61
Liverpool Chamber of Commerce Blyden's
  address to (1901) 30–1
Liyong, Taban lo 45, 247, 258–62
  biography and important works 379
  The Cows of Shambat 260–2
  Culture is Rutan 259, 262
  Eating Chiefs 259
  Frantz Fanon's Uneven Ribs 259, 260
Lokotown and Other Stories (Ekwensi) 80,
  136
Lonely Village, The 75
Longman 86, 87
Longman Drumbeat series 79, 80
Longman (Kenya) Crime Series 99
Lover in the Sky (Kahiga) 99
Lubega, Bonnie 129
Luganda (language) 45, 75, 92
Lugard, Lord 43, 72
Luo (language) 92
Luthuli, Albert 216

McHardy, Cecile 77
McKay, J. 61
McLuckie, Craig 231, 233
Macmillan 79
Maddy, Yulisu Amadu 251–2, 379
Madmen and Specialists (Soyinka) 235, 236–7
Madubuike 173
Maduokor 78
magazines 77–8
Mahjoub, Jamal 87, 309–13
  biography and important works 380
  In the Hour of Signs 312–13
  Navigation of a Rainmaker 309–10
  Wings of Dust 310–12
Maillu, David G. 97–8, 131, 136–7, 204
  After 4.30 98
  biography and important works 380
Maimo, Sankie 277–8, 380
Maitu Njugira (Mother Sing to Me) 212
Maja-Pearce, Adewala 147, 324
Majangwa: A Promise of Rains (Serumaga) 208
Maji-Maji Rebellion (1905–7) 225, 226–7
Major Gentl and the Achimoto Wars (Laing) 333
Makerere Free Travelling Theatre 207
Makerere University 42, 45, 77, 207
Malawi 130
Man Died, The (Soyinka) 115, 185, 235
Man of the People, A (Achebe) 126, 143, 144, 145
Man Who Came in from the Back of Beyond, The (Bandele- Thomas) 331–2
Mangua, Charles 99–101, 380
Maps (Farah) 271
Maranda, Kongas 195
marriage
  books on 239–40
Marriage of Anansewa, The (Sutherland) 296, 297
Married Love is a Plant (Kagwema) 101
Mask, The (Maimo) 277–8
Masquerade (Clark) 114–15
'massa talk' 7
Master and the Frauds, The (Sowande) 182
Matigari (Ngũgĩ) 102, 118, 127, 215–16, 217–20, 228
Mau Mau movement 46
  rebellion (1952) 75
  representation of in writing 227–30
Maughan-Brown 229
Mazuri, Ali 203, 231, 380

Meet Me in Conakry (Sarr) 254
Memories of Our Recent Boom (Omotoso) 174–5
Men From Pretoria, The 98–9
Mengistu regime 265–6
Messages: Poems from Ghana 110
'Messed up by English' (Liyong) 262
Mezu, S. Okechukwu 231–2, 380–1
Mfukwe, W. E. 240–1, 381
Midnight's Children (Rushdie) 320
Mūkarrire ya Agikuyu (Gathigira) 212
Miller, Christopher 118–19
Mine Boy (Abrahams) 80
'Mirage' (Angira) 202
mission presses 50–69, 71, 76, 79, 84, 211–12
  establishment of 54–5
  influence of texts sponsored by 62–3
  literary forms of narratives produced by 55
  and Little Books for Africa 58–60, 61
  patrons of first generation of nationalist leaders 36, 54–5
  'release narratives' published by 55–8, 60–1, 62
  'resistance' against control 63–6
  suppression of material not appropriate 61
  texts produced under control of 50–4
missionaries 15, 16, 33, 50, 64, 74
Mister Johnson (Cary) 117
Mockere, Parmeneo Gĩthendu 45
Mocking Stones, The (Palmer) 252
Mohamed, Jan 113
Moll Flanders (Defoe) 137
Mombasa 74
Money Doubler, The (Moore) 256
Moodie, Susannah 21
Moore, Bai T. 255, 256, 381
Moore, Gerald 291
Morountodun (Osofisan) 175, 176, 182, 187
Mude, Mude Dae 239, 381
Mūgo, Micere Githae 78, 228
Muhando, Penina 381
Muigwithania (newspaper) 46
Mukasa, Ham 44, 45, 381
mulatto children 17, 18
Munonye, John 80, 126
  biography and important works 381–2
  A Wreath for the Maidens 233
  Murder in the Cassava Patch (Moore) 255
Mutesa, Sir Edward 204
Mutia, Ba'bila 275

Mwangi, Meja 100, 102, 166–8, 213, 239
  biography and important works 382
  Carcass for Hounds 229–30
  The Cockroach Dance 167–8
  embracement of popular forms 168
  Going Down River Road 167
  Kill Me Quick 136, 166–7
  representation of Mau Mau movement
    229–30
  Taste of Death 229
My Bondage and My Freedom (Douglass)
  14
My Dear Bottle! (Maillu) 98
My Life in the Bush of Ghosts (Tutuola)
  325, 334
My Life in Crime (Kiriamiti) 99
My Life with a Criminal: Milly's Story
  (Kiriamiti) 99
My People of Kikuyu (Kenyatta) 63, 66,
  67–8
Myth, Literature and the African World
  (Ṣoyinka) 151

Nagbe, K. Moses 256, 382
Nagenda, John 206–7, 382
Naipaul, V. S. 319
Nairobi University 77, 259
Naked Needle, A (Farah) 269
nationalism
  early writings on 27–8, 33–4
Navigation of a Rainmaker (Mahjoub)
  309–10
Nazareth, Peter 209, 382
Ndaanan (journal) 253
Neustadt International Prize for Literature
  273
Never Again (Nwapa) 287
'new African writing' 116, 118
'New Farmer's Bank, The' (Osundare) 191
New Patriots, The (Easmon) 248
newspapers 1, 35, 55, 103
Ngoh, John 96
Ngũgĩ wa Thiong'o 169–70, 211–21, 259
  attacks fatalist and pessimistic vision of
    Africa 212–13
  biography and important works 382–4
  The Black Hermit 207
  and decolonisation of African writing
    203, 211, 213, 215, 220, 227, 309
  Devil on the Cross 102, 118, 213–15,
    216–17, 228
  A Grain of Wheat 100, 160, 227, 229
  I Will Marry When I Want 212, 215, 228
  imprisonment and exile 212, 213, 220,
    228

  and indigenous languages 199, 211–12,
    213, 309
  and Kamiriithu Community Centre 93,
    212, 228
  Matigari 102, 118, 127, 215–16,
    217–20, 228
  opposition to KANU politics as focus of
    later writing 203, 229
  Petals of Blood 160–4, 213, 227
  and politics of corruption 160
  and popular writing 102
  representation of Mau Mau movement
    227–9
  The River Between 12, 118, 119, 126–8,
    289
  strength of work 216
  themes in novels 160
  Weep Not, Child 84, 119, 122, 126
  writing in Gĩkũyũ 46, 91, 92, 211, 212,
    215, 220
Nicol, Davidson (Abioseh) 34, 248, 384
Nigeria 85, 103, 248
  books on post-independence disillusion
    143–54
  civil war 115
  poetry 191, 195
  policy of indirect rule in 43
  and popular writing 97, 101–3
  theatre 92–3
  themes of opposition and resistance in
    novels 173–92
  women writers 297–9
  Women's War 225
  see also individual writers
Nigerian Civil War 173, 183
  history 230–1
  representation of in literary accounts
    136, 145, 230–9
Nigerian National Democratic Party 183
Nigerian Trumpeters books 101
Night Before, The (Sowande) 181
Night of My Blood (Awoonor) 154
1960 Masks (theatre troupe) 147, 295
Nkrumah, Kwame 28, 210
'No Coffin, No Grave' (Angira) 200–1
No Longer at Ease (Achebe) 119, 143–4,
  150, 239, 300
No New Land (Vassanji) 323
No Past, No Present, No Future (Maddy)
  252
No Sweetness Here (Aidoo) 293
noble savage 8
Northern Nigerian Literature Bureau 71,
  72, 73, 74, 75
Nsukka school 173

Ntiru, Richard 207
'Nunya' (Anyidoho) 194, 195
Nwachukwu-Agbada, J. O. J. 195
Nwamife Publishers 77
Nwanko, Nkem W. 136, 384
Nwapa, Flora 129, 269, 281–9
  biography and important works 384
  criticism of work 287
  Efuru 79, 125–6, 131, 281–7, 288–9,
    301, 305
  establishes own local press 104, 159,
    288
  Idu 287
  Never Again 287
  and Nigerian Civil War 287
  One is Enough 287–8, 294
  Women are Different 288
Nyerere, Julius 227

Obasai and Other Plays (Maddy) 251
Obeng, R. E.
  biography and important works 384–5
  Eighteenpence 37, 40–2
Obi (Munonye) 126
Obiechina, Emmanuel 95, 96, 97, 113
Obote, Dr Milton 204, 207
Oculi, Okello 385
Ofeimun, Odia 174, 185–9
  biography and important works 385
  *A Handle for the Flautist and Other
    Poems* 187–8
  interview with Jemie 186–7
  The Poet Lied and Other Poems 185–6
  themes of later poems 188
  'We Hurtle Down' 187
Ogali, Ogali A. 97
Ogbunigwe 237
Ogoni people 102
Ogot, Grace 129, 199, 269, 289–92
  biography and important works 385
  The Island of Tears 289
  The Promised Land 131, 281, 289–92
  themes of books 289
Ogunde, Hubert 92, 176
  biography and important works 385–6
  Yoruba roni 183
Ogundipe-Leslie, Molara 385
Ogunyemi, Wale 93, 176, 386
Ojaide, Tanure 174, 195–6, 386
Ojukwu, Colonel 231
Okara, Gabriel 133, 386–7
Okigbo, Christopher 114, 133–5, 174, 195
  biography and important works 387
  'Heavensgate' 134
  homage to by Angira 200

  influences on poetry 133–4, 173
  and Nigerian Civil War 115, 173
  'Path of Thunder' series 133, 134–5, 173
Okike: An African Journal of New Writing
  77
Okpewho, Isidore 78, 192
  biography and important works 387–8
  The Last Duty 233–4
  The Victims 241–2
Okri, Ben 87, 118, 135, 323–7
  biography and important works 388
  criticism of work 326
  The Famished Road 326, 327
  Flowers and Shadows 323–4
  Gurnah on 309
  'magical realist' label 309, 326–7
  other works 326
  short story collections 324–5
  Stars of the New Curfew 324–5
  success of 326
  The Landscapes Within 187, 324
  and Yoruba narrative technique 325–6
Okyema (journal) 77
Olisa, Okenwa 97
Omiyale, Oma 101–2
Omotoso, Kole 102, 173, 174–5
  biography and important works 388
  Just Before Dawn 174, 175, 203, 204
  Memories of Our Recent Boom 174–5
'On Market Day at Ugunja' (Angira)
  199–200
On Trial for my Country (Samkange) 203
Once Upon Four Robbers (Osofisan) 178
'One Country' (Clark) 116
One is Enough (Nwapa) 287–8, 294
'One Pot' (Angira) 200
Onitsha Market Literatures 1, 95–7
Only Son, The (Munonye) 126
Onwueme, Tess 298–9, 388–9
oral forms
  influence of 91, 195
  and literary forms 93–4, 109, 133, 195,
    333–4
Oriki of a Grasshopper, The (Osofisan)
  176–7, 324
Oroonoka (Behn) 8
Osiris Rising (Armah) 102, 159
Osman, Abdirazak Y. 273, 389
Osofisan, Femi 92, 103, 173, 174, 175–81,
  187, 279
  Altine's Wrath 177
  Another Raft 115, 179, 180
  Aringindin and the Nightwatchmen 179,
    180
  biography and important works 389

Esu and the Vagabond Minstrels 178–9
failure to attract large audiences 176–7
Fires Burn, and Die Hard 177
Morountodun 175, 176, 182, 187
The Oriki of a Grasshopper 176–7, 324
performance style 176
television plays 177
Yungba-Yungba and the Dance Contest
  179, 180–1
Osundare, Niyi 135, 174, 189–91, 193
biography and important works 389
concern with ecology 191
The Eye of the Earth 191
on newspapers 103
respect for traditional 190–1
review of *Hopes of the Living Dead* 184
rhythm of verse 190
Songs of the Season 103, 190
themes 191
Village Voices 190, 191
Oulogouem, Yambo 158
'Our Birth-Cord' (Anyidoho) 193
'Our Earth Will Not Die' (Osundare) 191
Our People of the Sierra Leone
  Protectorate (Garvie) 66
Our Sister Killjoy (Aidoo) 293
Outcasts, The (Lubega) 129
overseas commercial presses 78–9, 80–6
Ovonramwem Nogbaisi (Rotimi) 183
Oxford University Press 86
Oyende, J. P. 76
Oyono, Ferdinand 276

Palm-Wine Drinkard, The (Tutuola) 116,
  325
Palmer, Prince Down 252
Palangyo, Peter 128, 389
Panya 56–8, 59–60
Paradise (Gurnah) 313–16
Pascal, Captain 7–8
'Path of Thunder: Poems Prophesying War'
  (Okigbo) 133, 134–5, 173
p'Bitek, Okot 204, 259, 261
biography and important works 390
Song of Lawino 130–1, 291
'Peasants' (Cheney-Coker) 249
PEC Repertory Theatre (Lagos) 115
pélegrinage tradition 63
Pemba 42, 43
Penpoint (magazine) 77
People of the City (Ekwensi) 80, 136, 233
Per Ankh 102, 159
Petals of Blood (Ngũgĩ) 160–4, 213, 227
Peters, Lenrie 253, 254, 390
pidgin 94, 196–7, 198

Pidgin Stew and Sufferhead (Aig-
  Imoukhuede) 196
Pilgrim's Progress (Bunyan) 63, 118, 213
Pirandello 112
Play of Giants, A (Soyinka) 183, 185
Play, The (Serumaga) 207–8
Playtime in Africa (Sutherland) 295
Poems (Clark) 114
Poems (Peters) 253
Poems from the Grassroots (Moore) 255
Poems on Various Subjects: Religious and
  Moral (Wheatley) 10
Poet Lied and Other Poems, The
  (Ofeimun) 185–6
poetry 133, 135
and indigenous languages 112
and local presses 114
and newspapers 103
Nigerian 191, 195
use of pidgin 196–7
'Poetry Is' (Osundare) 189–90
Poetry and Prose of Phillis Wheatley, The
  (Wheatley) 9
'Politician's Two Mouths, The' (Osundare)
  191
polygamy 64, 138, 239–42, 241, 293
popular writing 95–104, 136–7, 212, 240
copies of Western genres 97
and elite writers 101, 102, 241
emergence of new popular series from
  established presses 98–9
influence of successful writers 102
and Onitsha Market Literatures 1, 95–7
popularity of crime- thrillers and
  romance 97
values and causes embraced by 96
Presbyterians 54
Prince, Mary 21–2, 390
Promised Land, The (Ogot) 131, 281,
  289–92
Proverbial Poems 110

Quaque, Philip 8, 14–18, 390
Quayson, Ato 36
Strategic Transformations in Nigerian
  Writing 93–4, 325–6, 327
Queen of Gems (Erapu) 99

Raft, The (Clark) 115, 180
Rain and the Night, The (Sankawulo) 256
'Raising of Lazarus, The' (Ofeimun) 188
'Rape 1' (Angira) 200
Rape of Shavi, The (Emecheta) 300
Real Drum Daddy is Back!, The (Nagbe)
  256

Rebellion (Kinteh) 253
Red is the Freedom Road (Osofisan) 175
Rediscovery and Other Poems (Awoonor) 133
Reed in the Tide, A (Clark) 114
relationships, problem texts dealing with 239–40
'release narratives' 55–7 59, 60–1, 62, 63, 64, 65, 66
Renga Moi (Serumaga) 209
Requiem for a Futurologist (Soyinka) 183, 185
'rescue' narratives 50, 59–60
'Resolve' (Ofeimun) 187
Return to the Shadows (Serumaga) 209
Richards, Charles 74
riddle mode 195
Riding the Whirlwind (Selassie) 263
Ring Finger (Omiyale) 101
Rip Van Winkle (Irving) 75
River Between, The (Ngũgĩ) 12, 118, 119, 126–8, 289
Road, The (Soyinka) 55, 86, 150–1, 152, 208
Road to Freedom (Hunter) 251, 327
Road to Jamaica, The (Cheney-Coker) 249
Road to Romeo, The (Nagbe) 256
Roberts, Gabriel J. 253, 390
Roberts, Shabaan 391
Roots (Haley) 159, 254–5
Rotimi, Ola 93, 182–4, 391
Rubadiri, David 205–6, 210
Ruganda, John 207, 209, 391
Ruhumbika, Gabriel 203, 391
Rushdie 320

St Charles Lwanga (Kawadwa) 210
St John's Episcopal Mission (Liberia) 63
Salih, Tayeb 391–2
Sallah, Tijan M. 254, 255, 392
Sambrook, Keith 81, 82
Samkange, Stanlake J. T. 203, 392
Sancho, Ignatius 8–9, 10, 392
Sanctus for Women, A (Sowande) 182
Sankawulo, Wilton 256
Sankoh, Foday 252
Sarbah, John Mensah 27, 34
Sardines (Farah) 269, 270, 272
Saro-Wiwa, Ken 102–3, 197–8
   background 197
   biography and important works 392–3
   execution 102, 196, 197, 198
   A Forest of Flowers 198
   founding of own publishing company 102, 104, 159

'Jebs Prison' books 198
Sozaboy 133, 197, 237–9
   and television 103
Saros International Productions 103
Saros International Publishers 102
Sarr, Sheriff 254, 393
Satellites (Peters) 253
Sawyer, President Amos 256
Schön, Rev. J. F. 51, 52
Seacole, Mary 22
Search Sweet Country (Laing) 332
Season of Anomy (Soyinka) 150, 235–6
Seasons of Thomas Tebo, The (Nagenda) 206–7
Second Class Citizen (Emecheta) 299
Second Dream (Omiyale) 101–2
Second Round, The (Peters) 253
Secrets (Farah) 272–3
'See Me Lakayana-Again' (Liyong) 261
Seed of Redemption: A Political Novel (Deng) 204, 257
Sekyi, Kobina 27
   biography and important works 393
   The Blinkards 35, 37–9, 39–40
   other writings 39
Selassie, Bereket Habte 263, 393
self-publishing 102, 104, 159, 197
Sellassie, Sahle 263, 393
Senegal 254
Sentongo, Nuwa 207, 209
Serumaga, Robert 207–9, 393
Seyyid Said, Sultan 42
Shadows in the Horizon (Omotoso) 174
Sharks and Soldiers (Askar) 268
Sharpe, Granville 12, 25, 26
Sheldon Little Books for Africa 58–60, 61
Shinega's Village (Sellassie) 263
Shuttle in the Crypt, A (Soyinka) 235
Sierra Leone 42, 85, 247
   civil strife in 252
   founding of 25
   Sharpe's scheme to set up colony for freed slaves in 12, 25, 26
   writing from 248–52, 256, 327–8
Sierra Leone Trilogy (Johnson) 250–1, 328–31
Silent Voices (Angira) 200–2
Singler, J. V. 64, 65
Six Characters in Search of an Author (Pirandello) 112
Slave Girl, The (Emecheta) 300
slave narratives 7–23
   and anti-slavery movement 8, 11, 50
   and autobiographical form 13–14

comparison between European-educated
  slaves and less formally educated West
  Africans 18–19
and *The Diary of Antera Duke* 18–21
interest in noble savage 8
master-slave exchanges 7
references to African world before
  European rule 12
and *The Letters of Philip Quaque* 14–18
transcription through amanuensis 8, 12,
  21–2
slaves/slavery 7–8, 62
  abolition of trading 25
  emancipation and return of freed 25
  perception by masters of ability to write
    as threat 7–8
  repatriation of 25–6
Slums, The (Akare) 168–70, 240
Smith, Venture 8, 393
Society in the Dock (Kagwema) 101
Society for Promoting Christian Knowledge
  (SPCK) 15, 17
Sofola, Zulu 297–8, 393–4
Soft Corals (Angira) 202
Somalia 78
  oral tradition 267
  political history 267
  writing from 267–74
Son of Woman (Mangua) 99–100
Son of Woman in Mombasa (Mangua)
  100
Song of Lawino (p'Bitek) 130–1, 291
Song of Ocol, The (p'Bitek) 131
Songs of the Season (Osundare) 103, 190
'Songs of Sorrow' (Awoonor) 133, 135,
  154
Sons of Adam: Stories of Somalia, The
  (Eby) 268
Sons and Daughters (de Graft) 111, 112
Sons of Somal, The (Hanghe) 268
South Africa 80, 220
Sov Mbang, the Soothsayer (Maimo) 277
Sowande, Bode 102, 173, 174, 181–2,
  187
  The Angry Bridegroom 183
  The Babylon Trilogy 181
  biography and important works 394
  Tornadoes Full of Dreams 182
Ṣoyinka, Wọle 86, 92, 154, 173, 183,
  184–5, 195, 201
  activist stance 185
  The Beautification of Area Boy 185
  biography and important works 394–5
  concerns featured in works 86
  criticism of Clark 115

criticism of work 149, 173–4
A Dance of the Forests 86, 147–8, 150,
  175, 182, 326
Death and the King's Horseman 122,
  148–9, 151–4
'The Fourth Stage' essay 151
The Interpreters 86, 150, 324
and ki-Swahili 211
Kongi's Harvest 149–50, 175, 235
The Lion and the Jewel 86, 138, 241
Madmen and Specialists 235, 236–7
The Man Died 115, 185, 235
and Nigerian Civil War 115, 185,
  235–6, 237
not recruited by Heinemann 79–80
Osofisan on 175, 176
A Play of Giants 183, 185
presenting of past 135–6, 148
The Road 55, 86, 150–1, 152, 208
Season of Anomy 150, 235–6
theatre troupe 147, 295
Sozaboy (Saro-Wiwa) 133, 197, 237–9
Spear Books 99, 100, 101
'Stage, The' (Angira) 202–3
Stars of the New Curfew (Okri) 324–5
State of the Union, The (Clark) 115–16
Stockholm Conference on African Writing
  (1967) 86
Stories of Old Times 59
Strasser, Captain Valentin 252
*Strategic Transformations in Nigerian
  Writing* (Quayson) 93–4, 325–6,
  327
Stratton, Florence 131, 291–2
'Student Days' (Kayper-Mensah) 110
student magazines 1, 77
'Student's Lament' (Liyong) 260
Sudan 130
  civil war 256–7
  indigenous languages 247
  writing from 256–62, 310–13
'Sufferhead' (Aig-Imoukhuede) 196
Sunday Tribune 103
Sunset at Dawn: A Novel About Biafra
  (Ike) 232
Survive the Peace (Ekwensi) 232–3
Survivors, The (Butake) 279
Sutherland, Efua 77, 112, 295–7
  biography and important works 395
  Foriwa 295, 297
  The Marriage of Anansewa 296, 297
Swahili language *see* ki-Swahili
Swaray, Nabie Yayah 251, 395
Sweet and Sour Milk (Farah) 270
Sweet Trap, The (Sofola) 297

Taban lo Liyong *see* Liyong, Taban lo
'Taban woos Beccie' (Liyong) 260
Tahinta (Sutherland) 295
Tail in the Mouth, A (Mangua) 100
Tale of Rachel Dangilo 60
Tanganyika 45, 46, 226
Tanzania 46, 85
  and Maji-Maji rebellion 225, 226–7
  use of ki-Swahili 46, 225
  writing from 101, 128
Taste of Death (Mwangi) 229
Taylor, Charles 256
television 103, 177
*Tell it to Women: An Epic Drama for
  Women* (Onwueme) 298–9
Tesfay, Gebra Selasie 265, 395
The Edifice, The (Omotoso) 174
theatre 177–8, 252
  and indigenous languages 92–3, 112
  and Uganda 207–10
  and women writers 297
  see also individual playwrights
Theatre Limited 207
theatre troupes 92, 93, 183
They Shall be Chastised (Likmani) 289
Things Fall Apart (Achebe) 41, 116–17,
  118, 119, 119–21, 122, 131, 143,
  289, 301, 316
Thirteenth Sun, The (Worku) 263–5
This Earth My Brother (Awoonor) 155
Thompson, Rev. Thomas 17
Thoughts and Sentiments on the Evil and
  Wicked Traffic of *Slavery* (Cuguano)
  10–12
Through a Film Darkly (de Graft) 111,
  112
To Borrow a Wandering Leaf (Omotoso)
  174
To Monrovia Old and New (Dempster)
  255
Tolow Waa Talee Ma (Farah) 268
Tom Jones (Fielding) 40
'Tongue-twister, The' (Liyong) 261
Tornadoes Full of Dreams (Sowande) 182
Townsend, Henry 53
transcultural writers 308–34
Transistor Radio, The (Saro-Wiwa) 103
Translation Bureau (Northern Nigeria) 71,
  72
Trapped 55–6
Treasure Island (Stevenson) 75
*Tree for Poverty: Somali Poetry and Prose,
  A.* (Laurence) 268
Trial of Christopher Okigbo, The (Mazrui)
  203, 231

Trial of Dedan Kimathi, The (Ngũgĩ) 228,
  229
Trouble With Nigeria, The (Achebe) 145
*Truly Married Woman and Other Stories,
  The* (Nicol) 248
Tubman, President 256
Tuma, Hama 265–7, 395
Tutuola, Amos 80, 117, 118, 132–3, 325
  biography and important works 395–6
  My Life in the Bush of Ghosts 325, 334
  The Palm-Wine Drinkard 116, 325
Twilight Woman (Akare) 99
Twingle-Twangle A Twynning Tale
  (Osofisan) 179
Two African Tales (Nicol) 248
Two in One (Gicheru) 240
Two Thousand Seasons (Armah) 158

UCC (Ghana) 77
Uganda 44, 45, 85
  playwrights 207–10
  writing from 128, 129, 204–7
  writing in indigenous languages 207
Uganda Crisis (Adoko) 204–5
Ugandan National Theatre 209
Under African Skies (Ofeimun) 187
United Society for Christian Literature 63
universities
  courses in African English writing 83
University of Ghana School of Music,
  Dance and Drama 295
university publications 77
urban-rural conflict theme 85, 128–9, 239

Vai people 255
Valley Without Echo (Akar) 248
Vassanji, M. G. 87, 226–7, 319–23
  biography and important works 396
  The Book of Secrets 227, 321–3
  The Gunny Sack 227, 319–21, 322,
  323
  No New Land 323
Vatsa, Mamman 196
Veronica My Daughter (Ogali) 97
Victims, The (Okpewho) 241–2
Village in Uhuru (Ruhumbika) 203
Village Voices (Osundare) 190, 191
Violence (Iyayi) 80, 186, 192, 235
Voice, The (Okara) 133
Voices in the Dark (Kibera) 165
Vulture! Vulture! (Sutherland) 295

Wala, Obi 211
Walcott, Derek 251
Walker, Alice 251

Walters, Joseph J. 255
  biography and important works 396
  Guanya Pau 27, 63–6, 69, 139
Wangombe, Chief 68–9
Wangusa, Timothy 396
Wanjaū, Gakarra wa 212
Warburg, Fred 116, 117
Warrior King (Sellassie) 263
Washington, Booker T. 13, 396–7
Ways I have Trodden 58–9
'We Hurtle Down' (Ofeimun) 187
Weapon of Hunger (Mwangi) 102
Wedlock of the Gods (Sofola) 297, 298
Weep Not, Child (Ngugi) 84, 119, 122, 126
West African writing 248, 277
  and colonisation 225
  and Creole intellectuals 28–32, 33, 34, 43
  differences between East African writing and 225
  early writings 25–42, 128, 129, 230
  novels on post-independence disillusionment 143–59
  popular writing 95–6, 101 theme of personal and domestic conflict 241–2
  transcultural writers 323–34
  see also individual countries
West African Countries and Peoples 31
What God Has Put Asunder (Epie'Ngome) 279
Wheatley, Phillis 8, 9–10, 50, 397
When Love Whispers (Ekwensi) 97
When the stars are Scattered (Kahiga) 240
White Man of God, The (Jumbam) 277
Whitlock, Gillian 22
Why Are We So Blest? (Armah) 157, 158, 159

Wicked Walk, The (Mfukwa) 240–1
William Waddy Harris (Casely Hayford) 28
Wind Versus Polygamy (Egbuna) 138–9, 241
Winful, E. A. 77
Wings of Dust (Mahjoub) 310–12
Wolseley, Sir Garnett 32, 158
Women of the Aeroplanes (Laing) 332–3
Women are Different (Nwapa) 288
women writers 2, 132, 269, 281–305
  see also individual names
Women's War (Nigeria) 225
Wonderful Adventures of Mary Seacole, The 22
Word, the 55
Worku, Daniachew 263–5, 397
Worl' Do for Fraid (Swaray) 251
Woza Albert 216
Wreath for the Maidens, A (Munonye) 233
Wright 13, 272
Writers Fraternity Limited 101

Yankah, Kwesi 210
Yoruba 35–7, 61, 86, 118, 132, 151, 153
Yoruba (language) 92, 93, 94
Yoruba roni (Ogunde) 183
Yungba-Yungba and the Dance Contest (Osofisan) 179, 180–1

Zanzibar 42, 43, 74, 226
Zanzibari rebellion 227
Zimbabwe 225
Zirimu, Elvania
  Namukwaya 207
Zola 213
Zuka (journal) 77